SCIENTIFIC PROGRAMMING

C-Language, Algorithms and Models in Science

SCIENTIFIC PROGRAMMING

C-Language, Algorithms and Models in Science

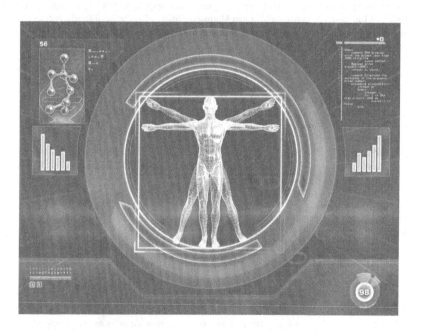

Luciano Maria Barone · Enzo Marinari
Giovanni Organtini · Federico Ricci-Tersenghi

"Sapienza" Università di Roma, Italy

World Scientific

NEW JERSEY · LONDON · SINGAPORE · BEIJING · SHANGHAI · HONG KONG · TAIPEI · CHENNAI

Published by

World Scientific Publishing Co. Pte. Ltd.

5 Toh Tuck Link, Singapore 596224

USA office: 27 Warren Street, Suite 401-402, Hackensack, NJ 07601

UK office: 57 Shelton Street, Covent Garden, London WC2H 9HE

Library of Congress Cataloging-in-Publication Data
Barone, Luciano M. (Luciano Maria), author.
   Scientific programming : C-language, algorithms and models in science / by Luciano M. Barone
(Sapienza Università di Roma, Italy), Enzo Marinari (Sapienza Università di Roma, Italy),
Giovanni Organtini (Sapienza Università di Roma, Italy) & Federico Ricci-Tersenghi (Sapienza
Università di Roma, Italy).
      pages cm
   Includes bibliographical references.
   ISBN 978-9814513401 (hardcover : alk. paper)
   1. Science--Data processing. 2. Science--Mathematical models. 3. C (Computer program
language) 4. Computer programming. I. Marinari, Enzo, author. II. Organtini, Giovanni, author.
III. Ricci-Tersenghi, F. (Federico), author. IV. Title.
   Q183.9.B37 2014
   502.85'513--dc23

                                                                   2013012751

British Library Cataloguing-in-Publication Data
A catalogue record for this book is available from the British Library.

Printed in Singapore

For Rossella
so patient with me and much more

For Margherita,
a flower indeed,
and for Chiara,
fair by name and by nature

For Federica, Lorenzo and Giulia
"the summum bonum was in the gifts of nature,
in those of fortune, in having many friends,
and many and good children"

Miguel de Cervantes Saavedra
"Don Quixote" (1615)

For my children Gaia and Marco
that make my life full of joy and fun,
bright colors and laughing sounds
...every day more and more!

Contents

Programming advanced algorithms   433

Preface

A book teaching how to program should help its readers to learn with minimal effort how to write properly working, efficient and interesting programs. Its potential readers may have very different interests, and the books that are currently available on the shelves generally do not take these needs into account. They mostly address a generic reader, whose interests the author is unaware of.

Books presenting a programming language in a specific context are much more effective and nicer to read, since the reader learns at the same time both the language and the basic concepts needed to formulate the problems one wants to solve. These books obviously address a more specialized audience. However, in many cases they are very precious and they are the right choice to teach professional and university courses.

The collection of programming manuals addressing a specialized audience is rather scarce and those dedicated to scientific programming even less numerous. Since computers play an increasingly important role in modern science this situation is very unfortunate. In many fields it is essential to both being able to express ideas into words or formulas and to translate them into a precise and rigorous programming language.

This book very nicely fills this gap in the current literature. The different parts of the C language are presented together with scientifically interesting algorithms, each one of which is then put into practice. Often the algorithms are not at all basic, and their theoretical motivation is explained in detail. Various implementations of a single algorithm are discussed in depth, keeping the different, sometimes opposing needs into account: precision, execution efficiency, code compatibility and readability. In this way the reader learns how to tackle a new problem while keeping these various aspects in mind, and how to select an optimal choice fitting his needs.

The topics have been carefully selected and the problems are very accurately discussed, as are the codes included in the book. Indeed, this book is the result of years of experience in teaching academic courses in scientific programming. Moreover, the authors have many years of experience addressing scientific problems with the use of the computer, introducing new techniques and designing algorithms which have become commonly used. It is hard to think of authors more qualified than the present ones to write this kind of book.

The original setup and the authors' extraordinary talent make this book an excellent product, a reference point for all those interested in scientific programming.

Rome, February 10, 2006

Giorgio Parisi

Giorgio Parisi is a full professor in Theoretical Physics at the *Sapienza* University of Rome. He is a member of the the the French and of the American Academy of Sciences and of the Lincei Academy. For his work in theoretical physics he received the International Feltrinelli prize in 1986, the Boltzmann medal in 1992, the Dirac medal and prize in 1999, the Fermi medal in 2002, the Nonino prize and the Dannie Heineman prize in 2005. the Galileo Prize in 2006, the Microsoft European Science prize in 2007, the Lagrange in 2009 and the Max Planck medal in 2011. He wrote three books and over 500 scientific articles.

Foreword

The decision to write a textbook is always a difficult and demanding choice for scientists engaged full-time in research activities. It is a very time consuming task, and it requires to have a clear idea about the direction to take in order to produce an innovative book.

Fortunately, some years ago, we started teaching, together with some other colleagues, a course about scientific computing to physics students of the Mathematical, Physical and Natural Science Faculty of the *Sapienza* University in Rome. These courses were a novelty. They were introduced in the context of the recent Italian and European reform, the so-called *three plus two*, aiming to provide students with skills which allow them to operate professionally in a scientific and technological environment.

The subject of these courses is based on our computer programming experience in various fields of scientific research. Throughout our teaching we realized that many fundamental notions about computing for scientific applications are never discussed in the standard manuals and textbooks. We were not able to find an adequate textbook for these kind of courses. Indeed, commonly used textbooks belong to one of the two following categories:

(1) programming language manuals;

(2) numerical analysis textbooks.

The former often contain examples on how to use a programming language without considering the application context. They contain plenty of examples and exercises, which are more game-like or have a concern a managerial context; the few examples written in a precise mathematical form are too simple for a university student and are therefore not appropriate for a scientific (engineering, mathematics, physics, chemistry, biology) faculty. On the other hand, numerical analysis textbooks are appropriate for advanced students and usually require a good knowledge of programming and of mathematical and physical notions. Using two textbooks, one of each category, does not solve the problem either, because the important topics are not correlated as they do not follow the same track.

Finally, we became convinced of the fact that the current survey of textbooks does not include an introductory programming manual for scientific university courses.

Forgetting all about the existing textbooks, we started working on an innovative scheme which we considered adequate for the new university courses. Moreover, the possibility to write a new textbook seemed interesting. We also felt that the project we were working on had an international feel and this stimulated us.

We conceived and built a scheme not just to teach students a programming language, but rather to give them the ability to build models to solve scientific problems by programming. The teaching method we chose takes into account the student skills evolution in time. The examples given are always accessible to the student. The first examples simply refer to mathematical problems in infinitesimal calculus. In the second part fundamental problems of both physics and mathematics are tackled, such as the study of differential equations and their application to problems in dynamics. Finally, in the third part, we discuss rather complex optimization problems.

The textbook is structured in three parts, reflecting the three teaching phases and corresponding more or less to three university courses. The complete journey goes hand in hand with a complete engineering or scientific graduate course. The three courses we propose are strongly linked, and guide the student from the condition of illiterate in computer science to an advanced and competent level. At the same time, the three parts are rather independent and allow a teacher to select only certain parts for particular courses.

The title of this textbook is short, but expresses various strong ideas. The *Programming* expresses the fact that we teach techniques on how to build models and generic algorithms to solve a problem, while creating a good executable code. The *Scientific* has a double meaning: it partly refers to the fact that we treat scientific problems, and partly refers to our way of introducing programming methods. Methods, statements and models are not given as *recipes*, but for each one of these we carefully examine their "raison d'etre", the mechanisms which make them useful, the possible alternatives and their pro and cons.

What this book is not

As we already mentioned, this book is not a C manual: there are already many manuals available in print and on the Internet. In *Scientific Programming* we introduce the C language as a tool to learn how to program: a process which is fully analogue to the one in which you learn how to talk. Just like you need a language when you learn how to talk, you need one to learn how to program. However, it is beyond the scope of this textbook to analyze the C language in-depth in all its aspects. For this kind of analysis, we refer the reader to the bibliography. Still, this textbook contains enough information to introduce the reader to the language without having to refer to a manual.

This textbook is not a generic programming manual either: no managerial, graphics or multimedia applications are discussed in detail. The scientific applications mainly consist in calculating and organizing data. The results are often represented in a graphic way, but these were mostly obtained with specialized programs. These programs are easily available on the Internet, and we do not discuss their setup.

Nor is this book a numerical analysis manual. It includes many, sometimes advanced, computation algorithms, but they are always presented in a simple and intuitive way. We do not want to discuss all aspects of numerical analysis from a mathematical point of view. We refer the reader to the bibliography for the proof of theorems, the detailed discussion of what certain choices imply and the theoretical aspects. Nevertheless, a diligent student will acquire all the tools needed to write complete, accurate and efficient programs.

How to use this textbook

This textbook consists of three parts. Each part reflects the contents of the courses we teach in the corresponding year of an undergraduate program. Therefore, each part contains the material of a first level, 6 credits university course.

The first part does not require any specific prior knowledge about programming. The student is guided along a track including the knowledge of the basic tools (the computer and the programming language), which is essential to understand the techniques to design the solutions. In the first part we aim to familiarize the student with the techniques by learning how to use them in simple and interesting examples. The student learns the elementary and fundamental C constructs and how to apply these in the basic numerical techniques (derivatives, integrals, sorting).

In the second part, we focus on the design aspect. In each chapter we consider the solution to a different problem. This is the right time to show, with examples, the general techniques to solve problems, to thoroughly analyze the advanced aspects of the language and to consider elements often neglected, such as the program's robustness and efficiency. The examined problems are original and stimulating.

In the third part we assume the student fully masters the tools (in particular the programming language). We discuss complex computation problems, which are common in engineering or science, along with code optimization techniques. Also in this part the topics we treat offer a generic overview of the techniques in use, but we frequently examine new and lesser known ones. In our opinion, the third part is more dense of what can be reasonably treated in a standard course and the teacher is free to choose which topics to discuss.

We hope that the student using this textbook becomes at least half as enthusiastic as we were while writing it. In which case our book will turn out to be, beyond any doubt, very useful.

Acknowledgments

At the end of this project, we first of all want to thank our colleagues, our collaborators, our PhD students and all those who depend on us in one way or the other, since in order to write the book we have taken away crucial time from them.

A special thanks goes to the Director and the personnel of the Physics Department of our University, and to the Directors and the personnel of the National Institute of Nuclear Physics and the National Institute of Matter Physics (now unfortunately no longer existing) Sections of Rome 1: without their help our job would have been impossible.

Thanks to our colleagues Zhen'an Liu of Beijing and Wu Hao of Shanghai, for helping us write the citation in Chapter 3 and to Anna Malerba for the citation in Chapter 2.

We also got some very important help from all our colleagues teaching the programming courses in the Physics Graduate Program of the *Sapienza*

University. The students attending our courses stimulated us and pressed us with questions and discussions which were often very important for the development of this textbook. Though they are far too many to quote them all here, we are very grateful to all of them.

Some PhD students and young researchers helped us during our courses throughout the years, and they corrected many, small and big, errors: we sincerely thank Tommaso Castellani, Tommaso Chiarusi, Jovanka Lukic and Valery Van Kerrebroeck.

Carlo Piano has been helping us with organizing the Italian version of the book, and his help has been for us very important.

Lisa Ferranti has been somehow the real responsible of all this. As the editor of the Italian version of the book she has believed in the book from the first moment, she has helped us, she has pushed us, she has brought us to print the book. We could not thank her more warmly.

Introduction to the English version

It took a little time, after we realized that we considered appropriate having this book available in English, finding the strength to go ahead with the project. We were indeed convinced it was a very good idea, since there is here an original approach that we hope will be useful to many students approaching the world of scientific computing. Also we had signals from many non-Italian colleagues, using the book (thanks to their brilliant knowledge of our language) as a trace for their courses but being unable to really give it, because of the language, as a source to the students.

We are very indebted to Valery Van Kerrebroeck that translated the text from Italian, with passion and dedication: without her our effort would probably have been vain. Many young colleagues close to our research groups have helped us in a final revision of the translation; even if they are too many to be quoted individually, they should know we are really grateful to all of them.

Rome, June 7th, 2013.

Luciano M. Barone, Enzo Marinari, Giovanni Organtini, Federico Ricci-Tersenghi.

Technical note

This textbook was written using LaTeX[Mittelbach and Goosens (2004)] version 3.141592-2.1 on a Linux operating system[1].

We used the `emacs` and `nedit` editors to write the text and the programs. We compiled the latter with `gcc` version 3.3.3. Generally we used the `-pedantic` option which generates a message in case the code is not compatible with the ANSI standard. We adopted this standard throughout the complete textbook, except for a few cases which we mentioned explicitly.

The figures were generated with the LaTeX `pstricks` package or the programs `gnuplot` and `xfig`, in Linux. We used different packages following the common habit in scientific environment to choose the best tools for a given problem; this is quite different from other environments, where usually the choices are dictated by conventions, convenience or imposition. This also allows us to show how versatile *open source*[2] programs are.

Typographical Conventions

We have quoted the programming language constructs and the system commands with a different font than the one used for the text. Its horizontal dimension is constant (*monospaced*) and does not vary with the character, as in

---

[1]Linux is a trademark registered by Linus Törvalds.

[2]Open source software is computer software whose source code is freely available and provided under an open source license allowing it to be studied, copied, changed and redistributed.

```
while
ls -la
return 0;
for (i = 0; i < 10; i++) {
```

We also used a similar font to represent URL names (*Uniform Resource Locator*) of Websites:

```
http://www.pearsoned.com
http://www.scientificprogramming.org
```

Characters that possibly cause confusion in the middle of the text (especially punctuation marks) are represented with a gray background: ., ;, {.

To show the syntax and the general definitions of commands, statements and functions we used a different monospaced character, as in

```
#define symbol [value]
```

In this scope words in italics, such as *symbol*, represent generic elements which have to be replaced by the actual ones. When they are included between square brackets, as in [*value*], they represent optional elements which may or may not be present. The example above describes several possible alternatives, as in

```
#define _DEBUG
#define MAX 100
```

In the first example *symbol* is replaced by _DEBUG and the optional value [*value*] is not present. In the second, *symbol* is replaced by the string MAX and an optional value 100 is present, described as *value* in the syntax example.

Program variable names are always chosen on the basis of what they represent.

Generally, programmers use a US keyboard. The reason is simply because programming languages often use the symbols present in this type of keyboard, which is considered to be international, and not in others. The C language is no exception to this rule and uses curly brackets and the tilde (~). In case one does not have a US keyboard, the required symbols can be created using certain combinations of the keys in order to avoid having to redefine the keyboard.

In the Microsoft Windows operating systems, the opening curly brackets can be obtained by holding the Alt key and pressing subsequently the keys 1, 2 and 3 of the numerical keypad. The closing curly bracket is obtained in the same way by pressing the keys 1, 2 and 5, while the tilde is composed with the keys 1, 2 and 6. Please note that this might get very complicated on portable computers which do not have the numerical keypad, but require it to be activated with yet another combination of keys. The curly brackets can alternatively be obtained by pressing the keys on which the square brackets are present while holding the `Alt Gr` and `Shift` keys.

In the operating systems using the graphic system X (X11 or X11R6), such as Linux or Cygwin in Windows, the opening and closing curly brackets are obtained by holding the `Alt Gr` key and pressing, respectively, the keys 7 and 0 on the first line of keys in the standard keyboard (i.e., the keys, respectively, on the left and right of the parentheses). The tilde can be obtained by pressing the `Alt Gr` key together with the ⌃ key.

There is a website accompanying this book at the web address `http://www.scientificprogramming.org/`, where one can find all the codes discussed here, and additional material.

The program listings are subject to the GPL license (`http://www.gnu.org/licenses/licenses.html`) allowing them to be copied, changed and redistributed.

Chapter 0

Programming to compute

It is true that software cannot exercise
its powers of lightness except through
the weight of hardware. But it is software
that gives the orders,
acting on the outside world
and on machines that exist
only as functions of software

Italo Calvino, *Six memos for the next millennium* (1984).

Students starting to program usually wonder about «How?» and «Why?».
This textbook aims to answer these two questions in a scientific applications context. Programming implies many things: to formalize a problem,
typically by reducing it into a series of smaller problems; to translate the formalization into a programming language, then writing the actual program;
to introduce checks which take all possible cases into account. Though
many university courses just follow a programming language manual, it is
fundamentally wrong to think that an expert programmer is someone who
knows well a programming language syntax.

In the majority of cases, a beginner immediately starts writing statements in the selected (or required) language, before trying to logically formalize the problem to be solved. However, only those more able in representing abstract concepts can write the code while defining the logical
flow of operations. Such an ability can be gained with practice. Beginners
should first write down the flow of operations needed to solve the given
problem. Coding comes only later. The study of algorithms, well defined

1

sequences of operations producing a result, is an important part of programming and helps in the logical formalization. Algorithms can have different levels of complexity. Despite some of them may appear as trivial, a careful analysis always reveals interesting aspects even in the simplest algorithm; their analysis is a good way to learn how to deal with more complicated problems.

Once the logical scheme of a program is established, the code can be written according to the rules of the selected language. Just like in any other language, the syntax of a programming language requires discipline. Even worse, in case of a programming language, discipline is mandatory as errors are not tolerated by the programs which translate and execute the code (the compiler and the operating system). Neglecting the syntactical rules is one of the first difficulties encountered by a beginner. Following these rules is sometimes boring, but there is no way out; the only solution is to learn the syntax up to the point that respecting the language rules becomes natural.

Finally, to become a good programmer one needs to know deeply several other aspects: how a computer works, number representation, the time needed for computation, the precision and approximation of mathematical operations.

In this textbook, we answer the question «How?» not only discussing the rules of a programming language (the C language in our case). We also discuss number representation, rounding problems, algorithms, computing efficiency and logical instruments. The student mastering these subjects knows how to program. The best way to acquire this knowledge is continuous practice on more and more difficult problems. We therefore invite the student to independently develop the topics treated in this textbook, besides carrying out the lab exercises.

In the first part of the text, "Basic Programming in C", we mainly focus on the rules of the language, on elaborating numbers and on the logical formulation of the problems.

At that point, the question «Why?» is still unanswered though. In most environments, the computer is now used as if it were a "black box" for graphic or multimedia office applications not requiring the least knowledge on how the software (and also the hardware) works. Whoever knows how to use an electronic sheet or an editor is considered *literate* in computer science. Actually, such a user relates to the software as a driver to his car. Indeed, owning a driver's license is quite different from being a mechanic or a car designer.

In a scientific research environment the computer is acknowledged as an essential tool to investigate the most varied fields, from biology to physics, from economy to engineering. The computer is a daily instrument in various disciplines and sometimes it is even the only way to study some phenomena. As an example, think of simulating systems consisting of many elementary particles: we cannot observe the single atoms and molecules, but we can simulate their collective behavior and compare the properties with the experimental macroscopic observations. The software developed in scientific research is always very specific and continuously needs to be updated to keep up with the rapidly changing demands. Apart from a few general programs (for graphics, statistics and few other applications) it is almost never possible to find commercial software adequate for scientific applications. The best solution to these problems certainly is being able to autonomously write programs for scientific applications.

Moreover, in several research fields, the computational approach has become a true alternative. It is considered a third possible way of investigating Nature, next to the more traditional theoretical and experimental approach. Whoever chooses this third way has to have a solid base in scientific programming. This textbook has the ambition to fill this gap, providing technical and logical tools to develop original scientific programs. Obviously it is not possible to treat exhaustively all scientific applications. Instead, it is possible to discuss the most important algorithms, explain how to translate them in computing code and progressively shape the mentality needed to face problems and algorithms not reported in this textbook. We hope to teach people how to fish, rather than to hand out them fishes.

The student applying himself to writing programs and solving exercises will be able to find a software solution to a scientific problem not explicitly discussed in this textbook. As a result, the student will be able to understand the meaning of the quote from Italo Calvino *it is the software that gives the orders.*

PART 1
Basic programming in C language

Chapter 1

Numbers and non-numbers

Novem figure indorum hae sunt
9 8 7 6 5 4 3 2 1
Cum his itaque novem figuris, et cum hoc signo 0,
quod arabice zephirum appellatur, scribitur quilibet
numerus, ut inferius demonstratur.

Fibonacci, *Liber Abaci* (1202).

In this chapter we show how to represent data (whether numerical or not) in the computer memory. The first step towards the creation of an automatic data manipulating machine is representing the information. The basic information, especially in case of scientific computation problems, consists of numbers. The representation of data of any other nature (characters, images, sounds, etc.) is based on that of numbers. Therefore, a considerable part of this chapter is dedicated to the ways of representing the latter.

1.1 Numeral systems

A *numeral system* is the set of rules determining how to graphically express numbers.

We need to distinguish between the abstract concept of number and the symbol representing it: symbols are called *numerals*. The number five, e.g., can indeed be written in various ways: 5 in Arab characters (those commonly used) or V in Roman numbers; Maya represented it as a horizontal dash —; the ancient Greeks as Π and so on. Whichever symbol is chosen, the number remains the same.

7

The first ingredient of a numeral system is a finite number of symbols or characters. These are then combined in different ways such that all numbers, which on the contrary are infinite, can be written. These characters are called *digits*. A numeral system also defines the digit composition rules and their sequence.

In the decimal numbering system there are 10 digits (from 0 to 9), and the number sequence is as following:

0	1	2	3	4	5	6	7	8	9
10	11	12	13	14	15	16	17	18	19
20	21	22	23	24	25	26	27	28	29
. . . . . .									
90	91	92	93	94	95	96	97	98	99
100	101	102	103	104	105	106	107	108	109
. . . . . .									

The first sequence is obtained by writing all available digits in a given, arbitrary, order (the first line of the series). Subsequently, this sequence is repeated while placing the number of repetitions before each digit. In this way 12 corresponds to the number obtained by counting all digits from 0 to 9 a first time and, next, repeating the digits up to number 2 one more time; 24 corresponds to the number obtained by counting up to 2 repetitions of the digit sequence, stopping at the number 4 during the second repetition; 106 is obtained by counting up to 10 repetitions of the digit sequence from 0 to 9, stopping at the number 6 during the last repetition, and so on.

Though this system might seem obvious, it is a mistake to think this way: this impression is due to habit. Every numeral system can arbitrarily define its own rules. For example, in the Roman numeral system, the numbers are obtained by algebraically adding the values of the digits, considering those preceding one with a larger value to be negative (the number four is written as IV ($-1 + 5 = 4$), while seven is represented as VII ($5 + 1 + 1 = 7$)).

1.2   Positional systems

The decimal numeral system has been borrowed from the Arabs who in turn took it from the Indians and Babylonians. It prevailed over the Roman one due to serious limitations of the latter. To figure out which are those limitations, try to add two Roman numbers or to write a very large number in this system. The problems you encounter are due to the fact that the Roman numeral system is not *positional*. In positional systems the value attributed to the digits depends on their position in the sequence representing the number: they have an increasing weight when moving in the leftward direction. For example, the numeral 1492 indicates the number obtained by carrying out the expression

$$1 \times 10^3 + 4 \times 10^2 + 9 \times 10^1 + 2 \times 10^0.$$

The numbers are expressed as a sum of digits multiplied by a power of 10, which grows from right to left. The explicit writing of these powers is omitted and only their coefficients are listed in the sequence. Such a system is said to be positional as the weight attributed to each digit depends on its position in the numeral.

In positional systems it is sufficient to choose a finite and arbitrary number b of digits (called *base*) to whom we assign a progressive value starting from 0. In the decimal system there are 10 digits and therefore, $b = 10$. In these systems the value of an integer number a is determined as

$$a = \sum_{i=0}^{M-1} c_i b^i, \tag{1.1}$$

where M is the *number* of digits composing a, c_i is the *value* of a digit and b is the *base* of the positional system. The corresponding numeral is indicated by writing the sequence of coefficients c_i. The rightmost digits are called the *least significant*, while the leftmost are the *most significant*.

Elementary operations, such as addition and subtraction, are simple to perform in these systems. Thanks to the distributive property of the multiplication with respect to the addition, we just need to align numbers in columns, while aligning the rightmost digits:

$$\sum_{i=0}^{M-1} \alpha_i b^i + \sum_{i=0}^{M-1} \beta_i b^i = \sum_{i=0}^{M-1} (\alpha_i + \beta_i) b^i. \tag{1.2}$$

Indeed, to add the number 1492 to the number 48, we start by adding the rightmost digit of the first addend to the corresponding digit of the second one as both of these express coefficients of the same power. In practice (Figure 1.1) this operation can be expressed as

$$1492 + 48 = \left(1 \times 10^3 + 4 \times 10^2 + 9 \times 10^1 + 2 \times 10^0\right) + \left(4 \times 10^1 + 8 \times 10^0\right)$$
$$= 1 \times 10^3 + 4 \times 10^2 + (9+4) \times 10^1 + (2+8) \times 10^0.$$

The operation 2+8 between parentheses multiplying the power 10^0 produces a *number* which needs *to be carried*. Indeed, the result is $10 \times 10^0 = 1 \times 10^1$. Thus, the digit 1 is, again thanks to (1.2), added to the digits of the respective addends with the same weight, namely 9 and 4. A similar technique is adopted for the subtraction where the digits on the right *borrow* an order of magnitude from those on the left. In this way, we add a number equal to the base value to the digit from which to subtract and subtract a unit from the lending column.

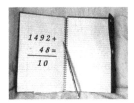  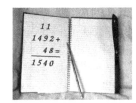

Fig. 1.1   The column addition operation starts at the right. Extra digits, if any, are placed at the top so they can be added to the corresponding powers. When adding the rightmost digits we obtain a number composed of two digits. The extra digit must be added to those multiplying the same power of the base. This is why it is *carried* to the line on top. The same occurs when adding the digits on the third column.

1.2.1   *The binary system*

The binary system takes its name from the fact that it uses only two digits: 0 and 1. The two digits of the binary system are called *bits*, short for *binary digits*. The base is $b = 2$ and the counting rule is the same as in the decimal system: first the available digits are written and then repeated. At each repetition they are preceded by the number of repetitions. The sequence starts with:

    0   1

The digits are then repeated preceding each of them by the number of repetitions (one):

    0   1
    10   11

The numeral 10 correspond to the number two, 11 to three. At this point, we need to repeat the sequence 0 1 a second time (recall that in binary two is indicated as 10) to continue counting:

0	1
10	11
100	101

and so on

0	1
10	11
100	101
110	111
1000	1001
1010	1011
1100	1101
1110	1111

Thus, the binary string 1101 is equivalent to the string 13 in the decimal system as both represent the number *thirteen*:

$$1101 = \sum_{i=0}^{3} c_i 2^i$$
$$= 1 \times 2^3 + 1 \times 2^2 + 0 \times 2^1 + 1 \times 2^0$$
$$= 1 \times 8 + 1 \times 4 + 0 \times 2 + 1 \times 1$$
$$= (8 + 4 + 0 + 1) \times 10^0 = 13 \times 1 = 13 \,.$$

For clarity, where the base is not evident from the context, we shall indicate it as a subscript: 11_2 is thus equivalent to the number 3_{10}. There are two rather simple ways to express decimal numbers in binary[1]. Let us, for example, express the number 10_{10} in base 2.

The fastest way consists in identifying the power of 2 which is closest to, though smaller than the number that is to be converted ($8 = 2^3$, in our case) and write a 1 in the position corresponding to this power in a binary number (in our case, the fourth starting from the right). Next, subtract this power from the original number and perform the same operation on the difference until this subtraction results in zero. For each missing power, a 0 is written. For the example under consideration, we wrote a 1 in the

---

[1] Both methods can actually easily be generalized to any other base

fourth position. Next we calculate the difference $10 - 8 = 2$, resulting in a 0 in the third position and a 1 in the second. Subtracting 2 from 2 we have 0. Thus, after placing a 0 at the first position, we have terminated the conversion: 1010_2.

A second, more algorithmic, method consists in iteratively dividing the number by 2, writing the remainders of these divisions from right to left, until the quotient is zero. In this way, we can express the number as a sum of multiples of 2, which is the representation we were looking for. Thus, to convert the number 10_{10} in base 2, we start by dividing it by this base: $10/2 = 5$ (or rewriting it as $10 = 5 \times 2$), with remainder 0. Next, we divide the result again by 2: $5/2 = 2$ with remainder 1 ($5 = 2 \times 2 + 1$). The integer part of the quotient (2), still needs to be divided by 2, giving the result 1, with remainder 0 ($2 = 1 \times 2$). The latter, divided by 2, results to be 0 with remainder 1 ($1 = 0 \times 2 + 1$). At this point we just need to write these remainders from right to left to obtain 1010_2. Indeed, the method is generally valid as the number N_i that is to be converted in base b can always be written as $N_i = bN_{i+1} + r_i$, with $r_i \in [0, b)$ and, in turn, N_{i+1} can be rewritten in the same way; the procedure can be iterated up to when we obtain a certain $N_k < b$. For example, for $k = 3$, we have $N_0 = bN_1 + r_0$, $N_1 = bN_2 + r_1$ up to $N_3 = r_3$ for which

$$N_0 = b\left(b\left(b\left(r_3\right) + r_2\right) + r_1\right) + r_0 = r_3 b^3 + r_2 b^2 + r_1 b^1 + r_0 b^0 , \qquad (1.3)$$

where b is the base in which the number is to be converted. From (1.3) it is clear that the sequence of remainders is exactly the desired number in base b.

The addition and subtraction operations in base 2 are executed similarly to those in base 10. Let us add two binary numbers, by writing them in columns: 11011 and 00101. Starting the addition from the right, the result should be $1_2 + 1_2 = 10_2$. Since this number consists of 2 digits it needs to be *carried*. Indeed, the magnitude of the value of the left digit 1 of 10_2 is a successive power of 2 and needs to be added to the digits of the same weight. Therefore, we *carry* it to the appropriate column at the top line:

$$1$$
$$11011 \; +$$
$$\underline{00101} \; =$$
$$0$$

Adding the second column, we have the same result, and the same occurs in the third and fourth column:

$$11$$
$$11011+$$
$$\underline{00101} =$$
$$00$$

$$1111$$
$$11011+$$
$$\underline{00101} =$$
$$0000$$

The last column requiring addition again results in 10_2. However, as no other digits need to be added, this result can immediately be included on the line of the sum:

$$1111$$
$$11011 +$$
$$\underline{00101} =$$
$$100000$$

Let us now check the result: $11011_2 = 27_{10}$, $00101_2 = 5_{10}$, $10\,0000_2 = 32_{10}$. Indeed, $27_{10} + 5_{10} = 32_{10}$. We leave the subtraction as an exercise to the reader.

Exercise 1.1 - Binary addition and subtraction

Perform the following addition and subtraction operations in the binary system, without converting them beforehand. Check the result by converting the numbers into decimals only after having performed the operations: $1100 + 0011$; $1110 + 0101$; $1010 + 0111$; $1100 - 0011$; $1110 - 0101$; $1010 - 0111$.

1.2.2 *The hexadecimal system*

As we see in Section 1.3, the binary system is convenient to represent numbers in electronic machines, however it is not very concise. To write down a relatively small number such as 27_{10} we need 5 digits! The number of digits increases at each power of 2.

Though the selected base is a completely arbitrary number, it is true that some are more convenient than others. If we choose the base to be a sufficiently high power of 2, we combine two advantages:

(1) if the base is larger than 10, writing numbers requires less digits than there are required in the decimal system;

(2) if the base is a power of 2, it is easy to convert the numbers in binary (which is the fundamental one used by computers).

The power of 2 larger than and closest to 10 is 16. In base 16 we need 16 symbols to represent the numbers. We can choose them freely, but the following are the most common choice:

0 1 2 3 4 5 6 7 8 9 A B C D E F

Obviously, the symbol A equals 10, B equals 11 and so on until F which equals 15. This numeral system is called *hexadecimal*.

Again, counting is achieved by repeating the digits and indicating the number of repetitions:

```
 0  1  2  3  4  5  6  7  8  9  A  B  C  D  E  F
10 11 12 13 14 15 16 17 18 19 1A 1B 1C 1D 1E 1F
20 21 22 23 24 25 26 27 28 29 2A 2B 2C 2D 2E 2F
...
90 91 92 93 94 95 96 97 98 99 9A 9B 9C 9D 9E 9F
A0 A1 A2 A3 A4 A5 A6 A7 A8 A9 AA AB AC AD AE AF
...
F0 F1 F2 F3 F4 F5 F6 F7 F8 F9 FA FB FC FD FE FF
```

The number FF is followed by the number 100_{16} and the counting continues. Let us try to convert the number 96_{16} using (1.1) to find out its value:

$$96_{16} = \sum_{i=0}^{1} c_i 16^i = 9 \times 16^1 + 6 \times 16^0 = 9 \times 16 + 6 \times 1 = 150_{10} \,. \qquad (1.4)$$

So, a number requiring three digits in decimal can be represented with only two symbols in hexadecimal. One digit less might appear a meager saving, however the real advantage of using the hexadecimal notation is that numbers can easily be rewritten in terms of powers of 2.

Analogously to what happens in base 10, if we multiply a hexadecimal number by a power p of 16, it moves p places to the left and p zeros need to be added on the right. The same occurs in base 2 where, multiplying a number by 2^q, is equivalent to adding q zeros on the right. Now, we also have that $16 = 2^4 = 10000_2$. Thus, moving a hexadecimal digit to the left is equivalent to moving its binary representation four places to the left. Moreover, all digits of the hexadecimal system can be expressed in binary using exactly four bits. Thus, by regrouping the digits of a binary number in groups of four starting from the right, each of these represents the hexadecimal digit which corresponds to the same number and vice versa.

Multiplying the digit 9 (1001 in binary) by 16_{10} (10 in hexadecimal and 10000 in binary), we have 90_{16}, as we are multiplying the number 9 by a power of the base; the result can be expressed by the number followed by an amount of zeros equal to this power (one in case of base 16 and four in base 2). If we add 6 (0110 in binary) to 90_{16} we have 96_{16} ($1001\,0110$ in base 2). So, to convert a number from hexadecimal to binary it is enough to write each digit in its binary notation using always 4 digits.

The other way round, given the number $1001\,0110_2$, it is enough to regroup its digits in 1001 and 0110 to transform them into hexadecimal. The desired representation follows easily by simply associating to each group the corresponding hexadecimal digit: 9 and 6, respectively.

The hexadecimal notation is used when it is important to highlight the composition of a number in terms of bits by means of a compact notation.

Hands on 1.1 - Conversion between numbers in different bases

Choose few numbers between 0 and 2000 and express them in base 2 and base 16. Compare the numbers written in binary notation to those expressed in hexadecimal, by regrouping the binary digits in groups of 4 starting from the right. Next, choose some random sequences of 8 bits and transform them in decimal and hexadecimal notation. The ancient Babylonians had a numeral system in base 60. Can you transform the chosen numbers into this base? What problem could you encounter in this new representation? Can you figure out the maximum number of digits required in this base for your numbers?

Exercise 1.2 - The creative Minister

A creative Minister of the Economy needs to make sure that the law he prepared governing the annual budget and demanding an extra effort of overall 43 billion euro from the taxpayers, gets approved. Confident that his colleagues know little about numeral systems, he writes the following Art. 1: «The quantities stated in the current law are all expressed in base 12». Which is the overall amount stated in the law?

Exercise 1.3 - License plates

The license plates of Italian cars have the format AA BBB AA where AA are two letters of the alphabet and BBB are three digits. Assuming all possible combinations of letters and numbers can be used, how many vehicles can be registered in this system?

Exercise 1.4 - The planet Htrae: numbers in base 12

The inhabitants of the planet Htrae have six fingers per limb and count in base 12. Write the first 50 numbers. A greengrocer of Htrae sold a customer a nolem and a bunch of ananabs (two types of local fruit). Their prices, displayed on the goods, are 77 and 870 orue (the local money), respectively. How many orues does the customer have to pay?

1.3 Representation systems

Deciding which numeral system is the more appropriate depends on the application. Once the base is determined, rules defining how to represent digits in practice and how to interpret their sequence to assign their meaning, need to be established. This set of rules defines the representation system.

In the usual typographic convention, as an example, digits are represented by adopting conventional graphic marks: for the negative numbers the symbol − precedes the digit sequence; a dot separates the decimal part of rational numbers from the integer one, and so on. However, this set of rules is completely arbitrary and can be superseded if we have to represent numbers in a different environment.

Suppose, for example, we were playing cards on a beach and needed some way to represent the scores of the two players throughout different games. Without any pen or paper, we could use a different representation system. Gathering a dozen of shells, we could decide to use base 2. Each team is given 6 shells. We *represent* the digit 0 by an *upright* shell and the digit 1 by one that is *upside down*. In this way we can represent the scores of each player up to a maximum of $2^6 - 1 = 63$. In this representation the number of digits is finite, and only a finite amount of numbers can be expressed.

The representation system of a computer works in base 2 as it is easy to construct devices assuming just two states: a switch can be open or closed, a capacitor is either charged or discharged, a transistor can either conduct or be disabled, and so on. Each of the two states can represent a binary digit. For example, the current RAM memories are nothing but large batteries of tiny capacitors etched on a silicon layer. As in the example of the card players on the beach, also in the case of computers it is impossible to represent all numbers. Indeed, computer memories are necessarily finite. In order to simplify its management it is organized such that each number is represented by a finite amount of digits. For historical reasons, the number of bits is usually a multiple of 8 (32 and 64 are the most common values, nowadays): a set of 8 bits is called a *byte* and is indicated by B. An adjacent group of bytes with a length in bit equal to n is called a *word* of n bits. If the length is not specified the term *word* indicates a group of bytes whose size is equal to that of the largest CPU register[2].

We also note that since the possible states of these devices are strictly two and not more, the various numbers can only be represented by means of just two symbols. The minus sign and a dot are not allowed and we need to represent them in a different way. As the numerals are of the binary type, using exactly n, and no more than n digits, we can represent integer positive numbers starting from 0 up to a value $N_{max} = 2^n - 1$. Larger numbers require more digits and cannot be represented as there is no memory available to store all of them. Moreover, the amount of digits representing each number is constant. The numbers requiring less digits than those available are represented by adding an appropriate number of non-significant digits 0 to the left of the first significant digit. Any attempt to represent a number larger than the number N_{max} gives an *overflow* error.

Exercise 1.5 - The birthday cake

If you have only 6 candles of two different colors, could you display your age on a birthday cake? Could lady Lisa, who is 96 years old and makes great cakes, use the same trick? Having numeral shaped candles, could she make use of a different base, to appear younger?

---

[2]A *word* is commonly identified with a group of 32 or 64 bits, depending on the size of the largest register in modern computers.

Computer measurement units

The size of a computer memory is measured in *bytes*, whose multiples are defined adopting the commonly used prefixes (k $= 10^3$, M $= 10^6$, G $= 10^9$), which are adjusted in order to become powers of 2. For example, 1 kB $= 1024$ B; 1 MB $= 1024$ kB $= 1048\,576$ B and 1 GB $= 1024$ MB $= 1073\,741\,824$ B.

A unit for the process speed is the FLOPS (*FLoating point OPerations per Second*), measuring the number of operations on floating point numbers (see Sec. 1.3.4) that the CPU is able to perform in one second . In most cases, however, the performance of a computer strongly depend not only on the CPU FLOPS, but also on the general architecture, the size of the RAM and the particular application. To define the performance of a computer taking into account all those aspects, SPEC (*Standard Performance Evaluation Corporation*) has been created: a non-profit organization defining a series of standard algorithms, called *benchmarks*, to evaluate the performance of computers by measuring their relative execution time (http://www.spec.org). From these execution times, metrics depending on a particular aspect for which the algorithm was designed, are derived. For example, the SPEC CINT2006 measures the overall process velocity on benchmarks performing operations on integer numbers.

In Table 1.1 on page 25 we display the minimum and maximum numbers that can be represented on a 32 bit architecture, using the techniques described in the next sections.

1.3.1   *Representing negative numbers*

We already noted that it is not possible to use a third symbol to represent the sign of a number, as all information must be conveyed in a unique way by means of the only two possible states of the devices composing the computer architecture. The sign of a number must then be represented with the same symbols 0 and 1 used to store the digits (i.e., with the two states of the physical device representing them): we could establish that the number is positive if the most significant bit is 0 and negative otherwise.

In this way, assuming that all numbers have a sign, the largest number that can be represented on an 8 bit architecture is 0111 1111 (equal to

$+127_{10}$), while the smallest is $1111\,1111$ (equal to -127_{10}). The zero would have two possible representations: $0000\,0000$ e $1000\,0000$.

More generally, n bits can represent positive and negative numbers ranging from $-(2^{n-1}-1)$ to $(2^{n-1}-1)$ with two possible representations of zero.

1.3.2 *Complement representation*

At the end of this section it will be clear that representing relative numbers with a sign is not the best solution on a computer. Remember that a fixed number n of bits allows us to represent numbers from 0 to $2^n - 1$. We could choose to divide this interval of representable numbers in two and interpret the numbers in one subinterval as positive numbers and the others as negative ones. The most common solution for representing negative numbers on computers is the two's complement representation.

To gain a better understanding of this type of representation it is useful to start from a visual model. Suppose we have a tape with the numbers from 0 to 99 printed on it, similar to a tailor's meter. If we fold the tape on itself, creating in this way a ring (Figure 1.2), we can interpret the numbers on the left of the zero as negative and the ones on the right as positive. Of course, as the tape is limited, both the positive and the negative numbers finish at a certain point, namely in the point that is diametrically opposed to the zero. Actually, what we do is we divide the interval of representable numbers into two sub–intervals and agree to use the upper half for negative numbers.

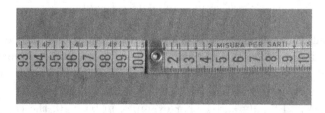

Fig. 1.2 A numbered tape folded onto itself to create a closed curve is an efficient way to visualize the representation of negative numbers in the base's complement.

It is easy to express a negative number with this notation, given that the sum of equidistant numbers from the zero (as $99 + 1$, $98 + 2$, etc.) is always equal to b^n where b is the base and n is the maximum number of digits composing the numbers under consideration. We also observe that

b^n is always written as 1 followed by n zeros for each b and thus takes $n+1$ digits. If the number of digits under consideration is limited to n, we can ignore the excess digit 1, and the sum will in fact always be 0.

The complement k of a number m, in a certain base b, represented by a fixed number n of digits, is the number obtained from the relation

$$m + k = b^n . \tag{1.5}$$

For example, in the decimal system, the ten's complement of the number 32 using 4 digits is

$$k = 10^4 - 32 = 9968 .$$

Obviously, $9968 + 32 = 10\,000$. However, if the number of digits is limited to 4, the leftmost digit 1 of the sum is omitted and the result is equal to 0. The same occurs in base 2 (10_2). The complement of the number 0110, with four digits, is

$$k = 10_2^4 - 0110_2 = 10000_2 - 0110_2 = 1010_2 .$$

Again, we have, in the appropriate base, $1010 + 0110 = 1\,0000$, such that the sum is a 5 digit number. If we ignore the first digit the result is equivalent to 0000.

The complement k of a number m is easily obtained rewriting (1.5) as

$$k = b^n - m = (b^n - 1) + 1 - m .$$

Note, in particular, that $(b^n - 1)$ is always expressed as a sequence of digits which are all equal to each other and to the last digit of the system in use (9 in base 10, 1 in base 2). So, to obtain k it is enough to write for each digit of m what is missing to reach the last digit of the base b (the complement to the base) and finally add 1. For example, in base 10, the complement of 0032 is the number 9968, obtained by adding 1 to 9967 which, in turn, is determined by noting that 9 is the complement of 0, 6 of 3 and 7 of 2. In base 2 things are even simpler as the last digit of the base is 1. Thus, the complement of 0 is 1 and that of 1 is 0. Thus, we just need to invert the digits to obtain the intermediate result; the two's complement of 0110 is obtained by inverting the digits (1001) and adding 1: $1001 + 1 = 1010$.

The interval of numbers that can be represented with this technique starts at $-\frac{b^n}{2}$ and ends at $\frac{b^n}{2} - 1$: in base 10, with 4 digits, this is from

−5000 to +4999; in base 2, with 8 digits, from −128 to +127. In this case there exists only one representation of 0. Taking this into account, it is easy to distinguish positive numbers from negative ones: in base 10 positive numbers start with a digit between 0 and 4 (9968 is a negative number and cannot be confused with +9968, which does not exist in this representation); in base 2 the negative numbers always have the most significant bit equal to 1.

Let us now also consider the fact that CPUs are equipped with electronic circuits to perform elementary functions. The number and size of these circuits are one of the parameters determining the amount of dissipated energy, the physical size of the CPU and its speed. Thus, it is clear that the representation of negative numbers in two's complement is extremely convenient. Indeed, the inversion operation of the digits can be done with a very simple circuit, and the subtraction operation is executed with the same, also relatively simple, circuit used for the addition. The advantages of this type of representation can be appreciated by those who solved the subtraction exercise of Section 1.2.1.

1.3.3 *Excess-N representation*

An alternative to the two's complement is the *excess-N* notation. The latter consists in representing the negative numbers by one part of the available numbers and the remaining part represent the zero and positive numbers. This just means that the origin of the axis of natural numbers is shifted and the negative numbers are represented by the numerals preceding this new origin.

In an n-bit representation we can write 2^n numbers (from 0 to $2^n - 1$) in total: by moving the origin N places, the bit sequence usually indicating the number N, represents the number 0. The sequences of digits preceding the origin indicate negative numbers, while those following express positive numbers, similarly to what has been done in two's complement. This representation is called excess-N. The value of each bit sequence is obtained by subtracting N from the number the sequence represents in binary. In this way all numbers from $-N$ up to $2^n - (N + 1)$ can be represented.

For example, in case $n = 8$, numbers from 0 to 255 (for a total of 256 numbers) can be represented. With $N = 127$ the numeral interval is divided in two. The numerals that in the usual notation represent numbers from 0 to 126 (0111 1110) represent negative numbers from −127 to −1, the numeral 127 (0111 1111) represents 0 and the remaining ones the positive numbers from 1 to 128. As N is arbitrary, the excess-N notation is preferred over the two's complement when it is necessary or suitable to freely choose the position of the origin on the numeral axes.

There exist other possible representations of negative numbers. Still, as they are only rarely used in practice, we do not cover them in this textbook.

Exercise 1.6 - Negative numbers in complement and excess-N

 Write the opposite of the following numbers in base 10 with the 3-digits complement and the excess-127 notation: 2, 28, 57, 128. Repeat the exercise in base 2, using an appropriate number of digits. Finally, express the given numbers in an uncommon representation such as excess-96.

1.3.4 *Rational number representation*

In the decimal system the integer part of rational numbers is generally separated from the fractional part by means of a *dot* or *decimal point*. The formula (1.1) is easily extended to include the case of rational numbers considering the fact that the weight of the digits to the right of the point are negative powers of the base that decrease as we move further to the right. A number a with N digits right of the point and M on the left equals to

$$a = \sum_{i=-N}^{M-1} c_i b^i . \tag{1.6}$$

For example, 45.127 has a value equal to

$$\sum_{i=-3}^{1} c_i b^i = 7 \times 10^{-3} + 2 \times 10^{-2} + 1 \times 10^{-1} + 5 \times 10^0 + 4 \times 10^1 .$$

As usual, the same is valid in base 2; the number 110.01101 is equal to

$$\sum_{i=-5}^{2} c_i b^i = 1 \times 2^{-5} + 0 \times 2^{-4} + 1 \times 2^{-3} + 1 \times 2^{-2} + 0 \times 2^{-1} +$$

$$+ 0 \times 2^0 + 1 \times 2^1 + 1 \times 2^2 = 6.406\,25_{10} .$$

Analogously to base 10, dividing or multiplying a binary number by a power of 2 means moving the point an appropriate number of places. For an architecture in which the K digits composing a number are fixed it could be convenient to reserve N of those digits to represent the integer part and the remaining ones, i.e., $M = K - N$, the fractional part. Fixing the number of digits after the point in this way is a waste though (all zeros following the last significant digit are useless). Indeed, it limits the potentially representable numbers to a rather low value, more or less equal to 2^N.

A better solution is offered by the floating–point representation, which expresses the numbers as in scientific notation. Indeed, the number 45.127 can always be written as 4.5127×10^1 or $0.451\,27 \times 10^2$. In scientific notation the number is written as a product of a *mantissa* (for example, equal to 4.5127) and an appropriate power of the base (1 in the given case). The base is the one of the adopted numeral system. Obviously, the possible floating–point representations are infinite: it is enough to choose a different power of 10 and change the mantissa correspondingly to change the representation. By convention, a standard notation has a mantissa with value always between 0 and the base and an as low as possible exponent. In this way the only proper representation is 4.5127×10^1.

This same representation, in base 2, is used in computers: each rational number is expressed as a product of an appropriate power of 2 and a mantissa. Having only a limited number of bits available (suppose 32), we reserve a certain (few) number n_e of bits for the exponent and the remaining ones ($n_m = 32 - n_e$) for the mantissa. Again, the possible representations are infinite. This is why a standard defined by an international organization, i.e., the IEEE 754, is followed, prescribing the following conventions:

- The most significant bit represents the mantissa sign (0 if positive, 1 if negative).

- The subsequent 8 bits represent the exponent of 2 in excess-127 notation.

- The last 23 bits represent the mantissa in normal form. This form is defined such that it represents $C + m$ with $m \in [0, 1)$ and C a constant, which does not require to be represented. Therefore, the 23 available bits represent only m. In the so–called normal form $C = 1$. However, if the exponent consists of 8 zeros (-127), $C = 0$ and it is more convenient to assign the value -126 to the exponent (denormalized form)[3].

---

[3]In the normalized form the smallest absolute value that can be represented is $1.000\ldots001 \times 2^{-127} = 2^{-127} + 2^{-23}2^{-127} \simeq 2^{-127}$. Instead, in the denormalized form, $1.000\ldots001 \times 2^{-127}$ becomes $0.111\ldots111 \times 2^{-126}$, and values up to $0.000\ldots001 \times 2^{-126} = 2^{-23}2^{-126} = 2^{-149}$ can be represented.

- The zero is represented by setting all the bits of the exponent and all those of the fractional part of the mantissa to zero.
- The values $+\infty$ and $-\infty$ are represented by setting all bits of the exponent equal to 1 and all those of the mantissa equal to 0.
- The value NaN (*Not a Number*) representing a non-real result (as $\sqrt{-1}$) is defined by an exponent equal to 1111 1111 and a mantissa different from 0.

Note that in this representation the minimum absolute value of the mantissa is 2^{-23} while its maximum is

$$1 + \sum_{i=-23}^{i=-1} 2^i = 1 + 0.5 + 0.25 + 0.125 + \ldots \simeq 2\,.$$

As the exponent ranges from -126 to 127, the representable values are comprised between (about) $2^{-23} \times 2^{-126} = 2^{-149}$ and $2 \times 2^{127} = 2^{128}$.

To represent the number 22.75 in floating–point binary notation, we could proceed as follows:

(1) transform the decimal number into binary keeping the decimal point: $22.75_{10} = 10110.11_2$ (the decimal part $0.75 = 0.5 + 0.25$ corresponds to the powers 2^{-1} and 2^{-2});

(2) translate the decimal point to the left such that the number becomes smaller than 2 (i.e., such that the decimal point is immediately to the right of the most significant bit): $1.0110\,11$;

(3) multiply the obtained number by a power of two equal to the number of places the decimal point has been moved: 2^4, whose representation in excess–127 is $4 + 127 = 131 = 1000\,0011_2$;

(4) write the bit of the sign (0), then the first n_e bits representing the exponent of 2 followed by the fractional part of the mantissa. For $n_e = 8$ and $n_m = 23$ we have: $0\ 1000\,0011\ 011\,0110\,0000\,0000\,0000\,0000$.

According to the IEEE 754 Standard rational numbers can be represented in *double precision*. In this way they follow the convention described above, using 64 bits, of which 11 are allocated to the exponent. In 2008, the *quadruple precision* representation was defined, as part of the IEEE 754 2008 Standard, using 15 bits for the exponent and 112 bits for the mantissa, for a total length of 128 bits.

Table 1.1 shows the minimum and maximum values of numbers representable in the memory of a 32 bit computer.

Table 1.1 Minimum and maximum values of the representable numbers on a 32 bit computer. For rational numbers the IEEE 754 representation has been used.

Number classes	Minimum	Maximum
integer		
unsigned	0	4294 967 295
signed	$-2147\,483\,647$	2147 483 647
two's complement	$-2147\,483\,648$	2147 483 647
rational (in modulus)		
in single precision	$1.401\,298 \times 10^{-45}$	$3.402\,823 \times 10^{38}$
in double precision	$4.940\,656 \times 10^{-324}$	$1.797\,693 \times 10^{308}$

1.4 The approximation problem

Since the available number of digits is limited, a computer can only represent those numbers whose fractional part can be expressed as a limited sum of powers of 2 exactly. If this is not the case, it is approximated by the nearest one. While 22.75 can be represented exactly, other cases, such as 0.1, cannot. To understand this try to write the latter number in binary notation considering a 32 bit computer.

The same occurs for non–rational, real numbers (such as $\sqrt{2}$, π, etc.): these numbers have an infinite amount of digits after the decimal point, for which there is not enough space in the computer memory. They can only be approximated by the closest rational number.

This limitation causes a problem which is to be faced each time a computer performs a computation: the rounding error. In practice, all non integer numbers are approximated by the nearest rational number having a finite representation, with a precision of the order of 2^{-n_m}, where n_m is the number of bits reserved for the mantissa. Two numbers that differ less than this quantity from each other are considered to be equal on the computer and a number smaller than the smallest representable number equals 0 (this is the case of an *underflow* error).

Care should be taken with this type of approximation. Though it is harmless in many cases, the error could propagate dramatically in some algorithms, especially the iterative ones, and may become important (a concrete example is given in Chapter 4). Frequent causes of such a catastrophic error are either very different or very similar operands. In the first case, the smaller of the two numbers is less precise because the mantissa needs to be represented with a larger exponent. Consider adding two numbers $a = 68\,833\,152$, i.e., 0 1001 1001 000 0011 0100 1001 1111 0000 in the IEEE 754 representation, and $b = 2309\,657\,318\,129\,664$ (0 1011 0010 000 0011 0100 1001 1111 0000). To carry out this addition, we need to organize these numbers in columns. To this purpose, we need to express the smallest of the two (a) with the same exponent of 2 as the biggest (b) in IEEE 754 notation. The exponent of a is 26, while that of b is 51. The difference between these two numbers is 25. Thus, we need to rewrite the mantissa of a moving the digits 25 places to the right. As the maximum number of digits of the mantissa is 23, the resulting mantissa of a is represented by a sequence of zeros:

$$0\ \ 1011\,0010\ \ 000\,0000\,0000\,0000\,0000\,0000 + \ldots$$
$$0\ \ 1011\,0010\ \ 000\,0011\,0100\,1001\,1111\,0000 =$$
$$\overline{0\ \ 1011\,0010\ \ 000\,0011\,0100\,1001\,1111\,0000}$$

and the sum is $a + b = b$, which obviously is nonsense!

The second type of error often occurs when subtracting two numbers that are close to each other. This is easily understood by considering some examples in the more familiar base 10 (though similar examples can be found in any other base). Suppose we represent floating–point numbers with 3 significant digits after the decimal point. The number 1000 is represented as $a = 1.000 \times 10^3$, while the number 999.8 as $b = 9.998 \times 10^2$.

The difference is $(a - b) = 0.2$. However, to perform this calculation in floating–point representation, the smallest number first needs to be expressed with the same power of 10 as the one of the higher number. This causes a loss of significant digits: $b \rightarrow b' = 0.999 \times 10^3$. Consequently, the difference becomes

$$(1.000 - 0.999) \times 10^3 = 10^{-3} \times 10^3 = 1.0\,.$$

Though the precision of each single number is of order 10^{-3}, the approximate value is larger by a factor 5 with respect to the true value! In some cases, this type of error can be avoided (or at least reduced) by reformulating the expression which is to be calculated. Suppose, $x = 3.451 \times 10^0$ and $y = 3.45 \times 10^0$ are given, and we need to calculate $\Delta = \left(x^2 - y^2\right) = 0.006\,901 = 6.901 \times 10^{-3}$. If we first calculate the squares $x^2 = 11.909\,401 = 1.190 \times 10^1$ and $y^2 = 11.9025 = 1.190 \times 10^1$, we find $\Delta = 0$. A disastrous result, especially if Δ is the denominator in some expression. Instead, by reformulating the expression as $\Delta = \left(x^2 - y^2\right) = (x - y)(x + y)$, we find $(x - y) = (3.451 - 3.450) \times 10^0 = 0.001 \times 10^0 = 1.000 \times 10^{-3}$, while $(x + y) = (3.451 + 3.450) \times 10^0 = 6.901 \times 10^0$, and thus, $\Delta = 1.000 \times 10^{-3} \times 6.901 \times 10^0 = 6.901 \times 10^{-3}$.

In numerical computation, unlike analytical calculus, the order in which operations are executed is extremely important, as is the order of magnitude of the terms subject to arithmetic operations. Depending on these operations, they should be neither too different from each other, nor be too similar.

The birth of positional systems

In ancient times, calculations were performed using an instrument called *abacus*: a slab with several parallel grooves where pebbles (*calculus* in Latin) were placed. The grooves represented the powers of the base and the number of pebbles they contained the weight assigned to each of them. The positional system for writing numbers imitates the way the abacus works. The first known positional system dates back to ancient Babylonia and was in base 60. The symbol corresponding to our 1, reproducing the presence of a single pebble in the appropriate groove of the abacus, was a vertical cuneiform sign. Each time there was just one pebble in a groove of the abacus, the Babylonians marked this sign in the corresponding position. They were also the first to introduce a symbol representing the absence of pebbles, the zero, which was shaped as two inclined parallel signs.

Fibonacci's *Liber Abaci*

For a long time, the way of writing numbers and the way of using them in calculations were different. For example, the Europeans only started using the positional system in 1202, the year in which Leonardo Fibonacci published his *Liber abaci*. In those times, writing numbers principally served to track money loans. To register the amount of money lent or deposited, cuts or roman numbers on sticks were engraved. These sticks were then halved longitudinally and one piece was given to the debtor, while the other served the creditor. The word *stockholder* derives from this practice and quite literally means the owner of a credit bill or stick (i.e., *stock* in old English).

1.5   Non-numbers on computers

Performing a task, whether it scientific or not, may require manipulating data other than numbers, such as images, sounds, etc. Today this might seem obvious because we can see images or watch a movie on a computer all the time; we can listen to music by means of the loudspeakers; a microphone allows us to use our voice to communicate with users far away through the Internet; we can use a video camera to organize a video conference.

When the computer era began, in the Forties of last century, their only purpose was to perform calculations. Numbers represented practically the only form of information available. Programs were built by operating switches. Their results were visualized by light bulbs whose status (on/off) indicated the bit sequence in binary. When it became possible to produce written results (on paper, and later, on screen) and to give commands by means of a keyboard, the problem of how to represent other types of information, such as characters, needed to be solved. As more refined techniques became available and computer architectures evolved, the necessity to represent information of different nature constantly grew. This process is still ongoing today, and it is natural to expect it will give rise to yet other representation forms. Indeed, nowadays, computers can, more or less faithfully, reproduce visual and audio information in their memory. Sooner or later, also odours, flavours and touches will be electronically manipulated, thus requiring an appropriate representation.

Whatever their nature, all information must be represented in binary form on a computer. Thus, the definitions of these representations closely follow the one of numbers.

1.6   Logical value representation

In mathematical logic, a *proposition* is any statement that can take on the values *true* or *false*. We assume the concepts of true and false to be primitive. For example, the sentence «*my Professor is boring*» is a proposition (the reader may judge whether it is true or false), while the sentence «*complete the exercises of chapter 1!*» is not, as no truth value can be assigned to it.

A logical expression is the combination of several propositions by means of *operators*, mostly in the form of a conjunction, which, in turn, can only assume the two values *true* or *false*. For example, the expression «*the professor is boring* **AND** *it is too hot in the room*», take on the value *true* if both propositions composing it are true.

The necessity to represent these two values in the computer memory derives from the fact that programs may need to take decisions depending on whether certain conditions occur. The representation of a logical value in the computer memory is rather simple: it is enough to establish the convention that the value 0 is interpreted as *false*, and the value 1 as *true*.

Manipulating numbers require a fixed number of bits in a computer. Indeed, it is difficult to design a computer that uses a variable number of bits, depending on the type of data to be manipulated. Therefore, even if logical values can be represented by a single bit, often they are represented by a larger number of bits equal to the amount used for numbers. A logical value is typically expressed as a bit sequence. Its representation is equivalent to that of an unsigned integer. If the latter assumes the value 0, the corresponding logical value is *false*. Depending on the cases, a logical value *true* is represented by an unsigned integer equal to 1 or an unsigned integer different from 0.

1.6.1 *Logical operators*

As arithmetical operators work on one or more numbers, the logical operators (or boolean, after the name of George Boole, an English mathematician of the XIXth century who formulated the corresponding theory of Boolean algebra) operate on one or more logical values. Their result is again a logical value. Therefore, these operators define an algebra. The operators combine logical propositions to form expressions. In these expressions, they play the role of the connective to which they correspond in common language.

Boolean algebra is based on three logical operations:

(1) **AND** is a binary operator that, applied to two elements of the set of logical values, returns the value *true* (1) if and only if both of the elements on which it operates are true;

(2) **OR** is the binary operator that, applied to two elements of the set of logical values, returns the value *true* (1) if at least one of the elements on which it operates is true; [4];

(3) **NOT** is a unary operator that, applied to an element of the set of logical values, returns its complementary value (false returns true and true returns false); it represents the negation of a proposition.

---

[4]Note that in common language the conjunction "or" is ambiguous: it may express a mutual exclusion or not. The OR operator is *inclusive*: it admits both propositions to which it is applied to be true.

Any element of the set on which the logical operator is applied, can assume only a finite amount of potential values. Therefore, their results can be expressed in a table. The table summarizing all possible combinations of logical values on which an operator applies, together with the result of the operation is called the operator *truth table* of the operator.

The AND and OR operators can be applied to two logical values which can be combined in four different ways. Therefore, their truth tables have four rows and three columns (Tables 1.2 (a) and (b)).

Table 1.2   Truth tables of the AND (a) and OR (b) operators.

A	B	A **AND** B	A	B	A **OR** B
0	0	0	0	0	0
0	1	0	0	1	1
1	0	0	1	0	1
1	1	1	1	1	1

Instead, the NOT operator is unary. Therefore, the values on which it operates are only two: 0 and 1. The corresponding truth table (Table 1.3) is then composed of two rows and two columns.

Table 1.3   The truth table of the NOT operator.

A	NOT A
0	1
1	0

The logical operators can be combined to create new operators. For example, the NAND operator is the result of applying the AND operator before the NOT operator.

The XOR (exclusive-OR) operator, returns the value *true* only if just one of the operands is *true*[5], and is made by combining the basic logical operators. One of the combinations resulting in XOR is

$$(A \textbf{ XOR } B) = (A \textbf{ OR } B) \textbf{ AND NOT } (A \textbf{ AND } B). \qquad (1.7)$$

We leave it to the reader to write the corresponding truth table and check it by means of the logical expression 1.7.

---

[5]In common language, the exclusive-OR corresponds to the conjunction "or" with disjunctive value. It expresses the mutual exclusion of the two possibilities composing the proposition.

We can always define new logical operators. However, it can be proven that all possible combinations of logical values always lead to truth tables which can be obtained by successively applying AND, OR and NOT. So, the existence of only these three operators guarantees the possibility of defining any other logical function[6].

1.7   Character representation

Another type of data which certainly need to be represented in a computer memory are characters. A character is a graphic symbol representing a phoneme (as the letters of the alphabet), a punctuation mark, a number (the symbols representing the 10 digits of the decimal system) or an entire word (as the characters of some oriental languages or, without going that far, symbols indicating the currency). In the case of computers, some control elements (whether graphic or not) are defined as characters. Some examples are the "new line" signal, the emission of a sound by a loudspeaker or the declaration that data transmission has started or finished.

Note that in this context characters act as information carriers. If the information remains constant, their representation does not change. As an example, let us consider the character representing the lowercase letter "a". The corresponding graphic sign (a glyph) may vary depending on the selected printing style, which could be italic, underlined, bold, etc. In this case, the information carried by the character consists in the fact that it is the first letter of the Latin alphabet, in lowercase form. Independent of its graphic appearance it always remains the same character, and therefore, is always represented in the same way.

A simple way to represent this type of information consists in associating, in a conventional way, an integer number (code) to each character. The character is then represented by the binary equivalent of its code.

1.7.1   *Character strings*

Words are character sequences which carry more information than the single characters composing them do individually. More generally, a character sequence, even if it does not represent a word out of the vocabulary, defines a *string*. A string is easily represented by a sequence of the codes of the

---

[6]Actually it is possible to build all logical operators starting only from the NAND operator. However, it is more convenient to use the three operators described in this chapter.

characters composing it. To distinguish adjacent strings from each other we need a distinctive sign indicating its end. In written text this is the blank space. From an information content point of view, the blank space, in turn, is also a character. As such it cannot be used to define the end of a string (a string might consists of several blank spaces).

By convention, a code indicating a character with empty meaning (NULL or *null character*) is established, namely 0. This code can indeed serve as a distinctive sign. A string of length n (i.e., consisting of n characters) then has a representation of total length equal to $n+1$ characters: the first n are represented by the integer numbers corresponding to the characters composing it and the last by the number zero.

1.7.2   *The ASCII code*

The only way to establish a correspondence between characters and integers is to define an internationally recognized *standard* to which everybody adheres.

A successful standard of today is the ASCII code (American Standard Code for Information Interchange), defined in 1968. This standard provides 256 characters whose codes start from 0 (NULL) and continue up to 255. In order to represent each one of these characters, 8 bits are required. The standard only defines the first 128 characters (from 0 to 127) unambiguously; the remaining 128 may vary depending on the particular chosen encoding (which depends on the language). One of great importance is the ISO 8859-1 code, also called "Latin Alphabet no. 1", providing the characters typical of the European alphabets (e.g., letters with diacritical marks such as accents, dieresis, etc.).

Table B.1 in Appendix B lists the characters corresponding to the integer numbers from 0 to 127 according to the ASCII code. The characters with codes smaller than 32 are special, non-printing control characters. The most important ones are: 0 (NULL), 10 (*newline*), abbreviated to NL, and 13 (*carriage return*)[7], abbreviated to CR.

The correspondence between codes and characters are defined such that the codes of uppercase characters only differ by a single bit from those of their lowercase counterpart[8].

---

[7]The name of this character derives from the carriage of a typewriter, which moves a sheet of paper from right to left as characters are printed on it. The carriage can be returned allowing to overwrite the characters already printed on the paper. The carriage return together with a lever (*newline*), lets the paper to advance one line.

[8]This simplified the generation of the code by means of mechanical devices, such as

1.7.3 *UNICODE*

Recently the inadequacy of the ASCII code, based on a set of characters used in the western world, has become evident. Indeed, the limited number of bits representing a single character do not allow to define all possible characters of other alphabets (Arab, Chinese, Japanese, etc.). Another problem is the ambiguity deriving from the various ISO encodings representing its variants. Indeed, two different symbols could be represented by the same code, which might entail problems when exchanging programs or data between computers using different ISO encodings.

A remedy for this problem has recently been defined by an open consortium of companies and individuals participated by the major hardware and software producers, namely the *UNICODE* standard [The Unicode Consortium (2003)]. The scope of UNICODE is to associate to each existing character in the world an unambiguous character. This is possible because the UNICODE standard defines a space of 1 114 112 possible characters of which about 96 000 are currently in use. The first 255 codes are identical to those defined by the ASCII/ISO 8859-1 standard to guarantee the compatibility between the two systems.

The standard defines 17 code segments called *planes*, each one of which consists of 65 536 (2^{16}) characters. Thus, in total there are $17 \times 2^{16} = 1\,114\,112$ characters. At present, all modern and special characters are defined in Plane 0 (called BMP: *Basic Multilingual Plane*). Plane 1 is dedicated to ancient alphabets, musical and mathematical symbols. Plane 2 contains about 40 000 less commonly used Chinese ideograms. The last two planes are reserved for private use.

1.8 Representing other information

Electronic processors must be able to represent also other types of information, such as images (static ones such as drawings or photographs, or moving ones as in videos) and sounds.

As we have learned, all information manipulated by this kind of machines should be representable in binary form. Non-numerical data are represented by the binary equivalent of an integer number which unambiguously corresponds to the information the data carry.

Multimedia data are no exception to this rule. Nevertheless, this type

---

keyboards, which in the sixties were rather popular. Today almost all devices connected to computers are electronic.

of data often is represented in different ways both for historical as technical reasons.

Images are usually represented by dividing them in many tiny rectangles called *pixels*. The original image is represented by the set of pixels, each of which has a color corresponding to the dominating color of the original. If the size of the pixel is sufficiently small and the image format is limited (the actual limit obviously depends on the pixel size), the human eye is not able to distinguish any difference between the original image and its pixel based reproduction. Colors are obtained by combining some basic colors with the appropriate intensity. The basic colors used on screen are red, green and blue. Thus, each pixel can be represented by a threesome of numbers (e.g., between 0 and 255), each of which represents the relative intensity of the corresponding color. The various formats (BMP, GIF, JPEG, etc.) all use this basic technique (called *bitmap*). The difference between them is essentially due to the compression algorithm used to reduce the overall number of bits needed to represent the whole image.

An alternative way to represent an image consists of vector graphics. Graphics based on vectors do not represent an image as a sequence of pixels. Rather it describes its aspect using *primitive* components, such as points, lines, curves, described in an analytical way. Vector graphics is more accurate than graphics based on pixels because it does not depend on the resolution. Often the vectorial format is also more compact. While the bitmap format necessarily requires all of the pixels in which the image is divided, in the vectorial format it is enough to possess the necessary information to reconstruct the image (for a circle, e.g., it is enough to have the coordinates of the center, the radius and potentially the color and style of the circumference and surface). On the other hand, vector graphics is rather complex. Devices employing this technique should be able to elaborate sometimes complicated operations in reasonably short times. Also, while this technique can easily be used to represent technical drawings, it is usually difficult to describe photographs or an artwork in terms of primitives. Therefore, this technique cannot universally be applied to any type of graphics.

Analogously as to what occurs in film-making, videos are represented by sequences of frames. In case of digital videos, signal compression techniques may be used. They take advantage of the fact that often only a (possibly small) part of the image changes from one frame to the next (in a take with a fixed camera, the background remains invariant and only the image around the close-up moving subjects change). In these cases we can just store the information relative to those parts of the frames that have changed with respect to the previous one.

Sound is represented in a similar way by reducing the overall information while limiting the perceived difference by the human ear with respect to the original sound as much as possible. The basic technique is the one used to produce musical Compact Discs (CDs) . The analog waveform of sound is sampled at a certain frequency f and the intensities of the sampled wave are digitalized (transformed in number or *digit* sequences). The sound is then represented by the binary counterpart of this number which is proportional to the waveform magnitude. Each second of sound becomes a sequence of f binary numbers (to which often additional information is added allowing to reveal or possibly correct reading errors made by the devices). For example, in case of CDs, songs are sampled with a frequency $f = 44.1$ kHz and the digital sequences contain data allowing to establish whether single samples have even or odd parity. Parity data allow the device to correct possible reading errors caused by scratches or dust on the disk surface.

There also exist different formats for sound representations. These essentially differ from each other by the compression techniques used. The MP3 format takes advantage of the reduced capacity of the human ear to perceive certain nuances in sound. It accurately represents the sound of a CD while reducing the size of the digital representation by a factor 12.

Chapter 2

Programming languages

> The piston engine [...] is now something quite
> antiquated and because of all the improvements it
> has become highly complicated, whereas the jet
> engine is much simpler because it is still at the
> beginning, then it too will become highly
> complicated and something else will have to be
> invented.
>
> Luigi Malerba, *The Serpent* (1989).

To fully comprehend the meaning of the word *programming* we should at
least have a vague idea of the principles on how computers work. We
dedicate the beginning of this chapter to this topic. Next, we tackle the
problem of how to define a language to program a computer. Finally, we
show some distinct features of the language selected for this course, namely
C. At the end of this chapter we briefly comment how this language is used
in the most popular operating systems in use today: Linux, Mac OS® and
Windows®.

2.1 The necessity of a programming language

In this section we show how an electronic processor or computer works in
order to introduce the concepts of *programming* and *language*. We do not
want to discuss the construction details of any specific product, but rather
the general working principles.

The main element characterizing a computer is its CPU (*Central Processing Unit*) or processor: a device able to execute an ordered sequence of

statements operating on data stored in a memory together with the program itself.

The CPU communicates with the exterior by means of devices for data *input* and *output* (I/O) or peripherals. Modern computers have rather many of these devices: the keyboard and the mouse, the screen and the printer, but also the loudspeakers, the microphone and the video camera. Also disks are I/O devices as their aim is to exchange data with the CPU.

Contrary to popular belief, CPUs can perform just few basic operations, which can be classified in three categories. More specifically, they can

(1) move data (from the memory to the CPU and vice versa, between two different memory locations, etc.)[1],

(2) compute simple operations (addition, subtraction, multiplication, division[2], logical operations: AND, OR, NOT),

(3) control flow (we see below that CPUs execute operations sequentially; the control flow allows us to alter this sequence).

These operations are realized by miniature electronic circuits and are executed one after the other, timed by a device sending a periodic impulse, called *clock*[3]. The frequency of the clock is expressed in GHz. It is one of the most important features determining the process speed. At each impulse, the CPU executes an elementary operation. Thus, the higher the clock frequency, the more single operations are executed per second when the CPU is operative[4].

The computer memory is an ordered series of elements (cells or locations) fit to store bit sequences. The ordinary memory is called the RAM (*Random Access Memory*; each element of the memory can be accessed in the same way and with the same speed). A memory element is made out of a group of bits of fixed length N. A number, called *address* is associated to each memory element. The address unambiguously identifies an element and indicates its position inside the sequence. A typical element

---

[1]Some CPUs have functions allowing to move entire data blocks and communicating directly with the output peripherals, thus giving rise to graphic manipulation statements.

[2]Today, the CPU of any computer contains an FPU (*Floating Point Unit*) inside, which evaluates complex mathematical functions as the trigonometric ones, roots, logarithms, exponentials.

[3]For practical reasons, the clock generating circuit is often built inside the CPU chip, though logically speaking it is not part of it.

[4]The clock frequency is not the only feature determining the effective process speed though. Other important factors are the memory access speed, the performance of the I/O devices, the CPU capacity to execute elementary operations on certain data types (integers or rationals), etc.

of modern memory consists of a battery of capacitors (Figure 2.1). The capacitor charge indicates the status of the corresponding bit (0 or 1). In

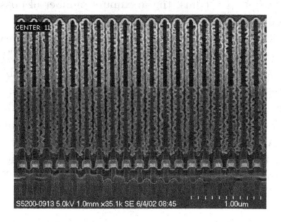

Fig. 2.1 Microphotograph of a section of RAM. Several cylindrical capacitors are aligned. The external conductor, common to all capacitors, is the *curly* structure and it is connected to ground. The internal conductor are the dark cylinders visible inside each capacitor (courtesy of Micron® Technology, Inc.).

these memories $N = 8$. Thus, a memory location corresponds to a *byte*. The CPU always has an internal memory, whose locations are called *registers*. The data of the RAM are copied in these registers in order to execute the operations.

The architecture of modern CPUs, the ways of accessing the memory and how its content is interpreted vary a lot depending on the model. Despite these differences we can assume that all processors, when turned on, collect a sequence consisting of an integer multiple m of N bits at a certain memory location L_0[5]. This sequence is interpreted as a *statement* or, more precisely, a request to execute a certain operation[6]. Statements are expressions consisting of an *operation code*, usually abbreviated to *opCode*, followed by zero or more parameters. The opCode defines the type of operation which is to be performed ("add two numbers", "move a byte from

---

[5]The address of this memory location in the CPUs of most Personal Computer is FFFF0 in hexadecimal.

[6]In the so-called RISC architectures (*Reduced Instruction Set Computer*) m is fixed and typically goes from 1 to 4. Instead, the CISC architecture (*Complex Instruction Set Computer*), uses statements of variable length. The CPUs of today Personal Computers are hybrid: they use CISC statements that are reduced to groups of *RISC* statements before they are executed.

one location to another", etc.). As all information saved to memory, also opCodes and their parameters are represented in binary as integers of fixed length k, with $k < mN$ (thus, the maximum number of possible opCodes defined per CPU is 2^k).

First (Figure 2.2), the CPU collects k bits at the memory location L_0 and interprets them as an opCode (e.g., "add two numbers"). If this code requires parameters (in our example the two numbers to be added), the $mN - k$ successive bits are collected and interpreted as such. Once a statement has been executed (requiring one or more clock cycles), the CPU accesses the following bit sequence, saved at mN memory locations from the current one. Again, it interprets this sequence as a statement. This is how a *program* is executed. Thus, a program is composed of a sequence of bits indicating which actions the CPU must perform on the data. These data are also expressed as bit sequences and form an integral part of the program.

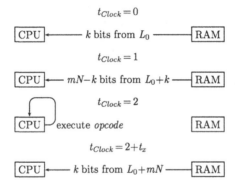

Fig. 2.2   Diagram of how a CPU works. In this example, the execution of the *opCode* requires t_x clock cycles.

The programming language is the way of expressing the sequences of operations which need to be carried out by the computer by means of statements. The latter follow a certain syntax, i.e., rules allowing to combine opCodes and parameters. The allowed combinations are those producing valid constructs to which an unambiguous semantics can be attributed (i.e., the meaning of each statement must be unmistakable). The language used by the CPU is called *machine language*.

As an example, let us create a program to add two numbers. To keep this example generic (and simple), we do not consider the language of a specific

A bit of history

The design of the first computer in history has been assigned to the English mathematician Charles Babbage (1792-1871). In the beginning of the XIXth century Babbage proposed to build a machine [Babbage (1822)] (analytical engine) able to memorize data in mechanical registers, read a program consisting of a sequence of statements impressed on special punched cards and execute them on the memorized data. The machine was never built because it resulted too complex. Only in the thirties of the XXth century a working machine based on the same principle was realized: the Mark I of the University of Harvard [MARKI (1946)], in which the mechanical elements had been substituted by electronic devices. The Colossus, built by the English during the second world war, is often indicated as the first European computer. However, almost nothing is known of its architecture as its documentation, classified as military secret, was destroyed in the sixties of the XXth century by order of W. Churchill. Indeed, we do not know whether it was a true computer (able to execute whatever program was loaded in its memory) or a device specifically built to decode the secret German codes. Between 1943 and 1946, some physicists of the University of Pennsylvania in the United States built the ENIAC (Electronic Numerical Integrator And Computer) [ENIAC (1946)] to cover the computation needs related to the design of the atomic bomb. Ten years earlier Alan Turing (1912-1954) conjectured [Carpenter and Doran (1986)] to store data and programs in the same *memory*. The construction of the ENIAC confirmed this intuition. Indeed, at that time, the technology had already advanced up to a point where the execution time of the program became negligible compared to the reading time. In 1946 John von Neumann (1903-1957) proposed [von Neumann (1946)] to realize a Turing machine, in which data and programs were saved in the same memory, a solution which is still in use today.

CPU. In this chapter we assume to have a processor (and its language) which was designed on purpose. Its opCodes are represented by the 8 bit sequences listed in Table 2.1. For practical purposes, we assigned to each numeric code an alphanumeric mnemonic code which is used in the text to comment the program. For this CPU we assume $L_0 = 0$, $N = 8$ and $k = 8$.

Table 2.1   List of the available opCodes in a simple exemplary CPU. Each statement is represented by a sequence of bits composed of the *opCode* possibly followed by parameters, the number of which is indicated in the *Parameters* column. For convenience, each *opCode* has been assigned a mnemonic *Code*.

opCode	Meaning	Code	Parameters
0000 0000	assign to the register a the value contained in the memory location indicated by the parameter which follows	set_a	1
0000 0001	assign to the register b the value contained in the memory location indicated by the parameter which follows	set_b	1
0000 0010	sum the content of the registers a and b, next place the result in the register a	sum_ab	0
0000 0011	jump to the location indicated by the parameter which follows	goto	1
0000 0100	write the content of the register a in the graphic memory (causing it to appear on screen)	out_a	0
0000 0101	increase the content of the register a by 1	inc_a	0

Any problem needs to be solved by a program executing an appropriate sequence of available statements operating on given memory locations. Considering the statements of Table 2.1, a program summing two numbers, say 2 and 3, should define the data on which it has to operate and the tasks to be carried out, as in the following list:

(1) insert the values 2 and 3 (the constants on which to operate) in two different memory locations;

(2) assign the content of the first address to the register a;

(3) assign the content of the second address to the register b;

(4) sum the content of the two registers, placing the result in register a;

(5) show the value contained in register a on screen.

The program consists of a sequence (words) of bits which is to be interpreted as a series of 8 or 16 bit *words*. Each of these words represent either a statement or data or both. A possible program resolving the problem is given in Table 2.2, showing the memory locations, their binary content and the corresponding mnemonic code.

When executing the program, the CPU collects the byte at the location $L_0 = 0$ and interprets its content as an opCode. In this case, the Code is 00000000 corresponding to the operation assigning the value contained in location 1111 1110 to the register a. The address of the value to be

Table 2.2 For each memory *Location* the stored value (*Content*) and, if any, corresponding *Statement* consisting of the mnemonic *op-Code*. If required, parameters are given.

Location	Content	Statement
0000 0000	0000 0000	set_a, 11111110
0000 0001	1111 1110	
0000 0010	0000 0001	set_b, 11111111
0000 0011	1111 1111	
0000 0100	0000 0010	sum_ab
0000 0101	0000 0100	out_a
1111 1110	0000 0010	
1111 1111	0000 0011	

assigned is indicated as a parameter in the next location. At the next clock impulse the CPU reads the contents of the byte $L_0 + 1 = 1$ (1111 1110), interprets it as an address and places the value it contains (0000 0010) in the register a. The statement composed of the bytes with addresses 2 and 3 is interpreted analogously. Reading the fifth byte (with address 4) causes the two registers a and b to be summed. The result is stored in a. The content of the latter appears on screen once the statement corresponding to the code 00000100 has been executed. Indeed, the latter statement simply copies the contents of the register a in a memory zone called the *graphic memory*. The contents of the color screen of a computer is represented by a sequence of pixels (Section 1.8). Each one of these pixels is associated to a threesome of graphic memory locations. Any changes to the content of one of these graphic memory locations, causes a change in the color of the corresponding pixel. To simplify our example, we assumed that simply writing a value in the graphic memory causes it to appear on screen.

2.2 High-level languages and elementary statements

Each CPU, because of how it is built, can only execute programs written in its own machine language and expressed as a long sequence of 0 and 1. The first computers were indeed programmed in this way. The statements in binary code were arranged on a panel by means of a series of switches and loaded into the memory by pressing a button. Obviously such a language is particularly difficult to handle by humans. However, at that time, it was the natural way to proceed.

To simplify a programmer's job, more comprehensible languages were introduced. Then these had to be translated into machine language before being loaded into the memory and executed. Initially, programming languages were made of simple rules with an almost mathematical character, to be applied to the sequences of bits representing them. They continuously transformed more and more into a set of constructs borrowed from the natural language. As a consequence, the resulting languages are much more independent on the underlying technology.

The natural language is, by nature, sometimes ambiguous and tolerates a creative use: the meaning of a sentence may depend on the context and may contain synonyms (different words with the same meaning) or polysemes (identical words with different meanings). This is why it is not fit to program a device requiring formal rules. Here, the term "formal" expresses the need for this system of rules to be unambiguous[7].

The abstraction degree of a given language is qualitatively indicated by the term *level*: a low-level language is very similar to the machine language, while a high-level language is "closer" to the natural language. Obviously, the level of a language is a relative concept. For example, the C language, is considered to be high-level with respect to the machine language and low-level with respect to the Java™ language. Generally, high-level languages are more concise. However, their biggest merit is the fact that their lexicon includes forms expressing articulate meanings, independently of the elements composing the CPU on which the programs are executed. In other words, in high-level languages, problems are no longer resolved by moving and manipulating data saved in binary in the memory. Rather, algorithms operating on complex data structures, are formulated with a higher degree of abstraction with respect to the *hardware* architecture.

2.2.1   *The assembly language*

Immediately above the machine language, there is a language whose statements are composed of alphanumeric strings, each one of which has a one-to-one correspondence to some elementary CPU statement[8]. This is called

---

[7]The very fact that we need to specify this, indicates how ambiguous the natural language is. Indeed, in the latter, the term "formal", may also indicate a *register* used to communicate (a letter to an Authority requires a more "formal" tone than an SMS to a friend).

[8]In modern assembly languages statements can be translated in several sequences of machine statements. For simplicity, we omit this case which only occurs in very specific circumstances.

the *assembly* language.

If we write the program of Table 2.2 using the mnemonic code instead of the bit sequences of the statements, it becomes as following:

```
set_a, 2
set_b, 3
sum_ab
out_a
```

The program is now definitely more comprehensible and almost self-explanatory. To each symbolic instruction of the assembly language, represented by the mnemonic code, generally corresponds a single machine language statement. Apart from the machine language, it is the language of the lowest possible level. Processors cannot execute programs written in assembly. Before the processor can execute an assembly program it must save it as a bit sequence into the memory, i.e., the program must be translated into machine language.

This operation entails both the translation of the statements in bit sequences, as the decision on which memory locations should be used. For example, in order to translate the statement set_a, 2, the memory address L_x where the value 2 will be saved, and an address to save the operation code 00000000 corresponding to the code set_a, followed by the value L_x, need to be determined. The translation is carried out by a program called the *assembler*. The input could be for example the code we just discussed. The corresponding output is then made of opcodes.

Hands on 2.1 - Use of the assembly language

Using the assembly language of Table 2.1, write a program printing the numbers from 0 to 5 on screen. Translate it into machine language by associating the corresponding opcode to each statement. Note how difficult it is to understand the purpose of the machine language program with respect to the one written in assembly language. Change the program such that it only prints the odd numbers on screen.

2.3   The role of the compiler

The translation from a high-level language into machine language is an extremely well-defined process. It can be described by a finite series of elementary steps. As a result, it is always possible to write a program performing such a translation. More precisely, such a program first acquires a sequence of alphanumeric characters and generates from it a bit sequence representing the corresponding set of machine statements. This type of program is called a *compiler*.

The introduction of compilers fostered the definition of more advanced and abstract languages. Though the assembly language is more comprehensible then binary code, it still has some undesired features: it is verbose, depends on the specific CPU architecture on which it is executed and forces programmers to design a solution to each, possibly complex, problem in terms of elementary objects such as registers and memory locations. This clearly shows the need for new languages.

A more "intelligent" compiler allows us to formulate programs in a more natural language, associating automatically one or even more machine language instructions to each of the statements in the new language. The production of a compiler for very high-level languages is an arduous, though not impossible task. Today, many compilers are even able to optimize the code written by the programmer. Indeed, compilers for the assembly language (also known as *assemblers*) are generally distinguished from compilers translating more advanced languages.

The invention of the compiler

Grace Brewster Murray Hopper (1906-1992) developed the first compiler in programming language history, known as the A-0 compiler. Hopper used it to program the UNIVAC (UNIVersal Automatic Computer), the first commercial computer built in the USA. She also introduced the term *bug* to indicate a programming error. Indeed, in 1945, while working on the Mark II computer, Hopper and her colleagues discovered an insect which had sneaked into the machine and in this way broke a relay preventing the computer to work properly. The *debugging* operation (localizing and removing that bug and substituting the relay) was successful, and ever since, this same term has been used to indicate the search for errors and the correction of their code.

Using a higher level language, the program we first wrote in machine language and next in assembly language, can be rewritten as

```
print 2 + 3
```

An appropriate compiler could read this program and reformulate it into machine language, thus changing just one line in a set of statements. Using the appropriate algorithms, it produces a program, called *object*, containing only machine code.

Who compiles the compiler?

The compiler itself is a program. Thus, before it can be executed, it must also be compiled. To this purpose, we again need a compiler, which in turn must be compiled. How can we resolve this apparent chicken-and-egg problem? The answer is actually relatively easy. Namely, the first compilers were written in machine language. Once we have a simple compiler written in machine language and able to translate a more advanced language, we can write and subsequently compile a more complicated translation program. Continuing this process, we create more and more advanced compilers and finally have the possibility to compile the compiler *B* with a program *A* which are both written in the same language.

The first *self-hosting* compiler, i.e., a compiler able to compile its own source code, was written in Lisp in 1962 at the MIT by Timothy Hart and Michael Levin.

Today, almost all compilers are written in C, which does this job well: the C compiler is almost always written in the C language. Making a compiler is a typical *bootstrap* process, i.e., a process in which an initially simple system activates itself by passing through several degrees of complexity. In other words, the system activates itself even if it is not yet fully up and running. Another example of a *bootstrap* process is the sequence of operations which need to be executed by a computer when it is turned on in order to activate itself: for the computer to work, a program needs to be loaded into its memory, but a program must be loaded into the memory to load other programs!

The term *bootstrap* was borrowed from the like-named strap sewed at the rear top of *cowboy* boots, helping to get them on easily. It is commonly believed that the *bootstrap* process recalls the legend of the Baron of Munchhausen. Depending on the version, he was said to be able to lift himself by pulling himself either by the hair or by his shoelaces, thus alluding to the undertaking of lifting himself without any external help.

Note that, in order to function correctly, the machine language program of Table 2.2 must contain statements preventing the CPU to continue acquiring bit sequences and interpret them as statements. Indeed, once the statement 00000100 (`out_a`) stored in location 5, is executed, the CPU would want to read the content of location 6 to interpret it as an *opCode*. However, the location with address 6 could contain any kind of code making the development of the program unpredictable. If the *object* program is equipped with all necessary elements to work well (in our example these are all necessary statements to interrupt the normal program execution flow and return the machine to the state in which it awaits to execute a new program), it is said to be *executable*. This means it can be loaded directly into the memory and executed by the CPU.

High-level programs have the advantage of being independent of the machine architecture. Without applying any changes, they can be used on CPUs with different architectures as long as they are translated by an appropriate compiler. Instead, the executable code generated by different processors for the same program can differ a lot.

2.3.1   *Interpreters and compilers*

To be useful, all high-level languages need to be translated into machine language. In natural languages, a translation, for example of a book, from one language into another can be carried out just once and re-used several times later on. Instead, the translation work during a simultaneous interpretation of a speech is repeated each time it is held. In computer science, the ordinary translation is called *compilation*, while simultaneous translation is called *interpretation*. *Compilers* are programs performing the compilation, while *interpreters* are simultaneous translators.

In practice, one often hears about interpreted and compiled languages, though the terms *interpreted* and *compiled* strictly apply to the implementation of the languages and not to the languages themselves. Indeed, for one single language there can both exist a compiler and an interpreter[9]. This practice is due to the fact that usually languages are only available in one flavour or the other for historical reasons.

An interpreter gives the impression that a high-level program does not need to be translated into machine languages before being executed. Actually, the translation is still performed. It is the interpreter which transforms

---

[9]For example, there exist C interpreters such as CINT: `http://root.cern.ch/root/Cint.html`.

the program into machine code, loading it into the computer memory and executing it.

Interpreters are used when a program execution speed is not critical. Indeed, in this case, we need to sum the interpreter translation time to the program execution time. On the contrary, the translation is carried out just ones for compiled programs. Therefore, the total execution time is less[10].

However, programs that are meant to be interpreted are more *portable*, i.e., they can easily be executed on different architectures. Compiled programs, on the other hand, are sequences of machine statements and thus depend on the specific CPU for which they were compiled. For programs designed for many users using it in different environments and architectures, it is preferable to use an interpreter. In this way, a unique version of the source code can be distributed. In theory, we could do the same for a program which needs to be compiled. However, the compilation process is often not that obvious and many users might not possess the necessary technology. To avoid the source code distribution, an executable code for each architecture possibly executing the program would need to be created.

A particular case are those languages that are partially compiled and completed by an interpreter during their execution. This is the case, for example, in the *Java*™ language: the Java code is first compiled in low-level statements which are independent of the specifically used CPU. The resulting code (called *bytecode*) is a set of conventional elementary statements. A specific interpreter (the JVM: *Java Virtual Machine*) interprets this bytecode and transforms it into processor specific machine statements. In this way the portability advantage of the interpreter is combined with the efficiency of a partial compilation.

2.4 The linker

When building a computer, we never just start from a pile of mechanical (screws, bolts, bearings) and electronic (resistors, capacitors, transistor, etc.) components which need to be welded onto a printed circuit. Generally, semi-processed components (motherboard, processor, fans, expansion cards) of various producers are assembled.

The same occurs when writing a program. Indeed, usually we do not

---

[10]Nevertheless, the same operation might take less time in an interpreted program with respect to a compiled program, because some languages are more suited to perform certain operations. Thus, the statement is true only on average.

start from scratch by building the code using only the native language statements. Instead, we use components performing complex functions. To understand how this works, let us extend the program of Table 2.2 such that it also performs the addition of the numbers 5 and 8. The simplest solution consists in repeating the assignment and addition statements twice. However, there is a way to reuse part of the existing code. To this purpose we add some new concepts to the language. Let us consider for example the Listing 2.1.

```
1   A = 2
2   B = 3
3   goto SUM
4   A = 5
5   B = 8
6   goto SUM
7   return
8  SUM :
9   set_a , A
10   set_b , B
11   sumab
12   out_a
13   return
```

Listing 2.1   An assembly language program for performing two additions.

A new concept has been introduced in this program, namely that of a *variabile*. A variable is a symbol to which a value is assigned. Clearly it has no equivalent in the machine language. During the translation, a memory location is associated to each variable, where the variable content is saved. We also defined a symbol (SUM) representing a *label* and a new statement (return). When the object code is generated, the compiler substitutes the SUM string of the goto statement with the memory address where the first statement corresponding to line 9 is saved. The return statement, in turn, causes a jump to the memory location following the one from where the last jump started. These memory locations, where jumps start and end, are not explicitly indicated in the program and need to be evaluated at the time the program is loaded into the memory. In this case we assume that the program started its execution by jumping to the memory location where the program started being loaded.

The sequences of operations performed by the program are:

(1) initialize the memory locations corresponding to the symbols A and B, say L_a and L_b, respectively;

(2) jump to the memory locations corresponding to the SUM label;

(3) registers a and b are filled with the content of the memory locations L_a and L_b which, in this case, have value 2 and 3;

(4) sum the content of the two registers;

(5) the result of the addition is written on screen;

(6) execute the **return** statement which jumps to the memory location containing the statement following the last jump (line 4);

(7) the next statements assign the value 5 to the location L_a and the value 8 to L_b;

(8) again perform a jump to the location corresponding to the SUM label;

(9) as before, the registers a and b assume, respectively, the value contained in the locations L_a and L_b which now have values 5 and 8;

(10) again, sum the values of the registers a and b;

(11) the result is written on screen;

(12) again execute the jump statement **return** which brings the execution to the memory location corresponding to line 7;

(13) finally, a jump causes the CPU to execute the statement following the memory location from which the program was started (we suppose that this next location contains the code required to stop the program).

In this example we created a so-called *function*: a piece of code (starting at the label identifying it and ending at the **return** statement) which can be reused. Functions not only allow us to create more compact programs, but also guarantee them to work more properly. Indeed, the repetition of long sequences of identical statements might entail transcription errors generating erroneous code. Instead, each time a function is called, the executed code is the same. Thus, the program will always perform the same operations. The concept of functions and its implications are shown in Chapter 7. For now, this example is enough to understand the role of the *linker*.

The addition function can be used in numerous programs. Therefore, it would be useful to the programmer to keep it as an independent component which can be included in various programs. Obviously, to be useful, the function needs to be compiled. If the programmer only compiled the addition function, all the code following the SUM label could be translated into machine language. The `return` statement, however, cannot be translated completely as it is impossible to determine the address of the statement from which the jump to the function was executed. Moreover, the memory addresses corresponding to the variables that were used in the function cannot be determined. To establish these we need to know which memory locations are still free to host the values of the data, and thus the total length of the program[11]. The assembler necessarily only performs an incomplete job, thus generating a non-executable object code. The object code contains machine language statements and undetermined symbols whose value can only be established when the function is actually used by a program.

To determine the symbols that remained undetermined after compilation the programmer has to *link* the portions of object code by means of an appropriate program: the *linker*. Indeed, the linker reads the codes which need to be linked and works out the values that were left undetermined during compilation. The *linker* produces a complete executable program, which can be loaded into the computer memory and executed.

The same occurs for a program written in a more advanced language. In this case, the role of the *linker* is even more important as it is almost never possible to write a complete program without linking functions supplied by the language manufacturer. These functions are called *library functions*, or briefly *libraries.*

Thus, the production process of an executable code starting from a program written in whatever language, is composed of a set of compilation and *linking* operations. Often though, to be concise, the term compilation is used to refer to the successive application of both operations. In the following we will often use this convention, unless otherwise specified.

2.5   Procedural and object-oriented languages

Modern high-level languages can be divided into two large categories: *procedural* and *object-oriented* languages.

Procedural languages act on and alter data sets in a sequential way. During program execution, the data are passive subjects and the program is a succession of actions.

---

[11]Modern compilers profit of the functions offered by the operating system, thus generating *relocatable* code. The memory addresses of this relocatable code are represented as differences (*offsets*) with respect to a basic address. Upon execution, the operating system determines this basic address, while taking the currently occupied memory into account.

Instead, in *Object Oriented Programming* (OOP), the concepts of statements and data are superseded and substituted by the concept of *object* possessing a *state* and *methods* to communicate with other objects. The state of an object can be changed by its own methods or those of other objects. The program consists of interacting objects which perform their tasks and thus change each others states.

Let us analyze a program allowing to manipulate geometric figures. To move them across the screen we could use the following set of statements in a procedural language:

```
moveSquare(squarePos, diag, delta);
moveCircle(circlePos, R, delta);
```

where **squarePos** and **circlePos** could represent, respectively, the coordinates (x, y) of the center of a square and a circle and **delta** their displacement vector. **diag** represents the length of the diagonal of the square, while **R** is the radius of the circle. In this case the functions **moveSquare** and **moveCircle** act on the data represented by **squarePos**, **circlePos**, **diag** and **R**, changing them as prescribed by **delta**. Note that functions treating different geometrical figures are necessarily different. Moreover, the programmer can always introduce a statement of the type:

```
moveCircle(squarePos, R, delta);
```

which is syntactically correct, but presumably wrong from the semantic point of view.

Instead, in an object-oriented language we could introduce the concept of **shape** representing all objects of the class of *geometric figures*. Each of these objects has its own *state* defining, among others, the position. We can create the objects **square** and **circle** belonging to this class. To move them we could use statements of the following type:

```
circle->move(delta);
square->move(delta);
```

In this way we no longer need to indicate the initial position because it is included in the description of the object state, and because the method allowing the action to be carried out carries the same name. Each object stores its own state and it is not explicitly shown to the programmer. Such a property is called *encapsulation*. In object-oriented programming, despite the fact that the name of the invoked method is the same in both cases, they could result in a different action, depending on their context. To draw a figure on screen, there might exist a method **draw()**

```
circle->draw();
square->draw();
```

which behaves in a different way depending on whether it is a circle or a square invoking it. The ability to recognize the correct method is called *polymorphism*.

We can think of the state of an object as a set of data representing it. However, the state does not depend on the particular chosen representation. For example, suppose a programmer wants to write a statement to move a circle. With procedural programming, he needs to express a vector `delta` in the initially selected convention (for example, a couple of rational numbers representing its Cartesian coordinates). On the contrary, in OOP, the vector representation is completely inside the object. Indeed, in well-made software the programmer should have the choice between employing the Cartesian, polar, cylindrical, and so on, representations, independently of the internal representation of the vector state.

This simplicity of OOPs is only apparent as large part of the complexity remains hidden. It requires a good abstraction capacity and much experience in problem analysis. In the procedural paradigm even beginners are able to produce good results. Instead, even expert programmers often write dreadful applications in object-oriented languages. This greater complexity of the object-oriented technology is compensated by the vast possibilities of reusing successful code in case of very structured programs. A detailed description of the properties of object-oriented programming languages is beyond the scope of this textbook. We refer the interested reader to the numerous specialized textbooks available, among which [Deitel and Deitel (2011)] and [Koenig and Moo (2000)].

However, we support the reader who is willing to learn object oriented programming, providing a free addendum to this textbook, available at our website at `http://www.scientificprogramming.org`. The addendum is organized in chapters whose numbering follows the one of this textbook, marked with ++, e.g. Chapter 5++ of the OOP addendum is intended to be read after Chapter 5 of this textbook.

Supporters of procedural programming consider its intrinsic simplicity to be an obvious advantage with respect to object-oriented programming. Instead, enthusiasts of the latter appreciate how natural object-oriented programming comes. Indeed, the concepts used in object-oriented languages are the same as the ones used to describe a problem in spoken language. Actually, as often occurs, which programming model is selected depends much on the context. OOP enforces greater formal rigor, allows several programmers to work independently but coherently and promotes to reuse the code by means of the *inheritance* property: all classes derived from another class "inherit" the code of the latter as if it belongs to them. Therefore, OOP is preferred for developing large and complex applications on which many programmers are working. Smaller applications of possibly reduced complexity[12] is a lot more complicated and tedious in the object paradigm with respect to the procedural one. On the other hand, the implementation of algorithms is intrinsically procedural. It is then worth learning a procedural programming language, given that methods are intended to manipulate the state of the objects, represented, in any case, by data.

2.6   Why C?

Learning to program is a bit like learning how to talk. A newborn baby is not able to communicate his needs with a language. However, with time he learns to talk, and everyone does so in his own mother tongue (in Italian, in English, in French, etc.). Learning how to talk is different form learning a language. Once one is able to talk, it is not so difficult to learn a new language. The difficulty is not in understanding the words or the grammatical and syntactical rules of a language, but rather in building the logical processes allowing to formulate sentences that make sense. The latter should be such that once they are defined, they can be expressed and understood in many different languages.

The same occurs in software development. Indeed, learning to program means acquiring the most efficient methods and techniques to formalize the solution of a problem or reach a purpose through a finite series of well-defined steps, called an algorithm. Once we know how to do this, the algorithm can be expressed in any of various languages. In order to start talking we need a language. Similarly, to learn how to program, we need a programming language. Once we know one programming language, it is not difficult to learn others and implement the same algorithm with different programs. To this purpose we chose the C language which was created in 1972, but today is still used in all fields, including scientific applications. The basic structure is relatively simple and its syntax is the same as the one of C++ (so, once one masters the C syntax, the C++ syntax also comes natural)[13]. Also, the scientific problems discussed in this textbook

---

[12]By complexity, here, we understand a measure of the number of existing relations between the various concepts required to describe the nature of the problem.

[13]This is why some consider C++ an evolution of C. Actually, the two languages are

can be solved by algorithms which are often intrinsically procedural, even if they can be better described in terms of objects. Thus, it is appropriate to write them in a language such as C. Moreover, many other languages, from Perl over Java to Python, have a syntax borrowed from the C syntax. Therefore, the latter is a good investment. Even the more modern languages used to develop *apps* for mobile devices and tablets adopt a syntax very similar to that of C. Thanks to statements which may manipulate the computer memory directly, the C language is a high-level language "close" to the hardware. It makes easier to understand some computer mechanisms which are hidden in other languages.

Obviously, we could have chosen other languages. For example, many introductory courses in programming adopt Pascal or BASIC. These languages are generally not really used though by researchers. Therefore, we did not consider them. The same goes for languages such as MATLAB, often adopted for introductions to scientific computation. We also excluded languages that are not very widespread (Ada, Forth, Ruby and many others) and, obviously, those used mainly in specific, non-scientific applications (such as COBOL, oriented towards management applications).

For decades FORTRAN 77 has been one of the most used programming languages for scientific applications. Indeed, it is particularly fit to solve mathematical problems (FORTRAN stands for FORmula TRANslator). However, since a few years now, the software of big scientific experiments (particle physics, astrophysics, molecular biology, etc.) is being developed in object-oriented languages such as C++. Moreover, FORTRAN is rarely used in other areas (commercial, *real-time*, basic software and general use applications). Therefore, we also excluded this language.

On the other hand, to learn how to program an object-oriented language seemed a bit too extreme for those who want to learn how to write computer programs for scientific applications. Indeed, object-oriented programming is particularly abstract. Also, it hides some intrinsic characteristics of how the machine works which we retain useful to know. For this reason, we have excluded both C++ and Java. You can learn the basics of the C++ language with the addendum freely available at our website. There is a clear advantage in learning that language together with C, being the basic syntax the same. Java, on the other hand, is very similar to C++, and can be easily learnt after it.

---

profoundly different. The syntax of the basic statements is the same, thus allowing to create programs apparently written in C, yet compilable with a C++ compiler. However, the two compilers are not compatible.

2.7 History and characteristics of the C language

The C language was created in 1972 by Dennis Ritchie to program the DEC PDP-11, a machine produced by the Bell Laboratories in the USA.

It was actually an evolution of the B language [Thompson (1972)] defined by Ken Thompson and used to create the first operating system: UNIX®. In turn, the B language was formulated starting from BCPL (*Basic Combined Programming Language*) [Richards (1967)], developed in 1967 by Martin Richards to write basic software (operating systems and compilers).

In the late seventies of the XX century, Dennis Ritchie and Brian Kernighan established the version which is currently in use [Kernighan and Ritchie (1988)][14]. Later, the various software producers, often tied to hardware producers in competition with each other, gave rise to a series of variants considered "dialects" of C. Due to this proliferation of languages, a program written for a certain hardware platform required corrections such as eliminating or substituting special statements used for the original version, before being executable on another. In order to facilitate the process of adapting programs to various platforms (*porting*), producers and programmers set up a committee for standardization. The competent organisms (ANSI and ISO) defined a standard of the language in 1990. The C defined in the document published by this organization [ANSI (1995)] is indicated today as ANSI-C. The use of standard ANSI allows one to write portable programs, compatible with any operating system without running into errors.

C is a procedural language, not fully structured and typed. We already know what procedural means. A language is said to be structured if certain rules are obeyed when expressing the sequence of actions in the code. In Chapter 4 we discuss these rules for C in detail. In particular, structured programs do not allow to transfer the control of operations from one portion of code to another non-adjacent one by means of operations of the goto kind. C possesses a certain number of these statements allowing the execution flow to jump from one part to another. Therefore, it is not strictly structured. However, a program in C can always be rewritten without making use of these statements, resulting in a structured C program.

C is a typed language. This means that all data need to be declared before they can be used in a program and this declaration should spec-

---

[14]In 2003 B. Kernighan declared in an interview on the Linux Journal [Dolya (2003)] that his only contribution to the development of C was to help Ritchie write the book, and that the latter should get all the merit.

ify their type (integer, rational, string, etc.). Still, C is not considered a *strongly typed* language. Indeed, it is always possible to interpret a bit sequence corresponding to data of a certain type as if they belonged to another type. In C, errors due to bad programming can always be eliminated by using the methods of structured programming. However, it is not always possible to avoid the use of so-called *type casting*, i.e., the transformation of one type to another (Section 3.2).

Nevertheless (and, in some cases, even thanks to this flexibility), C is quite adapted as a first language to learn the scientific programming methods.

2.8   C compilers in their environment

The *operating system* is a program that, when a computer is turned on, is loaded into its memory and immediately executed (*bootstrapped* in technical jargon). It takes care of the management of the computer resources (the CPU, the memory, the peripherals) and allows the programmer to interact with these by giving instructions (in the form of text, signs, sounds, etc.) without knowing the particular hardware structure of the machine or how the memory is organized[15].

In theory, many different operating systems can be loaded on each CPU (not at the same time though). The most widespread ones are Microsoft® Windows®, Mac OS® and Linux. These are actually classes of operating systems as there exist many versions of each one of them. The versions may be more or less compatible, but they all have some common features. The Mac OS operating system is based on FreeBSD [Urban and Tiemann (2001)] (FreeBSD is a registered trademark of the FreeBSD Foundation). Like Linux, it is one of the many operating systems belonging to the UNIX family. We do not treat the Mac OS operating system separately, as the considerations made for Linux equally apply to Mac OS. In order to be able to write and compile C programs on a Mac OS computer you need to install the `Xcode` app. Depending on the version you may be required to install the "command line tools".

To develop C programs it is essential that the operating system of our machine is advanced enough. In these environments the concept of *file* is

---

[15]The operating system is loaded into the computer memory through a series of successive steps, starting with the execution of the BIOS (*Basic Input-Output System*). The BIOS, in turn, resides in a memory called ROM (*Read-Only Memory*) whose memory locations contain fixed statements and data.

defined as an ordered collection of data of whichever nature, registered in a permanent way on an appropriate physical medium, such as a (magnetic, optical or solid state) disk or a flash memory. Each file is identified by a name consisting of a possibly long string of characters[16] and a *path* identifying its position inside logical divisions of the disk called *directories*, which in turn carry a name. We can think of a file as if it were a sheet for notes with a title representing the file name. The directory is then a folder possibly containing several such sheets (file), but also subfolders[17]. The path indicates the sequence of folders that need to be opened to find the file. A C program is a file containing a sequence of strings, each one of which is a syntactically valid expression of the language. The names of the files are usually completed with an *extension*, i.e., a (usually short) character sequence separated from the actual name by a period ▪. The extension usually identifies the content of the file by its name. By convention, text files have the extension `txt`, files containing C code carry the extension `c`, `C` or `cc`. Generally, self-explanatory extensions are used[18].

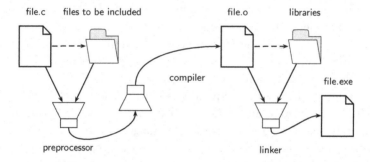

Fig. 2.3   The process starting from a C program up to its executable is composed of various steps, each one of which generates the necessary files for the next step.

Now, the steps leading to an effective C program (Figure 2.3) are the following.

---

[16]Not all available characters of a computer may be used to compose the name of a file. The list of legitimate characters depends on the operating system. Generally, all alphanumerical characters are allowed.

[17]Indeed, in some systems, due to this analogy a file is referred to as a *Document* and a directory is called a *Folder*.

[18]In some systems, extensions are optional and arbitrary, while in others they are mandatory and possibly fix the way a file is used.

(1) The code is written with a program (*editor*) used to insert the characters with the keyboard. The text is generally saved as a *file* (source file) on one of the computer disks.

(2) The source file is read by another program, called the *preprocessor*, executing statements, the so-called *directives*. These directives are not actually part of the language. Rather, they give instructions to the preprocessor to perform some operations on the input file. For more details we refer the reader to Section 3.5 of this textbook. In particular, the preprocessor can include the content of one or more files in the C code.

(3) The preprocessed file is passed on to the compiler who translates it into machine language and produces object code in a binary file (object file). The standard extension of the object file is o.

(4) The object file (or, if more than one, object files) is given as an input to the *linker*. The linker produces the executable by resolving the remaining undetermined symbols during compilation and adding the system libraries. As mentioned in footnote 18, in some systems the extension of the file fixes its behavior and is mandatory. Generally, executable files have the extension exe. In any case, it is good practice to follow a coherent convention and thus, to assign a file either names without any extension or always use the same meaningful extension (for example, exe).

In the easiest of cases, these operations occur in automatic. Compilers generally verify whether all the lines of text contained in the source file are syntactically correct expressions of the language. A syntax error stops the translation process and the error is reported to the programmer. Obviously no compiler is able to track down semantic or logical errors. Therefore, a successfully compiled program does not guarantee correct results. It is important to note that errors reported by the compiler may depend on each other. Indeed, a long sequence of error messages does not always imply many corrections are needed. This is why it is better to correct one error at a time, in the order in which they are listed by the compiler and recompiling the program each time. Often it is sufficient to correct the first error to get a working program.

2.8.1 *Linux and Windows*

Linux is an *Open Source* operating system, i.e., a system whose source code (written in C) is available to anyone, and can be downloaded for free from the Internet. It belongs to the family of UNIX operating systems and was initially developed by Linus Törvalds. Thanks to the collaboration of thousands of programmers around the world it evolved rapidly as they had access to the source code, could change, recompile and redistribute it. The main interface between the system and the machine is a program called *shell*, which is based on text. The input accepted by the shell are commands inserted with the keyboard. The shell interprets and execute them. Since several years also graphic environments (with windows) interfacing with the shell have been available. These are generically referred to as *Desktop Environments*. Strictly speaking, these environments are not part of the operating system. They are set up as additional applications and the user can freely select one of the many available ones or even just choose not to use them. A large part of the available Linux software is released with the same GPL license (*General Public License*) of the operating system and therefore, freely available together with the source code.

Instead, the Windows system is a commercial Microsoft product. Its name reflects the interface allowing the user to interact with the machine, which is almost exclusively graphic. The control elements are geometric figures (often rectangular, and thus called *windows*) with various functions which can be selected by means of a pointing device (a *mouse* or a *trackpad*) or activated by pressing a key. Although there does exist a textual interface in Windows (*Command Prompt*) available through a dedicated window, the graphic interface is used in most circumstances. Opposed to Linux, the source code of the Windows systems is secret. The user can only buy the user license of the compiled program.

2.8.2 A first example, in Linux: gcc

The C compiler is commonly installed on almost all Linux machines. Apart form the standard (*default*) compiler, others can be installed. These might be different in use or more capable of optimizing the code. There also exist graphic interfaces acting as IDE (*Integrated Desktop Environment*). The IDE is a kind of operating environment integrating all the functions of the software development: from text editing to loading the executable program into the memory.

The predefined compiler is the GNU compiler[19]. The `gcc` command, written in the shell, invokes the compiler to read the file passed on as a

---

[19]GNU is a recursive acronym invented by Richard Stallmann, father of the free software movement. It stands for "Gnu is Not Unix": the acronym is an open challenge to the AT&T who decided to make the source code of the UNIX operating system a secret, though its initial release was for free.

parameter and compiles it; `gcc` acts as an interface for the preprocessor, the compiler and the *linker*. Strictly speaking, the preprocessor is invoked by the `cpp` command, while the *linker* with the `ld` command.

In summary, in the simplest of cases, the programmer writes the program with an editor and assigns a name to the file. By convention, the name of the file, always ends with `.c` and should always be related to its contents. Once it is saved to disk, the file can be compiled with a command like:

`gcc -o programname.exe programname.c`

where `programname` is the name selected for the application. To load the compiled program into the memory and execute it, it is enough to invoke the command corresponding to the name of the executable file, preceded, if needed, by the path. In Linux, the path corresponding to the current working directory is indicated by a period . . The filename is separated form the path by a *slash*:

`./programname.exe`

In this way the program is executed and possible messages appear on screen.

Hands on 2.2 - Using the compiler in the Linux operating system

Copy the text of the Listing 3.8 in a file and name it `program.c`. To this purpose, use the `emacs` or `nedit` editor. For the time being it is not important to understand its contents. Just copy character by character (pay attention not to forget any as the expressions may become invalid!). Invoke the following command

`cpp program.c`

A long series of C statements, among which also the ones contained in the file `program.c` will appear on the screen. Indeed, the preprocessor executes the directives and directs the result to the *standard output* (`stdout`), i.e., the predefined output peripheral, which is usually the screen. In particular, note what happens to the symbol `G` and the characters enclosed between `/*` and `*/`. The `gcc` compiler always assumes that the input file first needs to be passed on to the preprocessor (an already preprocessed file will remain invariant under this action). Therefore, a command like

`gcc program.c`

automatically calls the preprocessor, who in turn sends its output as an input to the compiler. In turn, this invokes the *linker* which completes the object code with the system standard libraries to produce the executable. If no specific options were included, the name of the executable file is a.out (a list of the files contained in the directory in which we are working should include a file with this name). This name does not suggest in any way the name of the source file from which it was generated, nor the aim of the program. It is always recommendable to assign a name to the executable file which recalls its function. The option[20] -o changes the name of the executable file into the one specified after this option:

```
gcc -o program.exe program.c
```

The disk will now include a file with the name program.exe. In case we want to avoid the linking process, the compiler needs to be invoked with an appropriate option, excluding the linker to be called. The option avoiding automatic invocation of the *linker* is -c:

```
gcc -c program.c
```

In this case, the object file that was produced has a name after the source file name, whose left part is followed by a period and the extension o: program.o.

The *linker* can be called separately or, more commonly, by means of the gcc command itself. Indeed, if we invoke the compilation command on an object file, the latter is passed on to the *linker* during the last phase of compilation:

```
gcc -o program.exe program.o
```

In some cases it is necessary to indicate the libraries which are to be linked to the compiler. For example, if we copy the program of the Listing 3.8, the compilation command does not produce any executable. Some messages informing the user that some undefined symbols were included (the names of trigonometric functions, defined in the mathematics library) are displayed. To link a library to the object, the option -l, followed by the library name is used. The name of the mathematics library is plainly m. Thus, the compilation command will be:

```
gcc -o program.exe program.o -lm
```

Often it is useful to include the options -Wall -pedantic. The first option is responsible for visualizing *warning* messages in all cases in which the expressions used by the programmer could possibly generate errors during execution. The option -pedantic produces warning messages when the chosen format of the statements is not compatible with the ANSI standard.

---

[20]Command options of the UNIX operating system are specified on the same command line by means of characters preceded by one or two minus signs -. Options alter the way in which a command is executed.

For further information we refer the reader to the manuals available in bookstores, as [Gough (2005)], on the Internet or on line (using the `man gcc` command).

2.8.3 *Compiling C in Windows*

There are many different C compilers for Windows. Many of them are complex tools integrating various functions within an IDE (Integrated Development Environment). An IDE appears as a window including an editor, a debugger and menu–driven tools to compile, link and run the programs. Each product is different from the other and it is impossible to give details about how they work, however they are rather intuitive and should not deserve detailed explanation.

Usually, in these environments, a programmer defines a *project*. The project is contained in a directory called after the project name. All the source files needed to build the executable (apart from standard libraries), as well as other resources that may be needed (data files, images, etc.), are included in the project.

Once all the source files are saved in the project, the programmer can *build* or *make* the project: a process that automatically consists of preprocessing, compilation and linking.

Chapter 3

Basics of C programs

千里之行始于脚下

A journey of a thousand miles
begins with a single step

Lao Tsu, *Tao Te Ching*.

In this chapter we discuss the basic elements that are needed to build a computer program which solves a concrete problem; a discussion that will be continued and expanded throughout the following chapters. It is important to stress that this text aims more at formalizing a problem and encoding it rather than describing the programming language. This is why we progressively introduce basic elements of the C language by using simple, but realistic programs. We do not cover the syntactical aspects of the C language in an exhaustive way, but just illustrate their most common use. For a complete description of the C syntax, we refer the reader to manuals like [Kernighan and Ritchie (1988); Kelley and Pohl (1998)].

This text contains both solved as to be solved examples of problems encountered in general physics, logics and mathematics. It does not cover operational or systems theory programs, which are beyond the scope of this book.

3.1   Starting to program

Given a solvable problem, generally its solution is an algorithm, i.e., a finite series of well-determined steps. A computer program is the translation of one or more algorithms in some programming language. It is also a symbolic and abstract way to represent problems, theoretical models and experimental phenomena. Each program needs a *starting point*. Independent of the complexity, the aim or the structure of the program, for both technical and logical reasons it is necessary to have a beginning.

The starting point of a program generally consists of a block of statements, which are identified by a specific name and differ in various programming languages. For instance, FORTRAN requires a statement `PROGRAM` which is then followed by the name of the program; in Java there exists one sole class `main`; in the C language (as in C++) the starting point is a *function* called `main`, mandatory to correctly compile being the program execution starting point. For now, we do not explain what is a function in the C language, as the subject is treated in Chapter 7. We limit ourselves to defining a function as the constituent block of a C program, syntactically expressed as

```
type name ([arguments]) {
...statements   ...
}
```

where `name` is the name we assigned to the function, `type` is the type of value returned by the function (Section 3.2) and `[arguments]` indicates a list of optional values which are passed onto the function by the calling program. The curly brackets `{}` include the *body* of the function, namely the C code performing the function tasks.

Given the requirement of a `main` function for each C program, the successive development of the program itself depends on its complexity. For simple programs consisting of up to few hundred lines of code, the `main` function usually coincides with the entire program. For more complex programs, the `main` function usually is very short. It is reduced to several lines of code, which typically call an initialization function, and successively delegate the execution of the program to other parts of it by calling other functions.

Note that there is no structural difference between the `main` function and other functions written in a C program, apart from the fact that the `main` function cannot be omitted, and the execution of a program starts with `main`. Indeed, in order to to avoid any ambiguity the name `main` is reserved to this initial function.

To conclude this section we recall that in the C language (as in C++ [Deitel and Deitel (2011)], in Perl [Wall *et al.* (2000)] and almost all other modern languages) upper and lowercase letters are not equivalent (*case sensitive language*); it is thus mandatory to have a `main` function, while a function `MAIN` or `Main` is acceptable, but not sufficient to compile a complete program.

The statements in C do not require any specific formatting: C is a free format language. The only rules which must be followed are:

- non-reserved words other than keywords follow composition rules which are discussed in detail in Section 3.2;
- each single statement must end with the character `;` (as in a = 2;);
- several instructions can be grouped by a couple of curly brackets `{}` and thus constitute a *composite statement* or *block*; in this case no character `;` is required after the curly bracket `}` as is clear from the example

    {a = 2; b = 3; c = a + b;}

In conclusion, a C program is composed of at least a `main` function and possibly some other functions; each function is made of statements which follow the syntactical rules of the language. In the next section we discuss the nature of these statements.

3.2   Statements, variables, types

The statements in the C language are sequences of symbols the compiler translates into executable code. A statement may contain variables, constants, operators, keywords and functions. Keywords are reserved, they are recognized by the compiler and cannot be used under a different meaning. For instance, the word `while` is a reserved word in C: it corresponds to an iterative instruction and thus cannot be used to denote a variable as in the statement

    while = 2;

A syntactically correct combination of operators, variables and constants defines an *expression*.

Variables and constants are fundamental elements of programming: they represent the components of a problem in the logic context of a program. Physical, numerical or abstract quantities, counting indices, etc. are all represented by variables or constants. A *variable* is defined as a symbolic name associated to a quantity or a memory location; the reserved memory location is determined by the *type* of the variable. For instance, an *integer* variable is generally associated to 32 bits; a variable of the *character* type is associated to a byte (8 bits). By definition the variable may take on other values throughout the execution of a program. Instead, a *constant* is a quantity associated to a symbol and a memory location whose size is always determined by the type of constant, and its value remains fixed throughout the entire duration of the program. Any attempt to change the value of a constant provokes a fatal error when compiling the program. Some examples of constants are, for instance, 2 (the integer 2), 2.0 (the decimal 2.0), 2.(the same decimal 2.0 where we omitted the 0 after the period).

When programming in the C language (as is the case in C++) you always need to declare all variables and functions in order to make sure the program compiles. A variable always needs to be declared before it can be used. The *declarations* inform the compiler of the existence of variables and functions, the space they take in memory and the *type* of representation of their value. A language which follows this rule is called *typed*. Often C is defined as a *strongly typed* language. However, as it is possible to change the type which was originally assigned to a variable, it is more appropriate to consider it a *weakly typed* language.

The fundamental types of variables are `int`, `float`, `double`, `char`, which respectively refer to integer variables (`int`), variables representing rational numbers, also called floating-point numbers (`float` and `double`), and characters (`char`). There exist specifiers of the fundamental types who change the precision by assigning a smaller or larger number of bits to the memory of the variable. The specifiers are `signed`, `unsigned`, `short`, `long`. Only some combinations make sense, such as `unsigned int` or `long double`. Note that the number of bits associated to a certain type of variable has lost its original meaning in today versions of the C language on a 32 bit architecture. For instance, today the declarations `int`, `long int`, `signed long int` all correspond to integers of 32 bits with a sign; `float` and `double` to rational numbers of 32 and 64 bits with sign, respectively. The declaration of an integer word of 64 bits, i.e., with extended precision, requires a `long long int` type; the `long double` type represents a floating-point variable of 96 bits. Note that the `long long int` type is not defined in ANSI C [ANSI (1995)]. The number of bits assigned to these types can be different on 64 bit architectures or may depend on the compiler. This text is based on an architecture and compiler as defined in the Technical Note.

In table 3.1 we list some of the allowed combinations, the corresponding meaning and the number of bits allocated in memory on a typical 32 bit architecture.

Table 3.1   Types of variables.

Type	Variable	Number of bits
char	character	8
short	integer	16
int	integer	32
long	integer	32
float	rational	32
long long int	integer	64
double	rational	64
long double	rational	96

For all **int** types listed in Table 3.1, the **unsigned** prefix does not change the number of bits; it represents only positive numbers by assigning the highest bit a power of 2 instead of a sign (see Section 1.3.1). The interval in which integer and rational numbers are represented for a specific given system can be deduced from two system files **limits.h** and **float.h**, called *header* files (Section 3.5). How the floating-point variables **float** and **double** are represented in memory is discussed in Chapter 1. The floating-point constants use the sign . (dot) as a separator between the integer and the decimal part as in

```
pi = 3.1415;
```

A rational numerical constant whose decimal part is zero still needs to be written with a decimal point, otherwise it is interpreted as an integer (Section 3.3.1 describes a consequence of this type of error);

```
b = 2.;
```

indicates that the variable **b** has value 2.0 . The variables of the character type are defined by delimiting the character by a pair of quotes ' . . . ' as in

```
char a;
a = 'Z';
```

where the variable **a** assumes the value of the character Z , i.e., 90 in ASCII code (Appendix B). In C the character strings are represented in a different way than in other languages; we discuss them in detail in Chapter 5. Finally, it must be noted that in the ANSI version of C [ANSI (1995)] the variable declarations inside a function or a block must be declared at the beginning of the function or the block in which they are used. In so-called C99 [ISO (1999)], as in C++, it is possible to declare a variable at any point within a function or block, as long as it precedes its actual use.

As in all programming languages, C follows a convention on how to name variables. In particular, the name of a variable may start with any letter, uppercase or lowercase, or with the *underscore* sign _ and can contain uppercase or lowercase letters, numbers and the underscore sign _. Instead, the following characters are not allowed

.   , ; :   + - = / \ * < > !   ?   ~ @ # $ % ^ & | " ` '

all types of brackets, the "blank" and all special characters. Finally, the name of a variable cannot start with a number. Examples of both valid and non-valid names in C are given in Table 3.2.

Table 3.2 Valid and non-valid variable names.

Valid name	Non-valid name
car_of_Bob	Bob's car
_1F	1F
xyzyzy	xyz:zy
x4756	.4756
__a	+a

At the end of this section we want to address the reader's attention to the conversion rules between variables and constants of different types. The C language adopts a general criterion aimed at avoiding any loss of information in expressions involving different types. More specifically, a variable of the **double** type potentially contains more information than a variable of the **float** type, which in turn contains potentially more information than one of the **int** type[1]. The reason is obvious: in a **double** variable for instance there are more decimal digits available, and therefore it has a higher precision. From this it is clear that an operation, for instance, between an integer and a **double** constant results in a **double**. The same holds for operations between constants and variables or between variables of different types. In general, an operation between different types produces a result of the type which is richer in information; for this reason the conversion

---

[1]It is not always true that a variable of the **float** type contains more information than one of the **int** type. Indeed, as only 23 bits are available for the significant digits of a **float**, an integer larger than 2^{24} represented in **float** could cause the loss of precision.

criterium is often defined as type *promotion*. In any case, as described in
Section 3.3.1, in an expression some operations are executed before others,
and this together with type promotion can cause some unexpected results.

3.3 Operators

Variables and constants are manipulated by *operators*. Note that the meaning of operators in a programming language differs from what is intended
by operators in a mathematics context. In mathematics the term *operator* is synonymous with *function* and it is used to indicate an application
which associates an element $x \in A$ to an element $y \in B$. The sets A and
B are called the *domain* and *co-domain* of the operator, respectively. You
can have operators which correspond to simple applications, such as the
sum operator, symbolized by the $+$ sign. Its domain is the set of number
pairs and it associates to each pair (a, b) a number c which is obtained by
adding a to b. There also exist operators which correspond to complex
applications, such as the derivative operator d/dx, acting upon the space
of derivable functions $f(x)$ and associates to each of these the derivative
$f'(x) \equiv \frac{df(x)}{dx}$.

In a programming language, an operator is a *symbol* (not necessarily one
sole character) associated to an *elementary* mathematical or logical operation; in programming languages there do not exist any operators playing the
role of the mathematical derivation operator or other operators of similar
complexity. There do exist operators which play the role of the mathematical sum (or product, division, etc.) operator. In programming an operator
acts on a single operand (*unary* operators) or two operands (*binary* operators). In C there also exists one single *ternary* operator, which is discussed
in Section 4.2.2. In this section, we illustrate the most commonly used
operators.

3.3.1 *Arithmetic Operators*

In Table 3.3 the elementary operators corresponding to the four arithmetic
operations are shown. All of these are binary operators.

A fundamental binary operator is the assignment operator $=$. The latter
is deeply different from the analogous symbol in mathematics: the mathematical expression $a = 2$ indicates the value of a and therefore it does not
make sense to write $k = k + 1$ in a mathematical expression. In the C lan-

Table 3.3   Arithmetic operators.

Operation	Symbol	Example
addition	+	a + b
subtraction	–	a - b
product	*	a * b
division	/	a / b

guage the expression a = 2 means *set the value* 2 *in the memory location allocated to the variable* a. Hence, the statement k = k + 1 makes perfect sense and implies *set* k *equal to its current value plus* 1, i.e., *increment the variable* k *by 1 unit*. This is a very frequently occurring operation.

Another interesting operator is the modulus operator % which returns the rest of a division between two integers. For example 5 % 2 is equal to 1, while 32 % 6 is equal to 2.

Among the unary operators, there are the increment ++ and decrement -- operators, which can be placed either before or after the operand. In the first case (pre-increment or pre-decrement) the operand is modified before the expression is evaluated, in the second case (post-increment or post-decrement) the operand is first evaluated and then modified:

```
a = 2;
b = ++a;
```

In this example (pre-increment) the variable a in the second statement is first augmented to 3 and then assigned to b, which also has the value 3. Instead, in

```
a = 2;
b = a++;
```

the variable a is first assigned to b, which takes on the value 2, and next augmented to 3 (post-increment). The - sign applied as a unary operator is called the negation operator and returns the value which is opposite in sign with respect to the variable on which it operates. For example, in

```
a = 2;
a = -a;
```

a takes on the value −2 after the application of the - operator. The expressions in which the value of a variable is modified by means of a mathematical operation can be written in a more compact way, for example

```
b += 2;
```

which is equivalent to

```
b = b + 2;
```

and similarly for `-=`, `*=`, `/=`. This notation is more synthetic and evaluates the variable on which it operates one single time, resulting in a faster execution.

We can now illustrate the use of arithmetic operators and types by means of a simple example. We consider a program converting the degrees of temperature from the Fahrenheit scale into the Celsius scale. Recall that

$$T_C = (T_F - 32) \times \frac{5}{9}, \tag{3.1}$$

where T_F indicates the temperature in degrees Fahrenheit and T_C the temperature in degrees Celsius.

```
1 main () {
2     double tc, tf, conv;
3     double offset = 32.;
4
5     conv = 5./ 9.;
6     tc = (tf - offset) * conv;
7 }
```

Listing 3.1   Conversion of measurement units.

As mentioned above, the program Listing 3.1 starts with the **main** function, which encloses its constituent statements between curly brackets. The first two statements are declarations of variables, followed by assignments and expressions. In particular, note that we declared the following variables to be of the **double** type as they correspond to rational numbers: `tc` and `tf`, which represent the temperature in degrees Celsius T_C and degrees Fahrenheit T_F, respectively, and the conversion constant `conv`. Next, we both declared and initialized at the same time the variable `offset`. This procedure of declaring a variable and contemporarily assigning a value to that variable is always allowed in the C language. The constants `32.`, `9.` and `5.` all contain a dot, indicating that they implemented in the floating-point representation (Section 3.2). Following the declarations, the other two statements both contain arithmetic operations and assignments of their results to new variables: `conv = 5./ 9.`, `tc = (tf - offset) * conv`. The variables `conv` and `offset` are not strictly necessary as we could have written straight away `tc = (tf - 32.) * 5./ 9.;`. Our choice highlights that `32.` is a scale variable, while the fraction `5./ 9.` is a conversion factor. Finally, note the choice of significant variable names, such as `tf` for T_F etc., which is just an example of a programming *style* resulting in easily readable programs. For instance, the Listing 3.2 performs the same computation of Listing 3.1, though its meaning is a lot less clear.

```
1 main () {
2    double x1, x2, y;
3
4    y = 32.;
5    x1 = (x2 - y) * 5./ 9.;
6 }
```

Listing 3.2   Cryptic conversion of measurement units.

If we delete the variable `conv` in Listing 3.1 and directly insert the conversion factor $\frac{5}{9}$ into the computation of T_C, we obtain the Listing 3.3.

```
1 main () {
2    double tc, tf;
3    double offset = 32.;
4
5    tc = (tf - offset) * 5./ 9.;
6 }
```

Listing 3.3   Conversion of measurement units.

If we omitted the parenthesis in the statement on line 5, writing `tc = tf - offset * 5./ 9.;`, the resulting computation would be wrong! The reason is that in this case the product `offset * 5./ 9.` would be carried out before the subtraction `tf - offset` since the addition `+` and subtraction operators `-` have a lower priority than the product `*` and division operators `/`. This is just a particular instance of a general rule as all operators follow *priority* rules establishing which operator is executed first in an expression. The order of priority of arithmetic operators (including the assignment operator `=`) is listed in Table 3.4, where the first line contains the operator with the highest priority. Operators with the same priority are executed from left to right.

As listed in Table 3.4, the operators `*`, `/`, `%` have a higher priority than the operators `+`, `-`. Thus, in the expression `a + b * c`, the product `b * c` is computed first and then added to `a`. If the Listing 3.1 had contained the following expression

```
tc = tf - offset * 5./ 9.;
```

this would have been interpreted as

Table 3.4   Order of priority of arithmetic operators.

- (negation, unary)
* (multiplication) / (division) % (modulus)
+ (addition) - (subtraction, binary)
= (assignment)

```
tc = tf - (offset * 5./ 9.);
```

instead of the correct expression

```
tc = (tf - offset) * 5./ 9.;
```

The parentheses are redundant if the operations respect the right order of priority. Instead, parentheses ( ) can be used to change the priority order as expressions contained within the most internally parenthesis are evaluated first.

Let us consider some examples on the priority of arithmetic operators.

```
a = 2; b = 3; c = 5;
d = a + b * c;
```

The variable d has value 17.

```
a = 2; b = 3; c = 5;
d = (a + b) * c;
```

The variable d has value 25.

```
a = 2; b = 3; c = 5;
d = a + (b * c);
```

The variable d has value 17. The parentheses are optional as they do not change the result.

Finally, let us return to the topic of type conversion, taking into account the different operators priority. As mentioned above, C automatically *promotes* types:

```
double a;
a = 9;
```

a has value 9.0, i.e., the decimal representation of the constant 9, which is here used without the decimal separator .. Consider

```
double a;
a = 5 / 9.;
```

the integer constant 5 is *promoted* to the rational number 5.0 as the second operand of / is the rational constant 9.. Thus, the ratio is correctly computed as 0.555 556 and assigned to a. Instead

```
double a;
a = 5 / 9;
```

results in the value 0 for a as the ratio between the two integer constants 5 and 9 is the integer part of 0.555 556. Similarly,

```
int k;
k = 5 / 9.;
```

assigns the value 0 to k. The integer constant 5 is *promoted* to the rational number 5.0, the ratio equals 0.555 556 but is assigned to an integer variable, truncating the value to 0.

What happens if we write (tf - offset) * 5 / 9 without the decimal separator in 5 and 9 in Listing 3.1? In this case the result is less obvious than it seems. The multiplication * and division operators / have the same priority. However, as the compiler evaluates the expression form left to right, i.e., in (tf - offset) * 5 the constant 5 is promoted to double, everything is divided by the constant 9, which is also first promoted to a double, the result is correct.

Summarizing, in this case the expressions

```
(tf - offset) * 5./ 9.
(tf - offset) * 5./ 9
(tf - offset) * 5 / 9.
(tf - offset) * 5 / 9
```

all give the same result. This does not exempt us from paying particular attention to the use of the decimal separator . in rational constants. By now it should be clear that rewriting the previous conversion as

```
5 / 9 * (tf - offset)
```

gives 0 as a result. Likewise, let us examine the code

```
int k = 3;
double a, b;
a = k * 4 / 5;
b = 4 / 5 * k;
```

In arithmetics the fraction $\frac{4}{5}$ equals 0.8 and both a and b equal 2.4. In C, however, the order of the operations is important and only the integer part of the expression $k * 4/5 = 2.4$ is evaluated, resulting in 2, which is then promoted into a double in a. For the variable b the difference is even more striking as b results to be 0! It suffices to introduce the . after the constant 4

```
int k = 3;
double a, b;
a = k * 4./ 5;
b = 4./ 5 * k;
```

to obtain the correct result for both a and b, i.e., 2.4 .

Exercise 3.1 - Conversion and priority

Evaluate the result of the following expressions in the C language, then explain the obtained results.

```
int i = 10, j = 4, k, n;
double a, b, c;
a = i + 3.5 * j;
k = (a - i) / j;
n = a - i / j;
b = (a - i) / j;
c = a - i / j;
```

3.3.2 *Logical operators*

In this section we discuss the operators corresponding to the logical operations described in Section 1.6.1. In C the binary operator **AND** is expressed by the symbol && and the binary operator **OR** by the symbol ||. Obviously, the rules explained in Section 1.6.1 and the corresponding truth tables remain valid. Also the unary logical negation operator ! exists, which produces the opposite logical value of the operand to which it is applied.

Some languages define a dedicated variable type, so-called *boolean* or *logical*, to treat values which are either true or false. In C, any expression which is equal to 0 when evaluated as an integer is defined as *false*, and everything which has a value *different* from 0 is defined as *true*. On the other hand, a true result produced by a logical expression has value 1. In Section 3.3.3 we discuss how this convention can be adopted in a non-obvious way.

Note that there does not exist an operator which corresponds to the **XOR** or exclusive **OR**. As mentioned in Section 1.6.1, there exist various ways to obtain a similar logical operation, one of which is a **XOR** b = ((a && !b) || (!a && b)).

3.3.3 *Other operators*

To complete the C operator overview, we must include the comparative or relational operators and the sizeof() operator. We refer the reader to Chapter 14 for the discussion of operators on a single bit.

The relational operators listed in Table 3.5, serve to compare the values of variables. The expressions containing them result in either a true or false value depending on the outcome of the comparison.

Table 3.5   Relational operators.

Operator	Relation
>	larger than
>=	larger than or equal to
<	smaller than
<=	smaller than or equal to
==	equal to
!=	not equal to

Note that the equal operator is defined as == and not as =, which is the assignment operator. Mixing up these two operators is one of the typical mistakes of newbies to programming in C.

We can now discuss the global priority hierarchy of the operators we discussed so far, which is given in Table 3.6. Remember that operators of the same priority are executed from left to right in the order in which they appear in a statement.

Table 3.6   Order of priority for all operators.

```
++ (post) -- (post)
++ (pre) -- (pre) ! -(unary)
* / %
+ - (binary)
< <= > >=
== !=
&&
||
= += -= *= /=
```

It is interesting to discuss some examples which include both logical and relational operators. What is the value of the variable **b** after executing the following statements ?

```
a = 2;
b = a == 2;
```

The answer is easy. First the expression **a == 2** is evaluated since the equal operator **==** has a higher priority than the assignment operator **=**, and it is true. This result is set to the variable **b**, which therefore takes on the value 1.

```
a = 2; b = 3; c = 5;
b = a >= c ;
```

In this case the variable **b** takes on the value 0, as the variable **a** is smaller than the variable **c**, hence the expression **a >= c** is false.

The logical operators **< <= > >=** all have the same priority. Instead, the operators **==** and **!=** have a lower priority than the former ones, but between them have an equal priority.

The **sizeof()** operator returns the number of bytes in memory for a given expression or variable type. For instance, the number of bytes of an **int** variable on a given system can be retrieved by including the following lines of code

```
a = sizeof(int);
```

where the variable **a** contains the desired information. The use of the **sizeof()** operator is discussed in more detail in Chapter 10.

Finally, we discuss the *cast* or conversion operator. In Section 3.3.1 we discussed implicit type conversion or promotion in mixed expressions. It is possible to perform an explicit type conversion to use, for example, an integer variable in decimal format without changing the variable in a permanent way. The *cast* operator is a unary operator which has a higher priority than the binary operators, as is the case for all unary operators. The syntax of the *cast* operator is

```
(new type) operand
```

Consider the following statements:

```
int i = 3;
double a;
a = (double) i / 2;
```

Without the (double) *cast* operator, the variable a would take the value 0. Instead, by including the *cast* operator the integer variable i is converted into a double only in the context of the expression where (double) operates, while the integer variable i itself remains equal to 3. The expression is promoted to a double and a takes the value 1.5.

3.4 Input/Output for beginners

Let us compile the Listing 3.1. The compilation does not give any errors and the program is executed without any problems. Nonetheless, we do not observe any effect of this execution. The reason is simple: the Listing 3.1 does not contain any *input/output* statements, (I/O), i.e., statements which receive external data or return data from the program to an external device. The most obvious extension of the program Listing 3.1 consists in asking the user to supply a value of T_C for the variable tc and print the computed value of T_F (tf) as this is simply the aim of a measurement unit conversion program!

Before entering the details of the syntax of I/O statements, we briefly discuss what receiving input or producing an output means in practice. In today computers an interactive program can receive input from any device that has been designed for this aim, for instance, from the keyboard or a file on a disk. In both cases, the program receives data through a communication channel which is managed by the operating system. Programming languages supply *native* functions which operate as an interface between I/O services of the system. The same holds for producing output. A program may write on devices, such as a terminal or a file, by using output functions of the language which depend on the operating system services.

The C language uses the **scanf** function to receive input from the keyboard and the **fscanf** function to receive input from a file. The output functions are **printf** to write to a terminal and **fprintf** to write to a file. These functions have a very complex syntax allowing one to use a variety of formats. In the remainder of this section, we illustrate just a part of the existing options and refer the reader to a C language manual for a complete overview [Kernighan and Ritchie (1988); Kelley and Pohl (1998)]. We anticipate that when using the **scanf** function a symbol of the C language is included whose meaning shall be clarified in Chapter 6. For now it suffices to follow the syntax of the command.

```
1 main() {
2     double tc, tf, offset, conv;
3     offset = 32.;
4     conv = 5./ 9.;
5     printf("Value in degrees Fahrenheit = ");
6     scanf("%lf", &tf);
7     tc = (tf - offset) * conv;
8     printf("Value in degrees Celsius = %f", tc);
9 }
```

Listing 3.4 Measurement unit conversion with I/O.

Reconsider the Listing 3.1 adding the I/O statements: examine the `printf` statement on line 5 in Listing 3.4. Between the parentheses ( ) there is a string of characters which is delimited by double quotes on each side "···". On line 5, the string is `Value in degrees Fahrenheit =`, and this string is printed on the output device (for instance the terminal). The aim is to be able to write informative messages that indicate what the program is computing, or what operations it is performing and similar information. On line 8 the syntax of the string included between the parentheses ( ) is slightly different: besides the message to be printed, it also includes a term `%f`. This term is called a *format specifier* as it serves to *specify the format* of the variable which follows the message. In this case the format specifier `%f` informs the compiler that the variable `tc` is of the `double` type, such that it can be correctly printed out onto the output. The `printf` function admits a variable number of arguments, separated from each other by a comma `,`. Its generic format is

```
printf("character string"[,exp1, exp2,...]);
```

The `character string` is always enclosed between double quotes "···", and, in case it is followed by one or more expressions which need to be printed out, it contains a format specifier for each expression which follows: the format specifier has the form `%characters` and reflects the type of the expression it corresponds to. The expressions `exp1, exp2,...` are optional and their number may vary. We use the term *expressions* as `exp1` could be either a simple variable or a complex expression since we could have written `printf("Value in degrees Celsius = %f",(tf - offset) * conv);` i.e., we could have computed the value of `tc` directly in the arguments of `printf`. The format specifier `%f` refers to a quantity which is represented in floating-point format. In Table 3.7 the most frequently used format specifiers are listed for `printf`.

Table 3.7   Output format specifiers.

Format specifier	Type
%f,%e,%g	float,double
%d,%i	int
%c	char (single)
%s	char (string)

The `scanf` function, on line 6 of Listing 3.4, serves to read the value of one or more input variables (for instance from the keyboard). Its format is similar to that of the `printf` function. However, there are some important differences between the two. A first difference is that in the `scanf` function only format specifiers of the variables which are to be acquired can be included between the double quotes "···". A second difference is the presence of the **&** symbol in the `scanf` function which must preceed every such variable.

The general syntax of the `scanf` statement is

```
scanf("character string",&var1[,&var2,...]);
```

The *character string* enclosed between double quotes "···" contains all format specifiers of the variables which are to be acquired in var1, var2,...and only those. Also in this case, the number of variables which follow the *character string* are not fixed and each variable must be preceded by the **&** character. On line 6 of Listing 3.4 the format specifier %lf for the `double` type variable tf is used. Note that if a format specifier %f corresponding to the `float` type were used, the program would behave differently. In Table 3.8 we list the most frequently used format specifiers for reading purposes.

Table 3.8   Input format specifiers.

Format specifier	Type
%f	float
%lf	double
%Lf, %llf	long double
%d, %i	int
%u	unsigned int
%Lu	unsigned long long int
%c	char (single)
%s	char (string)

The I/O functions for files are discussed in Chapter 6.

Finally, let us underline that the program Listing 3.4 actually does not compile correctly[2]; The reason is connected to the considerations made in Section 2.4, i.e. the necessity to *link* the code written by the programmer (Listing 3.4) to the already existing code, which in this case concerns the code for the `printf` and `scanf` functions. Indeed, the I/O functions `printf` and `scanf` are not written by the person who encodes a program to solve a given problem; rather they are already available from the C compiler, which is why they are generally called *system functions.*

Exercise 3.2 - I/O statements

 Write down `printf` and `scanf` statements to read the input from a `double` type variable a and a `long int` type variable k, based on a message that is printed by the program. Next, print out the values of a and k multiplied by the constant `3.14`, preceded by an explanatory message.

However, the fact that these functions are available from the compiler does not imply they are automatically linked to the remainder of the code. In order to achieve this link between the "personal" code and the "system" code, we at least need *to include* the file with all the references to external code in the "personal" code. This file is a first example of a *header* file, i.e., a file consisting of generally used declarations and definitions which must be included in the program to complete it. In Chapter 7 we discuss the technical details of the functions in the C language, which clarifies the necessity to include header files. There exist both library *header* files for system functionalities or user *header* files for functionalities which are specific to the application under consideration. The library *header* files are defined by a name enclosed between angular brackets as in `<stdio.h>`; for the user *header* files we need to specify their complete path between double quotes as in `"/home/include/myInclude.h"`[3]. Thus, the program of Listing 3.4 needs to be corrected as in Listing 3.5.

---

[2]As explained in the next section there do exist compilers configured in such a way that they do not give any errors. However, in general, this affirmation is true.

[3]The compiler searches for the *header* files enclosed between angular brackets in either the predefined or the optionally specified *directory.*

```
1 #include <stdio.h>
2
3 main() {
4    double tc, tf, offset, conv;
5
6    offset = 32.;
7    conv = 5./ 9.;
8    printf("Value in degrees Fahrenheit= ");
9    scanf("%lf",&tf);
10   tc = (tf - offset) * conv;
11   printf("Value in degrees Celsius= %f",tc);
12 }
```

Listing 3.5   Measurement unit conversion with I/O.

The statement #include <stdio.h> on line 1 includes a system *header* file which makes all I/O functions of the C language available to the program. The format of this statement is discussed in Section 3.5. Note that in some cases the inclusion of a header file is not always sufficient to link the user's code to the system code. In these cases specific options must be included in the compilation command, such as the one given in Section 2.8.2 for the Linux operating system, gcc -o program.exe program.c, following the syntax of the operating system employed.

3.5   Preprocessor directives

Let us now discuss the statement #include <stdio.h> of Listing 3.5 in more detail. It has quite a different format compared to the lexical rules of the other C statements we have encountered so far since it starts with the character # and does not end with the character ;. Indeed, as all statements which start with the character #, it is not a C statement, but rather a *preprocessor directive*.

The *preprocessor* is a software component which elaborates the C code before it is compiled. The preprocessor directives are usually included for two reasons:

- to include generally, though not necessarily, system declarations or definitions; they are synthetically expressed in one line of code and expanded by the preprocessor into several lines of code;
- to define, by means of the directives #define, #if, #ifdef, #ifndef, #endif, #undef, constants or expressions which depend on the context, for instance on the operating system, the precision, the hardware architecture, etc.

Some directives #include are in fact mandatory to build a complex program. For instance, as we saw in Section 3.4, a program communicating with some external device requires the directive #include <stdio.h>, a program which uses non-elementary mathematical functions requires the directive #include <math.h>, <limits.h> contains the numerical limits for precision in a given version of the C language[4].

The definition directives are generally used to make the code more comprehensible and avoid explicit dependencies on constant values. For instance, the statement

```
#define MY_MAX 100
```

enforces that the character string MY_MAX is replaced by the numerical constant 100 throughout the rest of the code which follows this statement. This means that a program which uses the constant MY_MAX can be changed in various instances by performing one single modification in the code, such as

```
#define MY_MAX 500
```

Although this is a useful way of defining constants, care must be taken to avoid possible unwanted collateral damage. For instance, the directive

```
#define MY_MAX 10 + 5
```

corresponds to a substitution of the MY_MAX string by the expression 10 + 5 in the program.

```
1 #define MY_MAX 10 + 5
2
3 int a = 3, b;
4 b = a * MY_MAX;
```

Listing 3.6   Effects of #define.

In Listing 3.6 it is clear we want to obtain b = a * 15;, i.e., b = 45 but the statement on line 4 becomes

---

[4]Some compiler versions allow the most common include such as <stdio.h> to be omitted; we invite the reader to avoid such practices as they might cause to loose control over the code.

```
b = a * 10 + 5;
```

after substitution, which results in b = 35, due to the fact that the operator
* has priority over the operator +. To avoid this type of undesired effects, a
useful practical rule is to always enclose expressions in #define directives
between parentheses as in

```
#define MY_MAX (10 + 5)
```

The other typical use of definition directives concerns the conditional
compilation of certain parts of the code depending on variable contexts. To
this purpose, let us rewrite Listing 3.5 in a more general way such that it
converts from either temperature Fahrenheit into temperature Celsius or
vice versa, based on the presence of one unique variable. Obviously the
program has to be compiled in two different ways in order to be able to
handle these two different cases.

```
1 #include <stdio.h>
2
3 #define TF2TC
4
5 main() {
6    double tc, tf, offset, conv;
7
8    offset = 32.;
9 #ifdef TF2TC
10   conv = 5. / 9.;
11   printf("Value in degrees Fahrenheit= ");
12   scanf("%lf",&tf);
13   tc = (tf - offset) * conv;
14   printf("Value in degrees Celsius= %f\n",tc);
15 #endif
16 #ifndef TF2TC
17   conv = 9. / 5.;
18   printf("Value in degrees Celsius= ");
19   scanf("%lf",&tc);
20   tf = tc * conv + offset;
21   printf("Value in degrees Fahrenheit= %f\n",tf);
22 #endif
23 }
```

Listing 3.7   Use of #define.

In this version, if the variable TF2TC is defined as in the statement on line 3,
the program converts from T_F into T_C; by deleting the statement on line 3,

the variable TF2TC is no longer defined and the program executes the inverse conversion. Note the use of the parentheses on line 13, (tf - offset), which enforces the subtraction to be executed before multiplying by the conversion factor and thus changing the natural priority of the operators. Moreover, we have used the \n string in the printf statements, which stands for *newline* and causes a new line to be used when printing the string argument in printf; \n is a control string which makes printed messages more easily readable.

If a #define directive contains a string with parameters, it is said to define a *macro*. For instance, suppose we would like to define a string associated to the computation of the sum of the squares of two parameters. If we write

```
#define SUMQ(a, b) ((a*a) + (b*b))
```

after this directive, all SUMQ strings of the code are substituted by the expression present in the directive before compilation. For instance, the statement

```
c = SUMQ(7, k);
```

is substituted by the statement

```
c = ((7*7) + (k*k));
```

by the preprocessor. As mentioned before, the use of parentheses avoids any operations to be executed in an order different from the desired one, due to the priority rules. Note that, although macros appear useful and handy, they do complicate corrections of the code. In particular, omitting or insufficient parentheses may cause collateral damage to the code which is extremely difficult to identify.

There exist other, less used, preprocessor directives (#error, #pragma, #line) for which we refer the reader to [Kernighan and Ritchie (1988); Kelley and Pohl (1998)].

3.6 Notes on library functions

In this section we discuss how to extend the functionalities of a program by making use of possibly complex operations which are available in the so-called library functions of the language itself. These can be mathematical functions, control functions, or variable manipulation functions. The basic mathematical functions of the C language are present in the *mathematics library* which is included by the preprocessor directive

```
#include <math.h>
```

The *header file* `math.h` contains the definition of the basic functions listed in Table 3.9, and many others.

Table 3.9   Basic mathematical functions.

Function name	Operation
sqrt(x)	$\sqrt{x}$
pow(x,y)	x^y
exp(x)	e^x
log(x)	$\ln x$
sin(x)	$\sin x$
cos(x)	$\cos x$
tan(x)	$\tan x$
fabs(x)	$|x|$

All functions listed in Table 3.9 receive an input of the **double** type and return a result of the **double** type. Moreover, they verify whether the inserted values are correct from a numerical analysis viewpoint. For instance, the code

```
a = -2;
b = sqrt(a);
```

returns the value NaN which is an abbreviation for Not a Number, since the C compiler does not work with imaginary numbers. The mathematics library <math.h> is an example of the case quoted in Section 3.4 where including the header file is not enough to link the user's code to the system code. In fact, in this case one needs to add the -lm option to the compilation command on a Linux operating sytem, thus writing

```
gcc -lm -o program.exe program.c
```

The directive

```
#include <stdlib.h>
```

allows the use of functions such as exit(), where a number or an integer variable can be included between the parentheses. When the program encounters an exit() function, it is immediately interrupted and the value included between parentheses is returned. The following functions are also defined in <stdlib.h>: **malloc** e **calloc** which directly allocate memory and are discussed in Chapter 10, the random number generating functions which are treated in Chapter 5, and, finally, the conversion functions between character strings and numerical strings.

There exist many more system libraries, which become available upon inclusion of the corresponding *header files*, and supply the programmer with a vast set of useful functions. A systematic overview of these libraries is beyond the scope of this book. However, all library functions which appear throughout this text are described and discussed in detail.

3.7 First applications

We are now ready to consider a first, less trivial problem which uses mathematical functions and performs some more complicated computations. However, we are not yet equipped to write a real complex program as we did not yet introduce logical constructs allowing to perform cyclic or conditional operations. These constructs are discussed in Chapter 4. However, we are able to perform sequential numerical computations by including parameters in the program which represent data given by the user.

Consider the problem of launching a mass in presence of gravity and absence of friction. This is a two-dimensional kinematics problem where the x-component of the velocity is constant, while the y-component is uniformly accelerated with acceleration $-g$. The position (x, y) of the mass can be calculated as a function of t, at each moment t. The concept of how to solve this problem is quite simple, though solving it manually is quite tedious. The program in Listing 3.8 asks for the initial parameters of the motion, the launching angle θ, the initial velocity v_0 and the time t that has passed since the beginning of the motion, at which to compute the position of the mass. The latter is then printed out as a result.

Note that the measurement units are not mentioned in Listing 3.8, though they clearly are relevant to perform a computation which makes sense. It is the programmer's responsibility to inform the user about what measurement units are used in the program (in the example the gravity acceleration g is in m/s^2, and thus the velocity has to be in m/s). We also introduced *comments* in the program, i.e. statements which are ignored by the compiler, but are useful to whomever gets in touch with the source code to clarify the meaning of the variables, algorithms, or, as we just mentioned, add information on how to execute and use the program.

```
 1 #include <stdio.h>
 2 #include <math.h>
 3 #include <stdlib.h>
 4
 5 #define G 9.82
 6 /* this program computes the coordinates x,y of a mass
 7 launched at an angle theta with the x-axis, and initial v
 8 v0. All quantities are in the MKS system */
 9 main() {
10    double t = 0;            /* time */
11    double theta;            /* launching angle */
12    double v0, v0x, v0y;     /* initial v */
13    double xt, yt, vx, vy;
14
15    printf(" Insert the launching angle in radiants: ");
16    scanf("%lf", &theta);
17    printf("\n Insert the initial velocity in m/sec: ");
18    scanf("%lf", &v0);
19    printf("\n Insert the time value t: ");
20    scanf("%lf", &t);
21 /* Compute the components of  v */
22    v0x = v0 * cos(theta);
23    v0y = v0 * sin(theta);
24    vx = v0x;
25    vy = v0y - G * t;
26 /* now compute the coordinates */
27    xt = vx * t;
28    yt = v0y * t - 0.5 * G * pow(t, 2.0);
29    printf("\n the coordinates at time %lf are x = %lf,
30           y = %lf\n", t, xt, yt);
31    exit(0);
32
33 }
```

Listing 3.8   Launching a mass.

The format of the comments in C are

```
/* ...comment... */
```

Everything that is enclosed between /* and */, even if spread over several lines of code or immediately after a C statement is considered to be a comment.

The Listing 3.8 has a linear structure: preprocessor directives, declaration of all required variables, I/O messages to acquire the necessary parameters such as theta, v0 and t, computation of the intermediate variables v0x, v0y, vx and vy and, finally, computation of the desired coordinates xt and yt at time t and the printing out of this final result. Note that the statement on line 29 continues on the next line; it is always possible to split long statements over more than one line, as the compiler assumes several lines belong to a single statement until a ; is encountered.

It is very easy to write a similar program for a different type of problem once we know the formulas that describe the problem. Try to formalize and write the code for the problems listed here below, always keeping a clear and readable program in mind.

Hands on 3.1 - Mechanical energy

Write a program that calculates and prints the values of the kinetic energy $T = \frac{1}{2}mv^2$ and the potential energy $U = mgh$ as a function of time of a pointlike mass m subject to the gravity force mg. The program first needs to acquire the mass, the initial velocity v_0 and the initial height h_0 of the point mass, and the time t at which the energies need to be calculated. Remember that in presence of an acceleration g, the velocity is given by $v(t) = v_0 - gt$ and the height is $h(t) = h_0 + v_0 t - \frac{1}{2}gt^2$.

Hands on 3.2 - Computing the Profits

Write a program computing the interest to be paid on a loan. The program must first acquire the exact amount of the loan, the interest rate, specifying the measurement unit, and the duration of the loan in months. Next calculate the monthly rate summing up the amount of the loan and the interest divided by the number of months.

Chapter 4

Logic management

«Two Stones make two Houses. Three Stones make six Houses. Four Stones make twenty–four Houses. Five Stones make one hundred and twenty Houses. Six Stones make seven hundred and twenty Houses. Seven Stones make five thousand and forty Houses. Beyond this point, think of what the mouth cannot say and the ear cannot hear. »
You know what this is called today?
Factor analysis.

Umberto Eco, *Foucault's Pendulum* (1988).

The devil will take
any home with two gates

Granma Celeste.

In this chapter we introduce decision making constructs and iterative cycles in programs. The former allow to choose between two or more possibilities, while iterative cycles admit a block of statements to be repeated several times.

First we show how to design an iterative algorithm or the choice made by a part of the program in generic terms. Next, we discuss how to implement them by using the statements of the C language.

4.1   Flow control

Any program is executed sequentially starting from the first statement. Statements are executed in the order in which they are written. The solution to certain problems might require certain statements to be repeated in a cyclic way (possibly with different parameters) or the choice between different actions after verifying whether certain conditions are satisfied. In these cases it must be possible for the program to follow different paths, which are not necessarily determined beforehand. An exception to the sequential execution can be obtained by means of a *jump* statement which continues the execution starting with a statement different from the next one.

One way of designing an algorithm transforming a number from the decimal to the binary system consists in dividing the number by two and write down the rest of the division; next, repeat this operation applying it each time to the integer part of the previously obtained quotient and write the remainder of the divisions from right to left, until the quotient is zero. When the C language was being developed it was customary for programmers to design algorithms by means of flow charts composed of directed graphs[1]. The vertices of the graph represent the elementary operations which need to be executed to achieve the solution. Its edges (called control flow lines) define the sequence in which the statements need to be executed. The use of flow charts allows us to better *visualize* the sequence of operations. Some textbooks still recommend to always use this technique before starting to write any code, though over the years this technique has lost importance. Today almost nobody uses this tool, apart for documenting some code[2]. This is the case in this chapter, where flow charts are used to explain algorithms and make them more readable. Figure 4.1 contains the flow chart corresponding to the algorithm to convert an integer number N into the binary system.

The rectangles in the flow chart represent operations performed on data. The diamond shaped boxes play the role of a predicate determining which operations are to be executed depending on whether or not a certain condition occurs ($N = 0$ in the example). The ovals represent the starting and

---

[1]The rigorous definition of a graph is given in Chapter 17. In this context the notion of a graph should be sufficiently intuitive.

[2]The flow charts technique became less important when programming languages allowing recursion (Chapter 15) first appeared, as it is not fit to visualize these new type of programs.

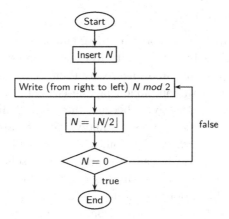

Fig. 4.1   The flow chart of an algorithm transforming the decimal notation of numbers into the binary one. The integer part of the number x is indicated by the symbol $\lfloor x \rfloor$.

ending point of the algorithm[3]. This illustrates the importance of both a way to repeat statements cyclically (dividing the quotient, obtained from the previous operation, by two and printing the remainder of this operation), as well as a mechanism to make a choice (continue dividing or not depending on whether the quotient equals zero or not).

Etymology of mathematical terms

The name algorithm for a sequence of operations resolving a problem originates from the name of an Arab mathematician, Mohammed ibn-Musa al-Khuwarizmi. In the IX–th century he collected the techniques allowing quick execution of calculations. Al-Khuwarizmi is also the author of *Kitab al-giabr*. The latter work was dedicated to equation solving methods. The name *algebra* indicating the mathematics of these types of problems, derives precisely from this book title.

---

[3]Often these symbols are omitted, in which case the starting and ending point are, possibly, represented by the rectangle on top and at the bottom, respectively.

4.1.1 *Nonlinear flows*

During the years in which the programming languages were developed, the statement flow included the possibility to execute jumps (the `goto` statement) inside the program, allowing to transfer the control to a portion of code different from the one following the current statement. As programming needs grew, the codes became increasingly more complicated and the number of jumps increased. Finally, with the appearance of programming languages allowing recursion, managing the jumps became that confusing and complex that it lead to a rather drastic solution: the abolishment of `goto` statements. Programmers soon were able to avoid this statement, and the possibility of its complete elimination was formally proved by two Italian mathematicians: Corrado Böhm and Giuseppe Jacopini. They proved [Bohm and Jacopini (1966)] that the flow of any program can always be written in terms of only three *control structures*: sequential execution, selection and iteration.

(1) In sequential structure or execution the program evolves by executing the statements in the order in which they are written. This is the normal way of proceeding.

(2) With the selection structure the program reaches a point where a logic expression is evaluated whose result (true or false) determines which statements are executed in the following.

(3) The iteration structure is used to execute a series of identical statements in a cyclic way, until certain conditions occur.

The control structures are represented by flow charts with a single starting and a single ending point. The Böhm-Jacopini theorem guarantees that any program, no matter how complex, can be written using only three control structures. Jumping from one statement to another is no longer necessary. This is the case of a *structured* program. Nevertheless, most existing programming languages (including C) permit to write not completely structured programs. A structured program allows us a better control of the flow with respect to a non structured one. Therefore, it is good practice to use this type of programming as much as possible. As often occurs, a rigorous application of a system of strict rules can sometimes provoke other kinds of problems[4]. Therefore, we will sometimes, in some very specific circumstances, deviate from what the Böhm-Jacopini theorem prescribes,

---

[4] In some cases the use of non-structured statements may give rise to a more efficient program. These cases are extremely rare as modern compilers can optimize the performance of the code very efficiently. In other cases the structured code may appear less clear.

though we try to stick on the rules of structured programming. In particular, statements as `break`, `continue` and `switch` are subjects of discussion as to whether or not they can be used in a structured program. We do not enter this discussion, but rather avoid their use.

4.2 Taking a decision

The selection structure identified by the Böhm-Jacopini theorem makes a part of code to be executed depending on the truth value of a proposition. Let us call I_a and I_b two groups of mutually exclusive statements, and C the proposition which needs to be checked. The control structure can be symbolically represented by the flow charts of Figure 4.2 (a).

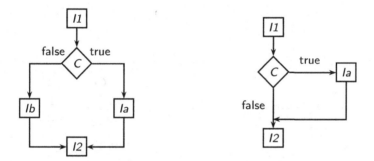

Fig. 4.2 (a) The general selection structure. (b) A simple selection structure, obtained from the fundamental one by substituting the I_b statement with the empty statement.

The program starts with the I_1 statement. Next, the truth value of the proposition C is evaluated: if it is true the group of statements I_a is executed, otherwise the block I_b is executed. At the end of the execution of one or the other set of instructions, the program continues by executing the statements I_2. The flow chart of Figure 4.2 (a) can be informally translated into: «If C is true, execute I_a, otherwise execute I_b».

The structure 4.2 (a) is the fundamental one, from which all others can easily be generated. For example, under some circumstances, the set of statements I_b is empty. In this case a more simple selection structure, not containing any alternatives, is generated, as the one shown in 4.2 (b). In this case the program starts by executing the statements I_1 and then evaluates the proposition C. If it results to be true, the commands in I_a are executed before the statements I_2 are executed. Otherwise, I_2 is executed immediately.

By combining several selection structures we obtain constructs allowing more complicated choices, as the one shown in Figure 4.3 (a). This is a chain of structures as the one shown in Figure 4.2 (a). By connecting the output of a first control structure with the input of a successive one, the block I_b is effectively substituted by a selection structure. Between the statements I_1 and I_2 a set of statements I_k are executed depending on whether one of the conditions C_j occurs. In case all conditions are false, the statements J are still executed (the set of these statements may be empty, of course). This structure corresponds to the one generated by the `switch` statement of the C language (Section 4.4). Another possibility, shown in Figure 4.3 (b), consists of a chain of non-mutual exclusive structures, generated by a sequence of the selection structures of Figure 4.2 (b).

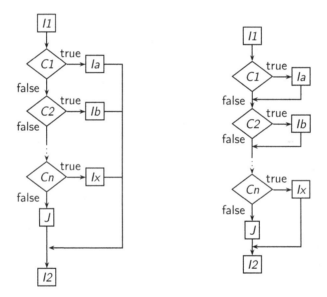

Fig. 4.3   To obtain multiple choice structures we can link several selection structures together. In the structure on the left the choices are mutually exclusive, while in the one on the right one choice does not exclude the others.

The difference between the two structures is only apparently small. Indeed, the program execution may vary drastically. In case of 4.3 (a), one true condition excludes all the others to occur. Once the statements corresponding to the true conditions are executed, the program immediately continues to execute the I_2 statements. Instead, in case of 4.3 (b), a true condition does not exclude others to occur. Thus, it is possible that several statement groups I_k are executed. Also, while in the former case only the conditions starting from C_1 up to the first true condition are evaluated, in the latter all conditions are evaluated. Thus, if the clauses are mutually exclusive, it is always convenient to choose a construct as the one shown in Figure 4.3 (a). Moreover, to improve performance, it is better to first insert the conditions which have a higher probability of occurring.

4.2.1 *if/else*

In C, the selection control structure can be achieved with the `if` construct, as shown in the Listing 4.1.

```
18    printf("Value in degrees Celsius= ");
19    scanf("%lf", &tc);
20    if (tc < -273.16) printf("Warning! T<0 K...\n");
```

Listing 4.1   A example of the `if` statement.

This Listing contains a part of the program of Listing 3.7. We inserted line 20, to check the value of the variable `tc`, which must not be smaller than $-273.16\,°C$ as it represents a temperature in degrees Celsius. The `if` statement on line 20 checks the value of `tc`: if it is smaller than -273.16, the program writes the message of the `printf` statement following it. The syntax of the `if` statement is the following:

if (*expression*) *statement_1* [else *statement_2*]

When this statement is executed, the *expression* is evaluated and the corresponding result is interpreted as a logical value. If the expression is true, the program executes *statement_1*. Otherwise, if the `else` clause is present, *statement_2* is executed. The alternative statements can be compound, i.e., they may consist of several statements enclosed between curly brackets. Despite each statement must end with the character ;, the latter is not required after the curly bracket as they mark off the end of a block.

A common error consists in inserting the ; character after the logical condition[5]. In this case the compiler does not report any errors as the statement if (*expression*); *statement* is syntactically correct. It means that if the logical value of the *expression* is true, no statements are executed. Indeed, the semicolon signals the end of the `if` statement

---

[5]This error almost always occurs when a condition is followed by a single statement that is not enclosed between curly brackets (a good reason for using them...).

containing an empty statement. The next statement is interpreted as a normal statement following the `if`. Thus, it is executed even in case the logical value is false. Writing

```
if (tc < -273.16); printf("Warning! T<0 K...\n");
```

the program behaves the same way independently of the value of `tc` and always prints the warning message even if `tc` has an acceptable value. This error is usually avoided by using curly brackets. Therefore, we shall always write

```
if (tc < -273.16) {
    printf("Warning! T<0 K...\n");
}
```

Another common error consists in mixing up the assignment = and the comparison == operator. Indeed, quite often a condition like the following is included

```
if (a = 5) {
    ...statements...
}
```

In this case the error is due to the use of the assignment operator = instead of the comparison operator ==. In C, every logical or mathematical expression has a value equal to the result of the expression. In this case, the = operator assigns the value 5 to the variable `a`. Therefore, the result of the expression included between parentheses is 5. In Section 1.6 we saw that the logical value *true* is represented in the memory by a bit sequence containing at least one 1. Therefore, in this case the expression is always equal to *true* and the condition is always satisfied. Moreover, the value of the variable `a` is always changed into 5 after this statement is executed. Note that from a syntactical point of view, the expression is correct. Indeed, the compiler would easily finish its job without warning about any possible disaster this expression might entail.

We now reformulate the Listing 3.7 with the selection control structure in order to avoid recompilation each time we want to change the type of conversion. Consider the Listing 4.2.

```
1 #include <stdio.h>
2
3 main() {
4     double tIn, tOut, offset, conv;
5     int option = 0;
6
7     offset = 32.;
8     printf("Press\n'1' to convert from F into C\n"
9             "'2' to convert from C into F\n\nChoice:");
10    scanf("%d", &option);
11    if (option == 1) {
12      conv = 5./ 9.;
13      printf("Value in degrees Fahrenheit= ");
14      scanf("%lf",&tIn);
15      tOut = (tIn - offset) * conv;
16      printf("Value in degrees Celsius= %f\n",tOut);
17    } else {
18      conv = 9./ 5.;
19      printf("Value in degrees Celsius= ");
20      scanf("%lf", &tIn);
21      tOut = tIn * conv + offset;
22      printf("Value in degrees Fahrenheit= %f\n",tOut);
23    }
24 }
```

Listing 4.2   Temperature conversion with if/else.

First of all, note that we introduced an integer variable option allowing us to store a conventional value defining the type of conversion (from Fahrenheit into Celsius or vice versa). The value of the variable option is acquired on line 10, after an initial message looking like the following (try to understand why) appears on screen:

```
Press
'1' to convert from F into C
'2' to convert from C into F

Choice:
```

Note that the argument of printf on the preceding line is composed of a single string. Indeed, the C compiler interprets two succeeding character sets delimited by double quotes " as a single string (this technique is used to obtain a more readable program). On line 11, the value of option is compared to the constant 1. If the two values coincide, the lines starting from 12 up to line 16 are executed. Otherwise, the lines 18 up to 22 are executed. Even though it is not necessary, we changed the names tc and tf of the variables into tIn and tOut (*in* and *out* temperature). Indeed, in this context the meaning of the variables is different from the one in Listing 3.7. For coherence, it is appropriate to give names which reflect the correct meaning.

4.2.2   *The selection operator*

When the selection control is used to determine the value of an expression which depends on whether a condition occurs or not, it is sometimes preferable to use a single, ternary C operator: the operator **?**. For example, a structure determining the maximum between two values **a** and **b**, could be the following:

```
(a > b) ? (max = a) : (max = b);
```

First, the expression to the left of the question mark (a > b) is evaluated. If this expression is true, the expression to the left of the colon is evaluated. Otherwise, the one to the right. Note that we are not dealing with statements, but rather with expressions. Therefore, the semicolon and the parentheses are compulsory. Indeed, a completely analogue statement is

```
max = (a > b) ? a : b;
```

where the parentheses are not required as each expression simply consists of the variable value. This statement can be read like this: «Is **a** larger than **b**? If yes, evaluate the value of **a**, otherwise that of **b**». The expression to the right of the = operator assumes the value of either **a** or **b** and the result is assigned to **max**.

4.3   Iterations

The third structure foreseen by the Böhm-Jacopini theorem is the iteration allowing the cyclic repetition of a block of statements. It can appear under various forms, which are all equivalent to each other. Indeed, it is possible to pass from one form to another by appropriately modifying the conditions. A first case is shown in Figure 4.4 (a). In this so-called *while-do* form, once the statement block I_1 has been executed, the condition C is checked. If the condition C is true, the block I_a is executed, at the end of which the program checks the validity of the condition C again. If it is still true, the statements I_a are executed again. At a certain point, they may alter

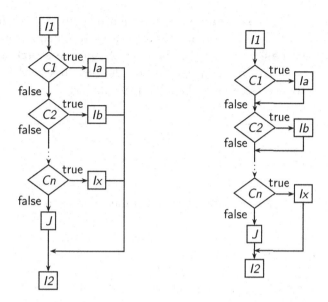

Fig. 4.4   Two forms of the iteration structure: *while-do* (a) and *do-while* (b).

the value of the condition C. In this case the iterative cycle terminates and the program jumps to execute the statements I_2. The flow chart of Figure 4.4 (a) can be read as following: «As long as C is true, I_a will be executed».

In this form, the condition C is evaluated at least once. In case it is false at the beginning of the cycle, the statements I_a are never executed. Alternatively, the iterative structure could have the *do-while* form, as the one represented in Figure 4.4 (b). Here, the statements I_a are executed at least once in any case. Only when these are completed, the value of the logical expression C is determined. If it results to be true, the statements I_a continue to be executed. On the contrary, if it is false, the iterative cycle is exited and the I_2 statements are executed. The two forms, *do-while* and *while-do*, are completely equivalent. Reformulating the condition C allows one to move the statement block I_a and change the form of the structure.

In C the iteration control structure can be achieved in both forms provided by the Böhm-Jacopini theorem. To build the first iteration form, C provides the `while` statement. Its syntax is

```
while (expression) statement
```

In this form the **do** term is *not* explicitly required. First, the logical value corresponding to the *expression* is determined. Only if it results to be true, the *statement* is executed. This sequence is repeated indefinitely as long as the *expression* results to be true. Again, the *statement* can be compound and it is recommended to use the curly brackets even when it is not strictly necessary as in the following example:

```
int i = 0, S = 0;
while (i < 10) {
    S += i++;
}
```

where the variable S will contain the sum of the numbers from 0 to 9 at the end of the cycle.

If the value of the *expression* remains permanently true, the cycle continues indefinitely. In this case the program execution can only be stopped by sending it a so-called *kill* signal (on many systems this is achieved pressing the key combination Ctrl+C). This behavior could be desirable, as in

```
while (1) {
    ...
}
```

Using the constant 1 as an expression (or whatever other constant apart from zero) guarantees the condition is always true. Sometimes it happens that this behavior is due to an erroneous formulation of the expression. In the latter case, the program seems to be stuck. To understand what is going on, we can insert some appropriate print statements[6]. The program of Listing 4.3 contains an obvious cycle management error. Indeed, the initial value of i must be different from zero in order to stop the cycle.

```
1 #include <stdio.h>
2
3 main() {
4    int i = 0;
5    printf("i: %d-", i);
6    while (i < 1000) {
7      i *= 2;
8    }
9    printf("%d\n", i);
10 }
```

Listing 4.3   A program with an infinite cycle.

---

[6]To this purpose so-called *debugger* programs, allowing to analyze the memory content at each instant during the execution of another program, are sometimes used.

In any case, we expect to see at least a part of the messages to be printed on screen (i: 0-). On some systems, this may not occur, causing the programmer to erroneously search for the problem in the statements preceding line 5. This happens because I/O operations are generally slower than memory operations. This is why the operating system does not immediately execute the printing operations. The characters to be printed are instead sent to a memory *buffer*, i.e., a reserved area of the operating system where these characters are temporarily stored. The *buffer* is emptied when full or when certain characters are to be printed. Emptying the *buffer* coincides with the effective printing of the messages. The `fflush(0)` statement enforces the *buffer* to be emptied. We do not discuss this function in detail as it requires some of the notions described in Section 6.7. For now, we are only interested in knowing that if we insert the statement

```
fflush(0);
```

after line 5, the `printf` function is executed completely (i.e., the characters are actually printed on screen).

If the block of statements needs to be executed at least once, the *do-while* construct might be more appropriate. This control structure has the following form :

```
do statement while (expression);
```

In this way, the *statement* is executed at least a first time in any case, before the truth value of the condition represented by the *expression* is evaluated. If it results to be true, the *statement* is repeated, and otherwise the successive statements are executed next. Note that, as usual, the *statement* must end with a semicolon. If curly brackets are used, the statement is, apart from safer, also more comprehensible:

```
do {
  statement
} while (expression);
```

The `do-while` construct may serve to check whether the input supplied by a user during execution is valid. Let us consider once more the program of Listing 4.2. If the user inserts an undefined option (e.g., 3) the program interprets it as a request to proceed with the conversion from degrees Celsius into degrees Fahrenheit. To avoid this and, in case this error does occur, to offer the user at the same time the possibility to insert his choice again, we could use the code shown in Listing 4.4.

```
5    int option;
6    offset = 32.;
7    do {
8      printf("Press\n1) to convert from F into C\n"
9             "2) to convert form C into F\n\nChoice:");
10     scanf("%d", &option);
11     if ((option != 1) && (option != 2)) {
12       printf("Wrong input. Repeat selection...\n");
13     }
14   } while ((option != 1) && (option != 2));
```

Listing 4.4   Use of the do-while construct.

In this example, the initial value of option is completely irrelevant. Indeed, once the program has reached line 7, it executes the lines between curly brackets anyway, thus acquiring the value of option from the keyboard. The condition on line 11 is true on the whole if and only if option assumes a value different from the expected ones. In this case, a message inviting the user to repeat the input is printed on the screen. The same condition is included in the do-while construct, and if the user made a mistake, the lines between curly brackets are executed again. This continues until the user correctly selects either 1 or 2. In cases like these, the break statement may be included to make the code more compact and clear (Listing 4.5).

```
1    do {
2      printf("Press\n1) to convert from F into C\n"
3             "2) to convert form C into F\n\nChoice:");
4      scanf("%d", &option);
5      if ((option == 1) || (option == 2)) {
6        break;
7      }
8      printf("Wrong input. Repeat selection...\n");
9    } while (1);
```

Listing 4.5   Use of break.

As soon as the condition on line 5 occurs (i.e., when the user selects a correct option) the cycle is interrupted at the break statement. The latter generates a jump to the statement following the while, which therefore no longer needs to contain a condition depending on what takes place inside the cycle. As mentioned before, some consider the use of the break statement unfortunate and it can actually easily be replaced by an alternative and, to some degree, more elegant technique as the one of Listing 4.6.

```
1    char incorrectInput = 1;
2    ...
3    do {
4      printf("Press\n1) to convert from F into C\n"
5             "2) to convert form C into F\n\nChoice:");
6      scanf("%d", &option);
7      if ((option == 1) || (option == 2)) {
8          incorrectInput = 0;
9      } else {
10         printf("Wrong input. Repeat selection...\n");
11     }
12   } while (incorrectInput);
```

Listing 4.6   Alternative to the **break** statement.

C does not provide a type representing only logical values. Therefore, they are represented by character variables as these occupy the least memory space (8 bit). By defining the variable `incorrectInput` which is set to true until the user does not insert a valid character, we can write the cycle as in the Listing 4.6.

C provides yet another statement to perform an iterative cycle, namely the `for` statement. The syntax of this statement is as follows:

```
for (expression_1; expression_2; expression_3)
statement
```

or, adopting a more readable style:

```
for (expression_1; expression_2; expression_3) {
   statement
}
```

This construct is fully equivalent to the following:

```
expression_1;
while (expression_2) {
   statement
   expression_3;
}
```

Indeed, first the value of `expression_1` is evaluated. Next, if the logical value of `expression_2` is true, the `statement` is executed (remember the final semicolon), before `expression_3` is evaluated. Of course, evaluating the expressions might require the execution of some statements.

Though all iteration structures are interchangeable, the `for` construct is preferred in cycles controlled by the value of a variable representing an index or counter.   In these cases the number of times the statements should be repeated is known beforehand.

Hands on 4.1 - The `for` construct

Rewrite the temperature conversion program using `for` cycles instead of the `while` construct, considering both iterative methods are equivalent. Note that even though they are, semantically speaking, equivalent, the `for` construct is not appropriate to represent the type of cycle of this program in a clear way.

4.3.1   *The factorial*

As an example of an iterative structure controlled by a counter, let us calculate the factorial $n!$ of a positive integer number n. Recall that

$$n! \equiv \prod_{i=1}^{n} i, \quad \forall n \in \mathbb{N}^{+}; \text{ with } 0! \equiv 1 .$$

The program of Listing 4.7 computes the factorial of a number chosen by the user with a `for` cycle. The variable p registers the value of the product. We set its initial value to 1 and declare it as an **unsigned long long int**. As a factorial of a relatively small number can reach high values, it is indeed appropriate for its representation to have many bits. By preceding the type declaration by the **long long**[7] specifier we are sure that 64 bits are allocated to the corresponding variable, such that numbers up to $2^{64} - 1 = 18\,446\,744\,073\,709\,551\,615$ can be represented.

If i lies between 1 and n, the statement included between curly brackets is executed. It multiplies the current value of the product by i, thus redefining its value. The value of i is increased by the `for` cycle third expression. When i is equal to n the cycle stops and the statement of line 12, responsible for writing the result, is executed. The modifier ll before the format specifier u indicates a **long long unsigned int** is to be written. Note that the result is correct even if n is 0.

---

[7]Remember that the **long long** specifier is not allowed by ANSI-C compilers. Therefore, it is not always possible to use it.

```
1 #include <stdio.h>
2
3 main() {
4   int n, i;
5   unsigned long long int p = 1;
6
7   printf("Insert a nonnegative integer number: ");
8   scanf("%d", &n);
9   for (i = 1; i <= n; i++) {
10      p *= i;
11  }
12  printf("%d!=%llu\n", n, p);
13 }
```

Listing 4.7   Computing a factorial with a `for` cycle.

Obviously an analogous program can be written using the `while` statement instead of the `for` statement. In cases like this, the usage of the `for` statement emphasizes the fact that the cycle is performed a preset number of times. Often programs become more comprehensible if we choose to use one statement rather than others. The use of the `for` statement in other cases is certainly allowed, but inappropriate.

Hands on 4.2 - Computing a factorial

 The Listing 4.7 is incomplete as it does not check whether the input is correct. Change the program such that a similar check is included. If the user did not insert the data correctly, do not allow the computation to continue. What happens if the factorial of **n** exceeds the maximum representable integer? Change the code such that this case is taken into account. Do not simply check the value of n. A more general way to verify this is by comparing the product value at a given iteration to its previous value. Also try to rewrite the program by substituting the `for` cycles with `while` and `do-while` cycles.

4.3.2   *Solving equations*

A useful example using the `while` construct is the *bisection method* to solve equations. Suppose we want to resolve the following equation numerically

$$f(x) = 0. \tag{4.1}$$

This is a very common problem as the equations describing scientific problems often cannot be resolved analytically. Suppose the equation (4.1) has N solutions x_i, $i = 1, \ldots, N$. If we are able to estimate the limits of the intervals $I_i \equiv (a_i, b_i)$ containing each one single solution x_i, we can approximate all these solutions. Let us also assume that neither a_i nor b_i are solutions of (4.1). Of course, due to the limited precision with which numbers can be stored into the memory, each solution x_i is approximated with a precision ϵ. In the best case, this precision is of the same order as that of the used representation.

The bisection method is an iterative method which works as following:

(1) calculate the midpoint c_i of the interval I_i: $c_i = (a_i + b_i)/2$;

(2) evaluate the product $p_i = f(a_i)f(c_i)$;

(3) if $p_i = 0$, then obviously c_i is the wanted solution[8];

(4) if $p_i < 0$, $f(a_i)$ and $f(c_i)$ have the opposite sign and the solution x_i lies on the left of c_i; in this case the search is repeated in the left subinterval by redefining $b_i = c_i$;

(5) if $p_i > 0$, the solution x_i lies to the right of c_i and the search is repeated in the other subinterval by setting $a_i = c_i$.

Steps 1 to 5 need to be repeated until $|b_i - a_i| < \epsilon$. In this way, the solution x_i lies in the interval (a_i, b_i). Generally, it is assumed that the solution value is equal to the midpoint of this interval with an uncertainty equal to half the size of this interval: $x_i = c_i \pm \epsilon/2$.

The Listing 4.8 contains one possible implementation of this algorithm. To make the program concrete let us consider an equation (4.1) for which we know the solution, thus allowing us to verify whether the algorithm is sound:

$$f(x) = \cos x = 0 \,.$$

The required precision is dictated by a **define** directive. The "core" of the program are the lines 12 up to 26. First, a check is performed to see if the desired precision has not already been reached. To this purpose we define **delta** as the absolute value of the difference between the two endpoints of the interval in which the solution is searched (the function **fabs**, defined in the mathematics library, returns the absolute value of a rational number). If this difference is still too large (**delta > EPSILON**), **c** is defined as the average of **a** and **b**, and the variable **p** is set equal to the result of the product $f(a)f(c)$, and the procedure is iterated.

---

[8]This is a lucky case in which the precision is sufficient to exactly represent the desired solution.

```
 1 #include <math.h>
 2 #include <stdio.h>
 3
 4 #define EPSILON 1.e-5
 5
 6 main() {
 7    double a = 0., b = M_PI, c;
 8    double delta = fabs(a - b);
 9    int i = 1;
10    printf("This program solves "
11           "the equation cos(x)=0 in (0, PI)\n");
12    while (delta > EPSILON) {
13      double p;
14      c = 0.5 * (a + b);
15      p = cos(a) * cos(c);
16      if (p > 0.) {
17        a = c;
18      } else if (p < 0.) {
19        b = c;
20      } else {
21        a = b = c; /* exact solution */
22      }
23      printf("Iteration n. %d: x = %f\n", i++,
24             0.5 * (a + b));
25      delta = fabs(a - b);
26    }
27    printf("The found solution is equal to: %f\n", c);
28    printf("The exact solution is equal to: %f\n", 0.5 * M_PI);
29    printf("The difference is equal to       : %e\n",
30           fabs(0.5 * M_PI - c));
31 }
```

Listing 4.8   Use of the **while** construct to solve an equation with the bisection method.

Note that the variable p is only used inside the cycle. Therefore, it makes sense to define it inside the block it defines (Section 3.2). The area in which a variable is "visible" is called its *scope*. The variable p may be used inside its scope defined by the block. Whereas, outside of the block, it is as if it did not exist. It is even possible to define another variable with the same name in the **main** environment. This is not a good idea though as it might cause confusion, however there are cases in which this is even recommendable (e.g. when different variables have the same meaning). The variable p is said to be *local*.

Depending on the value of p, the new value is assigned to either a or b, as established by the algorithm. During a cycle, the value of delta is recalculated until the condition of the **while** statement is satisfied. If $p_i = 0$ (line 20), the solution found is exact. In this case the interval (a_i, b_i)

is reduced to a point. The statement

```
a = b = c;
```

should be read as «Set b equal to c, and, in turn, a equal to b». Indeed, as mentioned before, in C a logical or mathematical expression takes on the value that is obtained when it is evaluated. The expression b = c takes on the value received by the variable b, which in turn is assigned to a. Also note that in the multiple selection structure, the alternative condition (the last one checked) is the least probable. The statements comprised between lines 12 and 26 are repeated until delta takes on a value smaller than EPSILON. To achieve a better understanding of the algorithm, we also included the line 24. It causes the solution approximation to appear on screen as the iterations progress.

Hands on 4.3 - Solving equations

Use the bisection method with various approximations to solve some other equations. Start from different endpoints delimiting the interval $I_i = (a_i, b_i)$. How does the number of necessary iterations vary as a function of the size I_i of the interval or as a function of the precision ϵ? What is the maximum precision possible?

There exist many equation solving algorithms. One of these is *Newton's method*. Let x_n be an approximation of the equation solution (4.1). The successive approximation x_{n+1} is obtained by expanding $f(x)$ in series up to the first order:

$$f(x_{n+1}) \simeq f(x_n) + f'(x_n)(x_{n+1} - x_n) = 0,$$

where $f'(x)$ is the first derivative of $f(x)$. The successive approximation is then obtained as following:

$$x_{n+1} = x_n - \frac{f(x_n)}{f'(x_n)}.$$

A solution is said to be found when $|x_{n+1} - x_n| < \epsilon$. Newton's method converges faster than the bisection method, though the initial estimate must be rather good. If the derivative $f'(x)$ is not known, the *tangent method* can be used. This method consists in approximating the derivative with the incremental ratio:

$$x_{n+1} = x_n - f(x_n)\frac{x_n - x_{n-1}}{f(x_n) - f(x_{n-1})}.$$

Try writing a program solving the same equation using different methods. Compare their performance in terms of convergence speed and dependence on the initial choice.

4.3.3 *Searching prime numbers*

Another example in which the `for` construct may be appropriate is when searching for the prime numbers between 1 and N, shown in Listing 4.9.

```
1 #include <math.h>
2
3 #define N 100
4
5 main() {
6   int i;
7   printf("The prime numbers between 2 and %d are\n", N);
8   for (i = 1; i < N; i++) {
9     int j = 2, jMax = (int)sqrt(i) + 1;
10    while ((j < jMax) && (i % j)) {
11      j++;
12    }
13    if (j == jMax) {
14      printf("%d\n", i);
15    }
16  }
17 }
```

Listing 4.9   Use of the `for` construct to search for prime numbers.

To check whether a number is prime we need to make sure it can only be divided by 1 and itself. The code performing this check must be repeated N times which is why the `for` construct is used (line 8). For each of the numbers i we need to check whether it can be divided by any of the numbers j between 2 and the integer larger than, but closest to its square root jMax (it is useless to try to divide by numbers larger than this one). With the % operator we compute the remainder for each potential divisor j. If the remainder is zero, the expression controlling the `while` on line 10 is altogether false. In this case j divides i. Therefore, the latter is not prime, and we may quit the internal cycle. The number i is prime only if the internal cycle did not end because the remainder of the division by any j was zero, but rather because j is equal to jMax.

Again, note that we defined some variables inside a smaller environment within the program. Also, a cycle may be present within another cycle (the internal cycles are said to be *nested*).

Hands on 4.4 - The average of a distribution

A biologist is doing a research on the length of mullets throughout the year. During each i–th period of the year, he measures N_i mullets, and subsequently calculates the average value of the length l_i, its variance σ_i^2 and the error on the average $\sigma_i^l = \sigma_i/\sqrt{N_i}$. Write a program computing these quantities, given the measures l_i. The biologist should first give the number of measurements he made during each period and then, one by one, the lengths of the mullets. Remember that if $\langle X \rangle$ indicates the average value of X, its variance is $\sigma^2 = \langle X^2 \rangle - \langle X \rangle^2$.

4.4 Deprecated statements

We already alluded to the fact that inside a C program there exist *unfortunate* statements related to the rules of structured programming. We duly note that the opinions regarding these statements are not unanimous. So, probably not everyone would agree with the considerations following now. Let us therefore clarify the idea behind this section. Obviously, any available construct of a programming language may be used when writing programs. Nevertheless, some constructs can be completely substituted by others that are universally accepted to be *legitimate* (in structured programming). Adopting solely the latter constructs guarantees that everyone will consider the programs good programming examples.

We already mentioned the **break** statement, whose legitimacy is subject of a (heated) debate. Indeed, this statement can easily be circumvented by rewriting the cycles.

Another contested statement is **switch**. The reason is that the **switch** statement demands the use of the **break** statement, which in turn many consider a regrettable choice. The **switch** construct creates a selection structure of the kind shown in Figure 4.3 (a). For example, the Listing 4.2 can be rewritten with this construct, thus allowing the user to select which type of conversion is to be performed, as shown in Listing 4.10. The expression following the **switch** statement must be of the integer type. In this case, the value of **option** determines which block defined by the label **case** will be executed. Namely, the one having the same value as the expression. At the end of each block, a **break** statement must be included to bring the program execution to the end of the **switch** construct, i.e., after the last curly bracket. The **default** label is reached when the value of the expression following **switch** does not coincide with any of the values of the other labels. It is easy to understand that the use of this statement does not simplify a programmer's job (the corresponding statement **if** is just as simple) and is less versatile (the control expression must be of the integer type and its value must be equal to one of the labels). For this reason we can easily live without it. On the other hand, the fact that all possible cases can immediately be identified is the reason why many programmers use the **switch** statement. At least, this is true if the program is written in an orderly way (using the inset of the statements and writing the possible cases in increasing order, placing the **default** case at the end).

```
1    switch (option) {
2      case 1:
3        conv = 5./ 9.;
4        printf("Value in degrees Fahrenheit= ");
5        scanf("%lf",&tIn);
6        tOut = (tIn - offset) * conv;
7        printf("Value in degrees Celsius= %f\n",tOut);
8        break;
9      case 2:
10        conv = 9./ 5.;
11        printf("Value in degrees Celsius= ");
12        scanf("%lf", &tIn);
13        tOut = tIn * conv + offset;
14        printf("Value in degrees Fahrenheit= %f\n",tOut);
15        break;
16      default:
17        printf("Wrong option: %d\n", option);
18        exit(-1);
19    }
```

Listing 4.10   Use of the switch construct.

To be complete, the last statement we discuss here is **continue**, which causes a jump to the evaluation of the control expression of the cycle that contains it.

```
int n = 1, S = 0;
while (n > 0) {
    scanf("%d", &n);
    if (n % 2) continue;
    S += n;
}
printf("%d", S);
```

This piece of code gets integer numbers from the keyboard and sum only the even ones. Indeed, the condition of the `if` statement is true when the remainder of the division by two of the inserted number is 1. In this case, the `continue` statement skips the remaining lines and return to the evaluation of the control expression (n > 0). Also this construct can easily be substituted. It is enough to rewrite the condition with a different structure:

```
int n = 1, S = 0;
while (n > 0) {
    scanf("%d", &n);
    if (!(n % 2)) {
        S += n;
    }
}
printf("%d", S);
```

In this way everybody considers it a good program snippet.

4.5   A rounding problem

In this section we discuss an apparently trivial problem which turns out to be particularly instructive: adding N numbers x_j, $j = 0 \ldots N-1$. It is not a coincidence that we postponed this problem till the end of this chapter. Indeed, the numerical problems we want to discuss occur when the result implies performing many iterations.

```
1 #include <stdio.h>
2
3 #define N 10000000
4
5 main() {
6    float S = 0., x = 7.;
7    unsigned int i, iS = 0, ix = 7;
8    for (i = 0; i < N; i++) {
9       S += x;
10       iS += ix;
11    }
12    printf("Using floats   : %.0f x %d = %.0f\n", x, N, S);
13    printf("Using integers: %d x %d = %d\n", ix, N, iS);
14 }
```

Listing 4.11   A program with unexpected results.

To simplify things we assume the numbers we want to add are all equal to each other. In particular, we consider the case where $N = 10\,000\,000$

and $x_j = 7$, $\forall j$. The expected result S is trivially $S = 70\,000\,000$. Let us consider the Listing 4.11.

Before discussing the algorithm, note the format of the `printf` statement on line 12: `%.0f x %d = %.0f`. The standard behavior of the format specifiers can be changed by placing modifiers between the `%` character and the specifier (`f` in this case). The modifier of rational variables specifiers generally have the form `n.m`, where `n` is the minimum number of characters required to print the result (including the possible decimal point) and can be omitted. In case the number consists of less than `n` characters, blank spaces are automatically added to its left such that it occupies exactly `n` characters. If `n` is omitted, the necessary digits are printed and aligned on the left. Instead, `m` represents the maximum number of digits that are printed after the decimal point. In this case, we are asking the rational values to be printed without any digits after the decimal point. In case of integers, the modifier is usually an integer number `n` representing the minimum number of characters that are to be printed. The possibilities offered by the modifiers are obviously many more and we refer the reader to the references for more details.

If we compile and execute the program of Listing 4.11, we get the following result:

```
Using floats   : 7 x 10000000 = 77603248
Using integers: 7 x 10000000 = 70000000
```

What happened? How come the sum S is wrong by more than 10 percent in case we compute it with rational numbers? The answer is easy: due to rounding errors (Section 1.4). Contrary to what happens with integers, the computer memory representation of rational numbers is not exact, as only a limited number of digits are available. Remember that rational numbers are represented as IEEE 754 floating-point numbers.

Following the program step by step, we discover that the first deviation from the true value already occurs at $i = 2396\,746$, when the variable S representing the sum S should be $16\,777\,229$. At the previous step, S $= 16\,777\,222$ which in standard IEEE 754 notation is represented as

$$0 \ 1001\,0111 \ (1) \ 000\,0000\,0000\,0000\,0000\,0011$$

The number between parentheses is implicit (i.e. not represented), the mantissa consists of 23 digits, the exponent of 2 is obtained by interpreting the 8 bits on the left in excess–127 and the sign is given by the first bit. In this case the exponent is 24 ($151 - 127$) and the mantissa is obtained by summing $1 + 2^{-22} + 2^{-23}$, from which S $= 2^{24}(1 + 2^{-22} + 2^{-23})$. Instead, the number 7 is simply written as $1.75 \times 2^2 = (1 + 0.5 + 0.25) \times 2^2$, i.e.,

0 1000 0001 (1) 110 0000 0000 0000 0000 0000

When this number is to be added to S $= 16\,777\,222$, it must be expressed as a multiple of 2^{24}. The bits of the mantissa (including the implicit bit 1) must be translated by 22 places. In this way, the rightmost digit is lost as there is no room for it in the 4 bytes provided for a `float`. The result is

0 1001 0111 (0) 000 0000 0000 0000 0000 0011 $= 6$

Summing the two numbers, we have

0 1001 0111 (1) 000 0000 0000 0000 0000 0011 $= 16\,777\,222\ +$
0 1001 0111 (0) 000 0000 0000 0000 0000 0011 $=\qquad\qquad 6\ =$
0 1001 0111 (1) 000 0000 0000 0000 0000 0110 $= 16\,777\,228$

We obtain a number which differs by one unit from the correct result. Though the difference is quite contained, the final result is disastrous. This is because the error is accumulated many times during the iterations and finally leads to an error of the size shown. From what we just saw, one might expect the final result to be smaller than the correct one. Indeed, the loss of bits should lead to summing smaller numbers (first, several times 6 and then 2) to the variable S. However, modern CPUs contain an FPU (*Floating Point Unit*) responsible for treating floating-point numbers. To reduce the possibility that these errors occur, the FPU uses 80 bits to represent results internally. When they are returned to the memory, these are truncated to 32 bits, in case of a `float`.

Table 4.1   Contents of the variables i and S and the registers R7 and P of the FPU during execution of the program in Listing 4.11.

i	R7	S	P
2396 745	16 777 222	16 777 222	0
2396 746	16 777 229	16 777 228	1
2396 747	16 777 235	16 777 236	1
2396 748	16 777 243	16 777 244	1
2396 749	16 777 251	16 777 252	1

Let us have a look at Table 4.1 listing the values of the variables i and S, the contents of the FPU register R7, keeping the result of the last performed operation, and the value of the FPU bit P, indicating whether a precision error occurred. When i $= 2396\,745$, R7 $= 16\,777\,222$, representing the correct value, is copied in the variable S. As shown above, during the next iteration the last bit is lost. However, the result in the FPU is correct as it has 80 bits, namely R7 = 16 777 229. When this value is copied into the memory, the truncation to 32 bits causes the variable S to take on the value 16 777 228 and the bit P is assigned the value 1. During the next iteration the (wrong) value of S is copied into the FPU. Adding the value 7, the register R7 takes on the value 16 777 235. Again, this value is not representable in an exact way with 32 bits, and the variable S takes on the value 16 777 236, which is the closest one near it. Due to rounding, P again equals 1. The successive iterations have an analogous effect. At each step, the value of S resulting from the previous iteration is copied into R7, to which 7 is added. The result is never representable with just 32 bits and must be approximated by the closest value when expressed in terms of powers of two, i.e., the correct one increased by 1. Analyzing all successive steps, we discover that almost always the value 8, and in one sole case, the value 4, is added to the variable S, instead of 7. Finally, the obtained result is

$$S = 7 \times 2396\,746 + 4 + 6 + 8 \times (10\,000\,000 - 2396\,746 - 1 - 1) =$$
$$= 16\,777\,222 + 4 + 6 + 8 \times 7603\,252 =$$
$$= 77\,603\,248\,.$$

The essential cause of this unexpected result is that the addends are too different from each other (16 777 222 against 7). Obviously, the same might occur if the numbers x_j which are to be added were all different from each other, but small. The only difference is that in the latter case the result is more difficult to check and understand. The danger can be avoided if

$$\log_2 S - \log_2 x_j \ll p\,,$$

where p is the mantissa precision in numbers of bit. In the case under examination $p = 23$, $N = 10^7$ and $x_j = 7, \forall j$, and therefore

$$\log_2 7 \times 10^7 - \log_2 7 \simeq 23.253\,,$$

which is of the order of p. Using a **double** variable, the problem would have emerged for larger N, of the order of 10^{16}. Still, it would not have disappeared. Note that integers instead are never approximated. However, as the interval of representable numbers is highly reduced, it is not always possible to use them.

It is useful to note that modern compilers can optimize a code making it faster or consume less memory. In some cases, this optimization may hide this type of problem. For example, compiling the program in Listing 4.11 on a Linux system, using the 3.3.3 (or higher) version of the gcc compiler with the option -O1, the problem vanishes.

The reason is that the optimization consists, among other things, in extracting the cycle invariants,i.e., it extracts all quantities that do not depend on the cycle. Indeed, the optimization directly transforms the cycle in

```
S  = x  * N;
iS = ix * N;
```

Note that we used a constant value for x to simplify our discussion, while in practice all values x_j are different from each other. In the latter case the optimization is not beneficial.

To avoid this inconvenience we must try to limit the difference between the addends. One way is to perform the additions in various steps (e.g., first summing M values x_j at a time and then summing these K results, with $K \times M = N$). The most extreme choice would then be to first sum all couples of adjacent numbers x_j and x_{j+1} ($M = 2$), then add these results by iterating this operation until we end up with one single result. To this purpose, we set $x_i = x_{2i} + x_{2i+1}, i = 0 \ldots N/2$ at each iteration[9], thus reducing the number of components which are to be added by a factor 2.

```
1    float sum=0., corr=0., x = 7.;
2    int i;
3    for(i=0; i<N; i++) {
4      float tmp, y;
5      y = corr + x;
6      tmp = sum + y;
7      corr = (sum - tmp) + y;
8      sum = tmp;
9    }
10   sum += corr;
```

Listing 4.12   Kahan summation algorithm.

A more general method is the Kahan summation algorithm [Kahan (1965)], given in Listing 4.12.

Obviously, from an algebraical point of view, the sequence of operations performed by the algorithm is completely equivalent to that of Listing 4.11. In Listing 4.12, the variable corr represents, at each step, the correction which is to be made to the element x that is to be summed as it compensates for the error made during the previous step. The error on this correction

---

[9]Care needs to be taken when the number of addends are odd.

value is negligible (asymptotically zero) as the numbers which are to be subtracted have the same order of magnitude.

Until the sums are exact, the value of `corr` remains zero and thus `y = x`. The variable `tmp` represents the temporary approximation to the sum. Indeed, in this variable it is possible that the precision is not maintained due to the information loss we discussed above. If the result were exact, the difference (`sum - tmp`) evaluated on line 7 would be exactly `-y` and thus `corr` would continue to remain zero. Instead, in case the result is approximated, the latter takes on a value equal to the quantity lost due to this approximation[10].

For the example discussed above, when `sum` = $16\,777\,222$, `tmp` = $16\,777\,228$. In this case `corr` = (`sum` − `tmp`) + `y` = $(16\,777\,222 - 16\,777\,228) + 7 = -6 + 7 = 1$. At the next step, instead of the value 7, the value 8 is added to the sum, compensating for the error.

Always keep in mind that computer arithmetic is not so easy. Special care needs to be taken when treating numerical problems, particularly when a program contains many iterations.

Hands on 4.5 - Summing many small numbers

 Write an algorithm computing the sum of 10^7 numbers x all equal to each other. Analyze how the error behaves as a function of x. For which values of x is the result exact? Why? Compute the sums again with the Kahan summation algorithm. Can you predict how the execution time increases with respect to the direct algorithm? When you know how to use arrays (Chapter 5), you can rewrite the algorithm such that it sums N different numbers x_j. Then compare the performance of Kahan's algorithm with the iterative one summing pairs of numbers as described above.

---

[10]This value cannot always be fully recovered. However, it can be proven[Goldberg (1991)] that the final obtainable result with the Kahan summation algorithm can be expressed as $\sum x_j(1 + \delta_j) + \mathcal{O}(Np^2) \sum |x_j|$, with $|\delta_j| \leq 2p$.

Chapter 5

Fundamental data structures

> The core data begin to emerge,
> exposed, vulnerable...
> they tower around us
> like vertical freight trains,
> color-coded for access

William Gibson, *Burning Chrome* (1986).

In the previous chapters we considered only scalar variables already allowing us to write rather complicated programs. Still, a vast class of problems can only be formalized and resolved by introducing more complex data structures. In this chapter we discuss some of these data structures: vectors, matrices and strings (vectors of characters). In programming, these structures are called *arrays*. The names *vector* and *matrix* have been borrowed from mathematics to allow a more direct identification. An array is characterized by its number of indexes. The concept of an array with one index is similar to that of a vector representation. An array with $M > 1$ indexes may represent a matrix or a tensor. The number of indexes of an array is often called the array *dimension*. Thus, an array with one index is said to be one-dimensional. In this context the term dimension does not correspond to the mathematical concept of a dimension, where a vector with N components describes an N-dimensional quantity. In a programming language, an array *dimension* corresponds to what we refer to as a tensor *rank* in mathematics (a tensor of rank 1 is a vector). In the following, the term *dimension* expresses the number of indexes of an array, and the terms vector and one-dimensional array are used interchangeably.

5.1 One-dimensional arrays

A one-dimensional array is a set of variables of the same type. It is represented by a unique symbolic name and a nonnegative integer index. The syntax to declare a one-dimensional array is

```
type name [length];
```

as in

```
double coord[3];
```

(Note that the square brackets **[ ]** used here do not indicate an optional element, but are part of the syntax). The array `coord`, of type `double`, has length 3, i.e., consists of three elements. Each element is associated to the name of the array and an index value, which is always included in square brackets **[ ]**. The index of an array takes on consecutive values starting from 0. Thus, the three elements of the array are indexed `coord[0]`, `coord[1]` and `coord[2]`, just like the components of a vector. This convention, typical of C, but also of C++ and Perl, might be confusing to beginners. If the length of an array `x` is N, its last element is *always* `x[N-1]`; the element `x[N]` *does not belong to the array.*

Note that an array of length N fills N contiguous positions in the computer memory. The size of these positions in bytes depends on the type of the array elements. The majority of C compilers do not check whether the declared length of an array and the indexes of its components are consistent. Therefore, it is possible that during execution, the index of an array takes on values larger than the declared array length. This action causes an unpredictable behavior. Indeed, instead of causing a compilation or execution error, it "blindly" uses the memory location with the address corresponding to the array index, which might contain any possible value during execution. Care must be taken to avoid array indexes to exceed their declared maximum value. In case of an array of length N this is $N - 1$.

It is possible to declare the length of an array with an expression as in

```
#define LEN 10
double x[LEN * 2];
```

This example also shows the commonly used way of defining the length of an array by means of a constant specified in a `#define` directive. This makes it easier to apply some changes to the code in case, for example, we only want to modify the size of an array in a program.

It is worth pointing out immediately that standard C does not provide arrays of variable length. For example, it does not accept the following code:

```
int n, data[n];
printf("give the length of the data ");
scanf("%d", &n);
```

This does not necessarily produce a compilation error[1] but it causes a fatal execution error (*segmentation fault*). The reason is simple: the declaration causes, among other things, the allocation of the right amount of bytes in memory to the declared array. In the previous lines of code the variable n does not have a defined value at the time of declaration. Therefore, the compiler does not know how much room to reserve for the vector `data`. There exist "extended" compilers accepting this syntax. Remember though that this kind of code is not portable: there is no guarantee other compilers might accept it. Instead, the code

```
int n = 3, data[n];

printf("give the length of the data ");
scanf("%d", &n);
```

is compiled and executed correctly. Indeed, the array `data` is assigned the length 3. Indexing beyond the third element of the array `data`, i.e., `data[2]`, is possible, though, as always, causes unpredictable behavior. In none of the above cases we are allocating a variable length to the array during its declaration. Obviously, this limiting feature of the language creates problems when in our program we want to include arrays of a length which is not known beforehand. For now, the only way to solve this problem is to declare a large array with the `#define` directive, which we can possibly change (and re-compile) depending on our needs. However, this solution often occupies more memory than is needed; in Chapter 15 we examine some alternative solutions.

An array can be filled in various ways. Upon its declaration we can specify the number of elements and explicitly list them,

```
double x[3] = {1.2, 3.5, 2.7};
```

or simply list the elements, without specifying their total number,

---

[1]The given example does possibly causes a compilation error depending on which version of the compiler and which options are included during compilation.

```
double x[] = {1.2, 3.5, 2.7};
```

In the latter case, the compiler computes the length of the array based on the number of elements included between curly brackets **{ }**. We can also implicitly fill an array by declaring it as follows:

```
double x[3] = {1.0};
```

In this example, x[0] is set equal to 1.0 and the other two elements of x are automatically set to zero. Thus, an array can easily be reset with the declaration

```
int k[100] = {0};
```

Finally, we can use a cycle to fill an array.

```
#define LEN 100
int k[LEN];
for (j = 0; j < LEN; ++j) {
  k[j] = j + 1;
}
```

In this example, the array k is filled with consecutive integer numbers starting from 1 up to 100.

The array indexes used in statements may be constants or integer variables or expressions. This results in large flexibility when operating on arrays, as shown in Section 5.2.

5.2 Algorithms with arrays

In this section we examine some logical operations on arrays. We will see how to use and manipulate these type of data structures. At the same time, though, it introduces some generic problems which are fully developed in Chapter 16. For simplicity, we consider arrays of integers. Still, all of the following observations can be extended to **float** or **double** numbers or any other derived type.

As a first example, we consider the problem of computing the minimum, the maximum and the average of a list of numbers entered, for instance, from the keyboard (this example becomes more interesting when applied to numbers read from a file or generated in a random way).

The program of Listing 5.1 solves this problem. It fills the array **data** with N integer numbers read from the keyboard (lines 10-13). To identify the minimum and maximum, each element is examined in the **for** cycle on line 20. Note the following features of the program:

```c
#include <stdio.h>
#include <stdlib.h>
#define LEN 20

main(){
  int data[LEN], i, N = 0;
  int min, max;
  double average;
/* acquire N data, N <= LEN */
  do {
    printf("number of data = ");
    scanf("%d", &N);
  } while (N <= 0 || N > LEN);
  for (i = 0; i < N; i++) {
    printf("data %d = ", i + 1);
    scanf("%d", &data[i]);
  }
/* data array analysis */
  min = max = average = data[0];
  for (i = 1; i < N; i++) {
    if (data[i] < min) {
      min = data[i];
    }
    else if (data[i] > max) {
      max = data[i];
    }
    average += data[i];
  }
  average /= N;
  printf(" The minimum is %d\n", min);
  printf(" The maximum is %d\n", max);
  printf(" The average is %lf\n", average);
  exit(0);
}
```

Listing 5.1   Average, minimum and maximum.

- the **do-while** construct on lines 10-13 checks whether the number N of the input data is positive and less than LEN, the maximum length of the array;
- on line 19 the values **min**, **max** and **average** are initially set to have the same value as the one of the array first element (this is obviously an arbitrary choice);
- the **average** is computed in two steps: on line 27, in the **for** cycle, the data are summed, on line 29, outside the **for** cycle, the sum is divided by the number of data (applying implicit type conversion).

Exercise 5.1 - Calculating the right quantities a the right time

 Explain what happens in the program of Listing 5.1 if the statement `average /= N;` were included inside the `for` cycle (lines 20-28). Instead, if the statement on line 27 were replaced with `average = average + data[i] / N;`, the computation of the average would be wrong and inefficient. Explain why (pay attention to the declarations and remember the remark on type conversion).

5.2.1 *Sorting: Bubblesort*

We are now ready to discuss a more complicated problem: read a series of numbers and sort them, for example, in increasing order. *Sorting* a series of numbers is an important problem with numerous applications. There exist complex algorithms for sorting numbers: Chapter 16 of this textbook discusses this subject in depth. Here, we discuss an easier, rather inefficient sorting method, known as *Bubblesort*, as efficiency is obviously not an issue when sorting small series of numbers. The Bubblesort algorithm works in the following way:

- the larger numbers progressively move from the beginning to the end of the array (as bubbles rise in a liquid, hence the name to the algorithm);
- we compare contiguous pairs of numbers: if the two numbers are not sorted we swap their positions; thus, N numbers require $N-1$ comparisons;
- each number is examined at most N times.

To simplify things, data declaration and acquisition have been omitted in Listing 5.2 and can be considered analogous to those of Listing 5.1. Here, we focus our attention on the sorting algorithm.

```
1 /* the array data contains NUM unsorted numbers */
2
3 for (i = 0; i < NUM - 1; i++) {
4     for (j = NUM - 1; j > i; j--) {
5         if (data[j-1] > data[j]) {
6             temp = data[j-1];
7             data[j-1] = data[j];
8             data[j] = temp;
9         }
10    }
11 }
```

Listing 5.2   Bubblesort example.

The vector **data** of Listing 5.2 is read from the keyboard and contains NUM elements in random order, possibly including repetitions. The given algorithm implements two nested cycles to sort the vector. The external cycle simply performs NUM steps; at each step the internal cycle is repeated, starting from the end of the array towards its beginning and comparing pairs of adjacent elements. Each repetition of the internal cycle stops at the current value of the external index **i**: the first one ranges from NUM - 1 to 1, the second one from NUM - 1 to 2, etc. In the internal cycle, each time an element in position **j** - 1 is larger than the one in position **j**, the two elements need to be swapped. This swap is carried out using a so-called *auxiliary* variable **temp**. The combined effect of the two cycles is to move the larger values towards the end of the array **data**, thus achieving a sorted array. Table 5.1 contains a simple numeric example of the first steps of the Bubblesort algorithm applied to an array of NUM = 5 elements. The first column contains the value of the index **i** of the external cycle, the second column the value of the index **j** of the internal cycle and the remaining columns the sequence of the array elements. The initial sequence is 21, 17, 23, −5, 17.

Table 5.1   Successive steps of *Bubblesort*.

i	j	data[0]	data[1]	data[2]	data[3]	data[4]
0	4	21	17	23	−5	17
0	3	21	17	−5	23	17
0	2	21	−5	17	23	17
0	1	−5	21	17	23	17
1	4	−5	21	17	17	23
1	3	−5	21	17	17	23
1	2	−5	17	21	17	23
2	4	−5	17	21	17	23
2	3	−5	17	17	21	23
3	4	−5	17	17	21	23

The second last line of Table 5.1 shows the array is sorted at this point (with **i** equal to 2 and **j** equal to 3). Still, the two cycles continue to compare the already sorted values without performing any swaps (in this specific example only one pointless iteration is performed, but the consideration is generally valid). When sorting very long number sequences, similar useless operations and, in particular, examining already sorted values, should be avoided.

Hands on 5.1 - Variations on the same theme

Change the Bubblesort algorithm in such a way to quit the cycle if no swap whatsoever has been made. Try to change the logic of Listing 5.2 such that the internal cycle runs through the whole vector from beginning to end. Change the order criteria: sort the entire array in decreasing order, separate the even from the odd numbers in two distinct, ordered arrays (0 is even).

Hands on 5.2 - "Merging" two arrays

Write a program sorting two disordered arrays of the same type and merging them, thus filling a third array containing the complete, fully sorted sequence. This operation is the idea behind the *Mergesort* algorithm.

5.2.2 *Binary search*

Another interesting problem with several applications consists in searching for a given element in a sequence. If the sequence is not sorted, all its elements need to be read to find the desired one. In this case, the program executes a number of operations proportional to the number of elements N. Instead, let us consider the case in which the sequence has already been sorted, for example with Bubblesort. Let us discuss which criteria may be used to increase the efficiency of the search. For simplicity, we assume the sequence of numbers is sorted in an increasing order.

An efficient method is called the *binary search*. It first takes the central element of the sorted sequence and checks whether it is larger or smaller than the desired element (obviously, also the case in which the central element is equal to the desired one should be considered). For example, if the central element is larger, the $N/2$ elements larger than the central one no longer need to be considered in the search. Next, we perform the same comparison operation on the central element of the first $N/2$ elements of the sequence, applying the same principle. Iterating this procedure, our search field is narrowed down without checking all elements. It can be proven that this algorithm locates the desired value (or not, if it is not part of the sequence) in at most $log_2(N) + 1$ operations (we leave the proof as an exercise to the reader). An example of binary search applied to an integer array, sorted in increasing order, is given in Listing 5.3 (not all statements are included).

```
 1   int end = LEN - 1, start = 0, middle;
 2   int target, found = 0;
 3 /* the array data[LEN] contains the numbers to be examined
 4   the variable target identifies the number we are looking for
 5   the variable found signals that the number has been found */
 6   do {
 7       middle = (int) (end + start) / 2;
 8       if (data[middle] == target) {
 9           found = 1;
10       }
11       else if (data[middle] < target) {
12           start = middle + 1;
13       }
14       else {
15           end = middle - 1;
16       }
17   } while (!found && start <= end);
18   if (found == 1) {
19       printf("The number %d has been located in position %d\n"
20               ,data[middle],middle);
21   }
22   else {
23       printf("The sought number has not been found\n");
24   }
25 }
```

Listing 5.3   Example of a binary search.

The algorithm is easy. On line 9 the variable **found** is set equal to 1 if the sought value was found. As a consequence, the logical expression **!found** in the **while** statement on line 17 becomes false. If the array **data** does not contain the sought value, the condition **start <= end** becomes false at a certain point, since **start** becomes larger than **end**, or the other way around depending on the search direction. It is worth writing the logical expression of the **while** statement in the given order to stop the search as soon as the sought value has been found, thus avoiding further pointless comparisons.

5.3   Multidimensional arrays

As already mentioned in the introduction, an M-dimensional array is defined as a set of variables of the same type represented by a single symbolic name and M indexes. A two-dimensional array is perfect to represent a matrix. Similarly, multidimensional arrays may represent multidimensional mathematical quantities or tables. Let us first consider two-dimensional arrays, such as

```
int a[5][7];
```

The array a consists of 35 elements arranged in 5 *rows* and 7 *columns*. Note that the use of the terms rows and columns is nothing but a convention. Indeed, the array a actually occupies 35 consecutive locations in memory (in this case, each one consisting of 4 bytes). It is practically the same as a one-dimensional array, such as `int a[35];`. In C it is better to talk about arrays of arrays rather than multidimensional arrays. In the above example, the array `a[5][7]` may be interpreted as 5 arrays of length 7, stored in consecutive memory locations. Having two indexes, instead of one, we can refer to the elements relative to the first index (the *rows*) while keeping an element of the second index (the *columns*) fixed, or the other way around. This principle allows us, in a program, to represent matrix operations or mathematical operations on quantities which can be associated to matrices. A classic example is the product of two matrices: the element ij of the product matrix (C_{ij}) is defined as $C_{ij} = \sum_k A_{ik}B_{kj}$ where A_{ik} and B_{kj} are, respectively, the elements of the matrices A and B with indexes ik and kj. The code fragment given in Listing 5.4 performs exactly this operation.

```
1 #define ROW1 5
2 #define COL1 7
3 #define ROW2 COL1
4 #define COL2 4
5 int a[ROW1][COL1], b[ROW2][COL2], c[ROW1][COL2];
6 int i, j, k;
7 for (i = 0; i < ROW1; i++) {
8     for (j = 0; j < COL2; j++) {
9         c[i][j] = 0;
10         for (k = 0; k < COL1; k++) {
11             c[i][j] += a[i][k] * b[k][j];
12         }
13     }
14 }
```

Listing 5.4   Product of two matrices.

The statement on line 11 performs the summation over index k computing thus the element i, j of the matrix C. The length of rows and columns have been parametrized by `#define` directives to keep the code general. Obviously, in order for the matrix product to be well-defined, `ROW2` is set equal to `COL1`.

5.4   Solving systems of linear equations

In this section we describe a numerical application requiring the use of arrays, namely solving systems of linear equations. A general linear system

$$\begin{cases} a_{00}\, x_0 + a_{01}\, x_1 + \ldots + a_{0n}\, x_n = b_0 \\ a_{10}\, x_0 + a_{11}\, x_1 + \ldots + a_{1n}\, x_n = b_1 \\ \quad\vdots \\ a_{n0}\, x_0 + a_{n1}\, x_1 + \ldots + a_{nn}\, x_n = b_n \end{cases}$$

can always be rewritten in matrix form as

$$A\vec{x} = \vec{b}, \tag{5.1}$$

where A is a two-dimensional $(n + 1) \times (n + 1)$ matrix, whose elements are a_{ij}, $\vec{x}$ is the vector $(x_0, x_1, \ldots, x_n)^T$ of unknowns and $\vec{b}$ the vector of known terms with components b_i, $i = 0, \ldots, n$. In the following discussion, we obviously assume the system to be determined and, thus, to have one unique solution. The values of the solutions x_i can be found using an iterative method called *Gaussian elimination*. The method is based on the property that the solutions of the system (5.1) are invariant under linear combinations of its equations. This property is equivalent to substituting the rows of matrix A and the corresponding elements of the vector b with other rows obtained by subtracting a row by another one multiplied by a certain factor.

Let us start by dividing the first row of A and the first element of b by a_{00}. The matrix A and the vector b become

$$A = \begin{pmatrix} 1 & a_{01}^{(1)} & a_{02}^{(1)} & \cdots & a_{0n}^{(1)} \\ a_{10} & a_{11} & a_{12} & \cdots & a_{1n} \\ a_{20} & a_{21} & a_{22} & \cdots & a_{2n} \\ \vdots & & & \cdots & \vdots \\ a_{n0} & a_{n1} & a_{n2} & \cdots & a_{nn} \end{pmatrix}, \; b = \begin{pmatrix} \frac{b_0}{a_{00}} \\ b_1 \\ b_2 \\ \vdots \\ b_n \end{pmatrix} \equiv \begin{pmatrix} b_0^{(1)} \\ b_1 \\ b_2 \\ \vdots \\ b_n \end{pmatrix},$$

where $a_{0j}^{(1)} = \frac{a_{0j}}{a_{00}}$. If we subtract the first equation multiplied by a_{10} from the second equation (i.e., from the second row of matrix A and vector b), we get

$$
A =
\begin{pmatrix}
1 & a_{01}^{(1)} & a_{02}^{(1)} & \cdots & a_{0n}^{(1)} \\
0 & a_{11} - a_{10}a_{01}^{(1)} & a_{12} - a_{10}a_{02}^{(1)} & \cdots & a_{1n} - a_{10}a_{0n}^{(1)} \\
a_{20} & a_{21} & a_{22} & \cdots & a_{2n} \\
\vdots & & & \cdots & \vdots \\
a_{n0} & a_{n1} & a_{n2} & \cdots & a_{nn}
\end{pmatrix},
$$

$$
b =
\begin{pmatrix}
b_0^{(1)} \\
b_1 - a_{10}b_0^{(1)} \\
b_2 \\
\vdots \\
b_n
\end{pmatrix}
\equiv
\begin{pmatrix}
b_0^{(1)} \\
b_1^{(1)} \\
b_2 \\
\vdots \\
b_n
\end{pmatrix}.
$$

Let us set $a_{1j} - a_{10}a_{0j}^{(1)} \equiv a_{1j}^{(1)}$. Repeating this same operation on all rows (i.e., subtracting the first equation multiplied by a_{k0}, from the kth equation), we obtain a matrix A whose first column contains only zeros except for its first element which is equal to 1. In this way, we eliminated the variable x_0 from all equations except the first one:

$$
A =
\begin{pmatrix}
1 & a_{01}^{(1)} & a_{02}^{(1)} & \cdots & a_{0n}^{(1)} \\
0 & a_{11}^{(1)} & a_{12}^{(1)} & \cdots & a_{1n}^{(1)} \\
0 & a_{21}^{(1)} & a_{22}^{(1)} & \cdots & a_{2n}^{(1)} \\
\vdots & & & \cdots & \vdots \\
0 & a_{n1}^{(1)} & a_{n2}^{(1)} & \cdots & a_{nn}^{(1)}
\end{pmatrix}, \quad
b =
\begin{pmatrix}
b_0^{(1)} \\
b_1^{(1)} \\
b_2^{(1)} \\
\vdots \\
b_n^{(1)}
\end{pmatrix}.
$$

If we ignore the first row and column of the matrix A and the first element of vector b we obtain a system of n linear equations in n unknowns, to which we can apply the same procedure we just described. In this way we eliminate the variable x_1 from all equations except the first of the resulting minor of A

$$A = \begin{pmatrix} 1 & a_{01}^{(1)} & a_{02}^{(1)} & \cdots & a_{0n}^{(1)} \\ 0 & 1 & a_{12}^{(2)} & \cdots & a_{1n}^{(2)} \\ 0 & 0 & a_{22}^{(2)} & \cdots & a_{2n}^{(2)} \\ & \vdots & & \cdots & \vdots \\ 0 & 0 & a_{n2}^{(2)} & \cdots & a_{nn}^{(2)} \end{pmatrix} , \quad b = \begin{pmatrix} b_0^{(1)} \\ b_1^{(2)} \\ b_2^{(2)} \\ \vdots \\ b_n^{(2)} \end{pmatrix} .$$

We iterate this procedure for all possible minors of A until we obtain an upper triangular matrix

$$A = \begin{pmatrix} 1 & a_{01}^{(1)} & a_{02}^{(1)} & \cdots & a_{0n}^{(1)} \\ 0 & 1 & a_{12}^{(2)} & \cdots & a_{1n}^{(2)} \\ 0 & 0 & 1 & \cdots & a_{2n}^{(3)} \\ & \vdots & & \cdots & \vdots \\ 0 & 0 & 0 & \cdots & 1 \end{pmatrix} , \quad b = \begin{pmatrix} b_0^{(1)} \\ b_1^{(2)} \\ b_2^{(3)} \\ \vdots \\ b_n^{(n+1)} \end{pmatrix} .$$

At this point we can easily retrieve the solution. Starting from the last row, the value of x_n is

$$x_n = b_n^{(n+1)} = \frac{b_n^{(n)}}{a_{nn}^{(n)}} .$$

The second last row contains only two variables x_n and x_{n-1},

$$x_{n-1} + a_{(n-1)n}^{(n)} x_n = b_{n-1}^{(n)} .$$

As the value of the first one is known, we have

$$x_{n-1} = \left(b_{n-1}^{(n)} - a_{(n-1)n}^{(n)} x_n \right) . \tag{5.2}$$

In general, we have

$$x_k = \left(b_k^{(k+1)} - \sum_{i=k+1}^{n} a_{ki}^{(k+1)} x_i \right) . \tag{5.3}$$

Let us now consider how to translate this iterative procedure in a C program.

```
1 #include <stdio.h>
2 #include <math.h>
3
4 #define N 100
5
6 main() {
7 /* solving a system of equations with
8        Gauss elimination */
9    double A[N][N], b[N], x[N];
10   double C, S;
11   int n, i, j, k;
12 /* give the initial data */
13   printf(" Give the number of equations (<100): ");
14   scanf("%d", &n);
15   printf("\n Now insert the coefficients and the known terms "
16          "of the system\n");
17   for (i = 0; i < n; i++) {
18     for (j = 0; j < n; j++) {
19       printf("A[%d, %d] = ", i, j);
20       scanf("%lf", &A[i][j]);
21     }
22     printf("b[%d] = ", i);
23     scanf("%lf", &b[i]);
24   }
25 /* triangulate the matrix */
26   for (i = 0; i < n; i++) {
27     /* divide the i-th equation by the diagonal element C */
28     C = A[i][i];
29     for (j = i; j < n; j++) {
30       A[i][j] /= C;
31     }
32     b[i] /= C;
33 /* subtract the normalized equation from the others */
34     for (k = i + 1; k < n; k++) {
35       C = A[k][i];
36       for (j = i; j < n; j++) {
37         A[k][j] -= A[i][j] * C;
38       }
39       b[k] -= C * b[i];
40     }
41   }
42 /* resolve */
43   for (k = n - 1; k >= 0; k--) {
44     S = 0.;
45     for (i = k + 1; i < n; i++) {
46       S += A[k][i] * x[i];
47     }
48     x[k] = b[k] - S;
49   }
50 /* print the result */
51   for (i = 0; i < n; i++) {
52     printf("x[%d] = %lf\n", i, x[i]);
53   }
54 }
```

Listing 5.5   Solving systems of linear equations.

The program of Listing 5.5 is easy and short compared to the previous explanation of the algorithm, showing the power of iterative constructs in programming languages. We do not comment the entire program in detail as it rather faithfully follows the previous algorithm. We just note that the `for` cycle on lines 43-49 is the translation of equation (5.3) into C code. We also want to draw the reader's attention to the fact that on line 30 the matrix element `A[i][j]` is divided by the variable `C`. Thus, if `C` were equal to 0 the program would be terminated by a fatal error (*overflow* due to the division by 0). Of course this also is a limit of the algorithm itself and we should verify whether none of the diagonal elements of the given matrix are zero. In case this does occur, the order of the rows is changed such that any zero on the diagonal is avoided.

Hands on 5.3 - Check Gauss' method

 First, check the correctness of the program in Listing 5.5 with a simple numerical example of, say, three equations in three unknowns x_1, x_2 and x_3, which can be solved manually in few steps. Next, use the same program to solve a large system of 30 equations. Are there any numerical precision problems when the matrix diagonal elements are zero?

Hands on 5.4 - Avoid zeros on the diagonal

 Change the program in Listing 5.5 so to avoid any possible elements `A[i][i]` with a value equal to zero. As suggested in the text, check the diagonal elements and in case some diagonal element is zero, swap the rows of the equations.

5.5 Generating random numbers

In the previous sections, in order to show how the algorithms work, we always needed to read number sequences (typically from the keyboard). Clearly this is a painstaking task which does not allow to acquire very long sequences (try to insert 10 000 numbers in a program!). It is legitimate to wonder which other methods could be used to insert long number sequences in a program. An easy way is to read a data file written by another program; reading files in C is discussed in Chapter 6. Another very efficient way is to generate random numbers adequate for the given problem. Generating random numbers is a vast and complex argument we treat in detail in Chapter 11. To make the execution of the programs discussed in this chapter simpler, we give here some easy recipes, without pretending to be rigorous, allowing to generate a data set we can work with.

In C, the functions **rand()** or **random()** , included in the **stdlib.h** library, allow to generate random number sequences. The **rand()** function is guaranteed by the ANSI C [ANSI (1995)] standard; in some versions of the compiler both functions use the same algorithm to generate random numbers. If the **rand()** function is called several times during a program execution, it returns at each call a different integer number. In the context of this discussion, this number can be considered to be random. The integer returned by the **rand()** function lies between 0 and a maximum value defined in **stdlib.h** and called **RAND_MAX**. On a typical 32 bit architecture **RAND_MAX** equals $2\,147\,483\,647$. Most of the time, we want to generate random rational, rather than integer, numbers in a given interval. For example, the code of Listing 5.6 generates **MAX** random numbers between 0 and 1.

```
1 #include <stdlib.h>
2 #define MAX 1000
3
4 main() {
5     double x[MAX];
6
7     for (i = 0; i < MAX; i++) {
8         x[i] = (double) rand() / RAND_MAX;
9     }
10 }
```

Listing 5.6   Generating random numbers with the **rand** function.

The value 1 can be excluded from the interval by changing the division in

```
x[i] = (double) rand() / (RAND_MAX + 1.);
```

In this case it is not strictly necessary to include the *casting* as the constant **1.** is represented as a floating point. Nevertheless, to avoid common errors, we strongly recommend the use of casting. To generate a random integer between 1 and N, we can write

```
z =  rand() % N + 1;
```

or, alternatively,

```
z = (double) rand() / RAND_MAX * N;
```

where the variable **z** is of the **int** type. If the variable **z** were of the **double** type, the expression

```
z =   rand () % N + 1;
```

would still produce an integer number between 1 and N, but in the **double** representation. Instead, the expression

```
z = (double) rand () / RAND_MAX * N;
```

produces a random rational number in the interval $[0, N]$.

Note that the algorithm for generating random numbers needs to be initialized. Usually, the function **rand()** is initialized internally, but always in the same way. Thus, two executions of a program using **rand()** always generate the same random number sequence. This problem can be circumvented by calling a different function called **lrand48()**, which has to be initialized explicitly. The initialization phase of an algorithm for random number generation requires a starting number, called *seed*. Different sequences are generated by initializing the algorithm with different values of the *seed*. An example with this function is given in Listing 5.7.

```
1 #include <stdlib.h>
2 #include <time.h>
3 #define MAX 1000
4
5 main() {
6     double x[MAX];
7     int seed;
8
9     seed = time(0);
10     srand48(seed);
11
12     for (i = 0; i < MAX; i++) {
13         x[i] = (double) lrand48() / RAND_MAX;
14     }
15 }
```

Listing 5.7   Random number generation with the **lrand48** function.

The statement **seed = time(0);** always sets the **seed** to a different value. This value is obtained from the **time** function returning the computer clock time, in seconds, at the program execution time. The statement **srand48(seed);** initializes the random number generating algorithm.

5.6   Character strings

In Section 3.2 we discussed variables of the character data type `char`. It is natural to wonder how to manage a character sequence (a sentence, a series of names, an entire text). To this purpose we introduce the concept of a *string* of characters. A character string is an array of the `char` type. A simple example is

```
char  line [10];

line [0]  =  'a';
line [1]  =  'b';
line [2]  =  'c';
```

Here we defined a string `line` of length 10 and assigned the characters a, b and c to the first three elements.

5.6.1   *C string syntax*

In C, character strings follow rather peculiar syntactical rules. To avoid common errors related to the use of this type of data structures, it is worth discussing them in detail.

The length of a string can be defined explicitly:

```
char  line [100];
```

or implicitly, initializing the string when declaring it:

```
char line [] = "To be or not to be, that is the question";
```

In the latter case, the length of the array is computed by the compiler and equal to the number of characters included between double quotes `"` (including the blank spaces the above example contains 40 characters) plus one, not included explicitly. The latter terminates the string and is added by the compiler. The terminating character is the null character representable as `'\0'` and in binary notation corresponds to 0000 0000. The null character is equal to the first eight bits of the integer 0, and not to the character 0 which in binary is equal to 0011 0000 and has ASCII code 48. In C the terminating character is *mandatory* for strings. Thus, the array `line` of the example `char line [100];` contains at most 99 useful characters, as the hundredth must contain the null character.

Let us clarify the syntax of how to assign values to variables of the `char` type:

- to assign a value to a scalar variable of the `char` type, we write `a = 'Z'`; with a couple of single quotes `'...'`;
- to assign many values to a string all at once, we write `char line[] = "To be or not to be, that is the question"`; with a couple of double quotes `"..."`, and the compiler terminates the string with the character `\0`;
- to assign a value to an element of a string, we write `line[0] = 'N'`; as is the case for a scalar variable of the `char` type;
- using the name of an array of the `char` type as in the following code

```
char line[100];
line = "To be or not to be, that is the question";
```

is not allowed as the compiler considers the declaration of `line` as an array and the following assignment inconsistent [2];

- it is possible to explicitly assign the null value to an array last element, both as a character, `line[99] = '\0';`, or as an integer, `line[99] = 0;` (in the latter case, it is essential not to include the quotes).

5.6.2 *I/O of character strings*

A character string can be entered with the keyboard by calling the `scanf` function with the format specifier `%s`, as in

```
char line[100];
scanf("%s", line);
```

This example contains two particular features. First of all, the character `&` has been omitted before the name `line`; this appears a violation of the rule given in Section 3.4. A full explanation of this format is included in Chapter 6. Here we just take as an empirical rule that to read an array of the `char` type with `scanf`, we just need to include its name as an argument. The second peculiarity is the way the array in input is terminated. Namely, a blank space entry ends the input of the string, and the terminating char-

---

[2]More precisely, the inconsistence is due to the fact that the name `line` is a pointer, a concept which is introduced in Chapter 6. For the same reason it is possible to write `line[0] = "To be or not to be, that is the question";`, which we do not consider here to avoid any confusion.

acter \0 is added by the compiler in the array last element. The `scanf` function provides more detailed and complicated format specifiers to read character strings. These might, for example, allow to overcome the problem of the blank space interrupting the data input. We refer the reader to the C manuals [Kernighan and Ritchie (1988); Kelley and Pohl (1998)] for a complete treatment of these format specifiers. Let us note once more that the compiler does not check whether the string exceeds the declared length.

```
1 #include <stdio.h>
2 #include <stdlib.h>
3
4 main() {
5    char c, line[100];
6    int i = 0;
7    printf("Enter the input string: ");
8    while ((c = getchar()) != '\n') {
9       if (i < 99) {
10         line[i++] = c;
11      }
12      else {
13         printf("The maximum string length has been reached\n");
14         exit(1);
15      }
16   }
17 }
```

Listing 5.8   Use of `getchar`.

Printing a string is very easy. It suffices to call the `printf` function with the same format specifier `%s` as in

```
char line[] = "We are such stuff as dreams are made on";
printf("Shakespeare lets Prospero say: \"%s\" \n", line);
```

There does exist a more flexible way to manage single characters in I/O. Namely, by making the program interpret them and make the appropriate decisions involved. This consists in using the two functions `getchar()` and `putchar()`[3].

With `getchar()` a program reads a single character entered with the keyboard and with `putchar()` it prints it on screen. The advantage of this approach is that an unforeseen character does not cause any unexpected effect, which instead is very common with the `scanf` function. The downside is that the code has to check the input, thus explicitly doing the work

---

[3]Technically speaking `getchar()` and `putchar()` are not functions, but rather *macros*. We defined a macro in Section 3.5.

scanf does based on the included format specifiers. The program of Listing 5.8 is a rather general example of reading and managing the input. With the **getchar** function the program reads the characters entered with the keyboard until it comes across the character \n (*newline*), corresponding to the *Enter* key. As the characters are being read, it assigns them to the array **line**. In this way, blank spaces or special characters can be included in the array **line**, which is not an easy task with the **scanf** function. Moreover, it is possible for the program to evaluate or select single characters as they are being inserted, for example, neglecting blank spaces or accepting only non-numeric characters.

5.6.3 *Multidimensional strings and arrays*

We now apply what we discussed in the previous sections to a text manipulation problem. For example, let us get a list of words from the keyboard and order them alphabetically. To solve this problem we need to apply the sorting algorithm to the characters and have a two-dimensional array to keep the words in memory.

More precisely, we need to write a program reading a text, dividing it in *words*, i.e, character sequences separated by blank spaces, and store these words in an array. Once this has been done, we sort the words in alphabetic order. The program structure is the following:

- get the characters one by one and immediately check whether the end of a string has been reached;
- load the alphanumeric characters in a two-dimensional array, whose first index (rows) counts the words and the second (columns) the characters composing a single word;
- cycle through the words and compare the characters of each pair of adjacent words in order to sort the latter;
- print the result.

The program of Listing 5.9 is neither simple, nor compact. We have chosen to present this example because the Bubblesort algorithm applied to arrays rather than scalar variables requires language tools, such as pointers and functions, we have not yet introduced. Without these tools we need auxiliary variables and it is not easy to fully compare all words with a compact code.

```
1  #include <stdio.h>
2  #include <stdlib.h>
3
4  #define MAX_STRING 256
5  #define MAX_WORDS  100
6
7  main() {
8     char c, line[MAX_STRING], temp[MAX_STRING];
9     char words[MAX_WORDS][MAX_STRING];
10    char separator = ' ';
11    int i = 0, j, k = 0, jchar, kchar;
12    int templen, wordcount, charcount;
13    int wordlength[MAX_WORDS], swap = 0;
14    printf("\n Insert a phrase to decompose and sort"
15       " (press RETURN to end the input, max 255 chars):");
16    while ((c = getchar()) != '\n' && i < MAX_STRING) {
17       line[i++] = c;
18    }
19    charcount = i;
20 /*
   we place consecutive characters different from the blank space
21    in the array words
22    we do not directly use the cycle index j,
23    but rather jchar to manage consecutive blank spaces   */
24    for (j = 0; j < charcount; j++) {
25       if (line[jchar] != separator) {
26          words[wordcount][k++] = line[jchar];
27       }
28       else {
29          words[wordcount][k+1] = '\0';
30          wordlength[wordcount] = k+1;
31          wordcount++;
32 /*   ignore consecutive blank spaces */
33          if (line[jchar+1] == separator) {
34             jchar++;
35          }
36          k = 0;
37       }
38       jchar++;
39    }
40    words[wordcount][k+1] = '\0';
41    wordlength[wordcount] = k+1;
42 /*   compare the words two by two and decide whether
43       to swap them redefining the value of the variable swap
44       swap = 1  to be swapped
45       swap = -1 to leave as is
46       swap = 0  to be examined   */
47    for (k = 0; k <= wordcount; k++) {
```

```
48        for (i = wordcount; i > k; i--) {
49          kchar = 0;
50          while (swap == 0 ) {
51            while (words[i][kchar] != '\0' &&
52                   words[i-1][kchar] != '\0' &&
53                   words[i][kchar] ==  words[i-1][kchar]) {
54              kchar++;
55            }
56            if (words[i][kchar] == '\0' &&
57                words[i-1][kchar] == '\0') {
58              swap = -1;
59            } else if (words[i][kchar] == '\0' ||
60                       words[i][kchar] < words[i-1][kchar]) {
61              swap = 1;
62            } else {
63              swap = -1;
64            }
65          }
66  /*    compare the words and sort them using an
67        auxiliary array temp     */
68          if (swap == 1) {
69            for (j = 0; j < MAX_STRING; j++) {
70              temp[j] = words[i-1][j];
71              templen = wordlength[i-1];
72              words[i-1][j] = words[i][j];
73              wordlength[i-1] = wordlength[i];
74              words[i][j] = temp[j];
75              wordlength[i] = templen;
76            }
77          }
78          swap = 0;
79        }
80      }
81  /*    print the sorted array      */
82      for (i = 0; i <= wordcount; i++) {
83        printf(" Word number %d ", i);
84        for (j = 0; j <= wordlength[i]; j++) {
85          printf("%c", words[i][j]);
86        }
87        printf("\n");
88      }
89  }
```

Listing 5.9   Text manipulation.

This problem is reconsidered in Chapter 6 to show how an easier and more versatile program resolving it can be written, once pointers have been introduced.

Let us explain how the code of Listing 5.9 works. The program reads a text consisting of at most `MAX_STRING` characters, in a character type array `line`. Usually this array contains a text like `Jingle bells jingle bells, jingle all the way` (an so on). The aim of the program is to separate the words and sort them. The separation of words requires what we define a *separator*, the blank space in this case, assigned to a character type variable `separator`. Using the separator we fill the two-dimensional array `words` with text characters (lines 24-41). This is already not an easy operation as we need to take into account the possibility that there are many consecutive blank spaces, and that the last character of a string may itself be a blank space. The variable `wordcount` counts the number of words, starting from 0. The auxiliary array `wordlength` holds the length of each word, using an index which has a one-to-one correspondence to the first index of the two-dimensional array `words`. On lines 47-80 the words are sorted with Bubblesort. The sorting consists of the following operations:

(1) the consecutive comparison of all characters in a word, in the j-th row of the array `words`, with all corresponding characters of the previous word, in the row j-1-th row of the same array; in this way we can decide whether, for instance, the word `bells` precedes or follows the word `jingle`;

(2) swapping the lines of the `words` array if this is required.

Let us recall that comparing characters in C translates into comparing integer numbers, namely the ASCII values corresponding to the characters. Thus, the character L, equal to 76 in ASCII, is less than the character l which is 108 in ASCII. Solving point 1 above is not easy without using functions. The Listing 5.9 requires two `for` cycles and two `while` cycles, one nested in the other, to analyze all letters of all words. The second operation is easy if the swap is made, as on lines 69-76, until the maximum length `MAX_STRING`. Instead, swapping two words of different length, taking their respective length into account, is a completely different matter. Finally, to decide whether two words should be swapped or not, we need an auxiliary variable `swap` initially set equal to 0. It assumes the value 1 if `words[i][j]` is less than `words[i - 1][j]` (swap needed), −1 in the opposite case or if the two words are equal to each other (no swap is needed). It is reset after each swap. On the one hand, this example shows how the language elements we have seen so far allow to resolve complicated problems. On the other hand, it shows the limits of these kinds of solutions.

Measuring time in computers

In C, the function `time(0)` returns the number of seconds that have passed ever since a conventional date, called *Epoch*, coinciding with the time 00:00:00 UTC (*Universal Coordinated Time*) of January the 1st, 1970. The first use of this measurement unit dates back to the UNIX programming manual, published at the end of 1971 and adopting the 1st of January of that same year as starting instance. The current definition dates back to 2001. The time interval returned by the `time` function does not really coincide with the true elapsed time. Indeed, a day does not have a fixed length, while in Epoch measure it has been set to 86 400 s. The UTC time measure is regulated by atomic clocks managed by the IERS (*International Earth Rotation and Reference Systems Service*). To keep the official and the solar time synchronized, the IERS may decide to add or remove a second (*leap second*), when necessary. This always occurs at UTC midnight of the day fixed by the IERS (the last day of the month during which the correction took place). In these occasions, the time 23:59:60 does not coincide with the time 00:00:00 of the next day, as is usually the case. This correction is made simultaneously all over the globe, and thus the local time at which it occurs varies from country to country. When this correction is made, a single Epoch time value represents two separate time instances, namely, 23:59:60 and 00:00:00 of the next day. The first correction dates back to June 30, 1972. Ever since then up to June 2005, 22 corrections have been made. The last time was at midnight of December 31, 1998. As is clear from the table included in this box, in Epoch the value $t = 915\,148\,800$ indicates two different time instances. The website of the IERS is available at `http://www.iers.org`.

UTC time	Epoch
31/12/1998 23:59:59	915 148 799
31/12/1998 23:59:60	915 148 800
01/01/1999 00:00:00	915 148 800
01/01/1999 00:00:01	915 148 801

The unsynchronized instances between Epoch and UTC are governed by the POSIX rules (*Portable Operating Systems Interface for computer environment*) issued by the IEEE. To keep the algorithms of the standard functions simple, they assume any possible correction is accounted for by the user.

Usually, the Epoch is represented by a 32 bit signed integer. The smallest value corresponds to December 13, 1901 at 20:45:52, while the largest value will be reached on January 19, 2038 at 03:14:07 (covering a total of about 136 years). On that day, the Epoch representation will have to be changed (for example, by extending the number of bits to 64). This is why this date is anxiously awaited as the event might create a lot more problems than the notorious *Millennium bug* did.

Chapter 6

Pointers

«Would you tell me, please,
which way I ought to go from here?»
«That depends a good deal
on where you want to get to»
said the Cat

Lewis Carroll, *Alice in Wonderland* (1865).

Throughout the previous chapters we often talked about memory locations occupied by a variable or an array. In this chapter we discuss how to access these memory locations and change their content in a program. In other words, we introduce the concept of a *pointer* in the C language and discuss how to use it when programming.

6.1 Pointers and pointed variables

Imagine the memory allocated to a program to be a series of post office boxes. Each box is identified by a progressive number marked on the door. We assume that initially all boxes are empty. Each box can contain an object (a parcel, a letter). The addressee of the object is associated to the box by means of a list, informing, for example, that Mr. Smith's object is in box 137. To access an object we do not need to open the preceding 136 boxes. Rather, we immediately go to box 137, open it and collect its content. The boxes represent the memory locations, the names on the list represent the variables of a program and the objects in the boxes their values[1]. Finally, the numbers on the doors of the boxes are the *addresses* of the memory locations. A *pointer* to a variable is defined as the address of the memory location allocated to that variable. More precisely, the term pointer defines a variable of the pointer type containing the address of another variable (in what follows, to be concise, we use simply the term *pointers*). Like all variables, also pointers need to be declared.

The declaration syntax is

```
type *name_pointer;
```

where the symbol * identifies the variable as a pointer in the declaration. We need to specify the type of variable that is pointed by the pointer variable as the number of bytes allocated to a variable depend on its type. To put it in terms of postal boxes, imagine there are both smaller boxes for letters and larger ones for parcels.

For example, the statement `double *pd;` declares a variable with name `pd` of the type pointer to `double`. At this point, the variable `pd` does not yet have a defined value. We can assign it a value by means of the *reference* operator &, a unary operator returning the address of the operand on its right. After this assignment the variable `pd`, occupying 4 byte on a 32 bit architecture, contains the address of the memory location containing a `double` variable (equivalent to the number 137 of the postal box). In the example

```
double a, *pd;
a = 3.14;
pd = &a;
```

the variable `pd` contains the address of the memory location of variable `a`. It is possible to define a pointer to any C type. In particular, it is possible to define a pointer to the `void` type, as in `void *pv` to use a pointer without knowing beforehand which type of variable it has to point. We can assign the value of any other pointer to a pointer to `void`. This does not imply a cast operation. Moreover, it is possible to temporarily change the type of a pointer to `void` with an explicit cast operation.

It is important to understand that the pointer `pd` *has nothing to do with the value of* `a`, just like the postbox number is not related to its content. Moreover, we can safely assign a value to a pointer, as in `pd = &a;`, before the pointed variable `a` has been defined, or assign an undefined pointer to

---

[1]As explained in Chapter 2, the memory locations allocated to a program not only contain variables, but also statements of the program itself. Here we concentrate only on the memory locations containing variables.

another. Therefore, the following lines of code,

```
double a, *pd, *pe;
pd = &a;
pe = pd;
a = 3.14;
printf("Pointers pd = %p,pe = %p,variable a = %f\n",pd,pe,a);
a = 2.73;
printf("Pointers pd = %p,pe = %p,variable a = %f\n",pd,pe,a);
```

produce the following print[2]

```
Pointers pd = 0xbffff7a0,pe = 0xbffff7a0,variable a = 3.14000
Pointers pd = 0xbffff7a0,pe = 0xbffff7a0,variable a = 2.73000
```

showing how the value of a changes while the value of pd and pe remains unchanged. Note that to print the value of the pointers, we use the format specifier %p in printf. This prints out the 8 digit, i.e. 32 bit, address to which pd or pe are pointing, in hexadecimal (the string 0x indicates that the following value is expressed in hexadecimal).

Pointers also allow to access or change the value of the variable they point to by means of the *indirection* operator[3], a unary operator whose symbol is the asterisk *. When the indirection operator * is applied to a pointer, it returns the content of the memory location that the pointer points to. In general, given a pointer pd, the expression *pd is equal to the value of the pointed variable. For example, in the following lines of code,

```
double a, b, *pd;
pd = &a;
a = 3.14;
b = *pd;
```

by indirection of the pointer pd, the variable b takes on the value 3.14, which was previously assigned to the variable a . If *pd is included to the left of the assignment operator, a value is assigned to the pointed variable, as in the code

---

[2]In this example, and all the following ones reporting memory addresses, the values of these addresses is the one the authors obtained by executing the code given in the examples. Executing this code in different moments or on different computers may produce different values.

[3]The indirection operator is sometimes also called the *dereference* operator. Indeed, as the operator & *refers to* the pointed variable it is sometimes also called the *reference* operator. Instead, the operator * has the opposite effect.

```
double a, b, *pd;
pd = &a;
*pd = 3.14;
b = a;
```

The result is the same as before, apart from the fact that we did not explicitly assign the value 3.14 to the variable a, but rather by means of indirection of its pointer pd.

In Section 3.4 we introduced the scanf function. We already pointed out that the variable names read by scanf from the keyboard have to be prefixed by the sign &. It is now clear why we need to do this. The scanf function actually reads numerical values or characters and writes them in the memory locations assigned to the variables appearing in the argument list. To access these memory locations, scanf needs the respective addresses, i.e., the pointers to these variables. Instead, the printf function prints the values of the variables specified in the argument list. To perform this task, it does not need to access the memory locations, which is why its arguments are included without the operator &.

Although the symbol is identical, we need to be careful not to mix up the binary multiplication operator * and the unary indirection operator or the symbol used for the indirection of a pointer. Table 6.1 contains three examples of code containing the symbol * together with its meaning in that context.

Table 6.1   Meaning of the symbol.*

Statement	*Meaning*	*Context*
c = a * b;	multiplication operator	in expressions
double *pd;	declaration of a pointer type	only in declarations
b = *pd;	indirection operator	in expressions

It is common to make syntactical mistakes when using pointers. In particular, declaring a pointer and using it before assigning an address to it leads to unpredictable results. It is good practice to initialize a pointer, upon declaration, with the special value NULL, which is generally represented in binary by all zeros. We invite the reader to train in basic usage of pointers by doing the Exercise 1.

Exercise 6.1 - Common programming errors

Decide whether the following expressions are correct or not and explain why. Note that among the incorrect expressions, some produce a compilation error, while others compile correctly, but cause a fatal error upon execution (generally, a *segmentation fault*). Pay attention to assign a defined address to pointers and make sure the type pointed to by the pointer and the type of the pointed variable are coherent.

```
int a;
double b, *pd;
pd = &a;
```

```
double b, c, *pd;
b = 3.14;
c = &(*pd);
```

```
double b, *pd;
pd = &b;
*pd = 3.14;
```

```
double b, c, *pd;
b = 3.14;
pd = &c;
*pd = &b;
```

```
int a;
double b = 3.14, *pd;
pd = &b;
a = *pd;
```

```
double b, c, *pd;
b = 3.14;
pd = &c;
*pd = b;
```

```
double b, *pd;
*pd = 3.14;
b = *pd;
```

```
double b, *pd;
*pd = 3.14;
&b = pd;
```

```
int a;
a = &2;
```

```
double b, *pd;
*pd = *&b;
```

6.2 Arrays and pointers in C

In C, pointers are particularly interesting and useful when they are applied to arrays. Indeed, in C the name of an array is a pointer to the memory location containing the array first element. Let us clarify this aspect better as it is often not well understood by C programming beginners. In Section 5.1 we defined an array as a set of variables of the same type, all associated to a single symbolic name. The declaration `int data[10];` asks the compiler to allocate ten integer elements (of 32 bits each) occupying ten contiguous memory locations, from `data[0]` to `data[9]`. We can define the pointer to the first of these positions as a pointer to any other variable

```
int data[10], *pd;
pd = &data[0];
```

Obviously, defining `pd` as a pointer to `data[0]`, the expression `*pd` is equal to `data[0]`.

The next elements of the array, which we have characterized up to now with an index between square brackets `[ ]`, can be addressed by incrementing the pointer to the first element. If `pd` is the pointer to the array first element `data[0]` and considering that the successive elements of the array `data` are contiguous in memory, the address of `data[1]` can be expressed as `pd + 1`, that of `data[2]` as `pd + 2` and so on. This becomes particularly clear if we print the value of a pointer incremented by a variable index `i`, as in Listing 6.1.

```
1 #include <stdio.h>
2 #define LEN 5
3 main() {
4   float data[LEN], *pd;
5   int i;
6   pd = &data[0];
7   for (i = 0; i < LEN; i++) {
8     printf(" pd + %d = %p, &data[%d] = %p\n",
9     i, data + i, i, &data[i]);
10   }
11 }
```

Listing 6.1   Augmenting a pointer to an array.

The result of the program of Listing 6.1 is for example

```
pd + 0 = 0xbffff780, &data[0] = 0xbffff780
pd + 1 = 0xbffff784, &data[1] = 0xbffff784
pd + 2 = 0xbffff788, &data[2] = 0xbffff788
pd + 3 = 0xbffff78c, &data[3] = 0xbffff78c
pd + 4 = 0xbffff790, &data[4] = 0xbffff790
```

It shows how changing the index `i` causes the address `pd + i` to increase by 4 bytes. This 4 bytes increment is due to the fact that the array `data` is of `float` type. Moreover, the value of the expression `pd + i` and that of `&data[i]` are identical.

Thus, the values of the array first elements take the form `data[0]`, `data[1]`, `data[2]`, `*(pd)`, `*(pd + 1)`, `*(pd + 2)` or, finally, `*(&data[0])`, `*(&data[0] + 1)`, `*(&data[0] + 2)`. The C language always defines the name of an array *without any square brackets* `[ ]` *identical to the pointer to its first element*. This makes more explicit the connection between an array index and the increment of the pointer to the first element of that array. Thus,

```
pd = &data[0];
```

is equivalent to

```
pd = data;
```

As a consequence, we can simply write `data` instead of `&data[0]` in all previous expressions, and `data[1]` is equal to `*(pd + 1)` and also to `*(data + 1)`.

It is now legitimate to ask the following question: how can the compiler correctly compute the address of the successive elements of arrays of different types, given that for `int` type arrays, the pointer must advance 32 bits, while for `double` type arrays it must move forward 64 bits? The answer lies in the fact that, when we declare a pointer variable, we always have to specify the type it points to. By writing

```
double data[10], *pd;
int x[10], *pi;
pd = data;
pi = x;
```

we inform the compiler that the pointer type variable `pd` points to a `double`, while the pointer variable `pi` points to an integer. In that same program a compiler will translate the expression `pd + 2` in machine code statements addressing the memory location contained in `pd` plus 2 × 64 bits. Instead, the expression `pi + 2` generates a machine code addressing the memory location contained in `pi` plus 2 × 32 bits. In conclusion, declaring the type to which a pointer points, allows us to correctly address successive memory locations: the pointer value will always be augmented by the correct amount for any size, in bit, of the pointed variables. Care needs to be taken when using pointers which are names of an array. For these pointers, some operations, which are generally allowed, try to change the memory map of the program and are therefore forbidden. These operations generate compilation errors.

Such a case is included in Listing 6.2. On line 4, the expression `a = d` assigns the address of the first position of the array `d[3]` to the pointer `a`, containing the address of the first position of the array `a[3]`. The two pointers `a` and `d` are constant though, as they address a part of the memory in a static way. Therefore, it is not possible to change their value. The expression `a = &d[0]` on line 5 does the same operation by applying the reference operator `&` to the element `d[0]`; also in this case the operation is illegal. Instead, it is allowed to assign the same address of the first position of the array d[3] to the pointer variable `pointer`, as we saw at the beginning of this Section.

```
1 main () {
2   int a[3], d[3];
3   int *pointer;
4   a = d;        /* forbidden operation */
5   a = &d[0];    /* forbidden operation */
6   pointer = d;
7 }
```

Listing 6.2   Forbidden operations between array pointers.

6.2.1   *The const qualifier*

When a constant value is repeated several times throughout a program, it is convenient to replace it with a parameter. In this way, we can simply change the parameter value in case we need to change the value of the constant. Up to now, we have used the #define directive to define constants. This directive replaces a character string with an expression (Section 3.5). It is often preferable to use variables which cannot be modified. In some way we can consider these *constant variables*, i.e, names associated to memory locations containing constant values (the term *variable* is rather misleading in this case).

In C, we can define constant variables by preceding their declaration by the qualifier const. The value assigned to a variable declared in this way cannot be changed by any part of the code. Let us consider the example

```
int b = 2;
const int a = b;
b = 3;
a = 1;
```

The variable b is a common integer variable initially set to the value 2. Instead, the variable a, preceded by the const qualifier, takes on a value which, once it has been fixed, can no longer be changed. In this case, the variable a takes on the value 2. The statement b = 3; is legal. Instead, a = 1; is illegal because the variable a has been declared to be constant and cannot take on any value different from 2 throughout the program. Indeed, the statement a = 1; produces a compilation error.

The const qualifier is often useful when dealing with pointers. In these cases, we need to pay special attention to the qualifier position with respect to the other elements in the declaration.

Let us consider the following three statements:

```
char * const p1;
char const *p2;
const char *p3;
```

The first statement declares p1 to be a constant pointer to characters; the second and third statements declare p2 and p3 to be pointers to constant characters. The variable p1 contains a memory address which cannot be changed, while the content of the pointed memory can change. Instead, the variables p2 and p3 can point to different memory locations (as they are no constants). However, the content of the pointed locations cannot be changed. Indeed, applying the trick of reading the declarations from right to left, we have that p2 is a pointer to constants of the character type, and p3 is a pointer to constant characters. The Listing 6.3 shows how the const qualifier can be applied to character strings pointers.

```
1  main () {
2     char string1 [50] = "Lucy in the sky with diamonds";
3     char string2 [50] = "Hey Jude";
4     char * const p1 = string1;
5     printf ("%s\n", p1);
6     p1 [17] = 's';
7     printf ("%s\n", p1);
8     p1 = string2;
9     printf ("%s\n", p1);
10 }
```

Listing 6.3   Use of constant pointers.

All lines of Listing 6.3 are correct, except for line 8, as it attempts to assign a different value to the pointer variable p1 whose initial value has been defined as the address of string1. If we substitute the statement on line 4 with the following

```
char const * p1 = string1;
```

line 6 becomes incorrect. Indeed, in that case it is legitimate to assign a different value to p1 (for example p1 = string2;). However, it is not allowed to change the content of the pointed memory location. This is also the case if p1 is declared as

```
const char * p1 = string1;
```

The **const** qualifier allows us to protect the content of a memory location. It is more general and flexible than the **#define** directive as it makes possible, for example, to extend the parametrization of constants to pointers.

6.2.2   *String pointers*

In Section 5.6 we discussed character strings or character arrays. A pointer to a string is not any different from a pointer to an array; the name of the string is the pointer to the string itself and all syntactical rules applying to array pointers remain valid. We can write

```
char *pc;
char line[] = "I can't get no satisfaction";
pc = line;
*(pc + 21) = 'i';
```

spoiling in this way the Rolling Stones verse by changing **satisfaction** into **satisfiction**. It is possible to write into a character string with the I/O function **sprintf**: the **sprintf** function, included in the header file **<stdio.h>**, takes as a first argument the pointer to the string on which we want to write, and allows one to write a numerical value or any other character string into this string. An example is

```
char string1[50] = "";
char string2[] = "%lf";
int n = 15;
sprintf(string1, "%c%d%s", string2[0], n, &string2[1]);
```

where the first argument **string1** is the pointer to the string element which is to be changed. The following arguments are analogous to the corresponding arguments of **printf**. In the example, we build the string **%15lf**, which is a printing format, starting from the string **string2**, equal to **%lf**, and the variable **n**, set to 15. This operation allows us to decide the printing format (in this case **%15lf**) as a function of the analyzed data; this possibility is particularly useful when printing scientific data. For example, we can read data and define part of a printing format, such as the total number of digits and the number of decimal digits, based on the order of magnitude of the read data. We can print these data in the most suitable format by building a string with one or more calls to the **sprintf** function which is then used as format specifier.

Hands on 6.1 - Variable printing format

 Write a program building a format specifier for the `printf` function based on the order of magnitude of the data. To this purpose, generate a set of random data as explained in Section 5.5. It is handy to generate integers between 0 and `RAND_MAX`, thus having orders of magnitude ranging from one up to 10^9. Evaluate the order of magnitude of the generated data by computing their logarithm in base 10. Use this value to define the printing format of the generated numbers by means of the `sprintf` function. Print the data with all and only the significant digits in decimal form multiplied by the appropriate power of 10. For example, in case of 14 567, generate the printing format `%7.5e` such that the number is printed as `0.14567e05`.

6.3 Pointer arithmetic

Since we can express the value of an array element, `data[3]`, as `*(data + 3)`, is it possible to apply whichever C operator to the pointer `data`? The answer is "NO". We can only perform additions or subtractions on a pointer, and even these operations are subject to some limitations. Once we have declared an array, we can add or subtract values, whether constant or variable, to or from that array pointer. Thus, all operations on pointers described in Listing 6.4 are valid.

```
1 #define LEN 10
2
3   double data[LEN] = {3.14, 1.57}, *pd;
4   double a, b, c;
5   int k = 2;
6
7   pd = data;
8   a = *(pd + 1);
9   pd++;
10  b = *(pd - 1);
11  c = *(pd + k);
```

Listing 6.4   Operating on pointers in an array.

On line 8 the constant 1 is added to the pointer `pd`; on line 9 the pointer `pd` is post-incremented, on line 10 the constant 1 is subtracted and, finally, on line 11 the variable `k` is added to `pd`. The result of these operations is a shift, *forward* or *backward*, in memory with respect to the current value of the pointer `pd`.

Exercise 6.2 - Pointer check

To briefly check whether you have understood the operations of Listing 6.4, compute the final values of the variables a, b and c. Check whether your answers are respectively 1.57, 3.14 and 0. Explain why.

As we mentioned several times in Chapter 5, the C compiler does not check whether the declared array length and the address of an element of that same array are consistent. Thus, accessing array elements by pointers requires the same, if not more, caution as when addressing them explicitly.

Once we have defined a pointer to a scalar variable, we can also add or subtract a preset quantity to the pointer value and access the resulting memory location. We need to be particularly careful when accessing memory locations by operating on pointers. Indeed, adding or subtracting quantities to a pointer such that the resulting address lies outside the memory allocated to the program when it is executed, always produces unpredictable results. In some cases the program can even be terminated with a fatal error (segmentation fault) caused by an attempt to access a forbidden memory area. The Listings 6.5 and 6.6 clarify this point.

```
1   double a, b, *pd;
2
3   a = 3.14;
4   pd = &a;
5   pd++;
6   b = *(pd - 1);
7   printf ("We get a = %f, b = %f, a, b);
```

Listing 6.5   Risky pointer operations.

```
1   double a, b, *pd;
2
3   a = 3.14;
4   pd = &a;
5   pd++;
6   b = *(pd - 1000);
7   printf ("We get a = %f, b = %f\n", a, b);
```

Listing 6.6   Fatal pointer operations.

The only difference between line 5 of Listing 6.5 and the same line of Listing 6.6 is the value of the constant which is subtracted from the value of the pointer pd. In the first case, the constant is 1, in the second 1000. It is very likely that the memory address (pd - 1000) lies outside the memory allocated to this program. Therefore, while the Listing 6.6, completed by the file #include <stdio.h> and the main statement, compiles correctly, it generally produces an error upon execution. Instead, the code of Listing 6.5 does not cause any errors when executed, but assigns an unpredictable value to the variable b.

Finally, we discuss the priority of the operators that can be applied to a pointer. Remember that the unary operators have the highest priority. Thus, expressions like *pi++, where pi is a pointer to an integer for example, are not obvious. Without parentheses, the expression *pi++ is equivalent to the expression *(pi++). Although the two unary operators have the same priority, they are associated from right to left. Thus, the post-increment operator ++ has a higher priority than the indirection operator *. Nevertheless, the effect of this operation is not obvious: the expression *pi++, or *(pi++), returns the indirection of the pointer pi, considering its current value; next, the pointer is augmented. As ++ has a higher priority it is applied to the pointer pi rather than the variable *pi. In comparison, the expression (*pi)++ takes the value of the variable pointed to by pi and increments it.

The code fragment of Listing 6.7 shows these cases.

```
1 int k[2], *pi;
2 k[0] = 137;
3 pi = k;
4 *pi++ = 100;        /* increment the pointer */
5 k[0] = 137;
6 pi = k;
7 (*pi)++;            /* increment the variable */
```

Listing 6.7   Operator priority applied to a pointer.

For example, if the address of the element k[0] equals 0xbffff7a0, the variable pi on line 3 takes on this value. On line 4 k[0] equals 100, while the pointer pi is augmented by one position (four bytes) and now equals 0xbffff7a4. Finally, on line 7, the variable pointed to by pi, i.e., k[0], is increased from 137 to 138. Instead, the pointer pi maintains its value 0xbffff7a0.

6.4   Efficiency issues

It might seem less "natural" to access the elements of an array by means of pointers, rather than the usual indexes. A good reason to opt for the pointers anyway is that they are more efficient. Let us consider the following code

```
double data[10] = {0}, a;
data[3] = 3.14;
a = data[3];
```

Each time we refer to an element of the array `data` by means of its index, the compiler needs to compute the memory position of `data[3]`. To this purpose, it must first read the value of the address in the variable `data`, compute the correct increment performing a multiplication (3×8 bytes) and finally, add the increment to `data`. If, on the opposite, we use pointers, the number of operations remains the same:

```
double data[10] = {0}, a;
*(data + 3) = 3.14;
a = *(data + 3);
```

Things are different in case of a cycle sequentially passing through all elements of an array. In the latter case it is less efficient to use indexes rather than pointers. To prove the latter statement, we consider an array of a hundred elements. We examine it in a cycle to search for elements with negative values. The Listing 6.8 contains the code cycling through the array elements.

This cycle, apart from the operations in the `for`, entails the computation of the address of `data[i]` for each control `if (data[i] < 0.)` that is performed during its execution; this amounts to executing 100 additions (`data + i`) and 100 multiplications (for each addition $i \times 8$ bytes).

```
1 double data[100];
2 int i;
3 ... omitted code ...
4 for (i = 0; i < 100; i++) {
5   if (data[i] < 0.) {
6     printf("Negative value found %f \n", data[i]);
7   }
8 }
```

Listing 6.8   Accessing an array by means of indexes.

Instead, consider the Listing 6.9. In this case, the arithmetic of the cycle is the same. However, for none of the controls `if (*pd < 0.)` we need to compute anything to access the current element of the array *pd. We also introduced an auxiliary variable lastpd to avoid computing 100 times the addition data + 100 in the condition to exit the for cycle on line 4.

```
1 double data[100], *pd, *lastpd;
2 ... omitted code ...
3 lastpd = data + 100;
4 for (pd = data; pd < lastpd; pd++) {
5   if (*pd < 0.) {
6     printf("Negative value found %f \n", *pd);
7   }
8 }
```

Listing 6.9 Accessing an array with pointers.

In conclusion, it is preferable to perform sequential operations on an array, particularly long ones, by means of pointers to the array, rather than explicit indexes of the array. The price we pay for this greater efficiency is that the code in Listing 6.9 is less clear and, in general, the use of pointers is more prone to programming errors.

6.5 Multidimensional arrays and pointers

In Section 5.3 we studied multidimensional arrays. Let us now show at how to access these arrays with pointers. Recall that an array with two indexes a[4][7] (for instance of the double type) fills 4×7 contiguous memory locations. Therefore, in some way, we could consider it as a one-dimensional array of length 28. The order of the array elements in the memory is such that the leftmost index of a multidimensional array grows more slowly, similar to how the digits of a car odometer change.

Thus, in the memory, after the element a[0][0] we have a[0][1], next a[0][2] and so on. From the operator priority viewpoint, the operator [ ], appearing twice in a two-dimensional array, is evaluated as always from left to right. We can think of the array a[4][7] as a 4 elements array a[4], whose elements are, in turn, a 7 elements array. In this viewpoint, the name a or also a[0] is a pointer to the first element of the two-dimensional array, i.e., to the first *subarray* of length 7; thus a + 1 or a[1] points to the second subarray of length 7 and so on. Figure 6.1 shows this in a diagrammatic way. The expression *(a + 1) is equal to the content of the memory location to which a + 1 points. This location contains the address of the second subarray. Thus *(a + 1) *is not an array element, but another*

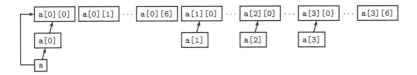

Fig. 6.1   A two-dimensional array expressed as an array of arrays.

pointer. Analogously, the expression *(a + 1) + 1 is a pointer as well, namely the address of the second element of the second subarray. Finally, the expression *(*(a + 1)) dereferences the pointer *(a + 1) returning the content of the pointed memory location, which corresponds to the first element of the second subarray. In terms of indexes, this would be a[1][0]. In the same way, the expression *(*(a + 1) + 3) is equal to a[1][3].

So, how can we run across a multidimensional array with a pointer? To this purpose we need to make the starting point, i.e., the initial address, explicit, as in &a[0][0], or *a and not a. Also, we need to take the memory map into account, i.e., the fact that the fastest changing index is the rightmost, then the one immediately to its left and so on. The following code explains what the algorithm should look like. We can write either

```
double a[4][7];
*(&a[0][0] + 1)     = 3.14;       /* set a[0][1] = 3.14 */
*(&a[0][0] + 7)     = 6.28;       /* set a[1][0] = 6.28 */
*(&a[0][0] + 7 + 1) = 2.73;       /* set a[1][1] = 2.73 */
```

or

```
double a[4][7];
*(*a + 1)       = 3.14;     /* set a[0][1] = 3.14 */
*(*(a + 1))     = 6.28;     /* set a[1][0] = 6.28 */
*(*(a + 1) + 1) = 2.73;     /* set a[1][1] = 2.73 */
```

In general, as we declared a multidimensional array a[N1][N2], we can dereference one of its elements a[i][j] by writing either

```
*(&a[0][0] + N2 * i + j)
```

or

```
*(*(a + i) + j)
```

In conclusion, we note that in case of multidimensional arrays the efficiency considerations of Section 6.4 are largely compensated for by the complicated pointer syntax. Nevertheless, we believe that for multidimensional arrays it is preferable to use explicit indexes between [ ] to minimize possible programming errors and create a more comprehensive code. Moreover, many problems dealing with complex data structures cannot be treated in an adequate way with static multidimensional arrays. In these cases, the arrays should be declared in a dynamic way; this type of data structure is discussed in Chapter 10.

6.5.1 *Pointer arrays*

Just like with any other type of variable, it is possible to create an array of pointers. An array of pointers is particularly useful to manipulate complicated data structures. A classic example are the two-dimensional arrays of character strings we considered in Section 5.6.3. In Listing 5.9 we saw how to elaborate a text by dividing it into words which are then sorted according to the alphabet. The logic of the program in Listing 5.9 is rather complicated and the program has certain limitations. The use of pointer arrays simplifies the solution to the problem and produces a more efficient and elegant code, as given in Listing 6.10.

```
1 #include <stdio.h>
2 #include <stdlib.h>
3
4 #define MAX_STRING 256
5 #define MAX_WORDS   100
6
7 main() {
8    char c, line[MAX_STRING];
9    char *wordaddress[MAX_WORDS], *pc, *temp, *p0, *p1;
10   char separator = ' ';
11   int i = 0, j = 0, k = 0, min;
12   int templen;
13   int wordcount = 0, charcount = 0;
14   int wordlength[MAX_WORDS], swap = 0;
15   printf("\n Give a phrase to be broken down and re-sorted\n "
16      " (the ENTER key to end the input, "
17      "max 255 characters)\n --> ");
18   while ((c = getchar()) != '\n' && i < MAX_STRING) {
19      line[i++] = c;
20   }
21   charcount = i;
22   line[charcount] = '\0';
23   for (pc = &line[0]; pc < &line[0] + charcount; pc++) {
24      if (*pc == separator && *(pc + 1) != separator) {
25         wordlength[k] = j;
26         wordaddress[k] = pc - j;
27         k++;
```

```
28       j = 0;
29     }
30     else if (*pc == separator && *(pc + 1) == separator) {
31     }
32     else {
33       j++;
34     }
35   }
36   wordlength[k] = j;
37   wordaddress[k] = pc - j;
38   wordcount = k;
39   for (k = 0; k <= wordcount; k++) {
40     for (i = wordcount; i > k; i--) {
41       swap = 0;
42       min = wordlength[i];
43       if(min > wordlength[i - 1]) {
44         min = wordlength[i - 1];
45       }
46       p0 = wordaddress[i - 1];
47       p1 = wordaddress[i];
48       j = 0;
49       while (swap == 0 && j < min) {
50         if (*(p1 + j) < *(p0 + j)) {
51           swap = 1;
52         } else if (*(p0 + j) < *(p1 +j)) {
53           swap = -1;
54         }
55         j++;
56       }
57       if (swap == 1) {
58         temp = wordaddress[i - 1];
59         templen = wordlength[i - 1];
60         wordaddress[i - 1] = wordaddress[i];
61         wordlength[i - 1] = wordlength[i];
62         wordaddress[i] = temp;
63         wordlength[i] = templen;
64         swap = 0;
65       }
66     }
67   }
68   for (i = 0; i <= wordcount; i++) {
69     printf(" Word number %d ", i + 1);
70     for (j = 0; j < wordlength[i]; j++) {
71       pc = wordaddress[i];
72       printf("%c",*(wordaddress[i] + j));
73     }
74     printf("\n");
75   }
76 }
```

Listing 6.10   Dictionary using pointers.

We encourage the reader to compare the Listing 6.10 with the Listing 5.9 to realize the different programming logic. Unlike Listing 5.9, Listing 6.10 does not contain any two-dimensional arrays to store the words the program acquires. Instead, we first analyze the string `line` containing the characters read from the keyboard. Next, we identify the words defined as character sequences separated by one or more characters equal to the `separator`. For each word, we store the address of its first character and its length in two separate arrays, the pointer array `wordaddress` and the integer array `wordlength`, respectively. At that point, in the `for` cycle on lines 39-67, we apply the Bubblesort algorithm (Section 5.2.1). The comparison between two words is limited to the minimum number of characters they have in common. It is interrupted as soon as a different character has been found, allowing the respective words to be sorted. The interesting fact is that we do not swap the words, but rather *their addresses* in the array `wordaddress` (lines 57-65). Obviously we also need to swap their respective lengths in the array `wordlength`. The string `line` is never altered. Swapping pointers is much more efficient than swapping strings as in Listing 5.9. Indeed, swapping pointers does not depend on the length of the words that need to be swapped. Moreover, additional cycles on the characters of each single word are avoided in this way. Pointer arrays are a very useful tool to treat problems in which many arrays need to be compared or manipulated.

6.6 Pointers to pointers

From the previous considerations it is clear that a pointer type variable also has an address in the memory allocated to the program. Therefore, we can define a pointer pointing to another pointer. The following code shows how to do this.

```
int a[5];
int *pi, **pk;
a[0] = 137;
pi = a;
pk = &pi;
```

We declare the variable `pi` as a pointer to an integer and define it to be equal to the pointer `a` to the array `a[5]`. The same variable `pi` occupies an address in the memory. The operator & applied to `pi` returns this address, which can be assigned to the variable `pk` of the type *pointer to a pointer to an integer*. Try to imagine what happens if we print the expression `*pk`.

The indirection operator * applied to the pointer pk returns its contents, i.e, the value of the pointer pi (for example, let us assume it is equal to 0xbffff770). Note how *pk is equal to *&pi which is equal to pi, as if the two operators * and & cancel each other out. So, is it possible to trace the value of a[0] from pk? Since *pk returns a pointer, let us apply once more the indirection operator, defining **pk which is equal to *pi. Let us consider the following lines of code

```
int a[5];
int *pi, **pk;
a[0] = 137;
pi = a;
pk = &pi;
printf("First try %p \n",*pk);
printf("Second try %d \n",**pk);
```

and its result

```
First try 0xbffff770
Second try 137
```

Despite the non-obvious syntax, the expression **pk returns, as expected, the content of the variable pointed to by *pk, i.e., of pi, which is the element a[0].

In case pointer arrays are not sufficiently flexible to deal with certain variable data structures, pointers to pointers can be useful as they do allow to manipulate the latter. A typical use regards text elaboration. An even more interesting application concerns hierarchical data structures, a subject treated extensively in Chapter 16.

6.7   Input/Output with files

In Section 3.4 we saw how to receive input or create output in a C program. In the many examples we considered so far, we often had to fill an array with numerical values or print the results of operations on arrays (e.g., print a sorted array or a triangular matrix). The language tools we discussed throughout the previous chapters do not allow the data resulting from these computations *to persist*. The most obvious way to do this on a computer is to write them to a file. Moreover, a file output by one program can become input to another. For example, we could generate a sequence of random numbers, write them to a file, sort them with the Bubblesort algorithm, write this sorted sequence to a file, reread the original sequence and sort it with a different algorithm. Or we could read the experimental data resulting from some measurement, analyze them with a program, represent them graphically, and finally, compute quantities which cannot be measured in a direct way. In this Section we explain how to read and write data to a file in the C language. The concept of a pointer is essential to access a file to either read or write on it.

In C, a file is considered to be a sequence of bytes. A file can be of the *formatted* type, also called *text file*, or the *binary* type. The bytes of a formatted file are interpreted as characters represented by the corresponding ASCII code. Such a file may be structured in *lines* defined as sequences of zero or more characters followed by the character *newline*, \n (ASCII code 10). It is possible to visualize formatted files directly on the screen by means of operating system commands (such as `cat` in UNIX/Linux and `type` in the *prompt* of the Windows commands). They can also be directly modified with an *editor* program. Instead, a binary, non formatted file contains a sequence of bytes whose meaning is defined when the file is being written. A binary file can be read with a program. If an editor is used, it generally results to be incomprehensible. In C a binary file containing characters is considered a text file (this is not the case in other programming languages). Bear in mind that a program interprets the content of a file in a correct way only if it knows its format, i.e., both the type of file (formatted or binary), as its internal structure (type of variables, their layout, etc.). Nevertheless, a text file is generally comprehensible even if a detailed description of its format is lacking. Instead, for a binary file a detailed description must be supplied along with it.

In C, any operation on a file occurs by means of a pointer of a special type, called *pointer to file*, as in

```
FILE *fp;
```

The variable `fp` is a pointer (recognizable by the presence of the character `*` in its declaration) to the type `FILE`; the use of uppercase letters for the type `FILE` is *mandatory*. A file pointer such as `fp` is often called a *stream* or *channel*. Once it has been declared, a file pointer takes on a value only after a function *opening* the file has been called, as in the following code

```
FILE *fp;
fp = fopen("myfile.dat","r");
```

Unlike with the more common pointers, a file pointer must be used exclusively in operations regarding the file itself; its value and its representation, generally depending on the system, are not of any interest to the average programmer. We can consider the pointer fp as a pointer to the element of the file (*record*) which will be accessed during the next reading or writing operation.

The function fopen, included in the header file <stdio.h>, takes two arguments[4]. The first argument is a string of characters containing the name of the file which is to be opened, in the example myfile.dat. The second argument is a string of one or more characters representing the opening mode of the file, in the example the character r (short for *read-only*). If the file has been successfully opened the pointer fp points to the file and can be accessed in other successive calls. Otherwise, the pointer fp takes on the value NULL. For example, the value NULL could be the result of an attempt to open an inexistent file or because it is impossible to write in an already existing file. In Table 6.2 we list the main options for opening a file. We do not discuss the meaning of the options in Table 6.2 in detail, but rather refer the reader to [Kernighan and Ritchie (1988); Kelley and Pohl (1998)]. Once the file has been opened, we can access its content in

Table 6.2   File opening modes.

String	Mode
r	read-only
w	write-only
a	append-only
r+, w+	read and write
rb	binary read-only
wb	binary write-only

reading with the functions fscanf, fgetc or fread. To write to the file, we call the functions fprintf, fputc or fwrite.

For formatted files, the I/O functions have a very similar syntax to the one of the functions discussed in Section 3.4. They also have the same name together with the prefix f. Let us consider an example of writing and modifying a file called random.dat. We assume to store into the file 100 randomly generated numbers. We then read back the numbers from the file, next invert their order and append this inverted sequence at the end of the same file (Listing 6.11).

---

[4]As we did when discussing printf and scanf, in this section we anticipate some of the terminology concerning C functions, which are discussed in depth in Chapter 7.

In Listing 6.11, on lines 8-11, we open the formatted file with the name random.dat, in writing mode (option w) and immediately check whether this operation was successful. At this point, the pointer fp points to the beginning of the file. In the for cycle on lines 12-15, we generate LEN random values comprised between 0 and 1 with the algorithm discussed in Section 5.5. At each step of the cycle we write an integer and a rational number in the file with the function fprintf. The latter function follows the exact same syntactical rules as the printf function, together with an additional argument in the beginning, namely the pointer fp to the file in which we are writing. On line 16 we close the file by means of the fclose function.

We can now reopen the file in reading and writing mode (option r+), and reread

```
1 #include <stdio.h>
2 #include <stdlib.h>
3 #define LEN 100
4 main () {
5   FILE *fp;
6   int i, k;
7   double x, data[LEN];
8   if ((fp = fopen("random.dat", "w")) == NULL ) {
9       printf("Error when opening the file random.dat\n");
10      exit(EXIT_FAILURE);
11  }
12  for (i = 1; i <= LEN; i++) {
13    x = (double)rand() / (double)RAND_MAX;
14    fprintf(fp, "%d %f\n", i, x);
15  }
16  fclose(fp);
17  fp = fopen("random.dat", "r+");
18  for (i = 1; i <= LEN; i++) {
19    fscanf(fp, "%d %lf", &k, &x);
20    *(data + LEN - k) = x;
21  }
22  fprintf(fp, "\n INVERSION \n");
23  for (i = 1; i <= LEN; i++) {
24    fprintf(fp, "%d %f\n", i, *(data + i - 1));
25  }
26  fclose(fp);
27 }
```

Listing 6.11   Writing and reading formatted files.

the data in the for cycle on lines 18-21 calling the fscanf function. Also the latter is completely analogous to the scanf function, apart from an extra first argument, the file pointer `fp`. In the same cycle we fill the array `data`, starting at the end, with the random data read from the file. In this way we immediately invert the original order to write them to the file. The option `r+` leaves the file pointer positioned at the last read element and allows a successive writing operation. Obviously, we must pay particular attention to the order in which these operations are performed: in Listing 6.11 we first read all the lines we wrote at an earlier stage and then write the values in the inverse order.

Note that for the reading operation we need to know exactly which file format has been used to write it. Generally, this information is communicated in a separate way, as in a manual for example. Without this knowledge we can of course read a file, but we need this information to *decode* it, just like if it were written in an unfamiliar language or a cryptographic code.

Let us now consider an example using a text file in a context which is more realistic than the previous ones. The Listing 6.12 reconsiders the sorting problem with the tools we have introduced so far.

The program of Listing 6.12 contains many interesting features we only discussed separately so far. To start with, the program generates 10 000 rational numbers between 0 and 1 in a random way (line 22), as explained in Section 5.5. It might be useful to save the original sequence of unsorted numbers, and given their number, the most indicated way to do this is to write them to a (formatted) file (line 23). The name of the file is not fixed, but rather determined by the user. The program checks whether the file is successfully created (lines 16-19). The program keeps the numbers in the usual array `data`. For efficiency purposes, pointers are used to fill the array (line 22) and sort it (lines 27-35). The array is sorted with the Bubblesort algorithm of Section 5.2.1. Finally, the program writes the sorted sequence of numbers to file (lines 37-39) allowing a comparison with the original sequence. Exclusively for clarity purposes, the program also writes a message line identifying the end of the original sequence and the beginning of the sorted one (lines 20 and 36). Also to improve the file readability (though not strictly necessary, the file would be incomprehensible otherwise) each index-number pair is followed by a *newline* character.

The actual writing to file occurs when the file is being closed or with a call to the function `fflush(fp)`, where `fp` is the file pointer. If the `fflush` function argument is 0 the writing is performed on all open files (Section 4.3).

```
1 #include <stdio.h>
2 #include <stdlib.h>
3
4 #define MAX_NUM 10000
5 #define MAX_FNAME 100
6 main() {
7   char outputFile[MAX_FNAME + 1], c;
8   FILE *fp;
9   int i = 0, j, n;
10  double data[MAX_NUM], temp, *lastpd, *pd, *qd;
11  printf("Give the name of the output file: ");
12  while ((c = getchar()) != '\n' && i < MAX_FNAME) {
13    outputFile[i++] = c;
14  }
15  outputFile[i++] = '\0';
16  if ((fp = fopen(outputFile, "w+") == NULL) {
17    printf("Error when opening the file %s\n", outputFile);
18    exit(EXIT_FAILURE);
19  }
20  fprintf(fp, "**** ORIGINAL DATA SEQUENCE ****\n");
21  for (i = 0; i < MAX_NUM; i++) {
22    *(data + i) = (double)random() / (double)RAND_MAX;
23    fprintf(fp, "%d %f\n", i, *(data + i));
24  }
25  fprintf(fp, "**** END OF THE ORIGINAL DATA ****\n");
26  lastpd = data + MAX_NUM - 1;
27  for (pd = data; pd < lastpd; pd++) {
28    for (qd = lastpd; qd > pd; qd--) {
29      if (*(qd - 1) > *qd) {
30        temp = *(qd - 1);
31        *(qd - 1) = *qd;
32        *qd = temp;
33      }
34    }
35  }
36  fprintf(fp, "**** SORTED DATA SEQUENCE ****\n");
37  for (i = 0; i < MAX_NUM; i++) {
38    fprintf(fp, "%d %f\n", i, *(data + i));
39  }
40  fclose(fp);
41 }
```

Listing 6.12 Sorting random numbers.

Hands on 6.2 - More sorting

Change the program in Listing 6.12 in order to save the data at intermediate steps of the sorting algorithm as given in Table 5.1. To this purpose open a second auxiliary file where you can write the status of the array **data** every

N steps, where N is defined by the user. Choose an appropriate format allowing to check the sorting status at a glance. Note that this is not an easy job when sorting 1000 numbers. To ease this task, you can divide the numbers in four intervals each of size 0.25. Associate to each interval a symbol of one single character, e.g., – between 0 and 0.25, + between 0.25 and 0.5, * between 0.5 and 0.75 and finally ! between 0.75 and 1. You can now write the intermediate sorting status in the auxiliary file as 20 lines of 50 symbols each. This allows us to view how the sequence becomes more sorted as similar signs tend to cluster together.

6.7.1   *Binary files*

The reading and writing functions for files in binary format have a slightly different syntax. Instead of reading or writing one or more variables at a time, they act on arrays, thus allowing to read or write many elements with a single operations. First, let us examine the function `fwrite` allowing to write data in a binary file. For example, let us consider the program in Listing 6.13: this program generates 1000 random numbers between 0 and 1, filling the array `data`. On line 14 the program writes, in the binary file `random.bin`, only 100 of these numbers, in particular those starting from `data[500]` up to `data[599]`.

```
1 #include <stdio.h>
2 #include <stdlib.h>
3 #define LEN 1000
4 main () {
5   FILE *fp;
6   int num, bytes, i, n;
7   double data[LEN];
8   fp = fopen("random.bin", "wb");
9   for (i = 0; i < LEN; i++) {
10     *(data + i) = (double)random() / (double)RAND_MAX;
11   }
12   bytes = sizeof(double);
13   num = 100;
14   n = fwrite(data + 500, bytes, num, fp);
15   fclose(fp);
16 }
```

Listing 6.13   Writing to binary files.

The arguments of the **fwrite** function are, in the order given on line 14, the pointer **data + 500** to the first element we want to write; the variable **bytes** representing the length in bytes of the elements we want to write; the variable **num**, here set equal to 100, indicating how many these elements are; and finally, the file pointer **fp**. The variables **bytes** and **num**, of the integer type in Listing 6.13, are actually interpreted by the **fwrite** function as a result of the **sizeof** operator. This means that the **fwrite** function writes **bytes * num** bytes starting from the position specified by the pointer included as a first argument. The **fwrite** function returns the number of elements actually written in the file, thus allowing to check whether the writing operation was successful. In Listing 6.13 this value is assigned to the variable **n**. Reading a binary file occurs in an analogous way, as given in the code fragment in Listing 6.14. The arguments of the **fread** function have the same meaning as in Listing 6.13.

```
1  ...omitted code
2    fp = fopen("random.bin","rb");
3    bytes = sizeof(double);
4    num = 50;
5    n = fread(data, bytes, num, fp);
6    for (i = 0; i < n; i++) {
7      printf("data[%d] = %f\n", i, data[i]);
8    }
```

Listing 6.14   Reading binary files.

After line 5 the array **data** contains 50 values read from the file **random.bin**. Therefore, the program can operate on them, by printing their elements for example. In this case, the integer variable **n** contains the effective number of elements read from the file. In case the function encounters the end of the file, **EOF**, before having completed the reading, this number can be less than the array actual number of elements. This number can also be equal to zero, if the file is empty, or negative, in case a reading error occurred.

Chapter 7

Functions

Adde parvum parvo magnus acervus erit
(Add little to little there will be a great heap).

Ovidius.

In this Chapter we give a full treatment of the *functions*. We already mentioned functions several times, e.g., the `main` function (Section 3.1) or the I/O functions, such as `printf` and `scanf` (Section 3.4), or mathematical functions, such as `sqrt` (Section 3.6). It would have been impossible to discuss everything we did so far without mentioning functions. Indeed, C is based in a structural way on the concept of functions. As a matter of fact, programming in C first of all means decomposing a problem in independent logic units with a well-defined task, and next, translate these units in blocks of code. The latter are the functions used in the program. In this chapter we do not only treat the technical aspects of using functions in C, but also the aspects related to *good programming*, i.e, how to write modular, reusable and easily comprehensible programs.

7.1 Declaration and definition

In C a function consists of a name, a type and a list of *arguments* or *parameters* included between parentheses ( ), and a block of code included between curly brackets { }, called the *body* of a function. When the body of a function A contains the name of another function, B, the function A is said to *call* the function B[1]. This means that the function A transfers the

---

[1]This is not the case when the name of a function appears in the declaration.

177

control of the program to the function B, passing on one or more values needed by B to accomplish its task. When the function B has completed its operations, it can return a *return value* to the calling function A. The return value can be considered the result of calling B, though there exist functions not returning any value. Generally, a function can call another or many other functions, and, as discussed in Chapter 15, it can also call itself.

To ease the discussion on the use of functions in C, let us first introduce some technical terms. In a program, a function first needs to be *declared* and then *defined*. The concept of declaration is not new. We already saw that all variables and arrays must be declared before being used in a program. This also applies to functions as they must be known to the compiler for a correct program compilation. Declaring a function is equivalent to signaling the compiler it exists, by specifying its name, its type and the type and number of the arguments. The declaration syntax is

type name ([*type argument1*] [,*type argument2*]...);

as in

```
unsigned long long int factorial(int n);
```

where we declared a function with the name **factorial**, of the type **unsigned long long int**, taking one single argument, of the **int** type. Another example is

```
double squareSum(double x, double y);
```

where we declared a function with the name **squareSum**, of the **double** type, with two arguments of the **double** type. The name of a function must be unique throughout a program; two different functions or a variable and a function carrying the same name cannot coexist. The type of a function may be any valid C type. It corresponds to the type of the value the function returns. The arguments serve to communicate input to the function. For example, if **factorial** computes the factorial of a number, it should know this number. Upon its declaration, we are informing the compiler that **factorial** takes an argument, of the integer type, which is precisely the number of which we want to compute the factorial.

Let us now consider what is meant by the definition of a function. A function is defined when, after the type, the name, and the argument list, the body of statements appears. Let us consider the computation of the factorial to exemplify the syntactical aspects. The function `factorial` in Listing 7.1 uses the code already shown in Section 4.3.1.

```
1 unsigned long long int factorial(int n) {
2    int i;
3    unsigned long long int p = 1;
4    for (i = 1; i <= n; i++) {
5       p *= i;
6    }
7    return p;
8 }
```

Listing 7.1   The factorial function.

We immediately note that the type of a function is related to the result it produces. When computing the factorial we want the integer result to be as large as possible, i.e., using the most number of bits possible. To this purpose we define (and elsewhere we declare) the `factorial` function of the type `unsigned long long int`. The function input is the integer number n of which we want to compute the factorial. The function output is the number p, of the type `unsigned long long int`, which is precisely $n!$. The `return` statement is a new statement of the C language. It immediately returns the control to the calling function, passing on, at the same time, the value of the variable or expression following the `return`. The `return` statement is the *only way* to directly communicate output from the called function to the calling function. It is now clear why declaring the type of a function is mandatory. Indeed, a function can only return, thanks to the `return` statement, values of the same type as the one declared for the function. This is why `factorial`, of the type `unsigned long long int`, returns the value calculated in the variable p.

Let us reconsider the function declaration; when defining a function (line 1 of Listing 7.1), we give the compiler the same elements of the declaration. Then why is it mandatory to declare a function? If the *definition* of a function, with its body of statements, precedes the use of the function itself in the code, the compiler can do its job without any problems even if the function is not declared separately. In this case the program will execute correctly. Still, there are two good reasons not to omit a function declaration. First of all, a program does not always contain the definition of the functions it calls. This is the case, for example, when system or user libraries are used or various files are compiled together. As in these occasions the function necessarily needs to be *declared*, it is better to get used to always include it. The second reason is related to the concept of scope discussed in Section 7.1.1. In conclusion, the practice of not explicitly declaring a function by substituting it, when possible, with its definition in a specific point in the code is a bad habit and we strongly disapprove it.

With the introduction of ANSI C [ANSI (1995)] the declaration took on the name of *prototype* of a function. A prototype necessarily includes information on the returning type and on *all* arguments of the function itself (type, number and order). Therefore, today it is said that, before we can use a function, we first need to specify its prototype. The prototypes of the system library functions are specified in the header files included by the #include directive, such as <stdio.h>, <stdlib.h>, etc. The prototype is needed to inform the compiler on the nature and the number of arguments of a function. Therefore, it is not necessary, though allowed, to specify the names of the arguments. For example, a valid prototype in case of the factorial is

```
unsigned long long int factorial(int);
```

where we left out the name of the variable n between the parentheses ( ), or, in the other example,

```
double squareSum(double, double);
```

Having the possibility to specify the argument names in the prototype or not, one may wonder which option is better, considering that it does not make any difference to the compiler. A program is correctly compiled if the compiler has checked the existence of a function by its name; if the function arguments are consistently used, via the number and type of parameters; and if the returned type corresponds to the type of the function. Including the parameter names in the prototype is only useful to the programmer as a mnemonic help or for sake of clarity.

If the return type of the function is not specified, the compiler assumes the function returns an integer value int. In case the function does not return any value, it is declared to be of the void type. This same type is used in the argument list if the function does not receive any external input. For example, the prototype of a function printing a fixed error message is

```
void printError(void);
```

A possible definition could be

```
void printError(void) {
  printf("FATAL ERROR\n");
}
```

It is called with the statement

```
printError();
```

The `main` function follows these same rules. In all examples given so far we have never included the type of `main`, which is an integer. Whenever the type of main is not specified[2], it is implicitly assumed to be of the integer type. In any case, the `main` function returns an integer value to the operating system. If the `main` terminates with a `return` statement followed by an expression, the expression value is the `main` return value. If the `return` statement is missing, `main` returns the value 0. It is good practice to use the two macros `EXIT_SUCCESS` and `EXIT_FAILURE`, defined in `<stdlib.h>`, as arguments of `return`. They are respectively used to exit a program in case of correct termination or generic error. The `main` function can be defined without arguments, `main()` or `main(void)`, or with two arguments allowing the final user to pass on variables to the program. In the latter case, the `main` argument list may depend on the operating system. In case of the UNIX family operating systems, including Linux, the two arguments take on the following form

```
int main(int argc, char *argv[]) {
  ... body of main ...
}
```

The first argument `argc` is an integer. It corresponds to the number of character strings passed on during execution, augmented by one unit. The second argument `argv[]` is an array of pointers to character strings. Generally, each string is an execution argument or option. The first string `argv[0]` contains the name of the executed program. The strings `argv[k]`, with k ranging from 1 up to `argc` − 1, contain the program arguments or options. For example, having created an executable program with the name `myprogram.exe` accepting in input the name of the file which is to be read and a printing option, we can give the following command

```
myprogram.exe random.dat -p=1
```

---

[2]In C99 [ISO (1999)] it is mandatory to declare the type of each function, and therefore also of the function `main`. Nevertheless, the majority of modern compilers, also in order to be compatible with ANSI C [ANSI (1995)], tolerates the type of the `main` function is omitted.

In the program, the string `argv[0]` contains the name of the program being executed, i.e., `myprogram.exe`, the string `argv[1]` the name of the input file `random.dat` and the string `argv[2]` the option `-p` = 1 which the program needs to interpret.

In conclusion, once the task of a function is defined and the relative code is written, we need to decide which and how many input arguments it needs and its type of output. We need to include its prototype, either explicitly or with an `#include` directive. Finally, its definition must be included in one of the files which will be compiled.

7.1.1 *Scope*

Let us discuss the concept of the *scope* of a variable in C, introduced in Section 4.3.2, more in depth. In Chapter 3 we explained how a variable must be declared before using it in any context, whether it is the `main` function or any other compound statement. Let us consider a variable declared inside a block included between a couple of curly brackets **{ }**. Its name and the value it assumes at any moment are visible in each, possibly compound, statement included in that same block. The Listing 7.2 contains a simple application of the scope rules.

```
1  #include <stdio.h>
2  main() {
3    int a, b;
4    a = 137;
5    b = 2;
6    {
7      int x;
8      double a;
9      a = 3.14;
10     x = 137;
11     printf(" internal block a = %f, b = %d, x = %d\n", a, b, x);
12   }
13   printf(" external block a = %d, b = %d\n", a, b);
14 }
```

Listing 7.2   Visibility example.

The result of the program in Listing 7.2 is

```
internal block a = 3.140000, b = 2, x = 137
external block a = 137, b = 2
```

The variable **a** in the internal block *hides* the same variable in the external block. This means that it is possible to declare a variable with the same name, possibly of a different type, inside the internal block. We can assign it values which are visible only inside the block. When the program exits the internal block, the name **a** again identifies the previous variable with the value it had before the internal block, 137 in Listing 7.2. The variable **b** is declared in the external block and automatically visible in the internal block with its current value. The variable **x** is only declared in the internal block, and therefore not visible in the external block where it is not defined.

The scope rules for functions are similar. By declaring the prototype of a function **A** before the **main** and other functions **B**, **C**, etc., the function **A** is visible both in **main** as in all other functions following it. Instead, by including the prototype of the function **A** inside the **main** function or inside another function **B**, the function **A** is visible only in that environment. For this reason it is better to specify all prototypes before the **main**, at the beginning of the file containing it, as we do for the **#include** directive. A possible structure of a program consisting of a **main** and four other functions **A**, **B**, **C** and **D** could be such that functions **A** and **B** are defined in the same file containing the **main** program (**myprogram.c**), while functions **C** and **D** are defined in a separate file, as follows:

File **myprogram.c**

```
prototype of A
prototype of B

#include "myFunctions.h"
\* the file myFunctions.h contains the prototypes of
   the functions C and D *\

main() {
...calls the functions A,B,C,D...
}
A(...){...}
B(...){...}
```

File `myFunctions.c`

```
C(...){...}
D(...){...}
```

where the symbol `(...)` indicates the possible argument list of each function, and the symbol `{...}` indicates the function body. In the Linux operating system, the compilation and *linking* command for this program is

```
gcc -o myprogram.exe myprogram.c myFunctions.c
```

Note how the file `myFunctions.h` does not appear in the compilation command as it is already present in the `#include` directive of the file `myprogram.c`.

7.2   Formal parameters

In this Section we discuss the important issue of communication between the calling and the called function. Generally, a function receives input from the calling function, uses that input and returns a result to the calling function. The input that is passed on to the called function consists of a list of arguments or parameters included between parentheses `( )`. We already saw that the result is the value of an expression, whose type is the one specified in the called function prototype. It is passed on to the calling function with the `return` statement.

The communication of data between functions or independent code modules, occurs *by value* or *by reference*. Data are said to be passed on *by value* if the calling function receives the current value of the data, independent of the name of the associated variable or its location in the memory. If the calling function receives the address of the memory location currently containing the data, the latter is said to be passed on *by reference*.

Without any exceptions, the C language only allows functions to pass data by value. More precisely, the argument list included between parentheses `( )` following the function name is considered to be a list of expressions which are evaluated when the function is called. The expressions are converted respectively to the types declared in the prototype and the resulting values are passed as input to the called function. It is important to fully understand this C feature. Therefore, we again consider the function

squareSum which receives two rational data a and b and computes the sum of their squares $a^2 + b^2$. The function prototype is

```
double squareSum(double, double);
```

The function definition is

```
double squareSum(double a, double b) {
  return (a * a + b * b);
}
```

The Listing 7.3 gives some examples using this function, showing how to pass its arguments by value.

```
1 #include <stdio.h>
2
3 double squareSum(double, double);
4
5 main() {
6   double x, y, q;
7   int k;
8   x = 3.14;
9   y = 2.;
10   q = squareSum(x, y);
11   printf(" first sum of squares = %f\n", q);
12   q = squareSum(5, 2 * 2);
13   printf(" second sum of squares = %f\n", q);
14   k = 2;
15   q = squareSum(x, k);
16   printf(" third sum of squares = %f\n", q);
17 }
18
19 double squareSum(double a, double b) {
20   return (a * a + b * b);
21 }
```

Listing 7.3 Examples of passing arguments by value.

The result when executing the program of Listing 7.3 is

```
first sum of squares = 13.859600
second sum of squares = 41.000000
third sum of squares = 13.859600
```

On line 10 of Listing 7.3 the function **squareSum** is called with arguments x and y of the double type. Correspondingly, the function receives in input the values of x and y in that moment, i.e, 3.14 and 2, already in double representation. It computes the sum of their squares and returns it to the calling program, assigning it to the variable q. On line 12, the same function is called with a list of constant integers, namely 5 and the product 2×2. The two integer numbers are converted into double before the function computes the sum of their squares. Finally, on line 15 the argument list consists of a double type variable x and the int type variable k equal to 2. The input of the function is the value 3.14 of x and the value 2.0 resulting by converting the integer value 2 to a double. The result is the same as the one of line 10.

The Listing 7.3 also shows another important aspect of the call-by-value mechanism. Namely, there does not exist any relation between the names of the variables used in the function definition and the names included to call that same function. The definition of squareSum contains the variables a and b, while other variables or constants appear in the various function calls. What is important are the values of the arguments when the function is called. The names assigned to the arguments of a function in its definition are called *formal parameters* or sometimes *actual parameters*. These names are only visible in the function scope, so they may be duplicates of names already used in the main or other functions without further consequences. When a function is called, an *effective parameter* is associated to each formal parameter of its argument list. This effective parameter, which can be a constant as well, is only visible in the scope of the calling function. The value of each effective parameter is passed on to the called function and assigned to the corresponding formal parameter.

A possibly obvious, though important detail is that the order of the argument list is essential. A function elaborates the input values by associating them to the variables that are visible only inside the function. The association is established by the order in which the parameters appear between parentheses ( ). The function squareSum computes $a^2 + b^2$ (which obviously is equal to $b^2 + a^2$), associating the first received value to the variable a and the second to the variable b. If we consider a function computing the difference of squares $a^2 - b^2$, as in Listing 7.4, the importance of the parameter order is more evident.

The program in Listing 7.4 uses the names a and b both in the main, as in the squareDiff function expressely to stress the importance of order in the function arguments. The purpose of the program is to compute the difference $5^2 - 4^2$, which is obviously equal to 9. The function squareDiff computes the difference between the square of the first argument and the square of the second. These arguments of the squareDiff function are generically called a and b.

```
1 #include <stdio.h>
2
3 double squareDiff(double, double);
4
5 main() {
6   double a, b, q;
7   a = 4.;
8   b = 5.;
9   q = squareDiff(b, a);
10  printf(" difference of squares = %f\n", q);
11  q = squareDiff(a, b);
12  printf(" difference of swapped squares = %f\n", q);
13 }
14
15 double squareDiff(double a, double b) {
16   return (a * a - b * b);
17 }
```

Listing 7.4   Order of arguments in a function.

On line 9 of Listing 7.4 the program calls the function squareDiff with first argument b, equal to 5, and second argument a, equal to 4. The names used on line 9 are irrelevant for the function squareDiff, receiving in input the values 5 and 4. The function assigns these values to its variables a and b according to the parameters name sequence, returning 9. On line 11 of Listing 7.4 we swapped the order of the variables a and b. The order of arguments on line 11 might seem consistent with that on line 15. However, the first argument is now equal to 4 and the second 5, and the function returns the value −9 instead of 9.

The call-by-value mechanism has two important consequences:

(1) it is not possible to change the value of variables in the calling function, even if they are input parameters of the called one;

(2) it is not possible to directly pass an array to a function (unless you want to explicitly specify the elements of the array among the formal parameters, which is often impossible in practice).

The first point requires a more in-depth discussion. Let us consider a classic example, namely swapping the content of two variables. Listing 7.5 contains a program which seems to swap the value of two variables x and y.

The output of the program is

```
before the swap, x = 3.140000, y = 2.720000
after the swap, x = 3.140000, y = 2.720000
```

```
1 #include <stdio.h>
2
3 void wrongSwap(double, double);
4
5 main() {
6    double x, y;
7    x = 3.14;
8    y = 2.72;
9    printf(" before the swap, x = %f, y = %f\n", x, y);
10   wrongSwap(x, y);
11   printf(" after the swap, x = %f, y = %f\n", x, y);
12 }
13
14 void wrongSwap(double a, double b) {
15    double temp;
16    temp = a;
17    a = b;
18    b = temp;
19 }
```

Listing 7.5   Wrong program to swap variables.

As the variables x and y have the same value before and after the function call to wrongSwap, they were not actually swapped. The reason is simply that the swap occurs between the variables a and b in the scope of the function wrongSwap, which does not have any influence on the variables x and y visible in the main function. Note that wrongSwap has been declared void as it does not return any value to the calling function. Could we change the type of wrongSwap to return the swapped values? Unfortunately, this is not possible with the types of variables we have studied so far. Indeed, the return statement returns one single value of an expression or a variable, while in this example two variables change their value. It is possible though to return many values to the calling function with a single return statement, namely with a structured type of variable called struct. The struct makes possible to manipulate many data all at once. It is discussed in Section 9.3, which is why we do not analyze this possibility at the moment. Both problems reported above (changing the input variables and passing on arrays) can be solved by using pointers as function arguments. How this mechanism works is explained in Section 7.3.

7.3   Pointers and array parameters

Suppose we have a pointer as an argument to a function. As always, the value of this pointer is passed on to the called function. Let us consider once more the case of swapping two variables, by defining another function `swap` receiving in input the addresses, rather than the values, of the variables which are to be swapped.

```
1 void swap(double *a, double *b) {
2    double temp;
3    temp = *a;
4    *a = *b;
5    *b = temp;
6 }
```

Listing 7.6   The correct function to swap variables.

First of all, we need to redefine the prototype of the function. Indeed, the list of formal parameters should contain two pointers to `double` changing the prototype into

```
void swap(double *a, double *b);
```

This can also be written as

```
void swap(double *, double *);
```

as it is not mandatory to indicate the name of the formal parameters in the prototype, but only their number and type. The syntax `double *` means that parameter is a pointer (indicated by the asterisk `*`) to `double`. We now rewrite the program of Listing 7.5 calling the `swap` function in `main` and passing it the pointers to the variables x and y as arguments,

```
swap(&x, &y);
```

We also write the code of the `swap` function such that it swaps the content of the two addresses it receives in input, as in Listing 7.6.
The result of executing the program of Listing 7.6 is

```
before the swap, x = 3.140000, y = 2.720000
after the swap, x = 2.720000, y = 3.140000
```

as desired. On line 10 of Listing 7.5 we call the `swap` function with two effective parameters &x and &y, i.e., the pointers to the two variables which need to be swapped. For example, suppose &x is equal to 0xbffff7a0 in hexadecimal. The `swap` function receives the two values of the pointers in input (thus, the pointer a is equal to 0xbffff7a0). It accesses the pointed variables with the indirection operator *. The swap occurs, with the help of an auxiliary variable, by changing the content of the addresses supplied by the pointers on the lines 16-18. The pointers a and b are visible only in the scope of the swap function. However, their value refers to the actual map of the program memory. Therefore, the expression *a returns the content of the memory located at the address 0xbffff7a0, which is the actual value of the address of the variable x in main. Note that if we changed the value of a pointer in the swap function, writing for example a++;,the value of &x in the main would not have changed, according to the scope rules discussed in Section 7.1.1.

In Section 7.2 we saw that passing an array from one function to another by value is rather problematic. Still, it is fundamental to encode complex problems in a modular way. The solution is again to use pointers as function parameters. Remember that, given for example an array a[10], the name a is a pointer to the array itself and a generic element a[j] has the address (a + j). As was the case for the swap function, we include a pointer, to an array in this case, as a parameter of the function. In this way the entire array becomes accessible to the called function by indirecting the transmitted address and the successive ones. In particular, we can change the values of the array elements. We can also write algorithms on arrays which are not dependent on the length of the array declared in the calling program. Similarly, we can declare a function of the type pointer to an array and return to the calling function an array that has been filled inside the called function. In conclusion, including pointers to arrays as parameters or return arguments of a function extends a lot a program computing capability. Still, this mechanism has a peculiar, rather complicated, syntax in C. This is why we discuss the syntax as well as the mechanism of array passing between functions.

7.3.1   *Array in input and output*

Let us consider a function f of the void type receiving in input an integer array int data[10] declared in the calling function. We can declare this array as a formal parameter of f in three different ways all having the same result.

```
void f(int data[10]);
void f(int *data);
void f(int data[]);
```

In either way, the value passed to the function is *always* the value of the pointer to the array. The first expression, f(int data[10]), clearly shows that the argument of the function is an array, but the nature of the value passed to f is misleading. Moreover, the length of the array data *is not passed* to the function f, even if it explicitly appears as a parameter. In the second case, the parameter is a pointer to an integer with the name data. There is no explicit indications that it is a pointer to an array. Also in this way the function f does not know the current length of the array data. The third expression clearly indicates that the argument of f is an array because of the square brackets []. The length of the array is again not indicated though. Thus, an array can be passed to a function as a formal parameter in various syntactical forms. However, in practice the mechanism *always* consists in passing to the function the current value of the pointer to the array. The information on the current length of the array is never implicitly transmitted. If this information is required (which is often the case) it needs to be communicated explicitly by means of an additional parameter.

```
1  void bubblesort(int data[], int n) {
2    int i, temp, *pd;
3    for (i = 0; i < n - 1; i++) {
4      for (pd = data + n - 1; pd > data + i; pd--) {
5        if (*(pd - 1) > *pd) {
6          temp = *(pd - 1);
7          *(pd - 1) = *pd;
8          *pd = temp;
9        }
10     }
11   }
12 }
```

Listing 7.7   The Bubblesort function.

Let us consider a more realistic case of a function sorting an array, of integers for example, with the Bubblesort algorithm of Section 5.2.1. The function may have two input parameters: the array to be sorted, passed via its pointer; and the number of elements to be sorted, which should be equal to or less than the array length declared in the calling function. The function returns the sorted array without explicitly returning any value. Instead, it directly sorts the array by operating on the pointers to its elements. The function code is shown in Listing 7.7.

Listing 7.7 contains the Bubblesort algorithm in its generic form: the sorting is independent of the array length and the function can be used as a "black box" taking a disordered array and returning the sorted one. Obviously, the type of arrays that can be sorted with this function is limited. For example, to sort an array of the `double` type, we need to write a new function, with a different name, whose first parameter is `double data[]`. The function is declared to be of the `void` type because it does not return any argument. Its prototype can be written as

```
void bubblesort(int *, int);
```

which does not contain any indication to the fact that the first parameter is linked to an array. Instead, if we want to be more clear, we could write

```
void bubblesort(int data[], int n);
```

where the nature of the arguments is conveyed more explicitly. We could rewrite the `bubblesort` function, using array indexes rather than pointers. However, this would only be an apparent change as the syntax `data[j - 1]` translates into `*(data + j - 1)` in any case.

Let us consider a more complex example. Suppose we want to divide an array of integer numbers in two sorted arrays of, respectively, even and odd numbers. In order to return two arrays as the output of a function, we can declare the pointers to the two output arrays as input parameters. In this case, the function is of the `void` type and the result is obtained by changing the content of the two arrays by means of their pointers, as in Listing 7.7. A possible encoding of the function resolving this problem is given in Listing 7.8.

```
1  void sortByParity(int data[], int odd[], int even[], int n) {
2    int *pd;
3    bubblesort(data, n);
4    for (pd = data; pd < data + n; pd++) {
5      if (*pd % 2) {
6        *odd++ = *pd;
7      } else {
8        *even++ = *pd;
9      }
10   }
11 }
```

Listing 7.8   Sorting and partitioning by parity.

In Listing 7.8 it starts to become more clear what is meant by dividing a problem in independent modules and translate these into functions. The function `sortByParity` has two tasks: divide the input array in even and odd numbers and sort them. The function delegates the sorting task to the `bubblesort` function (Listing 7.7), and limits itself to the separation of the even from the odd numbers. Note that the `bubblesort` function does not necessarily have to be defined in Listing 7.8. It could for example be contained in a library which is to be linked during compilation to the executable program. Instead, the file containing the `main` function has to include the prototypes of the two functions we are using, as in the following lines of code:

```
void bubblesort(int *, int);
void sortByParity(int *, int *, int *, int);
main() {
... omitted code ...
}
```

As we already mentioned before, if the function code is not directly available, the information on the parameters of `bubblesort` must be supplied separately, usually in the related documentation. In Listing 7.8 we applied the pointer arithmetics rules discussed in Section 6.3 to scroll through the array `data` in a more efficient way. We also run through the arrays containing `even` and `odd` numbers by incrementing the respective pointers. Note that the way in which we wrote the function `sortByParity` does not return to the calling function any information on how many even or odd numbers have been found. In case we want this kind of information, we at least have to define an integer variable counting the even or odd numbers. We could write, for example, for the odd numbers,

```
*(odd + ko) = *pd;
ko++;
```

instead of line 6 in Listing 7.8. Obviously, in this case, we need to return the value of the counter `ko` to the calling function (the number of even numbers is `n - ko`).

Hands on 7.1 - Returning more than one value

Suppose you need to classify a numeric sample in more than two categories. In this case, the function sorting the sample has to return more than one value to the calling function. Adapt the function `sortByParity` such that it returns for example the number of even numbers, the number of multiples of 3, and the number of multiples of 5, using what we just discussed. This problem can be solved in different ways. Find these solutions and examine their advantages and drawbacks.

7.3.2   *Passing multidimensional arrays*

Passing a multidimensional array to a function via pointers is syntactically more complicated than passing a one-dimensional array. Let us remind the reader that we can consider a multidimensional array to be an array of arrays (Sections 5.3, 6.5). Taking into account what said in Section 7.3.1, we need to specify the limits of all indexes but the first one, when passing to a function a formal parameter which points to a multidimensional array. An example may clarify this issue more. Let us consider a function `transform` performing a transformation on a 5×7 matrix representing a two-dimensional array `a[5][7]`.

```
void transform(int [][], int);
main() {
  int a[5][7];
... omitted code ...
  transform(a,5);
}

void transform(int data[][7], int n) {
... function body ...
}
```

We declared the array `a[5][7]` in the `main` function. The `transform` function has two formal parameters, a pointer to a multidimensional array and an integer, representing the length of the sub-array addressed by the array first index. We call this function and specify the pointer `a` as a first argument. In the prototype of `transform` we cannot write

```
void transform(int *, int);
```

because the first argument is not a simple array, nor can we write

```
void transform(int [], int);
```

because its first argument refers to a one-dimensional array. The correct prototype is

```
void transform(int [][], int);
```

where we explicitly indicated that the function first parameter is a two-dimensional array.

When defining **transform** we necessarily need to declare that the second index of **data** is equal to 7 in the parameter list. In this way, the compiler knows that the function **transform** receives a pointer to an array of n. arrays of 7 elements. In general, it is convenient to specify the value of all dimensions of a multidimensional array both in the function definition as in the function call.

We apply this rule and change the code of Listing 5.5 to resolve a system of linear equations (Section 5.4). More precisely, we delegate the operations performed on the matrices of coefficients to two separate functions: one triangulating the matrix, and another resolving the system. These functions are of the **void** type. They directly operate on the one-dimensional and multidimensional arrays by means of the pointers to these arrays. This version of the program is given in Listing 7.9.

```c
 1 #include <stdio.h>
 2 #include <math.h>
 3
 4 #define N 100
 5 void triangle(int, double [][], double *);
 6 void solve(int, double [][], double *, double *);
 7 main() {
 8 /*  solving a system of equations with
 9     Gauss elimination */
10   double A[N][N], b[N], x[N];
11   int n, i, j;
12 /*  give the initial data */
13   printf(" Give the number of equations (<100): ");
14   scanf("%d", &n);
15   printf("\n Now insert the coefficients
16          and the known terms\n");
17   for (i = 0; i < n; i++) {
18     for (j = 0; j < n; j++) {
19       printf("A[%d, %d] = ", i, j);
20       scanf("%lf", &A[i][j]);
21     }
22     printf("b[%d] = ", i);
23     scanf("%lf", &b[i]);
24   }
25 /*  triangulate the matrix */
26   triangle(n, A, b);
27 /*  resolve the system   */
28   solve(n, A, b, x);
29 /*  print the result   */
30   for (i = 0; i < n; i++) {
31     printf("x[%d] = %lf\n", i, x[i]);
32   }
33 }
```

```
35 void triangle(int n, double a[N][N], double *b) {
36    int i, j, k;
37    double c;
38    for (i = 0; i < n; i++) {
39 /* divide the i-th equation by the diagonal element C */
40      c = a[i][i];
41      for (j = i; j < n; j++) {
42        a[i][j] /= c;
43      }
44      *(b + i) /= c;
45 /* subtract the normalized equation from the others */
46      for (k = i + 1; k < n; k++) {
47        c = a[k][i];
48        for (j = i; j < n; j++) {
49          a[k][j] -= a[i][j] * c;
50        }
51        *(b + k) -= c * (*(b + i));
52      }
53    }
54 }
55
56 void solve(int n, double a[N][N], double *b, double *x) {
57    int i, k;
58    double s;
59    x[n] = b[n] / a[n][n];
60    for (k = n - 1; k >= 0; k--) {
61      s = 0.;
62      for (i = k + 1; i < n; i++) {
63        s += a[k][i] * x[i];
64      }
65      x[k] = b[k] - s;
66    }
67 }
```

Listing 7.9   Solving a system of linear equations with functions.

Comparing the Listing 7.9 with 5.5, the algorithm is the same and the lines of code are even more. Nevertheless, the main function is more simple and the two functions triangle and solve are completely generic, as long as the length of the arrays is less than N. The part of the arrays a and b that is used, is defined during the execution by passing the value of the variable n. The function calls in main occur by including the names of the arrays as pointer arguments. In the function triangle we explicitly referred to the elements of the array b with pointers, while in the other functions we use the syntax with indexes to demonstrate the two possible ways.

7.3.3 *Global and local variables*

To end the discussion on passing data structures, we again consider the problem of the visibility of variables in C programs. Remember the rule that a variable (or an array) declared in a block is visible in that entire block and also in any blocks that one contains (as long as it is not *hidden* by the declaration of an homonymous variable). So, a variable (or array) declared before the main function is visible anywhere, also in all functions composing the program, as long as they are part of the same file. It is now legitimate to ask why we do not simply declare arrays outside of the main function, instead of passing data structures to functions by means of pointers? Once more, let us consider the example of the bubblesort function. We could write

```
int data[100];          /* global declaration of data */
void bubblesort(int);   /* Bubblesort prototype*/

main() {...}                 /* array data is visible*/
void bubblesort(int n) {...} /* array data is visible */
```

In this way any operation performed on the array data is always visible in any part of the program. A variable (or array) that is declared before the main function is called a *global variable*, while a variable (or array) declared with a limited scope is called a *local variable*.

Even though the use of global variables seems easier, it is generally discouraged. There are several reasons for this, but they can all be ascribed to the necessity of writing general, reusable programs behaving in a controlled way. Here we quote two possible undesirable effects of global variables.

(1) We want to change a global variable in a function and the name of this global variable is the same as a local variable of that same function; the scope rules state that the local variable hides the global one such that no changes are carried out on the global variable.

(2) Functions acting on global variables are not general because they depend on the names of these variables. For example, in case the array data in the bubblesort function were declared globally, we would always need to use the name data in each program calling this version of bubblesort. Of course it is possible to do this, but it certainly is not in line with the concept of modularity and code recycling!

In conclusion, it is better to renounce to the comfort of global variables to maintain more control over the code and write modular programs which are easily reused.

7.4   Applications

In this Section we discuss two easy, but interesting, applications of modular programming of general utility by defining some functions which can be reused in possibly very different contexts.

7.4.1   *Histograms*

A common problem in data analysis is the need to represent data by histograms. There exist numerous, very complete and professional programs to do this job. Often though, they force the user to work in a given environment. There also exist histogram library packages where the user can call only those functions that are needed in the program. Nevertheless, it is an interesting exercise to create an original program to produce histograms. The basic version of such a program, at least the algorithmic part, is rather easy to write. The Listing 7.10 contains a complete program filling a histogram with variable limits and number of intervals, and printing it with ASCII characters.

```
 1 #include <stdio.h>
 2 #include <stdlib.h>
 3 #include <time.h>
 4 #define MAX_NUM 10000
 5 #define MAX_BINS 100
 6 int defineInput(double buf[], int max);
 7 void fillDist(double *data, int *bin, double min, double max,
 8                int n, int nData);
 9 void printHisto(int *bin, int n);
10 main() {
11    int k, bins, entries, content[MAX_BINS] = {0};
12    int seed;
13    double xmin, xmax;
14    double data[MAX_NUM];
15    seed = time(0);
16    srand48(seed);
17    entries = defineInput(data, MAX_NUM);
18    printf("Give the limits of the histogram\n xmin = ");
19    scanf("%lf",&xmin);
20    printf(" xmax = ");
21    scanf("%lf",&xmax);
22    do {
23      printf("Give the number of bins = ");
24      scanf("%d",&bins);
25    } while (bins <= 0 || bins > MAX_BINS);
26    fillDist(data, content, xmin, xmax, bins, entries);
```

```
27    printHisto(content, bins);
28    exit(EXIT_SUCCESS);
29 }
30
31 int defineInput(double buf[], int max) {
32    int k, N;
33    do {
34      printf("Number of events = ");
35      scanf("%d", &N);
36    } while (N < 0 || N > max);
37    for(k = 0; k < N; k++) {
38      buf[k] = (double)lrand48() / (RAND_MAX + 1.);
39    }
40    return N;
41 }
42 void fillDist(double *data, int *bin, double min, double max,
43                int n, int nData) {
44    int i, j;
45    double invWidth = (double)n / (max - min);
46    for (i = 0; i < nData; i++) {
47      j = ((*(data + i) - min) * invWidth);
48      if (j < n && j>=0) (*(bin+j))++;
49    }
50 }
51 void printHisto(int *bin, int n) {
52    int i, j, max;
53    int maxChar = 100;
54    char c = '*', empty = ' ', hist[n + 2][maxChar + 1];
55    for (i = 0; i < n + 2; i++) {
56      for (j = 0; j < maxChar; j++) {
57        hist[i][j] = empty;
58      }
59    }
60    max = bin[0];
61    for (i = 1; i < n; i++) {
62      if (bin[i] > max) {
63        max = bin[i];
64      }
65    }
66    if (max > maxChar) {
67      max = maxChar;
68    }
69     for (j = 0; j <= max; j++) {
70      hist[0][j] = '|';
71    }
72    hist[0][0] = hist[1][0] = '_';
73    for (i = 2; i < n + 2; i++) {
74      hist[i][0] = '_';
75      for (j = 0; j < *(bin + i - 2); j++) {
76        hist[i][j + 1] = c;
```

```
77      }
78    }
79    for (j = max; j >= 0 ; j--) {
80      for (i = 0; i < n + 2; i++) {
81        printf("%c", hist[i][j]);
82      }
83      printf("\n");
84    }
85 }
```

Listing 7.10   A simple program for histograms.

The program in Listing 7.10 was clearly built according to the principle of modularity of the required operations. With this program we can fill and subsequently print a histogram of the data stored in an array. We can divide the operations in several logically independent phases: data acquisition, filling the histogram, printing the histogram.

Data acquisition is preliminary and obviously independent of the histogram. Therefore, the filling of the array **data** is delegated to the **defineInput** function. In this way we are free to decide whether the data are generated in a random way, as in Listing 7.10, or whether they are read from a file, entered by means of the keyboard or in any other way. The only functional aspect of our interest in **defineInput** is that it returns to the calling function, in this case **main**, an array **data** filled with values and the relative number of data elements. We also want **defineInput** to check whether the number of data does not exceed the maximum length **MAX_NUM** of the array **data**. In this case the latter check occurs when this number is entered with the keyboard, though in other situations it could occur in a different way. The important thing is that from now on we no longer need to consider whether we could exceed the maximum limit of the array **data**.

The second phase consists in filling the histogram. This operation requires to define a sequence of intervals or bins, in this case evenly spaced, and assign the data to these bins according to their numerical value. In Listing 7.10 the function **fillDist** performs this phase. The function receives in input the pointer to the array containing the data, the number of these data, and the parameters defining the horizontal axis, i.e., the minimum and maximum values of the scale and the number of intervals. Its output is the integer array **bin**: in each of its elements the number of entries in that bin is stored. As the pointer to the array **bin** is one of the function parameters, it does not need to return any value explicitly. So **fillDist** is declared as a **void**. Let us highlight some technical tricks optimizing the execution time. On line 45 we computed, once and for all, the inverse of the total size of the interval, in order to avoid computing this costly division over and over again in the `for` cycle on lines 46-49. On line 47 we establish to which bin the value `*(data + i)` belongs simply by considering the integer part of the division between this number, diminished by the lower limit of the interval, and the size of the interval. Note we could have passed the size of the interval, instead of the distribution lower and upper limit, to the function. Also, we could have computed the limits of the interval from the data. Generally, which type of histogram parameters are passed to a function, such as `fillDist`, depends both on the problem and the reason for creating the histogram. In professional applications there typically exist several filling functions accepting a set of various parameters.

Finally, we need to print the histogram. Though conceptually easy, this is the most complicated part from a programming point of view. The input of the `printHisto` function is the array containing the number of entries per bin and the number of bins. It returns nothing to the calling function as its output consists in printing the histogram. Therefore it is declared as `void`. In the version of Listing 7.10 we chose to represent the histogram in memory as a two-dimensional character array `hist[n + 2][maxchar + 1]`, where `n` is the number of bins and `maxchar` is the maximum number of entries that can be visualized per bin (in Listing 7.10 `maxchar = 100`). The first index represents a generic bin of the histogram, while its second index represents the number of entries of each bin. The entries are represented by repeatedly printing a character, in Listing 7.10 we used the asterisk `*`. It is better to print the histogram by first performing a cycle on the rows and then one on the columns of the array `hist`. Also we need to draw the axes. The first index of the array `hist` is defined as `n + 2` because we need two extra rows other than `n`: one for the vertical axis and another to graphically separate the latter from the content of the first bin. To this end, note that in the double `for` cycle on lines 79-84, where we print the content of the histogram, we scroll more "slowly" through the rightmost index of the array `hist` (the columns) with respect to the left index (the rows).

If we execute the program in Listing 7.10 with the following input values

```
Number of events = 300
Give the limits of the histogram
 xmin = 0
 xmax = 1
Give the number of bins = 40
```

it produces a histogram similar to the one in Figure 7.1.

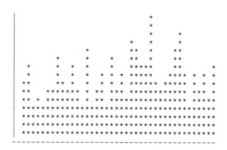

Fig. 7.1   A simple histogram.

The program in Listing 7.10 is rather easy to write. However, it would still take quite some work before obtaining a scientific histogram or one that is worth including in a professional presentation.

Hands on 7.2 - Improve the histogram

The program in Listing 7.10 does not make use of any scaling factor to represent the histogram content. If, for example, we were to execute the program with 10 000 events in 50 bins, we would have 200 events per bin on average. In the current printing version, this would lead to columns of 200 * spread over several pages (in this case we would also need to adapt the limit of 100 in the array `hist` in `printHisto`). The correct way to build a histogram is first to find the interval with the maximum number of entries. Next, we establish the maximum acceptable number of printable rows (for example 50). This then allows us to define the weight of the printed symbol (in this case *) as the ratio between the maximum number of entries and the maximum number of rows. For example, if the maximum number of entries per bin is 200 and the maximum number of rows is 50, each * represents 4 events. If the content of a bin is not an exact multiple of this weight, we could also print "on top" of each bin an integer number smaller than this weight, instead of the * character. In this case, we also need to print the numeric scales of both axes. Change the program of Listing 7.10 such that it includes these improvements we just discussed.

7.4.2 *Computing the χ^2 of a distribution*

Another interesting application consists in computing the χ^2 (chi-squared) of an experimental distribution. In general, experimental measurements of a quantity suffer errors. If we are measuring continuous quantities and the errors are random and independent, the result differs from the actual value by a random quantity following the *normal* or *Gaussian distribution*. Determining whether or not a hypothesis regarding the type of probability distribution experimental data follow is of great interest. This is the aim of the χ^2 test.

To compute the χ^2 of a distribution, we need to split up the experimental data over K intervals, as we did for the histogram. In each interval $k = 1, \ldots, K$ we drop O_k experimental data. To compare this distribution with the one we expect from a given hypothesis on the probability distribution, we need to build an expected distribution E_k, where $E_k = N P_k$: N is the total number of data and P_k is the probability that a datum falls in the kth interval. Note how the values O_k are integers, while generally the values E_k are real numbers. We now build the χ^2 estimator defined as

$$\chi^2 = \sum_k \frac{(O_k - E_k)^2}{E_k} \, . \tag{7.1}$$

How to compute χ^2 is explained in more detail in Section 11.4.1. Here, we assume the probability distribution of the number of data in the kth interval is a Poisson distribution with average E_k and variance $\sigma^2 = E_k$. The value of χ^2 allows us to establish whether this hypothesis should be rejected or not. When the number of degrees of freedom d, i.e, the number of experimental parameters minus the number of constraints on them, is high, a hypothesis is not rejected if $\chi^2 \simeq d$ or better if $|\chi^2 - d| \simeq \sqrt{d}$.

It is easy to encode this problem with functions and, in particular, using some functions already introduced in Listing 7.10, such as `defineInput` and `fillDist`.

In Listing 7.11 we have recycled the functions `defineInput` and `fillDist` of Listing 7.10 and do not show them in the new code. The function `chiSquare`, defined as a `double`, computes the χ^2 and returns it to the calling function. The input of `chiSquare` are the pointers to the arrays `obs`, the observed distribution, and `exp`, the expected distribution, and the number n of intervals of the two distributions, which obviously is the same in both cases. In the program of Listing 7.11, we assume the expected distribution to be the uniform distribution with $E_k = \frac{1}{K} \sum_k O_k$. The array `expected` is filled in the `main` function.

```
1 #include <stdio.h>
2 #include <stdlib.h>
3 #include <time.h>
4 #define MAX_NUM 10000
5 #define MAX_BINS 100
6 int defineInput(double buf[], int max);
7 void fillDist(double *data, int *bin, double min, double max,
8                int n, int nData);
9 double chiSquare(int *obs, double *exp, int n);
10 main() {
11   int k, bins, entries, content[MAX_BINS] = {0};
12   int seed;
13   double xmin, xmax;
14   double average = 0., chi2, data[MAX_NUM];
15   double expected[MAX_BINS] = {0.};
16   seed = time(0);
17   srand48(seed);
18   entries = defineInput(data, MAX_NUM);
19   printf("Give the limits of the distribution\n xmin = ");
20   scanf("%lf", &xmin);
21   printf(" xmax = ");
22   scanf("%lf", &xmax);
23   do {
24     printf("Give the number of intervals\n bins = ");
25     scanf("%d", &bins);
26   } while (bins < 0 || bins > MAX_BINS);
27   fillDist(data, content, xmin, xmax, bins, entries);
28   for (k = 0; k < bins; k++) {
29     average += (double)content[k];
30   }
31   average /= (double)bins;
32   for (k = 0; k < bins; k++) {
33     expected[k] = average;
34   }
35   chi2 = chiSquare(content, expected, bins);
36   printf(" Chi2 = %f\n", chi2);
37   exit(EXIT_SUCCESS);
38 }
39 double chiSquare(int *obs, double *exp, int n) {
40   double S = 0., t1, t2;
41   int k;
42   for (k = 0; k < n; k++) {
43     t1 = (double) *(obs + k);
44     t2 = *(exp + k);
45     S += (t1 - t2) * (t1 - t2) / t2;
46   }
47   return S;
48 }
```

Listing 7.11   Computing χ^2.

In case the assumed distribution were more complex, it would be appropriate to include a separate function to compute E_k. To optimize the number of operations in `chiSquare` we used two auxiliary variables `t1` and `t2`. Moreover, we assume, by definition, that `t2` is never zero such that the quotient on line 45 is always well-defined.

Hands on 7.3 - Computing χ^2 in function of the number of intervals

Use the Listing 7.11 to compute χ^2 for a uniform distribution while varying the number of intervals. Fix N, the number of observations which, as usual, can be generated in a random way. Vary the number of intervals K between minimum 4 and maximum $\frac{N}{10}$. Study how χ^2 and the ratio χ^2/d varies. Take the number of degrees of freedom d into account. For a uniform distribution, there is only one constraint on the degrees of freedom, namely the normalization condition $\sum_k O_k = N$. Therefore, for this distribution we have $d = K - 1$. Observe how, for a single observed distribution, the results of the test are worse when the intervals are too few or too many (and therefore, each one of them contain few results).

7.4.3 *Programming style and reusability*

In Listing 7.10 and 7.11 we gave a small example of programming style: the problem is decomposed in independent subproblems, each subproblem is delegated to a function, the names of the functions refer to the task they perform, the names of the variables reflect what they represent. Moreover, the functions are written in such a way that they can be reused in different contexts. It is certainly not necessary to program in this way, and it can even be very tiring to keep it up. However, it offers great advantages in terms of reusability. We want to stress how important it is to make this effort as it pays off on the long run and in big projects. Not only is it important to logically separate independent operations in order to progressively build better versions of the code (for example, printing always more complete histograms by only changing the `printHisto` function), it is also essential to slowly but surely create a library of commonly used functions which may ease our work. This is why it is fundamental to write code foreseeing all possible errors and protected against unexpected input (a classic example in the `chiSquare` function is to find E_k is equal to zero).

We invite the reader not to neglect this programming aspect and to actively apply it when learning how to program. Nevertheless, in this text it has sometimes willingly been left out to favor algorithmic and efficiency aspects.

7.5   Pointers to functions

We now treat the subject connecting variables of the pointer type to functions. We have already mentioned several times that the memory allocated to a program not only contains variables but also the program statements themselves. Each statement occupies one or more memory addresses and, in particular, there exists a memory address which is the function entry point. In C, this memory address is associated to the name of the function itself just like the basic address of an array is associated to the array name.

We can define a *pointer to a function* as a variable of the pointer type containing the address of the function to which it points. An example declaration of a function pointer is

```
int (*pf)();
```

where **pf** is a pointer variable pointing to a function *which currently is not yet defined* returning an integer. Note the particular syntax: the character ***** defines **pf** as a pointer, the second pair of parenthesis **()** associates **pf** to a function, the first couple of parentheses enclosing ***pf**, is *necessary* to avoid any ambiguity with the declaration

```
int *pf();
```

referring to a function with the name **pf** returning a pointer to an integer. A pointer to a function takes the same values as the pointer to any other type of variable. For example, in the code fragment

```
int defineInput(double *, int);
main() {
  int (*pf) ();
  pf = &defineInput;
}
```

the pointer to a function **pf** contains the basic address of the memory space in which the function **defineInput** is loaded; this address is defined with the indirection operator **&** as for any other variable. Once the address of a function has been assigned to the pointer, we can use either one without any difference, i.e.,

```
entries = defineInput(data, MAX_NUM);
```

is identical to

```
pf = &defineInput;
entries = pf(data, MAX_NUM);
```

Introducing pointers to functions might seem very technical and of little importance. On the contrary, without this type of pointers it would be impossible to write functions executing algorithms on other functions which have not been defined beforehand. We discuss this interesting case in Section 7.6.

7.6 Functions of functions

There exist many situations in which it is useful, and sometimes necessary, to pass a function to another function as an input parameter. For example, suppose we want to translate the basic mathematical operators, such as the integral, the derivative, the summation, the product of a sequence operator, etc., into code. As mentioned in Section 7.5, we can pass a function to another one by pointers to a function. Once the syntactical rules have been understood, it is very easy to build this kind of application.

Let us consider, for example, the numeric computation of the derivative of a function. The derivative of a fuction $f(x)$ is defined as

$$f'(x) \equiv \frac{df(x)}{dx} \equiv \lim_{\epsilon \to 0} \frac{f(x+\epsilon) - f(x)}{\epsilon} . \tag{7.2}$$

In equation (7.2) we need to compute the limit of the incremental ratio $\frac{f(x+\epsilon)-f(x)}{\epsilon}$. We can write a function computing this ratio numerically as a function of a variable parameter ϵ and define the numerical derivative as this incremental ratio. For sufficiently small ϵ, the ratio should coincide with $f'(x)$. One of the input arguments of this function computing the numerical derivative necessarily is a pointer to the function for which we want to compute the derivative.

The Listing 7.12 contains a possible way to create such a function, applied to the library function `sqrt(x)` computing the square root, $\sqrt{x}$.

In Listing 7.12 we defined a generic function `func(double x)` representing the function which is to be derived. In this specific example, the function `func` simply returns `sqrt(x)`. However, it is clear that it could contain any possible complicated function.

```
1 #include <stdio.h>
2 #include <math.h>
3 double func(double);
4 double derivative(double (*)(double), double, double);
5
6 main() {
7   double epsilon = 1.;
8   printf("epsilon      derivata\n\n");
9   while (epsilon > 1.e-18) {
10    printf("%e %f\n", epsilon, derivative(func, 1., epsilon));
11    epsilon /= 10.;
12  }
13 }
14 double func(double x) {
15   return sqrt(x);
16 }
17
18 double derivative(double (*f)(double), double x, double epsilon) {
19   return ( f(x + epsilon) - f(x) ) / epsilon;
20 }
```

Listing 7.12   Computing the numerical derivative.

The function **derivative** computes the incremental ratio. Its input parameters are a pointer to the function **f**, for which we want to compute the derivative, the value of the variable with respect to which we want to perform the derivation, and the increment of the variable **epsilon**. In Listing 7.12 we assume **epsilon** is always larger than 0. Nevertheless, it would be appropriate to protect the **derivative** function against the occurrence of such a zero. In the **main** we start from $\epsilon = 1$ and divide it iteratively by 10. At each step we compute the value of the derivative and stop the iteration when $\epsilon \leq 10^{-18}$. We expect that for smaller and smaller values of ϵ the computed derivative is increasingly more precise. The result we obtained is listed in Table 7.1 and is somewhat surprising.

The given example is the computation of the derivative of $\sqrt{x}$ with respect to $x = 1$, which is equal to 0.5. It is clear from Table 7.1 that for values of $\epsilon \geq 10^{-5}$ the derivative is not yet correct because the value of ϵ is not yet small enough. When ϵ takes on a value comprised between 10^{-6} and 10^{-11}, the function always computes the correct value. For $10^{-15} \leq \epsilon < 10^{-11}$ the computed derivative moves farther and farther away form the correct value, until finally for $\epsilon < 10^{-15}$ the result is 0! The latter effect is due to the fact that the difference between **f(x + epsilon)** and **f(x)** cancels out because of the limited precision of the numerical representation (remember that $10^{-16} \simeq 2^{-48}$): this is true when the derivative of the

Table 7.1 Computing the derivative in function of ϵ.

ϵ	derivative
1.000 000e+00	0.414 214
1.000 000e−01	0.488 088
1.000 000e−02	0.498 756
1.000 000e−03	0.499 875
1.000 000e−04	0.499 988
1.000 000e−05	0.499 999
1.000 000e−06	0.500 000
1.000 000e−07	0.500 000
1.000 000e−08	0.500 000
1.000 000e−09	0.500 000
1.000 000e−10	0.500 000
1.000 000e−11	0.500 000
1.000 000e−12	0.500 044
1.000 000e−13	0.499 600
1.000 000e−14	0.488 498
1.000 000e−15	0.444 089
1.000 000e−16	0.000 000
1.000 000e−17	0.000 000
1.000 000e−18	0.000 000

function is small, as is the case with $\sqrt{x}$. In particular, by printing the values of x + epsilon, x, f(x + epsilon) and f(x), as they come along, we can verify that, even if the variable epsilon is different from 0, the computed function returns the same value in x as in $x + \epsilon$, such that its difference is zero. A similar effect may occur when the variable epsilon takes on values which are a lot less than the variable x. Using the same code of Listing 7.12, this effect can be verified by computing the derivative for $x = 1000$. In this case we dot not have enough bits for the mantissa of the variables epsilon and x to compute the incremental ratio in an adequate way. We conclude that a correct computation requires we do not exaggerate when reducing the increment ϵ, even if ϵ should be small, as this does not guarantee a greater precision.

Hands on 7.4 - Precision of the derivative

Verify the effect of the precision we just described by computing the derivative of the function $\sqrt{x}$ for increasing values of x, $x = 10, 100, 1000$, and printing the values of the variables x + epsilon and x, as well as f(x + epsilon) and f(x), during the cycle. Compute the derivative of other more complicated functions numerically. Start for example with the function $\sin(x)$ for various values of x in the interval $[0, \frac{\pi}{2}]$. Next, try with a function of the type $(1 + x^2)^{-1}$ or similar. Study the behavior of the derivative when varying ϵ and check whether the obtained result is correct when ϵ lies in the same interval of values as the one of the example discussed in the text. Study whether the interval of values of ϵ for which a correct derivative is obtained depends on the fact that the function to be derived is "flat" or irregular.

Hands on 7.5 - Mathematical operators

Write the code for a summation function $\sum_k f_k(x)$, summing N terms $f_k(x)$, with N given by the user. Next, write a function computing the difference between the exact value of a function $f(x)$ and its expansion in Taylor series for a given value of x. For example, chose $f(x) = \sin x$ and a small value of x different from 0. Remember that $\sin x = \sum_{k=0}^{\infty} (-1)^k \frac{x^{2k+1}}{(2k+1)!}$. Stop the series expansion at the third or fourth term.

Chapter 8

Numerical interpolation and integration

> If in any figure [...] any number of parallelograms
> [...] are inscribed [...]; if then the width of these
> parallelograms is diminished and their number
> increased indefinitely, I say that the ultimate ratios
> which the inscribed figure [...] the circumscribed
> figure [...], and the curvilinear figure [...], have to
> one another are ratios of equality
>
> Isaac Newton, *Principia Mathematica* (1725).

In this chapter we discuss how to translate nontrivial mathematical operations in algorithms and thus, in C programs. It is therefore of a more mathematical nature compared to the previous ones: it is dedicated to the basic techniques of numerical analysis to interpolate and integrate functions. There are many ways to numerically interpolate or integrate a function. Each one of these is either more appropriate to treat a certain class of functions or optimized with respect to certain characteristics (speed, precision, etc.). In the following we only consider the basic techniques.

8.1   Interpolation

The value of many mathematical function is known with infinite precision only in a finite number of points. For example, the values of the trigonometric functions are only known exactly for certain particular angles. To evaluate these type of functions in a point intermediate to these ones where the function is known exactly, we can *interpolate* the values: we can estimate the unknown values taking into account the general properties of the function (continuity, derivability, etc.) and the values it takes in the known points.

This technique is sometimes also used in daily practice. Even if we do not have a computer or a calculator with us, we can be certain that the value of the function $f(x) = \sqrt{x}$ for $x = 5$ lies between the values $\sqrt{4} = 2$ and $\sqrt{9} = 3$, since $f(x)$ is continuous and monotonic in this interval. It is also reasonable to expect the value of $\sqrt{5}$ to be closer to 2 rather than 3. But how much closer is it? The techniques collected in this chapter allow us to answer this question. Indeed, an algorithm exists to compute $\sqrt{5}$ without any calculator, though in certain cases its application is complicated and long[1]. Instead of wasting energy to apply this algorithm, it is enough to estimate the function value with a certain precision. We encounter the same problems when trying to estimate the value of a function with a computer. As in the cases given above, it could be that the function to be evaluated cannot be expressed analytically (and, therefore, cannot be expanded in a Taylor series either) or that evaluating it in an exact way is extremely expensive in terms of CPU time.

Another case requiring interpolation consists in determining the behavior of a quantity y as a function of another quantity x, $y = f(x)$, known in a limited number of points. For example, we can measure the values of the quantity y in correspondence with certain values of x. Sometimes we have a model establishing the shape of the function $f(x)$, possibly depending on a certain number of parameters $\vec{\alpha} = (\alpha_1, \ldots, \alpha_m)$, therefore $f = f(\alpha_1, \ldots, \alpha_m; x) = f(\vec{\alpha}; x)$. In these cases the interpolation consists in determining the values of the parameters $\vec{\alpha}$. For example, classical mechanics states that a body falling from standstill moves in a uniformly accelerated way. If y is the time it takes to fall and x the initial height, we have that

$$y = \sqrt{\frac{2x}{g}}, \tag{8.1}$$

where g is the gravitational acceleration. By measuring the time y at various heights x attained during the fall, we can determine n pairs of values (x_i, y_i) supplying the values of the function $y = f(g; x)$ (here, the vector $\vec{\alpha}$ has one sole coordinate $\alpha_1 = g$). Knowing the relationship between y and x, we can determine the value of g from the data. In these cases, the interpolation does not consist in describing the shape of a function, but

---

[1]This algorithm is due to Rafael Bombelli (1526-1572). It is studied during the first years of high school, though usually nobody remembers it.

rather in determining the best possible parameters. This is called a *best fit* or regression.

In even other cases we do not yet have a model describing the data. In this case, we fall back to the case given at the beginning of this section. If the values of the function describing the data are known in some points x_i, we can only approximate its value in an intermediate point taking into account the known values and some general properties we assume based on reasonable hypotheses (for example, we could assume that certain quantities vary in a continuous way or are derivable, etc.). For example, suppose we have the temperature of our city at 8 and 11 o'clock. Common sense tells us that this quantity varies slowly, in a continuous way and, if no atmospheric phenomena occur, grows monotonically in the considered interval.

8.1.1 *Determining the parameters of a function*

Consider we have a set of experimental points (x_i, y_i), $i = 1, \ldots, n$ following a known functional behavior. We limit ourselves to the simple case of a linear function $f(\vec{\alpha}; x)$: $y = f(A, B; x) = A + Bx$. This example is not too restrictive. Indeed, in many cases the function can be *linearized*. The function (8.1) can be rewritten as

$$y' = \frac{2x'}{g} \text{ where } y' = y^2 \text{ and } x' = x \, .$$

Measurements of a physical quantity always suffers some error. In the following we assume, for simplicity, that the uncertainty on the quantity x_i can be neglected with respect to that on each y_i, σ_i. To determine the parameters A and B we use the least squares method [Taylor (1996)]. According to this technique the best function describing the experimental data is the one minimizing the quantity

$$\chi^2 = \sum_{i=1}^{n} \frac{(y_i - f(\vec{\alpha}; x_i))^2}{\sigma_i^2} \, . \tag{8.2}$$

In practice, we require that the *distance* between the known points (x_i, y_i) and the line interpolating them be the minimum possible. In case $f(\vec{\alpha}; x) = A + Bx$, it is relatively simple to determine the parameters A and B. The function $\chi^2(A, B)$ has a minimum in the point where its partial derivatives with respect to A and B vanish:

$$\begin{cases} 0 = \dfrac{\partial \chi^2}{\partial A} = -2 \displaystyle\sum_{i=1}^{n} \dfrac{y_i - A - Bx_i}{\sigma_i^2} \,, \\[3mm] 0 = \dfrac{\partial \chi^2}{\partial B} = -2 \displaystyle\sum_{i=1}^{n} \dfrac{x_i(y_i - A - Bx_i)}{\sigma_i^2} \,. \end{cases} \tag{8.3}$$

Defining the quantities

$$S \equiv \sum_{i=1}^{n} \frac{1}{\sigma_i^2} \,, \quad S_x \equiv \sum_{i=1}^{n} \frac{x_i}{\sigma_i^2} \,,$$

$$S_y \equiv \sum_{i=1}^{n} \frac{y_i}{\sigma_i^2} \,, \quad S_{xx} \equiv \sum_{i=1}^{n} \frac{x_i^2}{\sigma_i^2} \quad \text{and} \quad S_{xy} \equiv \sum_{i=1}^{n} \frac{x_i y_i}{\sigma_i^2} \tag{8.4}$$

the system (8.3) can be rewritten in a more compact way. The corresponding solution is

$$\begin{cases} A = \dfrac{S_{xx}S_y - S_x S_{xy}}{SS_{xx} - S_x^2} \,, \\[3mm] B = \dfrac{S_{xy}S - S_x S_y}{SS_{xx} - S_x^2} \,. \end{cases} \tag{8.5}$$

Taking into account how the errors propagate, it can be proven that the variances of the parameters A and B are, respectively:

$$\begin{cases} \sigma_A^2 = \dfrac{S_{xx}}{SS_{xx} - S_x^2} \,, \\[3mm] \sigma_B^2 = \dfrac{S}{SS_{xx} - S_x^2} \,. \end{cases} \tag{8.6}$$

A program performing a linear regression is extremely simple. Indeed, it is enough to write the code computing the quantities (8.4), (8.5) and (8.6). We need to keep in mind that these computations may suffer rounding errors. In particular, equation (8.5) contains four subtractions of possibly large and similar quantities. To limit possible rounding effects, it is worth rewriting everything in terms of the quantities

$$t_i = \frac{1}{\sigma_i} \left(x_i - \frac{S_x}{S} \right) \quad \text{and} \quad S_{tt} = \sum_{i=1}^{n} t_i^2 \,.$$

It is easy to verify by substitution that

$$
\begin{cases}
B = \dfrac{1}{S_{tt}} \displaystyle\sum_{i=1}^{n} \dfrac{t_i y_i}{\sigma_i} \,, \\
A = \dfrac{S_y - S_x B}{S} \,.
\end{cases} \tag{8.7}
$$

with variances

$$
\begin{cases}
\sigma_A^2 = \dfrac{1}{S}\left(1 + \dfrac{S_x^2}{SS_{tt}}\right) \,, \\
\sigma_B^2 = \dfrac{1}{S_{tt}} \,.
\end{cases}
$$

As usual, the most elegant mathematical expression (8.5) is not necessarily the most indicated one to implement to perform the numerical computation. The most efficient way to compute the quantities we need is by summing the data when they are inserted, as in Listing 8.1. In this program, all quantities are initialized to zero, and declared as **double**, except for i and n which are integers. We need two cycles to compute all quantities, since the computation of t_i requires the values of S and S_x. Note that we could have used separate functions to compute, for example, the various summations. It is not too difficult to write a single function returning any of these. It would make the program far more elegant, but less efficient. Indeed, a similar function would be called at least four times to compute S, S_x, S_y and S_{tt}, performing every time a cycle of n steps. Dividing a program in modular elements, such as functions, is always a compromise between execution speed, code readability, reusability and compactness.

```
1    for (i = 0; i < n; i++) {
2        printf("Insert x[%d], y[%d] and sigma[%d]: ", i, i, i);
3        scanf("%lf %lf %lf", &x[i], &y[i], &sigma[i]);
4        s2 = sigma[i] * sigma[i];
5        Sx += x[i] / s2;
6        Sy += y[i] / s2;
7        S  += 1./ s2;
8    }
9    for (i = 0; i < n ; i++) {
10       t[i] = (x[i] - Sx / S) / sigma[i];
11       Stt += t[i] * t[i];
12       B += t[i] * y[i] / sigma[i];
13    }
14   B /= Stt;
```

```
15   A = (Sy - Sx * B) / S;
16   sigmaA = sqrt((1. + Sx * Sx / (S * Stt)) / S);
17   sigmaB = sqrt(1./ Stt);
```

Listing 8.1   Computing the summations for the least squares regression.

Unfortunately, things are not always that simple. Sometimes, the function describing the data cannot be linearized or depends on more than two parameters. In these cases, some general considerations are still valid. However, we do not always know how to analytically solve a system obtained by setting all partial derivatives of χ^2 equal to zero. The only way out is to minimize χ^2 numerically. This is a more complex task, tackled in Chapter 18.

Hands on 8.1 - Linear fits

Write a program performing a linear regression on n experimental points, where each one is a set of three numbers (x_i, y_i, σ_i). Change the given algorithm so that the data are read from a file. Try to decompose the program in functions and compare the performance of the two versions. Be aware that the differences are tiny! To measure the effective times use a system function able to measure the elapsed time and a high number of experimental points. One way to do that is the function `clock()` included in `time.h`. The function `clock()` returns the elapsed time in cycle units of conventional clocks. The symbol `CLOCKS_PER_SEC` defines the number of conventional CPU cycles per second. Note that to measure the length of a time interval we need to make two calls to `clock()`: one at the beginning and one at the end of the interval. Also pay attention to the fact that this time measure is reset each time it reaches the value `CLOCKS_PER_SEC`. Write a function which, given the values A and B and the set of numbers (x_i, y_i, σ_i), returns the value of χ^2. Use this function to print the values of χ^2 as a function of A and B.

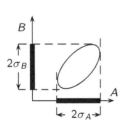
Observe that χ^2, as a function of A and B, is shaped like a paraboloid. The intersection of this paraboloid with a horizontal plane of height z is an ellipse in the plane (A, B) (figure on the side). Fixing $z = \chi^2_{\min} + 1$, where $\chi^2_{\min}$ is the minimum value of χ^2, it can be shown that the uncertainty on the estimate of A is obtained by projecting the ellipse on the A–axis (and analogously for B). You can then obtain an estimate of the errors on

parameters finding for which values of A and B the χ^2 increases by 1 with respect to its minimum value. Compare these error estimates with the ones obtained with equations (8.7).

8.1.2 *Interpolation with Lagrange polynomials*

When we do not have a model describing the functional form of the data or we need to estimate the value of a mathematical function in points where its value is difficult to obtain, we interpolate it by means of polynomials. In this case, the interpolation problem consists in estimating the values of a given function $f(x)$, given its values in a finite set of points $\{x_i\}$, where $i = 1, \ldots, n$, approximating it with another function L.

The interpolating function L approximating the function f in the best way, depends, apart from the variable x, on one or more parameters to be determined according to the specific interpolation method. We indicate them by $\vec{a}$. L, then, is a function of both x and $\vec{a}$: $L = L(x, \vec{a})$. Obviously, we need to have that

$$L(x, \vec{a}) \simeq f(x), \tag{8.8}$$

at least inside the interval $[x_{\min}, x_{\max}]$, where $x_{\min}$ and $x_{\max}$ are, respectively, the minimum and maximum of the set $\{x_i\}$. To find an interpolating function $L(x, \vec{a})$ adequately representing the unknown function $f(x)$, we can proceed in the following way. First of all, we require the interpolating function L to be identically equal to f in the set of points $\{x_i\} \equiv (x_1, x_2, \ldots, x_n)$ for which the value of f is known:

$$L(x_i, \vec{a}) \equiv f(x_i), \quad \forall i = 1, \ldots, n. \tag{8.9}$$

We can always chose the function $L(x)$ to be a linear combination of other functions $\phi_i(x)$:

$$L(x, \vec{a}) \equiv \sum_{i=1}^{n} a_i \phi_i(x), \tag{8.10}$$

where the coefficients a_i are determined by imposing the condition (8.9). The functions ϕ_i, unknown for the time being, can be chosen arbitrarily as long as they satisfy the condition (8.8). Thanks to this dose of arbitrariness, we can always require that

$$\phi_i(x_j) \equiv \delta_{ij}, \tag{8.11}$$

where δ_{ij}, called the Kronecker symbol, is defined by the relation

$$\delta_{ij} = \begin{cases} 0 & \text{if } i \neq j, \\ 1 & \text{if } i = j. \end{cases}$$

The equation (8.11) fixes in this way the coefficients a_i,

$$f(x_j) = L(x_j, \vec{a}) = \sum_{i=1}^{n} a_i \phi_i(x_j) = \sum_{i=1}^{n} a_i \delta_{ij} = a_j.$$

Again, thanks to the arbitrariness with which the functions ϕ_i are defined, we can choose the following polynomials for them

$$\phi_i(x) \equiv \alpha \prod_{j \neq i} (x - x_j). \tag{8.12}$$

This choice automatically satisfies the condition (8.11). Indeed, for each point $x_j \neq x_i$ the value of the function $\phi_i(x_j)$ is zero because at least one factor of the product is zero. Instead, for $i = j$, we have

$$\phi_i(x_i) = \alpha \prod_{j \neq i} (x_i - x_j) \equiv 1 \qquad \Rightarrow \qquad \alpha = \prod_{j \neq i} \frac{1}{(x_i - x_j)}. \tag{8.13}$$

By substituting (8.13) in (8.12) we have

$$\phi_i(x) = \prod_{j \neq i} \frac{x - x_j}{x_i - x_j}.$$

In this way we have determined all necessary parameters to build the interpolating polynomial $L(x, \vec{a})$, called the *Lagrange polynomial*. By substituting the expressions of a_i and ϕ_i in (8.10) we obtain the explicit expression of the Lagrange polynomial of degree $n - 1$ approximating the function $f(x)$ in the best way:

$$L_{n-1}(x, \vec{a}) = \sum_{i=1}^{n} f(x_i) \prod_{j \neq i} \frac{x - x_j}{x_i - x_j}. \tag{8.14}$$

In the case $n = 2$ the interpolation is said to be linear because geometrically the polynomial represents the straight line passing through the two points, in the Cartesian plane, where the function $f(x)$ is known. Indeed, the Lagrange polynomial of degree 1 is

$$L_1(x) = f(x_1) \frac{x - x_2}{x_1 - x_2} + f(x_2) \frac{x - x_1}{x_2 - x_1}.$$

We can easily check whether all required conditions are verified, and whether the formula corresponds to the straight line passing through the points $(x_1, f(x_1))$ and $(x_2, f(x_2))$.

Generally, the term interpolation is used when the point x where the function $f(x)$ is to be evaluated belongs to the interval $[x_{\min}, x_{\max}]$, otherwise we talk about *extrapolation*.

In those cases, it is very important to know how to evaluate the maximum possible error we are making. It can be proven [Bachvalov (1977)] that, in the case of the Lagrange polynomials, the maximum error Δ_n, called *remainder*, due to the approximation of $f(x)$ with $L_{n-1}(x)$ is given by

$$\Delta_n = |f(x) - L_{n-1}(x)| \le \sup_{\xi \in [x_{\min}, x_{\max}]} \left| f^{(n)}(\xi) \frac{\prod_{j=1}^{n}(x - x_j)}{n!} \right|, \quad (8.15)$$

where $f^{(n)}(\xi)$ represents the nth derivative of f with respect to x computed in the point ξ. Despite the fact that in many cases f is unknown, this formula is very useful. It tells us that the error diminishes like $1/n!$ if the derivatives are limited. It also tells us that the error is zero in the points where the function is known (of course, only in those cases in which they are known with infinite precision). We can hope that the derivatives of the function to be interpolated are limited if we can consider it to be sufficiently regular. This latter remark makes us understand that not all functions lend themselves to be approximated by a polynomial.

It is extremely easy to write a C–function computing the Lagrange polynomial of a generic degree. The Listing 8.2 shows a function returning the value of $L_{n-1}(x)$. It takes four input parameters: x (represented by the variable y), n, a vector containing the coordinates x_i and one containing the values of the function $f(x)$ to be interpolated computed in the points x_i. Note the double cycle to compute the summation of the products. The variable P storing the current value of the product is initialized to 1 at each iteration, while S, a sum, is initialized to 0 outside the cycle.

```
1  double Lagrange(double y, int n, double *x, double *f) {
2    double P, S = 0.;
3    int i, j;
4
5    for (i = 0; i < n; i++) {
6      P = 1.;
7      for (j = 0; j < n; j++) {
8        if (j != i) {
9          P *= (y - x[j]) / (x[i] - x[j]);
10       }
11     }
12     S += P * f[i];
13   }
14   return S;
15 }
```

Listing 8.2   A function computing the interpolating Lagrange polynomial.

Hands on 8.2 - Interpolation errors

Write a program comparing the values of a known function $f(x)$ with the Lagrange polynomial L_{n-1} of degree $n - 1$ approximating it. Compute the difference $R(x) = |f(x) - L_{n-1}(x)|$ while varying x and n and make plots of such a difference as a function of x and as a function of n. Study how $R(x)$ changes as a function of x and n (remember the error behaves like $1/n!$). For example, consider a regular function like $\sqrt{x}$, $x \in (0, 5)$, for $1 \leq n \leq 5$. Observe what happens outside the interval $(0, 5)$. Next, consider other functions, such as a trigonometric one, in the same interval. Estimate the maximum errors using the relation (8.15). Compare this estimate to the numerical result.

Hands on 8.3 - Interpolating experimental data

Bioassays are systems for toxicological assays to measure the action of certain substances based on the effect they have on living organisms. For example, the toxicity of some pesticides in marine waters is measured by determining the percentage p of anomalous larvae in bioassays of the embryos of certain bivalve shellfish (such as the *Mytilus Galloprovincialis*). Bioassays are calibrated by exposing N of them to a known solution of pesticides prepared in the laboratory, with a variable ratio of substance T_i, $i = 1, \ldots, N$, and determining the percentage of anomalous larvae p_i found in each of them. To measure an environment toxicity T_x, the test is repeated with a bioassay determining again the percentages p_x of anomalous larvae. Write a program to determine the degree of toxicity T_x by interpolating the data measured in the laboratory with a generic Lagrange polynomial of degree $N-1$. The input consists of a file containing two columns which represent, respectively, the values p_i measured in the laboratory for the corresponding T_i and the values of p_x measured in the latter test. The output is the value of T_x. Graphically compare the obtained Lagrange polynomial with the experimental data.

Hands on 8.4 - Interpolating functions

Euler's Γ function, used to define many statistical functions, is defined by an integral, whose primitive is not known analytically. On the other hand, evaluating this integral with numerical methods is a particularly burdensome task in terms of CPU time. The function, defined as

$$\Gamma(x) = \int_0^\infty u^{x-1} e^{-u} du \,,$$

has the following property: if x is a positive integer, $\Gamma(x) = (x-1)!$. Thus, one way to obtain the values is by interpolating it using a finite number of finite points $x_1, \ldots, x_n$ with x_i integer. Write a program estimating the values of the function $\Gamma(x)$ by means of Lagrange polynomials of different degrees (try both with polynomials of low degree, such as 1, 2 or 3, and degrees greater than 10). Compare the obtained values with the ones listed in mathematics textbooks. In particular, we have that $\Gamma\left(\frac{1}{2}\right) = \sqrt{\pi}$, $\Gamma\left(\frac{3}{2}\right) = \frac{1}{2}\sqrt{\pi}$ and $\Gamma\left(\frac{5}{2}\right) = \frac{3}{4}\sqrt{\pi}$.

8.2 Numerical integration

Problems of a scientific nature often require that we evaluate defined integrals. In this section we study the methods to compute integrals of the type

$$I = \int_a^b f(x)\, dx \,. \tag{8.16}$$

Of course, if we know the antiderivative $F(x)$ of $f(x)$, we can always write a function returning its value and compute the definite integral as a difference

$$I = F(b) - F(a) \,.$$

Unfortunately, the antiderivative of the integrand is not always known analytically. This is the case, for example, for numerous, frequently used probability distributions, from the Gaussian distribution to the χ^2 and the Student's t-distribution. In other cases it might be necessary to create a generic integrating function, independent of the particular form of the function f, to include it, e.g., in a mathematical library. In these cases, the integral I can only be approximated to its true value. This is referred to as numerical integration.

Before we show the methods for numerical integration, we observe that due to the additive property of integrals, setting $c_0 = a$, $c_M = b$, we can write

$$I = \int_a^b f(x)\,dx = \sum_{i=0}^{M-1} \int_{c_i}^{c_{i+1}} f(x)\,dx = \sum_{i=0}^{M-1} I_i \,,$$

with $c_k \in [a, b]\ \forall k$. Therefore, we can limit ourselves to select one single term of the summation by choosing an interval which can be, within the limits of the computer architecture, as small as we want.

In these cases, the most natural operation is to substitute the integrand with another function. The latter should approximate the integrand well and be a function of which we know the antiderivative. Such a function exists, namely the Lagrange polynomial. Computing the integral I thus is equivalent to the evaluation of the integral of a polynomial,

$$I_i = \int_{c_i}^{c_{i+1}} f(x)\,dx \simeq I_i^{(n)} \equiv \int_{c_i}^{c_{i+1}} L_{n-1}(x)\,dx \,. \tag{8.17}$$

The expression (8.17) represents an entire family of different integration methods, depending on the degree of the Lagrange polynomial. The remainder of the Lagrange polynomial, given by equation (8.15), allows us to evaluate the maximum error, or remainder, we make using such an approximation. For simplicity, we suppose all intervals composing $[a, b]$ have the same size $h = c_{i+1} - c_i$. Let us set

$$\delta_i^{(n)} = \left| I_i - I_i^{(n)} \right| \leq \int_{c_i}^{c_{i+1}} |\Delta_n|\,dx \,.$$

By substituting Δ_n with the right–hand member of the inequality of expression (8.15) and performing the following substitution

$$x = \frac{c_{i+1} + c_i}{2} + \frac{c_{i+1} - c_i}{2}t = \frac{c_{i+1} + c_i}{2} + \frac{h}{2}t \qquad \Rightarrow \qquad dx = \frac{h}{2}\,dt\,,$$

we have

$$\delta_i^{(n)} \le \left| \sup_{\xi \in [c_i, c_{i+1}]} f^{(n)}(\xi) \right| \frac{1}{n!} \int_{-1}^{+1} \prod_{j=1}^{n} |t - t_j| \left(\frac{h}{2} \right)^{n+1}$$

$$\times\, dt = A_i^{(n)}(f) \left(\frac{h}{2} \right)^{n+1} D_n\,,$$

where $A_i^{(n)}(f)$ represents the maximum value of the function nth derivative in the interval and

$$D_n \equiv \frac{1}{n!} \int_{-1}^{+1} \prod_{j=1}^{n} |t - t_j|\, dt\,.$$

Finally, summing the various contributions and considering that $Mh = b - a$, we obtain the error δ on the integral, given by equation (8.16), is

$$\delta^{(n)} = \sum_{i=0}^{M-1} \delta_i^{(n)} = \left(\frac{h}{2} \right)^{n+1} D_n \sum_{i=0}^{M-1} A_i^{(n)}(f) \le \frac{A_n(f) D_n}{2^{n+1}} h^n (b - a)$$

$$= \frac{A_n(f) D_n}{2^{n+1}} \frac{(b - a)^{n+1}}{M^n}\,, \qquad (8.18)$$

where

$$A_n(f) \equiv \max_i A_i^{(n)} = \left| \sup_{\xi \in [a,b]} f^{(n)}(\xi) \right|\,.$$

As expected, this relation tells us that the error with which we can estimate the value of the integral decreases as the size of the single integration interval h decreases (it decreases if the number M of points in which we divide the interval $[a, b]$ increases). Instead, for larger integration intervals the error may increase a lot.

8.2.1 *The rectangle rule*

If the integrand can be approximated with a constant C in the integration interval (i.e., if the integration interval is small enough such that we can consider $f(x)$ to be constant in that interval), we can write

$$\int_{c_i}^{c_{i+1}} f(x)\, dx \simeq I_i^{(1)} = C(c_{i+1} - c_i) = Ch,\qquad (8.19)$$

where $C = f(\xi)$ and $\xi \in [c_i, c_{i+1}]$ is arbitrary. This corresponds to substituting the integrand with a Lagrange polynomial with degree 0 passing through the point $(\xi, f(\xi))$.

The relation (8.19) is called the rectangle rule[2]. It takes this name because from a geometric point of view, calculating I_i is equivalent to calculating the area of a rectangle with base $h = (c_{i+1} - c_i)$ and height C (as shown in Figure 8.1). The remainder of this quadrature formula is easily derived using equation (8.18) with $n = 1$ and is

$$\delta^{(1)} \leq \left| \sup_{\xi \in [a,b]} f'(\xi) \right| D_1 \frac{(b-a)^2}{4M} = \left| \sup_{\xi \in [a,b]} f'(\xi) \right| D_1 \frac{b-a}{4} h,\qquad (8.20)$$

where D_1 may vary, depending on the choice of the point ξ, between 1 and 2. In general, this method is used when the function to be integrated is unknown, but its value is known in some points (for example, as a result of some measurement). Instead, when the function to be integrated is known, the midpoint method is used.

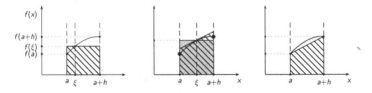

Fig. 8.1   From a geometric point of view, the rectangle rule corresponds to substituting the integral of the curve $f(x)$ with the outlined area in the figure on the left. Instead, the trapezoidal rule approximates the curve integral with the area of the trapezoid shown in the rightmost figure. The midpoint method is shown in the figure in the middle. The area of the outlined trapezoid (with the oblique side tangent to the curve in ξ) is equal to the one of the gray rectangle (with one side passing through ξ).

---

[2]The formula (8.19) is also called Newton's quadrature formula. Indeed, Newton introduced this method to evaluate the area of the portion of the plane included between the horizontal axis and the curve described by the integrand, when differential calculus did not yet exist.

8.2.2 The midpoint method

The midpoint method is a special case of the rectangle rule. It consists in choosing for ξ the midpoint of the interval or, in terms of the variable t, $t_1 = 0$. The performance of the integration method can be improved exploiting the symmetry properties of the interpolating polynomial. If we choose ξ as the midpoint of the interval, $\xi = (c_{i+1} + c_i)/2$, it is easy to understand that the rectangle with base h and height $f(\xi)$ is equivalent to any trapezoid of height h, with the oblique side passing through $f(\xi)$. So, instead of approximating the function f with a constant, we approximate it with a straight line passing through the point

$$\left(\frac{c_i + c_{i+1}}{2}, f\left(\frac{c_i + c_{i+1}}{2} \right) \right).$$ (8.21)

The quadrature formula remains the same, namely (8.19), but the error is smaller. Indeed, expanding the function $f(x)$ in series around the midpoint, we have that

$$f(x) \simeq f\left(\frac{c_i + c_{i+1}}{2} \right) + f'\left(\frac{c_i + c_{i+1}}{2} \right) \left(x - \frac{c_i + c_{i+1}}{2} \right) +$$

$$+ \frac{1}{2} f''\left(\frac{c_i + c_{i+1}}{2} \right) \left(x - \frac{c_i + c_{i+1}}{2} \right)^2 + \dots$$

The first two terms of the series represent precisely a straight line passing through the point (8.21). Therefore, the error we made with this approximation is given by

$$\delta_i^{(1)} \leq \left| \frac{1}{2} f''\left(\frac{c_i + c_{i+1}}{2} \right) \right| \int_{c_i}^{c_{i+1}} \left| \left(x - \frac{c_i + c_{i+1}}{2} \right)^2 \right| dx =$$

$$= \frac{1}{24} \left| f''\left(\frac{c_i + c_{i+1}}{2} \right) \right| (c_{i+1} - c_i)^3,$$

from which we obtain that

$$\delta^{(1)} \leq \frac{1}{24} \left| \sup_{\xi \in [a,b]} f''(\xi) \right| h^2 (b - a) = \frac{1}{24} \left| \sup_{\xi \in [a,b]} f''(\xi) \right| \frac{(b - a)^3}{M^2},$$ (8.22)

This is identical to (8.18) for $n = 2$, apart for a factor 2. Thus, even if we only used a single point to approximate the integrand in each interval, the estimate of the error is of the same order as the one obtained when we use two points. Indeed, the midpoint method derives from the integrand approximation with a Lagrange polynomial of the first degree passing through two coinciding points lying in the center of the interval.

8.2.3   *The trapezoid rule*

Using a Lagrange polynomial $L_1(x)$ of the first degree passing through the points $(c_i, f(c_i))$ e $(c_{i+1}, f(c_{i+1}))$ we obtain the trapezoid or Bézout[3] rule (we leave the determination of $L_1(x)$ as an exercise):

$$I_i = \int_{c_i}^{c_{i+1}} f(x)\,dx \simeq I_i^{(2)} = \int_{c_i}^{c_{i+1}} L_1(x)dx = \frac{f(c_{i+1}) + f(c_i)}{2}\,(c_{i+1} - c_i)\,,$$

Its name is due to the fact that from a geometric point of view the integral consists, in fact, in calculating the area of a trapezoid whose bases are equal to $f(a)$ and $f(b)$ with height $(c_{i+1} - c_i)$, as shown in the rightmost plot of Figure 8.1. The error we make when approximating with the trapezoid rule, computed with (8.18), is

$$\delta^{(2)} \leq \frac{1}{12}\left|\sup_{\xi \in [a,b]} f''(\xi)\right| h^2(b-a) = \frac{1}{12}\left|\sup_{\xi \in [a,b]} f''(\xi)\right| \frac{(b-a)^3}{M^2}\,, \qquad (8.23)$$

i.e., (8.18) with $D_2 = 2/3$. Even if the Lagrange polynomial of degree 1 describes the integrand better than the polynomial of a smaller degree, this does not imply the trapezoid rule is more precise than the rectangle rule. Indeed, the midpoint method, which is a special case of the latter, is a clear case of this. Even if the behavior of δ with n is different, the possible symmetry properties of the interpolating polynomial and the size of the maximum of the n–th derivative of f in the interval $[a,b]$ may produce results which at first sight seem unexpected. To understand this better, let us observe Figure 8.1. In the integration interval the function is shaped such that it overestimates the left subinterval and underestimates the right subinterval. The final result could be that on average the integral of $f(x)$ evaluated in this way is more or less correct. Instead, in case of the trapezoid rule, the integral in Figure 8.1 is underestimated. It must be said that this is not a general rule and which technique is more suitable depends on the type of function. This occurs when the integrand is almost linear, since in that case we have that

$$f\left(\frac{a+b}{2}\right) \simeq \frac{1}{2}(f(a) + f(b))\,.$$

Thus, in this case both methods are essentially equivalent.

---

[3]Étienne Bézout (1730-1783) was a French mathematician.

If we know how the error behaves with h, we can adopt a relatively simple technique to estimate the true value of I. By writing

$$I = \sum_{i=0}^{M-1} I_i^{(n)} + R(h), \qquad (8.24)$$

the error $R(h)$ is given by the relations (8.20), (8.22) or (8.23), depending on the used method. In all cases, we have that $R(h) = Ah^n$ ($n = 1$ for the rectangle rule and $n = 2$ in the other two cases) and the following relation is valid

$$\lim_{h \to 0} R(h) = 0.$$

In this limit, we can extrapolate the true value of the integral. By evaluating $\sum_i I_i$ for different sizes h of the interval, we can plot the results as a function of h^n and perform a linear regression on the data obtained in this way. Relation (8.24) tells us that the intercept of the straight line interpolating the data represents the best estimator of the value I.

If the integrand is sufficiently regular, the method allows us to limit M to few points, thus limiting the computational cost. So, it is not always true that the size h of the interval should be very small. Due to rounding errors, actually, the contrary can be true.

Hands on 8.5 - Comparing integration methods

Write a program to numerically evaluate the integral of a function you are able to integrate also analytically, with the three different methods described in this section. Allow the user to give the integration interval $[a, b]$ and the minimum $M_{\min}$ and maximum $M_{\max}$ number of parts in which it should be divided. Compute the integral $I(m)$ for m comprised between $M_{\min}$ and $M_{\max}$ and plot the values of $I(m)$ as a function of h or h^2, depending on the cases. Perform a linear regression on the resulting behaviors and compare the intercept with the true value of the integral. Try with the functions $\sin(x)$ and $\sin(1/x)$ in the interval $[0, \pi]$ with $1 < m < 100$. The first is approximately equal to 0.4597, the second to 1.5759.

When we write a function for numerical integration, we always need to pay attention to possible rounding problems we already discussed several times. Indeed, if the number M of points dividing the interval is large, it is appropriate to adopt accurate summation algorithms, like the Kahan algorithm (Section 4.5). A sloppy encoding could cause problems when M is small. Let us consider Listing 8.3, where the arguments of the `midpoint` function are the endpoints of the integration interval of the function `f`, the number of points in which it is divided and the pointer to the integrand. The integration step `h` is evaluated and a summation cycle is performed until the variable `x` exceeds the value `b` of the right end. For example, if we apply this algorithm to evaluate $\int_0^1 \sin x \, dx$ (this is the integral of a very regular function for which we expect few points should be enough) we find $I_i(M)$ to behave as a function of the number M of points as is given in Figure 8.2. The cause of this strange behavior is once more due to approximation problems. Indeed, certain values of M are completely inadequate, because the corresponding values of h are not exactly representable in the computer memory.

```
1 double midpoint(double a, double b, int m,
2                 double (*f)(double)) {
3    double I = 0., x = a;
4    double h = (b - a) / (double) m;
5    while (x < b) {
6      I += (*f)(x + 0.5 * h);
7      x += h;
8    }
9    return I * h;
10 }
```

Listing 8.3   A bad coding of the midpoint algorithm.

For example, the value $M = 10$, leads to a value $h = 0.1$, which unfortunately cannot be represented with a finite number of bits in the computer memory[4]. Even though `h` is defined as a `double`, its value is approximated and results are slightly less than the true value. This small difference is sufficient to satisfy the condition on line 5 of the Listing 8.3 at each step, also at the one (the eleventh one) in which we expect it to become false. In this way, the integration interval increases by about 10 percent. Again, a tiny error (of the order of 2^{-64}) causes a disastrous result.

---

[4]The only numbers which can be represented in an exact way are those which can be written as a finite sum of powers of 2.

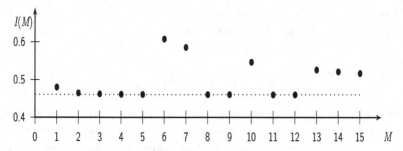

Fig. 8.2 Behavior of the integral $\int_0^1 \sin x \, dx$ (whose true value is about 0.4597, represented by the dotted line) as a function of M. The estimate is obtained with the midpoint method, dividing the interval $[0, 1]$ in M parts.

To avoid this type of errors it is better to control the number of steps rather than the value of x, as is done in the algorithm of Listing 8.4.

```
1 double midpoint(double a, double b, int m, double (*f)(double)) {
2   double I = 0., x, h = (b - a) / (double) m;
3   int i;
4   for (i = 0; i < m; i++) {
5     x = a + h * i + 0.5 * h;
6     I += (*f)(x);
7   }
8   return I * h;
9 }
```

Listing 8.4   A good encoding of the midpoint algorithm.

8.2.4   *Other integration methods*

To enhance the precision with which the integrand is described inside the integration interval, we can interpolate it with a parabola passing through the integration limits and the midpoint of the interval. Performing this exercise, it is easily proven that

$$I_i = \int_{c_i}^{c_{i+1}} f(x) \, dx \simeq I_i^{(3)} = \frac{c_{i+1} - c_i}{6} \left[f(c_i) + f(c_{i+1}) + 4f\left(\frac{c_{i+1} + c_i}{2}\right) \right],$$
$$(8.25)$$

known as the Cavalieri–Simpson formula[5]. Using the formula (8.25) the value of $\sum_i I_i$ converges more rapidly to I when increasing M. Indeed, we have that

$$\delta^{(3)} \leq (b-a)A_3 h^4 = A_3 \frac{(b-a)^5}{M^4},$$

where A_3 contains all factors not depending on the number of steps. Note that also in this case, the formula seems to converge faster compared to when we use the error estimate of the degree–2 Lagrange polynomial. Again, this is due to the symmetry properties of the polynomial. Indeed, we obtain the same integral with a Lagrange polynomial of four points, two of which coincide with the midpoint of the integration interval.

The integration methods we have analyzed so far, unfortunately depend rather strongly on the choice of points in which we divide the integration interval. Indeed, a wrong choice of the integration points can lead to disastrous results (think of a strongly oscillating periodic function, for which we choose the integration points which are separated exactly by a period). The other way around, a good choice of these points leads to an improvement of the precision without increasing the order of the interpolating polynomial (Simpson's method and the midpoint method). By optimizing the choice of points dividing the integration interval we determine an entire class of quadrature formulas known as the *Gaussian formulas*. The Gaussian quadrature formulas all have the following form

$$I(f) \equiv \int_a^b f(x)\,dx \simeq S_n(f) \equiv \frac{b-a}{2} \sum_{i=1}^n w_i\,f(x_i)\,. \qquad (8.26)$$

The points x_i are called *fundamental points*. The various quadrature formulas differ by the number and position of points dividing the interval $[a, b]$. To determine the values w_i and x_i we require the quadrature formula (8.26) to be exact for the polynomial P_m of degree m with m as high as possible. This means we require

$$S_n(P_m) \equiv S_n\left(\sum_{k=0}^m a_k x^k\right) = I(P_m)\,.$$

---

[5]Bonaventura Cavalieri (1598-1647) was a disciple of Galilei. He first calculated the quadrature formula of a parabola. The British mathematician Thomas Simpson (1710-1761) applied this result to the evaluation of an integral of any possible continuous function.

In order for the quadrature formula (8.26) to be exact for a polynomial of degree m it is necessary and sufficient that for each x^k with $k = 0, \ldots, m$:

$$R_n(x^k) \equiv \int_a^b x^k \, dx - \frac{b-a}{2} \sum_{i=1}^n w_i x_i^k = 0 \,. \tag{8.27}$$

This relation must be true for each k and represents a system of $m + 1$ equations in $2n$ unknowns (n values of w_i and as many x_i). The system can be solved for $m \le 2n - 1$. Therefore, we can find exact quadrature formulas at n points for polynomials of maximum degree $m = 2n - 1$. The midpoint formula is a special case of the Gaussian quadrature formula. Even though we assume the function to be constant within the interval, it is also exact for degree–1 polynomials. Indeed, for $n = 1$ we have $m = 2n - 1 = 1$. It is easily verified that the quadrature formula (8.26) with $n = 1$ is exact for degree–1 polynomials:

$$\int_a^b P_1(x) \, dx = \int_a^b (Ax + B) \, dx = \left(A \frac{x^2}{2} + Bx \right) \Big|_a^b =$$

$$= \frac{A}{2} (b^2 - a^2) + B (b - a) = (b - a) \left(A \frac{b+a}{2} + B \right) = (b - a) P_1 \left(\frac{b+a}{2} \right) ,$$

This is exactly the Gaussian quadrature formula with $w_0 = 2$. More generally, the system (8.27) can be solved for $m = 2n - 1$. However, its solutions are not guaranteed to be such that $x_i \in [a, b] \; \forall i = 1, \ldots, n$. We write the polynomial of maximum degree $m = 2n - 1$ as $P_m = (x - x_1) \ldots (x - x_n) P_{n-1}$. If the Gaussian quadrature formula has to be exact for this polynomial, the following relation must be true

$$\int_a^b (x - x_1) \ldots (x - x_n) P_{n-1} \, dx = \frac{b-a}{2} \sum_{i=1}^n w_i P_{2n-1}(x_i) = 0 \,. \tag{8.28}$$

This equality derives from the fact that, by construction, $P(x_i) \equiv 0 \; \forall i = 1, \ldots, n$. Due to equation (8.28) the fundamental points coincide with the zeros of the polynomial $\Psi_n(x) = (x - x_1) \ldots (x - x_n)$. Multiplying the expression (8.27) of the remainder by $\Psi_n(x)$ we have

$$\int_a^b \Psi_n(x) x^k \, dx = \frac{b-a}{2} \sum_{i=1}^n w_i \Psi_n(x_i) x_i^k \,. \tag{8.29}$$

It can be shown [Smirnov (1964)] that it is always possible to find a polynomial of degree n which is *orthogonal* to all other polynomials of lower degree with all zeros lying inside the interval $[a, b]$. Two polynomials $\Psi_n(x)$ and $\Psi_m(x)$ are said to be orthogonal in $[a, b]$ if

$$\int_a^b \Psi_n(x)\Psi_m(x) \, dx \propto \delta_{nm} \, .$$

If we can find a base of orthogonal polynomials in $[a, b]$ whose zeros all lie within this interval, we can use the zeros of the degree–n polynomials as fundamental points of the Gaussian quadrature formula of order n. In this way, the system (8.27) is automatically satisfied. The techniques used to determine these polynomials are beyond the scope of this book. The interested reader can find their derivation in [Smirnov (1964)]. A good base of orthogonal polynomials consists of the Legendre polynomials. We can generate a Legendre polynomial $P_j(x)$ of degree j with the relation

$$j \, P_j = (2j - 1) \, xP_{j-1} - (j - 1) \, P_{j-2} \, , \qquad (8.30)$$

with $P_0(x) = 1$ and $P_1(x) = x$. All its zeros are contained in the interval $[-1, 1]$. For this reason the integral is rewritten by substituting the variable

$$y = -\frac{2}{a - b} \, x + \frac{a + b}{a - b} \, ,$$

and we obtain

$$\int_a^b f(x) \, dx = \frac{b - a}{2} \int_{-1}^1 f(y) \, dy \, .$$

In this case, always indicating the roots of the polynomial with x_i, it can be shown that

$$w_i = \frac{2}{(1 - x_i^2) \left(P'_{n+1}(x_i) \right)^2} \, ,$$

where $P'_{n+1}(x_i)$ is the first derivative of the Legendre polynomial of degree $n + 1$ evaluated in the point x_i.

Hands on 8.6 - Gauss-Legendre integration

 Using the relation (8.30), write a function returning the generic Legendre polynomial of degree j for a given value of x. Use the bisection method to find its j roots in the interval $[-1, 1]$. To this purpose, keep in mind that the zeros of the Legendre polynomials are symmetric with respect to the origin. Thus, it is enough to find $j/2$ roots in the interval $[0, 1]$ to know all of them. Moreover, the zeros of the polynomial $P_{j+1}(x)$ are distributed such that each one of them lies in an interval given by dividing the segment $[a, b]$ by the roots of $P_j(x)$. Use this property to determine the endpoints delimiting the zeros.

Write a function filling an array with the zeros of the Legendre polynomial of degree $n + 1$ found in the interval $[-1, 1]$ and another array containing the corresponding values of its derivative in those points. The derivative can be approximated with the finite difference ratio

$$P'_{n+1}(x_j) \simeq \frac{P_{n+1}(x_j + \epsilon) - P_{n+1}(x_j)}{\epsilon},$$

where ϵ is the tolerated error when applying Newton's method to find the roots x_j. However, in this case, equation (8.30) supplies us with a way to compute the exact derivative, namely as

$$jP'_j = (2j - 1) P_{j-1} + (2j - 1) xP'_{j-1} - (j - 1) P'_{j-2}.$$

Another function could fill an array containing the coefficients w_i, if the polynomial zeros and its derivatives are given in input.

At this point, you can compute the integral of any function with the Gauss–Legendre method. Use the program to determine the values of x_i for $n = 2$. If the code is well written, you should find the values $\pm\sqrt{3}/3$. Compare this to your results. Compare the value of the integral of any function computed with the 2-point Gauss-Legendre method and the trapezoid rule (in particular, try to integrate a second degree polynomial). Note how the trapezoid method takes the same number of points, but the choice of the abscissa of these points is not optimal.

8.3   The Monte Carlo method

The deterministic methods of the previous sections cannot always be applied because the integrand is not always well–approximated by polynomials. Periodic, strongly oscillating functions with discontinuities or asymptotes could create serious problems. To overcome the latter we can use a stochastic method which is less dependent on the choice of points where we want to compute the function to be integrated, namely the Monte Carlo method. Moreover, this method is easily implemented. The corresponding error can be estimated in a statistical way, and can be shown to decrease as $1/\sqrt{N}$, where N is the number of points where the integrand has been evaluated. With the deterministic methods described in the previous sections, the function is evaluated $N = Mn$ times, with M equal to the number of intervals in which the integration interval is subdivided and n the order of the Lagrange polynomial interpolating the integrand. The method is particularly useful to estimate the integrals of complicated functions, and systematic errors due to badly chosen points dividing the interval $[a, b]$ are more under control.

Suppose we want to compute the integral of a function $f(x)$ between the points a and b. We randomly chose the points x_i, $i = 1, \ldots, N$, which are distributed according to a certain probability distribution $P(x)$, which, by definition, is positive–definite and such that

$$\int_a^b P(x)\,dx = 1\,. \tag{8.31}$$

We define a new function $s(x)$ as $s(x) \equiv f(x)/P(x)$, whose expectation value $\langle s \rangle_P$ on $P(x)$ is given, by definition, as

$$\langle s \rangle_P \equiv \int_a^b s(x)P(x)\,dx = \int_a^b \frac{f(x)}{P(x)}P(x)\,dx = \int_a^b f(x)\,dx\,,$$

which is exactly the integral we wanted to compute. The best estimator of the expectation value of a random variable is its average value. Thus, if we extract N points $x_i \in [a, b]$ in a random way with the distribution $P(x)$, we have that

$$I \equiv \int_a^b f(x)dx \simeq \frac{1}{N}\sum_{i=1}^{N} s(x_i)\,.$$

To estimate the value of I it is enough to extract a number N of points $x_i \in [a, b]$, with a certain probability distribution $P(x)$ and compute the average value of $s_i = f(x_i)/P(x_i)$. In the limit $N \to \infty$ the method is independent on the particular choice of the distribution $P(x)$. So, we can choose it to be a simple one, such as the uniform distribution[6]

$$P(x) = \begin{cases} c & : & x \in [a, b], \\ 0 & : & x \notin [a, b], \end{cases}$$

where, due to (8.31), we have that the constant $c = 1/(b - a)$.

In Section 5.5 we learned how to generate pseudo–random numbers. It is easy to create a simple function performing an integration with the Monte Carlo method, as the one of Listing 8.5. On line 7 of Listing 8.5 a pseudo–random number comprised between a and b is generated. On the next line, the values of the function in the N extracted points are summed and accumulated in the variable S. Since the selected distribution is constant and equal to $C = (b - a)^{-1}$, we just need to divide the variable S by C to obtain the sum $s(x_i)$ and divide by N to obtain the average (line 10).

```
1 double mcIntegration(double a, double b, int N,
2                      double (*f)(double)) {
3     int i;
4     double S = 0.;
5     double x;
6     for (i = 0; i < N; i++) {
7         x = a + (b - a) * (double)lrand48() / (double)RAND_MAX;
8         S += (*f)(x);
9     }
10    return S * (b - a) / N;
11 }
```

Listing 8.5   Monte Carlo integration.

Of course, before calling the `mcIntegration` function, we need to initialize the random number generator with a call to `srand(unsigned int seed)`. We only need to do this once to avoid generating non–random sequences. A very common error consists in initializing the random number generator in the function, or even worse, in the integration cycle.

If the seed is fixed, the generator always returns the same number sequence. Instead, if the seed is computed with an algorithm or with the

---

[6]Obviously, the choice of the distribution function could influence the result when N is finite. How to select the most appropriate distribution function is discussed in Chapter 19.

value returned by the `time(0)` function, the numbers could be different (however, they may not be randomly distributed).

Hands on 8.7 - The Monte Carlo method

 Write a program evaluating the integrals of the Hands On exercise 8.5 with the Monte Carlo method. Vary the number N of points and write the values of N and the corresponding integrals $I(N)$ to a file. Plot $I(N)$ as a function of N and observe how $I(N)$ oscillates above and below the true value of the integral, though the fluctuations diminish as N increases. Perform a linear regression on the obtained data. What do you expect for the value of the intercept? What about the slope?

8.3.1   *Multiple integrals*

In case we need to integrate a function of one variable, the Monte Carlo method is rather inefficient with respect to deterministic methods. Already the simple rectangle method converges much faster.

This is not the case for multiple integrals, for which the Monte Carlo methods are successful. The reason is that the error decreases as $1/\sqrt{N}$ independently of the number of dimensions of the integral. Moreover, it is rather easy to write a stochastic algorithm for multiple integrals, while it is much more complicated with deterministic methods. Indeed, in order to evaluate the volume of a complicated shape, such as the intersection of a sphere of radius R with its center in $(0,0,0)$ and a cube with edge length 2 with its center in $(1,1,1)$, we would need to carry out the integral

$$\iiint_\Omega dx \, dy \, dz \,, \qquad (8.32)$$

where Ω represents the limits of integration, which cannot be expressed easily, but with a system of equations:

$$\begin{cases} x^2 + y^2 + z^2 < R^2 \,, \\ 0 < x < 2 \,, \\ 0 < y < 2 \,, \\ 0 < z < 2 \,. \end{cases} \qquad (8.33)$$

This integral is easy to evaluate, even with a deterministic method (passing, for example, to cylindric coordinates). However, this is a particularly simple case we selected to show a method which, instead, is completely general. With the Monte Carlo method it is easy to evaluate the integral (8.32). It is enough to extract N random points distributed in a uniform way in a cube of volume V containing the one which is to be integrated. We then determine the wanted integral as

$$I = V \frac{k}{N} \, ,$$

where k is the number of points contained inside the volume to be integrated. For example, the volume $V_{S \cap C}$ of the portion of the sphere S of radius $R = 1$ intersecting the cube C with edge length 2 centered in $(1, 1, 1)$, manifestly is

$$V_{S \cap C} = \frac{1}{8} \frac{4}{3} \pi R^3 \simeq 0.523\,904 \, .$$

The few lines of code of Listing 8.6 are enough to compute it numerically with the Monte Carlo method.

```
1   #define L      2
2   #define R      1
3   #define N  10000
4   ...
5   double x, y, z, V;
6   int i = 0, k = 0;
7   for (i = 0; i < N; i++) {
8     x = L * (double)lrand48() / RAND_MAX;
9     y = L * (double)lrand48() / RAND_MAX;
10    z = L * (double)lrand48() / RAND_MAX;
11    if ((x * x + y * y + z * z) < (R * R)) {
12      k++;
13    }
14  }
15  V = (double)(L * L * L) * k / N;
```

Listing 8.6   Computing a volume with the Monte Carlo method. In this example the volume of the space region defined by the system (8.33) is computed.

The symbol L represents the edge of the cube, while N is the number of points which need to be extracted. R is the radius of the sphere. In the cycle we extract N sets, consisting of three values each, contained in the integration volume. The variable k counts the points falling inside the sphere volume. Therefore, the volume is estimated as prescribed.

It is not difficult to extend the method to the multiple integral of any other function. Suppose, for example, we need to determine the mass of a body with variable density $\rho = \rho(x, y, z)$, shaped as a sphere of radius $R = 1$. The integral we need to evaluate in this case is:

$$\iiint_\Omega dx \, dy \, dz \, \rho(x, y, z), \qquad (8.34)$$

where Ω represents the constraint $x^2 + y^2 + z^2 \leq 1$. Whichever is the expression of ρ, to compute that mass it is enough to extract N points $\vec{x_i} = (x_i, y_i, z_i)$ uniformly distributed within a cube of size 2 containing the sphere. If the point $\vec{x_i}$ is contained by the latter, the value of $\rho(\vec{x_i})$ is added to the variable k. You can still use the symmetry properties of the problem, if any, to reduce the number of points $\vec{x_i}$ to generate. For example, if ρ is spherically symmetric, you can compute the mass of $1/8$ of the sphere and multiply the result by 8.

Hands on 8.8 - Integrating with the Monte Carlo method

Repeat the Hands On exercise 8.5 with the Monte Carlo method. Verify whether the error varies as $1/\sqrt{N}$ (remember the value of the integral itself is a random variable and to estimate the error we need to repeat the evaluation many times in the same conditions to compute its variance). Apply the Monte Carlo method to evaluate the multiple integral given in (8.34) assuming a constant density. Compare the value with the expected one (if ρ is constant the mass is proportional to the sphere volume).

PART 2

Advanced programming and simple algorithms

Chapter 9

Integrating differential equations

> If a non-negative quantity was so small that it is smaller than any given one, then it certainly could not be anything but zero.
>
> Leonhard Euler.

In this chapter we discuss how to numerically integrate differential equations: we consider the basic example of a harmonic oscillator. When introducing the different methods of numeric integration we focus on how to control the systematic error due to the discretization of the time interval. In particular, we consider the simple and basic methods of Euler and of Euler-Cromer. We analyze their merits and limitations. We learn how to organize data inside a construct of the type `struct`. We discuss a code that solves numerically the equations of motion of a harmonic oscillator.

In this chapter we discuss concepts that are particularly important: the numeric integration of differential equations is fundamental to study many physical, chemical, biological and geological phenomena, and to analyze static structures and electronic circuits.

9.1   The harmonic oscillator

We are now ready to discuss a first, rather easy, yet very important application of scientific programming, namely the harmonic oscillator. We examine how to numerically integrate its equations of motion. We discuss a number of potential problems and difficulties: this helps us to approach this discussion on numerical integration. First of all, we introduce the relevant equations. Next, we discuss the numerical integration algorithms and we introduce *new* and stimulating questions that one can ask thanks to the potential of numerical calculus. We should not act too fast though: indeed, it is important that we proceed in small steps.

The harmonic oscillator is the starting point of many models and fundamental theories in physics. The harmonic oscillator can be solved exactly, which is rarely the case for more complex physical models. The motions repeating themselves belong to the class of the so-called periodic or harmonic motions. Oscillators are physical systems characterized by periodic motions between two points in space. Probably the most important model in which the harmonic oscillator plays a fundamental role is the one of the oscillations of atoms in solids (together with field theory).

A generic equilibrium point of a physical system can often be approximated by a parabolic behavior: the Taylor expansion around a function minimum does not include a first order term. In this case, if we consider the dominating term near the minimum, we basically approximate the system behavior with the one of a harmonic oscillator. Such an approximation may be sufficient to describe motions close to the potential energy minimum.

We consider a body of mass m connected to a spring (Figure 9.1). We identify the origin of the axis x with the position in which the body is at rest. In this way, x is the variable defining the displacement from the mass point of equilibrium. The body moves without any friction, while a spring tries to pull it back to the point where it is at rest, $x = 0$, i.e., the body equilibrium point. The force acting on the body is an elastic restoring force:

$$F = -K\,x\,,$$

where K is the (positive) elastic constant, measuring how rigid the spring is. The negative sign is very important and indicates that we are dealing with a restoring force. As we are treating a one-dimensional problem we do not include the vectorial symbols appearing in problems defined in more than one dimension.

In order to understand how the system moves we consider Newton equations. Namely, if the system mass is constant in time, we have that

$$F(t) = m\,a(t)\,. \tag{9.1}$$

This is an extremely important relation, telling us that two measurable quantities (a force and an acceleration) are linked to each other by a proportionality constant, namely the mass, which is exactly the body gravitational mass. More explicitly, the relation tells us that

$$\frac{d^2x(t)}{dt^2} = -\omega_0^2\,x(t)\,, \tag{9.2}$$

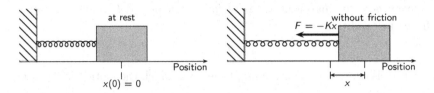

Fig. 9.1 A first easy diagram. A mass m oscillates without any friction along the x-direction, connected to a spring with elastic constant K.

where we defined

$$\omega_0^2 \equiv \frac{K}{m} .$$

The dimensions of ω_0^2 are $[T^{-2}]$, i.e., the dimensions of the square of an inverse time (remember that it is always very important to use dimensional analysis), and its square root has the same dimensions of a frequency. So, we have that

$$\ddot{x}(t) = -\omega_0^2 \, x(t) . \tag{9.3}$$

This is the definition of a simple harmonic motion. The differential equation (9.3) is very easily solved. Its general solution is of the form

$$x(t) = A \cos(\omega_0 t + \delta) , \tag{9.4}$$

where A and δ are two constants determined by the motion initial conditions (this is a second order differential equation, so we have two constants). A is the motion amplitude, δ is the phase at time zero. Note that the cosine argument is expressed in radians.

Exercise 9.1 - A simple check

This is a very simple exercise. Verify that (9.4) solves (9.2). To do this you can simply substitute the former in the latter. Also consider some other differential equations describing other simple physical systems.

The initial conditions of the problem can be given in different ways. For example, A and δ can be substituted by an initial position and velocity:

$$(A, \delta) \longleftrightarrow \left(x_0, v_0 = \left. \frac{dx}{dt} \right|_{t=t_0} \right) .$$

The harmonic oscillator motion is *periodic*. The period T can be determined from the condition

$$x(t + T) = x(t) ,$$

where T is chosen as the minimum time after which the motion is repeated. In our case

$$A \cos \left(\omega_0 \left(t + \frac{2\pi}{\omega_0} \right) + \delta \right) = A \cos \left(\omega_0 t + \delta \right) .$$

This implies that

$$T = \frac{2\pi}{\omega_0} = 2\pi \sqrt{\frac{m}{K}} .$$

The *frequency*

$$\nu \equiv \frac{1}{T}$$

is the number of cycles completed per unit of time. Note that the period T does not depend on A and δ (or, equivalently, on x_0 and v_0), but only on the ratio $\frac{K}{m}$. Even if, formally speaking, we included two parameters, m and K, in our equation of motion, the latter only depends on a specific combination of m and K, namely their ratio.

The harmonic oscillator energy E consists of a kinetic term $\mathcal{T}$ and a potential term $\mathcal{V}$. Its energy does not vary with time:

$$E = \text{ constant } = \mathcal{T}(t) + \mathcal{V}(t) = \frac{m \, v(t)^2}{2} + \frac{K \, x(t)^2}{2} .$$

This conservation law is violated in our numeric integration (which is necessarily based on a finite time integration steps). Checking whether or not this conservation law is violated is precisely one of the ways we can use to verify how well the integration algorithm performs. The knowledge of whether there exists a conserved quantity in the original differential equations (which is not necessarily the energy: think for example of the angular momentum, or of any other conserved quantity, i.e., one of the motion integrals) is a very important tool to check the consistency of a numerical approach.

9.2   Integration algorithms

We now study how to numerically integrate the equations of motion characterizing a physical system. We consider the simple harmonic oscillator, easy to integrate in an exact way, as a first exercise. It allows us to define a method and to develop some techniques that will be useful to analyze more interesting physical systems.

We discuss the properties of a number of integration algorithms. The list of names of algorithms is impressive: Euler, Euler-Cromer, interior-point, mid-point, Verlet, velocity Verlet, predictor-corrector, Runge-Kutta.

The numerical integration allows one to reconstruct the system trajectory in its phase space. Starting from the initial conditions at a time t_0 and incrementing the time variable with small steps, we obtain the system trajectory, i.e., its position and velocity for a discrete sequence of times included in the interesting time interval. Our main goal is to understand how to judge an algorithm performance, and how to chose the appropriate parameters to optimize its accuracy.

In Chapter 8 we introduced some basic elements of numerical integration. In this section we elaborate this subject further. The basis of any numerical integration consists in approximating the infinitesimal calculus formalism with finite differences. In some way we travel along the road introducing the infinitesimal calculus moving in the opposite direction, in the hope that this will allow us to enhance our understanding of the most important mechanisms. We are approximating time derivatives and we want to evaluate how efficient this is. A second important issue, as we already mentioned, is to check how the conservation laws, valid in the continuous theory, are violated in the numerical integration. We verify here this aspect by considering as an important example the energy of the system.

In one spatial dimension, defining $\phi(t) \equiv \frac{F(t)}{m}$, Newton equations are of the form

$$\ddot{x}(t) = \phi(t) .$$

This second order differential equation can be rewritten as a system of two coupled first order differential equations:

$$\begin{cases} \dot{v}(t) = \phi(t) , \\ \dot{x}(t) = v(t) . \end{cases} \tag{9.5}$$

It is easy to check, by deriving the second equation and substituting it into the first one, that these two formulations are equivalent. Indeed in the first order formulation both first order equations allow for an arbitrary constant, so that we have, as in the first case, two free constants. We will discuss here the second formulation, as it is easier to resolve these equations numerically.

To study these equations with a computer we need to discretize the time variable. We consider very small, though finite, time increments Δt, and we are interested in the limit in which this increment tends to 0, i.e., $\Delta t \longrightarrow 0$. Starting at a given time t_0 (which we usually set equal to zero) we compute the solution of (9.5) at the times: $t_1 = t_0 + \Delta t$, $t_2 = t_1 + \Delta t = t_0 + 2\Delta t$, ... $t_n = t_{n-1} + \Delta t = t_0 + n\Delta t$.

To simplify the notation, we also define

$$\begin{cases} x_n \equiv x(t_n) \,, \\ v_n \equiv v(t_n) \,, \\ \phi_n \equiv \phi(t_n) \,, \end{cases} \tag{9.6}$$

and, as we mentioned before, we want to study the regime in which $\Delta t \longrightarrow 0$, but is still finite. Let us elaborate on the operational interpretation of $\Delta t \longrightarrow 0$ in this procedure. In Chapter 8 we already discussed two fundamental aspects.

- When varying Δt, the amount of which our results (i.e., what we measure, such as, $x(t)$ or $v(t)$ at a given time t) change should not be larger than a given value. We can compare the trajectories in phase space for various values of Δt, and verify that they do not vary too much.

- The quantities that are conserved in the continuous limit and that are time-dependent in our numerical integration instead should not change more, at the time $\bar{t}$, than by a maximum preset quantity. In case of the energy, for example, we want the quantity $(E(\bar{t}) - E(0))/E(0)$ to be smaller than a predetermined quantity (for example, of no more than 0.01, meaning that at time $\bar{t}$ the energy has not changed of more than one percent).

Another fundamental notion we need to define in a more precise way is the *stability* of the system. At the same time we need to establish how we can verify the stability during the integration process. By stability we mean that if we make a small error when computing the system phase space trajectory, the error reduces with time instead of being amplified, thus closing in onto the correct trajectory (or at least not moving away from it). This is important since computer always commit small (rounding) errors when operating on non-integer numbers. Indeed, as all numbers are represented with a finite number of bits (see the discussion in Chapter 1), non-integer numbers are necessarily rounded.

9.2.1   *Euler and Euler-Cromer: convergence and stability*

We start by expanding the two equations (9.5) as a Taylor series. Since it will be useful when writing more accurate and efficient algorithms, we keep the term of the order dt^2 when expanding $x(t)$ and only the one of order dt in the expansion for $v(t)$. We find that

$$\begin{cases} v(t + dt) \simeq v(t) + \phi(t)dt + O(dt^2) \,, \\ x(t + dt) \simeq x(t) + v(t)dt + \frac{1}{2}\phi(t)dt^2 + O(dt^3) \,, \end{cases}$$

where, in the term in dt of the first equation and in the term in dt^2 of the second equation, we replaced the second derivative of x with respect to time by $\phi(t)$.

In the Euler method only the first order terms are taken into account and the infinitesimal dt is substituted with the small but finite term Δt. This is equivalent to applying the rectangle integration method and assuming the force and the velocity to be constant within the time interval Δt. We start from time t_0, add Δt at each time step, such that the time t_n is reached after n steps. After the next step, we have reached $t_{n+1} = t_n + \Delta t$ and, according to the definitions given in (9.6), we find the following iterative scheme

$$\begin{cases} v_{n+1} = v_n + \phi_n \Delta t \,, \\ x_{n+1} = x_n + v_n \Delta t \,, \end{cases}$$

that defines the Euler method.

The top plots of Figure 9.2 help to clarify what is happening. The left plot shows the system velocity, the right one its position. Since we discretized the time variable, our time steps start at time $t_n = t_0 + n\Delta t$ and end at the time $t_{n+1} = t_0 + (n + 1)\Delta t$. We do not consider what happens in between these two times. Using this discretization procedure, we just want to estimate the true trajectory as well as possible. In the Euler method, both $v(t)$ and $x(t)$ are estimated by the tangent to the true trajectory in the point t_n. This tangent is then used to extrapolate the value of the trajectory to the next time instance. The error we make in this way decreases as Δt decreases.

In order to better evaluate the intrinsic error of the Euler method, we start by noticing that at each integration step an error of the order $O(\Delta t^2)$ is made. Indeed we only kept terms of the order dt in the Taylor series. This is called the method local error. It accumulates throughout the numerical integration, as an integration over a time interval t takes $t \cdot \Delta t^{-1}$ integration steps. If, for example, t is equal to 60 seconds, with $\Delta t = 0.1$ seconds, we need 600 integration steps. If we improve the integration precision bringing Δt to 0.05 seconds, we need to perform 1200 elementary steps to cover the same 60 seconds.

So, we need to consider a global error, whose order of magnitude is given by the product of the local error and the number of steps needed to reach the desired (fixed) time. Therefore the global error decreases with Δt as $\Delta t^2 \cdot \Delta t^{-1} = \Delta t$. So, the Euler method is of the first order in Δt. This, together with some other reasons we discuss next, is why it is considered an awful integration method).

Hands on 9.1 - The harmonic oscillator with the Euler method

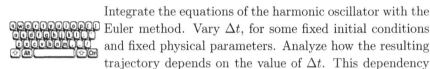
Integrate the equations of the harmonic oscillator with the Euler method. Vary Δt, for some fixed initial conditions and fixed physical parameters. Analyze how the resulting trajectory depends on the value of Δt. This dependency can also be studied as a function of ω_0. Verify how the system energy varies with time, by analyzing the ratio

$$\frac{\Delta E_{(\Delta t)}}{E(0)} \equiv \frac{E_{(\Delta t)}(t) - E(0)}{E(0)} .$$

For $\Delta t \longrightarrow 0$ this difference should be linear in Δt at a fixed time instance t. Check whether this is the case. Even if we mathematically derive the answer to these questions in the following sections, try to answer them now. Another interesting quantity is the parametric plot of $x(t)$ as a function of $v(t)$. What should be the shape of this plot? Instead, what shape does it have when integrating with the Euler method?

Note, as it is clear from Figure 9.2, that this is an asymmetric method. Indeed, it treats the starting point t_n and the ending point t_{n+1} in a different way. In order to compute the terms of order Δt, we approximate the velocity and the acceleration with their value at time t_n, and use these to bring the system to time t_{n+1}. Moreover, as we shall see throughout the following pages, its solution is unstable.

A small change leads to the Euler-Cromer method (often this change is even due to a programming error, because of updating a variable too soon: spend a few moments pondering this statement, and try to be sure you really got its meaning):

$$\begin{cases} v_{n+1} = v_n + \phi_n \Delta t , \\ x_{n+1} = x_n + v_{n+1}\Delta t , \end{cases}$$

where we substituted v_n by v_{n+1} on the right hand side of the equation for x_{n+1}. We first calculate the new velocity and then compute the increment

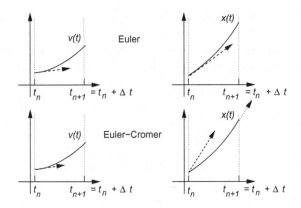

Fig. 9.2 Iteration in a time interval Δt with the Euler method (on top) and with the Euler-Cromer method (bottom). The dashed lines indicate the directions in which the system moves, the dotted lines the way in which these displacements have been calculated (see discussion in text).

for the position precisely with this new value (and not with the original one). As we shall see next, this method is not unstable when integrating oscillating systems, even if it is, as the Euler method is, of the order Δt (i.e., a "bad" method).

This new method uses the starting and ending time in a more balanced way. Indeed, while the acceleration, used to update the velocity, is calculated at the starting time t_n of the integration step, the velocity, used to update the position, is computed in the ending point t_{n+1}. In this way we hope to approximate the trajectory better. In order to estimate the system new position in the phase space at the time t_{n+1} we used more than just the information at the time t_n (leading to an awful approximation of the true motion trajectory).

This situation is shown in the lower half of Figure 9.2. The velocity changes exactly as in the case of the Euler method. However, the tangent of $x(t)$ is no longer estimated at time t_n, but rather at the time t_{n+1} (dotted line). The latter is used to increment $x(t_n)$. The dashed line is in the direction of the update. Its direction coincides with the one of the dotted line, which has been displaced in t_n.

Hands on 9.2 - The harmonic oscillator with the Euler-Cromer method

 Repeat the same operations you performed for the Euler method in case of the Euler-Cromer method. Compare the answers. Some behaviors are very similar, while others are

quite different. Which ones?

As a first elementary stability analysis of the Euler method, we consider a first order, rather than a second order differential equation:

$$\dot{y}(t) + f(y(t), t) = 0 ,$$

i.e.,

$$\dot{y}(t) = -f(y(t), t) .$$

Applying the same discretization procedure we described before (to obtain the Euler method), this leads to the iterative rule

$$y_{n+1} = y_n - f_n \Delta t , \tag{9.7}$$

where we defined $f_n \equiv f(y_n, t_n)$.

An integration method is stable if a small perturbation of the solution does not grow if we continue to iterate this solution. Suppose that at a given instant the numerically iterated solution (i.e., the system trajectory) differs by a given quantity ΔY from the correct solution of the discretized equation with finite differences (not the one of the original differential equation). So, we have that

$$y_{n+1} + \Delta Y_{n+1} = y_n + \Delta Y_n - \left[f_n + \frac{\partial f}{\partial y} \bigg|_n \Delta Y_n \right] \Delta t , \tag{9.8}$$

where the term enclosed between square brackets includes the change of f_n due to the change of y_n by ΔY_n.

Subtracting the members of equation (9.7) from equation (9.8), we obtain

$$\Delta Y_{n+1} = \left[1 - \frac{\partial f}{\partial y} \bigg|_n \Delta t \right] \Delta Y_n \equiv G \, \Delta Y_n , \tag{9.9}$$

where

$$G \equiv \left[1 - \frac{\partial f}{\partial y} \bigg|_n \Delta t \right] .$$

We are now able to understand what is going on. The error at time t_{n+1} is obtained by multiplying the error at time t_n by a factor G. If $|G| > 1$ the difference is amplified by the integration method. Instead, if $|G| < 1$ the difference reduces when applying the method.

Therefore, the Euler method is stable only if $|G| < 1$, i.e., if

$$-1 < 1 - \frac{\partial f}{\partial y} \Delta t < +1 .$$

First of all, note that Δt is larger than zero. Therefore, the inequality on the right implies the Euler method is stable only if

$$\frac{\partial f}{\partial y} > 0 .$$

Instead, the inequality on the right tells us that in order for the solution to be stable the time interval should be small enough:

$$\Delta t < \frac{2}{\frac{\partial f}{\partial y}} .$$

Three important, simple and interesting cases are those in which f is proportional to y:

$$\begin{cases} \dot{y}(t) + \alpha^2 y(t) = 0 \implies y(t) = y_0 \, e^{-\alpha^2 t} \quad \text{decay;} \\ \dot{y}(t) - \alpha^2 y(t) = 0 \implies y(t) = y_0 \, e^{+\alpha^2 t} \quad \text{growth;} \\ \dot{y}(t) \pm i\alpha^2 y(t) = 0 \implies y(t) = y_0 \, e^{\mp i\alpha^2 t} \quad \text{oscillations.} \end{cases} \tag{9.10}$$

For instance, the solution of equation $\ddot{x} = -\omega^2 x$ is $x \sim e^{i\omega t}$ (oscillating solution), for which $\dot{x}(t) = i\omega x(t)$.

In general, if the function $\frac{\partial f}{\partial y}$ is complex, it is convenient to consider whether

$$|G|^2 \leq 1 . \tag{9.11}$$

In case of the oscillating solution, we find

$$|1 - i\alpha^2 \Delta t|^2 = 1 + \alpha^4 \Delta t^2 > 1 .$$

Therefore, since the condition (9.11) can never be satisfied, the Euler method is unstable for oscillating systems.

Exercise 9.2 - Euler method stability

Show that for the systems defined in (9.10), the Euler method is unstable in case of growing or oscillating solutions, while it is stable for decaying solutions if $\Delta t \leq \frac{2}{\alpha^2}$.

Hands on 9.3 - Euler method instability

Numerically verify what is stated in Exercise 2. The error can be introduced in various ways. Reflect on how to implement this in an efficient way.

Exercise 9.3 - An interpretation problem

Think of a counterexample. Is the observation made in Exercise 3 meaningful in case of growth? If not, why? Note that we are trying to understand whether the method instability amplifies the error, thus causing two nearby trajectories to move away from each other.

9.2.2 *Other methods: midpoint and leapfrog*

So far, we have tried, respectively with the Euler method and with the Euler-Cromer method, to compute the new value of x_{n+1} starting either from v_n or from v_{n+1}. A third possibility, as prescribed by the midpoint method, is based on the use of the quantity

$$\frac{v_n + v_{n+1}}{2} .$$

This leads to the following iterative procedure

$$\begin{cases} v_{n+1} = v_n + \phi_n \Delta t , \\ x_{n+1} = x_n + \frac{v_n + v_{n+1}}{2} \Delta t . \end{cases} \tag{9.12}$$

We should not forget that all these algorithms lead to the correct solution in the limit $\Delta t \longrightarrow 0$. What we want to know is how large is the error that we are making when Δt is small but finite.

An elementary time step in this new scheme is shown in Figure 9.3 (analogous to Figure 9.2 for the Euler and the Euler-Cromer method). The way in which the velocity is incremented remains the same. However, the tangent to $x(t)$ is computed both in the initial point and in the endpoint (dotted lines), and we move in the intermediate direction (dashed line).

The true reason why we introduce this new scheme is immediately clear. If we substitute the first equation of (9.12) in the second one, we find that

$$x_{n+1} = x_n + \frac{v_n + v_n + \phi_n \Delta t}{2} \Delta t = x_n + v_n \Delta t + \frac{1}{2} \phi_n \Delta t^2 ,$$

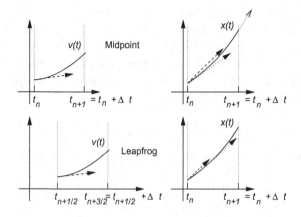

Fig. 9.3 Iteration in a time interval Δt for the midpoint method (on top) and the leapfrog method (bottom). The dashed lines give the directions of the displacements. The dotted line show how the displacements have been calculated (see discussion in the text).

correctly reconstructing the first and second order terms when developing x in series. So, the midpoint method is of the order $O(\Delta t^2)$ as far as the part in x is concerned and of the order $O(\Delta t)$ for the part in v.

Finally, we introduce the so-called leapfrog method. The velocities are defined at times which are halfway the steps bringing us from one value of x to the next. The algorithm is defined by

$$\begin{cases} v_{n+\frac{1}{2}} = v_{n-\frac{1}{2}} + \phi_n \Delta t \,, \\ x_{n+1} = x_n + v_{n+\frac{1}{2}} \Delta t \,. \end{cases}$$

Note that the method is not able to start the iterative procedure in an autonomous way (it is not *self-starting*). Given the initial conditions x_0 and v_0, we cannot start the iteration cycle (as we do not know the value of $v_{\frac{1}{2}}$). A simple possibility (even though one should consider the consequences of this approach) is to make a first step with the Euler method, leading to

$$v_{\frac{1}{2}} = v_0 + \frac{1}{2}\phi_0 \Delta t \,.$$

One can also use a more accurate method (see later) only for this first step. Once this first step has been made, one can proceed according to the iterative cycle we defined before.

This iterative scheme is shown in the lower half of Figure 9.3. Note that the horizontal axis of $v(t)$ (in the left part of the figure) has changed. In case of the velocity we no longer start from the time t_n, but rather from time $t_{n+\frac{1}{2}}$, and, moving of the usual time step Δt, we reach time $t_{n+\frac{3}{2}}$. Therefore, the tangent of $x(t)$ is calculated in the midpoint of the interval (dotted line), and it is used to move from time t_n to time t_{n+1} (dashed line). Note that for sufficiently regular trajectories, the midpoint method is very similar to the leapfrog method.

Hands on 9.4 - Midpoint and leapfrog

 Repeat the studies you carried out for the Euler and the Euler-Cromer method in the case of the midpoint method and of the leapfrog method. Compare the results. Obviously all these methods have a serious limitation in common.

9.2.3 *Physical results of a simple integration*

We now discuss some first results obtained by numerically integrating the equations of the harmonic oscillator. In Section 9.4 we analyze a program computing the quantities we define here. A very careful student should already have obtained the results we are about to discuss (actually we only examine some facts which are observed with a numerical integration).

First of all, we chose the parameters of the problem. We give ω_0^2 (as mentioned before, K and m only appear through their ratio in the problem, so the physical system is characterized by just one free parameter), fix the initial conditions and choose the value of Δt. Moreover, we want to follow the integration up to a fixed given time indicated by $\bar{t}$. In the following example, we have $\omega_0^2 = 3$, $x(t=0) = 2$, $v(t=0) = 1$, $\Delta t = 0.01$, $\bar{t} = 100$.

Figure 9.4 shows a plot of $x(t)$ and $v(t)$, obtained by integrating the equations with the Euler method (with the parameters we have given before). The result is obviously a disaster. The two curves, that in the limit $\Delta t \longrightarrow 0$ should be two sinusoids, now show a motion with growing amplitude. In less than 30 periods, the motion amplitude has become four times its original size. Also note that the period T does not vary perceptibly at these time scales.

At first sight, the results shown in Figure 9.5, obtained in the same conditions, but integrated with the Euler-Cromer method, seem to be more reassuring. The amplitudes of $x(t)$ and $v(t)$, and the period, appear to be

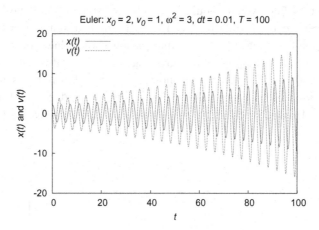

Fig. 9.4 $x(t)$ and $v(t)$ as a function of t for a harmonic oscillator integrated with the Euler method.

essentially constant.

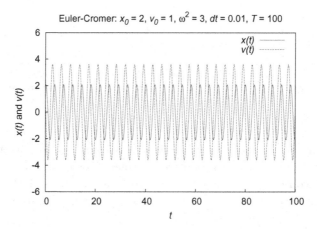

Fig. 9.5 $x(t)$ and $v(t)$ as a function of t for a harmonic oscillator integrated with the Euler-Cromer method.

It is extremely interesting to observe Figure 9.6, where we plot the position $x(t)$ at time t as a function of the velocity $v(t)$ at the same time t. Such a so-called *parametric* plot is often very useful. The curve resulting for an Euler integration, in the same conditions than before, is shown in Figure

9.6 with a thin line. What should be an ellipse (the motion is periodic and the phase space trajectory is closed) has become a spiral growing away from the points which a "correct" integration should have produced. As we shall see this corresponds to a growing, severe violation of the energy conservation law. The thick line shown in Figure 9.6 is the same curve in case of an Euler-Cromer integration. The latter does not reveal any divergence of x and v. Soon, we will discuss what is really going on.

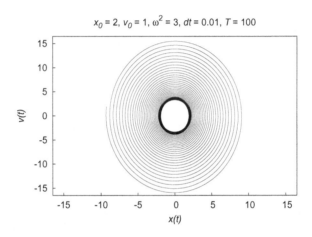

Fig. 9.6 $x(t)$ as a function of $v(t)$ for an Euler integration (thin spiraling curve) and for an Euler-Cromer integration (thick curve, concentrated on the innermost part of the spiral).

In Figure 9.7 we show the value of $\frac{\Delta E}{E(0)}$ as a function of the integration time, for both the Euler and the Euler-Cromer algorithm. The violation of the energy conservation law seems enormous in case of the Euler method, while on this scale the Euler-Cromer method does not seem to be problematic at all.

At this scale (induced by the size of the energy conservation violation produced by Euler integration) the energy in the Euler-Cromer integration appears to be perfectly conserved. In spite of this apparent perfection it is worth not to give up immediately, and to try to find out whether we can observe some effect by using a better resolution.

Hands on 9.5 - Violation of the energy conservation law

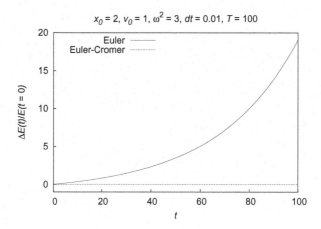

Fig. 9.7 $\frac{\Delta E(t)}{E(0)}$ as a function of time for the two integration algorithms of the Euler (continuous line) and the Euler-Cromer (dashed line).

Try to establish, for example by using the program **gnu-plot** (Section 10.5), the functional dependence of $\frac{\Delta E}{E(0)}$ on t. Do this for a given, small enough, Δt in order to find significant results.

Analyzing the system at different scales is often a necessary and useful exercise. In Figure 9.8 we show the same results of Figure 9.7, at a much smaller scale. The energy conservation violations of the Euler method are too large for this scale, and they grow immediately out of the plot range. However, this scale allows one to observe that the energy conservation violation of the Euler-Cromer method are periodic. Indeed, the system first loses energy, but then regains it back and oscillates around a value close to the original energy. This certainly is an interesting fact, and we we will explain it in mathematical terms in the following.

Finally, we want to analyze how $\frac{\Delta E_{(\Delta t)}(t)}{E(0)}$ depends on Δt at fixed t. Figure 9.9 clearly shows this dependency is linear in Δt for both methods (the lines are the best fits to a linear behavior). Both the Euler and the Euler-Cromer method are of the order Δt. So, both are "bad" integration methods. Even if for a given Δt the Euler-Cromer method is superior compared to the Euler method, this gain is somehow fictitious. For example, if we want to halve the error we are making, in both methods we need to halve Δt, thus doubling the integration effort.

Finally, we note that the same (linear) law applies at different times. So,

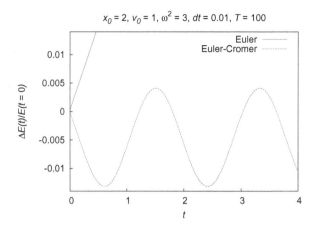

Fig. 9.8   As in Figure 9.7, but on a much smaller scale.

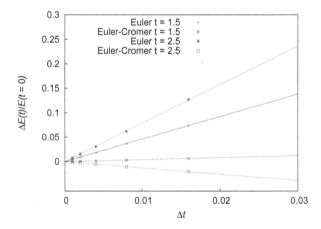

Fig. 9.9 $\frac{\Delta E_{(\Delta t)}(t)}{E(0)}$ as a function of Δt for the Euler and the Euler-Cromer method, and for two different times $t = 1.5$ and $t = 2.5$. The continuous curves represent the best linear fit.

the scaling law that characterizes the integration method does not depend on the time at which we observe it.

9.3 The struct

The structure is a C language construct: it is a group of one or more variables, possibly of different types, such to allow the user an easier use of these variables. In the case of the harmonic oscillator it could be reasonable to group x and v together, thus creating a structure, say xV. This is not only for aesthetic or indexing purposes. It also allows, among others, one to manage functions in a more efficient way.

In some way we can consider structures to be an integration and an enrichment of predefined types. They are very useful in a scientific programming context, but they are also especially useful to manage heterogeneous databases, which are very important in many areas (also in scientific programming). A typical example, that has little to do with scientific matters, concerns a university administration. For example, it might be useful to store a list of student names (represented by a string of variable length), together with the student birth date (three integers), the enrollment number (integer), the number of exams already passed, examination scores (two integers) and the average mark obtained so far (a **float** type variable) organized in a **struct**. Usually the average mark is not stored, as it can be easily computed given the other data, but we would like to memorize it by including a **float** variable in our example. The birth date might be a structure **birthDay** consisting of three integers, which will be one of the elements of the structure **students**. The number of exams already passed and the corresponding scores, together with their average could be grouped in another elementary structure, called **marks**.

We can perform several operations on structures: we can assign them, we can pass them to functions, or we can have functions returning structures or pointers to structures.

Let us start by discussing the simple case of a point in a plane. Such a point is characterized by two coordinates of type **double**, x and y. We can define a structure of the type **point** as

```
struct point{
  double x;
  double y;
};
```

The final ; of the declaration is very important, but easily forgotten. Note that with the previous statement we only create a *type of structure* (the type of structure we named **point**). We do not define any true structure in this declaration (we will do this later on). Indeed, we have not allocated any data memory location. It is as if we were creating the type int, that allows us to create integer variables later on (a declaration of a structure defines something very similar to a type). The variables included in the structure declaration (x and y in the example) are the structure members.

We can declare one or more variables of the type struct upon defining this structure. For instance, in the following lines we define a structure of the point type and we create two structures position1 and position2:

```
struct point{
  double x;
  double y;
} position1, position2;
```

We can also define such variables further on in the code by using the structure type we created:

```
struct point position3, position4;
```

We can initialize a structure when we define it with the command

```
struct point position5 = {7, 13};
```

One possible way to refer to a given structure member is by means of the construct

```
structure_name.member
```

The operator . links the structure name to the name of its member. In this way, we can, for example, compute the ratio between the coordinates x and y as following

```
double xOverY = position3.x / position3.y;
```

The structures can be concatenated. We can define a new structure whose members are previously defined structures (note that the structure definition operation is rather abstract):

```
struct twoPoints {
  struct point firstPoint;
  struct point secondPoint;
} couple;
```

We can access the element x (which is a variable of type double) of the structure secondPoint, which in turn is an element of the structure couple, as

```
couple.secondPoint.x;
```

We can copy or assign values to structures, only by means of a pointer pointing to them. They cannot be compared in a direct way. They can be used as function arguments, though, as well as be a function return value. Structures are different from arrays. Indeed, their name does not represent the pointer to the structure, but rather it represents the full structure.

It is possible (and an interesting exercise for the reader) to write functions performing mathematical operations on structures of a given type. For example, we can use the following function to sum the coordinates of two points

```
struct point sumPoints(struct point pa, struct point pb) {
    struct point temporary;
    temporary.x = pa.x + pb.x;
    temporary.y = pa.y + pb.y; return temporary;
}
```

Note that in this function we used the entire structure and not just its pointers. This is often not the best choice. It is now easy to sum two structures.

```
struct point xPlusY = sumPoints(position1, position2);
```

Hands on 9.6 - Operations on a **struct**

Write other functions performing interesting mathematical operations on a structure of the type **point**. For example, compute the square modulus of a given vector, or write functions performing a scalar or a vector product of three-dimensional vectors.

Structures can be manipulated by means of their pointers:

```
struct point *pPoint;
pPoint = &position1;
```

assigning the address of the structure **position1** to the variable **pPoint**. We can call a structure member with the structure pointer followed by the symbol -> and the name of the member:

```
pPoint->x
```

For example, the three following statements are equivalent:

```
position1.x
(*pPoint).x
pPoint->x
```

The third form is probably the most commonly used one.

Just like for variables of the predefined types, we can define arrays of structures. For example, we can write:

```
struct point position5[1000];
```

9.4   A complete program as a simple example

We now analyze a program listing: comments will help us to understand what it does. The program integrates the equations of motion of a harmonic oscillator with either the Euler or the Euler-Cromer method. The program computes and writes, at each time instance of the integration procedure, the system energy.

```
 1 %%%%%%%%%%%%%%%%%%%%%%%%%%%%%% OA.C %%%%%%%%%%%%%%%%%%%%%
 2 /* We introduce structures, we freshen up the use of the I/O
 3 /* and of the functions, we learn how to avoid any side */
 4 /* effects when using functions */
 5
 6 #include <stdio.h>
 7 #include <math.h>
 8
 9 #define EXIT_SUCCESS      0
10 #define EXIT_FAILURE     -9
11 #define EULER            0
12 #define EULER_CROMER     1
13
14 /* Note how the semicolon included   */
15 /* at the end of the following lines is fundamental! */
16
17 struct phaseSpace {
18    double x;
19    double v;
20 };
21
22 struct phaseSpace *initHarmonicOscillator(double x0,
23                                           double v0);
24 struct phaseSpace *euler(double dt, double omega2,
25                     struct phaseSpace *pXAndV);
26 struct phaseSpace *eulerCromer(double dt, double omega2,
27                          struct phaseSpace *pXAndV);
28 double energy(double omega2, struct phaseSpace *pXAndV);
29 double forceHarmonicOscillator(double omega2, double x);
30 double potentialEnergyHarmonicOscillator(double omega2,
31                                          double x);
32 double myReadDouble (char *printMessage);
33 long int myReadLong(char *printMessage);
```

```
1
2  /*********************************/
3  /* THE PROTOTYPES */
4
5  int main(void) {
6    double x0, v0, dt, omega2, totalTime, energy0, energy1;
7    long int  numberOfSteps, algorithm, i;
8    struct phaseSpace xAndV;
9
10   /* The symbols # help gnuplot, for instance,  */
11   /* or help us when using a filter to eliminate */
12   /* the lines which are not needed when we plot the data */
13
14   printf("# Harmonic oscillator integration\n");
15   printf("#v1.1.1, June 1, 2013\n");
16
17   /* We use this myRead to avoid some code */
18
19   totalTime =
20     myReadDouble (
21       "Enter the total integration time");
22   algorithm =
23     myReadLong("Insert 0 for Euler, 1 for Euler-Cromer");
24   dt = myReadDouble ("Enter dt");
25   x0 = myReadDouble ("Enter x0");
26   v0 = myReadDouble ("Enter v0");
27   omega2 = myReadDouble ("Enter omega2");
28
29   /* We explicitly perform the cast, to keep */
30   /* things under control! */
31
32   numberOfSteps = (long int)(totalTime/dt);
33   printf("# dt = %g total time = %g\n",
34           dt, totalTime);
35   printf("# omega2 = %g number of steps = %d\n",
36           omega2, numberOfSteps);
37
38   /* A function without any side effects. What is changed */
39   /* is changed with a return statement */
40
41   xAndV = *initHarmonicOscillator(x0, v0);
42   printf("# Initial conditions x0 = %g v0 = %g\n",
43           xAndV.x, xAndV.v);
44   energy0 = energy(omega2, &xAndV);
45   printf("# The energy at time t = 0 is %g\n", energy0);
46   if (algorithm == EULER) {
47     printf("# Using the Euler algorithm\n");
```

```
1    for (i = 0; i < numberOfSteps; i++) {
2
3      /* Another function without side effects */
4
5      xAndV = *euler(dt, omega2, &xAndV);
6      energy1 = energy(omega2, &xAndV);
7      printf("%g %g %g %g\n",
8             (double)i*dt, xAndV.x, xAndV.v, energy1 - energy0);
9    }
10  } else if (algorithm == EULER_CROMER) {
11    printf("# Using the Euler-Cromer algorithm\n");
12    for (i = 0; i < numberOfSteps; i++) {
13
14      xAndV = *eulerCromer(dt, omega2, &xAndV);
15      energy1 = energy(omega2, &xAndV);
16      printf("%g %g %g %g\n",
17             (double)i*dt, xAndV.x, xAndV.v, energy1 - energy0);
18    }
19  } else {
20    printf("# THUNDER AND LIGHTNING:");
21    printf("Algorithm n. %ld unexpected. Error.\n",
22           algorithm);
23    exit(EXIT_FAILURE);
24  }
25  energy1 = energy(omega2, &xAndV);
26  printf("# The energy at time t = %d is %g\n",
27         numberOfSteps, energy1);
28  return EXIT_SUCCESS;
29 }
30
31 /********************************/
32 struct phaseSpace  *initHarmonicOscillator(double x0,
33                                            double v0) {
34   static struct phaseSpace xAndV;
35   xAndV.x = x0;
36   xAndV.v = v0;
37   return &xAndV;
38 }
39
40 /********************************/
41 struct phaseSpace *euler(double dt, double omega2,
42                          struct phaseSpace *pXAndVOld) {
43   static struct phaseSpace xAndVNew;
44
45   /* What happens if the first couple of parentheses */
46   /* on the next line is omitted? */
47
48   xAndVNew.v = (*pXAndVOld).v +
49     forceHarmonicOscillator(omega2, (*pXAndVOld).x) * dt;
```

```
 1
 2
 3   xAndVNew.x = pXAndVOld->x + pXAndVOld->v * dt;
 4   return &xAndVNew;
 5 }
 6
 7 /********************************/
 8 struct phaseSpace *eulerCromer(double dt, double omega2,
 9                                     struct phaseSpace *pXAndVOld) {
10
11   static struct phaseSpace xAndVNew;
12   xAndVNew.v = (*pXAndVOld).v +
13     forceHarmonicOscillator(omega2, (*pXAndVOld).x) * dt;
14   xAndVNew.x = pXAndVOld->x + xAndVNew.v * dt;
15   return &xAndVNew;
16 }
17
18 /********************************/
19 double energy(double omega2, struct phaseSpace *pXAndV) {
20
21 /* We do not compute E but compute 2 E / m */
22
23   double localEnergy;
24   localEnergy = (*pXAndV).v * (*pXAndV).v
25     + potentialEnergyHarmonicOscillator(omega2, (*pXAndV).x);
26   return localEnergy;
27 }
28
29 /********************************/
30 double forceHarmonicOscillator(double omega2, double x) {
31   return - omega2 * x;
32 }
33 /********************************/
34 double potentialEnergyHarmonicOscillator(double omega2,
35                                     double x) {
36   return omega2 * x * x;
37 }
38
39 /********************************/
40 long int myReadLong(char *printMessage) {
41   long int inputData;
42
43   printf("# %s\n",printMessage);
44   fflush(stdout);
45   scanf("%ld",&inputData);
46
47   return inputData;
48 }
```

```
 1
 2 /**********************************/
 3 double myReadDouble (char *printMessage) {
 4   double inputData;
 5
 6   printf("# %s\n",printMessage); fflush(stdout);
 7   scanf("%lg", &inputData);
 8
 9   return inputData;
10 }
```

Listing 9.1   Integration of the equations of motion of the harmonic oscillator, with either the Euler or the Euler-Cromer method.

We use the above listing to discuss in detail how to structure a rather complete program. In some cases, we will be repeating some things that have already been mentioned before, but at this point a few repetitions can help us.

First of all, notice the commands #include to include system files. In this case, these are I/O and mathematical library files. Do not forget that if you make use of mathematical functions such as sqrt() or pow(), we not only have to include math.h, but we also have to specify the option -lm upon compilation. With a generic compiler, say cc, a typical compilation command is

```
cc -o myfile.exe myfile.c -lm
```

specifying that the name the compiler gives to the executable program it generates should be myfile.exe.

Immediately afterwards we define an object called EXIT_SUCCESS which takes the value 0. We use this as an argument to quit the program in a regular way. It is worthwhile to proceed in this way. Indeed, if we wrote -3 to quit in case a specific error occurred, -5 in case of another error, and 1 in a regular case, the resulting code would be less comprehensible. Anybody else (but even ourselves at a later time) reading the code, possibly in order to change it, would have more difficulty in understanding how it works. Instead, a structured code, appropriately defining the numerical values is certainly more clear

```
#define EXIT_SUCCESS 0
#define OPEN_FILE_ERROR -3
#define MEMORY_ERROR -5
```

Indeed, in this way, we can include statements like exit(OPEN_FILE_ERROR) to quit the program in case an error occurred when opening a file, `exit(MEMORY_ERROR)` to quit it in case an error occurred when trying to allocate memory, and `exit(SUCCESS)` in case the program exited in a regular way. The time it takes to write a clear and "clean" code pays far better of what it costs, in the form of large savings of time when we have to improve, change or reuse the code. In this example we only included one type of code to quit the program upon an error. The other `#define` directives have been included for the same reason.

On line 20 of the listing in page 262 we define a `struct` of the type `phaseSpace`. Here, we only define the type of structure. The actual variable declaration of structures of this type occurs later on in the program. Here, we decided to group the position and the velocity of our physical system into a `struct`. This choice comes natural, because we often need to use these two variables together (e.g., when updating the position and the velocity in the same integration step).

Next, we include the function prototypes. It is very important we do this in a clear way. Here, we even used dummy names for variables, that tell us something about what is the function of the arguments of the functions. Deciding precisely the types of the different variables (the ones we define, those we pass to functions, and the ones returned by functions) is referred to as *strong typing* (see also Chapter 3). It is very important that we make sure that the variables are of the correct type. For example, we advise to always include an explicit *cast* when we need to change a type of variable. Indeed, why should we confide in a compiler if we can guarantee certain things ourselves?

On line 5, p. 263, we define the `main` function. One of the variables we defined immediately afterwards is the `struct phaseSpace xAndV` containing, as indicated by its name, the system position and velocity at time t. Next, we included the name of the program, its version and the corresponding date.

The functions `myReadDouble` and `myReadLong` have as argument a message that will be given to the user, and return the read data item, thus saving us some code.

On line 32, p. 263, we compute the number of steps needed to integrate over the entire selected time interval (note the explicit cast, choosing again to strongly type, i.e., keeping a tight control over, the variable). Remember that when we change δt (the variable `dt` in the program) the number of steps needed to cover the given physical time changes accordingly.

We print all the variables we have read in order to check the results and to make sure we can reproduce them. It is easy to make a mistake when entering a number or when writing the `scanf()` statement (remember that while the arguments of the `printf()` function are values, the `scanf()` functions take pointers for arguments).

Our first function, called on line 41 of page 263 and defined on line 33 of page 264, initializes the position and the velocity of the harmonic oscillator. It is a very simple function. Nevertheless, we want to discuss it in detail as the general idea behind it has been applied to all of the functions. The two arguments are passed by means of their *value* and not by means of their address, i.e., not by means of the pointer to the memory location containing the initial data. The function returns a pointer to a structure consisting of the initial position and velocity. This structure should be `static`, because once it is returned by the function it will be used by other functions of the code. The structure this pointer points to is copied into `struct phaseSpace xAndV`. Thanks to this mechanism this function cannot, not even if the programmer had been uncareful, change the data of the problem: the function knows the values of the initial data, but it does not know where they are located. It can only carry out a computation, which in this case is limited to building a structure starting from two `double` type variables, and return the corresponding result.

The function `energy()` uses the structure we just initialized and the value of ω^2 to compute the energy. Here, to include a different construct, we used the structure pointer as an argument (making the code less safe, but more efficient). The function `energy()` sums the values of the kinetic and the potential energy (computed in case of the harmonic oscillator from `forceHarmonicOscillator()`) and returns the total energy which is saved in `energy0`. The function `energy()` is generic as it does not include any information regarding the fact that we are studying a harmonic oscillator. It only depends on the single parameter ω^2: in a different system the number of needed parameters might be different.

With the variable `algorithm` we choose which integration algorithm we want to apply. In this code we have implemented the Euler and the Euler-Cromer algorithm. For example, let us consider the case of the Euler algorithm (the Euler-Cromer method is completely analogous). We iterate the procedure a number of times equal to `numberOfSteps`. The function `euler()` performs a time step (i.e., advances by a time Δt). The function reads as inputs the values of `dt`, `omega2` and the pointer to the structure containing the position and the velocity. In the function, on line 42 of page 265 , we use, to give an example, other constructs. First we compute the new velocity (with the function `forceHarmonicOscillator`) and next, the new position (with the old value of the velocity, otherwise we would have coded the Euler-Cromer method!). The function `euler()` behaves well, and changes the surrounding environment only by returning the pointer to a structure. The `main()` function then copies the latter into the structure containing the position ad the velocity. This is what we mean by avoiding side effects.

At each step, the program computes the system energy and prints on the video terminal the value of the time, the position and the velocity, and the difference between the current and the system initial energy (if we want to run the code under the control of a shell program the writing on the terminal can be redirected into a file).

Hands on 9.7 - Optimization options

Once you wrote a program (nicer and more efficient than the one discussed here) try to change the compilation options, increasing and decreasing the required optimization level (for example, for `gcc` we can include the options -O0, -O1, -O2, or -O3). Does the program performance change in any way? How can you make sure you measure the time needed by the program to integrate the equations of motion (for example, in the function `euler()`), rather than the time it takes to print the information on screen or write it to a file?

Chapter 10

In-depth examination of differential equations

Being determined by custom to transfer the past to the future, in all our inferences [...] we expect the event with the greatest assurance, and leave no room for any contrary supposition.

David Hume, *An Enquire Concerning Human Understanding* (1748).

The basic numerical integration methods that we have applied to study the differential equations allow us to analyze many different physical systems: for example we can analyze the motion of a pendulum, of damped and forced oscillators, of planetary motions and discuss how satellites can be launched

Here we improve our knowledge on the C language by learning how to include in our codes system command calls via the `system()` function, by dynamically allocating memory with the function `malloc()`, and by defining new variable types with the command `typedef`. We discuss how to use a graphics program to visualize our results.

Finally, we discuss some other interesting applications such as the motion of a falling body and some dynamical systems with chaotic behavior.

10.1 More algorithms

We are now ready to discuss some more efficient algorithms, which are at least of the second order in Δt. First, we discuss the the Verlet procedure (also called the position Verlet method, necessarily activated by first performing a preliminary step with some other algorithm) and one of its velocity versions. Next, we analyze the predictor-corrector method and the second and fourth order Runge-Kutta schemes. Finally we discuss the stability of integration methods, examining the Euler and the Euler-Cromer methods in detail.

10.1.1   *Verlet and velocity Verlet*

In Section 9.2.1 we saw that (if we substitute the infinitesimal dt with the small, but finite term Δt) the Taylor development up to the second order in dt leads to :

$$x_{n+1} = x_n + v_n \Delta t + \frac{1}{2} \phi_n (\Delta t)^2 + \mathcal{O}\left((\Delta t)^3\right) . \tag{10.1}$$

Analogously, taking one step back in time, i.e., integrating over a time $-\Delta t$, we find that

$$x_{n-1} = x_n - v_n \Delta t + \frac{1}{2} \phi_n (\Delta t)^2 + \mathcal{O}\left((\Delta t)^3\right) . \tag{10.2}$$

By summing (10.1) and (10.2) we find that

$$x_{n+1} + x_{n-1} = 2 \, x_n + \phi_n (\Delta t)^2 + \mathcal{O}\left((\Delta t)^4\right) ,$$

where the coefficient of the cubic term in Δt cancels out due to parity. This last formula can be rewritten as

$$x_{n+1} = 2 \, x_n - x_{n-1} + \phi_n (\Delta t)^2 + \mathcal{O}\left((\Delta t)^4\right) . \tag{10.3}$$

Instead, by subtracting (10.2) from (10.1) we find an estimate the velocity given by the following expression:

$$v_n = \frac{x_{n+1} - x_{n-1}}{2 \, \Delta t} + \mathcal{O}\left((\Delta t)^2\right) . \tag{10.4}$$

Let us note that the expression for v_n is not directly used, in this case, during the integration of the motion equations. The positions and the velocities of the Verlet algorithm defined by equations (10.3) and (10.4) are, respectively, of third order and of second order.

    The algorithm that we have just described is not self-starting. Indeed, given the initial conditions, at time $t = 0$, such as x_0 and v_0, we cannot compute x_2, and therefore we cannot start the Verlet integration, since the latter needs the value of x_1. We can for example use the Euler algorithm to compute x_1, and systematically continue the integration with the Verlet method.

The velocity v in the Verlet algorithm is obtained from equation (10.4) as a difference between two numbers (x_{n+1} and x_{n-1}) of the same order of magnitude. This difference decreases as Δt becomes small. This might lead to serious rounding errors, possibly invalidating the numerical integration (as discussed in detail in Section 1.4).

To avoid these problems at least partially, we can derive and use a different integration scheme, starting from the Verlet method. We add and subtract the quantity $\frac{x_{n+1}}{2}$ on the right side of equation (10.3), and we divide the terms x_{n-1} and x_n in two equal parts:

$$x_{n+1} = x_n + \frac{1}{2}(x_{n+1} - x_{n-1}) - \frac{1}{2}x_{n+1} - \frac{1}{2}x_{n-1} + x_n + \phi_n \Delta t^2 .$$

Using equation (10.4), we find that:

$$x_{n+1} = x_n + v_n \Delta t - \frac{1}{2}(x_{n+1} - 2x_n + x_{n-1}) + \phi_n \Delta t^2 .$$

The term between parentheses in the previous expression is a discrete approximation (up to the order we are considering) of the second derivative:

$$\ddot{x}(t) \xrightarrow[\Delta t \to 0]{} \frac{x_{n+1} - 2x_n + x_{n-1}}{\Delta t^2} .$$

Therefore, we can write that

$$x_{n+1} = x_n + v_n \Delta t + \frac{1}{2}\phi_n \Delta t^2 ,$$

that is the new iterative relation to compute x. This is precisely the result that we would obtain if we truncate the Taylor expansion after the second order.

We now derive the new scheme to compute v_{n+1} in the new Verlet algorithm. Writing (10.4) for v_{n+1} we have that

$$v_{n+1} = \frac{x_{n+2} - x_n}{2\,\Delta t} .$$

To eliminate x_{n+2} from the previous formula we write equation (10.3) for x_{n+2}, i.e.,

$$x_{n+2} = 2\,x_{n+1} - x_n + \phi_{n+1}\Delta t^2 .$$

This results in the following expression for v_{n+1}:

$$v_{n+1} = \frac{1}{\Delta t}\left(x_{n+1} - x_n + \phi_{n+1}\frac{\Delta t^2}{2}\right) .$$

Now we just need to isolate x_n in equation (10.3) to obtain an expression for v_{n+1} as a function of v_n:

$$x_n = \frac{1}{2}(x_{n+1} + x_{n-1}) - \frac{1}{2}\phi_n \Delta t^2 ,$$

giving

$$v_{n+1} = \frac{1}{\Delta t}\left(\frac{x_{n+1} - x_{n-1}}{2} + \frac{\phi_n + \phi_{n+1}}{2}\Delta t^2\right) = v_n + \frac{\phi_n + \phi_{n+1}}{2}\Delta t \ .$$

We have obtained the following two iterative equations

$$\begin{cases} x_{n+1} = x_n + v_n\Delta t + \frac{1}{2}\phi_n\Delta t^2 \ , \\ v_{n+1} = v_n + \frac{\phi_n + \phi_{n+1}}{2}\Delta t \ . \end{cases}$$

that define the velocity Verlet method. If in the previous equation to compute the new velocity we would have used the new force (instead of the average of the force at the previous step and of the new force), the asymptotic error of the method would have been larger. The mathematical steps we have used have been important to achieve this more accurate results, compared to, for example, Newton method.

Hands on 10.1 - The Verlet algorithm

 Apply the two Verlet algorithms, and compare their performance. As in Exercises 1 and 5, follow how the energy behaves with time. Verify how the energy conservation law is violated when $\Delta t \to 0$.

As the equations defining the algorithm depend on an index n, we might think that in our numerical implementation of the problem we need to use one or more arrays. Instead, if there are no better reasons to do so, we do not need to define arrays (with a size equal to the number of simulated time steps) containing all values of the positions and the coordinates. The values at a given time step only depend on the values of the positions and the velocities at the previous step. So we just need two scalar variables for each one of these variables (or a **struct**, or a two-dimensional array).

10.1.2   *Predictor-corrector and Runge-Kutta*

We now define two important integration methods, but we will not analyze them in detail. The first one is the predictor-corrector method. It is of great importance because it belongs to a vast category of methods, where a first estimate of the quantities that will have to be integrated is used to build the true numerical integration step. In one version of these method, we define a *prediction*

$$x_{n+1}^{(p)} = x_{n-1} + 2v_n\Delta t \ ,$$

from which we can obtain a preliminary estimate for the predicted force $\phi_{n+1}^{(p)}$, that is in our case a function of the position x (this is not the value we will actually find for the force ϕ_{n+1} at step $n+1$). So, $\phi_{n+1}^{(p)}$ is computed using the value $x_{n+1}^{(p)}$ which will not be the value of the coordinate at time $n+1$. Instead, using $\phi_{n+1}^{(p)}$ we compute v_{n+1} and we define x_{n+1} as:

$$v_{n+1} = v_n + \frac{\phi_{n+1}^{(p)} + \phi_n}{2} \Delta t \ ,$$

$$x_{n+1} = x_n + \frac{v_{n+1} + v_n}{2} \Delta t \ .$$

The method is not self-starting. A first step needs to be made, for example with the Euler method. The predictor-corrector method can be generalized to higher orders. The idea behind all these methods is to first "predict" a value and then correct it. Remember Figures 9.2 and 9.3: we are trying to get the most out of our knowledge on the function's behavior in the interval Δt.

Last, but certainly not least, we mention the *Runge-Kutta method* and we discuss its *second order* version. This is a very popular approach, and its results are precise enough for real simulations. The integration step consists of two parts. We write

$$x^+ = v_n \Delta t \ ; \quad v^+ = \phi_n \Delta t \ ,$$

and next we compute

$$\begin{cases} x_{n+1} = x_n + \left(v_n + \frac{1}{2}v^+\right) \Delta t \ , \\ v_{n+1} = v_n + \phi\left(x_n + \frac{1}{2}x^+ \ , \ v_n + \frac{1}{2}v^+\right) \Delta t \ . \end{cases} \tag{10.5}$$

The Runge-Kutta method can be generalized to higher orders. As far as the physical problems that we discuss in the following are concerned, it is preferable to use the Runge-Kutta algorithm (the simple second order version defined by equation (10.5) or, even better, a more accurate version).

Hands on 10.2 - Predictor-corrector and Runge-Kutta

Use the predictor-corrector algorithm or the Runge-Kutta method to study the equations of motion. It could be interesting to search in one of the textbooks cited in the bibliography or on the Internet for the equations defining the Runge-Kutta method of a higher order. Try to implement it and to analyze the resulting behavior.

We have considered the Runge-Kutta method applied to a single differential equation. It is then straightforward to extend it to the case of a couple of differential equations. To solve the first order differential equation

$$\dot{y}(t) = f\left(y(t), t\right)$$

we set

$$\begin{cases} y_1 = f\left(y_n, t_n\right) \Delta t \ , \\ y_2 = f\left(y_n + \frac{1}{2}y_1, t_n + \frac{1}{2}\Delta t\right) \Delta t \ , \\ y_3 = f\left(y_n + \frac{1}{2}y_2, t_n + \frac{1}{2}\Delta t\right) \Delta t \ , \\ y_4 = f\left(y_n + y_3, t_n + \Delta t\right) \Delta t \ , \end{cases} \tag{10.6}$$

and

$$y_{n+1} = y_n + \frac{1}{6}\left(y_1 + 2y_2 + 2y_3 + y_4\right) + \mathcal{O}\left((\Delta t)^5\right) \ . \tag{10.7}$$

The method defined by the equations (10.6) and (10.7) is easy to implement and it is robust.

10.1.3   *Stability analysis*

In Section 9.2.1 we discussed in very simple terms the problem of the stability of a numerical integration algorithm. We analyzed the Euler method applied to a single first order differential equation. We computed the value of a coefficient that gives information about the procedure's stability.

We now discuss how this computation is generalized in case of a system of two first-order differential equations (i.e., our laws of motion, defined by a second order differential equation which can be rewritten in terms of two first order differential equations). We analyze both the Euler and the Euler-Cromer methods, and we clarify the different nature of their behavior.

The Euler integration method for the harmonic oscillator is written as

$$\begin{cases} x_{n+1} = x_n + v_n \Delta t \ , \\ v_{n+1} = v_n + \phi_n \Delta t \ = v_n - \omega^2 x_n \Delta t \ . \end{cases}$$

Let us write this iterative procedure in terms of a two-dimensional matrix:

$$\begin{pmatrix} x_{n+1} \\ v_{n+1} \end{pmatrix} = \begin{pmatrix} 1 & \Delta t \\ -\omega^2 \Delta t & 1 \end{pmatrix} \begin{pmatrix} x_n \\ v_n \end{pmatrix} \equiv \mathcal{T}_E \begin{pmatrix} x_n \\ v_n \end{pmatrix} \ ,$$

where we have defined the transition matrix $\mathcal{T}_E$ as

$$\mathcal{T}_E \equiv \begin{pmatrix} 1 & \Delta t \\ -\omega^2 \Delta t & 1 \end{pmatrix} \ .$$

Applied to (x_n, v_n), this transition matrix generates (x_{n+1}, v_{n+1}).

The method's stability properties are linked to those of the transition matrix, and, more precisely, to those of its eigenvalues.

The determinant of $\mathcal{T}_E$ is equal to $1 + \omega^2 \Delta t^2$, and is therefore larger than one for any value of Δt. This precisely implies the growth of a random error as discussed in Section 9.2.1. The stability analysis is completely analogous to the one we have done in the case of a single equation, as discussed in Section 9.2.1. As in the case of equation (9.9), where the modulus of G determines a possible expansion or reduction of the error (depending on whether it is smaller or larger than 1), here the determinant of $\mathcal{T}_E$ decides about this expansion or contraction. We can think of the two eigenvalues as two amplifying or damping coefficients in the two directions corresponding to the two eigenvectors.

Exercise 1 - Perturbation of the solution

Apply the method of Section 9.2.1, perturbing the solution of the difference equation by a small quantity, to our case of a two by two matrix.

We can obtain a more precise information by computing the eigenvalues of $\mathcal{T}_E$. To this end we need to resolve the equation

$$\det\left(\mathcal{T}_E - \lambda I\right) = \det\begin{pmatrix} 1 - \lambda & \Delta t \\ -\omega^2 \Delta t & 1 - \lambda \end{pmatrix} = 0 \,,$$

i.e.

$$(1 - \lambda)^2 + \omega^2 \Delta t^2 = 0 \,,$$

leading to

$$\lambda_{\pm} = 1 \pm i\, \omega \Delta t \,.$$

Both eigenvalues have a modulus which is strictly larger than one. Therefore the directions defined by the corresponding eigenvectors are unstable. In Figure 10.1 we show the unit circle of the complex plane λ and the position of the two eigenvalues $\lambda_{\pm}$. For any value of Δt the eigenvalues lie outside of the unit circle, and the difference between the numerical and the correct solution is amplified more and more as the iteration with the Euler method proceeds. Again, this is completely analogous to the simple case of a equation (9.9). The modulus of each eigenvalue is the coefficient of

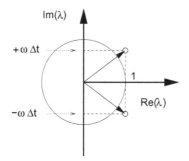

Fig. 10.1   The circles represent the eigenvalues of the transition matrix for the Euler method. The circumference shown in the figure has unit radius in the complex plane.

the expansion or reduction of the error in the direction of each of the two eigenvectors.

Things are different in case of the Euler-Cromer method. The iterative equations are

$$\begin{cases} x_{n+1} = x_n + v_{n+1}\Delta t = x_n + v_n\Delta t - \omega^2 x_n \Delta t^2 \,, \\ v_{n+1} = v_n + \phi_n\Delta t \ = v_n - \omega^2 x_n \Delta t \,. \end{cases}$$

Therefore, in this case, the transition matrix is equal to

$$\mathcal{T}_{EC} \equiv \begin{pmatrix} 1 - \omega^2\Delta t^2 & \Delta t \\ -\omega^2\Delta t & 1 \end{pmatrix} \,.$$

The determinant of $\mathcal{T}_{EC}$ equals one. Noise is not amplified nor reduced; this is a marginal case, leading to systematic oscillations, as we already saw.

Let us now compute the eigenvalues of $\mathcal{T}_{EC}$. In this case we need to solve the equation

$$\det \begin{pmatrix} 1 - \omega^2\Delta t^2 - \lambda & \Delta t \\ -\omega^2\Delta t & 1 - \lambda \end{pmatrix} = 0 \,,$$

i.e.,

$$1 + \lambda \left(\omega^2\Delta t^2 - 2 \right) + \lambda^2 = 0 \,,$$

whose solutions are

$$\lambda_\pm = \left(1 - \frac{\omega^2\Delta t^2}{2} \right) \pm i\,\omega\Delta t\sqrt{1 - \frac{\omega^2\Delta t^2}{4}} \,.$$

The two eigenvalues now lie on the unit circle (compute explicitly, for example, the value of the two eigenvalues when $\omega^2\Delta t^2 = 1$). Note that there exists some "particular" values of Δt. Which ones?

Exercise 10.2 - Stability analysis

When integrating an oscillating equation, the Euler-Cromer method behaves in a more complex way than the Euler method. Does something happen, and if so, what, when $\omega^2 \Delta t^2 = 2$? And when $\omega^2 \Delta t^2 = 4$? What is the correct limit we should implement when integrating in this way the equations of motion?

A general, very important observation that we need to remember at all times is that Δt should be smaller than all the relevant time scales of the phenomenon under study. For example, when integrating a periodic motion, an integration step Δt should be order of magnitudes smaller than the period of the oscillations.

10.2 system, malloc and typedef

We now introduce some new elements of the C language. We discuss a fundamental topic, namely the dynamic memory allocation by means of a statement of the type `malloc()`. We also examine in detail some other topics, such as the function `system()` and the use of derived types with the command `typedef`.

10.2.1 *The interaction with the operating system: the function system*

The function `system()` allows our C codes to interact with the operating system. Its prototype is

```
int system(char *s);
```

and it is defined in the system file `stdlib.h`. The function executes a command of the operating system, and returns the status variable returned by the command, or it returns -1 in case an error occurred. The statement (under Linux)

```
system("ls");
```

or the statement (under Windows)

```
system("dir");
```

prints to the `stdout` a list of the files present in the directory where the program is working. For example we can use this command to delete a file with a C program. The return variable allows one to verify whether the command has been executed correctly, as in:

```
i = system("rm badFile.txt");
if (i != 0) {printf("Error upon deletion.\n");}
```

10.2.2 *Dynamic memory allocation: malloc and calloc*

So far, in order to guarantee that the program can count on some given amount of memory space (for example, to store a vector containing a thousand `float` variables) we had to act before the program was being executed (by statically allocating memory). With commands such as `float x[100];`, the memory is assigned at compilation time.

It is very important and useful to learn how to allocate memory blocks dynamically. In this section we discuss various reasons why a static allocation of the memory is frequently unsatisfactory.

The function `malloc`, whose prototype is

```
void *malloc(size_t n);
```

returns a pointer to `n` bytes of (uninitialized!) memory space, or `NULL` if the request to allocate new memory could not be satisfied. The function returns a pointer to `void`. Essentially this means that the returned pointer is undetermined. Therefore, we need to specify its type with an explicit cast.

We always need to remember that after each call to `malloc()` we need to explicitly verify that the operation was correctly brought to an end (i.e., that the function did not return a value equal to `NULL`). For example, if we want to store 100 steps of the spatial trajectory of a material point moving in one dimension we can use the following code:

```
float *xFloat;

xFloat = (float *) malloc(100 * sizeof(float));
if (xFloat == NULL) {
  printf("failed malloc of xFloat.\n");
  exit(EXIT_FAILURE);
}
```

Remember that we can also interpret `xFloat` as an array consisting of 100 `float` type elements, starting from `xFloat[0]` up to `xFloat[99]`. In this way, we allocated enough memory to store a part of the trajectory during the program execution. This could be, for example, the steps performed during one period of the motion. Indeed, this is a useful application because the period is not known beforehand, and only after its computation we can allocate the correct amount of memory space.

We still need to discuss a number of important features. First of all, the unary operator `sizeof` (see also Chapter 3) computes the size of a generic object (for example, of an array or of a `struct` or of a type). The syntax of the statement is

```
sizeof(object);
```

and

```
sizeof(type);
```

The function `sizeof` returns an integer equal to the size in byte of an object (e.g., a variable, a vector, a structure) or a type (a basic type or a derived type). For example, the code

```
int x[99];
printf("%d\n",sizeof(x));
```

prints the value 396 (the number of bytes contained in x), which can be used in this case to check whether when asking for an element of the array x we are using an index that has a value included within the allowed bounds. It is fundamental that the vector x is declared in a static, and not a dynamic way by means of a `malloc` or a `calloc`. Only in this way, its size is known to the compiler, and the `sizeof` operator returns the correct result.

`size_t` is the unsigned integer type returned by the `sizeof` operator. It is defined in the system file `<stdef.h>`. In practice, this is a generic type, for which it is best to make an explicit cast, as we have shown in the example above.

There are various occasions in which a dynamic memory allocation has to be preferred to a static one. Often, even when we can know a priori the amount of memory needed by the program, we do not want to recompile the program each time we change the parameter values. When simulating a system with 100 variables or a system consisting of 1000 variables the memory needs are different, and it is a useless waste of time to recompile the program each time. It would be inefficient to reserve the maximum possible memory upon compilation, as we would create a slow, and potentially even malfunctioning, executable code.

On the other hand, note that the dynamic memory allocation procedure is a slow process. Therefore, it is very important to try to allocate a high number of bytes (e.g., ten or one hundred thousand) at the time, rather than reserving a few words at a time.

The function `malloc()` does not initialize the memory it reserves. There is a function that initializes to zero all bytes it reserves:

```
void *calloc(size_t n, size_t size);
```

The function `calloc()` is used in a very similar way as the `malloc()` function. To store the 100 positions of a point, represented by `float` variables (that we need to be initialized to zero) we write:

```
float *xFloat;
xFloat = (float *)calloc(100, sizeof(float));
```

Note that `xFloat` is completely equivalent to a `float` array consisting of 100 elements, just like in case of a `mallloc()`. So, it is for example possible to ask for the element `xFloat[12]`.

The memory allocation mechanism is important. The programs receive, if possible, the memory space they request from the operating system. To this end, the operating system keeps a list of free memory blocks (i.e., a contiguous sequence of memory locations). When the program receives the information about the location of the requested amount of memory, the operating system subtracts the memory blocks corresponding to the assigned memory space from this list. The requirement that the memory space needed to execute the program be contiguous is often relaxed by the operating system by using techniques such as paging and segmentation of the memory, or most of the time with a combination of both of these. If the operating system does not have the required operating blocks to satisfy the memory request of a program, it returns a pointer to NULL.

To summarize: memory space is a limited resource, like water, and we need to use it in a parsimonious way. Unlike in the case of water, though, the allocated memory can (and must) be directly returned to the system, who can reuse it without further processing. Think of a function reserving memory by means of a `malloc()`. When we exit from the function the allocated memory space is not automatically freed. If the function is called too many times, the program will terminate with an error. Why? Each time the function is called we allocate new memory, while keeping with us the one allocated at an earlier instance. Even though we are no longer using the latter, it remains available to us. After a sufficiently large number of function calls the system no longer has any memory available which can be allocated, and the program cannot operate normally anymore.

Hands on 10.3 - The memory disaster

Allocate memory (for example 100 kbyte at the time) in a function. Count the number of calls and verify when the program stops working (in a more or less disastrous way, where the size of the disaster is inversely proportional to the amount of care we took). Is this always the same number? Does it depend on the system load? And on the computer itself?

In short, it is important to free the memory space which is no longer needed. To this end, it is essential to use the system function

```
void free(void *p);
```

The function **free()**, included in the library **stdlib.h**, does not return any value. When the memory reserved with a **malloc()** or a **calloc()** is no longer needed, it should be immediately freed with a function call to **free()**:

```
free(xFloat);
```

If needed, the size of a vector that has been allocated dynamically can be enlarged with a call to a **realloc**. This is actually one of the major advantages of dynamically allocating memory. The syntax is

```
void *realloc(void *p, size_t size);
```

realloc changes the size of the object pointed to by the pointer p to the new quantity of **size** byte (if its size in byte is already larger than or equal to **size**, it remains unchanged). The additional memory is not initialized. If p is NULL the call to **realloc(p, size)** is equivalent to a call to **malloc(size)**. In this case, the function **realloc(p, size)** creates new memory space. If **size** equals 0 the call is equivalent to a call to **free(p)**, and the previously allocated memory is freed. Except for the case in which p is NULL, p should have been returned at a previous instance by a call to **malloc()**, **calloc()** or **realloc()**.

realloc() returns a pointer to the newly allocated memory, which might be different from p, or returns NULL if the request could not be satisfied. If **realloc()** fails, the original memory block is remains unchanged. It is neither freed or deleted, nor moved.

The short program of Listing 10.1 helps to clarify this matter. Namely, we reserve an array to register the system's position throughout 100 steps with a `calloc`. Later on we realize we need to store 200 steps instead. Therefore, we enlarge the array with a `realloc`. Only in the first case we expect the array to be initialized to zero.

```
1  #define NUMBER_OF_STEPS 100
2  main() {
3    long int i;
4    float *xFloat1, *xFloat2;
5
6    xFloat1 = (float *)calloc(NUMBER_OF_STEPS, sizeof(float));
7    printf("calloc:   NUMBER_OF_STEPS = %d xFloat1 = %d\n",
8           NUMBER_OF_STEPS, xFloat1);
9    printf("The calloc() initializes to zero: ");
10   for (i = 0; i < 10; i++) {
11     printf("%g ", xFloat1[i]);
12   }
13   printf("\n");
14   xFloat2 = (float *)
15     realloc(xFloat1, 2 * NUMBER_OF_STEPS * sizeof(float));
16   printf("realloc: NUMBER_OF_STEPS = %d xFloat2 = %d\n",
17          2*NUMBER_OF_STEPS, xFloat2);
18   printf("The calloc() initialized to zero: ");
19   for (i = 0; i < 10; i++) {
20     printf("%g ", xFloat2[i]);
21   }
22   printf("\n");
23   printf("The realloc() does not (but could have 0 by chance): ");
24   for (i = NUMBER_OF_STEPS; i < NUMBER_OF_STEPS + 10; i++) {
25     printf("%g ", xFloat2[i]);
26   }
27   printf("\n");
28 }
```

Listing 10.1   Dynamic memory allocation.

Finally, to sum things up, remember the following general rules:
  (1) always perform explicit cast operations when handling pointers returned by a dynamic memory allocation operation;
  (2) always verify that the memory space you requested was actually reserved, i.e., that the returned pointer is different from NULL;
  (3) always free the memory which is no longer needed.

10.2.3 *Defining derived types: typedef*

In C we can define new types, obtaining in this way the so-called derived types. This construct does not have very profound underlying basis. Yet, it is useful in many contexts.

A typical example could be when we need an **unsigned** integer type consisting of 64 bits, i.e., 8 bytes (no more and no less). With some compilers this type can be obtained with a **long int** declaration, while with others we might need a declaration like **long long int**.

In case we want to define a type **float** characterizing the positions of the system particles (this type might become a **double** when a more precise description is needed) we use the statement

```
typedef float position;
```

From now on **position** is a type, (coinciding with the **float** type). We can now declare for example

```
position x1 = 0.0, x2 = 0.0;
```

Actually, it is often useful to define, upon compilation, a variable telling us how the **position** type is defined. A short code using this construct is given in Listing 10.2.

```
1 #define MYFLOAT   0
2 #define MYDOUBLE  1
3 #define MY_SUCCESS 1
4 #define MY_FAILURE -9
5 #define POSITION MYFLOAT   /* to be changed line */
6 #if POSITION == MYFLOAT
7 typedef float position;
8 #elif POSITION == MYDOUBLE
9 typedef double position;
10 #endif
11
12 int main() {
13   if (POSITION == MYFLOAT) {
14     printf("#The variables of the POSITION type are float.\n");
15   } else if (POSITION == MYDOUBLE) {
16     printf("#The variables of the POSITION type are double.\n");
17   } else {
18     printf("The program terminates due to an error:\n");
19     printf("   unexpected value of POSITION.\n");
20     exit(MY_FAILURE);
21   }
22 exit(MY_SUCCESS);
23 }
```

Listing 10.2   Use of **typedef**.

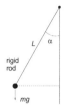

Fig. 10.2   A simple pendulum.

We can use the value of POSITION (which might be MYFLOAT or MYDOUBLE) also to define the printing formats used by the program, to decide whether or not to execute a printing statement, to decide which type of computation we need to perform. So, in a different situation, we just need to write

```
#define POSITION MYDOUBLE
```

and the rest of the code is left unchanged.

Since the types defined with **typedef** are completely identical to the native types, we can (and typically do) perform a cast to the derivative types:

```
x = (position)y;
```

Moreover, we can use the **sizeof** on the derivative types.

We have discussed the use of **typedef** to select the types of an appropriate size. Another typical and important way of using **typedef** is aimed at making the code more readable, synthetic and compact. For example, the construct **typedef** is extremely useful to simplify the management of the structures.

Actually with **typedef** we do not really create a new type. We just create a new name for a type which is already defined in standard C. Still, this operation gives us additional flexibility, allowing us to write better code. In short, we could say the main reason to use **typedef** are the portability and the clearness of the code.

10.3   The simple pendulum

So far we have mostly analyzed what is considered to be the ancestor of all problems in physics, i.e. the simple harmonic oscillator. The problem of the simple pendulum, depicted in a diagrammatic way in Figure 10.2, is interesting since it behaves as a harmonic oscillator in the limit of small oscillations. Unlike for the harmonic oscillator here we do not have a simple analytic solution. It is a nonlinear systems, for which the numerical computation plays a very important role.

We consider a pendulum of fixed length L (the rod of the pendulum can considered to be rigid), and the angle $\alpha(t)$ specifies the pendulum's position at time t: we are dealing with a one-dimensional problem. The linear velocity and the acceleration, both measured along the arc (α is measured in radiants) are given by the expressions

$$\begin{cases} v(t) = L\frac{d\alpha(t)}{dt} = L\dot{\alpha}(t) \ , \\ a(t) = L\ddot{\alpha}(t) \ . \end{cases}$$

We are describing a physical situation in which the friction can be neglected. The forces we need to take into account are the gravity force, mg, pointing downwards, and the constraining force given by the rigid rod that holds the pendulum's mass. This implies we need to consider the component of the gravity force acting tangentially on the point of the arc along which the mass is moving. The motion equations are given by

$$m \, L \, \ddot{\alpha}(t) = -m \, g \, \sin\left(\alpha(t)\right) \ ,$$

or also

$$\ddot{\alpha}(t) = -\frac{g}{L}\sin\left(\alpha(t)\right) \ .$$

This is a nonlinear equation, more complex than the one of the harmonic oscillator. Let us immediately point out though, that in the limit of small oscillations, i.e., for small $\alpha(t)$, we obtain that

$$\sin\left(\alpha(t)\right) \simeq \alpha(t) \ ,$$

and, therefore,

$$\ddot{\alpha}(t) \simeq -\frac{g}{L}\,\alpha(t) \ .$$

In this limit we find the equations of the harmonic oscillator. For small oscillations the motion of the simple pendulum coincides with the one of a spring attached to a mass.

The system's total energy is conserved and it is given by the sum of a kinetic energy term $K(t)$ and a potential energy term $V(t)$:

$$E = K + V = \frac{m \, L^2}{2}\dot{\alpha}(t)^2 + m \, g \, L\left(1 - \cos\alpha(t)\right) \ .$$

Hands on 10.4 - The simple pendulum

This Hands on consists of three different problems. Numerically calculate T. First of all, verify that, for $\alpha(t) \ll 1$, the pendulum's period T is very well approximated by the expression

$$T \simeq 2\pi \sqrt{\frac{L}{g}} \, .$$

For example, determine the maximum angle for which the percentage difference between the previous expression and the measured value is smaller than a given threshold, say ten or one percent. Note that in order to estimate T it is easier to determine the zeros of $\alpha(t)$ rather than estimating the distance between two maxima.

Second, compare the performances of different integration algorithms, as you already did in case of the harmonic oscillator. Determine the typical amount of violation of the energy conservation and the scaling laws as a function of Δt. All results should be coherent with the ones already obtained for the harmonic oscillator.

Finally, compare in detail the case of a force of the type $-\omega^2 x(t)$ with a force of the type $\sin(\omega x(t))$. We want to accurately quantify how similar the trajectories are. It could be interesting to store the entire trajectory during one period of the motion (this could be the right moment to implement for the first time a dynamic memory allocation with the `malloc()` function, explained in detail in Section 10.2.2). In this way, the difference between the two trajectories during an entire period or during part of it can be evaluated in a second moment. Try to use both graphical analysis methods and quantitative ones.

It is interesting to consider the case in which a friction term is added to the harmonic oscillator's restoring force. This friction term can be represented by a force which is proportional to the velocity:

$$\ddot{x}(t) = -\omega^2 x(t) - \gamma \, \dot{x}(t) \, ,$$

where γ is the damping coefficient. Unlike the harmonic force, the damping force, is always opposite to the motion's direction. The system dissipates energy through the friction term. So, the oscillator looses energy and asymptotically stops.

Hands on 10.5 - The damped oscillator: frictional forces

Choose, for instance, $\omega^2 = 9$, $x_0 = 1$ and $v_0 = 0$, and study the system for various values of γ. Compute the period $T(\gamma)$ and study its behavior as a function of γ also analyzing the case without any friction, where $\gamma = 0$. There exists a critical value of $\gamma = \gamma_c$ for which the spring is not able to complete its first oscillation. Determine this value numerically, by automating the code searching for γ_c.

The motion's amplitude is reduced in time. Let A_n be the amplitudes of the different maxima of the system, that decrease with time (and with n). Compute the time it takes to halve it a first time (this calls for at least a linear interpolation) and call it $\tau(1)$. Let $\tau(2)$ be the time needed before the amplitude is halved a second time, and so on. In this way, we obtain a series of values $\tau(n)$. Does this sequence have a limit? If so, estimate this limit numerically.

How does the energy decrease with time? Given its numerical values, make a hypothesis of a functional rule governing $E(t)$. Estimate from the numerical data the corresponding parameters.

It is interesting to add to the oscillator an external forcing term. This could be, for example, a sinusoid with frequency $\overline{\omega}$ (i.e., a term of the type $f_0 \cos(\overline{\omega}t)$. we shall use this term also in what follows to study chaos in the pendulum). Make a numerical study of this type of system.

The aim of Lab Exercise 5 is to write a clear, efficient program, that should be easy to read and understand. Try the C constructs we have discussed so far. For example, use variables of the **struct** type and dynamically allocate memory by means of the **malloc()** function.

10.4 Two planets revolving around the sun

We now discuss Kepler's problem. We consider two planets revolving around a "sun" with a very large mass. We consider the two-dimensional version of this problem, i.e., the sun and the planets reside and orbit in a plane with coordinates x and y. We indicate the two planets respectively with the symbols A and B. In this way their motion equations have the following form:

$$\begin{cases} m_A \ddot{\vec{r}}_A(t) = -\frac{m_A MG}{r_A(t)^3}\,\vec{r}_A(t) + \frac{m_A m_B G}{r_{AB}(t)^3}\,\vec{r}_{AB}(t)\,, \\ m_B \ddot{\vec{r}}_B(t) = -\frac{m_B MG}{r_B(t)^3}\,\vec{r}_B(t) - \frac{m_A m_B G}{r_{AB}(t)^3}\,\vec{r}_{AB}(t)\,, \end{cases} \tag{10.8}$$

where m_A and m_B are the masses of the two planets, M is the solar mass, G is the gravitational coupling constant (with dimensions $\left[\frac{L^3}{MT^2}\right]$), $\vec{r}_A(t)$ and $\vec{r}_B(t)$ are the vectors pointing from the sun to the planets, while $\vec{r}_{AB}(t)$ is oriented from planet A to planet B. For each vector the corresponding symbol without the arrow indicates its modulus. For example, $r_A(t) = \left(x_A(t)^2 + y_A(t)^2\right)^{\frac{1}{2}}$ is the modulus of the vector $\vec{r}_A(t)$, where $x_A(t)$ and $y_A(t)$ are the two components of $\vec{r}_A(t)$. The four second order scalar differential equations are coupled.

Before elaborating on the equations (10.8), we first mention some fundamental facts. In the simple case of the one body problem, Newton's force takes the simple form $\vec{F}(t) = -\frac{mMG}{r^3(t)}\,\vec{r}(t)$, and the angular momentum in the direction z, perpendicular to the plane of motion, has the form $L = (\vec{r} \wedge m\vec{v})_z = m(xv_y - yv_x)$, and is conserved. In this case, the system can be solved analytically.

In order to avoid any problems due to large numbers creating possible *overflows*, it is useful to introduce the astronomical units. In astronomical units (AU), the unit length is close to the length of the larger semi-axis of the orbit of the Earth around the sun. By convention it takes on the value 1 UA $= 1.496\ 10^{13}$ cm (we do not need a number with more significant digits). The time unit is equal to a year, i.e., $3.156\ 10^7$s. In Table 10.1 we give some interesting data concerning the planets of the solar system (note that the solar mass is about $1.989\ 10^{33}$g). In astronomical units we have that

$$GM = 4\pi^2\,\frac{(\text{UA}^3)}{\text{year}^2}\,,$$

i.e., a reasonable number of order 10. In these units, it is easier to keep the code under control.

We rewrite (10.8) by dividing the first and the second relations by the solar mass M. At the same time we also insert a factor M in both the numerator and the denominator of the contributions proportional to $\vec{r}_{AB}(t)$:

$$\begin{cases} \frac{m_A}{M}\ddot{\vec{r}}_A(t) = -\frac{m_A}{M}\frac{MG}{r_A(t)^3}\,\vec{r}_A(t) + \frac{m_A}{M}\frac{m_B}{M}\frac{MG}{r_{AB}(t)^3}\,\vec{r}_{AB}(t)\,, \\ \frac{m_B}{M}\ddot{\vec{r}}_B(t) = -\frac{m_B}{M}\frac{MG}{r_B(t)^3}\,\vec{r}_B(t) - \frac{m_A}{M}\frac{m_B}{M}\frac{MG}{r_{AB}(t)^3}\,\vec{r}_{AB}(t)\,. \end{cases}$$

Table 10.1   Mass, radius, period and the larger semi-axis of the planets of the solar system.

planet	mass (g)	radius (cm)	period (years)	max semi-axis (AU)
Mercury	$3.303 \ 10^{26}$	$2.439 \ 10^8$	$2.409 \ 10^{-1}$	$3.871 \ 10^{-1}$
Venus	$4.870 \ 10^{27}$	$6.050 \ 10^8$	$6.152 \ 10^{-1}$	$7.233 \ 10^{-1}$
Earth	$5.976 \ 10^{27}$	$6.378 \ 10^8$	$1.000 \ 10^0$	$1.000 \ 10^0$
Mars	$6.418 \ 10^{26}$	$3.397 \ 10^8$	$1.882 \ 10^0$	$1.524 \ 10^0$
Jupiter	$1.899 \ 10^{30}$	$7.140 \ 10^9$	$1.186 \ 10^1$	$5.205 \ 10^0$
Saturn	$5.686 \ 10^{29}$	$6.000 \ 10^9$	$2.946 \ 10^1$	$9.575 \ 10^0$
Uranus	$8.66 \ \ 10^{28}$	$2.615 \ 10^9$	$8.401 \ 10^1$	$1.931 \ 10^1$
Neptune	$1.03 \ \ 10^{29}$	$2.43 \ \ 10^9$	$1.648 \ 10^2$	$3.021 \ 10^1$
Pluto	$1.000 \ 10^{25}$	$1.2 \ \ \ 10^8$	$2.477 \ 10^2$	$3.991 \ 10^1$

At this point it is natural to define mass ratios and a reduced coupling constant as

$$\mu_A \equiv \frac{m_A}{M} \ , \qquad \mu_B \equiv \frac{m_B}{M} \ , \qquad \Gamma \equiv MG \ .$$

If we insert these definitions in the previous equations, we find that

$$\begin{cases} \mu_A \ddot{\vec{r}}_A(t) = -\mu_A \Gamma \ \frac{\vec{r}_A(t)}{r_A(t)^3} + \mu_A \mu_B \Gamma \ \frac{\vec{r}_{AB}(t)}{r_{AB}(t)^3} \ , \\[2mm] \mu_B \ddot{\vec{r}}_B(t) = -\mu_B \Gamma \ \frac{\vec{r}_B(t)}{r_B(t)^3} - \mu_A \mu_B \Gamma \ \frac{\vec{r}_{AB}(t)}{r_{AB}(t)^3} \ . \end{cases} \qquad (10.9)$$

In this formulation, there are not very large or very small numbers: the numerical study of the motion equations is less risky.

Hands on 10.6 - Two planets

Write a numerical integration program that solves equations (10.9) (for example, use the Runge-Kutta method). A possible choice to keep things simple (though not very realistic) is $\mu_A = 0.01$ and $\mu_B = 0.001$: table 10.1 could help to choose more reasonable values. A possible approach could be starting by neglecting the interaction between the two planets (for example, by multiplying the two contributions in $\vec{r}_{AB}$ in the motion equations by a coupling constant ϵ, that we will set equal to zero in a first phase). This allows us to study the two planets orbiting independently around the sun. Finally, by adiabatically (i.e., very slowly) turning on the interaction, we can analyze its effects. Another interesting assignment could be to study numerically the conservation of the energy and of the momentum. It is also possible to plan the launch of a space probe such that it reaches a chosen (planetary) destination.

We have discussed here a problem for which the analytic approach does not provide us with all the interesting information: in this case the numerical approach makes a crucial contribution.

10.5   Software tools: gnuplot

We already saw some graphs, and we discussed how a graphical analysis of numerical data is often very useful.

Any graphics program should be able to satisfy our relatively small needs (even though some programs might be more appropriate than others): the details are not particularly important. Just to give an example, we discuss here **gnuplot**. This program is freely available on the Internet (http://www.gnuplot.info) For the experts, **gnuplot** is not a GPL licensed program, but, as mentioned on their site, «**gnuplot** is freeware in the sense that you don't have to pay for it». The advantage of **gnuplot** is that it is a simple and clear program. Moreover, it can be easily managed by means of control files (which are often very useful).

More specifically, to give an idea of what a truly free program entails, we quote the from the *Copyright* file of the **gnuplot** distribution: «Permission to use, copy, and distribute this software and its documentation for any purpose with or without fee is hereby granted, provided that the above *copyright* notice appear in all copies and that both that *copyright* notice and this permission notice appear in supporting documentation.»So, **gnuplot** can be downloaded from the Internet and installed on your computer without paying any fee. It is a freely distributed software. Various versions exist for Linux, Windows and other operating systems.

As an example, we discuss here some arbitrary[1] elementary **gnuplot** commands. After invoking **gnuplot** we obtain a command line with a *prompt*, **gnuplot>**. Here we can perform various tasks. For example, we can plot functions or data files in two or three dimensions, or perform fits of data to some functional behavior by means of interpolation operations.

We can plot a function defined by **gnuplot** itself,

```
gnuplot> plot sin(x)
```

or a user-defined function

```
gnuplot> f(x) = x * cos(x)
gnuplot> plot f(x)
```

---

[1]There are important commands that we do not mention here. Use the **help** command of **gnuplot** to search for commands and understand their syntax.

Note that, as a default, the output appears on screen, in a dedicated window. We can also plot the data contained in a file. By default, the first column of the data file is plotted on the x-axis ad the second one on the y-axis. A dot is drawn for each value:

```
gnuplot> plot 'file.dat'
```

Note that the quotes are crucial. **gnuplot** is very sensitive to the correct use of quotes. Moreover, the quotes are needed in many contexts.

To use the third column for the x-axis and the fifth for the y-axis and obtain a plot with lines instead of points, we need to write

```
gnuplot> plot 'file.dat' using 3:5 with lines
```

We can also plot functions of the values in the columns. In this case, we need to include the entire expression between parentheses and the number of the column should be preceded by a dollar sign. The following command plots four times the difference between the second and the third column on the x-axis and three times the product of the fifth and seventh column on the y-axis:

```
gnuplot> plot 'file.dat' u (4*($3-$2)):(3*$5*$7) with p 3
```

We abbreviated **using** simply to u and **points** to p. In **gnuplot** each command can be abbreviated to its minimal unambiguous length (keeping in mind its position: in different contexts p stands for **plot** or for **points**). If we insert a command in a file (say **first_file.gp**), we can execute it with the line (*scripting*)

```
gnuplot> load 'first_file.gp'
```

The **call** command is very similar to the **load** command. In the **call** command the columns need to be preceded by a double dollar sign as numbers preceded by a single dollar sign are interpreted as parameters. For more details we refer the interested reader to the program manual.

In the syntax we have shown so far, the limits of the plots are determined automatically by the program. These limits can also be specified by the user with the commands **xrange** and **yrange**. Alternatively, we can explicitly mention the limits for the x and y-axis by means of commands like

```
gnuplot> plot [2:3] [4:6] 'file.dat' u 6:(2*$7)
```

The first couple of parentheses contains the limits of the x-axis (first the minimum value of x is indicated, and after the colon, the maximum value), and the second the limits for the y-axis. In case we just want to specify the limits of the y-axis we need to use the syntax [:] [4:6]. The command `replot` works very similarly to the `plot` command and it is useful to overlap several plots. It does not remove anything from the screen before making a new plot and it cannot specify the intervals to define the axes.

We can label the axes (the label is only written when the plot is drawn with, for instance, the `plot` command) with commands like the following ones

```
gnuplot> set xlabel 't'
gnuplot> set ylabel 'x(t)'
```

As the legend should never overlap the data, its position can be regulated with the command **set key** followed by one of the following options: **left**, **right**, **top**, **bottom** or one of their combinations, as in

```
gnuplot> set key left bottom
```

These commands should be enough to get started. More important information can be obtained with the **help** command.

10.6   A falling body

Studying the harmonic oscillator and several variations on the same theme, we have learned how to integrate the motion equations of a physical system. It is interesting to apply these same techniques to simple physical systems which can be very different from the ones we analyzed so far.

We just give some basic facts about a simple problem that generates a large number of interesting questions, namely the two-dimensional motion of a body in a viscous fluid. We start form the hypothesis that the mechanism describing the friction is non linear in the velocity, and it is different from the one described in Section 10.3. Depending on the situation, i.e., on the nature, the shape, the energy and other factors of the materials playing a role, one or the other mechanisms is valid. We will start by studying numerically the motion in absence of any friction. Only at a second stage we consider the more complicated problem of friction.

The basic motion equations describing out problem are given by:

$$\begin{cases} \dot{v}_x = -A|v|v_x \,, \\ \dot{v}_y = -A|v|v_y - g \,, \end{cases}$$

where the velocity in the direction x is $v_x = |v| \cos(\theta)$, the one in the direction y is $v_y = |v| \sin(\theta)$, $\theta(t)$ is the angle between the trajectory and the x-axis at time t, $|v| \equiv \sqrt{v_x^2 + v_y^2}$, the coefficient A can be rewritten as

$\frac{k}{m}$, m is the body's mass and k the friction coefficient. The friction term couples the two differential equations as v contains both v_x as v_y. These two equations have to be considered together with the two equations for the positions $\dot{\vec{x}} = \vec{v}$.

The problem's kinematics is shown in the left part of Figure 10.3. The body starts at time $t = 0$ from a height h, with an initial angle $\theta_0 = \theta(t = 0)$ between the trajectory and the x-axis. In the right part of the Figure 10.3 we show the forces acting on the body at time t. The gravity force is oriented in the negative direction of the y-axis, while the frictional force always points in the direction opposite to the motion.

When performing a numerical integration of the motion equations, several interesting questions arise regarding the motion parameters needed to overcome a wall of a given height or to reach a certain distance. Let us stress that in this case we need to keep the numerical integration under control by implementing a good integration method, such as the fourth order Runge-Kutta method.

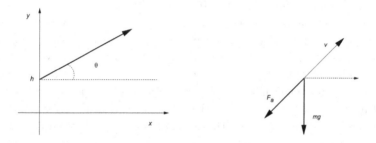

Fig. 10.3   On the left, the kinematics characterizing the moving body. On the right, the forces acting on a body moving in a viscous fluid.

Hands on 10.7 - The soccer player challenge

A soccer player, standing on a tower, launches a ball starting from a height h above the ground. For practical purposes we assume that the modulus of the ball's initial velocity (given by the strength of the soccer player) is always equal to $v_0 = 20\ m/s$, while the initial angle θ_0 (determined by the direction of the launch) varies. In a first numerical study, neglect the friction and study how the trajectory changes as the soccer player's height h from the ground is varied. The soccer player launches the ball starting from the ground level ($h = 0$). Vary θ_0 and verify that the maximum reachable distance is $R_{max} = v_0^2/g$ for $\theta_0 = \pi/4$. In case the soccer player stands on a tower of height $h = 100\ m$, what is the maximum reachable distance R_{max}? At which angle θ_0 is this distance reached? Determine numerically these values and compare the optimal trajectory with the one of the case in which $h = 0$. Next, include the action of the frictional force and, for simplicity, consider $h = 0$. For two values of the friction, $A = 0.1$ and $A = 1$, determine the maximum reachable distance R_{max} and the corresponding angle θ_0. Plot the trajectories of the ball in these cases and compare them to those obtained in the case without any friction.

10.7   The pendulum and chaos

Our simple pendulum may lead us far away. Here, we briefly mention the problem of chaos in dynamical systems [Gutzwiller (1990)], which can be studied in a simple context thanks to the pendulum.

We can define and study the chaos in a physical system in many ways. Probably the most intuitive (qualitative) definition is based on the fact that in a chaotic system two instances of the system, starting from very similar initial conditions or with very similar parameter values, rapidly separate. The system is no longer periodic, and it is practically impossible to predict its future position (given the fact that a tiny error, or a minor rounding, quickly and drastically changes the system trajectory). Let us try to treat this problem in a quantitative way.

We consider a pendulum under a friction force, also in presence of a periodic external force:

$$\ddot{\alpha}(t) = -\omega^2 \sin\left(\alpha(t)\right) - \gamma\,\dot{\alpha}(t) + f_0 \cos\left(\overline{\omega}t\right)\ , \qquad (10.10)$$

where ω is the simple pendulum natural frequency (in absence of any friction or external force), γ is the friction coefficient, f_0 is the external force amplitude and $\overline{\omega}$ is the frequency of the external periodic force.

Hands on 10.8 - Many copies for chaos

To simplify the parameter space when studying the forced pendulum with friction we can choose specific values for some constants, and vary some others. We can for example fix $\gamma = \frac{1}{2}$, $\omega = 1$, $\overline{\omega} = \frac{2}{3}$, $\alpha(t=0) = \frac{\pi}{2}$ and $\dot{\alpha}(t=0) = 0$, and vary f_0. For example, consider the cases $f_0 = 0.9$, 1.07, 1.15, 1.47, 1.50 (this should help you understand what is the *road leading to chaos*). In the remainder of this section, when referring to the motion equations defined in (10.10), we always have these parameter values in mind as a starting point. Write a program integrating, in parallel, different copies of our pendulum. Slightly change some parameters (for example, vary the initial condition, in a small interval around the values we just fixed), and plot the various trajectories as a function of time in a single graph. What happens? Are we able to identify various regions of the parameters?

The question we want to answer is whether our system is chaotic or not for a given value of the parameters. To this end we need to introduce some new techniques.

The first tool is a *Poincaré section*. Taking a Poincaré section is a bit like looking at a pendulum with a strobe light (as when you dance in a disco) which is synchronized with the external force. We now specify an operational definition of a Poincaré section. A Poincaré section is measured as following. After each period of the external force we record a point in phase space $(\alpha, \dot{\alpha})$. This point represents the pendulum configuration at a given moment. As time goes, we add points to our plot, with α on the horizontal axis and $\dot{\alpha}$ on the vertical one. The graph we obtain in this way is precisely a Poincaré section. In case of a chaotic system, the figure resulting from this procedure is very complex; for chaotic systems it is typically not a simple curve (i.e., an object with geometric dimension one), nor does it fill the plane. Its *fractal dimension* is nontrivial and lies between one and two.

A second interesting technique is based on studying the system *basins of attraction*. Also in this case we give an operational definition of attraction basins, and how to numerically measure them. After choosing a fixed value of f_0 we vary the initial conditions and check after a fixed time whether the system velocity is positive or negative. We mark each type of point in a different way. In this way define the basins of attraction, i.e., groups with similar initial conditions attracting the system towards a similar behavior. Also in this case, small modifications in the initial conditions possibly generate big changes in a chaotic system behavior.

The last technique we describe leads to a *bifurcation diagram*. In this case, the definition is somehow similar to the one of a Poincaré section. In this case we vary f_0 and we record $\dot{\alpha}(t)$ on the y-axis and f_0 on the x-axis. Here the aim is to understand how sensitive the system is to small changes in the periodic external force modulus.

Hands on 10.9 - An analysis of chaos

Compute the Poincaré section for the parameter values given in the Hands On 8. First of all, note that it might be convenient to ignore a *transient phase* of the moving pendulum. We are interested in the asymptotic regime, at large times, and the first steps of the motion might be atypical. Selecting the asymptotic regime is often an important (and unfortunately an empirical) part of a numerical simulation. Generally, we decide to have reached the asymptotic state when the system obvious features have become stationary. Typically, the measured quantities need to have reached a constant value. These quantities could be, for example, the period typical of an oscillating motion, or the velocity of a liquid moving in a stationary way, or the temperature of a thermometer used to measure fever and thus needing some time before reaching thermal equilibrium with our body. Therefore, it might be useful to ignore these first points in the plot. What results do you expect? For $f_0 = 0.9$ the motion should be periodic. For $f_0 = 1.07$ things start changing (technically speaking, a *period doubling* occurs). What changes in the Poincaré section? What happens for $f_0 = 1.47$? If $f_0 = 1.50$ the motion is chaotic. What is the shape of the Poincaré section? In the chaotic case something interesting happens when adding points to the plot (you should find a complex figure, not entirely covering the plane, but more than a regular curve, namely a *fractal curve*!). Always remember to plot $\alpha(t)$ and $\dot{\alpha}(t)$ as a function of time and in a parametric way.

Study the basins of attraction. For a given value of f_0, in a plane with the initial position on the horizontal axis and the initial velocity on the vertical one, place a red point if the velocity is negative at the given time t, and black otherwise. How does this plot change with f_0?

Finally, study the bifurcation diagram in the following way. For each value of f_0 (we choose several values in regions which seem interesting) first eliminate the transient regime (making the pendulum oscillate without recording the results for some time). Next, collect the values of $\dot{\alpha}(t)$ by sampling at each period of the external force and plot them (representing f_0 on the x-axis and $\dot{\alpha}(t)$ on the y-axis). What happens close to $f_0 = 1.07$ (period doubling)? What happens when chaos is about to arise ($f_0 \sim 1.50$)?

It is interesting to study two different systems possibly undergoing chaotic behavior. The equation describing a pendulum in which the hinge is forced to move vertically is

$$\ddot{\alpha}(t) = - \left(\omega^2 + g_0 \cos\left(\overline{\omega}t\right)\right) \sin\left(\alpha(t)\right) - \gamma\, \dot{\alpha}(t)\,.$$

We can apply the previous techniques to also study this system. What results do we find?

The second system is a double pendulum. Many of you probably observed "experimentally" that a double pendulum may behave in an unexpected way. Can you write the motion equations and study them with the methods we have introduced?

Chapter 11

(Pseudo)random numbers

The self-fulfilling prophecy is, in the beginning, a false definition of the situation evoking a new behavior which makes the original false conception come 'true'. This specious validity of the self-fulfilling prophecy perpetuates a reign of error. For the prophet will cite the actual course of events as proof that he was right from the very beginning.

Robert K. Merton, *Social Theory and Social Structure* (1968).

But Harry, never forget that what the prophecy says is only significant because Voldemort made it so. [... He] singled you out as the person who would be most dangerous to him - and in doing so, he *made* you the person who would be most dangerous to him!

Joanne K. Rowling, *Harry Potter and the Half-Blood Prince* (2005).

In this chapter we discuss the generation of random numbers, or better, of sequences of pseudo-random numbers, with a computer.

We analyze generators of uniformly distributed numbers in a given interval. In particular, we consider generators based on the linear congruence method (a relatively simple method allowing us to build accurate pseudo-random number generators). We study how to select the generator parameters: among them the modulo and the multiplier. We discuss in detail the purely multiplicative generator, and we analyze some practical examples.

We discuss the procedures that allow us to verify the generator quality: the χ^2 test and the Kolmogorov-Smirnov test, with some details on their practical application.

We discuss generators based on *shift registers*, and the generation of pseudo-random numbers distributed in a nonuniform way. We analyze in detail the important example of the normal distribution.

11.1   Generating random sequences

In this chapter we discuss how using a computer to generate good imitations of random number sequences. These numbers are not really random, but *pseudo-random*. Indeed it is impossible to generate truly random numbers with a computer. Even if a process seems random and we can measure it (consider for example current fluctuations) it could be affected by correlations, thus creating values that depend on each other. We try to give practical advice on how to build a generator, and especially, how to check whether a random number generator works properly. We recommend the reader to check this in detail during the Lab Exercises. We also want to understand how and why such a generator works. The main message we want to transmit in this chapter is that each time we use a random number generator we need to critically examine its features and be ready to identify its weak points.

Let us start from an elementary consideration, namely that random number sequences obtained with an electronic computer are one of the least random objects we could possibly imagine. This is why we refer to them as *pseudo-random number sequences*. Actually, these sequences are the result of often very simple algorithms. So, once this generating algorithm is known, it is easy to predict the sequence.

Still, these sequences are able to deceive us. If we take a look at one of these number series without knowing the simple algorithm behind them, the series seems really random. The key is that a random phenomenon is typically a phenomenon we do not understand. Imagine one of our friends behaves in an absurd way. For example, he often goes to another city in the most unexpected moments, learns how to walk a tightrope, studies

Etruscan. This seems like a random behavior. Next, we find out that our friend met an acrobat living in that city, that she is off from work each time in different moments (depending on the rehearsal and show times) and is passionate about ancient civilizations. All is clear now. Our friend acts absolutely in a normal way (he is now married and they have two wonderful children) and there was nothing random about his behavior.

A pseudo-random number sequence that has been generated with a good algorithm not only deceives us, but also the generic physical system under study. The system "does not understand" that behind that sequence there is a simple algorithm. Indeed, the sequence appears to be completely random, and successive random impacts, emissions at random times, magnetic impurities in an amorphous material, telephone switchboard breakdowns, or other phenomena implying randomness, simulated with our computer, appear to be fully random.

These considerations rapidly lead to a discussion of the *complexity*. Defining complexity is in itself a rather elaborated task, giving rise to a whole new research area. One possible definition of the complexity of a number sequence characterizes it as the length of the most simple program generating it. From this viewpoint, pseudo-random numbers have a very low complexity (the generating program essentially consists of one line of code). This definition does not wrap up the problem: the fact that they can be that deceiving, clearly shows that there is a more complicated side to pseudo-random numbers which this definition does not capture. The continuation of this discussion brings us to the analysis of the relations between disorder and complexity. The latter is of great importance in many issues, the most important of which are problems related to the behavior of dynamical systems and matters related to how glassy systems are organized (which is very different from the organization in crystalline structures).

In conclusion, there exist many situations where it is useful and sometimes necessary to use a computer to produce number sequences which seem random for all intents and purposes. The following are typical and important cases:

- Monte Carlo integration methods (in very different contexts: multidimensional, stochastic differential equations, simulations of particle interactions, statistical mechanics problems, as discussed in Chapters 8 and 19);
- creating disorder which does not change in time, to numerically study disordered systems (see Chapter 13);
- simulations of choices with a random component and simulations

of general models (see Chapter 12).

To conclude this introductive discussion we want to stress that choosing a method to produce pseudo-random numbers is a very delicate operation. In order for the results of a numerical simulation to be reliable, we need to use a generator of guaranteed quality which has been checked. Often it is also worthwhile to check whether the obtained results remain stable when another generator is used. A random number generator should never be changed or personalized. As is often the case, amateur-like behavior often causes disasters.

11.2   Linear congruence

We start our discussion by generating a sequence of random numbers distributed according to the uniform probability distribution $P(x)$ in the interval $(0, 1)$. From this starting point we then move to the generation of a uniform distribution in a generic interval (a, b), and eventually to a nonuniform distribution (Section 11.6).

In computers real numbers are always represented with a finite number N of bits (usually 32 or 64). Thus, to generate random real numbers R_n we can generate uniformly distributed integers I_n between 0 and $\Xi \equiv 2^N - 1$, and define the real random numbers R_n as

$$R_n = I_n/\Xi \ , \tag{11.1}$$

which lie, as desired, between zero and one. We must pay attention to what happens for the two endpoints of the interval, namely for $I_n = 0$ or $I_n = \Xi$. In these two cases R_n is, respectively, equal to 0.0 and 1.0. If, for example, we want to compute $\log(R_n)$ or $\log(1.0 - R_n)$, these cases should be excluded as they create problems.

The generators based on *linear congruence* (*LCG*) have the form

$$I_{n+1} = (aI_n + b) \bmod m \ ,$$

where a is called the *multiplier*, b the *increment*, and m the *modulo*. I_0 is the seed initializing the generator. The value of I at step $n + 1$ is obtained from its value at step n. Let us first consider an elementary, yet instructive example. Let $I_0 = a = b = 7$, $m = 10$. So, we start from the value 7, and the generated number sequence is 7, $6 = (7 \times 7 + 7) \bmod 10$, $9 = (6 \times 7 + 7)$ mod 10, 0, 7, after which the sequence repeats itself. The period of a number sequence is defined as the minimum number of values of the sequence after which the numbers are repeated in a periodic way. So, in this case the *period* T equals 4.

The maximum period a generator might assume is given by the modulo m. Beware though, that the period also depends on the choice of the other parameters, and therefore could be a lot smaller than the maximum value m. In the previous example, since $m = 10$, the generator period T could be maximum 10. However, given the values of the other parameters I_0, a ad b, the period is smaller, namely 4. In Section 19.2 we discuss Markov chains and some details on the attractors of a dynamical process and its asymptotic behavior (limit cycles, transient behavior, fixed points).

A good generator of pseudo-random numbers should always have a long period. A short period introduces spurious correlations in the system under study. Indeed, in the latter case, the values obtained in a certain point of the sequence are correlated to the values found in other parts of it. For example, if we wanted to study and simulate the independent failures in a telephone exchange system this correlation might appear to be a correlation between the failures, thus introducing an unwanted feature in the system.

Listing 11.1 contains a simple code that computes the period of a generator (not for a realistic generator, but for those generators with a small, unrealistic value of m). The main idea behind it is that we have reached the generator period when a number is repeated, since from that moment on the whole sequence is repeated.

```
1 #include <stdlib.h>
2 #include <stdio.h>
3 #include <math.h>
4
5 #define EXIT_SUCCESS      0
6 #define EXIT_FAILURE     -9
7 #define MAX_M 1024
8
9 typedef long int RANDOM_TYPE;
10
11 int main(void) {
12    long int i, j, successFlag;
13    RANDOM_TYPE a, b, m, seed, randomNumber, randomStore[MAX_M + 1];
14    a = 7;
15    b = 7;
16    m = 10;
17    seed = 7;
18    seed = seed % m;
19    printf("a = %ld b = %ld m = %ld I0 = %ld\n", a, b, m, seed);
20    randomNumber = seed;
21    randomStore[0] = randomNumber;
```

```
1   if (m > MAX_M) {
2     printf("Error: m is too large.\n");
3     exit(EXIT_FAILURE);
4   }
5   i = 1;
6   successFlag = 0;
7   while ((i <= m) && (successFlag == 0)) {
8     randomNumber = (a * randomNumber + b) % m;
9     randomStore[i] = randomNumber;
10    j = 0;
11    do {
12      if (randomStore[j] == randomNumber) {
13        successFlag = 1;
14        printf("Done: T = %ld\n", i - j);
15      }
16      j++;
17    } while ((j < i) &&
18             (randomStore[j - 1] != randomNumber) );
19    i++;
20  }
21  if (successFlag == 1) {
22    exit(EXIT_SUCCESS);
23  }
24  else if (successFlag == 0) {
25    printf("Error (major inconsistency): T not found.\n");
26    exit(EXIT_FAILURE);
27  }
28 }
```

Listing 11.1   A generator period.

In codes using random numbers it is good practice to define a specific type for them, as we did on line 9 (page 305) of Listing 11.1. This makes the code more flexible in case, for example, we compile it on a different computer, where the types may have a different size. The variables which are important for the generator are of the type RANDOM_TYPE. They are defined on line 13 and initialized on lines 14-17 of the listing shown in page 305.

The crucial part of the code computing a generator period is included on lines 5-20 in the same page. This clear, but rather inefficient method takes an array of size equal to the maximum possible period. Therefore, it cannot be applied to realistic generators, but only to examples with not too large values of m. The (pseudo-random) variable randomNumber is initialized on line 20 with the seed given on line 17 (page 305). It is copied and stored in randomStore[0] on line 21 (page 305), and recomputed on line 8 (page 306) with the LCG formula defined in (11.1). Each new random number is stored in the vector `randomStore[]` on line 9 (page 306), and compared to all other numbers that have already been produced on lines 11-18 in the same page. If the number has already been extracted, we have reached the end of the cyclic sequence! We print the value of the period as the distance between the two occurrences of the number and interrupt the program (thanks to the conditions in the two `while` constructs). This is not the most efficient of methods (see Lab Exercise 1), but it does store the information in such a way that, if necessary, we could easily reconstruct the generated number sequence.

Note we introduced the variable `successFlag`, initially set to zero, to exit the program once the period has been determined. When the internal `do-while` construct is successfully completed (because the period has been found) the variable `successFlag` is also set equal to one (the flag of success is raised). At this point it is pointless to continue the external `while`. Indeed, due to the presence of the variable `successFlag`, which is now equal to one, it is conditionally interrupted.

Obviously, choosing small values for m, though useful in the preliminary studies of these types of algorithms, is not very realistic. Indeed, it is not very suitable to claim the corresponding generators produce pseudo-random numbers as not even a very naive or distracted person could possibly mistake their sequences for random ones.

Hands on 11.1 - The period of a generator

Let us apply the ideas discussed in this section, and create a slightly different code from the one in Listing 11.1. For example, let us create a vector τ of m components, initialized to zero. When the generator produces the random number n at step t there are two possibilities. If the component $\tau[n]$ equals zero, we set it equal to t, such that $\tau[n]$ stores the first time in which the number n has been generated. Instead, if $\tau[n]$ is already different from zero, the number n has already been generated at the time $\tau[n]$. Therefore we found the period, which is precisely $t - \tau[n]$. Note that using the value of I_0 as a starting point, the generator stable cycle does not necessarily contain the value I_0 (unless the period of the generator is exactly $T = m$). Try with different generators and compute their period. Analyze their performance and prove how this code is more efficient than the one discussed in the text.

Generators with $b = 0$ are said to be *purely multiplicative generators*. They have the advantage of being faster than generic congruential generators because they only have to perform half the number of operations compared to the latter to generate a random number. Their period is smaller than the one of complete LCG, though it can still be sufficiently long.

11.2.1   *Choosing the modulo*

A good choice of the modulo is essential to implement a generator with a long period. First of all, the period T is necessarily smaller than or equal to m. Therefore, a necessary condition for T to be long is that m is large.

Second, we need to understand the following point. Imagine we want to generate a random sequence of (Boolean) values B_n, which are either equal to 0 or 1. Is it sufficient to choose $m = 2$? The answer is definitely no. Indeed, the most complex sequence we could possibly obtain in this way is $\ldots, 0, 1, 0, 1, 0, \ldots$ All other allowed sequences are even more monotonous (which ones are they?). The best way to proceed is the following. We need to choose a large value for m, generate good random numbers R_n, and take $B_n = 1$ when $R_n > 0.5$, and $B_n = 0$ when $R_n \leq 0.5$ (the case in which R_n is precisely equal to 0.5 has a very small probability for good random numbers, and we can include it without paying any particular attention).

It is important to choose the modulo m such that the operation of modulo is fast (or even in such away that we do not need it at all). For example, the values $m = 2^{32}$ for types consisting of 32 bits or $m = 2^{64}$ for types of 64 bits satisfy this condition. In this case we avoid a costly division, and the truncation is done automatically through the computer hardware. When the value takes more than 32 (or 64) bits, the most significant bits of the word are cut off. Note that often this is not an optimal choice for the generator quality. Indeed, when $log_2 m$ is equal to the number of bits of the word, the least significant bit (i.e., the rightmost digits) often present correlations which are stronger than the one that can be observed for the most significant bit (the one that code for the leftmost digits) because of how the multiplication works.

To build generators of good quality one further reasonable option is to choose the modulo in the form $m = 2^L \pm 1$, where L is the length (in bit) of the word of the type of choice. It is possible to program this type of generator in a very effective way (see [Knuth (1969)] for details). Moreover, it can be proven they have high quality properties.

11.2.2 Choosing the multiplier

Let us now discuss how to choose a reasonable value for the multiplier a. We can start by discussing how to determine which values of a generate the maximum period T of the generator (for a fixed value of the modulo m).

This is only a first criterion. Some others are also of great importance and not considering them could lead to disastrous results. Let us immediately analyze a counterexample by choosing the values $a = b = 1$. This might seem a clever choice. Indeed, the recurrence relation becomes

$$I_{n+1} = (I_n + 1) \bmod m ,$$

with period $T = m$, i.e., the longest possible period. However, it is also immediately clear that the random number sequence it produces is rather disastrous. For example, starting from $I_0 = 29$, we have

$$29, 30 \ldots m - 1, 0, \ldots 29 \ldots ,$$

which is clearly not a good random sequence. Remember, now and in the following, that formally the value 0 is a multiple of each number. It can be proven that the following theorem is valid, namely

Maximum period theorem (1961-1962). [Knuth (1969)] A linear congruence sequence has a period length $m = T$ (the maximum allowed length) if and only if

   (1) b and m do not have any divisors in common [1];

   (2) $\tilde{a} \equiv a - 1$ is a multiple of p for every prime p dividing m;

   (3) if m is a multiple of 4, $\tilde{a}$ is a multiple of 4. $\square$

The value 4 plays a particular role in this theorem. We do not give here a proof of this theorem, but we rather refer the interested reader to [Knuth (1969)].

To verify the theorem, we need to write a code that, given the values of a, b and m, checks whether the hypotheses are satisfied. Here, we only discuss the fundamental points of this code. Namely, it is based on two functions: one computing directly the period and another verifying the hypotheses:

```
period = findPeriod(a, b, m, seed);
proof = maxPeriodTheorem(a, b, m);
```

The function **findPeriod** returns the period computed in a direct way (as we saw in Section 11.2 and as we did in the Lab Exercise 1).

---

[1] b is said to be relatively prime to m.

The function `maxPeriodTheorem` analyzes the hypotheses of the theorem and returns an integer value which is copied into `proof`. This value is 1 if the hypotheses are satisfied and larger than 1 otherwise. The code ends with

```
if ((period == m) && (proof == 1)) {
  printf("OK: The system has the maximum period and "
         "the theorem has been verified.\n");
} else if ((period < m) && (proof > 1)) {
  printf("OK: The system does not have the maximum period and "
         " the theorem has been verified.\n");
} else {
  printf("Error: internal contradiction\n");
  exit(EXIT_FAILURE);
}
```

If the code reports that the period is not the maximum one and the hypotheses are satisfied, or that the period is maximum ($T = m$) and the hypotheses are not satisfied, there is a problem (in our code!): in this case an internal inconsistency is reported, and the program is exited with a negative code (which usually signals an error).

To verify the theorem hypotheses, we first of all need to be sure that the increment b is relatively prime to the modulo m. To this end, we compute the prime numbers comprised between 2 and m, for example with the algorithm given in Listing 4.9. The prime numbers we find are stored in the array `prime` and their number in the variable `numPrimes`. We are now able to check whether b and m have prime divisors in common with the code given in Listing 11.2.

```
1 commonDivisor(*prime, numPrimes, b, m){
2   for (i = 0; i < numPrimes; i++) {
3     if (((b % prime[i]) == 0) && ((m % prime[i]) == 0)) {
4       return 1;
5     }
6   }
7   return 0;
8 }
```

Listing 11.2   Searching common prime divisors.

The function `commonDivisor` returns 1 if it finds common divisors, i.e, if the theorem first hypothesis is violated. In this case the period T cannot take on the maximum value, m.

Analogously, we can check whether $a - 1$ is a multiple of all prime divisors of m. If m is a multiple of 4, we can easily check whether b is a multiple of 4, as shown in Listing 11.3.

```
1 if ((m % 4) !=0 ) {
2   printf ("3) OK: m is not a multiple of 4\n");
3   return 0;
4 } else {
5   if ((aTilde % 4) ==0 ) {
6     printf ("3) OK: m and a-1 are both multiples of 4\n");
7     return 0;
8   } else {
9     printf ("3) KO: m is a multiple of 4, but a-1 is not.\n");
10    return 1;
11  }
12 }
```

Listing 11.3   Verifying the maximum period theorem.

Hands on 11.2 - Linear congruential random number generators

Write a simple generator and verify the maximum period theorem by numerically computing the generator period. Consider rather small values of m (not appropriate for a real generator) because otherwise it would take a lot of memory and time to compute the period. Check the various cases considered in the theorem. This is the right moment to use a `malloc`. Indeed, we want to provide m from a keyboard input, so the compiler cannot know the array size beforehand.

Note that if the period is exactly equal to m, each integer number comprised between 0 and $m - 1$ appears in the sequence. Therefore, the choice of I_0 is irrelevant when determining the generator period.

11.2.3   *Purely multiplicative generators*

Let us consider the case of an increment equal to zero, $b = 0$. Due to the maximum period theorem stated in Section 11.2.2, we necessarily have $T < m$: this is obvious because the recurrence relation of a purely multiplicative generator has the form

$$I_{n+1} = (a\, I_n) \bmod m \,,$$

and the value $I_n = 0$ cannot be part of the sequence (as it is transformed in itself). So, in this case the maximum period is $m - 1$.

Table 11.1   An example of how to compute the
order of a modulo m. Here, we have $a = 3$ and
$m = 5$.

λ	a^λ	$a^\lambda \bmod m$
1	3	3
2	9	4
3	27	2
4	81	1

Before we continue, we need some more definitions. Let a be relatively prime to m. The smallest integer λ for which

$$\left(a^\lambda\right) \bmod m = 1$$

is said to be *the order of a modulo m*. In Table 11.1 we show as an example the case in which $a = 3$ and $m = 5$: the order of 3 modulo 5 is 4. Each value of a giving the maximum possible order modulo m is a *primitive element modulo m*. We define $\lambda(m)$ as the order of a primitive element.

The question we want to answer is then: how can we choose a multiplier a such as to obtain a maximum period, for a given value of the modulo m. The answer is based on the following theorem:

Carmichael theorem (1910) [Knuth (1969)]. The maximum period possible when $b = 0$ is $\lambda(m)$. $\square$

The value of $\lambda(m)$ can be obtained using the following results:

- $\lambda(2) = 1$;
- $\lambda(4) = 2$;
- $\lambda(2^z) = 2^{z-2}$ if $z \geq 3$;
- for p prime, $\lambda(p^z) = p^{z-1}(p-1)$ if $p > 2$;
- for $p_1, p_2, \ldots, p_k$ prime $\lambda(p_1^{z_1} p_2^{z_2} \ldots p_k^{z_k})$ = smallest common multiple of $\lambda(p_1^{z_1})$, $\lambda(p_2^{z_2})$ ..., $\lambda(p_k^{z_k})$.

This maximum period is obtained if I_0 is relatively prime to m and a is a primitive element modulo m.

Hands on 11.3 - Purely multiplicative generators

Build purely multiplicative generators with a long period using Carmichael theorem. Note that we are building these generators as an exercise and to understand their control mechanisms better. They should never be used in a true numerical computation. The generators used in real applications should always be professionally written, suggested and verified.

To carry out the Lab Exercise 3 it is useful to quote a last theorem allowing us to determine a primitive element modulo m. This allows us to explicitly identify the optimal values of a.

Primitive element theorem [Knuth (1969)]. a is a primitive element modulo p^z if and only if the following conditions are true:

- $p^z = 2$, a is odd; or $p^z = 4$, $a \bmod 4 = 3$; or $p^z = 8$, $a \bmod 8 = 3$ or 5 or 7; or $p = 2$, $z \geq 4$, $a \bmod 8 = 3$ or 5.
- Or p is odd, $z = 1$, $a \bmod p \neq 0$ and $a^{\frac{p-1}{q}} \bmod p \neq 1$ for any prime divisor q of $p - 1$.
- Or p is odd, $z > 1$, a satisfies the conditions of the previous item and $a^{p-1} \bmod p^2 \neq 1$. $\square$

The series of theorems we discussed allow us to analyze linear congruential generators and to start evaluating their behavior. It is an extremely useful analysis tool.

These theorems allow us to find generator parameters which are surely *bad*: a fast analysis can already allow us to eliminate some generators. What is even more important, though, is that the theorems show that a generator does not work in a mysterious way, but that its functioning is rather related to important theorems in number theory. Furthermore, for example, the concepts we discussed are at the basis of cryptography theory, guaranteeing a (hopefully) safe and secure way of communicating.

Hands on 11.4 - Primitive elements

 In a common, easy case (probably the first one worthwhile checking), where $m = 2^z$, if $z \geq 3$ the previous conditions give $a = 3$ or 5 modulo 8. In this case one out of four multipliers gives the maximum period. Verify this case, for not too large values of z. Try for example $z = 16$.

11.3 Some examples of generators and a first test

The first generator we consider (and which is to be evaluated, after learning how to test random number generators) is the so-called *minimal standard* due to Lewis, Goodman and Miller. It is characterized by the values [Hellekalek (2009)]

$$a = 7^5 = 16\,807 \;, \quad m = 2^{31} - 1 \;, \quad b = 0 \;.$$

This generator is often considered to be the minimum acceptable satisfactory tool for producing fair pseudo-random numbers (hence its name). It is a good starting point for comparing and evaluating other generators. It has a complete period, and m is prime. Therefore, due to Carmichael theorem (more specifically, because of the fourth point quoted immediately after the theorem) the order of any of its primitive elements is $m - 1$. Instead, the second point of the primitive element theorem shows how a is precisely a primitive element of m. Moreover, the minimal standard generator successfully pass the statistical causality tests.

We show how to code this generator, by analyzing statements similar to the ones of Listing 11.1. First of all, we initialize the increment, the modulo and the seed:

```
typedef unsigned long long int RANDOM_TYPE;
RANDOM_TYPE a, b, m, seed, randomNumber;
a = 16807;
m = 2147483647;
seed = 756431;
```

We choose the seed in an arbitrary way. It is important to check whether the type we have chosen has a sufficient number of bytes allowing us to correctly multiply two 32 bit numbers:

```
if (sizeof(RANDOM_TYPE)<8) {
   printf("Error: RANDOM_TYPE must have at least 8 byte,"
          " while it has  %d\n", sizeof(RANDOM_TYPE));
   exit(EXIT_FAILURE);
}
```

It is not difficult (we omit the details) to write this generator with types of only 32 bit. A pseudo-random uniformly distributed value between 0 and 1 is generated with the two statements

```
randomNumber = (a * randomNumber) % m;
r = (double)randomNumber / (double)m;
```

This procedure it used to program a generic LCG generator.

A second generator we mention here is a very particular case. Generally known as *the infamous RANDU* [Hellekalek (2009)] it was first adopted in 1968, and adapted and altered on many different computer systems. This generator is a disaster in many ways. Namely, it does not have a full period. Moreover, it generates sequences which are definitely and obviously not random. The infamous RANDU is defined by the relation

$$a = 2^{16} + 3 = 65\,539 \;, \quad m = 2^{31} \;, \quad b = 0 \;.$$

A typical way to test a generator is to consider v-dimensional vectors consisting of v consecutive random numbers $(R_n, R_{n+1}, \ldots, R_{n+v-1})$. An interesting theorem tells us that the maximum number of planes on which we can distribute these vectors is $m^{\frac{1}{v}}$. Since in our case $v = 3$, the maximum possible number of planes is 1300. If we choose $v = 3$ in the RANDU generator these vectors are distributed on few planes (always the fifteen same ones!) in a three-dimensional space. This denounces a very high and inappropriate correlation (this phenomenon is also evidenced by the so-called *spectral tests* [Knuth (1969)], which we do not discuss in this textbook). Note that it is not always easy to value this effect. In Figure 11.1 we show, on the left, how no effect can be observed if we watch the three-dimensional vectors from a random viewpoint. Instead, if we choose the correct point of view, the effect is visibly striking, as shown in the right plot.

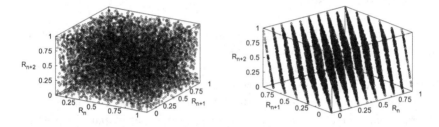

Fig. 11.1 Set of three numbers produced by the infamous RANDU generator. On the left, the point of observation is not the correct one, while from the viewpoint chosen on the right the condensation effect of the points on few planes is very clear.

Exercise 11.1 - Concentration exercise

After having read the box RANDU on page 316, think about the software help desk declaration, also in light of what we discussed in this chapter. Try to grasp its depth and implications. What do we truly mean when claiming a variable is random? Does it make sense when talking about one single variable?

The site mentioned in [Hellekalek (2009)] is the right place to search for efficient generators, verify their characteristics and find the results of the most important tests. For example, it is often safe and useful to use 64 bit generators (i.e., with $m = 2^{64}$). In this case, we need to make sure that the size of the type used in the program is sufficiently large (sometimes an `int` is not enough).

RANDU

At the times of the RANDU scandal, users calling some software help desks to denounce this inappropriate behavior, got to hear the following answer: «We guarantee one number to be truly random, not that a group of these numbers are.».

11.4 Statistical tests

We now focus on how to evaluate the quality of (pseudo)random number generators. Essentially we want to know whether the number sequence produced with our generator really appears to be random or if it introduces correlations. Whether the latter are weak or strong, the properties of the corresponding sequence are evidently different than those of a random sequence. To answer these questions with some quantitative parameters we consider here some basic tests (for more advanced tests, see [Knuth (1969)]).

First of all, we should check some basic facts. For example, do the probability distribution first moments coincide with those of the theoretical distribution, in the limits of a large number of generated events? Given N events, the average value is estimated to be

$$\overline{x} \equiv \frac{1}{N} \sum_{i=1}^{N} x_i \ . \tag{11.2}$$

An estimate of the variance, which can be studied instead of the second moment, is given by

$$\sigma^2 = \frac{1}{(N-1)} \sum_{i=1}^{N} (x_i - \overline{x})^2 \ . \tag{11.3}$$

Hands on 11.5 - Moments of a distribution

Compute the quantities (11.2) and (11.3) for growing values of N, for different pseudo-random number generators.

Do the measured values tend to the theoretical predictions for large N? First, verify analytically (with pen and paper) that for an uniform distribution between 0 and 1 $\bar{x}$ tends, for large N, to the exact value $\frac{1}{2}$ and σ^2 to the value $\frac{1}{12}$. Do not expect $\bar{x}$ and σ^2, computed with N iterations, to coincide exactly with the theoretical values. Indeed, both these quantities are, in turn, random variables, depending on the extracted random numbers. Only for large N ($N \to \infty$) they tend toward the exact values. It is better to study the dependency on N and estimate how the differences from the theoretical value tend toward zero for large N (i.e., to assess the statistical uncertainty characterizing the numerically estimated quantities).

It is important and necessary to also verify many other more complicated aspects. For example, the pseudo-random sequences could contain dynamic correlations. These could be rather obvious, as we saw when testing the infamous RANDU, but they might also be less noticeable in other generators. It is complicated to define objective tests telling us whether a certain *pattern*, i.e. a repetition of a group of elements arranged in a certain way, is a statistically relevant feature or whether it occurs by chance (as sometimes happens). For example, in a page full of random letters, it is possible that the series L E O appears three times. We recognize it as the word LEO, which coincidentally is the name of our best friend. Is this sequence the result of chance? Did somebody try to send us a message? It could be, but we need to decide with which probability. Probably, we just noticed the sequence LEO because we often pronounce the name of our best friend (this is typically why we remember predictions coming true, while we remove the false ones, thus letting ourselves get fooled by a horoscope and by astrology). Psychological effects strongly limit our capacity to analyze a sequence of events. Only mathematically rigorous tools can truly help us to build a coherent framework.

Let us therefore discuss objective criteria to evaluate the randomness of a sequence produced by a pseudo-random number generator.

11.4.1 χ^2 *test*

Imagine we have produced a sequence of pseudo-random numbers, and we want to know how much it resembles a sequence of truly random numbers. This amounts to solving the problem of comparing an observed distribution (the one of the numbers we are generating) to an expected one (whose properties we know a priori). We have introduced this technique in Section 7.4.2, and we use it now to analyze the reliability of the pseudo-random number sequence.

In particular, we discuss how to estimate the reliability of a numeric experiment in which each extraction has K possible results. This is not the case of an uniform distribution between 0 and 1, which is a continuous distribution with an infinite number of possible values. Still, even in this case we can apply the χ^2 test (Section 7.4.2). To this end, we need to divide the possible values of the random variable, that take values between zero and one, in K groups. For example, if $K = 100$, we can consider the first event to be the one of numbers between 0 and 0.01, the second event the one of those between 0.01 and 0.02, and so on. In this way we transform our problem to one with discrete states.

Let us start by generating n pseudo-random numbers (or, similarly, producing n independent measures). Let p_α be the theoretical, a priori, probability that a measure belongs to the αth interval. For example, rolling a dice ($K = 6$), all 6 possible results have the same probability: $p_1 = p_2 \ldots = p_6 = 1/6$. Instead, using two dices, we have $K = 11$ and the probability depends on the category: $p_2 = 1/36$ (two can only be obtained in one way, as the sum of two ones), $p_3 = 1/18$ (the value 3 is obtained if the first dice gives 1 and the second 2, but also if the first is 2 and the second 1), $p_4 = 1/12$ (4 can be obtained as 1 and 3, 2 and 2 or 3 and 1), and so on.

Let Y_α be the number of measures which actually fall into the αth interval. We also define the following quantity

$$\Phi = \sum_{1 \leq \alpha \leq K} \frac{(Y_\alpha - np_\alpha)^2}{np_\alpha} \,,$$

where the denominator is an important *weight* such that also less filled categories contribute in the right way to our reconstruction. The numerator can be rewritten as

$$(Y_\alpha - np_\alpha)^2 = Y_\alpha^2 - 2np_\alpha Y_\alpha + n^2 p_\alpha^2 \,,$$

and the entire argument of the sum as

$$\frac{Y_\alpha^2}{np_\alpha} - 2Y_\alpha + np_\alpha \,.$$

Using

$$\sum_\alpha p_\alpha = 1 \,, \quad \sum_\alpha Y_\alpha = n \,,$$

we find that

$$\Phi = \sum_\alpha \left(\frac{Y_\alpha^2}{np_\alpha} - 2Y_\alpha + np_\alpha \right)$$

$$= \frac{1}{n} \sum_\alpha \left(\frac{Y_\alpha^2}{p_\alpha} \right) - 2n + n = \frac{1}{n} \sum_\alpha \left(\frac{Y_\alpha^2}{p_\alpha} \right) - n \ .$$

Φ characterizes our specific draw of pseudo-random numbers. We need to establish a reasonable value for Φ. If the experimentally measured value for Φ is too small or too large, it is reasonably to suspect (and we are right to do so with a given probability) that the random number generator has some flaws, and does not faithfully represent the probability distribution we want to reproduce. First of all, remember that the degrees of freedom of the problem is

$$\nu \equiv K - 1$$

(a degree of freedom is constrained: $\sum_\alpha Y_\alpha = n$, and given $Y_2, \ldots, Y_n$ we also know Y_1). It can be proven that (see for example [Abramowitz and Stegun (1965)]) Φ follows the χ^2 distribution with ν degrees of freedom. The probability $P(\chi^2, \nu)$ that $\Phi \le \chi^2$ is

$$P(\chi^2, \nu) = \frac{\int_0^{\chi^2} t^{\frac{\nu}{2}-1} e^{-\frac{t}{2}} dt}{2^{\frac{\nu}{2}} \Gamma\left(\frac{\nu}{2}\right)} \ , \quad 0 \le \chi^2 < \infty \ , \tag{11.4}$$

where Γ is Euler Gamma function. In Table 11.2 we report the values of χ^2 corresponding to the various choices of ν (first column) and the probability $P(\chi^2, \nu)$ (first row). The integral of the formula (11.4) cannot be calculated analytically. It is evaluated with numeric integration methods discussed in Chapter 8. Table 11.2 tells us that (due to the random fluctuations) the quantity Φ is larger than the value indicated in a given position with the probability P given in the first row. For example, for 20 degrees of freedom, Φ is larger than 28.41 only in average one time over ten. Knuth [Knuth (1969)] tells us we can make the following statements:

- the generator is *obviously inaccurate* if Φ is less than or equal to the value corresponding to the probability 0.99 or if Φ is larger than or equal to the value corresponding to the probability 0.01;
- the generator is *suspect* if Φ is less than or equal to the value corresponding to the probability 0.95 or if Φ is larger than or equal to the value corresponding to the probability 0.05;
- the generator is *slightly suspect* if Φ is less than or equal to the value corresponding to the probability 0.90 or if Φ is larger than or equal to the value corresponding to the probability 0.10.

Table 11.2   Table of probabilities of the χ^2 test. Each line corresponds to the number of degrees of freedom indicated in the first column. The other columns correspond to various probability thresholds. For example, the probability that the value of Φ is larger than the number indicated in the second column is 0.995.

ν	0.995	0.99	0.975	0.95	0.9	0.1	0.05	0.025	0.01	0.005
2	0.01	0.02	0.05	0.10	0.21	4.61	5.99	7.38	9.21	10.60
3	0.07	0.11	0.22	0.35	0.58	6.25	7.81	9.35	11.34	12.84
4	0.21	0.30	0.48	0.71	1.06	7.78	9.49	11.14	13.28	14.86
5	0.41	0.55	0.83	1.15	1.61	9.24	11.07	12.83	15.09	16.75
6	0.68	0.87	1.24	1.64	2.20	10.64	12.59	14.45	16.81	18.55
7	0.99	1.24	1.69	2.17	2.83	12.02	14.07	16.01	18.48	20.28
8	1.34	1.65	2.18	2.73	3.49	13.36	15.51	17.53	20.09	21.95
9	1.73	2.09	2.70	3.33	4.17	14.68	16.92	19.02	21.67	23.59
10	2.16	2.56	3.25	3.94	4.87	15.99	18.31	20.48	23.21	25.19
11	2.60	3.05	3.82	4.57	5.58	17.28	19.68	21.92	24.73	26.76
12	3.07	3.57	4.40	5.23	6.30	18.55	21.03	23.34	26.22	28.30
13	3.57	4.11	5.01	5.89	7.04	19.81	22.36	24.74	27.69	29.82
14	4.07	4.66	5.63	6.57	7.79	21.06	23.68	26.12	29.14	31.32
15	4.60	5.23	6.26	7.26	8.55	22.31	25.00	27.49	30.58	32.80
16	5.14	5.81	6.91	7.96	9.31	23.54	26.30	28.85	32.00	34.27
17	5.70	6.41	7.56	8.67	10.09	24.77	27.59	30.19	33.41	35.72
18	6.26	7.01	8.23	9.39	10.86	25.99	28.87	31.53	34.81	37.16
19	6.84	7.63	8.91	10.12	11.65	27.20	30.14	32.85	36.19	38.58
20	7.43	8.26	9.59	10.85	12.44	28.41	31.41	34.17	37.57	40.00
25	10.52	11.52	13.12	14.61	16.47	34.38	37.65	40.65	44.31	46.93
30	13.79	14.95	16.79	18.49	20.60	40.26	43.77	46.98	50.89	53.67
35	17.19	18.51	20.57	22.47	24.80	46.06	49.80	53.20	57.34	60.27
40	20.71	22.16	24.43	26.51	29.05	51.81	55.76	59.34	63.69	66.77
45	24.31	25.90	28.37	30.61	33.35	57.51	61.66	65.41	69.96	73.17
50	27.99	29.71	32.36	34.76	37.69	63.17	67.50	71.42	76.15	79.49
55	31.73	33.57	36.40	38.96	42.06	68.80	73.31	77.38	82.29	85.75
60	35.53	37.48	40.48	43.19	46.46	74.40	79.08	83.30	88.38	91.95
65	39.38	41.44	44.60	47.45	50.88	79.97	84.82	89.18	94.42	98.11
70	43.27	45.44	48.76	51.74	55.33	85.53	90.53	95.02	100.43	104.22
75	47.21	49.47	52.94	56.05	59.79	91.06	96.22	100.84	106.39	110.29
80	51.17	53.54	57.15	60.39	64.28	96.58	101.88	106.63	112.33	116.32
85	55.17	57.63	61.39	64.75	68.78	102.08	107.52	112.39	118.24	122.32
90	59.20	61.75	65.65	69.13	73.29	107.57	113.15	118.14	124.12	128.30
95	63.25	65.90	69.93	73.52	77.82	113.04	118.75	123.86	129.97	134.25
100	67.33	70.06	74.22	77.93	82.36	118.50	124.34	129.56	135.81	140.17

In general, the test is performed a certain number of times (for example, five or ten) and all results are evaluated together. For large values of ν, the integrand appearing in the relation (11.4) becomes a Gaussian kernel with average ν and $\sigma = \sqrt{2\nu}$, with the correct normalization.

The central part of the code performing a χ^2 test for a generator of pseudo-random numbers between 0 and 1 is very simple. First of all, we initialize the vector y[] to zero,

```
for (i = 0; i < numBin; i++) {
  y[i] = 0;
}
```

(the number of degrees of freedom is numBin - 1). Next, we generate a sequence of pseudo-random numbers, and we update the frequency vector y[]:

```
for (i = 0; i < totNumber; i++) {
  double r;
  randomNumber = (a * randomNumber) % m;
  r = (double)randomNumber / (double)m;
  bin = (int)(r * numBin);
  y[bin]++;
}
```

As usual, randomNumber is initialized to seed. Finally, we can compute Φ with the following lines of code:

```
unsigned long long int tmpPhi = 0;
for (i = 0; i < numBin; i++) {
  tmpPhi += (y[i] * y[i]);
}
phi = (double)tmpPhi * (double)numBin / (double)totNumber
    - (double)totNumber;
```

Note that phi is a random variable. We can compute its average over various attempts of the test, and the corresponding statistical error. It is convenient to choose totNumber such that the error is sufficiently small, thus allowing us to accurately determine how the generator behaves. This can be achieved by making several attempts.

Hands on 11.6 - Two linear congruential generators

Compare the results obtained with two linear congruential generators by means of the χ^2 test. The first has $I_0 = 1$, $a = 663\,608\,941$, $b = 0$, $m = 2^{32}$; the second $I_0 = 1$, $a = 41\,475\,557$, $b = 0$, $m = 2^{28}$. Is one much better than the other? Continue to test other generators, both invented ones as popular generators many people rely upon.

11.4.2   *The Kolmogorov-Smirnov test*

If we want to evaluate a continuous distribution (such as the uniform distribution between 0 and 1) the Kolmogorov-Smirnov test is more natural than the χ^2 test (even if it is not clear whether it is more efficient). Indeed, the former does not require we artificially divide our distribution in K categories. Rather, we can directly work with the distribution of our interest. Apart form the tests we discussed so far, we only mention there also exist the very important *spectral tests*, which are too involved to be analyzed here. We refer the interested reader, for example, to Knuth textbook [Knuth (1969)].

The Kolmogorov-Smirnov test is particularly useful to check whether a continuous distribution is faithfully reproduced. The test is based on the *cumulative function* $F(x)$, also called *primitive function*, and defined as the probability that a random quantity X takes on a value less than x:

$$F(x) = \text{Prob } (X \le x) \, .$$

In Figure 11.2 we show the cumulative function $F(x)$ of a uniform distribution between 0 and 1. The cumulative function of the uniform distribution grows linearly with unit slope from $F(0) = 0$ up to $F(1) = 1$, and for large x values it has a constant value 1.

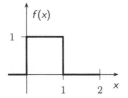
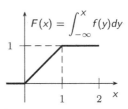

Fig. 11.2   Cumulative function $F(x)$ of a uniform distribution $f(x)$ in the interval $(0, 1)$. The distribution $f(x)$ is shown on the left.

Let us recall some general, important properties of the cumulative function $F(x)$. $F(x)$ is monotonous and non-decreasing (it is the sum of probabilities, which are non-negative by definition). It always starts at 0 and ends at 1 when x ranges from $-\infty$ to $+\infty$.

Table 11.3   Table of probabilities for the Kolmogorov-Smirnov test: the various entries, for different number of attempts, are the threshold which are not exceeded by the K outcomes with a certain probability (reported on the first row).

n	0.995	0.99	0.975	0.95	0.9	0.1	0.05	0.025	0.01	0.005
10	0.126	0.133	0.145	0.157	0.172	0.369	0.409	0.446	0.491	0.522
15	0.104	0.110	0.120	0.129	0.142	0.304	0.338	0.368	0.405	0.430
20	0.090	0.096	0.104	0.113	0.124	0.265	0.294	0.321	0.353	0.375
25	0.081	0.086	0.093	0.101	0.111	0.238	0.264	0.288	0.317	0.337
30	0.074	0.079	0.086	0.093	0.102	0.218	0.242	0.264	0.290	0.308
35	0.069	0.073	0.079	0.086	0.094	0.202	0.224	0.244	0.269	0.286
40	0.065	0.068	0.074	0.080	0.088	0.189	0.210	0.229	0.252	0.268
45	0.061	0.064	0.070	0.076	0.083	0.179	0.198	0.216	0.238	0.253
50	0.058	0.061	0.067	0.072	0.079	0.170	0.188	0.205	0.226	0.240
55	0.055	0.058	0.064	0.069	0.076	0.162	0.180	0.196	0.216	0.229
60	0.053	0.056	0.061	0.066	0.072	0.155	0.172	0.188	0.207	0.220
65	0.051	0.054	0.059	0.063	0.070	0.149	0.166	0.181	0.199	0.211
70	0.049	0.052	0.057	0.061	0.067	0.144	0.160	0.174	0.191	0.204
75	0.047	0.050	0.055	0.059	0.065	0.139	0.154	0.168	0.185	0.197
80	0.046	0.049	0.053	0.057	0.063	0.135	0.150	0.163	0.179	0.191
85	0.045	0.047	0.051	0.056	0.061	0.131	0.145	0.158	0.174	0.185
90	0.043	0.046	0.050	0.054	0.059	0.127	0.141	0.154	0.169	0.180
95	0.042	0.045	0.049	0.053	0.058	0.124	0.137	0.150	0.165	0.175
100	0.041	0.044	0.047	0.051	0.056	0.121	0.134	0.146	0.161	0.171

Exercise 11.2 - The cumulative function

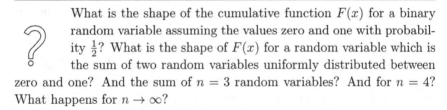

What is the shape of the cumulative function $F(x)$ for a binary random variable assuming the values zero and one with probability $\frac{1}{2}$? What is the shape of $F(x)$ for a random variable which is the sum of two random variables uniformly distributed between zero and one? And the sum of $n = 3$ random variables? And for $n = 4$? What happens for $n \to \infty$?

Suppose we measured the random variable X n times. Let X_1, X_2, ..., X_n be the values we obtained (i.e., the values of the generated pseudo-random numbers). In principle the correct ways of proceeding is as follows. Using the X_k, we build the *empirical distribution function*

$$F_n(x) \equiv \frac{(\text{ number of } X_k \leq x)}{n},$$

and we compare it to the theoretically expected one, $F(x)$. We compute the two quantities

$$K_n^+ \equiv \max_x \left(F_n(x) - F(x)\right) , \qquad (11.5)$$

$$K_n^- \equiv \max_x \left(F(x) - F_n(x)\right) , \qquad (11.6)$$

and we compare them with the Table 11.3, following the same procedure of the χ^2 test. We actually only computed the values of the empirical distribution function for some specific values of $x = x_j$ (namely, the results of the measurements). Therefore, the relations (11.5) and (11.6) cannot be applied in a direct way. This is why it is convenient to use an approach that is slightly different from the one we just discussed. Note that $F_n(x)$ is a step function, whose steps correspond to the values of the generated random numbers X_k. Therefore, the maximum distance $|F_n(x) - F(x)|$ will be reached on one of the values X_k. Let us sort the values X_k in increasing order, and check the values that the distribution function F reaches at each measured value of x_j. For example, for a uniform distribution we define

$$K_n^+ \equiv \max_k \left(\frac{k}{n} - F(X_k)\right) , \qquad (11.7)$$

$$K_n^- \equiv \max_k \left(F(X_k) - \frac{k-1}{n}\right) , \qquad (11.8)$$

and we compare the maximum of these values to the expected probability reported in Table 11.3. In this way we obtain for example the probability for which a sequence of pseudo-random numbers clearly exhibits a nonrandom character. If the cumulative function of the generated distribution is too different from or too similar to the expected one, there is a problem. The information needed to get Table 11.3 can, for example, be found in the textbook by von Mises [von Mises (1964)], containing the formulas that give the probabilities that the K_n are larger than a certain threshold ϵ. An interesting discussion is given in [Press *et al.* (1992)].

```
1   kPlusMax = -1.0;
2   kMinusMax = -1.0;
3   for (i = 0; i < totNumber; i++) {
4     double kPlus, kMinus;
5     kPlus = fabs((double)i * invTotNumber - vRandom[i]);
6     kMinus = fabs((double)(i - 1) * invTotNumber
7                    - vRandom[i]);
8     if (kPlus > kPlusMax) {
9       kPlusMax = kPlus;
10    }
```

```
1    if (kMinus > kMinusMax) {
2      kMinusMax = kMinus;
3    }
4  }
5  if (kPlusMax >= kMinusMax) {
6    kMax = kPlusMax;
7  } else {
8    kMax = kMinusMax;
9  }
```

Listing 11.4   Kolmogorov-Smirnov test.

The code performing this test starts by generating pseudo-random numbers which are stored in a vector and subsequently sorted. Sorting algorithms are discussed in detail in Sections 5.2.1 and 15.2.

The second part of the code, given in Listing 11.4, computes the quantities defined in equations (11.7) and (11.8) and determines the maximum between these two. For each extracted value, we compute K_n^+ and K_n^- and the difference between the expected and the empirical distribution.

On lines 5 and 6 the variable invTotNumber is equal to one over totNumber. In this way, we perform two multiplications instead of two divisions which take a lot more computation time with respect to the former.

Hands on 11.7 - The Kolmogorov-Smirnov method

 Use this method to verify whether pseudo-random number generators are correct. Compare the results with those of the χ^2 test after dividing the numbers in K discrete categories. Are the results of the two methods compatible? Is one of them clearly superior? To sort the X_k use, for example, the lists, discussed in Section 13.2.1 and Chapter 17 (at first, you can use any, even slow algorithm as we did in the code we just discussed).

11.5   Shift registers

A different type of generator, often of great use in practice, is the so-called *shift register*. In this context it is preferable to consider a random number as a sequence of random bits. The number of bits with which we work depends on the random variable (it also determines the maximum value the random

number can attain when represented for example as an **unsigned** integer).
It is always convenient to choose this type as an **unsigned** such that we do
not need to treat the last bit, the one that would give information about
the sign, with particular care. Here, the kth random number is generated
according to the rule (Figure 11.3)

$$R_k = (R_{k-b} \oplus R_{k-c}) \ ,$$

where $\oplus$ is the bitwise *exclusive-or* operator, XOR (discussed in Section
14.1). A common and appropriate choice for the *offsets* b and c is $b = 24$
and $c = 55$. The apparently random nature of the sequence (the results
of the standard tests of randomness are good) is guaranteed by the XOR
operation between faraway bits of the sequence.

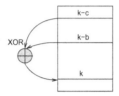

Fig. 11.3   Generating pseudo-random numbers with a shift register.

The generator independently acts on the single bits that form the number. This guarantees that the bits are really independent and uncorrelated.
In some applications, we need to pay a lot of attention to the problem of
possible correlations among the bits (even because of the way they have
been initialized). In order to be safer, a second operation mixing the bits
can be added to the shift register based generator.

A characteristic which has both positive as negative sides, is that this
generator needs to be initialized with another generator. In the case $c = 55$
we need to fill all bits of all 55 vector components in which we store the
pseudo-random numbers at the beginning of the procedure. The pseudo-random numbers are produced by means of another generator, for example,
of the LCG type. This might be a burdensome task. However, it is important to guarantee that the single bits are independent, and of uniform
quality. The most common approach is as follows. A linear congruential
generator (or the machine internal generator) is used to generate 55 times
the number of bits composing a word. The tables of the shift register are
filled using the *shift* operations (described in Section 14.1).

In practice, a shift register is usually programmed with one of two common methods. In the first approach three pointers run through an array of 55 components. Each time a pointer reaches one of the edges of the array, it is sent back to the beginning of the array, with a modulo 55 operation. In this way the desired operation, i.e., XOR between the number generated 24 steps earlier and the one generated 55 steps earlier, is executed. This is the more natural method, though it takes up a lot of machine time. Indeed, we continuously need to perform tests and many modulo operations are required to bring back the pointers to the beginning of the array. This approach can be optimized by always referring to the shift registers with indexes of the type `char` and setting the size of the array containing the register equal to $256 = 2^8$. In this case, the modulo operator is done without any added cost each time an index reaches the value 256. Nevertheless, this explicit use of an *overflow*, i.e., an error condition, to compute the correct index is not very safe.

As often occurs if we occupy more memory space, we can save CPU time. A second approach consists in storing a vector with a large number of components, many more than the 55 which are strictly necessary. For example we could allocate 10^4 or 10^5 memory positions (we have to be careful not too exit from the fast memory, the so-called *cache*, otherwise the speed of our code could be reduced several orders of magnitude). We now move the pointers. By keeping track of the number of performed operations, we can make sure that the pointers never reach the vector beginning or end. Only when we are close to its border, the active part of the vector of pseudo-random numbers (the 55 most recent components) is copied to the beginning of the memory space in which the shift register is stored. Correspondingly, the pointers are updated. In this way, the majority of updates of the pointers are simple additions (fast like the XOR which is the engine of our machinery), and only rarely we need to perform arithmetic tests or copies.

In this case, the code is mainly based on two principal functions, one to initialize the shift register, `shiftRegister[SHIFT_LENGTH]`, and another producing a new random number by updating the shift register:

```
typedef unsigned long int RANDOM_TYPE

void shiftInit(unsigned int seed);
RANDOM_TYPE callShift(void);

RANDOM_TYPE shiftRegister[SHIFT_LENGTH];
```

The function `shiftInit()` plays various important roles. First of all, it assigns starting values to `addressB` and `addressC`, that are addresses of the shift register components that we are using at a given moment. The shift register bits are one by one initialized with the machine generator, `rand()`.

First, `rand()`, which in turn is first initialized with a call to `srand(seed)`, is called a given number of times (for example, a thousand) to make sure that we have left a possible transient regime. A wrong choice of the value used to initialize the generator could generate inappropriate sequences.

```
1   addressB = 31;
2   addressC =  0;
3
4   srand((unsigned int) seed);
5   for (i = 0; i < 1000; i++) {
6     rand();
7   }
8   for (i = 0; i < SHIFT_LENGTH; i++) {
9     shiftRegister[i] = 0;
10   }
11   for (i = 0; i < SHIFT_LENGTH; i++) {
12     for (j = 0; j < 8 * sizeof(RANDOM_TYPE); j++) {
13       r = (double)rand() / (double)RAND_MAX;
14       if (r > 0.5) {
15         theBit = 0;
16       } else {
17         theBit = 1;
18       }
19       shiftRegister[i] = shiftRegister[i] | (theBit << j);
20     }
21   }
```

Listing 11.5   Initializing the shift register.

Next, we reset the shift register to all zeros, and we generate values between zero and one with calls to the function `rand()`. More precisely, for values smaller than 0.5 the new bit is set to zero, otherwise it is set to one.

On line 19 of Listing 11.5, a shift and bitwise OR operation allow us to set the value of the bit under consideration. These operations are repeated on all bits. We discuss the bitwise OR, XOR and AND operators and the left shift `<<` operator in Chapter 14. The logical operators compare the bits belonging to two separate words, while the left shift operator moves the word a given number of bits to the left.

It is now easy to produce a new pseudo-random number, by updating the shift register. The function `callShift()` performs exactly this task and returns a variable of the type `RANDOM_TYPE`. A bitwise XOR operations between the components of the `shiftRegister` pointed by `addressB` and `addressC` generate a new random number. Once this is done, the random number stored in `addressC` is no longer needed. So, we use it to store the value of the random number we just created. Finally, we update the pointers.

The only thing we need to worry about is that we need to stay within the array (of 55 components) we created. Once we have reached the end of the array, we start using it again at its beginning (but we never over-write memory locations which are still useful). Identifying in this way the array head with its tail, we look at it like a ring. Finally, the function `callShift()` returns the new pseudo-random number, which can directly be used (we do not need to fetch it from the array).

```
RANDOM_TYPE r;
r = shiftRegister[addressB] ^ shiftRegister[addressC];
shiftRegister[addressC] = r;
addressB++;
addressC++;
if (addressB == SHIFT_LENGTH) addressB = 0;
if (addressC == SHIFT_LENGTH) addressC = 0;
return r;
```

Hands on 11.8 - A shift register

 Program a random number generator based on a shift register. With the tests we defined before, verify whether it behaves in a correct way. Check its performance and efficiency, by implementing different ways of defining the array that hosts the shift register.

The fact that the shift register does not mix bits is an advantage in some applications, while for others it is a serious limit, that potentially can cause errors. In the latter cases, extra bit mixing procedures have been proposed.

Some generators which are generally believed to be of high quality are RANLUX, due to M. Lüscher in 1994 [Luescher (1994); James (1994)], and some generators described in an interesting comment by George Marsaglia [Marsaglia (1999)].

11.6   Generating nonuniform distributions

When implementing numerical simulations, codes integrating stochastic equations or decision making codes, we often need to generate pseudo-random numbers which are extracted according to probability distributions other than the uniform one (which we now know how to reproduce in various ways). Several standard techniques allow us to do this for a large number of distributions.

The most common case is that of the *Gaussian distribution* (also called *Normal distribution*). Here, we only discuss this important case. We refer the reader to, for example, [Knuth (1969)] and [Press *et al.* (1992)] for more details on the Gaussian distribution and on building other probability distributions.

One of the most well-known methods is based on the *Box-Müller transformation* [Press *et al.* (1992)]. We start by extracting, independently and uniformly two pseudo-random numbers ρ_1 and ρ_2 in the interval $(0, 1)$. We define

$$\gamma_1 \equiv \sqrt{-2\ln(\rho_1)} \cos(2\pi\rho_2) \ ,$$
$$\gamma_2 \equiv \sqrt{-2\ln(\rho_1)} \sin(2\pi\rho_2) \ .$$

γ_1 and γ_2 are two pseudo-random numbers which are normally distributed with average zero and variance one.

One negative aspect of this procedure is that it is not particularly efficient (it takes four, computationally heavy, library function calls). Moreover, the careful programmer should use only one of the two random numbers created in this way, in order to reduce the risk of enhancing small correlations between successive random numbers (this occurs when very small pseudo-random numbers are extracted).

```
1 double r1, r2, g1, g2, s1, s2, mySqrt, myArg;
2 randomNumber = (a * randomNumber) % m;
3 r1 = (double)randomNumber / (double)m;
4 randomNumber = (a * randomNumber) % m;
5 r2 = (double)randomNumber / (double)m;
6 mySqrt = sqrt(- 2.0 * log(r1));
7 myArg = 2.0 * M_PI * r2;
8 g1 = mySqrt * cos(myArg);
9 g2 = mySqrt * sin(myArg);
```

Listing 11.6   Generating Gaussian distributed random numbers.

The most important part of the code that generates normally distributed values with the Box-Müller transformation is very easy. Starting from two uniformly distributed numbers two Gaussian values are generated, as shown in Listing 11.6. The system constant M_PI is defined in the file included with the command include <math.h> and has the value $\pi \sim 3.141\,593$.

There exist efficient techniques to obtain random numbers distributed according to various probability functions. We only present the main, general ideas and refer for example to [Press *et al.* (1992)] for details and codes applying this approach.

Suppose we have a random variable x, uniformly distributed in the interval $(0, 1)$. We want to obtain a variable y distributed according to the probability distributed $P(y)$. Note that

$$P(y)\, dy = dx \ . \tag{11.9}$$

Let $F(y)$ be the primitive function of $P(y)$, i.e., the function such that

$$\frac{dF(y)}{dy} \equiv F'(y) = P(y) \ . \tag{11.10}$$

Then, from the relation (11.9) we have that

$$\frac{dF(y)}{dy} dy = dx \ ,$$

i.e., $x = F(y)$. By inverting this relation we get

$$y = F^{-1}(x) \ . \tag{11.11}$$

In order for the equation (11.11) to be useful, note that we should know the primitive function of P: this is rarely the case. For example, if the variable x is uniformly distributed between 0 and 1, the variable $z = -\log(x)$ is distributed according to the exponential $\exp(-z)$ between 0 and $+\infty$.

An extremely flexible method to obtain values distributed according to a generic probability distribution $p(x)$ is the *acceptance-rejection* method. Here we only describe the main idea behind this method, and again we refer the reader to [Press *et al.* (1992)] for more details.

The first step is to choose a function $n(x)$ such that, from an algorithmic viewpoint, it is easy to generate random numbers distributed according to this function $n(x)$. To this end, $n(x) \geq p(x)$ $\forall x$ and $n(x)$ should satisfy $\int_{-\infty}^{+\infty} n(x) = A < \infty$. This is always true given that $p(x)$ is a probability distribution, and thus, its integral in the real plane equals 1. It is always possible, though usually rather inefficient, to choose $n(x)$ to be a constant value which is a little higher than the maximum of $p(x)$.

The function $n(x)$ is called the *reference function*. In order for this method to be efficient the reference function $n(x)$ should be as similar as possible to $p(x)$. Therefore, we first choose a random value $\overline{x}$ distributed according to $n(x)$, and next a second, uniformly distributed random variable z between 0 and $n(\overline{x})$. The value $\overline{x}$ is accepted in the random sequence if and only if z is less than $p(\overline{x})$.

Hands on 11.9 - The acceptance-rejection method

 Choose different probability distributions $p(x)$ and reproduce them with the acceptance-rejection method, trying different reference functions $n(x)$. Evaluate the method quantitatively by varying the reference function.

Chapter 12

Random walks

SHE LOVES SHE LOVES ME NOT
If doubts in love
Too strong are for you
You better get a daisy
With a single petal.

Stefano Benni, *Margherita Dolcevita* (2005).

In this chapter we discuss random walks. An indecisive traveler elects to let chance determine his wandering, which, needless to say, drastically changes his life in an unexpected way. Perhaps the indecision is due to one glass too many, which is why we, somewhat mercilessly, refer to the traveler as *a drunk traveler*, and why he zigzags.

In Section 12.1 we define a simple version of this problem by constraining the traveler to move along one single dimension, for example on a narrow sidewalk. We verify that the drunk traveler moves quite a lot slower than a determined traveler, as the *random walk* is rather different from a deterministic walk. In Section 12.2 we discuss a more general version of the same problem by considering a drunk traveler which moves about in two or more dimensions. We introduce the powerful technique of the generating function, which supplies new information on the problem.

In Section 12.3 another interesting generalization allows us to study a lattice gas and the way in which its particles diffuse.

Finally, our drunk traveler, dreamer or slightly tipsy, explores the mountains in Section 12.4, where she moves in an environment with a preferential direction which depends on the site itself and does not change with time.

This causes yet another slowing down of the dynamics, which we try to explain qualitatively.

The random walk problems are ideal to test whether one has fully grasped how to treat random numbers. Indeed, these types of problems call excellent random number generators. Fortunately, we learned how to deal with such problems in Chapter 11.

12.1   A first simple crucial argument

Consider a straight line divided into discrete parts. We are thus considering a single spatial dimension. Consider equidistant sites, where the drunk traveler rests after each step (Figure 12.1). This is a discrete problem both in space and time. The latter is subdivided in elementary intervals since the traveler takes a step at each time instance. To solve this problem we need to know the traveler initial position, i.e., the *initial condition*, together with the rule governing the motion. The initial condition only influences the detailed route of the traveler and not the typical or average characteristics of the motion.

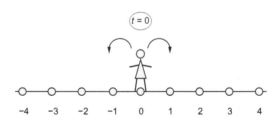

Fig. 12.1   The traveler moves randomly along a one-dimensional chain, starting at time $t = 0$ from position 0.

We define x_t to be the position of the random walker at time t. As can be seen from Figure 12.1 the x_t take values along a one-dimensional chain. We typically choose $x_0 = 0$ as initial condition, and x_t can take on the values $0, \pm 1, \pm 2 \ldots$ and so on. The positions x_t are integer variables, i.e., they take values in $\mathbb{Z}_n$. At each time unit the traveler makes a step moving with probability $\frac{1}{2}$ one interval to the right or with probability $\frac{1}{2}$

one interval to the left. More synthetically, we can write:

$$P\left(\text{right}\right) = \frac{1}{2} = P\left(\text{displacement} = +1\right) ,$$

$$P\left(\text{left}\right) = \frac{1}{2} = P\left(\text{displacement} = -1\right) . \qquad (12.1)$$

Each trajectory is different from the others as the motion of the walker is determined by extracting random numbers. Rather than studying such a motion single trajectory, it is therefore more interesting to analyze the average properties typical for this kind of dynamical process. For instance, the fact that the walker reached a certain position after twenty steps during his last journey, does not give us much information on what might happen during his next trip. Instead, it is more interesting to analyze the average distance the walker has traveled from the starting point after a certain number of steps. Average values mathematically correspond to expected values under the probability distribution P and they are represented with angular brackets $\langle \cdot \rangle$. It is easy to compute the expected value of the displacement of the traveler at a given time, or the expected value of its square. Since we assume that at each successive time step a shift Δx in the position occurs, which takes the values ± 1 with equal probability, we have

$$\langle \Delta x \rangle = \frac{1}{2}\left((+1) + (-1)\right) = 0 \ , \quad \langle \Delta x^2 \rangle = \frac{1}{2}\left((+1)^2 + (-1)^2\right) = 1 .$$

Let r_t be the increment of the traveler position at time t. Thus, the value of r_t can be ± 1. In order to obtain the expected values, we actually compute the average values of the *random variable* r_t. In practice, averaging comes down to repeating the traveler evolution several times, using different random numbers, then sum the results of these different histories and divide the latter by the number of histories considered. Therefore, we have

$$\langle r_t \rangle = \frac{1}{2}\left((+1) + (-1)\right) = 0 \ , \ \langle r_t^2 \rangle = \frac{1}{2}\left((+1)^2 + (-1)^2\right) = 1 . \quad (12.2)$$

The walker position at time $t + 1$ is obtained from the position at the previous time step, t, incremented by the (positive or negative) displacement which occurred at time t:

$$x_{t+1} = x_t + r_t .$$

If we square the previous expression and consider the expected value of both members, we have

$$\langle x_{t+1}^2 \rangle = \langle x_t^2 \rangle + 2 \langle x_t \, r_t \rangle + \langle r_t^2 \rangle .$$

Note that x_t does not depend on r_t, but only on all other random increments up to time $t - 1$, i.e., on r_0, r_1, ..., r_{t-1}. Thus, the random variable r_t

and the position x_t are uncorrelated. Translated into mathematical terms, we have $\langle x_t \, r_t \rangle = \langle x_t \rangle \langle r_t \rangle$. Therefore, using the two relations (12.2), we obtain

$$\langle x_{t+1}^2 \rangle = \langle x_t^2 \rangle + 1 \, .$$

This is a very interesting formula. For instance, if we set the initial condition to $x_0 = 0$, we get $\langle x_1^2 \rangle = \langle x_0^2 \rangle + 1 = 1$, $\langle x_2^2 \rangle = \langle x_1^2 \rangle + 1 = 2$ and, in general,

$$\langle x_t^2 \rangle = t \, . \tag{12.3}$$

If we choose a different initial condition, the previous relation would also contain an additional additive constant. However, this does not change anything in the following analysis as the interesting quantity is the traveler displacement from the starting point.

The relation (12.3) is very important and has enormous consequences in many scientific applications. Simulating a random walk in two spatial dimensions allows us to appreciate its importance even more. First, let us point out that in normal cases, i.e., cases which are not based on random dynamics, it is x_t and not x_t^2 which grows proportionally to the time t. The latter is defined as a *ballistic motion*. A good example is the motion of an object launched from the Earth and brought back to the Earth due to the gravity force. After two hours of traveling by car on a highway, the distance from the tollbooth where we entered the highway is more or less the double of the distance after one hour of traveling. Instead, the average distance traveled by the random walker (who should certainly not be drinking and driving at the same time!) grows a lot more slowly, namely as the square root of the elapsed time:

$$\text{distance} \sim \sqrt{\text{time}} \, . \tag{12.4}$$

Let us discuss this aspect in some more detail. The walker average position is always zero, due to the fact that the rule governing the displacement is symmetrical. The average distance from the origin grows as the square root of time. Let us consider the traveler position to be the result of a game. At time t we are either winning or loosing with equal probability. However, the average amount we lost or won at a given instant grows with time. At the start of the game we either loose or win rather little on average, while later on the average gain or loss is larger. The key is indeed the relation (12.4), which states that the typical distance from the origin grows only as the square root of time. Our walker moves only very slowly away from the origin, and, as we will discuss better further on, its motion covers a two-dimensional manifold rather than a simple curve.

These phenomena are mathematically described by *Wiener walks*. The equations describing these Wiener walks are stochastic equations [Gihman and Skorohod (1972)]. In the limit where the lattice spacing tends to zero, the discrete equations become continuous equations and the corresponding motion is described by continuous trajectories which are however never differentiable.

Hands on 12.1 - The drunk traveler

Simulate the motion of the drunk traveler and verify property (12.3). Start by observing a single trajectory (for instance a trajectory of 1000 or 10 000 steps). Next, average the results of various walks using the same initial condition, but different random number sequences.

Simulating a random walk requires the use of a good pseudo-random number generator. Bearing in mind that the bad quality of pseudo-random number generators reveals itself only occasionally, the standard generator used by gcc, i.e., rand() will do for now. However, in order to maintain a better control on the quality of the code, it is good practice to also program the generator which is to be used. In this way it is for instance easier to temporarily replace it by another one allowing us to verify whether the outcome is related to the choice of the generator. For instance, we can use one of the generators suggested by L'Ecuyer. A first one is based on 64 bits; remember that the type used for the random numbers must be of the same length. For clarity purposes, we advise to define a type typedef unsigned long long int RANDOM_TYPE, and to verify whether the RANDOM_TYPE type has the desired length with the sizeof operator. In this way, the rest of the code is not dependent on the number of bits used by the generator, and possible changes can be applied by changing only few lines of code. This specific generator is defined by the following parameters:

$$\text{L'Ecuyer type 1; } m = 2^{64} \quad a = 1181\,783\,497\,276\,652\,981 . \qquad (12.5)$$

Note that the compiler might not accept the definition of such huge constants. In this case an appropriate suffix must be added. For example, a word of the unsigned long long int type must end with the suffix ULL. If the random variable type is exactly contained in 64 bits, the modulo m operation is automatically carried out because the excess bits are lost.

In this way we avoid a costly division operation. Another good generator requiring a 64 bit type, in which the modulo has to be computed explicitly, is

$$\text{L'Ecuyer type 2; } m = 2^{31} - 1 \quad a = 1385\,320\,287 \,. \tag{12.6}$$

Let us discuss the Lab Exercise in some more detail. Given a certain initial condition, the traveler starts walking. We either save the trajectory in the memory (the required space can be reserved with a `malloc()`) or write it to a file. Both ways allow us to plot x_t as a function of time t at the end of the walk. For a single trajectory, we could also do the same for x_t^2. However, the key is to average these quantities over many trajectories (e.g., a hundred, a thousand or ten thousand). By studying the behavior of these averaged quantities, we obtain the most relevant information.

Finally, this Lab Exercise also allows us to appreciate *log-log* graphs, i.e., graphs where both axes are in logarithmic scale. In log-log representation a power law reveals a linear dependency, where the slope is exactly the power in question. For instance, if $|x(t)|$ grows as t^α, the logarithm of $|x(t)|$ grows as $\alpha \log(t)$. Thus, with the log-log plot we can estimate α from our numerical data. Can we also estimate the error on our best estimate of α?

```
1 randomNumber = seed;
2 position = 0;
3
4 for (i = 0; i < numberOfSteps; i++) {
5    double r;
6    fprintf(fDat, "%d %d\n", i, position);
7    randomNumber = a * randomNumber;
8    r = (double)randomNumber * iDoubleM;
9    if (r < 0.5) {
10      position += 1;
11   } else {
12      position -= 1;
13   }
14 }
15 fprintf(fDat, "%d %d\n", i, position);
```

Listing 12.1 The code simulating a random walker.

A program simulating the evolution of a single random walk on a discretized straight line is rather simple and is give in Listing 12.1. The program is essentially limited to the generation of a series of pseudo-random numbers. If the random number takes a value between 0 and $\frac{1}{2}$, the position is incremented by $+1$ (rightward step). Instead, when the random number lies between $\frac{1}{2}$ and 1, the position is diminished by -1 (leftward step). The case where the random number takes on exactly the value $\frac{1}{2}$ is not very significant and can be included in either one of the two cases.

The random number generator is initialized by the seed variable. We choose the traveler initial position (at time zero) to be zero. The generation of a random number does not require the modulo operation because the randomNumber type is exactly 64 bits and, therefore, taking the modulo of 2^{64} consists in truncating the variable. The for statement manages the cycle of the total number of the traveler steps. At each step, we write the current position to a file, we extract a random number r between zero and one (iDoubleM is the inverse of the generator modulo) and we modify the position variable accordingly. At the end of the for cycle, a final writing statement registers the traveler final position in the file pointed by fDat.

A typical trajectory generated in this way is shown in Figure 12.2. Obviously this graph depends on the choice for the initial value of the random number generator. Both the x-axis and the y-axis are in linear and not in logarithmic scale. The traveler first moves in the positive direction, then returns to $x = 0$ and travels in both positive and negative directions of x. Note the jagged pattern of the trajectory. In the limit of infinitesimal displacements the trajectory is always continuous, but never differentiable.

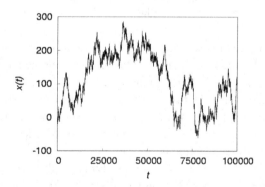

Fig. 12.2 The position $x(t)$ in function of time t for a generic trajectory of a one-dimensional random walk.

Also a plot of $x^2(t)$ for a single trajectory, given in Figure 12.3 for the same trajectory from before, turns out to be rather interesting. Again, the details of the motion are different for different numerical experiments: however, the general characteristics do not change. This time both axes have a logarithmic scale. The straight line with slope one identifies the following relation $x^2(t) = t$, i.e., $\log x^2(t) = \log t$. First of all note that in spite of severe fluctuations the walker squared position grows linearly with time, as expected. Sometimes the walker passes by the origin again, but this event becomes rarer as time passes (remember we are working in logarithmic scale). For the larger part of the time the traveler displacement from the origin is of the order $\sqrt{t}$, i.e., rather close to the straight line plotted in the graph.

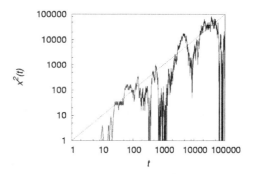

Fig. 12.3   The squared position, $x^2(t)$ as a function of the time t for a generic trajectory (the same of the previous figure), in log-log scale. The straight line has slope one.

Other features can be obtained by determining the averages for various instances of the traveler motion. To this end, we perform the walk several times, always starting from the origin, and we compute the averages of the desired quantities. For instance, at each of the time instances we want to analyze, let us sum the quantity $x^2(t)$ for the various trajectories and then divide this value by the total number of trajectories considered: this gives us $\langle x^2(t) \rangle$. In the example, we compute the value of $\langle x^2(t) \rangle$ together with its statistical error. It is useful to dynamically reserve the memory space inside the code. A `calloc` guarantees that the allocated spaces are reset, which is necessary because we use them to accumulate the interesting values. The use of `calloc` is shown in the following code fragment:

```
double *x2Average;
x2Average = calloc(numberOfSteps, sizeof(double));
if (x2Average == NULL) {
  printf("Error: calloc of x2Average failed\n");
  exit(EXIT_FAILURE);
}
```

As usual, we are careful about interrupting the program execution in case the dynamic memory allocation is unsuccessful (for instance because we ask too much memory space). As we are considering averages over different histories, we need to restart the traveler walk many times. We must not forget to execute the statement `position = 0;` at the beginning of each of these! At each time instance, we accumulate the information needed to compute the expected value of the quadratic distance and the corresponding statistical error using the `position` variable :

```
x = (double)position;
x2 = x * x;
x4 = x2 * x2;
x2Average[i] += x2;
x2Error[i] += x4;
```

At the end of the code, we compute the error using the correct combination of x^2 and x^4, normalize both the error and the expectation value of the quadratic distance and print them.

Figure 12.4 shows $\langle x^2(t) \rangle$ in function of time using a logarithmic scale for both axes. The average over different walks (in this case 5000) eliminates the strong fluctuations which are present in the single trajectory of Figure 12.3. The numerical measurements, shown here together with their statistical error, are perfectly distributed along a straight line (so well that they hide the reference with unit slope). Note that while the positions at different times in different walks are uncorrelated, the positions at different times of a single walk, and therefore also the average values at different times, are correlated. The reason is quite trivially that the traveler position at time t depends on all its positions at the previous times.

12.2 More than one dimension: the generating function

Let us elaborate some more on random walks. We want to determine the universal behavior of a random walk. For instance, the relation $|\vec{x}(t)| \sim \sqrt{t}$ is not only valid on a simple one-dimensional chain, but for every number of spatial dimensions on any lattice shape. In one dimension we discussed a discretized straight line. In two or more spatial dimensions the space can be discretized in different lattice shapes: square, triangular, simple cubic, face centered cubic and so on.

A typical and simple example is the square lattice in two dimensions (see Figure 12.5). In this case $\vec{x}$ is a couple of integer values, $\vec{x} = (x_1, x_2)$,

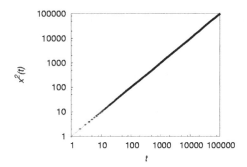

Fig. 12.4   The average value (computed from 5000 samples) of the quadratic position, $\langle x^2(t)\rangle$ as a function of time, in log-log scale. The straight line (visible only at short times) has unit slope.

while for a generic dimension D, $\vec{x}$ is D-plet of integer values. Let $P_t(\vec{x})$ be the probability that the walker is in position $\vec{x}$ at the (discretized) time t. At each step, the walker moves with equal probability in one of the four allowed directions. As an initial condition, we assume that the walker starts at time zero from the origin, $\vec{x}_0 = (0,0)$. Thus, $P_0(\vec{x}) = \delta_{\vec{x},\vec{0}}$, where δ is the product of two Kronecker delta distributions, one for the component x_1 and one for the component x_2.

We can now simply repeat the one-dimensional exercise in case of a walker on a two-dimensional grid. More specifically, in what follows, we discuss the case of a square lattice. First we perform a theoretical analysis of the problem, and then we discuss the details of a numerical simulation. We want to compute in which sites the walker should be after a given time, together with the probability that the walker arrives in a certain site.

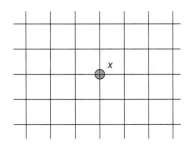

Fig. 12.5   A two-dimensional square lattice.

It is easy to derive a recursive relation for the function $P_t(\vec{x})$. The walker can only be at the site $\vec{x}$ at time $t+1$ if at time t he was at an adjacent site, and chance wanted that the subsequent displacement from the adjacent site was towards that site $\vec{x}$. Figure 12.6 shows the situation in which the walker at time t is at a site O and at time $t+1$ at site X. In order to remain as general as possible, we suppose that the distance between every two adjacent lattice points is the same and set it equal to a (up to now, we implicitly considered the case $a = 1$). In other words, we have

$$P_{t+1}(\vec{x}) = \frac{1}{2D} \sum_{\vec{y}} J_{\vec{x}\vec{y}} \, P_t(\vec{y}) \, , \qquad (12.7)$$

where the sum is over all sites, $\frac{1}{2D}$ is the probability that the walker moved in a certain direction, and $J_{\vec{x}\vec{y}}$ equals 1 if $|\vec{x} - \vec{y}| = a$ and 0 otherwise. This recurrence relation is given together with an initial condition, e.g.,

$$P_0(\vec{x}) = \delta_{\vec{x},\vec{0}} = \delta_{x_1,0} \, \delta_{x_2,0} \, .$$

An important step forward in the theoretical understanding of this model can be achieved by introducing the *generating function G* of the probability distribution $P_t(\vec{x})$:

$$G(z, \vec{x}) \equiv \sum_{t=0}^{\infty} z^t \, P_t(\vec{x}) \, , \qquad (12.8)$$

where z is a parameter which changes the weight with which the probabilities at different times contribute to the generating function. When $z = 1$, $G(z, \vec{x})$ is equal to the sum of all $P_t(\vec{x})$ without any weights.

It is straightforward and interesting to derive an equation for $G(z, \vec{x})$. We sum both members of the relation (12.7) over all times, after multiplying them with the weight z^t:

$$\sum_{t=0}^{\infty} z^t \, P_{t+1}(\vec{x}) = \frac{1}{2D} \sum_{\vec{y}} J_{\vec{x}\vec{y}} \sum_{t=0}^{\infty} z^t P_t(\vec{y}) \, ,$$

or,

$$\sum_{t=0}^{\infty} z^t \, P_{t+1}(\vec{x}) = \frac{1}{2D} \sum_{\vec{y}} J_{\vec{x}\vec{y}} \, G(z, \vec{y}) \, .$$

We now substitute the summation index in the term on the left-hand side by setting $\tau = t+1$. The sum for $t = 0, \ldots, \infty$ becomes a sum for $\tau = 1, \ldots, \infty$. Dividing and multiplying by z, we obtain

$$\sum_{\tau=1}^{\infty} z^{\tau-1} P_\tau(\vec{x}) = \frac{1}{z} \sum_{\tau=1}^{\infty} z^\tau P_\tau(\vec{x}) \, .$$

If we now add and subtract a term with $\tau = 0$, we have

$$\frac{1}{z}\left(\sum_{\tau=0}^{\infty} z^\tau P_\tau(\vec{x}) - P_0(\vec{x})\right) = \frac{1}{z}\left(G(z,\vec{x}) - \delta_{x,0}\right) .$$

In other words,

$$\frac{1}{z}\left(G(z,\vec{x}) - \delta_{\vec{x},\vec{0}}\right) = \frac{1}{2D}\sum_{\vec{y}} J_{\vec{x}\vec{y}}\, G(z,\vec{y}) ,$$

or

$$G(z,\vec{x}) - \frac{z}{2D}\sum_{\vec{y}} J_{\vec{x}\vec{y}}\, G(z,\vec{y}) = \delta_{\vec{x},\vec{0}} , \qquad (12.9)$$

which is the *equation for the generating function of random walks.*

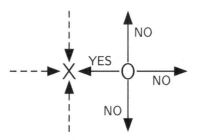

Fig. 12.6   Transition from site O to site X.

In order to obtain more information starting from the relation (12.9), we need some more refined mathematical instruments than the ones used up to now. We briefly introduce these techniques, the *spectral methods*, as they are crucial in many engineering, physical and biological applications. We introduce the *Fourier transform*, as a simple transformation allowing us to retrieve important result. We refer the reader to textbooks like [Morse and Feshbach (1953)] for further details and for a more general discussion on the general implications of these methods. We also discuss how to derive simple and accurate mathematical predictions in the limit of a large number of steps, i.e., at large times t, which we eventually verify numerically.

We define the *discrete Fourier transform* (on an infinite lattice) of the generating function as

$$\widetilde{G}(z,\vec{q}) \equiv \sum_{\vec{x}} e^{i\vec{q}\cdot\vec{x}} G(z,\vec{x}) , \qquad (12.10)$$

where the sum is over all lattice sites, and the argument of the exponential function is the scalar product of the new two-dimensional vector $\vec{q}$ and the position $\vec{x}$ multiplied by the imaginary unit constant i. In other words, we sum the generating function over all lattice sites, with a complex weight which depends on the site. Note that if we define the *inverse Fourier transform* for the infinite lattice as:

$$G(z,\vec{x}) = \left(\frac{a}{2\pi}\right)^D \int_{-\frac{\pi}{a}}^{+\frac{\pi}{a}} dq_1 \ldots \int_{-\frac{\pi}{a}}^{+\frac{\pi}{a}} dq_D \; e^{-i\vec{q}\cdot\vec{x}}\widetilde{G}(z,\vec{q}) \,, \qquad (12.11)$$

we find that it coincides with the function from which we started. We will use this fact during the following derivation, namely that the inverse Fourier transform (which is an integration over the above defined region) annihilates the effect of the Fourier transform (which is the infinite sum defined in (12.10)), thus allowing us to obtain the original function which we started from. As a proof, note that if we use (12.10) at the right-hand side of (12.11), we have

$$\int_{-\frac{\pi}{a}}^{+\frac{\pi}{a}} dq_1 \; e^{-iq_1(x_1-y_1)} = \frac{2\pi}{a}\delta_{x_1 y_1} \,.$$

When x_1 differs from y_1, the contributions of the integration cancel each other out and the integral is simply zero. Only in case $x_1 = y_1$, we integrate the constant 1 over the interval of size $2\pi/a$.

We multiply both members of equation (12.9) by $e^{i\,\vec{q}\cdot\vec{x}}$, and sum over $\vec{x}$. In this way we obtain that

$$\sum_{\vec{x}} e^{i\vec{q}\cdot\vec{x}} \, G(z,\vec{x}) - \frac{z}{2D}\sum_{\vec{x}\vec{y}} J_{\vec{x}\vec{y}} \, e^{i\vec{q}\cdot\vec{x}} \, G(z,\vec{y}) = \sum_{\vec{x}} e^{i\vec{q}\cdot\vec{x}} \, \delta_{\vec{x},\vec{0}} \,.$$

The first term on the left-hand side is the desired function $\widetilde{G}$, while the term on the right-hand side is one. Therefore, we have

$$\widetilde{G}(z,\vec{q}) = \frac{z}{2D}\sum_{\vec{x}\vec{y}} J_{\vec{x}\vec{y}} \, e^{i\vec{q}\cdot\vec{x}} \, G(z,\vec{y}) + 1 \,.$$

We still need to analyze the second term on the left-hand side. We rewrite it by multiplying and dividing it by $e^{i\,\vec{q}\cdot\vec{y}}$:

$$\frac{z}{2D}\sum_{\vec{x}\vec{y}} J_{\vec{x}\vec{y}} \, e^{i\vec{q}\cdot\vec{x}} \, G(z,\vec{y}) = \frac{z}{2D}\sum_{\vec{x}\vec{y}} J_{\vec{x}\vec{y}} \, e^{i\vec{q}\cdot(\vec{x}-\vec{y})} e^{i\vec{q}\cdot\vec{y}} \, G(z,\vec{y}) \,.$$

$J_{\vec{x}\vec{y}}$ is different from zero only if the distance between the two sites is exactly one lattice step, i.e., $|\vec{x} - \vec{y}| = a$. Therefore, for each value of $\vec{y}$, there are exactly two values of $\vec{x}$ in each of the two possible directions which have a nonzero contribution. Using the relation

$$\cos(x) = \frac{e^{ix} + e^{-ix}}{2} \ ,$$

we have that the contribution we want to estimate is

$$\frac{z}{2D} \, \widetilde{G}(z, \vec{q}) \sum_{\alpha=1}^{D} (2 \, \cos(aq_\alpha)) \ .$$

The equation for the generating function becomes

$$\widetilde{G}(z, \vec{q}) - \frac{z}{D} \, \widetilde{G}(z, \vec{q}) \sum_{\alpha=1}^{D} \cos(aq_\alpha) = 1 \ . \tag{12.12}$$

The big progress we made in this way is that it is rather easy to write down a solution for the latter equation. If we define

$$\Phi(\vec{q}) \equiv \frac{1}{D} \sum_{\alpha=1}^{D} \cos(aq_\alpha) \ ,$$

a solution to equation (12.12) is given by

$$\widetilde{G}(z, \vec{q}) = \frac{1}{1 - z \, \Phi(\vec{q})} \ . \tag{12.13}$$

Therefore, in *Fourier space* (i.e., when applying the transformation (12.10)) it is easy to evaluate the generating function of a random walk in an exact way in D dimensions. Obviously the next step then is to find out what happens in the $\vec{x}$ space by means of an inverse transformation.

Many important results can be deduced from expression (12.13). First of all, note that (12.13) is the sum of a geometric sequence, which can formally be expressed as

$$\widetilde{G}(z, \vec{q}) = 1 + z \, \Phi(\vec{q}) + z^2 \, \Phi(\vec{q})^2 + \ ... \ + z^t \, \Phi(\vec{q})^t + \ ...$$

A comparison with the definition (12.8) of the generating function, shows how the Fourier transform of $P_t(x)$ is given by

$$\widetilde{P}_t(\vec{q}) = \Phi(\vec{q})^t = \left(\frac{1}{D} \sum_{\alpha=1}^{D} \cos(aq_\alpha) \right)^t \ .$$

In other words, the Fourier transform of the generating function immediately gives us the Fourier transform of the probability that the walk has reached site $\vec{x}$ at time t. Still, we are interested in the probability itself, and not in its Fourier transform. Therefore, we need to compute

$$P_t(\vec{x}) = \left(\frac{a}{2\pi}\right)^D \int_{-\frac{\pi}{a}}^{+\frac{\pi}{a}} dq_1 \ldots \int_{-\frac{\pi}{a}}^{+\frac{\pi}{a}} dq_D \; e^{-i\vec{q}\cdot\vec{x}} \; \widetilde{P}_t(\vec{q}) \;. \tag{12.14}$$

In the large time limit, it is reasonable to suppose that a walk is composed of many independent random contributions. Therefore, it becomes possible to approximate this expression for large t. For large times t, the terms that contribute the most in the expression $\left(\sum_{\alpha=1}^{D} \cos(aq_\alpha)\right)^t$ are those with small $\vec{q}$. For these terms, we can expand the cosine around 0:

$$\frac{1}{D}\sum_{\alpha=1}^{D} \cos(aq_\alpha) = \frac{1}{D}\left(D - \frac{a^2}{2}\sum_{\alpha=1}^{D} q_\alpha^2\right) + \mathcal{O}\left(|q|^4\right) = 1 - \frac{a^2}{2D}\,|\vec{q}|^2 + \mathcal{O}\left(|q|^4\right) \;,$$

Rewriting the cosine for small values of its argument

$$\left(\frac{1}{D}\sum_{\alpha=1}^{D} \cos(aq_\alpha)\right)^t = \exp\left[t \, \log\left(\frac{1}{D}\sum_{\alpha=1}^{D} \cos(aq_\alpha)\right)\right] \;,$$

we obtain

$$t \, \log\left(\frac{1}{D}\sum_{\alpha=1}^{D} \cos(aq_\alpha)\right) \simeq -\frac{ta^2}{2D}\,|\vec{q}|^2 \;.$$

In the large time limit, the Gaussian nucleus cancels out the contributions far away from the region of small $\vec{q}$. Therefore, we can ignore the limits of integration in (12.14), and find:

$$P_t(\vec{x}) \simeq \left(\frac{a}{2\pi}\right)^D \int_{-\infty}^{+\infty} dq_1 \ldots \int_{-\infty}^{+\infty} dq_D \; e^{-i\vec{q}\cdot\vec{x} - \frac{ta^2}{2D}|\vec{q}|^2} \;.$$

Finally, we still need to compute the D integrals of the kind

$$e^{-t\frac{a^2 w^2}{2D} - i\,xw} dw \;.$$

With the correct normalization, we obtain that in the large time limit

$$P_t(\vec{x}) = \left(\frac{D}{2\pi t}\right)^{\frac{D}{2}} e^{-\frac{D|\vec{x}|^2}{2ta^2}} \;. \tag{12.15}$$

The relation (12.15) expresses the probability that the random walk, starting at site $\vec{0}$ at time $t = 0$, arrives at site $\vec{x}$ at time t. This expression is valid at large times. Only in this limit the probability is invariant under rotations and depends on $\vec{x}^2$ only. At large times, the traveler has explored a region which extends itself linearly with respect to the lattice space.

Given the relation (12.15), it is straightforward to compute the expected value of the squared position at a given large time. We have:

$$\langle x^2(t) \rangle \sim a^2 \frac{t}{D} \,.$$

Just like x^2, the dimensions of the factor a^2 are of a squared length.

Hands on 12.2 - Two-dimensional random walks

Analyze various two-dimensional random walks numerically. First average out the results, and then analyze the corresponding probability distribution. Save $x_1(t)$ and $x_2(t)$ at several chosen time instances (for instance $t = 10$, 100, 1000 and 10 000). Reconstruct $P_t(x_1)$ and find out its functional form. Is it a Gaussian distribution? Verify that for larger times the distribution resembles more and more a Gaussian distribution by comparing it to the expression we have derived in (12.15). Note that in case you consider only one component, the expression needs to be modified accordingly. Use programs allowing us to determine the best interpolation. (For example **gnuplot** allows us to perform a *best fit* with respect to some user-defined function). Also compute the first moments of these distributions from the numerical data. Compare them to those of a Gaussian distribution.

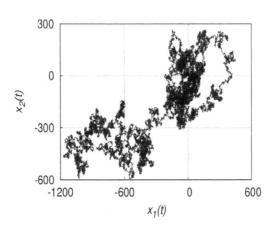

Fig. 12.7 $x_2(t)$ as a function of $x_1(t)$ for a generic two-dimensional random walk trajectory. A million steps of the walker are plotted.

The simulation of a single two-dimensional random walk trajectory is not very different from the one in one dimension.

We define the position vector as a **struct**

```
struct x {
    long int x1, x2;
} position;
```

At a given time, the position is incremented by means of the following statements

```
if (r < 0.25) {
    position.x1 += 1;
} else if (r < 0.5) {
    position.x1 -= 1;
} else if (r < 0.75) {
    position.x2 += 1;
} else {
    position.x2 -= 1;
}
```

where r is a random number uniformly distributed between 0 and 1. Figure 12.7 shows a parametric plot of the x_2- component of the walk in function of the x_1-component. Every black point drawn on the plane corresponds to a different time. For the example in question, we have a million points. The traveler first explored the region where both x_1 and x_2 are positive, he then wandered for a long time around the origin and finally moved into the opposite direction where both x_1 and x_2 are negative. Note that the traveler trajectory seems to cover a two-dimensional surface rather than a one-dimensional curve. Indeed, an important mathematical property of random walks is the fact that they visit a dense region in two dimensions. The property which says that the traveled distance is proportional to the square root of time can be interpreted in two ways. On the one hand, it implies that the walk slowly moves away from the origin. On the other hand, this means that within a given region "many" points are visited. In a time t, the random walk visits t points in a region which contains $\mathcal{O}\left(t^{\frac{D}{2}}\right)$ points. Therefore, for $D \leq 2$ the visited points are dense.

A code which helps to compute the probability distribution $P_t(\vec{x})$ does not represent any additional difficulty with respect to what we discussed so far. For example, we could save the two coordinates at some given time instances to a file. We then need a simple code to compute the corresponding histograms starting from the coordinate values, which are just the normalized probability distributions. For example, we choose to save the data of each time instance which is a power of 10. Performing a total of 10^5 steps (for each random walk) we write the positions at times $t = 10$, 10^2, 10^3, 10^4 and 10^5. The choice of tracking the time in a logarithmic way is often useful as it allows us to study time regions which are quite different. A typical line in the output file could be

```
S 4 T 10000 X1 -12 X2 90
```

where the number following the letter S indicates that this line describes walk number 4, the number which follows the T says we are at time $t = 10\,000$, and the values of the two coordinates at this time are preceded by X1 and X2, respectively. It is handy to save all data into one single file. Using the above illustrated format it is easy to filter the desired data. For example, the command

```
grep "T 99 " datafile.dat
```

selects only those lines of the file which contain information concerning the time $t = 99$. grep is a standard UNIX/Linux program. Also the Windows operating system allows us to build this kind of filters. Writing additional characters on each line requires and occupies disk space. However, subsequent analysis of these data may benefit considerably from such an approach. A second simple program computes the histograms. The probability distribution is found by normalizing them. First, we need to decide the number of intervals that compose the histogram[1]. Then, for each event, i.e., for each registered position at a predetermined time, the counter of the corresponding interval is increased by one. A correct normalization of the histogram, being a probability distribution, requires that its integral is one (and not the discrete sum of possible values). Therefore we need to divide by the size of the interval.

Figure 12.8 shows the probability distribution for the x_1-component of the two-dimensional random walk at various times ($t = 10^3$, 10^4 and 10^5). When considering a single component of the trajectory, the expected probability distribution at large times equals $\sqrt{1/\pi t}\exp(-x_1^2/(ta^2))$. Here and in the following numerical simulations we choose $a = 1$. The points in the figure are the numerical data, while the lines are best fits to a function of the kind $A\exp(Bx^2)$, where A and B are free parameters. The values we obtained for A and B in the best fits correspond to their expectation value at large times, considering a 2 percent error margin. As one can expect, at smaller times the discrepancy between the numerical data and

---

[1] It is good practice to make sure all intervals are reasonably filled.

the theoretical prediction is larger.

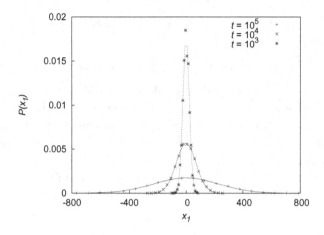

Fig. 12.8 $P(x_1(t))$ as a function of $x_1(t)$ at different times ($t = 10^3$, 10^4 and 10^5). The lines are best fits to the Gaussian behavior expected at large times. The data are averages over 10 000 instances of the random walk.

Figure 12.9 illustrates the complete probability distribution $P_t(x_1, x_2)$ as a function of x_1 and x_2. The continuous grid is the expected theoretical result (equation (12.15)). The vertical lines that end with a circle reflect the results of the numerical simulation. This histogram, based on the numerical data, needs to be normalized correctly. Note that the normalization constant in this case is different from the one used in case of, for example, $P_t(x_1)$. We chose to represent only the data at time $t = 10^5$. The results are averages over 10 000 histories of the traveler motion. The numerical analysis corresponds well to the theoretical prediction.

Hands on 12.3 - Random walks in continuous space

An important property of the behavior of random walks (which is valid for example for the relation $\langle x^2 \rangle \sim t$) is the *universality*, i.e., the same property is valid for random walks based on very different rules (in two or three dimensions, on a square or triangular lattice, and so on).

So far we only discussed random walks on a lattice. The random walk in continuous space is interesting to study as well as it has the same universal properties. In D dimensions (for example two or three) the position may assume arbitrary values and changes according to the following equation:

$$\vec{x}_{t+1} = \vec{x}_t + \delta\vec{x} \,,$$

where $\delta\vec{x}$ is a random variable, for which the following relation for its D components are valid:

$$\langle \delta x_\alpha \rangle = 0 \,, \quad \langle \delta x_\alpha \, \delta x_\beta \rangle = \epsilon^2 \, \delta_{\alpha\beta} \,,$$

for $\alpha, \beta = 1, ..., D$ and the values of all δx_α at different times are uncorrelated. A typical choice as to how to generate δx_α is by extracting a uniformly distributed number between zero and one, subtract a half from it and multiply it by an adequate constant (as part of the exercise, decide which constant).

Study this random motion numerically and determine its properties. First of all, verify the validity of the relation $\langle x^2 \rangle \sim t$.

Hands on 12.4 - Return probability and self-avoiding walks

 Study a three-dimensional random walk on a simple cubic lattice (for which every site has six nearest neighbors). Measure the various relevant characteristics, such as the distance traveled at time t, computing the corresponding statistical error.

Next, determine the probability that the traveler returns to the site where she started her walk. One possible approach to solve this problem is to choose a maximum testing time and compute how often the traveler does not return to the origin in this time window. Next, change the maximum testing time and determine the desired result asymptotically.

Consider a *Self-Avoiding Walk (SAW)* on a three-dimensional simple cubic lattice, i.e., a walk starts from the origin and never intersects with itself. A site which was already visited by the traveler once, cannot be crossed any more. To study this problem, we need to save the traveler trajectory in memory.

Note that there exists a strictly positive probability that the traveler gets blocked and can no longer move. This happens when the traveler arrives at a site whose neighboring sites have all been visited before. Considering various SAWs, compute for example the probability that she gets trapped at various times.

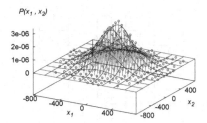

Fig. 12.9 $P(x_1(t), x_2(t))$ as a function of $(x_1(t), x_2(t))$ at $t = 10^5$. The vertical lines ending in a circle represent numerical data, while the continuous grid represents the mathematical result we obtain in the large time limit.

12.3   A lattice gas

A first extension to the study of random processes, which is more interesting though still extremely simple, is a lattice gas of free particles. Variations of this model have given rise to a major research area. For instance, the continuous hydrodynamic equations which are used in meteorologic prediction models and in car and airplane design are very complex. Approximating them by relations defined on a lattice, of which the lattice gas model discussed in this section is the starting point, leads to remarkable results.

Consider a a two-dimensional square lattice, i.e., $D = 2$. A fraction ρ of the lattice sites are occupied by particles. For now we consider the case where each site is occupied by a particle with probability ρ. The total number of sites of the lattice is V. In two dimensions, we have $V = L^2$, where L is the number of sites in one dimension.

Initially, the particles are randomly distributed on the lattice. In this case, the lattice gas density itself is a random variable, determined by the distribution of the particles on the lattice. The dynamics we study here does not alter the density. Another possible approach is to first fix the number of particles on the lattice ($N = \rho\,V$) and then distribute them randomly among the sites, taking the following *exclusion principle* into account: if a site is already occupied by a particle, it cannot be occupied by a second one. The particles are numbered, i.e., they are characterized by a label, and during the dynamics they keep this original label. A typical example is given in Figure 12.10.

The problem can be defined in terms of *occupation variables* η_{x_1,x_2} which can assume values 0 and 1: $\eta_{x_1,x_2} = 0$ says that site (x_1, x_2) is unoccupied, while $\eta_{x_1,x_2} = 1$ says the site is occupied. Note that the case in which

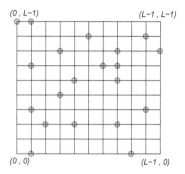

Fig. 12.10   A lattice gas of density $\rho = 0.2$. $D = 2$, $L = 10$ and $V = L^2 = 100$.

the variables take on values $+1$ or -1, i.e., $\sigma_{x_1,x_2} = \pm 1$, is equivalent. Due to the analogy with a two-state magnetic system, these variables are often referred to as *spin variables*. It is straightforward to verify that the transformation $\sigma_{x_1,x_2} = 2\,\eta_{x_1,x_2} - 1$ links σ_{x_1,x_2} to η_{x_1,x_2}.

The lattice we consider has *periodic boundary conditions*: a particle leaving the lattice on the right side border, reappears at the border on the left, one that leaves it on top, enters the lattice back at the bottom. In other words, the site with coordinates (i,j) is identical to the sites with coordinates $(i \pm L, j)$, $(i, j \pm L)$, $(i \pm L, j \pm L)$ and so on.

The dynamics which we are about to define conserves the particle density. Since the particles can only move to an adjacent empty site, and they are not allowed to disappear or reappear, the total number of particles

$$N = \sum_{x_1,x_2} \eta_{x_1,x_2}$$

remains invariant.

A time step is defined by various actions. First, randomly pick a particle. We already know how to do this, namely, we need a uniformly distributed integer random number between 1 and N. At this point, independently of whether the particle is eventually moved or not, we increase the elapsed time by one unit. Next, we randomly select one of the 4 nearest neighbors of the site occupied by the particle in question. If this neighboring site is empty, the particle moves onto this new site, otherwise a new step starts.

The squared distance the particle α has traveled can be expressed in function of its coordinates as

$$\Delta R_\alpha^{(2)}(t) \equiv (x_1^\alpha(t) - x_1^\alpha(0))^2 + (x_2^\alpha(t) - x_2^\alpha(0))^2 \ .$$

Considering the average with respect to the positions of the N particles, the *mean square distance* of the system is defined as

$$\Delta R^{(2)}(t) \equiv \frac{1}{N} \sum_{\alpha=0}^{N-1} \Delta R_\alpha^{(2)}(t) \ . \tag{12.16}$$

Note a first technical problem with the definition of the mean square distance (12.16). A direct application of (12.16) is not appropriate when periodic boundary conditions are used. Suppose a particle leaves at time zero from site $(0,0)$, and at the first step moves in the $-\hat{x}$-direction, thus reaching site $(L-1,0)$. In this particular case, the displacement of one lattice step appears to be of $L-1$ steps instead! In order to avoid this type of problem, we should keep track of two types of lattice positions. A first type which refers to the position on the basic lattice defined with its periodic boundary conditions, and a second type which does not take the latter into account, but simply increase or decrease by $+1$ if a displacement in the positive or negative direction, respectively, occurred. The latter type of positions are used in (12.16), while the former type are used to verify at each step whether a particle neighboring sites are occupied or not.

The most important quantity characterizing the system (diffusive) behavior is the *diffusion coefficient*, defined as

$$\mathcal{D}(\rho) = \lim_{t\to\infty} \mathcal{D}(\rho, t) = \lim_{t\to\infty} \frac{1}{2Dt} \left\langle \Delta R^{(2)}(t) \right\rangle \ , \tag{12.17}$$

where the expected value is computed by averaging over several histories of the system motion. Each time the system is reinitialized and the dynamics takes place starting at time zero up to a time which is large enough to allow an accurate prediction of the limit in (12.17). The diffusion velocity decreases with increasing density as in this case it becomes more and more difficult for the particles to move around. Obviously, a fully occupied lattice is completely blocked, while a single particle on a lattice behaves at each step exactly like a normal random walk. Note that also for the dynamics of a lattice gas, the square distance divided by a time asymptotically tends to a constant: this fact is the most important property of random walks.

Hands on 12.5 - The diffusion coefficient

Compute the diffusion coefficient $\mathcal{D}(\rho)$ for $\rho = 0.2$, 0.4, 0.6 and 0.8. Repeat the same computation for lattices of different sizes (for example with $L = 10$, 20, 40 and 80) and verify that for larger lattice volumes the results are independent from the volume. The computation has to be performed in the region where $\langle \Delta R_\alpha^{(2)}(t) \rangle^{\frac{1}{2}} < \frac{L}{2}$, as finite size effects may occur in the region where the square root of the mean square displacement becomes of the order of the size of the lattice. However, the finite size effects on this lattice are rather limited: try to quantify them. How does $\mathcal{D}(\rho)$ depend on ρ?

Study a two-dimensional triangular lattice, with connectivity six (each site has six nearest neighbors). How does this case differ from the previous one?

The code simulating a lattice gas is probably a bit more complicated with respect to the ones we have dealt with so far. This is a good reason to subdivide it into several functions. The prototypes of the functions we use are:

```
double myInit(void);
long int initLattice(double rho);
void updateLattice(long int thisNumberOfParticles);
double measure(long int thisNumberOfParticles);
void myEnd(double averageRho);
```

The function `myInit` is called one time when the execution starts. It carries out the necessary initialization procedures. For example, it opens the output files, which are controlled by some global variables. Further on, we discuss how to identify the nearest neighboring sites in an efficient way, and how to efficiently initialize an array. The function `initLattice` is called each time the lattice is initialized to extract a new initial configuration, simulate its dynamics and extract the corresponding sample properties which allows us to evaluate the corresponding averages and their statistical errors. The function `updateLattice` is the motor of the program. It lets the time increase by one unit, during which we try to move a particle. The total number of times we try to do this is equal to the number of particles in the lattice. The function `measure` computes the relevant quantities (in our case this is the mean square distance) for which we then compute the averages. The function `myEnd` performs operations which need to be executed only once at the end of the code (for example, normalize average values, calculate their errors and close open files). The more important arrays we choose to use are

```
long int particleOfSite[L][L];
long int positionOfParticle[VOLUME][DIM];
long int truePositionOfParticle[VOLUME][DIM];
long int zeroPositionOfParticle[VOLUME][DIM];
```

where `DIM` is the spatial dimension of the system, which in our case is 2. We are defining a double link between particles and sites: each particle is linked to a site and each site is linked to a particle. When a particle moves from one site to another, we need to adjust the vector containing the particle coordinates, and the two arrays indicating which particle was at the old site and which one is at the new site. The array `particleOfSite[x][y]` keeps track of the label of the particle that occupies the site with coordinates `x` and `y` at a given time. If the corresponding site is empty, it is given the value `MY_EMPTY`. We use three vectors for the particles positions: `zeroPositionOfParticle[VOLUME][DIM]` contains the position at time zero, `positionOfParticle[VOLUME][DIM]` keeps track of the position at the current time (taking the periodic boundary conditions into account, i.e., these coordinates have values from 0 up to $L - 1$, and a particle leaving the lattice, reappears at the opposite side of the lattice), and `truePositionOfParticle[VOLUME][DIM]` which keeps track of the "absolute" position obtained by neglecting the periodic boundary condition and used to compute the mean square displacement. The average values at various time instances calculated together with their respective statistical errors are kept in two arrays. We do not calculate the expected values at all times, but only at some selected time instances. To this end, we define the following two arrays

```
double averageDeltaR2[NUM_MEASUREMENTS];
double errorDeltaR2[NUM_MEASUREMENTS];
```

The constant `NUM_MEASUREMENTS` is defined as following

```
#define NUM_SWEEPS 1000
#define NUM_MEASUREMENTS 100
#define MEASUREMENT_PERIOD (NUM_SWEEPS / NUM_MEASUREMENTS)
```

In this way the total number of steps is guaranteed to be a multiple of the number of measurements. In the function `init` we include

```
if ((NUM_MEASUREMENTS * MEASUREMENT_PERIOD) != NUM_SWEEPS) {
  printf("Error: number of steps is not a multiple\n");
  printf("       of number of measurements\n");
  exit(MY_EXIT_FAILURE);
}
```

The measurements therefore only takes place after every MEASUREMENT_PERIOD time steps. After calling the function updateLattice in the main function, we write

```
if ((sweep % MEASUREMENT_PERIOD) == 0) {
   double deltaR2 = measure(trueN);
}
```

where trueN contains the exact number of particles composing the considered sample. The function measure computes and returns the mean square displacement at the considered time. The omitted code includes the update of the averages and the errors.

In a code which is slightly more complex than the ones we considered so far, it is useful to include and maintain some lines of code which verify its internal coherency. These are pieces of code which do not need to be executed in case we are sure everything works fine, but which help to identify incoherences or signs of programming errors. They prove to be very useful when changing the code in order to generalize it or to include other functions. However, the coherence checks slow down the execution of the code. A good possible solution to this dilemma is based on using the *preprocessor* of the C language, discussed in Section 3.5. In this way certain lines of code are only conditionally included depending on whether a certain constant has been defined or not. By including at the beginning of our C code,

```
#define MY_DEBUG
```

we define a constant MY_DEBUG to which we do not attribute a specific value. The important thing is to define and include it in our program dictionary. For example, in the function main, we write

```
#ifdef MY_DEBUG
if (numMeasure >= NUM_MEASUREMENTS) {
   printf("Error: numMeasure too large\n");
   exit(MY_EXIT_FAILURE);
}
#endif
averageDeltaR2[numMeasure] += deltaR2;
```

This stops the execution of the program with a message and an error code if numMeasure (a counter of the actually performed number of measurements) is too large. We know that if the program is correct this error should not occur as numMeasure cannot get to NUM_MEASUREMENTS. When writing or improving the program, we want to verify this condition to check whether we did not introduce any errors (e.g., logic or typographical) in the program. Program *debugging*, i.e, locating these errors, is a crucial aspect of programming. At the end of the debugging, we can simply remove the line which defines the variable `MY_DEBUG`, or add a line which cancels out its definition:

```
#define MY_DEBUG
#undef MY_DEBUG
```

The `myInit` manages (one single time, at the beginning) the *periodic boundary conditions*. Usually the nearest neighbor in the $+\hat{x}$-direction of the site with coordinates (x, y) has coordinates $(x + 1, y)$. However, for the site with coordinates $(L-1, y)$ this becomes the site with coordinates $(0, y)$. Managing this problem with `if` statements is extremely inefficient as it requires many operations for each site. A good solution consists in defining two vectors `plusNeighbor[L]` and `minusNeighbor[L]`, of type `long int`, which are initialized by the following statements

```
for (i = 0; i < L; i++) {
  plusNeighbor[i] = i + 1;
  minusNeighbor[i] = i - 1;
}
plusNeighbor[L - 1] = 0;
minusNeighbor[0] = L - 1;
```

Now, the neighbor of (x, y) in the $+\hat{x}$-direction has coordinates (`plusNeighbor[x]`,`y`).

The code defining the particles initial configuration is executed in `initLattice`, each time a new sample is started. After the vectors have been initialized to `MY_EMPTY`, the following lines of code are executed:

```
trueN = 0;
for (x = 0; x < L; x++) {
  for (y = 0; y < L; y++) {
    randomNumber = a * randomNumber;
    r = (double)randomNumber * iDoubleM;
    if (r < rho) {
      particleOfSite[x][y] = trueN;
      positionOfParticle[trueN][0] = x;
      positionOfParticle[trueN][1] = y;
      zeroPositionOfParticle[trueN][0] = x;
      zeroPositionOfParticle[trueN][1] = y;
      truePositionOfParticle[trueN][0] = x;
      truePositionOfParticle[trueN][1] = y;
      trueN++;
    }
  }
}
```

The function creates samples of variable density which on average is equal to ρ. `trueN` is the actual number of particles of the sample under consideration, and thus varies from sample to sample. A function initializing the configuration while keeping the number of particles fixed would be different. It is a good exercise for the reader to write such a function.

The earth of the updating procedure is contained in `updateLattice`, which manages the updates of the particles positions. First, one of the `trueN` particles is randomly chosen with a uniform probability and the time is increased by one unit, independently of whether a change in the particle position will occur. Then, after a possible direction in which the particle could move has been chosen (for example, if `thisDirection` equals 0 we move in the positive direction of the x-axis), we write

```
if (particleOfSite[nX][nY] == MY_EMPTY) {
  particleOfSite[nX][nY] = particleOfSite[x][y];
  particleOfSite[x][y] = MY_EMPTY;
  positionOfParticle[thisParticle][0] = nX;
  positionOfParticle[thisParticle][1] = nY;
  if (thisDirection == 0) {
    truePositionOfParticle[thisParticle][0]++;
  } else if (thisDirection == 1) {
    truePositionOfParticle[thisParticle][0]--;
  } else if (thisDirection == 2) {
    truePositionOfParticle[thisParticle][1]++;
  } else if (thisDirection == 3) {
    truePositionOfParticle[thisParticle][1]--;
  }
}
```

If the randomly chosen neighbor (`nX` stands for *neighbor x*) is empty, the particle moves to this neighboring site, and the previous site it occupied is emptied. Correspondingly, we update the particle position vectors, both the one which does as the one taking periodic boundary conditions into account as the one which does not.

Let us analyze the results one obtains with this code. Figure 12.11 shows the diffusion coefficient $\mathcal{D}(\rho, t)$ (defined in (12.17)) as a function of time t for several values of the density ρ. These data were obtained for $L = 80$ and a density which varies from 0.1 up to 0.9 at steps of 0.1. $\mathcal{D}(\rho, t)$ monotonously decreases with ρ. As expected, $\mathcal{D}(\rho, t)$ tends to a constant at large times. Instead, at smaller times there is a systematic variation, that can already be seen on the scale used in the figure. It is worth focusing on the behavior occurring at smaller times: this allows us to get a better understanding of the convergence of the diffusion constant.

Figure 12.11 is the result for a system with $L = 80$, i.e, a volume composed of 6400 sites organized on a two-dimensional square lattice with

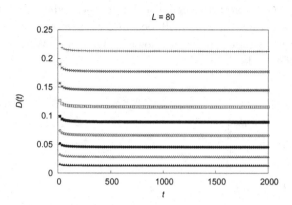

Fig. 12.11   The diffusion coefficient $\mathcal{D}(\rho, t)$ as a function of time t. $L = 80$ and $V = L^2 = 6400$. The larger coefficients correspond to the systems with lower density (from top to bottom: $\rho = 0.1$, 0.2, 0.3 up to 0.9, at steps of 0.1).

periodic boundary conditions. Why did we chose $L = 80$? Before opting for this choice, we studied various lattice sizes to ensure *finite size errors* were under control. Namely, the fact that we are dealing with a lattice of finite size brings about that the estimate for the coefficient depends on L. Only in the limit $L \to \infty$, we obtain the result typical of an infinite volume (which is the one we are interested in). In Figure 12.12 we show the diffusion coefficient $\mathcal{D}(\rho, t)$ as a function of time t for $\rho = 0.6$, computed on lattices of size $L = 10$, 20, 40 and 80. There is a 3 percent difference between the value obtained on a lattice composed of 100 sites and the correct one! Also the value obtained on a lattice with $L = 20$ is visibly different from the asymptotic value, while the values obtained on lattices with either $L = 40$ or $L = 80$ coincide (considering our statistical precision). This indicates that by using the lattices of this size we have reached a sufficient systematic precision. Note that this systematic precision is strictly related to the statistical precision of our numerical quantities. Therefore, it is useless to set one of these uncertainties a lot smaller than the other. Also note that the numerical results obtained for a lattice of a particular size can never provide us with any indications on how precise these results are. The precision can only be deduced by observing how the numerical results change when changing the size. Finite size effects are analyzed by comparing several lattice sizes and checking the behavior of the measured quantities as L increases. Finally, the scale used in Figure 12.12 allows us to observe a small remnant drift, indicating that the system has not yet fully reached the asymptotic regime at large times, where $\mathcal{D}(\rho, t)$ no longer depends on the time t. This drift becomes even more obvious on a plot where the time is represented on a logarithmic scale. We leave this as an exercise to the reader.

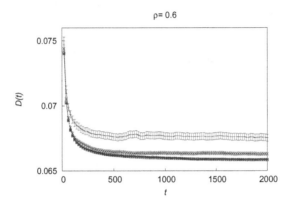

Fig. 12.12   The diffusion coefficient $\mathcal{D}(\rho, t)$ as a function of time t, for $\rho = 0.6$. The series of points from top to bottom correspond to lattices of size $L = 10$, $L = 20$, $L = 40$ and $L = 80$, where the latter two essentially overlap each other (the finite size effects are negligible).

Figure 12.11 shows how the diffusion coefficient decreases monotonously as a function of the density ρ, for each value of t. This is rather intuitive: when few particles are present on the lattice, it should be easier for them to move around. Instead, if many particles are present, often a nearest neighboring site will be occupied and therefore the particles are expected to move less. To study the behavior of $\mathcal{D}(\rho)$, we select those numerical data that have reached the asymptotic regime. Another more accurate, but also more complex approach consists in extrapolating the desired data at finite times using an appropriate functional form. We here avoid this more complicated approach as we assume to have gathered enough evidence that the asymptotic regime has indeed been reached. The data of Figure 12.13 are the result of an averaging procedure over times ranging form $16\,000$ up to $20\,000$, where each time step or unit consists in $\rho\,V$, i.e., `trueN`, attempts of moving a randomly chosen particle. This time scale is clearly larger than the one reported in Figure 12.11 and 12.12, in which we were mainly considered with demonstrating the existence of a transient phase. Figure 12.13 illustrates the behavior of the diffusion coefficient computed in this way, as a function of the density ρ.

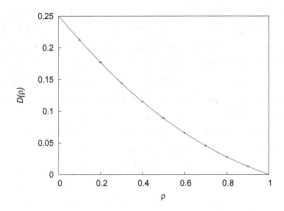

Fig. 12.13 The diffusion coefficient $\mathcal{D}(\rho)$ as a function of the density ρ, computed in the infinite time limit.

Which function describes the behavior of the data in Figure 12.13 in function of ρ analytically? A first, too simple attempt could be a linear behavior of $\mathcal{D}(\rho)$ in function of $(1 - \rho)$. Indeed, as a first approximation, increasing the density causes a decrease in the mean displacement of a particle at a given time step, thus effectively reducing a lattice step from a to $(1 - \rho)a$. This is a reasonable first approximation, given that a single particle on a lattice moves a distance a, while a particle with on average two neighbors moves on average one out of two times, i.e., a distance $\frac{a}{2}$.

However, this does not cover all aspects of the dynamics. Let us consider a rather dense system. A particle residing in a region with lower density (with respect to the average density), has a higher probability to remain there rather than moving to a denser region. There is a strong *correlation* correcting the first linear approximation. Namely, there exists a secondary effect connected to the case when two particles are close to each other, which must be dependent on ρ squared, or better on a term $(1 - \rho)^2$. The continuous curve in Figure 12.13 is a best fit to a functional form with four free parameters (two multiplicative factors and two powers of $(1 - \rho)$). We find two very similar coefficients close to the value $\frac{1}{8}$, an exponent close to 1 and another one close to 2: this is fully consistent with our previous reasoning.

12.4   Random walks in random environments

We now discuss how an apparently small modification to the problem of the drunk traveler actually changes all its main properties. For simplicity, we define the new problem on a one-dimensional discretized lattice. During one discrete time step, the walker no longer moves with equal probability, $p = \frac{1}{2}$, in the leftward or rightward direction. Rather, at each site he moves to the right with a given probability Π_x: Π_x is a value that depends on the site x and does not change in time. Correspondingly, the walker moves to the left with a probability $1 - \Pi_x$ [Sinai (1982)], [Marinari *et al.* (1983)]. We can consider *the drunk walker to travel in the mountains*, though it is not quite just a simple matter of climbing and descending. A difficult rightward step, i.e., a case in which the probability to go from site x to site $x + 1$ is small, could also be difficult in the leftward direction, i.e, the probability to go from site $x + 1$ to site x. Indeed, the latter probability is independent of the probability to go from site x to site $x + 1$, and could also be small. This problem describes a situation where the factors causing difficulties to move in one direction are independent of those which aggravate the motion in the opposite direction. For example, the difficulty with which you climb the steps of a mountain trail could be due to the height of these steps, while the difficulty with which you move downhill can be independent of the height, but rather depend on whether the soil is slippery, whether your foot can get a good grip on the soil or on the size of the rocks on which you walk. For the reader who does not appreciate the above example, we refer them to a more expert *mountaineering* friend. Actually, in the mountains one usually does not get trapped this way. However, let us not forget that our traveler is and remains drunk.

Mathematically speaking, we consider a dynamical rule such that for each site x a fixed probability has been given beforehand, thus defining the random environment. The fact that this probability does not undergo any changes in time is fundamental (we are dealing with a so-called *quenched disorder*), and determines the system properties. The relation (12.1) now becomes

$$P\,(\text{right}) = \Pi_x = P\,(\text{displacement} = \ +1) \ ,$$
$$P\,(\text{left}) = (1 - \Pi_x) = P\,(\text{displacement} = \ -1) \ , \qquad (12.18)$$

where Π_x is a new uniformly distributed random variable between zero and one. The new problem includes two different sources of random noise. The first one, of the *thermal* kind, generates a random walk and was in fact already considered in the simple random walk. The second is a source of frozen noise, which creates a non-homogeneous environment (the various sites of the chain). Thus, for a generic observable O we now have to define two types of averages. The usual one is taken with respect to the thermal noise (consider the walker to make several walks starting from the same point in a fixed environment), and we indicate it with $\langle O \rangle$ as before. A new average involves the study of the motion in *various environments* and is noted as $\overline{O}$.

The transition probabilities Π_x linked to each site need to be determined *before* starting a simulation of the dynamics: this needs to be done for each instance which contributes to the *average of the disorder, $\overline{O}$*. The Π_x do not change during a given walk, i.e, when the walker returns to the site x the probability to go right is always Π_x and the one to go to the left is always $1 - \Pi_x$. In other words, the points of the random landscape causing a slowing down of the motion do not change in time and the situation cannot improve: this is a very crucial issue. The fact that disordered traps do not move with time applies to many engineering applications. The random motion in a random environment is a lot slower than the usual random walk (which in turn is slower than a deterministic walk). Indeed, the mean squared distance traveled by a random walker in a random environment, as defined by (12.18), only grows logarithmically with time [Sinai (1982)]:

$$\overline{\langle x^2(t) \rangle} \sim (\log t)^4 . \tag{12.19}$$

Note that the average can also be computed by considering one single motion per random environment.

The mechanism causing the slowdown is due to the presence of *traps* which cannot disappear over time. The environmental disorder is frozen and is independent of the thermal motion. The presence of very deep traps causes the logarithmic slowdowns. Let us have a look at some examples. A simple trap could be $\Pi_x = 0.9 = 1 - \Pi_{x+1}$, where the traveler moves away from the sites x and $x + 1$ only after a certain amount of time (of order ten). This situation is illustrated on top in Figure 12.14. The traveler can encounter even more profound traps than this one. The drawing on the bottom of Figure 12.14 illustrates a trap where $P_{x-1} = P_x = 1 - P_{x+1} = 1 - P_{x+2} = 0.9$. Even if the traveler leaves the most internal trap with a small probability, at a higher level of the trap he moves back down with high probability. These kinds of traps can be very large. They occur with a probability that decreases for traps of growing size, buts stays different from zero. As time passes, the traveler encounters traps of growing size where he spends more and more time; the traveler spends almost all his time in a trap.

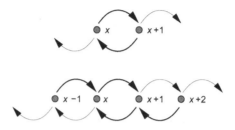

Fig. 12.14 On top, a simple trap. On the bottom, a double trap. The thick arrows represent a high probability to move in that direction (in the text example 0.9), while the thin lines represent a low value (in the example 0.1).

Hands on 12.6 - The random walk in a random environment

Verify the properties of a random walk in a random environment. Compute the value of $\overline{\langle x^2(t)\rangle}$ and verify the relation (12.19). Plot a few single trajectories and compare them to those of the simple random walk. Are there any obvious differences? Are you able to explain them based on the previous arguments, and to relate them to the asymptotic behavior of $\overline{\langle x^2(t)\rangle}$?

The code simulating a random walk in a random environment is very similar to the one we used to study the simple random walk. It requires the introduction of a new array containing the probability that the walker moves, say rightward, at a give site. To compute the average over the disorder we need to study several outcomes of this probability. Every time we study a new sample this new array needs to be initialized with new random numbers. The corresponding outcome for this sample is then used to compute the average over the environmental disorder. The traveler must not leave the array. This can be guaranteed by either dynamically reserving new memory in case the traveler reaches the pre-set boundary of the lattice, or by defining a distance at which the program execution is stopped. Given the fact that the motion is very slow, the traveler never moves very far away from the origin and defining such a maximum distance at which the code stops with an error message is safe. However, we need to define this maximum distance large enough to avoid running into an error, in which case we need to start all over. It is not allowed to just neglect the cases in which the walker moves farther away than usual. This would lead to systematic discrepancies.

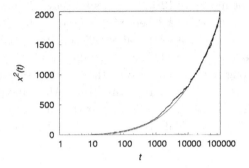

Fig. 12.15 $\overline{x^2(t)}$ as a function of t: average over 1000 environmental disorder samples. The x-axis is in logarithmic scale, the y-axis is in linear scale.

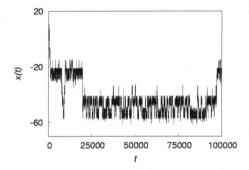

Fig. 12.16 $\overline{x(t)}$ as a function of t for a specific environmental disorder, in linear scale.

In Figure 12.15 we show $\overline{x^2(t)}$ as a function of t, where the average is taken over 1000 samples with different environmental disorder. For each sample of the transition probabilities we considered one single dynamical history. The x-axis is in logarithmic scale, the y-axis in linear scale. In this scale the theoretically predicted behavior is a power law with exponent four. The jagged curve is obtained by joining the numerical data. In order to allow for a clear comparison with the theoretical prediction, we omitted the statistical error. The regular curve is a best fit to the functional form $A \log(t)^4$, with free parameter A. After a few steps the agreement between the theoretical curve and the numerical data is already excellent.

It is interesting to also observe the dynamics of a single trajectory. We show a typical one in Figure 12.16. The walker leaves from 0, and soon gets trapped close to $x \simeq -25$. A brief excursion down to $x \simeq -50$ is rapidly absorbed again, but after a while (about 20 000 steps) the walker returns to the trap close to $x \simeq -50$. This is a bimodal trap, with a third attractor which is less strong than the other two: the traveler oscillates between two points which are sub-valleys of the same trap. After about 100 000 steps, at the end of the time window, the traveler returns back to the first trap. This *memory* effect is particularly interesting and is of great importance in the study of complex systems.

Chapter 13

Lists, dictionaries and percolation

The black 99 had been a *nozoki*: it aimed to the
center of the white triangle. The whites, with the
100, connected.

Yasunari Kawabata, *The Master of Go* (1954).

In this chapter we discuss different types of data structures, and some applications. We introduce a new C construct, namely the **union**, and we discuss linked *lists*. These data structures are very simple, but they fundamental in many contexts. We discuss how to build a simple dictionary with lists, suggesting how to lexically analyze a text. To this end we introduce doubly linked lists, which we can easily scroll through in both directions.

We define the concept of *recursivity*, and we apply to the *factorial*, and to a the design of a *tree* (in order to efficiently manage data). A useful application in various scientific and engineering contexts is the *reconstruction of connected components of a cluster*. After introducing an elementary algorithm that can do this, we use the lists to improve the code. These algorithms allow us to study the problem of *percolation*.

13.1 The union

A **union** is a type of C variable, which at different times, during execution, can contain elements of different types. This might seem incompatible with the paradigm we usually adopt, namely that a variable is of a well-defined given type, and that each environment knows which type it has to expect and return. A strict control of the used types (even in a simple multiplication) helps to avoid programming errors. Nevertheless, as we discuss in the following, there are some situations in which this flexibility is useful. In these cases the union construct is essential.

The syntax of a union is very similar to the one of a struct, though the object defined in this way is very different. Let us define a union of the chameleon type (as a chameleon easily changes color depending on its needs of the moment). We also define two instances of this union type, say theChameleonJohn and theChameleonMary, thus allocating the memory required to store them:

```
union chameleon{
    double green;
    int red;
    char yellow;
} theChameleonJohn , theChameleonMary;
```

Knowing that the double type takes eight bytes, the int type four bytes and the char type just one byte, each union of the chameleon type allocates eight bytes. Indeed, a union allocates the space necessary to store its largest possible member. Contrary to the case of a struct, in which a memory location is allocated to each one of its components, a single memory location, large enough to contain any member of the union, is allocated. The variables theChameleonJohn and theChameleonMary can contain, at different times during the execution, variables of the double, int or char type. As for the struct we refer to the members of a union by writing something like *name_ union.name_ element*, as in theChameleonMary.red.

At a given time, the type of a union is the one of the last piece of data it has been assigned. The program does not have any information on this type, and it is the programmer task to keep track of this (obviously an error could have catastrophic consequences). One possible way out is to define an associated variable which is updated each time the union is. For example, let us define the constants

```
#define GREEN 0
#define RED 1
#define YELLOW 2
```

and a new variable for each union we defined

```
int colorOfTheChameleonJohn , colorOfTheChameleonMary;
```

When we change the union we should always remember to update the associated variable as well, as in

```
theChameleonJohn.green = 256.32;
```

```
colorOfTheChameleonJohn = GREEN;
```

or, in case of an integer,

```
theChameleonJohn.red = 25632;
colorOfTheChameleonJohn = RED;
```

From the value of `colorOfTheChameleonJohn` we always know the type of value stored in the `union`. If, after the above statement has been executed, we would assume that the `union chameleon theChameleonJohn` contains a variable of the `double` type, we would probably run into a disaster. The allowed `union` operations and the ways of accessing its components are the same as for the `struct`. Moreover, it is possible to define `structs` or arrays of `unions`. The `union` construct is not used very often. We quote three cases in which they can be very useful.

(1) Sometimes we need to align short words (for example variables of the `char` type) delimiting long words (for example of the `long int` type). In this case an array of `unions` can be the most efficient solution.

(2) An `unions` can be useful to initialize different parts of a large word (consisting, for example, of eight bytes) with variables of shorter sizes (consisting, for example, of a single byte).

(3) Sometimes, we might need to communicate an object whose type might depend on the context. For example, depending on the result obtained in a function, the function return value might either be a variable of the `float` type or a variable of the `int` type.

Hands on 13.1 - A safe factorial and its logarithm.

The result of a factorial $n!$ can be represented as an integer variable of 64 bits only if $n \leq 20$. Write a function that returns a value of the `unsigned long long int` type containing the factorial, when called with an argument $n \leq 20$, while for $n > 20$ it returns a value of the `double` type containing the factorial logarithm obtained by using the Stirling approximation:

$$n! \simeq \sqrt{2\pi}\, n^{n+\frac{1}{2}}\, e^{-n}\,.$$

The function, returning a `union`, should be used by considering these two possibilities.

13.1.1 *A virtual experiment*

We now discuss a typical situation in which the `union` construct is particularly useful. We consider the *on-line* analysis of the results of an experiment. Often a computer is connected by means of an appropriate hardware interface to an experimental instrument collecting data. Here, we obviously limit ourselves to a simulation of an experiment and we analyze the random results that our code generates. Still, the procedure we show is the same when we want to check a real experiment.

For example, think of a detector measuring what happens to a particle traveling through a physical medium. We start from the hypothesis that one out of three possible situations occur in each one of our measurements. In the first case the particle travels in the medium without creating any other particle. In this case, the variable we want to measure and analyze is the particle speed. Correspondingly, the device returns a `double` value. In the second case the particle strongly interacts with the medium, and generates a swarm of particles. In this case, the device cannot measure the particles velocities, but rather counts their number and returns a value of the `int` type. In the third case, an error occurs. This is a rare case which nevertheless might occur. The error might have several causes: the detector electrical components possibly responded too slowly, the particle interaction occurred too close to the border of the material (i.e, outside the "confidence zone"), an error occurred in the memory of the device. In these cases we only want to write an error message on screen to notify the researcher performing the experiment. This error message, i.e., a character string, is produced directly by the device. In this situation the hardware interface returns a variable of the `double` or `int` type or a series of characters. Therefore, a `union` is the ideal data structure to manage these different cases when calling this function.

The relevant code for this operation is easy and compact, while the overall code simulating the experiment and randomly deciding which results to return is still easy, but a bit long. Therefore, we only describe the essential features and do not discuss it in detail.

The type of `union` we need is

```
union experimentData {
    double speed;
    int num;
    char *errorMessage;
};
```

The code simulating the experiment is of the form of the one given in Listing 13.1.

```
1 int main(void) {
2   int experimentOutput = 1;
3   int experimentNumber = 0;
4
5   srand(MY_SEED);
6   while (experimentOutput < 4) {
7     union experimentData scratchData;
8     experimentNumber++;
9     experimentOutput = setExperiment(experimentNumber);
10    scratchData = experimentBody(experimentOutput);
11    analyzeExperiment(experimentOutput, scratchData);
12  }
13  myEnd(experimentNumber);
14 }
```

Listing 13.1   The main function of the virtual experiment.

As we said before, we need to simulate the experiment, but do not want to discuss it in detail: the parts relevant for this discussion are the analysis of the experiment (in line 11) and the final output of the results (in line 13). In the remainder of the main function, we initialize the random number generator (line 5), and we iterate the experiment to have several independent tests. The function setExperiment on line 9 asks the user to insert a number; the value 4 ends the experiment, while the input value 3 causes the type of result to be random. The function setExperiment, which we do not report here, decides the type of result of a single experiment, and experimentBody, on line 10, randomly chooses the output values (the particle velocity in case 0, the number of particles in case 1 and the type of error in case 2). The experiment output is defined by the union experimentData scratchData and the value of experimentOutput, which is, respectively, equal to 0, 1 or 2 in the three cases.

The function analyzeExperiment of Listing 13.2 is very simple (thanks to the fact that it uses a union!). Its input is scratchData and experimentOutput.

```
1 void analyzeExperiment(unsigned long int experimentOutput,
2                        union experimentData newData) {
3   if (experimentOutput == EXP_SPEED) {
4     averageSpeed += newData.speed;
5   } else if (experimentOutput == EXP_JET) {
```

```
1    } else if (experimentOutput == EXP_ERROR) {
2        hystogramNumber[newData.num]++;
3        printf("ERROR IN EXPERIMENT: %s\n", newData.errorMessage);
4    }
5 }
```

Listing 13.2   The function `analyzeExperiment`.

The variable `experimentOutput` tells us of which type the experiment result is, and therefore, tells us which type of value is contained in `union experimentData newData`. In case of a velocity it is a `double`, and on line 4 of the listing in page 373 the new velocity is added to the `averageSpeed` to compute the average. In case of a group of particles it is an `int`, and on line 2 in the same page we update a histogram. In case an error occurred, we just print the error message, on line 3 in page 373.

Finally, the function `myEnd` prints the average velocity, the histogram of the distribution of particles produced during the interactions and the number of errors made.

Hands on 13.2 - A virtual experiment

Describe a problem analogous to the previous one, related to the control of an industrial production line. Write a simulator which takes various cases into account, and manage them with a `union`.

13.2   Linked lists

A problem appearing in many contexts and often leading to a dramatically narrow bottleneck is the management of small or large quantities of data. The interesting problems could be very different from each other: reading a text, creating a dictionary, inserting and storing addresses, managing a student *database* with time-dependent *records*. Also think of engineering applications, such as collecting data of industrial processes, or the control or analysis of experiments in any scientific field (signals obtained when treating biologically interesting molecules, information of chemical reactions, controlling experiments of collisions between highly energetic particles generating a multitude of new particles).

13.2.1 *Lists, strings and a dictionary*

Let us discuss how to organize words in a structure which can easily be consulted. We initially use a rather inefficient, though absolutely elementary structure, which helps us understand the concept of a *linked list*. We read the words from a data file and we progressively add them to our list. A first example consists in creating a list to which we add the words while we read them. In a second example we eliminate the repeated words, thus creating a dictionary starting from a text. The core of a structure referring to a structure of the same type is shown in the following definition of the struct of the word type,

```
struct word {
   char *pointerToString;
   struct word *pointerToNextWord;
};
```

The structure consists of two pointers. A first pointer points to a memory location where we write the word we have read as a character string (this is useful because the word length may vary and in this way the structure word does not depend on these details). The second pointer, pointing to a structure *of the same type*, is the crucial one. It points, in this case, to the next word of the list. Note that we do not reserve any memory for the data, but only the memory required for the two pointers. The memory for the data is reserved separately. An even simpler case consists in recording some sorted telephone numbers. In this case the memory space required to contain the data (the telephone number) could have been included in the structure itself,

```
struct phoneNumber{
   unsigned long int thisNumber;
   struct phoneNumber *pointerToNextPhoneNumber;
};
```

In this case the memory space needed to store the telephone number is allocated when declaring the structure of the phoneNumber type as it always has the same dimension. The fundamental feature of the linked list is still present at least one member of the structure is a pointer to a structure of the same type (in this case, the next element of the list). Figure 13.1 helps to clarify how the data are organized in the case of telephone numbers, with data containers and pointers to the next structure.

This type of list structure is more flexible than an array. In an array the data are classified in necessarily consecutive memory locations. It is not possible to change the order of the memory locations, as we need to do, for example, for dynamic structures, whose order changes throughout the execution. Adding memory locations to an array (by means of a `realloc` for example) is possibly a rather burdensome task due to the fact that the data need to be contiguous. It could be that the total space required by the `realloc` is only available in a different area than the used one. In this case, in order to be extended the array must be copied in a new part of the memory. In case of a very large array this can take a lot of CPU time.

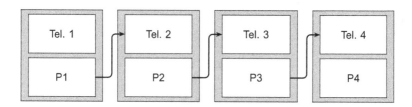

Fig. 13.1   A linked list of telephone numbers. The numbers are stored in the containers on top. The containers on the bottom store the pointer to the next structure.

Hands on 13.3 - A linked list

  Write a code reading a text (for example a Shakespeare poem), which recognizes the words it contains and organizes them in a linked list. The detailed organization of the list can be chosen in different ways. It is instructive to try several of these.

Let us take a look at the important points of the code analyzing a text. First of all, we define a structure of the `word` type:

```
struct word {
  char *pointerToString;
  struct word *pointerToNextWord;
} *wordList = NULL;
```

Apart from defining a type of structure, `word`, we also declared a pointer to this type of structure: `wordList`. Note we did not reserve a structure of the `word` type, but only a pointer to a structure. Because we have not yet read any word, our list is still empty. Therefore, the pointer is initialized to

NULL, a symbol defined by the compiler. The essential part of the program, typically included in the `main` function, has the following form

```
myEnd = 0;
while (myEnd != 1) {
  myEnd = readWord();
  buildInverseList();
}
printInverseList();
```

The function `readWord` reads a word, and the function `buildInverseList` inserts it in the list. This is an inverse list, because the links between two elements start from the last inserted element up to the first one. This is the easiest way to create a list. Note that for simplicity we did not include any arguments in the functions, and we rather use a certain number of global variables. When programming we always need to find a compromise between ease of writing and code robustness. In general, it is best to use as little global variables as possible as any function of the code could change their value, thus possibly causing programming errors.

The function `readWord` (Listing 13.3) reads the text from the global variable `fInput` (a pointer) to FILE and identifies the words. The function identifying the objects (in this case the words) in a context is called the *lexical analysis* function. It is an important component of the *parsing* process, i.e., the analysis of the grammatical structure of a character flow by decomposing the flow in more or less complex units (lexical elements) and interpreting them with respect to the grammatical rules.

The lexical analysis is a complex process, also because a word can be delimited in many ways inside a text. In most cases, one or more spaces appear at the end of a word, but also a punctuation mark (a comma, a period), parentheses or a simple "end of line" are allowed. Creating a complete lexical analyzer is a difficult task that goes beyond the scope of this textbook. For now, we only consider an elementary lexical analyzer. We leave any improvement to it as an exercise to the reader. To simplify the memory management, we assign a maximum number of characters per word, namely `MY_MAX` to the function `readWord`. If for some reason this maximum is exceeded, the program terminates with an error. The variable `myFlag` is reset when the word is complete. In this case the function transfers the control to the `main` function, while returning the value 0 unless the end of the file has been reached. In the latter case, the return value is 1. In our elementary lexical analyzer a word can only end with a single space or with the end of the file. We leave the case of more consecutive blank spaces as an exercise. The end of line characters are ignored and we do not consider that they can possibly signal the end of a word. Therefore, also the last word of a line must be followed by a blank space. At the end of the word we add the terminator "\0" to the string. The character array `myString` is declared as a global variable, and can be seen by all functions of the program. The variable `myString` is used to temporarily store the words we have read, before they are inserted in the list.

The characters of the word are read one by one with the `fgetc` function. The function `fgetc` (included in `<stdio.h>`) takes a file pointer argument (the file must be opened and be accessible) and returns the character read from the file as a `char` converted into an `int`, or, if the end of file has been reached, the end of file signal, i.e. `EOF`, defined in the system headers. Its prototype is

```
int fgetc(FILE *stream);
```

At this point, the function given in Listing 13.3 should be clear.

```
1  int readWord(void) {
2    char myFlag = 1;
3    int j, myEnd = 0;
4    j = 0;
5    while ((j < MY_MAX) && (myFlag == 1)) {
6      myString[j] = fgetc(fInput);
7      if (myString[j] == ' ') {
8        myString[j] = '\0';
9        myFlag = 0;
10     } else if (myString[j] == '\n') {
11       j--; /*to ignore the end of a line*/
12     } else if (myString[j] == EOF) {
13       myEnd = 1;
14       myString[j] = '\0';
15       myFlag = 0;
16     }
17     j++;
18   }
19   if (j >= MY_MAX-1) {
20     printf("Program interruption: "
21             "the word was too long.\n");
22     printf("Recompile with a new value of MY_MAX "
23             "larger than %d\n", MY_MAX);
24     exit(EXIT_FAILURE);
25   }
26   printf("Word of length %d: %s\n",
27           strlen(myString), myString);
28   return myEnd;
29 }
```

Listing 13.3   The function `readWord` to lexically analyze a text.

Note that it is much wiser to use the `fgetc` function than `fscanf`, which is more complex and sometimes deceiving, leading to reading errors.

The `buildInverseList` function builds the list (Listing 13.4). It is a simple and compact function calling `malloc` to reserve the required memory for the string that has just been read and is stored in the array `myString` of the global memory. The function `strlen` (included in `<string.h>`) takes a string pointer argument and returns the string length:

```
size_t strlen(const char *myString);
```

(`size_t` is discussed in Section 10.2.2).

The pointer `scratchPointer` points to the new permanent memory space (reserved by the program for as long as it is being executed) in which we store the new word. To permanently (until the code has stopped executing) store the words, we copy the content of `myString` in a memory location specifically allocated and pointed to by `scratchPointer`. If the memory request is unsuccessful, the pointer `scratchPointer` is set to NULL, and the program is terminated with an error. Once this is done, we store the pointer to the last `word` structure that is in this moment stored in `wordScratchPointer` (without this pointer the communication between the various elements of the list would be broken). We then ask for new memory for the new `word` structure to contain the new word. This is the only moment in which we reserve a new `word` structure (before we only reserved a pointer to a structure). Again, we check whether the `malloc` was successful.

We are almost done now. We copy the word we just read from the temporary buffer `myString` into the buffer pointed by `scratchPointer`. This can be done by means of the system function `strcpy` (included in `<string.h>`) copying a string (including its terminating character \0) from one location to another. Its prototype has the form

```
char *strcpy(char *destination, const char *source);
```

and the pointer it returns points to the destination string (which is left unused in our code).

All we have to do now is fill the `word` structure we just created by copying the pointer to the new word in `wordList->pointerToString` and by copying the pointer to the second last structure (which we had wisely saved on line 11) in `wordList -> pointerToNextWord;`. In this way the new structure that we added contains a pointer to the word we have just found, and a pointer to the structure we had created before. The first structure we created points to the value NULL we used to initialize the first pointer we declared in the beginning of the code. A pointer to NULL in the pointer list wordList->pointerToNextWord indicates that the list is complete. At this point the function buildInverseList should be clear to us.

```
 1 void buildInverseList(void) {
 2   char *scratchPointer;
 3   struct word *wordScratchPointer;
 4
 5   scratchPointer = (char *)malloc(strlen(myString));
 6   if (scratchPointer == NULL) {
 7     printf("Program interruption: "
 8            "malloc failure number 1\n");
 9     exit(EXIT_FAILURE);
10   }
11   wordScratchPointer = wordList;
12   wordList = (struct word *)malloc(sizeof(struct word));
13   if (wordList == NULL) {
14     printf("Program interruption: "
15            "malloc failure number 2\n");
16     exit(EXIT_FAILURE);
17   }
18   strcpy(scratchPointer, myString);
19   wordList->pointerToString = scratchPointer;
20   wordList->pointerToNextWord = wordScratchPointer;
21 }
```

Listing 13.4   The function buildInverseList to build a linked list.

A better understanding of how the linking of this list works can be obtained by looking at the function used to print it, given in Listing 13.5.

```
 1 void printInverseList(void) {
 2   struct word *wordScratchPointer = wordList;
 3   while (wordScratchPointer != NULL) {
 4     printf("%s\n", wordScratchPointer->pointerToString);
 5     wordScratchPointer =
 6       wordScratchPointer->pointerToNextWord;
 7   }
 8 }
```

Listing 13.5   The function printInverseList printing a linked list.

The function mechanism is clear. The pointer wordList (a global variable) points to the structure containing the last word that has been read. We print it and we continue with the previous word, by means of `wordScratchPointer->pointerToNextWord`, until we reach the pointer to NULL, indicating that the word list is finished and that the reconstruction has been completed.

Hands on 13.4 - More lists and dictionaries

The lexical analyzer we discussed is extremely simple. Improve it by taking into account possible punctuation marks and uppercase and lowercase characters. Also consider that the "end of line" character terminates a word (unless a selected symbol, for example '-', is present indicating the word has been divided in two parts). Include letters with accents, apostrophes and the fact that the accents are sometimes inserted by a symbol following the word, into account. More generally, this is the right time to take another look at the table of ASCII characters, discussed in Section 1.7.2 and in AppendixB, in order to build a lexical analyzer which takes the most interesting cases into account.

Write a code that implements a direct list, starting from the first read word up to the last one read. The code is very similar to the one described for the inverse list. Finally, change the code to eliminate repeated words.

To eliminate repeated words it suffices to add four simple lines of code at the beginning of **buildInverseList** (Listing 13.4). A local pointer scrolls through the words we found so far and compares them to the last one we read. If it coincides with one of the previous ones, it is not recorded. The two strings are compared by means of the system function **strcmp**, included in **<string.h>**, which has as prototype

```
int strcmp(const char *string1, const char *string2);
```

The function compares the two strings pointed by **string1** and **string2**. With the ASCII encoding (Section 1.7.2 and Appendix B), it basically associates a numeric value to each string such that a string preceding it in alphabetic order is assigned a smaller numeric value. Thus, the function returns an integer smaller than, equal to or larger than zero if **string1** is, respectively, smaller, equal to or larger than **string2**. Note that, in the following code, in this case the function is left by means of a **return** statement placed inside a block. Not everybody considers this to be a structured construct because it entails we have a block of statements that we can access only in one way, but that we can quit in two different ways, namely at the end or by means of the **return**. We should not abuse this form, though sometimes it is useful. With this so-called *safeguard clause*, we basically reserve the right to immediately quit the function if a certain condition is verified (in our case if the word is already included in the list).

```
struct word *wordScratchPointer , *pointerCheck;
for (pointerCheck = wordList; pointerCheck != NULL;) {
  if (strcmp(pointerCheck ->pointerToString , myString) == 0) {
    return;
  }
  pointerCheck = pointerCheck ->pointerToNextWord;
}
```

A single link list is the easiest example among many possible cases. In Figure 13.2 we give an example of a double link list. Thanks to the double pointer structure it can be scrolled in both directions, from head to tail and the other way around. In this case, each structure stores, apart from the relevant data, also a pointer to the preceding structure and a pointer to the next one.

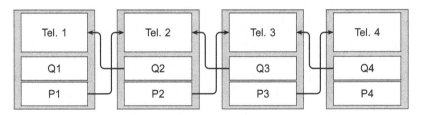

Fig. 13.2   A double link list. The structure is richer than a single link list. We can easily scroll through it in both directions, form head to tail and the other way around. The pointers P_i point to the next structure, the pointers Q_i to the preceding one.

13.2.2   *Recursive functions: computing the factorial*

To continue our analysis about how to organize data and how to build and manage lists, it is useful to briefly introduce the concept of *recursion*, which is treated in detail in Section 15.3.1.

A function is said to be recursive if it can call itself. Not all programming languages allow the use of this type of functions: C does, and this is one of its particularly interesting features. As an example we consider how to compute a factorial, $n! \equiv 1 \cdot 2 \cdot 3 \cdot \ldots \cdot n$, defined for integer, non-negative values n. The Section 4.3.1 contains a simple non-recursive code computing the factorial, while the recursive function is given in Listing 13.6.

```
1 unsigned long long int factorial(unsigned int n) {
2   if (n == 0) return 1;
3   return (n * factorial(n - 1));
4 }
```

Listing 13.6   Computing the factorial with a recursive function.

The key is the mathematical identity $n! = n \cdot (n-1)!$. When called with a positive integer, the function calls itself until it is called with the value zero. In the latter case, it returns one. So, when the function is called with argument 2 it returns in turn $2 = 2 \cdot 1$, when called with argument 3 it returns $6 = 3 \cdot 2$ and so on. A specific situation defines the condition ending the recursive chain, which in this case is the call to the function with argument equal to zero. Without this termination condition (or if the condition is wrong or never encountered) the function will call itself until it fills the computer memory and blocks it. A function like ours, based on variables of the **unsigned long long int** type, can compute factorials up to $n = 20$, i.e., until the result representation takes more than 64 bits. This is why the argument can be of the **unsigned int** type, which is sufficiently large.

A recursive function calling itself is completely analogous to calling a new function. The whole scope (local variables, parameters) must be stored, such that it can be recovered when returning to the calling function. An instructive way to think of a recursive function which is called many times is as if we wrote the function the same number of times, reproducing the same number of lines of code for each call to the function. In practice this is obviously not possible, given that a function could call itself recursively hundreds of times (and that we do not know this number a priori). Still, it helps us to figure out how complex this mechanism is. One of the main contexts in which a recursion is applied are *tree-like* data structures, which we discuss in Section 13.2.3.

13.2.3   *Binary trees and dictionaries*

The way we built the list in Section 13.2.1, storing one by one the (non repeated) words found in the text, may be very slow to sort. As the number of words increases, organizing the list, to sort it in alphabetic order for example, takes a large amount of computer resources. In the third part of this textbook, we analyze *scaling laws* describing how the execution time grows in function of the size of the input, which in this case is the number of words composing the list.

Building and managing a *tree* with recursive functions helps to create efficient dynamic structures. Trees are structures whose elements point to other elements of the same structure, as in lists. The elements of the trees, though, are organized in a more complex way. A list is a linear structure, while a tree is a branched structure with a ramification in each *node*. The initial node has k branches who all end in other nodes. Each of these k nodes can have again k branches, and so on. For example, think of a *binary tree* , i.e., a tree with $k = 2$. The first part of a binary tree is shown in Figure 13.3. The first word that has been read (word 1) occupies the first node; the (non repeated) words read next are placed along the branches of the tree. If, according to the alphabet, a new word precedes the word that has found its place in the first node, it follows the left branch, while a word following it in alphabetic order will follow in the branch on the right. This is done on every occupied node, and eventually the new word is placed in the first empty node along this path. This is a simple recipe to build a binary tree. We always consider and discuss trees which are upside down (as in Figure 13.3), i.e., with the root on top and the branches developing downward.

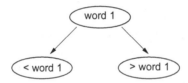

Fig. 13.3   The root of the tree. word 1 is the first read word. A word alphabetically preceding word 1 moves along the left branch, while a word alphabetically following word 1 moves along the branch on the right. The word stops in the first empty node along this path. The root of the tree is shown on top, while its leaves are shown at the bottom.

Hands on 13.5 - The binary tree

Write a code that reads a text and organizes it in a binary tree as the one we just discussed, eliminating the repeated words. Use a recursive algorithm. The task of the recursive function is to place the new word in the tree. It should call itself until it reaches the tree branch on which the word should be stored. Write a function printing the word list in alphabetic order.

The use of recursive functions makes the code reading a word list and organizing it in a binary tree much more compact. We want to write a function `addToTree` (Listing 13.7) calling itself up to when it has reached the leaf of the tree where it can deposit the new word.

Organizing words in a tree is extremely efficient. If the N words are read in a random order, the time it takes to sort them in alphabetic order only grows like $N \log(N)$. In this case, the tree is said to be *balanced*. This is for example also the case if the words were not picked in a random way, but rather taken from a novel. Typically even in this case we will obtain a balanced tree, since the author usually does not choose to only use words starting with the letter "a" in the first chapter, with the letter "b" in the second chapter, and so on. Instead, if the read words have a well-organized order, the tree is unbalanced, and searching the tree is a lot slower. For example, reading a dictionary which is already sorted, the words are all placed on a single branch, producing a completely unbalanced tree, whose depth grows linearly with the number of read words. In this case the tree structure is as inefficient as a list.

The node structure has two pointers to nodes of the same type,

```
struct word {
  char *pointerToString;
  struct word *nextWordLeft;
  struct word *nextWordRight;
} *treeRoot = NULL;
```

As usual, the first pointer points to the word stored in the corresponding character array, while the second and the third pointers allow us to find the following word on the tree, respectively, along the left or right bifurcation.

Upon execution, we start by creating a pointer to a structure of the **word** type pointing to NULL. The basic structure of the program is very simple:

```
fW1.myEnd = 0;
while (fW1.myEnd != 1) {
  fW1 = readWord();
  treeRoot = addToTree(treeRoot, fW1.scratchPointer);
}
```

The structure `fW1` contains the pointer to the word we have read and a control variable signaling when to terminate the program execution (because the last word of the text file has been read). It has the form

```
struct fromWord {
  int myEnd;
  char *scratchPointer;
} fW1;
```

The function declared as

```
struct fromWord readWord(void);
```

reads a word, whose pointer is returned, together with a control variable, or *flag*, which is equal to one if the end of file is read. Also in the latter case, the read word is a legitimate word and should be analyzed and possibly stored. This function structure is the same as the one for the management of the simple list discussed in Section 13.2.1. The function **addToTree** adds the read word to the tree starting from its root and moving along its branches until an empty node (a leaf) is found.

Note that in this simple example we are not treating lowercase or uppercase letters any differently, and we simply assume we only have to deal with lowercase letters. We leave the correct treatment of uppercase letters as an exercise.

```
1  struct word* addToTree(struct word* inputWord,
2                         char *localPointer)
3  {
4    int stringDifference;
5    if(inputWord == NULL){
6      inputWord =
7        (struct word *) malloc(sizeof(struct word));
8      if(inputWord == NULL){
9        printf("Program interrupted: malloc failure 1\n");
10       exit(MY_RUIN);
11     }
12     inputWord->pointerToString = localPointer;
13     inputWord->nextWordLeft = NULL;
14     inputWord->nextWordRight = NULL;
15   } else if((stringDifference =
16              strcmp(inputWord->pointerToString,
17                     localPointer)) != 0){
18     if(stringDifference > 0) {
19       inputWord->nextWordLeft =
20         addToTree(inputWord->nextWordLeft,localPointer);
21     } else {
22       inputWord->nextWordRight =
23         addToTree(inputWord->nextWordRight, localPointer);
24     }
25   }
26   return inputWord;
27 }
```

Listing 13.7   The function **addToTree** adding a word to the tree.

Let us have a look at how this function, given in Listing 13.7, works. If the function is called with an argument which is an empty location, the word can be added to the tree. In this case `thisWord == NULL`. We add a leaf to the tree, where we store the word and add a bifurcation leading to two empty positions (lines 12-14). A `malloc` (line 7) reserves the memory location required to store the word we just read, and we check whether the memory has been allocated correctly (if not, the program is terminated with an error). We assign to the string pointer the address of the word we have read and the two pointers to the left and the right are initialized to `NULL`. The latter information is then returned with a single `return` (line 26). The word has been inserted and all open calls in the recursive chain are closed, in a cascade. Instead, if the considered location is occupied, the function `strcmp` on line 16 (`strcmp` is discussed in Section 13.2.1) plays a fundamental role. If the new word is equal to the one in the considered node, nothing happens: the search is finished, without leading to any update of our list. In this case the function returns the address of the word already occupying the considered memory, and the recursive chain is closed.

Instead, if the considered tree node is not a leaf and does not contain a word equal to the one we just read, we check whether the new word alphabetically precedes or follows the one already present in the node. In this case, the function is called recursively to check, respectively, the next node on the left and the one on the right. For example, let us assume, without loss of generality, that the new word alphabetically precedes the one already contained in the node. In this case the recursive call has the following form

```
thisWord->nextWordLeft =
  addToTree(thisWord->nextWordLeft, localPointer);
```

Thus, we want to insert the new word in the next branch on the left. The recursive procedure runs along the tree and stops either when it finds an empty space (where it inserts the new word) or when a word equal to the read one has already been inserted. In Chapter 15 we discuss the recursive procedures in much better detail and we clarify how crucial the definition of the return condition is.

The power of a recursive procedure is probably most clear in the function that prints in alphabetic order the word list: this function is also recursive, and it is shown in Listing 13.8.

```
1 void printTreeInAlphabeticOrder(struct word* thisWord) {
2   if (thisWord != NULL) {
3     printTreeInAlphabeticOrder(thisWord->nextWordLeft);
4     printf("%s\n", thisWord->pointerToString);
5     printTreeInAlphabeticOrder(thisWord->nextWordRight);
6   }
7 }
```

Listing 13.8   The function `printTreeInAlphabeticOrder`.

The function consists of only four short lines, accomplishing an absolutely nontrivial task! Take your time to digest what is happening: this is the only way to fully comprehend what the recursive approach entails. The function first moves down along the left side of the tree. The word in the leftmost leaf is certainly the first one in alphabetic order. We then travel along all branches of the tree from left to right. Note that when printing a tree, its left half is printed before its right half (the first read word occupies the root of the tree and divides it in two). Moreover, this is true for each subdivision of the tree.

Also note how powerful and compact this code is with respect to the one discussed in Section 5.6.3, and to the one based on pointers discussed in Section 6.5.1.

13.3   Connected clusters

We now consider a lattice problem. In particular we try to understand what happens if we place objects on the sites of a lattice: when do they start to form large connected clusters which become infinite if the lattice is infinite? This leads us to the important subject of *percolation*. An algorithm based on lists allows for an effective treatment of this problem.

In this Section we consider a two-dimensional square lattice ($D = 2$): analogous considerations can be made for other lattice shapes, such as a triangular lattice, also in a different number of physical dimensions (for example in the $D = 3$ case). We place binary (or Boolean) variables on the lattice sites. By convention, we assume that the two possible values of these variables are $(-1, +1)$, or $(0, 1)$, or red and green. The problem can be interpreted in various ways and have different applications: however, the values we choose for representing our variables do not change the problem structure. For example, we could decide that the lattice represents our city telephone network with, in each site, a telephone exchange which could be either working or broken. We can associate the value $+1$ or the color green to a working telephone exchange and the value -1, 0 or red to a broken one. A second interesting application of our system deals with magnetism. In this case the lattice variables represent magnetic spins, which are either oriented in the negative directions (value -1) or in the positive one (value $+1$). This very simple model is a powerful instrument to study a complex phenomenon such as magnetism. Finally, we mention the example of a gas of particles (discussed in Chapter 12): if the variable of the site has value 1, the site is occupied by a particle, otherwise, if it has value 0, the site is empty. The absence of a particle can be described as the presence of a *gap*.

We now choose to examine the failures in a telephone network. If there are only a few breakdowns, there is no problem. We can bypass the few broken telephone exchanges, thus guaranteeing the communication between any two points in the city by using functional telephone exchanges. Now let the density of breakdowns increases. For example, there is a moment in which the city is divided in two by a connected set of broken telephone exchanges. From the northern part of the city, it is no longer possible to call to the southern part. Many local breakdowns had a global consequence, thus blocking the communication between two parts of the city. We say that the breakdowns *percolated*, thus dividing the city in two separate parts.

The fundamental concept in this discussion is the one of *connected component*. Before defining the latter, we first introduce the concept of *nearest neighbors*. Namely, two site variables (two breakdowns) are said to be *nearest neighbors* if the distance between them is one lattice step. For example, the breakdown in position $(x, y) = (5, 6)$ is close to the breakdown in position $(5, 7)$ and to the one in position $(4, 6)$, but not to the one in positions $(1, 23)$ or $(6, 7)$ (where one needs two lattice steps to go). A set of site variables is a connected component of the system if from each site of the set we can continuously reach any other site passing only through first neighbors with the same value of the variable, while none of the sites of the set has a nearest neighbor which does not belong to the set. A typical situation is shown in Figure 13.4, where the connected components (or *connected clusters*) are included in closed boundaries. Note that the problem should be defined together with its boundary conditions, as we explain when discussing the lattice gas in Section 12.3. In Figure 13.4 we assumed the borders to be empty. They do not allow the variables to be connected to each other, contrary to what happens, for example, in case of periodic boundary conditions.

We start by discussing an algorithm that allows us to reconstruct the

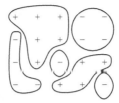

Fig. 13.4   Connected components of a two-dimensional lattice.

system connected components. For now, we consider an easy approach and neglect efficiency.

We consider a two-dimensional square lattice containing randomly placed breakdowns with density p. In each site we define a variable identifying the connected components. When we have finished applying the algorithm this variable should have the same value on all sites belonging to the same connected component and be different for each separate connected component. First of all we initialize the label for all sites with a breakdown with a site-dependent number which is different for each site. For example, if the lattice size is $L_x \cdot L_y$, we can choose the label of the site (x, y) to be $x + L_x \cdot y$. For all working sites we can choose one value, different from the previous one. By convention, all sites with this label (for example, a negative value) should not be considered.

We choose a site with a breakdown: for example we select the first one of the lattice in lexicographic order, and we examine the variables of its nearest neighbor sites. In Section 12.3 we discuss how to identify the nearest neighbors of a given site. For each broken nearest neighbor with a label different than the site under consideration, we copy the smallest label into the larger one. For example, if the label of the considered broken site is 6 and the broken nearest neighbor is labeled 18, the latter label is set equal to 6 and the label of the considered site remains the same. In the opposite case (18 on our site and 6 on the nearest neighboring site) we copy the label of the first nearest neighbor to our site. In both cases the result is that the smallest label characterizes, after this step, both breakdowns. If we copied a label we increase the number of changes we have made by one.

We repeat this procedure of comparing a broken site with all its broken nearest neighbors on all lattice sites. When the total number of changes performed during an analysis of all connections of the lattice is zero, the procedure has converged and we have achieved the desired property: now

the labels of sites belonging to the same connected component are the same
and those of different components differ, thus characterizing the connected
clusters. We can use these labels to study the clusters properties, such as
their size. Note that this is a *local* algorithm, that, in order to build the system structure, only takes information from the sites close to the considered
one. This is precisely why the algorithm becomes rather inefficient when
the system contains large structures. The study of percolation phenomena
helps to clarify this matter.

Hands on 13.6 - Connected components

 Use the local algorithm described here above to build connected components on a two-dimensional square lattice.
This problem has the same structure (lattice structure,
initialization) as the lattice gas problem discussed in Section 12.3. Evaluate the total execution time as a function of the breakdown
density.

Let us analyze the key points of this local algorithm. For the initialization of the random numbers, the random placement of the breakdowns and
the vectors identifying the nearest neighbors we refer the reader to Section
12.3. The connected components search is based on the main cycle shown
in Listing 13.9.

The function `siteUpdate(direction, site)` updates the labels of the
site

```
1   j = 0;
2   while ((somethingChanged != 0) && (j < MAX_ITER)) {
3     j++;
4     somethingChanged = 0;
5     for (i = 0; i < V; i++) {
6       somethingChanged += siteUpdate((long int)RIGHT, i);
7       somethingChanged += siteUpdate((long int)BOTTOM, i);
8       somethingChanged += siteUpdate((long int)LEFT, i);
9       somethingChanged += siteUpdate((long int)TOP, i);
10    }
11    printf("# number of changes %ld\n", somethingChanged);
12  }
```

Listing 13.9   The main cycle of the labeling algorithm.

`site` and of its nearest neighbor in the direction `direction`. It is performed
on all sites and in all four directions. If the reconstruction is finished, no

change is made. In this case, the condition `somethingChanged == 0` is true
after the cycle of all lattice sites has finished and the program has completed
its task. The update procedure is not executed more than `MAX_ITER` times,
thanks to the second `while` condition. Indeed, if after `MAX_ITER` attempts
the condition `somethingChanged == 0` is not verified the program is terminated with an error (this part is included in the program `main` function and
not reported here). Actually, the algorithm always converges and, for any
realistic case, it is not plausible it takes an enormous number of iterations
to converge. Nevertheless, it is always better to limit, to a very high value,
the computational effort that will be requested to a code solving some problem. In this way we also avoid the possibility of executing for days a code
that will eventually return a meaningless results, as often happens because
of programming errors.

The function `siteUpdate` is very simple and is shown in Listing 13.10.

```
1 unsigned long int siteUpdate(long int direction,
2                              long int site) {
3   long int i, j;
4   char weAreChanging = 0;
5   int n = neighbor[site][direction];
6
7   if (cluster[site].spin == cluster[n].spin) {
8     if (cluster[site].label < cluster[n].label) {
9       weAreChanging = 1;
10      cluster[n].label = cluster[site].label;
11    } else if (cluster[site].label > cluster[n].label) {
12      weAreChanging = 1;
13      cluster[site].label = cluster[n].label;
14    }
15  }
16  return weAreChanging;
17 }
```

Listing 13.10   The function `siteUpdate`.

The variable of the site under consideration is compared to the one of
the neighboring site. If the two variables are different the function returns
the value zero and the next couple of sites is evaluated. We assume the
breakdowns are represented by the value -1. Without loss of generality,
this program both reconstructs the connected clusters of breakdown and
the connected clusters of variables equal to $+1$. In this way it is easy to
identify only the clusters of the breakdowns. If the two variables are equal
to each other, the corresponding labels are read. If the latter are different,
the smaller label substitutes the larger one, and the value one is returned

(signaling a change has been made and the labels are still being modified). Otherwise, the function simply returns the value zero. This simple process converges to the correct identification of the system connected components. Note that the flag `weAreChanging` could be of the `char` type, as it only takes on the values 0 or 1. The use of types with few bits does not always enhance the program execution though. Often, it is convenient to use types which have the same number of bits as the number on which the machine hardware is based: this avoids the time-consuming conversions possibly imposed by the compiler.

The game *Go*

The Chinese game *Go* dates back to about 4000 years. It soon became very popular in Japan, and later in the rest of the world. It is a strategic game representing, as often is the case with oriental games, a refined life metaphor. Two players in turn place their pieces (black and white) on the intersection of the *goban*, i.e., a board consisting of a network of 19 horizontal lines and as many vertical lines. Once the pieces are placed on the *goban*, they are never ever removed again. The aim of the game is to define the *territories* whose borders are determined by pieces of the same color. The pieces cannot penetrate inside a closed territory of an opponents color. Essentially a territory is defined as a *connected component* of pieces on the *goban* lattice.

13.4 Percolation

We now discuss *percolation* a physical phenomenon of great interest [Stauffer and Aharony (1992)]. To define the problem we assume that the breakdowns of our telephone network are randomly distributed in an independent and uniform way with probability p. A somewhat different problem could be that of correlated breakdowns, because of a fire for example. The case we consider, though, represents random breakdowns and is a first interesting approximation to a realistic problem.

When the breakdown density p is small the problem is not too serious. It suffices to reconfigure the network to avoid broken exchanges. In this way it remains possible to call from one point of the city to another (Figure 13.5).

Fig. 13.5   The exchanges represented by white circles are operative, the gray ones are broken. In the left figure all exchanges work and the communication is established along the shortest connection. In the figure on the right, an exchange is broken. Nevertheless, the communication can take place along a slightly longer path of working exchanges.

Things get worse when the breakdown probability p increases (because the telephone company decided to save on maintenance). In this case, the number of broken connections which must be avoided increases, and it becomes difficult to connect two city parts which are far away from each other. For large enough p, the network is divided in many separate parts, and we can only call friends living close to us. A mathematical result of *percolation theory* says that when the network is really large, this phenomenon occurs at a precise value for p, called the *percolation threshold* p_c. When $p = p_c$, we have reached the *critical percolating point*, and the system behaves in a very peculiar way. Remembering our discussion on random walks in Chapter 12, we remark that the *percolating cluster* has a non-integer, effective *fractal dimension*, larger than one, but smaller than two (it is not a normal curve, but a very rugged object).

This percolation phenomenon is exactly the one of a coffee percolator. We can enjoy a good coffee thanks to this percolating cluster property. When moving through a porous medium like coffee powder, water takes a particularly twisting road. This allows it to capture the aroma of the warm drink.

Percolation has properties different from what we have discussed so far. Structures of macroscopic size, i.e., non-local structures, are created (breakdown clusters percolate and invade our city as if it were a science fiction movie). This is a *purely geometric* phenomenon. There is no interaction between its elements, apart from how they occupy the physical space, which in our simple case is a two-dimensional square lattice. Indeed, a breakdown at site x does not induce one at another neighboring site. Let us explicitly stress the fact that we assume that the number of breakdowns in the network under study remains unchanged. We assume the number and position of broken exchanges are given beforehand.

There are other examples, apart from the telephone network, which are applicable to our system. For example, one of great importance is a material with impurities. A certain level of impurities changes the interactions between the material components. Indeed, the disorder may drastically change the material properties.

Percolation with broken sites, i.e. with broken exchanges, is called *site percolation*. An analogous problem is *bond percolation*. Bond percolation is defined on a lattice in which some *bonds* are missing. We do not have to deal with broken exchanges in a lattice site, but rather with broken telephone wires connecting two sites.

The properties of both problems are similar. Also in this second case, there exists a critical threshold for the failure density $p_c^{(b)}$ at which a *percolation transition* takes place, and breaks the network in separate pieces (the superscript (b) stands for bond percolation).

In the limit of an infinite lattice, we can easily give a mathematical definition of the critical percolation density p_c. Namely, p_c *is the breakdown density at which an infinite lattice contains an infinite cluster of breakdowns.* Thus, when the density reaches the value p_c on an infinite lattice, we surely have an infinite, extensive cluster of breakdowns. In two spatial dimensions this cluster divides the network in various pieces. The so-called *infinite volume limit*, plays a fundamental role in many contexts. On the one hand it often describes the studied system well (a macroscopic sample of material consists of a number of atoms of the order of magnitude of 10^{23}, and is described rather well by the infinite volume limit). On the other hand, it allows us to apply powerful mathematical techniques allowing us to analyze the problem.

This definition is valid for an infinite lattice, but it is not directly applicable to the case of a large, but finite network, like the ones we can analyze on a computer. The problem is that, with the connected components reconstruction method we just described, a computer only allows us to study finite networks. Indeed, the available computer memory and computing time are necessarily finite quantities. The limited memory only allows us to store a certain quantity of information, and the limited available computing time only allow us to perform a given number of CPU operations. Even if we are interested in properties concerning an infinite system, when studying a lattice problem with a computer, we are always forced to work with systems of finite size. We need to evaluate ourselves the limit of interest. This is typically done by analyzing systems of various sizes and observing how their properties vary with increasing size.

Thus, we need a working definition of the percolation threshold $p_c(L)$ valid on a lattice of linear extension L, and tending to $p_c(L = \infty) \equiv p_c$ when $L \to \infty$. There exist many definitions satisfying this property. In the limit of large networks they all produce the same result. Different definitions may be more appropriate when studying different models or when using different parameter values. Deciding which one is most convenient demands a clever use of the available information about the model, and preliminary numerical studies.

Here we introduce a definition useful to our percolation study, namely the concept of an *extensive cluster* (*spanning cluster*) on a lattice of finite size L. We can choose among different definitions, all leading to the same result in the large lattice limit. An extensive cluster is defined as a cluster possessing one of the following properties:

- it touches the top and bottom of the lattice;
- it touches the left and right border of the lattice;
- it touches the four borders of the lattice.

How can we check one of these properties? This is very easy in our two-dimensional lattice example. We can verify the first property by checking whether there exists a label which is present in at least one site of the top row and in one site of the bottom row of the lattice. In this case, given we are dealing with connected clusters, the considered cluster is necessarily an extensive cluster. Analogously for the second property, we check whether a same label is present both in a site of the rightmost and leftmost column of the lattice.

With these definitions we can define the quantity $p_c(L)$ (the percolation density on a lattice of linear size L) as the density for which an extensive cluster is found with probability equal to $\frac{1}{2}$. For each value of the density smaller than $p_c(L)$ the probability to find an extensive cluster is smaller than $\frac{1}{2}$, while for each value larger than $p_c(L)$ the probability to find an extensive cluster is larger than $\frac{1}{2}$.

Determining $p_c(L)$ (for example for site percolation) is easy. For a given value of L, we choose a certain density p and a configuration of working telephone exchanges. With the simple algorithm given in Section 13.3, or even better with the more complicated one described in Section 13.5, we decompose it into connected components. We check whether it contains an extensive cluster, and repeat this operation on a certain number of randomly chosen possible lattice configurations. In this way we can compute the rate[1] of the event "presence of an extensive cluster". If this probability is smaller than $\frac{1}{2}$, no percolation has occurred yet. Otherwise, the system is said to have percolated. By repeating this operation for various values of p we obtain an estimate of $p_c(L)$. Finally, we vary the value of L. We estimate $p_c(L)$ for increasing values of the linear size, and we analyze the functional dependency on L in the limit of large L. We evaluate the value of the asymptote p_c and compute the shape of the corrections changing the asymptotic value when L is finite.

Let us summarize this rather complex approach we just described. We compute a sample average (with respect to the various configurations of site failures or, in the example of a material description, with respect to different configurations of the impurities). To estimate the critical density for fixed L, we do this for varying values of the density p. To numerically reconstruct the limit $L \to \infty$, we perform this operation for various values of L. A reliable analysis of the phenomenon requires all these steps together with an evaluation of the statistical error characterizing the studied quantities.

Once the structure of connected components has been reconstructed, the system can be characterized by means of a certain number of interesting quantities. First of all, we consider the *probability to find a connected cluster of given size* T, defined as

$$\mathcal{N}(T) \equiv \frac{\overline{(\text{number of clusters of size } T)}}{(\text{total number of clusters})} \ , \tag{13.1}$$

where the line on top indicates the average with respect to the different system configurations. The probability that a randomly chosen lattice site belongs to a connected cluster of size T is

$$\frac{T\mathcal{N}(T)}{\sum_T T\mathcal{N}(T)} \ .$$

Thus, the *average size of a cluster* is

$$S = \frac{\sum_T T^2 \mathcal{N}(T)}{\sum_T T\mathcal{N}(T)} \ . \tag{13.2}$$

It is essential to note that if we choose a density larger than the critical one, $p > p_c$, the extensive cluster *should not be included in the sums* of equation (13.2). This is necessary to obtain an interesting result both in the region with $p < p_c$, and the percolating region with $p \geq p_c$. The extended cluster would cause the average cluster size to be infinite everywhere in the percolating region. The same phenomenon occurs when defining the

---

[1] We are using the rate to estimate the probability.

magnetic susceptibility of a magnetic system. The probability of having a percolating cluster, i.e., $\mathcal{N}(T)$ of equation (13.1), and S defined in equation (13.2) are interesting quantities to compute numerically. They characterize the system properties, and determine, for example, whether it is possible or not to make phone calls in our city.

Finally, we define the density of sites belonging to an extensive cluster as

$$\pi_\infty \equiv \frac{\text{(number of sites in the extensive cluster)}}{\text{(total number of broken sites)}} \ . \tag{13.3}$$

π_∞ is a function of the impurity density p: $\pi_\infty(p)$. Below the percolation threshold we have that $\pi_\infty(p < p_c) = 0$ when the lattice size diverges (i.e., when $L \to \infty$). Obviously, for $p = 1$, we have that $\pi_\infty(p = 1) = 1$. Also the quantity defined in equation (13.3) is interesting to study numerically. It clearly distinguishes the percolating phase from the one with a low density of breakdowns. This is why it is said to be the *order parameter* of the percolation transition.

Hands on 13.7 - Percolation on regular lattices

Numerically study the percolation phenomenon on a two-dimensional square lattice. Use periodic boundary conditions. It is interesting to study all the definitions of an extensive cluster given above. Make a detailed study of the quantities (13.1), (13.2) and (13.3). Evaluate their statistical error and graphically analyze the results. Estimate $p_c(L)$ for various values of L. It is known that $p_c \simeq 0.593$ in the large volume limit [Stauffer and Aharony (1992)]. Verify this result. Study the phenomenon on a two-dimensional triangular lattice, and three-dimensional lattices with various types of connectivity.

The codes needed to study percolation are simple extensions of those reconstructing the connected components. The output of the program, i.e., the labels classifying each site by indicating to which connected component it belongs, allows us to compute all interesting quantities.

When $p \to p_c^-$, i.e., when, starting from small values the breakdown density p tends to the critical density p_c, there exists a length ξ characterizing the size of the lattice largest clusters, which diverges. When $p \to p_c^-$, $\xi \to \infty$. In Section 13.5 we see that understanding the physical properties of the problem (the presence of a length scale typically diverging if a system control parameter is varied) allows us to develop a more efficient algorithm than the local one we described before. This is generally true and important to remember. When we want to study a problem with a computer, it is very important to exploit our complete knowledge on the problem to develop a good numerical algorithm.

A natural way of defining this length ξ on our lattice system consists in associating it to the *radius of gyration* of the considered cluster. Consider a cluster of size T, and let $\vec{r}_\alpha$ be the coordinates of the site of variable α belonging to the considered cluster ($\alpha = 1, \ldots, T$). A particle at the origin has $r_\alpha = (0,0)$. We now define the *center of mass* of the connected cluster as

$$\vec{r}_{(b)} \equiv \frac{1}{T} \sum_{\alpha=1}^{T} \vec{r}_\alpha \; .$$

In Figure 13.6 we show a system consisting of 7 particles, indicated with small circles, and the vector pointing to its center of mass. We can associate the length ξ to the cluster gyration radius, R, by means of the relation

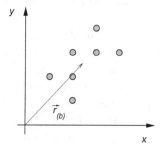

Fig. 13.6 A system of 7 particles and the vector pointing to its center of mass.

$$\xi^2 \sim R^2 \equiv \frac{1}{T} \sum_{\alpha=1}^{T} \left(\vec{r}_\alpha - \vec{r}_{(b)} \right)^2 \; . \tag{13.4}$$

To evaluate ξ we choose the largest cluster, except for the potential extensive cluster. If we were to include it, we would obtain a trivial result: in the infinite volume limit ξ becomes infinite. This cluster gives the correlation length ξ through (13.4). As the lattice grows, the behavior of ξ resembles more and more a divergence at p_c.

Hands on 13.8 - A diverging length of the percolation

 Study the correlation length ξ defined in (13.4) as a function of the density p for various values of L. For $p \to p_c$, we expect the correlation length to diverge like

$$\xi(p) \sim |p - p_c|^{-\nu} \ .$$

Verify this fact. Starting from the above hypothesis on the functional behavior of ξ, numerically estimate the exponent ν.

13.5 An algorithm based on lists

The ideas we introduced and discussed in Section 13.4 can help us to describe a new connected components reconstruction algorithm. When we approach the percolation density p_c, the performance of this new algorithm should be far superior to the ones of the local algorithm described in Section 13.3.

Why does the local reconstruction algorithm slow down as we approach the critical density? The reason is the fact that the length ξ that we defined earlier on diverges, i.e., some connected components become very large. Let us try to imagine how the local algorithm we discussed behaves. Initially, every site has a different label. Subsequently, the algorithm starts to copy these labels in the connected sites. Think of two large connected sets of variables in which, respectively, the label 2 and the label 5 diffused. It is possible that, after several iterations, the algorithm finds a connection between two sets of connected variables, because they are two parts of the *same connected component.* In this case, according to the rules we described earlier, the label 2 overrules the label 5. this occurs very slowly though. First, 2 is copied in the variable at the border between the two parts of the connected component. Next, it spreads out inside the part which originally carried the label 5. The problem is that this kind of situation occurs more frequently as the system connected components grow. The typical large clusters have many branches. They contain both groups of very interconnected sites and very weakly connected parts. Various parts of the same cluster grow with different labels. When they reach other clusters, we need to update the labels. With a local algorithm the latter process takes a considerable amount of time because it implies many complete inspections of the full lattice. In this case, a local algorithm converges very slowly, and undergoes a so-called *critical slowdown*.

Can we limit this effect? This is possible, by using concatenated lists. This is not the best known algorithm (for the two-dimensional percolation this would be a very accurate implementation of the Hoshen-Kopelman algorithm[Stauffer and Aharony (1992)], based on the same principles discussed here). Still, in the percolating limit it behaves much better than the local algorithm. It also clearly shows the ideas on which it is based. Instead, Section 17.5 contains a very efficient and compact implementation of the Hoshen-Kopelman algorithm. In the algorithm we introduce here for each site variable we store at least two pointers and a label. The first pointer points to the next variable of the same cluster (or to itself if it is the cluster last variable). The second pointer points to the cluster previous variable. The latter points to itself in case it is the first variable of the cluster. Thanks to these pointers, when two parts of a connected cluster meet, we can change the labels of all involved sites in a time which is proportional only to the size of the two parts. Obviously we also need to change the most important pointers, namely those of the two sites which met, such as to merge the two parts into one single new connected cluster.

This algorithm behaves differently than the local one when $p \to p_c$. In this case, the labels of the "big" clusters are quickly updated. Instead, before, each encounter between already formed parts of the same cluster, entailed several complete inspections of the entire lattice.

Deciding which type of pointers should be used is a project-related choice. It should take into account the fact that storing and updating a large amount of information takes more memory and could take more time to update the labels. Nevertheless, it allows us for an easier use of the obtained information, for example, to compute cluster properties, such as the gyration radius.

In our example, we stored four pointers for each lattice variable. We also included a site variable indicating whether a breakdown is present or not. Because of the analogy with magnetic materials, we called the latter **spin**. The pointer **next** points to the next variable of the same cluster, **former** to the previous one. The pointer **parent** points to the first site variable of the considered connected component and **son** to the last one.

Both the pointers **parent** and **son** play the role of cluster label. Indeed, all variables belonging to the same cluster have the same values for **parent** and **son**. This scheme is extremely redundant, but it makes a lot of information directly available.

The structure struct siteCluster, containing all these pointers, is defined as follows:

```
struct siteCluster {
  char spin;
  struct siteCluster *next;
  struct siteCluster *former;
  struct siteCluster *parent;
  struct siteCluster *son;
} cluster[L * L];
```

In this way, it is immediately possible, from any site, to get to the head or tail of the cluster, and we can run through the cluster both in the head to tail direction and in the tail to head one. Initially, each site is declared as a cluster on its own. All pointers point to a single site which is both the first and last site of the cluster:

```
for (i = 0; i < L; i++) {
  for (j = 0; j < L; j++) {
    cluster[j + i * L].next   = cluster + (j + i * L);
    cluster[j + i * L].former = cluster + (j + i * L);
    cluster[j + i * L].parent = cluster + (j + i * L);
    cluster[j + i * L].son    = cluster + (j + i * L);
  }
}
```

Note that we are using a one-dimensional array indexed by means of both lattice coordinates. This method is useful and often used, because it allows for an efficient memory access and an efficient computation of the indirect referencing.

The function siteUpdateList updating a site is obviously more complex than in the local algorithm, because it needs to update pointers. It is shown in Listing 13.11.

```
1 unsigned long int siteUpdateList(long int direction,
2                                  long int site) {
3   long int i, j;
4   unsigned long int weAreChanging = 0;
5   long int lowerSite, upperSite;
6   struct siteCluster *upperHead, *upperTail;
7   struct siteCluster *lowerHead, *lowerTail;
8   struct siteCluster *scratchSiteCluster;
9
10  unsigned long n = neighbor[site][direction];
11
12  if ((cluster[site].spin == cluster[n].spin) &&
13      (cluster[site].parent != cluster[n].parent)) {
```

```
1
2     weAreChanging = 1;
3
4     if (cluster[site].parent < cluster[n].parent) {
5       lowerSite = site;
6       upperSite = n;
7     } else {
8       lowerSite = n;
9       upperSite = site;
10    }
11
12    upperHead = cluster[upperSite].parent;
13    upperTail = cluster[upperSite].son;
14    lowerHead = cluster[lowerSite].parent;
15    lowerTail = cluster[lowerSite].son;
16
17    scratchSiteCluster = upperHead;
18    scratchSiteCluster->parent = lowerHead;
19    while (scratchSiteCluster != scratchSiteCluster->next) {
20      scratchSiteCluster = scratchSiteCluster->next;
21      scratchSiteCluster->parent = lowerHead;
22    }
23
24    scratchSiteCluster = lowerHead;
25    scratchSiteCluster->son = upperTail;
26    while (scratchSiteCluster != scratchSiteCluster->next) {
27      scratchSiteCluster = scratchSiteCluster->next;
28      scratchSiteCluster->son = upperTail;
29    }
30
31    lowerTail->next = upperHead;
32    upperHead->former = lowerTail;
33  }
34  return weAreChanging;
35 }
```

Listing 13.11   The function siteUpdateList.

The array **neighbor** and the structure array **cluster** are global variables, which are visible to the function. On line 12 in the listing in page 402 we evaluate whether the site and its neighbor have the same value for their site variable (if they are both operative or both broken). On line 13 in the same page we evaluate whether they have different labels. In the latter case, we need to change the labels, which is indicated by the statement **weAreChanging = 1**. Otherwise, the function has finished its task and returns the value 0. If the labels need to be updated, we first establish which of the two parts has the lowest label. We identify this label with

parent, which is thus the only one surviving. At this point, we store the value of the **parent** and the **son** of both parts in auxiliary variables and we copy the lowest **parent** on the cluster part who has the highest **parent**: we do the other way around for the **son**. Now, the two parts that before were considered separate clusters have the same **parent** and the same **son**.

To complete the fusion of the two clusters in a single one, we only need to change the pointers **next** and **former** pointing, respectively, to the last site of the prevailing cluster (the one with the smallest **parent** label) and the first site of the absorbed cluster. This is taken care with the statements on lines 31 and 32 in page 403.

Hands on 13.9 - Reconstructing the connected components

Program the non-local algorithm we just described. Compare its performance to that of the local algorithm. For example, compare the average CPU time and the average number of lattice inspections needed before the algorithms converge. Study various values of the density, while approaching the critical density. The lattice size should not be too small (for example, start with a lattice of size $V = 20 \times 20$).

Chapter 14

Bits and Boolean variables

Everything should be made as simple as possible,
but not simpler.

Albert Einstein.

In this chapter we introduce the operators acting on a single bit of a word.
On the one hand, we discuss the operators AND, OR, XOR and NOT, and
we clarify the difference between these *binary operators* and the logical ones
(that are discussed in Section 3.3.2). On the other hand, we introduce the
shift operators (*shift*), and we learn how to create "masks" to select parts
of a word.

We discuss how the basic operators of elementary algebra can be easily
built by only using binary operators. We define simple *cellular automatons*
in a single spatial dimension. We explain why we introduce these models
based on binary variables, and we discuss their implementation in C by
means of binary operators. We generalize these models to a two-dimensional
space and introduce John Conway *game of life*.

14.1 Single bit operators

The bit operators allow us to look at a word as a sequence of bits. In C,
words are composed of 8, 16, 32, 64 or more bits, i.e., of binary variables
which can take two possible values. In what follows we almost always
chose to indicate these values with, respectively, 0 and 1. However, as
we have already discussed a few times, in other contexts it can be useful

and it is absolutely equivalent to represent them in a different way. For example, when discussing the Ising model in Section 19.3, we represent the two values, respectively, with +1 and −1, or, even, with the *green* and with the *red* color.

Throughout the first chapters of this textbook we discussed how words are organized. Now we want to get a better understanding of how to act directly on the single bits. Figure 14.1 shows the 4 bytes and 32 bits of an int type variable. Let b_0 be the rightmost bit, b_1 the second one from the right, up to the leftmost bit, b_{31}. Each bit can take the values 0 or 1. The rightmost bit is said to be the low order bit, while the leftmost bit is the high order one.

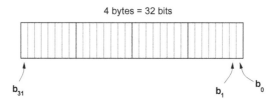

Fig. 14.1   A word of the int type (in this case consisting of four bytes). Each byte consists of eight bits: the word consists of 32 bits in total. Each bit can take the value 0 or 1.

Single bit operators are applied to entire operands of the char, short, int, long int or long long int type, with or without the unsigned qualifier (with this kind of operators it is always better to use unsigned types, and in what follows we will normally assume this is the case).

The binary operator & performs the bitwise AND operation between two variables of the integer type. We should not confuse it with the unary operator, which returns instead the operand address. The result is a word with bits equal to 1 only in those positions in which the bits of both operands are equal to 1. Let us consider, for example,

```
unsigned int a, b, c;
a = 11;
b = 13;
c = a & b;
```

The result of this operation is c = 9. Indeed, in Chapter 1 we saw that $11 = 2^3 + 2^1 + 2^0$: in other words the decimal number 11 in binary becomes 1011, preceded by twenty eight zeros. The decimal 13 becomes 1101 in

Table 14.1   Truth table of the bitwise AND operator.

AND	0	1
0	0	0
1	0	1

Table 14.2   Truth table of the bitwise OR operator.

OR	0	1
0	0	1
1	1	1

binary. The operator & acts on all bits of the word. The only bits which are equal to each other in both numbers and equal to 1 are the first on the right (b_0) and the fourth from the right (b_3). Thus, in binary, the result of the operation equals 1001 (preceded by twenty eight zeros), i.e., 9 in decimal.

In Table 14.1, we show the *truth table* of the bitwise AND operator (obviously it is the same as the truth table of the logical AND operator). For each of the two possible values of both the first and the second operand (we need to consider four possibilities) the truth table contains the corresponding result of the considered operation.

The second operator acting on single bits is the OR operator. It has the form | and gives a positive result if at least one of the two considered bits is equal to 1. Its truth table is given in Table 14.2.

An example for the use of the bitwise OR operator is

```
c = a | b;
```

In the case where a = 11 and b = 13 the result of this operation is c = 15 (since in the four rightmost bits at least one of the operands has value 1).

A third relevant operator is the XOR (or exclusive-OR) operator. It has the form ^ and gives as a result the value 1 only if *just one* of its operand equals 1 (XOR of 1 and 1 gives 0). Its truth table is given in Table 14.3. Note that the corresponding logical operator is not defined in C. We have

```
c = a ^ b;
```

Again, considering a = 11 and b = 13 the operation result is c = 6. Indeed, only the second and third bit starting from the right equal 1 in just one of the operands. The binary operators comparing two words bit by bit are

Table 14.3   Truth table of the
bitwise XOR operator.

XOR	0	1
0	0	1
1	1	0

Table 14.4   Truth table of
the multiplication between variables with the values $+1$ or -1.

$\times$	$+1$	-1
$+1$	$+1$	-1
-1	-1	$+1$

very different from the logical comparative operators (discussed in Section
3.3.2) which act on the value represented by the entire word.

It is interesting to note that there exists a particularly simple notation
for the XOR operator. The Boolean variables can, for example, be represented either by the values 0 and 1 or by the two values $+1$ and -1. For
example, let the symbol η indicate a Boolean variable represented by the
values 0 and 1. Repeating the arguments given in Section 12.3, we define
the variable

$$\sigma \equiv (1 - 2\eta) \ , \tag{14.1}$$

which can take the values $+1$ and -1. The XOR operation on two variables
of the type η has a one-to-one correspondence to the usual multiplication of
two variables with values $+1$ or -1. The multiplication truth table is given
in Table 14.4. If we identify the value 0 for η with the value $+1$ for σ and
the value 1 for η with the value -1 for σ, everything clearly coincides. This
correspondence allows us to treat very different problems with the same
techniques.

Even if this identification is generally valid, there are some important
differences between the two approaches. First of all, usually a XOR operation is faster than an a multiplication between integers. The second
difference is more substantial. Imagine to have a couple of two binary variables, η_1 and η_2. We store them in the first (rightmost) two bits of an
unsigned char type of variable. In binary, the two variables both have
value $0000\,0011$. Applying one single XOR operation we simultaneously
perform the *two desired operations* on both variables (this occurs for thirty
two variables if we fill words of the **int** type with Boolean variables). This
technique is called *multi-spin coding*. It allows us to save CPU time when

working with binary variables. We discuss this aspect further throughout the following pages. With a multiplication, this same approach cannot be applied in such a direct and optimized way.

Two other very important operators are the left and right shift operators, respectively. The left shift operator is indicated with ≪ while the right shift operator is indicated with ≫. The left shift operator is a binary operator applied as follows:

```
c = a << b;
```

It shifts the bits of the variable a, b bits to the left, filling the word on the right with bits of value 0. The bits leaving the word on the left are discarded. For example, 1 << 2 = 4. The reason for this is simple. The constant 1 only has the rightmost bit equal to 1, while all others are 0. Instead, for variables of the **unsigned char** type, we have, for example, 3 << 7 = 128, given that the first 1 on the left is eliminated. If we consider a **char** of eight bit, we have 0000 0001. Shifting all of them two positions to the left, we get 0000 0100, i.e., the value of 4 in base ten. Clearly, a left shift operation by b bits is equivalent to a multiplication by a factor 2^b until none of the bits equal to 1 reach the end of the word.

The right shift operator is applied as follows:

```
c = a >> n;
```

It shifts the bits of the word a, n places to the right. The lower bits on the right are eliminated. In the case of an **unsigned** variable, bits with value 0 are inserted on the left. In section 14.2 we give some more information on what happens for the leftmost bits of a word for variables with a sign. For now, though, we do not make any general assumption on their value. For example, (assuming zeros are inserted on the left) 21 >> 3 = 2 because 21 equals $16 + 4 + 1$ and, thus, in binary equals 10101. Moving these three bits to the right, we get 10 in binary which is precisely 2 in decimal.

Finally, we introduce the bitwise NOT operator, ~. This operator transforms each bit of the variable to which it is applied in its one complement. It is used as follows

```
b = ~a;
```

For example, in binary notation, the NOT of an **unsigned char** variable 4 is, ~0000 0100 = 1111 1011 equal to 251 in decimal.

The priority of the binary bitwise operators is lower than the mathematical comparative operators, such as == or !=, but higher than the corresponding logical operators. The unary negation operator has the same priority as the unary + and - (higher than the binary + and -), while the shift operators have a higher priority than the comparative operators. Also in this context a non parsimonious use of parentheses making the priorities more explicit leads to a better code and helps to reduce the number of programming errors.

14.2   How to operate on bits

The first important concept we want to discuss is the one of a *mask*. A mask is a word used to extract a group of bits from a number. In what follows we consider two **unsigned char** variables each including eight bits. The variable uc has value 91 in decimal, corresponding to 0101 1011 in binary. Imagine we want to know the number corresponding to the three least significant or low order bits (the three rightmost bits) of uc. Since the (decimal) value 7 is written as 0000 0111 in binary, it is immediately clear that the value we are interested in is given by r = uc & 7;. Indeed, the bitwise AND with *mask* 7 selects the three rightmost bits of uc. The (most) significant bits are certainly reset because in 7 those bits are 0, while in the low order bits the values of uc are copied because the value 7 consists of three bits equal to 1.

A second important remark concerns the difference between bitwise operators and logical operators. The bitwise operators & and | are very different from their equivalent logical operators && and ||. The bitwise operators compare the bits composing a word *one by one*, while the logical operators compare two complete numbers. For example, if a = 5 and b = 8 we have that a & b equals 0 while a && b equals 1. Indeed, the values 5 and 8 do not have any bits in common which are equal to 1. Therefore, the bitwise AND operation results to be zero. Instead, both values are *true* by convention (i.e., they are nonzero). Hence, their logical AND is true, and the result is set equal to 1 (again by convention: if the result is true, the value 1 is returned).

We already mentioned how a left shift, as in y << 3, is equivalent to a multiplication, in this example times $2^3 = 8$. The high order bits are dropped, while the zeros needed to complete the word are added on the right. On the contrary, a right shift of n bits is connected to a division by 2^n. The rightmost bits that leave the word are eliminated. Moreover, as we already mentioned, if the word is of the **unsigned** type, the empty spaces on the left are guaranteed to be filled with zeros. Instead, in case of a signed quantity (for example, a simple **int**), what is inserted in the leftmost bits may depend on the compiler, on the hardware and on the operating system (for example, sometimes, the bit of the sign is copied in all other bits). Therefore, we should not count on the value of these bits. Instead, with the help of a mask, we can make sure they all have the desired value.

It is often useful, especially when working with bits, to indicate the numerical constants in a base different from the decimal one. The compiler assumes that an integer constant starting with 0 (zero) is expressed in *octal*, i.e., base eight. The statement

```
unsigned int a = 013;
```

assigns the decimal value $11 = 1 \cdot 8^1 + 3 \cdot 8^0$ to the variable **a**. Instead, the compiler assumes an integer constant starting with $0x$ or $0X$ (the two notations are equivalent) is expressed in *hexadecimal*. The statement

```
unsigned int a = 0x13;
```

assigns the decimal value 19 to the variable **a**. Even if it only contains a single decimal digit (the zero on the left), the value **0XFFUL** is, for example, a legitimate hexadecimal constant (**U** stands for **unsigned** and **L** for **long int**) which in decimal notation equals 255. Specifying that the variable is of the **unsigned** type, allows us to also use the high order bit as part of the word (which otherwise is destined to indicate the sign). Instead, if we specify the variable to be of the **long int** type, we can represent values that are larger than if we were to use an **int** for example.

When working with bits, often the bitwise NOT operator, performing the one complement, is important. Let us analyze, for example, the result of the expression

```
y = x & (~0X7F);
```

The hexadecimal value $7F$ in decimal is expressed as 127 (which is completely irrelevant) and in binary as $\ldots 0001111111$ (with all initial zeros needed to fill the bits of the word). The NOT of this value equals $\ldots 1110000000$ (with all initial bits equal to 1). Therefore, the bitwise AND of this value and x selects all bits of x except for the seven low order ones, which are set equal to zero: y is equal to x with the seven rightmost bits set to zero.

Hands on 14.1 - Selecting a group of bits

Write and test a function

```
unsigned int fieldSelect(unsigned int word,
                         unsigned int position,
                         unsigned int size);
```

returning the field consisting of **size** bits at the position **position** of the word **word**. The field should be returned at the extreme right of the word. Write a function that puts the field back in its original place.

The function described in the Hands on 1 can be described in a single statement. In short, the function returns

```
word >> (position + 1 - size)
    &
  ~ (~0 << size);
```

Let us start by analyzing what happens on line 3. First of all, the NOT of 0 creates a word in which all bits are equal to 1. Subsequently, this word is shifted **size** bits to the left, by means of the shift operator (`<< size`). In this way we obtain a word with **size** zeros on the right and all other bits equal to one. The other NOT operation (also on line 3) computes the complement to one of these bits, thus creating a word with, on the right, **size** ones and all other bits equal to zero. This is the mask we use to extract the field of our interest. The mask has the correct length and selects the rightmost bits. We still need to select the correct field; this is done on line 1, where we move the field of our interest. The AND operation on line 2 applies the mask and stores precisely the desired field.

Hands on 14.2 - Bit rotation

Write and test the function

```
unsigned int rotate(unsigned int word,
                    unsigned int direction,
                    unsigned int size);
```

performing a cyclic shift of **size** bits in the word **word**. The bits leaving the word **word** on one side should reenter it on the other side. The variable **direction** allows us to rotate to the right (for example, if **direction** = 0) or to the left (for example, if **direction** = 1). The function returns the new, rotated word.

Hands on 14.3 - The bits of a `float`

Write a function that prints the values of the bits of a word of the `float` type. Test it with various values: positive, negative, integer, simple and non-simple rational fractions. Can you interpret the role of all 32 bits? This is a case where a `union` may come in handy.

14.3 A small multiple adder of bits

We want to discuss an extremely simple example showing how C is able to act on single bits and how to use these in parallel, with few elementary logical statements, to perform various operations (in our simple example we consider additions). Logical statements (applied to bits) are typically much more efficient than the usual operations between integers. This is an additional advantage together with the fact that a single group of statements acts on many variables. Let us see how this works in detail.

We consider binary variables η_i, which take the values 0 or 1. Each of these variables can be stored in a single bit of memory. We now want to add two of these variables and we need to perform this operation for a large number of couples of variables. For example, we want to know whether, in each one of many couples of telephone exchanges needed to guarantee redundancy, both are working (this is the optimal situation), one of the two is broken (in this case we immediately need to perform a quick maintenance operation) or both are broken (this is a very bad case). The sum $\eta_1 + \eta_2$ is necessarily equal to 0, 1 or 2, as the two operands are either 0 or 1. A variable which can take three possible values can be stored in two bits. The fourth and last representable value with two bits, 3, is not allowed.

In a word consisting of 32 bits we can store 16 such results. Even more crucial is the fact that, using words of 32 bits and a single group of elementary operations, we can compute 16 such additions at the same time. We only perform logical, single bit operations and no additions between integers, as the former are often more efficient.

We choose an `unsigned` type of 32 bits (and with a `sizeof` we check whether the type really occupies 32 bits!). In each variable of this type, we store 16 Boolean variables, indicated by $\eta_i^{(j)}$, where i takes the values 1 or 2 and characterizes the operand, and j characterizes the bit. The bit

b_0 (the rightmost one) contains $\eta_1^{(0)}$, the next bit, b_1, equals 0. Continuing in this way bit b_2 contains $\eta_1^{(1)}$, b_3 equals 0, up to b_{30} containing $\eta_1^{(15)}$ and b_{31} has value 0. A variable a defined in this way equals

$$a = 0\,\eta_1^{(15)} \ldots 0\,\eta_1^{(1)}\,0\,\eta_1^{(0)}\,,$$

where the symbols following each other do not indicate they are multiplied, but rather indicate the positional order in which they are stored in the 32 bits composing the word **a**. In other words, we can write

$$a = \begin{bmatrix} 0 & \begin{Bmatrix} 0 \\ 1 \end{Bmatrix} \end{bmatrix} \cdots \begin{bmatrix} 0 & \begin{Bmatrix} 0 \\ 1 \end{Bmatrix} \end{bmatrix} \begin{bmatrix} 0 & \begin{Bmatrix} 0 \\ 1 \end{Bmatrix} \end{bmatrix}.$$

In each couple of bits, the left bit is equal to 0, while the right one has value 0 or 1.

Again interpreting the sequence of symbols as the order in which they are written in the word, and not as a multiplication, the second operand can be written as follows:

$$b = 0\,\eta_2^{(15)} \ldots 0\,\eta_2^{(1)}\,0\,\eta_2^{(0)}\,.$$

To compute the sum between the 16 variables contained in **a** and the 16 variables of **b**, we want to use bitwise comparative operations. The possible results of each of these additions, in decimal, are

$$0+0 = 0\,;\ \ 0+1 = 1+0 = 1\,;\ \ 1+1 = 2\,.$$

Instead, in binary and explicitly writing both bits involved in the sum, we have

$$00 + 00 = 00\,;\ \ 00+01 = 01+00 = 01\,;\ \ 01+01 = 10\,.$$

This last result is important, since it tells us when we have to "carry" a one to an upper bit: the low order bit is set to 0, but a 1 is carried to the high order bit of the two bit word. If we just consider the low order bit of the word, we find the following rule:

$0+0 = 0\,;\ \ 0+1 = 1+0 = 1\,;\ \ 1+1 = 0$ with a 1 which is to be carried.

Ignoring the carrying problem, this rule corresponds exactly to the truth table of the XOR operation! Thus, the low order bit of the result can be determined with a simple XOR.

How can we determine the value of the bit that we will carry? We saw we need to carry a 1 if and only if both of the to be summed bits are equal to 1. So, obviously we need to use the AND operation, giving 1 if both bits in input are 1, and 0 otherwise. The bit supplied by the AND is then shifted by one position to the left by means of a shift operator.

In short, the operation we want to perform, is given by:

```
((a & b) << 1) | (a ^ b);
```

as should be clear by now. The XOR operation determines the low order bit, the AND determines the bit that will be carried, the shift moves the latter to where it belongs and the OR merges the two words. There can be no conflicts, because in one of the two words all even bits are zero, while in the other all odd bits are zero.

Let us reexamine how we can build and test this adder, highlighting the important steps.

- We start by creating 16 couples of random numbers, with the value 0 or 1. Remember that, even if this is just a test and the quality of the random numbers is not essential, this operation should, as is always the case with random numbers, be performed *well*. Thus, we need to use a good random number generator with a long period and choose the value 0 if the random number lies in the first half of the possible values and the value 1 otherwise. We define these variables $r_\alpha^{(i)}$, with $\alpha = 0, 1$ and $i = 0, \ldots, 15$.
- We print the couple of numbers and their sums computed in the usual way.
- We "wrap" the two groups of 16 variables in two variables of the **unsigned int** type consisting of 32 bits each:

$$A_\alpha \equiv \sum_{i=0}^{15} \left(r_\alpha^{(i)} << (2i) \right) ,$$

for $\alpha = 0, 1$.
- We use our small Boolean adder (we use the $\oplus$ to indicate the operator applying this type of addition) to calculate the sum

$$B = A_0 \oplus A_1 .$$

- We unwrap B and print the results, i.e., the 16 words

$$R^{(i)} \equiv (B >> (2i)) \,\&\, 3 \ .$$

The mask which in decimal equals 3 in binary equals 11 and the bitwise AND operation selects the two rightmost bits of the word.

Hands on 14.4 - Generalizations of the small adder

Create the small adder we just described, test it, and evaluate its efficiency. It is possible to write a code based on `unsigned char`, `unsigned int`, `unsigned long int`, or also `unsigned long long int` variables. Do this and again evaluate how effective these various approaches are.

Generalize the adder to deal with sums of three binary variables. Generalize it also to deal with sums of two variables which can take four, instead of two values. How many variables can we simultaneously add in an efficient way in this case? Try to write a generic adder of integers in this form. This is a bit more difficult, but certainly not impossible.

14.4   Von Neumann and Ulam cellular automatons

It is often possible to describe even very complex problems with Boolean variables. We already encountered some of these systems. For example, the lattice gas discussed in Section 12.3, which is a simple prototype of particles interacting only by means of the excluded volume effect. Lattice gases can be more complicated than this simple model, and they can describe realistic, interacting models. Another example is percolation theory discussed in Section 13.4. In usual models binary variables interact in a simple, local way. This is because the behavior of each such elementary variable only depends on the state of the *neighboring* variables and does not need to have a particularly complex functional form. This does not prevent the possibility of finding, for some values of the parameters, a collective and complex behavior, where elementary variables are correlated at long distances.

Formally simple rules are often sufficient to generate complex behavior. This apparent paradox lies in how we define these *simple* rules. They can considered to be simple, because they connect, by means of simple functional forms, variables that can only take two values. But the system consists of many variables, and this fact can be a crucial new element.

We start by considering the *cellular automatons* introduced by von Neumann and Ulam [von Neumann and Burks (1966)]. First of all, we analyze the one-dimensional case. We consider cells which can take the values 0, 1 arranged along a chain in one spatial dimension. We consider a dynamic process depending on a time variable t proceeding at discrete intervals of size 1. We assume that the value of a given cell at time $t + 1$ only depends on the value of that same cell and its two neighboring cells at the preceding time instance, equal to t. We show what happens in Figure 14.2. The dashed variable is the one that is changing. On the top we show all the variables that can possibly influence the dynamics at time t. This is a *cellular automaton*.

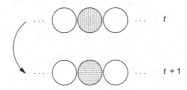

Fig. 14.2 A configuration at time t (on the top) evolves into a different configuration at time $t+1$ (at the bottom), by changing the central, dashed variable. The (deterministic) rule defining this change depends only on the state of the three variables shown in the figure at time t.

How can we study this kind of model? First of all, we choose an initial configuration which, for example, has a single cell turned on (with value 1), or an initial configuration initialized in a random way. This configuration evolves under application of a given rule, that characterizes the model, to all the cells of the chain. An important fact is that the cells are updated *in parallel*. So, all new values are calculated based on the values at the previous time instance. Only when we have calculated all values of the new variables we update their values. Remember that we defined the model such that the configuration of system variables at time $t + 1$ is determined using only the variables defined at time t.

If we define i to be the cell index, $C_i(t)$ the value at time t of the variable "living" on site i (ith cell) and $\{C_i(t)\}$ the configuration of all values of the variables at time t, the rule establishes the correspondence

$$\{C_i(t)\} \longrightarrow \{C_i(t+1)\} \,,$$

between the configuration at time t and the one at time $t + 1$. In some cases, the number of cells N, just like the boundary conditions, can play an important role. In this case, it is interesting to study the *finite size effects* by varying the value of N. In the following typical numerical experiment we study initial configurations for which at the initial time, $t = 0$, only the variable in $i = 0$ plays a role (we assume i can take values ranging from $-\frac{N}{2} + 1$ up to $\frac{N}{2}$). Moreover, we assume to be working in conditions guaranteeing that the boundary of the cellular automaton never touches the border. Thus, usually we choose a value of N such that all the dynamics is contained within the array used to store the variables and the border does not play any role. This strategy is valid only for particular initial conditions, which depend on the selected dynamical rule.

Two fundamental aspects characterize the cellular automatons. First of all, the systems we defined are discrete by nature. They have not been created to have a continuous limit, where they live in a space-time which cannot be represented by a lattice. The rules governing the discrete dynamics have a fundamental character and, in this way, they define the model. Second, the one-dimensional cellular automatons are a simple example of a dynamical system with a possibly very interesting behavior. Our numerical analysis should clarify this fact.

The cellular automatons have the following fundamental characteristics:

 (1) they are discrete systems (both in space and time);

 (2) they are local systems, since the dynamics of a variable only depends on the neighboring variables (and the values computed at the time step preceding the considered one);

 (3) they are synchronous systems since all new values of the variables are calculated before the system is updated.

The rule describing a variable value at time $t+1$ and how it is updated, is determined using at most 3 variables, as we mentioned before. Namely, it depends on the values of the variable that will be updated and on its two neighbors at time t. As each of these three (Boolean) variables can take two possible values, the possible number of different inputs is $2^3 = 8$. Our rule should take eight different input values into account and associate to each of these eight values one of the two allowed values for the new variable (the value at time t).

How many rules, associating two output values to eight input values, exist? There exist $2^{2^3} = 2^8 = 256$ possible rules, associating a Boolean output to a triple of Boolean input values. We can name each one of these 256 rules giving each a classification number. A natural way of doing this can be achieved with the very simple classification scheme proposed by Wolfram [Wolfram (2002)]. For example, let us consider the rule described in Table 14.5. According to this rule, to the configuration 1 1 1 at time t, we associate the value 0 at time $t+1$. So, if a variable at time t equals 1 (the second value of the threesome) and has a right neighbor which equals 1 (the third value) and a left neighbor with value 1 (the first value), it becomes 0 at the next time instance. We can list all correspondences in this way. Starting from, 1 1 1 which in decimal is written as 7, passing to

Table 14.5 The rule 90 of the Wolfram classes. The eight lines contain the chosen correspondences for the eight possible configurations of the input variables. The second value $(v(t))$ is the one of the to be changed variable at time t. The first $(s(t))$ is the one of the variable to its left, and the third $(d(t))$ the one of the variable to its right, always at time t. The fourth value is the one the considered variable takes at time $t + 1$.

$s(t)$	$v(t)$	$d(t)$	$\longrightarrow$	$v(t+1)$
1	1	1	$\longrightarrow$	0
1	1	0	$\longrightarrow$	1
1	0	1	$\longrightarrow$	0
1	0	0	$\longrightarrow$	1
0	1	1	$\longrightarrow$	1
0	1	0	$\longrightarrow$	0
0	0	1	$\longrightarrow$	1
0	0	0	$\longrightarrow$	0

1 1 0 which in decimal is 6 and so on, we write, from left to right, all values the output variable takes. For example, for the rule of the Table 14.5, this procedure gives the number 0101 1010, which in base ten is 90. This is why we call it the rule 90.

We now apply the rule 90 to the variable living at site i. The result produced by applying this rule does not depend on the value of the ith variable at time t, but only on its two neighbors living at sites $i-1$ and $i+1$ (at time t of course). The first and second output of Table 14.5 coincide with the third and fourth, and the fifth and sixth coincide, respectively, with the seventh and eight. So, changing the second of the three bits (representing the value of the to be changed bit) does not have any influence on the result. If the two neighbors of the considered variable are equal to each other the result is 0 (lines 1, 3, 6 and 8 of the table), otherwise it is 1 (lines 2, 4, 5 and 7 of the table). This table is identical to the one of the XOR operator that has as arguments the values at time t of the two variables spatially adjacent to the one that has to be changed. In other words the rule 90 consists of a single XOR.

Many of the 256 allowed rules are trivial and give predictable and dull results (think for example of the results of rule 0). It is worth noting, though, that some rules generate results which are absolutely non elementary and for which the *living* variables (equal to 1) and the *dead* ones (equal to 0) alternate in a complex way. For example, if we consider them in the space-time plane, they generate figures covering more than a one-dimensional curve, but less than a two-dimensional plane. They are said to have a non-integer dimension, i.e., a *fractal dimension* different from a surface natural dimension, namely two. From one of the most simple imaginable dynamics based on variables taking only two possible values, some extremely complex behavior emerges.

The cellular automatons we are describing are based on Boolean variables, that we can represent with a single bit[1]. In this case, a strategy in which various couples of automatons are studied in parallel comes absolutely natural. This can be achieved by storing a number of them in the same word, thus allowing us to study a single rule applied to various automatons with a computational effort similar to the one required in the case we were considering just one automaton. In a 32 bit word we can store 32 copies of one of the variables of the automaton. Suppose we want to study what happens when starting from random initial conditions. We fill the 32 bits of each variable with random bits. Using what we learned in Chapter 11, we need to make sure that these random numbers are generated with care, i.e., that they are independent of each other. Suppose we want to study rule 90. Performing a XOR operation on two variables at time t, we automatically get the 32 new values at time $t + 1$.

Hands on 14.5 - Rule 90 and not only

 Study a cellular automaton. Start by applying rule 90. Write a first simple code simulating the dynamics of a single copy of the automaton. Start at time $t = 0$ with a single variable, at the center of the lattice, equal to 1, and all other variables equal to zero.

Next, write a code implementing the dynamics of 32 copies of the system by using the bitwise logical operators. Analyze the statistical properties of the asymptotic state generated with different rules. What happens for rule 101? What happens for rule 20? Compare the results obtained with these two rules.

A simple version of a code implementing cellular automatons (monitoring one single copy) is simple and given in Listing 14.1.

```
1 #include <stdio.h>
2 #include <math.h>
```

---

[1]More generally, cellular automatons based on variables taking on more than two values can be defined. Still, these variables are anyhow discrete and can only take a finite, and not an enormous, number of values.

```
 1
 2 #define NUM_ITER 200
 3 #define L (2 * NUM_ITER)
 4
 5 typedef unsigned long long int RANDOM_TYPE;
 6 typedef char CELLULAR_AUTOMATON;
 7
 8 /* Random numbers might be needed upon initialization */
 9 #define MYR64  myr64 = (6364136223846793005ULL * myr64)
10 #define MAX_RAND64    0XFFFFFFFFFFFFFFFFULL
11 RANDOM_TYPE myr64;
12 double inverseMaxRand64 = 1.0L / (double)MAX_RAND64;
13
14 CELLULAR_AUTOMATON C[L], CP[L];
15 int rule = 90;
16
17 #define MY_FAILURE -9
18 #define MY_SUCCESS 1
19
20 /****************************************************/
21 int main(void) {
22   long int time, site;
23
24   for (site = 0; site < L; site++) {
25     C[site] = 0;
26     CP[site] = 0;
27   }
28
29   C[(int)(L / 2)] = 1;
30   printf("# rule n. %d\n", rule);
31
32   for (time = 0; time < NUM_ITER; time++) {
33     for (site = 0; site < L; site++) {
34       printf("X %ld T %ld CELL %d\n",
35              site - (int)(L / 2), time, C[site]);
36     }
37     /* synchronous update */
38     for (site = 1; site < L - 1; site++) {
39       if (rule == 90) {
40         /* rule 90: XOR of neighbors */
41         CP[site] = C[site - 1] ^ C[site + 1]; {
42       } else if (rule == 150) {
43         /* rule 150: XOR of neighbors,
44                      XOR with itself */
45         CP[site] = (C[site - 1] ^ C[site + 1]) ^ C[site];
46       } else {
47         printf("program error: rule not defined\n");
48         exit(MY_FAILURE);
```

```
1          }
2        }
3        /* set C to CP */
4        for (site = 0; site < L; site++) {
5          C[site] - CP[site];
6        }
7      }
8      for (site = 0; site < L; site++) {
9        printf("X %ld T %ld CELL %d\n",
10               site - (int)(L / 2), time, C[site]);
11     }
12     return MY_SUCCESS;
13 }
```

Listing 14.1   A cellular automaton.

Let us comment about the most relevant points of the code included in Listing 14.1. The random number generator defined on line 9 in the listing in page 421 is needed to create a random initial configuration. In our version we start with a configuration consisting of all 0, except for the variable at the center of the lattice which is equal to 1, as is clear from the lines 24-29 in the same page. So, we never use the generator, but we include it for completeness.

We define the type CELLULAR_AUTOMATON on line 6 in page 421 by means of the type char. It could be interesting, though, to use, for example, an int instead, and check whether the code performance changes. The two main arrays, C[L] and CP[L] are of the type CELLULAR_AUTOMATON. They are defined in the statement 14.

In the cycle on line 38 in the same page, we first of all compute the new values of all variables (as mentioned before, we are using a *synchronous* dynamics) for each of the NUM_ITER time steps. The array C supplies the values of the input variables, while the output values are temporarily stored in the array CP. Only at the end, the resulting values are copied in the array C with the cycle on line 4. In the code of Listing 14.1 we defined, as an example, the rule 90 and the rule 150. We remark that the way we wrote things down is clear, but very inefficient, given that a not very optimized compiler checks the selected rule at each step of the cycle. It would be more correct, but less clear and more error-prone, to use the #ifdef command (deciding upon compilation which lines of code should be included). For example, if we choose the rule 90, the if command on line 39 leads to a XOR operation between the two neighbors.

The rule 90 is simply written as CP[site] = C[site-1] ^ C[site+1] (line 41 in the same page), i.e., by means of a single bitwise XOR.

For each rule we can choose to explicitly use the truth table with its eight possibilities or a simplified notation (deduced case by case) as the one given. In what follows we also consider the example of rule 150.

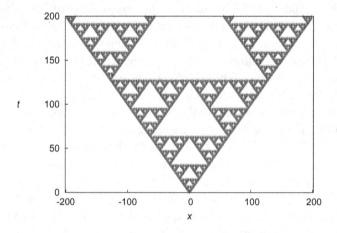

Fig. 14.3   On the horizontal axis we represent the sites of the chain. On the vertical axis we represent the discrete time of the dynamics (evolving according to rule 90 of Wolfram classification). Variables equal to 1 are represented by a black box, while the boxes of the variables with value 0 are kept white. Initially, only the variable at the central site of the chain equals 1, and all others are equal to 0.

In Figure 14.3 we show the results obtained by applying the rule 90. The sites of the chain are represented along the horizontal axis. The discrete time of the dynamics (evolving according to rule 90 of Wolfram classification) is represented along the vertical axis. The time increases towards the top of the leaf. The initial configuration is the bottom one, lying on the horizontal axis. The variables equal to 1 are represented by black boxes and those equal to 0 are kept white. Initially, only the variable at the central site of the lattice equals 1, while all others are equal to 0. It is easy to see that the geometric set generated in this way is *self-similar*. Whether we look at the figure at a given length scale, or at a scale which is two times smaller or two times larger, we always observe the same figure. A large triangle consists of three triangles which are smaller by a scale factor λ. In turn, these triangles contain themselves three triangles which are smaller by the same factor λ and so on. This is true for each triangle of the figure, however large, up to the scale induced by the discrete character of the elementary variables. This is what we define as a complicated rule.

The geometric shapes generated by the rule 90 have a nontrivial *fractal dimension*. This means that the space occupied by the black points increases with time according to a power different from one or two. If we consider the black points of Figure 14.3 to be a subset of a two-dimensional plane, with the space on the abscissa and the time on the ordinate, this subset does not fill the entire plane. Still, it is not simply a curve (of dimension one) on the plane either. It has an intrinsic dimension, generated by the dynamical process we defined, which is intermediate between one and two. Only some rules generate figures with a non-integer intrinsic dimension. This dimension depends on the used rule.

Another example of a rule producing an interesting dynamics is given in Table 14.6. Following the same reasoning as before, this rule takes the name of rule 150. Let us take a look at the truth table of the rule 150. We consider the three input variables (the variable to be updated and its two neighbors at time t). The output is precisely the sum of the three input variables modulo two. If the sum of the three inputs is even (zero or two inputs equal 1) the output value is zero, while if it is odd (one or three inputs equal 1) the output value is 1. In terms of the arrays C and CP, it is easy to see that the rule 150 can easily be rewritten, requiring very little computation power, as

```
CP[i] = (C[i-1] ^ C[i]) ^ C[i+1];
```

In Listing 14.1 we used a different, though fully equivalent formulation, to show how a single rule can be expressed in different ways. To understand this formula well, it is useful to remember the two-by-two bit adder. Indeed, here we are interested in the result modulo two, so we can omit the bit to be carried from the bit adder. In Figure 14.4 we show the results of the rule 150. Also in this case the intrinsic dimension is nontrivial. There are two groups of triangles repeated at all length scales. The intrinsic dimension is different from the one of rule 90.

Writing a code that simultaneously evaluates the dynamics of 32 systems is easy. First, we write the rule by means of bitwise comparative operators, taking the truth table of the basic operators as a reference. Next, updating an appropriately initialized 32 bit variable, the 32 copies of the system are updated automatically. Essentially, the 31 additional copies are analyzed, without any further work, by the system hardware. Once the numerical simulation has ended, the data analysis is clearly a bit more difficult than in case we only study a single copy of the system. The various copies

Table 14.6   Rule 150 of Wolfram classification.

$s(t)$	$v(t)$	$d(t)$	$\longrightarrow$	$v(t+1)$
1	1	1	$\longrightarrow$	1
1	1	0	$\longrightarrow$	0
1	0	1	$\longrightarrow$	0
1	0	0	$\longrightarrow$	1
0	1	1	$\longrightarrow$	0
0	1	0	$\longrightarrow$	1
0	0	1	$\longrightarrow$	1
0	0	0	$\longrightarrow$	0

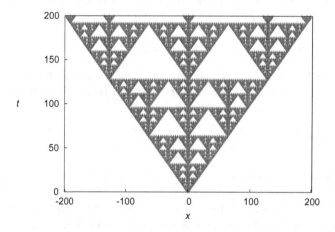

Fig. 14.4   As in Figure 14.3, but for rule 150.

first need to be *"unwrapped"* with the shift operators before they can be analyzed.

In case of the one-dimensional automatons with first neighbor interaction, Wolfram classification allows each of the possible rules to be easily named. Moreover, it allows us to catalog the rules based on the characteristics of their asymptotic state. The rules leading to a stable configuration, in which nothing changes, as time increases, are called *Class 1 rules* (the equilibrium configuration possibly consists of only zeros). These are the "dullest" rules. The Class 2 rules lead to simple configurations, without any local temporal oscillations in space. For example, a local variable may oscillate forever between the values 0 and 1. The rules of Class 2 are less dull than those of Class 1, though they are certainly not overwhelming.

The Class 3 rules possibly generate self-similar schemes and spatial arrangements with a nontrivial intrinsic dimension. These rules, of which we discussed two examples, are certainly interesting. Indeed, an articulate structure emerges from these extremely simple rules and variables. The Wolfram classification also introduces rules of Class 4, even if it is not fully clear whether this category is well-defined. Class 4 rules would be those, if they existed, generating an unpredictable asymptotic behavior which is "more complex" than that of the Class 3 rules (its behavior cannot even be predicted hypothesizing fractal structures). The *game of life*, discussed in Section 14.5 together with other automatons defined in two spatial dimensions are one of the rules typically considered to be Class 4. These "unpredictable" behaviors of the potential Class 4 could turn out to be less interesting of what we could hope.

Exercise 14.1 - The classes of the rules

Find rules of Class 1, 2 and 3. Does a small modification of the rule drastically change the system behavior, turning it, for example, from Class 1 into Class 3?

14.5   The game of life

The cellular automatons we discussed so far are defined in a single spatial dimension; we defined the system along a chain and then we let it evolve in time. The most fascinating feature of these models is their extreme simplicity. The case we considered only allowed for 256 possible rules.

A very natural way to generalize the one-dimensional cellular automatons is to build a network of cellular automatons in two spatial dimensions. For example, we could create a square lattice of Boolean variables evolving in discrete time. Each variable has eight neighbors (as is clear from Figure 14.5). Again, we consider local automatons for which the dynamics only depends on the value of the cell to be changed and its direct neighbors (not only adjacent along the sides, but also at the vertexes). So, the rule governing such a local automaton assigns a Boolean output value to nine Boolean input values (a variable and its eight neighbors). There are $2^9 = 512$ possible input values, and to each one of these we can assign one out of two possible output values. Thus, there are 2^{512} possible rules, which is an enormous number (in base 10 this is a number consisting of about 150 digits).

Even if we are still considering binary variables and local interactions both in time and in space, the fact that we are now considering two instead of one spatial dimension makes the number of possible rules explode from a value of order 10^2 to one of order 10^{150}. This is the miracle of exponential growth.

Fig. 14.5   A cellular automaton in two spatial dimensions. The central variable we want to change is drawn on a grid. The four nearest neighbors of the considered variables are filled with vertical lines, while the ones along the diagonals are filled with horizontal lines. Thus, the rule determining a new value of the central variable can depend on nine Boolean values.

An important two-dimensional cellular automaton is the so called *game of life*, or simply *Life*, due to John Conway [Gardner (1970)]. This epic model has been a source of wonder, fun and game for a long time.

The rules of the game of life are extremely simple. A living cell, i.e., with value equal to 1, survives if it maintains its value 1, or dies if it switches to the value 0. A cell with value 0 either remains inactive if it stays equal to 0, or it gets alive and becomes 1. To decide what occurs, we first of all compute the sum of the values of the eight neighbors, and we call it Σ. Σ can take a value ranging from 0 (in case of no living neighbors) to 8 (in case all neighbors are alive). Next, we evaluate what happens based on the following rules.

- A living cell, i.e., a cell with value 1, stays alive if Σ is equal to 2 or 3; otherwise it dies. A too crowded environment does not allow us to survive, because it implies that there is too much competition for the available resources. Nor can we survive if we are too lonely, because loneliness does not allow for a synergic organizational force to evolve.
- An inactive cell, i.e., with value 0, gets alive only if $\Sigma = 3$, and remains 0 in all other cases. A birth only occurs in optimal conditions, which here are considered to have three neighbors.

A certain number of configurations behave in a particular, possibly periodic or diffusive, way. An example could be three consecutive living sites which are isolated from the other cells. A figure of the transient status if a game of life configuration has *flying kites*, oscillating flip-flops and many other non-obvious patterns. These interact among themselves, change and mutate towards an asymptotic state. A typical numerical experiment starts from a random configuration containing the patterns one will analyze. We then iterate the system (generating many instantaneous images of two-dimensional figures evolving in time, as in a movie). Typically the final point is a configuration which is generally not alive, but does contain some surviving patterns.

Hands on 14.6 - The game of life

 Study the game of life. Analyze the dynamical states and the elementary configurations which are repeated over time. Which forms can you identify, classify and analyze? Which properties can you deduce?

In the game of life simple shapes can generate complicated structures, evolving in a complex way in time. By analyzing these structures we discover a virtual and two-dimensional world where we can study interesting events. A first noteworthy structure is the one that drew Conway attention to this model, and to which Martin Gardner dedicated his famous popular article [Gardner (1970)], namely the *R-pentomino* (shown in Figure 14.6). A pentomino is a group of five elementary squares in which each square has at least one side in common with another square of the group. We can draw twelve different shapes like this (considering the shapes obtained by rotation or reflection as the same). Usually they are indicated by the letters of the alphabet they resemble. The R-pentomino does not look too much like the letter R, but as it does not resemble any other letter, R is a good way to name it. While the other 11 pentominos have a trivial fate, the R-pentomino enjoys a glorious life. Its (isolated) evolution lasts for 1103 iterations in the world of the game of life. It undergoes a large number of interesting effects[2].

Exercise 14.2 - The pentominos

 Draw the twelve pentominos. For the 11 pentominos different from the R-pentomino-R, describe, without using a computer, how it evolves according to the dynamics of the game of life. Describe the endpoint of the dynamics.

---

[2]In Gardner original article, the faith of the R-pentomino-R was not yet known since only 460 steps had been simulated. The computers of those days were certainly not like today powerful machines.

Fig. 14.6   The so-called *R-pentomino* was the first *interesting* scheme, which motivated Conway to study the game of life in depth. It consists of only five living variables. The evolution starting from this pattern, reaches a stationary point only after 1103 iterations, after the variables propagated throughout a large region of the lattice and after having gone through a large number of intermediate states.

The R-pentomino is one of the many exceptions that make the game of life interesting. Other typical configurations have various levels of interest. The simplest and less dynamic configurations are stationary, i.e., they do not vary with time. They are called *still lives*, of which some are given in Figure 14.7. In order for a figure to be stationary, all living variables should have 2 or 3 neighbors and no dead cell should have 3 neighbors. Clearly a compact square (called *block*) is the simplest shape satisfying this condition. Each of the four living variables has 3 living neighbors, while the dead variables adjacent to the square all have 2 neighbors which are alive. For example, the R-pentomino, disseminates several blocks throughout its evolution. These remain abandoned in the two-dimensional world of the game of life. Figure 14.7 also includes some other stable shapes: a *beehive*, a *boat*, a *ship* (similar to a boat, but a bit bigger) and a *loaf*.

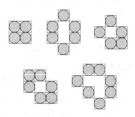

Fig. 14.7   *Still lives* (i.e., stable shapes which do not change throughout the game of life dynamics). On top, from left to right: a *block*, a *beehive* and a *boat*. On the bottom, again from left to right: a *ship* and a *loaf*.

A second category of noteworthy shapes are the *oscillators*, which periodically repeat elementary structures. The *blinker* and the *toad* are shown in Figure 14.8. For example, the *blinker* oscillates with a period equal to one between a horizontal bar of three living variables and a vertical one of three living variables. The moving shapes are extremely interesting. For

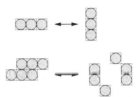

Fig. 14.8   *Oscillators* (i.e., shapes oscillating in place with a fixed period, which in this case is equal to one). On top, the *blinker*, on the bottom the *toad*.

example, in Figure 14.9 we show a *glider*. The glider, moving along the diagonal, is the simplest moving object. After four steps its shape is repeated, but has moved one step along one of the diagonals. This is why the glider is said to move at a fourth of the speed of light in the world of the game of life.

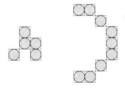

Fig. 14.9   Simple moving objects. On the left, a *glider*, moving along the diagonal. On the right, the *queen bee shuttle*, which first moves to the right, then to the left, next makes a long show and finally stops.

In Figure 14.9 we show another particular shape, called the *queen bee shuttle*. This shape in the end stops moving, but before becoming stationary, moves first to the right, then to the left and produces a certain number of remarkable effects. Combining the queen bee shuttle with other simple forms, we can build interesting shapes. The *spaceships*, shown in Figure 14.10, move along the system axes. In these systems the concept of transient plays an important role. Some shapes giving rise to transient effects are shown in Figure 14.11. For example, ten adjacent aligned living variables evolve into an oscillator with period 15 in which this initial configuration no longer occurs.

Finally, we mention some shapes which keep on growing. For example, with two queen bee shuttles we can build a *glider gun*. The fact that these structures exist is important in the game of life. Without the proof that the latter exist, the possibility that every initial configuration asymptotically

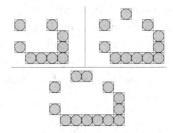

Fig. 14.10 The *spaceships*, moving along the horizontal or vertical axes. At the left top, a *lightweight*, at the right top a *medium weight*, at the bottom a *heavy weight space-ship*. The thin lines serve to delimit the three spaceships. These figures are especially interesting for astrophysics and aerospace engineering students.

comes to an end in a limited space would remain open.

At this point we have all the elements to write a code simulating the game of life. It is important to decide how the input is given to the program. It should be possible to give it both by means of the keyboard as from a file. On the Internet network enormous and very complex files of patterns can be read without any problems with a well-written code. It is also possible and easy to find Java applets efficiently simulating the game of life. We can use these to check our results.

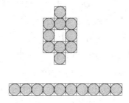

Fig. 14.11 Some transient configurations. The line on the bottom evolves into an oscillator with period 15, while the shape of top becomes a *pulsar*, an oscillator with period 3.

Simple models, such as the game of life, help to highlight the important features of a complex problem. In many situations it is not interesting to consider all details of a complicated problem (in order to build a skyscraper, it would be risky to proceed by resolving all the quantum-mechanical equations of the atoms composing all the cement needed to build 176 floors). Identifying the features allowing us to resolve the problem of interest is precisely the foundation of a scientific approach. So, the type of modeling we considered here could be useful in many contexts. Typical applications of analogous methods are traffic studies, dealing with how congestions arise and how they can be avoided. Another significant argument concerns how fires propagate in woods and how to limit the damage provoked by such a process. Finally, we mention the study of earthquakes for which it is of enormous practical importance.

Hands on 14.7 - The disordered life

 The game of life usually ends in stationary states, which possibly contain periodic repetition in time and infinite cycles, but are not so interesting. To make the game more passionate (and more realistic) we introduce some randomness into it. Study the game of life, while perturbing the system with a certain quantity of random noise: the rule should be applied, but is violated with a certain probability defined beforehand.

There exists an interesting regime, with a very small amount of randomness. For example, a rule is violated with probability 0.01 percent or smaller, even by a factor ten. Start with an R-pentomino and analyze the system in presence of randomness. What happens when there is more randomness, for example, of 2 percent?

In conclusion, we summarize our observations on the *cellular automatons*. They are certainly interesting systems. First of all, they can be fun to study, they are easy to program, their study does not take much computation time and interesting behaviors easily emerge from simple rules. We created a virtual (and somewhat magical) world evolving in our computer. Second, the *complexity* in these systems emerge from something *very simple*. Elementary rules which are local both in time and in space, and variables assuming only two values generate persistent behavior leading among others to nontrivial fractal dimensions. This is interesting. What is missing, though, is a link with a mathematical analysis explaining these phenomena. This clearly is a limit of this approach. Indeed, there is no corresponding quantitative theory explaining these phenomena, while much more complicated systems can be explained by appropriate mathematical theories, usually based on continuous variables and infinitesimal calculus. This is limiting because the most important role of a computer in quantitative scientific research is to proceed together with the analytic calculus, to open new roads for the latter, clarify the paths, provide quantitative and rigorous basis and create new questions and approaches.

PART 3

Programming advanced algorithms

Chapter 15

Recursion and data sorting

> What is recursion? It is [...] nesting, and variations
> on nesting. The concept is very general. (Stories
> inside stories, movies inside movies, paintings inside
> paintings, Russian dolls inside Russian dolls (even
> parenthetical comments inside parenthetical
> comments!)—these are just a few of the charms of
> recursion.)
>
> Douglas R. Hofstadter, *Gödel, Escher, Bach* (1979).

In this chapter we explore the concept of recursion. We show how efficient it is when applied to a simple problem, namely data sorting. A plain definition of a *recursive* function is a function which calls itself. The use of recursive functions is generally a delicate, but extremely efficient operation: indeed recursion optimally exploits computer features, but small programming errors may cause disastrous results. A good use of the recursive technique, even in case of very complex operations, allows one to create programs which are much shorter than those written without this technique.

Initially, it might seem less "natural" to use a recursive algorithm rather than a non-recursive one. This is probably due to the fact that we are essentially brought up with the sequential logic. Nevertheless, it is important to learn how to use the recursive logic. Anybody who ever tried to solve the problem of the "Tower of Hanoi" (box on page 453) surely agrees.

Let us consider the computer as a machine helping us to avoid repeating some simple operations many times. The advantage is to write a program of a restricted length compared to the number of operations that are finally executed by the computer. In this respect, the recursion is a program property which maximizes the ratio between the complexity of the executed machine operations and the programmer's work. Indeed, programming a single simple function and calling it in a recursive way, works at different levels of the algorithm to achieve the desired final result. Very often recursive algorithms perform better than non-recursive ones. Therefore, we start this chapter by recalling some basic concepts about the analysis of the computational complexity of an algorithm. We also introduce some simple sorting algorithms, and classify them according to the computational resources they require.

15.1   Analysis of the performance of an algorithm

An algorithm is a well-defined computational procedure transforming an *input* into an *output*. As an example, consider the problem of sorting data (discussed in this chapter). The input is a set of objects (for simplicity, though not necessarily, we presume they are numbers) and the output is the same set of objects, arranged in a different way (for example in increasing or decreasing order).

By definition, an algorithm is a deterministic procedure. Nevertheless, there exist *randomized algorithms* which make use of random numbers during their execution. In practice these random numbers are obtained with a pseudorandom number generator (Chapter 11), and the randomized algorithm together with the pseudorandom number generator again are a deterministic algorithm. Therefore, the difference between the two types of algorithms might seem only formal. In any case, the probabilistic analysis of a randomized algorithm assumes the random numbers to be completely uncorrelated (although the pseudorandom numbers, used in practice, may have some correlation).

The *computational complexity* theory (box on page 439) classifies computational problems based on the computing resources required to solve them. The following are the most common resources considered.

- The computation time (also called CPU time or machine time) is the number of elementary operations which need to be executed to solve the problem. This time does not coincide perfectly with the physical execution time because different elementary operations may have different execution times depending on the processor. Still, it is reasonable to assume that an algorithm requiring a smaller number of elementary operations finishes earlier than one requiring a larger number of operations.

- The memory required to store all data of the problem, which includes both the original data and the data generated during execution.
- The number of processors (nodes) in a parallel computer.
- The bandwidth (i.e., the amount of data that can be transmitted per time unit) of the communication channel between the memory and the processor in a single computer or between different nodes in a parallel computer.

In this textbook, we only consider the first two resources, as the other two depend on the computer architecture. For example, the communication bandwith might depend on the number of registers, *cache* levels and the communication protocol between the nodes of a parallel computer.

The complexity of a problem is inevitably connected to the complexity of the best algorithm solving that problem. However, the computational complexity is a formal theory classifying *problems* even before the best algorithm resolving them is known. Due to space limitations we do not expose the computational complexity theory in this textbook. Rather, we limit ourselves to the computational complexity analysis of *algorithms* (i.e., of their performance).

The computational resources required during the execution of an algorithm increase with the size of the input (sorting a million numbers is much more demanding than sorting a thousand numbers). For this reason the computational complexity theory classifies algorithms based on the *rate* with which the necessary resources increase with the size N of the input.

Let T be the generic computational resource required by the algorithm. An algorithm is said to be linear or quadratic in the size of the input if, in the limit $N \to \infty$, we have that[1] $T = \mathcal{O}(N)$ or $T = \mathcal{O}(N^2)$. In practical applications, the multiplicative coefficient of the power of N is also important. Suppose for example that we have two algorithms available, one with $T_1 = N^2$, and another with $T_2 = 1000N$. Therefore, for small input sizes, $N < 1000$, the first algorithm is more efficient. Nevertheless, the classification of algorithms is based on the asymptotic behavior when N tends to infinity. Therefore, from the theoretical viewpoint, the multiplicative constant can be ignored and the second algorithm is said to perform better.

---

[1]We write $T = \mathcal{O}(N^\alpha)$ if the limit $c = \lim_{N\to\infty} T/N^\alpha$ exists and it is different from zero ($0 < c < \infty$). In practice $T = \mathcal{O}(N^\alpha)$ indicates that T grows like N^α for very large N.

In order to correctly apply the theory it is crucial to make a good estimate of the input size N. Indeed, depending on the problem under consideration, the input size N should be defined in different ways. For example, in a data sorting algorithm, N is the number of objects to be sorted. However, for an algorithm computing the factorization of a number, N is the number of bits required to represent this number. The rule that N is the number of bits required to encode the complete input may be enough to classify a problem as P or NP (see box on page 439). However, in order to compute the exact power determining the growth of an algorithm complexity, a more precise definition of N is needed. This becomes clearer by considering an example.

Consider a quadratic sorting algorithm, i.e., its execution requires a number of operations proportional to M^2, where M is the number of input datapoints which need to be sorted. If all datapoints are composed of B bits, a single comparison operation between two elements takes a time which is proportional to B. Therefore, the total execution time is proportional to $B \cdot M^2$, which cannot be expressed as a function of the number of input bits, i.e., $N = B \cdot M$, only. Therefore, with this specific algorithm, sorting 100 numbers of 30 bits each requires more time than sorting 30 numbers of 100 bits each, even though the total number of input bits is the same in both cases.

Bear in mind that these kinds of situations are rather rare though. Typically, the computer memorizes every single input datapoint in a memory *word*, consisting of $B = 32$ or $B = 64$ bits in most of today's computers. Therefore, in the majority of the cases, the rule that N is either the number of bits, or the number of memory words to represent the input is perfectly fine.

From a practical viewpoint, the most useful classification is the one which divides the algorithms between the following two classes:

- polynomial (or subexponential) algorithms, whose execution time grows as $T = \mathcal{O}(N^\alpha)$, and that solve problems belonging to the P (polynomial) class;
- exponential algorithms[2], whose execution time grows as $T = \mathcal{O}(e^{aN})$, and that solve also problems belonging to the NP (nondeterministic polynomial) class.

The definitions of classes P and NP together with a short account on computational complexity theory are given in the box on page 439.

---

[2]We here neglect the superexponential algorithms, for which we have for instance $T = \mathcal{O}(N!)$, as these solve problems which are not treated in this textbook.

Computational complexity theory

Computational complexity theory is a branch of theoretical computer science which is mainly concerned with the classification of problems based on the resources required to solve them. The complexity of a problem is defined by how the resources required by the best solving algorithm increase with the size N, measured in bits, of the most difficult input (*worst case analysis*).

A large part of computational complexity theory deals with *decision problems*, i.e., problems whose solution consists of a simple answer Yes or No. It can be proven that more complicated problems can be reformulated as decision problems. For example, for an optimization problem (in which the minimum of a cost function needs to be determined) the question «What is the minimum cost?» is equivalent to a series of questions of the type «Is the minimum cost smaller than C?», for appropriate values for C.

Decision problems are grouped together in classes of equal complexity, the most important ones being P and *NP*. The complexity class P comprises all problems that, even in the worst case, can be solved by a deterministic Turing machine in polynomial time. The problems in the NP class can be solved in the worst case by a non-deterministic Turing machine in polynomial time. Indeed, NP stands for Non-deterministic Polynomial. A deterministic Turing machine is nothing but a mathematical formalization of a normal computer. Instead, its non-deterministic analogue is a hypothetical computer that can be programmed also using the `goto both` statement. In case the program gets to such a statement, the execution *contemporary* follows in both directions specified by the statement. A similar machine could potentially manage a number of processes exponentially large in N. An alternative definition is that a possible solution to a NP problem can be *verified* in polynomial time by a deterministic Turing machine.

The NP class certainly contains P, but the question whether «P=NP?» remains unanswered so far. The importance of this question is clear from the fact that there exists a one million dollar prize for whoever finds a mathematically rigorous answer. An interesting subset of NP is the *NP-complete* class. It suffices to find an algorithm 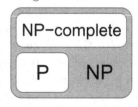 solving one of the NP-complete problems in polynomial time, to prove that all problems in NP are solvable in polynomial time. Thus, NP-complete contains the most difficult problems of NP. The figure illustrates a possible structure of the complexity classes (the one which is likely to hold, according to the opinion of experts in the field).

Exercise 15.1 - Computational complexity

Based on the simple classification of algorithms presented here above, make an estimate of the computational complexity of the following problems, or at least indicate to what complexity class they belong:

• verify whether N data are in decreasing order;

• given the positions of N planets, compute their potential gravitational energy;

• compute $N!$;

• list the permutations of N numbers;

• given a system composed of N spins (i.e., binary variables) $s_i \in \{-1, 1\}$ with $i = 1, \ldots, N$, whose energy is $E = \sum_{ij} J_{ij} s_i s_j$ (where all J_{ij} are given in input), find the histogram of the energy E considering all possible configurations of the system (this histogram is called the density of states).

In practice, the problems belonging to the P class are considered to be *tractable*. The fact that a polynomial algorithm exists ensures it can be solved even for large input sizes. Instead, problems belonging to the NP class, but not the P class, are considered *intractable*, as the best known solving algorithm takes an exponential time.

These definitions of tractable and intractable problems are obviously a bit arbitrary. For example, having to choose among two algorithms running in a time N^{10} and $e^{0.0001N}$ respectively, we would opt for the exponential one since it is faster for any reasonable value of N. The above definitions are very useful though. Indeed, experience teaches us that given a problem for which the best known algorithm is of the exponential type, finding a new polynomial algorithm which solves it, is very difficult. Nevertheless, once a polynomial algorithm has been identified (even with a large value for the exponent), improving this algorithm (by decreasing the value of the exponent) is relatively easy. It is not a coincidence that the vast majority of well-known polynomial algorithms has an exponent $\alpha \leq 3$. This justifies the division we introduced between tractable and intractable problems.

In the following sections we illustrate how to calculate the computational complexity of some polynomial sorting algorithms. In section 18.4 some exponential algorithms are described.

15.2   A first sorting algorithm: Insertion sort

Sorting a data set is a simple problem with many applications. Very often the sorting algorithm is called by a more complex algorithm which requires a part of the data on which it is working to be sorted. Formally, the data sorting problem can be defined as follows:

input: a set of N *datapoints to be sorted*, $\{x_i\}_{i=1,\dots,N}$, and a *binary* comparison *operator* which applied to a couple of data, returns a **true** value if they are in the right order and **false** otherwise;

output: a set of N *sorted datapoints*, $\{y_i\}_{i=1,\dots,N}$, which is a permutation of the input data set

For simplicity, but without loss of generality, we always use the larger than operator ($<$) as comparison operator in this chapter. The following discussion generally applies to any other comparison operator, as long as it has the transitivity property, i.e, if $A < B$ and $B < C$ then $A < C$.

Let us start with the most simple data sorting algorithm, *Insertion sort*. The following example explains how this sorting by insertion works.

Imagine having a deck of mixed cards which need to be sorted (this is the set $\{x_i\}$). Pick a first card and hold it in your hand. Pick a second card, and compare it to the one you are already holding: if it has a lower value, place it to the left of the first card, otherwise place it to its right. Pick a third card, after comparing it with the other two, insert it in the correct position. By continuing this process until you have finished the deck (and assuming you manage to hold all of them in one hand!) the cards result to be sorted and the set $\{y_i\}$ is represented by the cards you are holding.

Hands on 15.1 - Insertion sort

 Write a program which reads from a file a data set to be sorted, rearranges it in increasing order using the Insertion sort algorithm and prints the sorted data set on screen (or in `stdout`).

Hands on 15.2 - Analysis of Insertion sort

 The aim of this exercise is to numerically estimate how the execution time of the Insertion sort algorithm increases with the number N of data to be sorted. To this purpose, create some files containing an increasing number

of random numbers (generated with another program for example). A reasonable number of input data varies from $N = 100$ up to $N = 10^4$. Execute the program written in the previous exercise while keeping track of the execution time (if you use the Linux operating system, use the shell command time). Plot the execution time as a function of N and estimate how it grows by fitting with a power law function AN^B.

The Listing 15.1 contains an example of a function using the Insertion sort algorithm (the name of the function is due to the fact that in Section 15.2.2 we describe a better function).

```
1  void naiveInsertSort(float *input, float *output, int size){
2    int i, j, k;
3    float datum;
4
5    for (i = 0; i < size; i++) {
6      datum = input[i];
7      j = 0;
8      while ((j < i) && (datum > output[j])) {
9        j++;
10     }
11     for (k = i; k > j; k--) {
12       output[k] = output[k-1];
13     }
14     output[j] = datum;
15   }
16 }
```

Listing 15.1   A first version of the Insertion sort algorithm.

The arguments of the function naiveInsertSort are, respectively, the pointer input to the data vector which is to be sorted, the pointer output to the vector where the sorted data are stored, and the length size of both these vectors. It is not necessary to initialize the output vector before passing it to the function (nor it is initialized inside the function) because the function is written in such a way that only those elements of the output vector to which a value has already been assigned are read.

The index i runs along the input vector. Note that the element which is to be inserted at step i of the most external cycle, input[i], has been saved explicitly in a temporary or *auxiliary* variable, datum (line 6). In this way, if a not very refined compiler were to be used, the program does not recalculates the physical memory location where it is stored, i.e., input[i], at each step of the internal cycle (line 8), if a not very refined compiler were to be used.

To this purpose it is useful to recall that when reading an element of a vector (`input[i]` in this case) a program performs the following operations:

(1) it reads the memory location corresponding to the beginning of the vector, which is stored in the pointer to the vector (`input` in this case);

(2) it adds, to this memory location, a quantity which is the product of the index of the element to be read (`i` in this case), and the number of bytes required to store a vector element (in this case, the vector contains `float` types and therefore the number of bytes is 4);

(3) it reads the memory location resulting from the previous operations.

This explains why reading the content of a single variable is faster than reading the content of a vector element. For this reason, i.e., to avoid many repetitions of the operations listed above, it is preferable to copy the content of a vector element which is to be used several times throughout the program into an auxiliary variable.

Continuing the analysis of the code, note that the index j is increased until it reaches the point where the content of the variable `datum` needs to be inserted. The order in which the two conditions in the `while` are executed is important. Indeed, during step i of the external cycle, the `output` vector has been already filled up to index i − 1. When the index j reaches the value i, the internal cycle is interrupted because the first condition of the `while` command is no longer satisfied. This is crucial for the program to work properly. If, at that point, the program also checked whether the second condition is fulfilled, it would have to read the contents of `output[i]` which has not yet been defined and the result of this operation is unpredictable. The conditions are evaluated form left to right, and their evaluation is interrupted as soon as a condition is decisive. Thus, the order of the conditions inside a control flow command is fundamental.

Once it has been established that the element `datum` needs to be inserted in the position j, all elements of the `output` vector with index j ≤ k < i are moved one position to the right to make room for `datum` (lines 11-12). Care is needed to ensure this displacement starts from the rightmost element in order to avoid overwriting the elements which have not yet been copied in the new position.

15.2.1   *Insertion sort analysis*

We now analyze the number of operations which are to be performed inside the function `naiveInsertSort` to sort N data, i.e., when `size` $= N$. Assuming that each elementary operation is executed within the same number of computer *clock* cycles, this number of operations is proportional to the actual execution time. This approximation is not fully correct, but sufficient for the level of approximation used here.

The external cycle (line 5) is repeated N times. Therefore, the operations executed within it must be multiplied by a factor N. More specifically, we need to evaluate how many operations are involved in the i-th cycle and then sum them. Lines 6, 7 and 14 contain a fixed number of operations, that we call n_1.

The duration of the `while` cycle (line 8) depends on the position where the element `datum` is inserted, which in turn depends on the sequence of numbers which are read in input. Here, we can only make an estimate based on the hypothesis that the sequence of input numbers is a typical random sequence, i.e., it is neither partially nor completely sorted. During the i-th step of the external cycle, $i - 1$ data were already sorted. Assuming there are no correlations between these already sorted data and the element we want to insert, we expect `datum` to be inserted in a position around $i/2$. So, the first internal cycle (line 8) lasts for $i/2$ steps on average, and each one of these consists of a fixed number n_2 of operations. The second internal cycle (line 11) runs for more $i/2$ steps on average, and each one of these consists of a fixed number n_3 of operations.

A precise estimate of n_1, n_2 and n_3 is beyond the scope of this textbook. It depends on many details, such as the compiler and the hardware characteristics of the used computer. Omitting their exact values, we just recall that they are fixed numbers, i.e., of order $\mathcal{O}(1)$ (in this particular case, they are all not much more than about ten operations).

If we bring together the information gathered so far regarding the number of operations, and using the fact that $\sum_{i=1}^{N} i = N(N + 1)/2$, we have

$$\sum_{i=1}^{N} \left(n_1 + n_2 \frac{i}{2} + n_3 \frac{i}{2} \right) = n_1 N + \frac{n_2 + n_3}{2} \frac{N(N + 1)}{2} = \mathcal{O}\left(N^2\right) , \quad (15.1)$$

where the summation corresponds to the external cycle.

Thus, the Insertion sort algorithm is of order N^2. A correct execution of the Hands on 15.2 should have led to the same finding. In the following sections, the same data sorting problem is solved in much more efficient ways using faster algorithms, that make use of recursion.

First, however, let us comment on how the code can be optimized. A function executing a certain algorithm can be programmed in many different ways. Code optimization is the search for the most efficient one among these. In terms of the mathematical expressions in (15.1) this corresponds to minimizing the coefficients n_1, n_2 ad n_3 (if we did not write some awful code, the power of N should not vary!). Of course such a search has a cost, namely the time it takes the programmer to find it. It is therefore important to understand a priori where in the program optimization could lead to better results. For example, referring again to expression (15.1), it is clearly more useful to decrease the coefficients n_2 e n_3, which are multiplied by a term of order N^2, rather than n_1 which is multiplied by a term of order N. Several techniques (and many "tricks") exist to obtain such optimization: one of which we already saw, namely, using an auxiliary variable, and others will be shown throughout the following chapters.

15.2.2 *Improving Insertion sort*

Before passing on to more efficient algorithms, let us still discuss a little more the Insertion sort algorithm and show how it is possible to improve the performance of an algorithm with essentially little effort. We just saw how the execution time of this algorithm grows as $\mathcal{O}(N^2)$. The memory needed during execution is $2N$, as it uses one vector in input and another in output. Even if the powers of N with which these resources grow cannot be improved upon (unless we change algorithm), by optimizing the program we can decrease the coefficients.

Hands on 15.3 - Insertion sort with less memory

 Suppose that the main limitation of the computer we are using is the memory used by the Insertion sort algorithm. Adapt the program written in the Hands on 15.1 such that the data are kept in one sole vector. At the beginning this vector contains the input data, while at the end it contains the sorted data.

The required memory space can be decreased only down to N: below it is impossible as the N data have to be memorized! However, also simplifying by a simple factor 2 may be important for large N. All algorithms treated in the remainder of this chapter use a total memory of N locations, i.e., the minimum required. The Listing 15.2 contains a possible function using one sole data vector while executing Insertion sort.

The `data` vector is sorted from left to right, i.e., starting from the elements with smaller index. At the `i`th cycle the elements with index lower than `i` are sorted correctly and the algorithm is concerned with inserting `data[i]` in the correct position. To this purpose, a copy of this element, `datum`, is compared to the sorted elements starting from the largest one and going down. The elements which are larger than `datum` move one position to the right to make room for `datum`.

Also for this version of the algorithm there exists a parallel with the commonly used method for sorting cards: the only difference with respect to the one mentioned earlier is that here we start with all cards in our hands.

```
1  void insertionSort(float *data, int size) {
2    int i, j;
3    float datum;
4
5    for (i = 1; i < size; i++) {
6      datum = data[i];
7      j = i - 1;
8      while (j >= 0 && data[j] > datum) {
9        data[j + 1] = data[j];
10       j--;
11     }
12     data[j + 1] = datum;
13   }
14 }
```

Listing 15.2   A function executing Insertion sort using one sole data vector.

A calculation similar to the previous one allows us to obtain the number of operations this function takes to sort N datapoints. For each external cycle (line 5), lines 6, 7 and 12 execute a fixed number n_1' of operations. In turn, each time the internal cycle (lines 8-11) is executed, a fixed number n_2' of operations are executed. A similar reasoning to the one we made above suffices to establish that during the i-th step of the external cycle the internal cycle is executed $i/2$ times on average. Thus, the total number of operations becomes

$$\sum_{i=1}^{N} \left(n_1' + n_2' \frac{i}{2} \right) = n_1' N + n_2' \frac{N(N+1)}{4} = \mathcal{O}\left(n_2' N^2 \right) .$$

A quick analysis of the two functions `naiveInsertSort` and `insertionSort` suggests that the number of operations n_2' is very similar to the sum $n_2 + n_3$. Therefore the execution times of both programs should not differ very much. On the contrary, the second program (apart from occupying half the memory of the first) executes a lot faster. It sorts the same data in about 60 percent of the time required by the first program (for $10^3 \leq N \leq 10^5$).

This shows that even though a *theoretical* analysis of an algorithm is important, it may not capture its real performance. The latter must be verified *experimentally* by measuring the execution times.

15.2.3 *Estimating the execution times*

The analysis of the Insertion sort algorithm depends on the specific sequence of numbers that are supplied in input (which is often the case also in many other algorithms). The required resources and, in particular, the execution time T may vary a lot depending on the input. In general, we can assume there exists a probability measure in the space of all possible input data defining a probability that a particular input is given. This probability measure induces a probability distribution on the execution times T, which is in general broad, i.e., it is not concentrated around its average value. A typical example are distributions with so-called "fat tails", which slowly decay for values far from the average one. In these cases, the average of the distribution, and sometimes also of the first moments, is not enough to accurately describe the complete distribution.

Suppose we calculate the execution time T_i of all possible inputs (the index i runs over all inputs). In practice, this may end up being a really heavy computation. It is enough to notice that N numbers can generate $N!$ sequences, and already for $N = 15$ this amounts to $N! > 10^{12}$ sequences, which is a considerable number of operations for a PC. Even if it is not always possible to compute T_i for each input, some interesting observations can be made regarding the set of times $\{T_i\}$.

Let us consider figure 15.1 that contains a schematic example of a possible shape for the distribution of times T. Certainly the most interesting quantity is the average value $\langle T \rangle$, which defines the so-called *average case*. Indeed, a first simple estimate of how much time it takes the program to

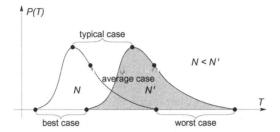

Fig. 15.1   Schematic representation of the execution times probability distribution of an algorithm with two different values for the input sizes N and N'. The typical case corresponds to the one with maximum probability (this is also known as the mode). The definition of the other cases is intuitive.

sort M randomly chosen sequences is given by $M \cdot \langle T \rangle$. However, this answer is sometimes not accurate enough, and it may generate annoying problems in case the computing time at our disposal is limited and we are not allowed to exceed it. Indeed, we should consider that the distribution $P(T)$ may have a long tail at large values of T, and it might be necessary to compute the variance of the distribution in order to understand the extent to which the execution time fluctuates from input to input.

Let us consider a somewhat paradoxical example showing that sometimes the average is not sufficient to correctly predict the execution time. Suppose we have the following distribution of times:

$$P(T) = 0.99\, \delta(T - 10) + 0.01\, \delta(T - 200)\,.$$

In other words, 99 percent of the sequences is sorted in 10 hours (the time measurement unit is irrelevant for the present purpose), while 1 percent of the sequences requires a lot more work, equal to 200 computing hours. The average of the distribution is $\langle T \rangle = 11.9$ hours. Thus, it would be reasonable to assume that 90 sequences can be sorted in 45 days: 45 days = 1080 hours $> 11.9 \cdot 90 = 1071$ hours. However, in 60 percent of the cases, a similar estimate would cause the program not to terminate! Indeed, this 60% is the probability that among 90 sequences there is at least one requiring 200 hours of computing time. The presence of a single "difficult" sequence causes the total execution time to become $89 \cdot 10 + 200 = 1090 > 1080$.

Though this example is slightly exaggerated (a more realistic example would be more complicated), it demonstrates that only the average might not be sufficient and we have to deal with rare and unexpected events. In the previous example, it would have been enough to save the sorted sequences on the hard disk each time they are computed, in order not to loose 45 days of work, when only a few hours of work remained.

In any case, it is useful to gather some more information on the time distribution $P(T)$. By defining the *best case* and *worst case* scenarios as those for which the required resources are minimum and maximum respectively, we define a time window in which the program necessarily terminates its execution. Let $T_{\min}$ and $T_{\max}$ be the times corresponding to the best and worst case scenarios, respectively. These two times depend on the input size N. Analogously to the analysis of Section 15.2.2 we can calculate how these two times grow with N.

Let us consider the function `insertionSort`. The best case occurs when we pass an already sorted data vector to the function. It is easy to verify that in this case the internal cycle is never executed. Therefore, the function executes $\mathcal{O}(1)$ number of operations at each step of the external cycle and we have $T_{\min} = \mathcal{O}(N)$. Note that it is impossible to sort the data in less than a linear time, as it takes a time N to verify whether N data are sorted.

In the worst case, the internal cycle is executed a maximum number of times, i.e, i times. This means `datum` is always copied into `data[0]` which occurs when the input sequence is sorted in a decreasing order. Thus, $T_{\max} \simeq 2\langle T \rangle = \mathcal{O}(N^2)$, and this means that this version of the Insertion sort algorithm behaves in the worst case only a factor 2 slower than the average case: in other words there are no rare events for which the performance drop down drastically.

Exercise 15.2 - Maximum and minimum times for Insertion sort

Calculate the execution time of the `naiveInsertSort` function described in Section 15.2 in the worst and the best case. Comment on the differences with the `insertionSort` function (and, in this way, find an extra reason to have written the second version).

15.3 The recursive "Divide and Conquer" strategy

Often, one of the most efficient strategies to solve a problem is to
- divide the problem in subproblems of smaller size;
- solve these subproblems;
- recombine the solutions of these subproblems into the solution of

the original problem.

This strategy has been known ever since ancient roman times as *divide et impera.*

At a first sight, this strategy might seem perfectly normal and not very ingenious. After all, all problems we considered so far that were of a certain complexity have been divided into subproblems and each single subproblem has been treated by a specific function. Here though, we want to focus on the innovating aspects of the *recursive* use of this strategy.

The real power of the "divide and conquer" (or in short D&C) strategy is that the subproblems can be solved with the same method, i.e., dividing them in even smaller subproblems. The D&C strategy can be applied recursively up to a point where the subproblems have reached a predetermined minimum size. Obviously this kind of strategy is almost exclusively programmed by means of recursive functions. Figure 15.2 contains a schematic representation of how the D&C strategy works. For simplicity, but without loss of generality, we never consider cases in which the number of generated subproblems is larger than 2.

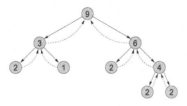

Fig. 15.2 Schematic representation of how a "divide and conquer" strategy works. Each node in the tree represents a recursive function and the number it contains is the size of the function input. For sizes larger than $N_{\min} = 2$, we apply the strategy: the input is divided into two parts and correspondingly, two recursive functions are called (downward arrows). The output of the functions called is sent back to the calling functions (dashed upward arrows), which use them to recompose the solution of the original problem.

The choices that have to be made when using this type of strategy essentially regard

- how to divide the problem in subproblems;
- the minimum size at which this strategy is no longer applied.

When deciding how to divide the problem in subproblems, we must both consider the difficulty of dividing the data of the original problem into subsets (to which we then apply the D&C strategy again), and the difficulty of reconstructing the solution of the original problem from the solutions of the subproblems.

The optimal minimum size beneath which it is no longer favorable to apply the D&C strategy often is difficult to calculate as it depends on the specific way in which the algorithms are programmed. Most of the time the minimum size up to which the D&C strategy is applied is decided by using common sense. For instance, let us consider the case of data sorting. When a recursive function for sorting a data vector consisting of $N = 2$ data is called, rather than dividing the vector in two subvectors of one element each and reapplying the D&C strategy to the smallest dimension possible ($N_{\min} = 1$), it is certainly more convenient to sort the 2 data inside the function and avoid any extra recursive calls (i.e., keeping $N_{\min} = 2$).

15.3.1 *The recursive logic*

There is a big difference between recursive and non-recursive functions. Namely, when we read the code of the latter it is easy to figure out all the operations that the computer will make upon execution: there is a direct correspondence between the lines of code and the computer operations.

This correspondence also exists for recursive functions, though it requires some level of abstraction. We have to imagine that at each point in which the recursive function is called, the whole code of the function has to be rewritten in order to obtain a code reflecting the effective number of operations the computer performs. This difference often complicates the programming of recursive functions.

```
1 unsigned long long int fact(int n) {
2   if (n > 0) {
3     return n * fact(n - 1);
4   } else {
5     return 1;
6   }
7 }
```

Listing 15.3   A recursive function computing the factorial.

Therefore, we start the study of the recursive D&C strategy by digressing first a bit on the logics of programming a recursive function. We reconsider the recursive function for computing the factorial from Section 13.2.2.

The recursive function of Listing 15.3 is particularly easy. Its correctness can be verified by performing a kind of "expansion": the expression `fact(2)` is equal to `2 * fact(1)`, which in turn is equal to `2 * 1 * fact(0)`, which has a value equal to `2 * 1 * 1`. In this way we expanded a recursive function, `fact(2)`, into a non-recursive form, 2 * 1 * 1. There is a direct relation between the latter expansion and the number of operations the computer executes in order to compute the factorial of 2, allowing us to assert the computation is correct.

Unfortunately, for more complicated recursive functions, especially the ones implementing a D&C strategy and thus including more than one recursive call, the previous expansion becomes undoable. We need a different kind of logic, namely the one of *proofs by induction*. For instance, in order to prove that a certain property is true for all natural numbers larger than or equal to n_{min} we can perform the following 2 steps:

(1) prove that the property is true for n_{min};
(2) prove that if it is true for n (with $n \geq n_{min}$) then it is also true for $n + 1$.

The same logic can be used when writing a recursive function or simply verifying its correctness. First one should check the case with input of size N_{min}. Then all inputs of size $N > N_{min}$ are considered and one must verify that the function returns the correct output by *assuming* it works properly for all inputs of size N' with $N_{min} \leq N' < N$.

More concretely, when reading or writing the code of a generic recursive function we can assume that all recursive calls to the same function return the correct result. Saying it with apparently contradictory words, we need to believe a recursive function is correct in order to demonstrate it works well! Actually there is no contradiction at all as a recursive function with an input of size N is only allowed to call itself with an input size smaller than N.

The box on page 453 contains an interesting example of how the recursive logic allows us to easily resolve problems which otherwise might be very complicated.

15.3.2 *A recursive algorithm: Quicksort*

Let us turn now to a concrete and very useful example using the D&C strategy to sort data: the *Quicksort* algorithm. Given a vector composed of N data which need to be sorted, the Quicksort algorithm divides it into two vectors: the first one containing all data that have a value less than some preset threshold and the second one containing all the rest. The choice of the threshold value is of fundamental importance. As described in section 15.3.3 the algorithm is more efficient if the division produces two subproblems that are of a comparable size. Unfortunately, the best choice

The Tower of Hanoi

The 'Tower of Hanoi' is a puzzle that was invented by the French mathematician Edouard Lucas (1842-1891) in 1883. The game consists of a tower composed of N disks of different diameters that are stacked in order upon a rod such that the  smallest one is on top. The scope is to construct a new pile, identical to the initial one, on a second rod, using a third auxiliary rod as a temporary store. We can move only one disk at a time, and each disk must always be stacked on top of a larger disk. The solution to this game is a typical application of the recursive strategy. Indeed, moving a tower composed of 3 disks is simple and requires few moves. Moving a tower of N disks (with $N > 3$), can be decomposed in moving $N - 1$ disks from rod A to rod B, subsequently move a disk from rod A to rod C and finally move the $N - 1$ disks from rod B to rod C.

Write a recursive algorithm describing the required moves and verify its correctness. Also think of a possible non-recursive version and consider what the advantages of the recursive solution are.

for the threshold, namely, the one producing two vectors of length $N/2$ each, is not easy to achieve since the data are not yet sorted!

A possible choice might be the average value of the data. Indeed, in case the data distribution is not too asymmetric, the average value should be close to the median (which by definition divides a data set in two subsets of equal size). Though this choice might seem quite reasonable at first sight, it is not always the most efficient one. Its principal weakness is that computing the average requires us to scroll through all the N data before starting the division. Moreover, for very large N, the average must be calculated in a smart way (see section 4.5) and thus, might necessitate more operations with respect to the method we want to adopt afterwards.

For recursive functions, a simple and fast, rather than an optimal choice is preferred in order to reduce the number of operations that are repeated at each new call of this recursive function. For instance, in case of the Quicksort algorithm, a fast choice is to randomly choose an element among the N data. For convenience, this usually is the first or the last element of the input vector.

Obviously the fastest choice is not perfect. With this choice, the worst thing that might occur is that the threshold element is the smallest or largest among the N input elements. In this way, a subproblem consisting of one sole element is created (this occurs more rarely when the choice for the threshold is given by the mean, though even in this case it might happen). This choice for the threshold generally generates a recursive process with less balanced binary trees. However, as we will see in what follows, this is not a major issue.

Here, we assume that the last element of the vector is the threshold value dividing the data. Then, the subvectors are generated by moving all elements with values smaller than or equal to the threshold value to the left side of the vector, and all the others to the right. This division is executed efficiently by performing a series of swaps between couples of elements, which were on the wrong sides. Once the two subvectors are generated, the Quicksort algorithm is applied to each one of these, and thus the two subvectors are sorted. The solution to the original problem, i.e, the fully sorted vector, still needs to be reconstructed, but this is a relatively easy task thanks to the way we divided the vector. Indeed, the left subvector contains all elements that are smaller than those on the right subvector. So, it is enough to concatenate the two subvectors to obtain the original vector sorted. This operation can be actually avoided if we manage to keep the two subvectors in the same memory locations of the original vector.

Figure 15.3 contains a simple example showing how the Quicksort algorithm works. Each gray rectangle represents a recursive function. Inside each rectangle, i.e., function, a first operation partitions the given input vector (the one on top) using the last element as a threshold. The two resulting subvectors (the ones in the middle) are passed onto the subsequent Quicksort functions (continuous downward arrows). The sorted vectors are returned to the calling functions (dashed upward arrows), where they are concatenated. In this version of Quicksort, we use $N_{min} = 2$. This means that functions with an input of size 2 or smaller directly sort the data vector without performing other recursive calls.

When conceiving a recursive algorithm it is particularly important to verify all *special cases*, i.e., all situations in which the general rule is not applicable. One of these special cases always is the one with an input of the minimum size N_{min}. The normal procedure described above is executed only if $N > N_{min}$. Instead, if $N = N_{min}$ a different operation takes place (and also for $N < N_{min}$ if $N_{min} > 1$).

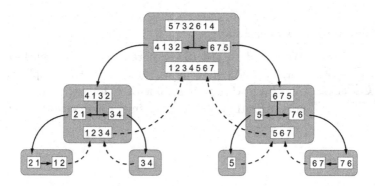

Fig. 15.3 Diagram showing how the Quicksort algorithm works.

Several choices can be made for the Quicksort algorithm. For $N_{\min} = 1$, we simply have to leave the function without performing any operation (a vector consisting of one sole element is already correctly sorted). Instead, for $N_{\min} = 2$, two data must be sorted (which can be done by performing a simple comparison) before exiting the function.

Choosing a larger value for $N_{\min}$ is preferable only if there exists a function, let us call it mySort, which for small values of N performs better than Quicksort (we assume that for large values of N Quicksort is faster otherwise we would always use mySort). Suppose that for $N < N^*$ mySort is faster than Quicksort. The optimal choice for $N_{\min}$ is then $N_{\min} = N^*$. In this way, the best algorithm is used for each value of N.

The other particular case which must be considered (or better, should be avoided!) is the one in which one of the subvectors has size zero. We leave it as an exercise to the reader to reflect on this case.

Exercise 15.3 - D&C with a subproblem of size zero

 Analyze what happens in a "divide and conquer" strategy in case a certain input generates a subproblem of size zero. Does it make sense to solve the issue by checking the size of the input of the recursive function? Or is it better to avoid a priori the generation of subproblems of size zero?

Hands on 15.4 - Quicksort

 Write a data ordering program using the Quicksort algorithm with a recursive function. For simplicity, set $N_{\min} = 1$. Use it for a value of N for which the Insertion sort algorithm took a long time. Does something change if $N_{\min} = 2$?

15.3.3 *Representations of a recursive process*

Let us recall how a computer manages recursive calls of a single function. When a recursive function, let us call it `quicksort` to be more specific, calls `quicksort` itself, the status of all variables declared in the first `quicksort` are saved in memory in a special structure called *stack* (defined in Chapter 17). Although the second function `quicksort` uses variables with the same name, the variables declared in the first function are not overwritten. In this way, when the program exits the second `quicksort` and returns to the first function, the variables of the latter are read from the stack and the execution of the first `quicksort` resumes from where it was left off.

The execution of a recursive function like `quicksort` can be efficiently represented by imagining each function to be a Chinese box containing another two boxes of smaller sizes. Only the boxes of the smallest size do not contain any other box. Initially, all boxes are closed. Each time a box is opened, a number of rice grains equal to the number of variables that are declared in that function are placed inside it (but outside of the boxes it might contain and which are surely still closed). Next, we proceed to open the first one of the boxes it contains (a recursive call) and we repeat the same operations described above. Only when reaching a box of the smallest size, which is always empty, it is opened and closed immediately afterwards. Each time a box is closed, it is sealed and not touch any more. The non-empty boxes are closed (and sealed) only when all the boxes it contains are sealed. Just before closing a box, we remove the rice grains from it.

In this analogy the number of open boxes represent the number of active recursive functions, i.e., the number of made calls whose execution has not yet ended. Moreover, the number of rice grains in the boxes correspond to the number of variables that have been stored in the stack.

Another useful way to understand a recursive algorithm is by using the tree representation (which is a binary tree in case each function makes at most two recursive calls). Here, each node represents a function and its children represent the recursive calls it makes. An example of such a tree is given in Figure 15.2, where for each node also the size of the input is given. In this representation the depth of the node is equal to the number of active functions at the time the corresponding function is called. The leaves of the tree, i.e., the nodes without children, are the functions with input size equal to or less than the minimum size.

It is important to estimate the maximum depth of this kind of tree as it corresponds to the moment in which the maximum number of functions are contemporary active. In other words, the maximum depth is proportional to the maximum amount of memory required to maintain all of the stack information. To this purpose we assume that the number of leaves is always equal to $N/N_{\min} = \mathcal{O}(N)$, where $N_{\min}$ is a fixed constant.

In the best case, the tree is perfectly balanced and the maximum depth is equal to $h_{\max} = \mathcal{O}(\log N)$, as shown in the following. Instead, in the worst case the tree is completely unbalanced to one side and the maximum depth is $h_{\max} = \mathcal{O}(N)$. Both cases are illustrated in Figure 15.4. Fortunately, it is easy to design an algorithm for which the typical case is much closer to the best case rather than to the worst case. Indeed, it can be proven that even a largely unbalanced algorithm has $h_{\max} = \mathcal{O}(\log N)$. Thus, it is unusual for this kind of recursive procedure to work so poorly!

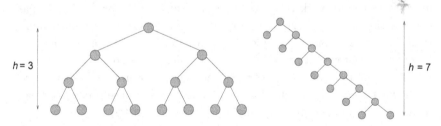

Fig. 15.4 Examples of binary trees: possible representations of a recursive process with input size $N = 8$. The tree on the left is perfectly balanced and has a maximum depth equal to 3. The tree on the right is completely unbalanced and has a maximum depth equal to 7.

As an example of the latter statement, we take a recursive function dividing an input of size N in two subproblems of size pN and $(1 - p)N$. For $p = 0.5$ the function is perfectly balanced, while for $p = 0$ or $p = 1$ it is completely unbalanced. For a generic $p < 0.5$ (the case with $p > 0.5$ is analogous for symmetry reasons) the node on the right-hand side is the one with larger input at each depth. The size of its input decreases with the depth h as Np^h. Therefore, the maximum depth can be derived by solving the equation

$$Np^{h_{\max}} = N_{\min} \quad \Longrightarrow \quad h_{\max} \simeq \log(N/N_{\min})/\log(1/p) \,.$$

For each "reasonable" value of p the depth of the tree is logarithmic with respect to the size of the initial input. As the number of consecutive recursive calls is at most logarithmic in N, we do not need to pay too much attention to the size of the stack. More generally though, the number of consecutive recursive calls is an important aspect when programming a recursive algorithm. Indeed, we need to take into account that each compiler assigns a maximum size to the stack of recursive calls: a recursive algorithm could exceed this maximum size if it is not controlled in an adequate way, and therefore it could be stopped during execution (not during compilation).

15.3.4   *How to write a good recursive function*

For instance, let us use the Quicksort algorithm to illustrate some important points when writing a recursive function. First, let us give some general advice. Always keep the number of declarations inside a recursive function to a strict minimum in order to avoid occupying too much memory. This is particularly true when dealing with large vectors or matrices. In case it is necessary to work on large data structures, it is preferable to pass the function the pointers to these large structures, rather than copying them locally. A typical example of how it should not be done is passing a large input vector to a recursive function which, after some elaboration, is rewritten in an output vector of the same size, which in turn is then passed to the next recursive call. In this way, the initial structure is copied at each recursive call and the memory might easily be exhausted.

Some other basic advice regards the readability of recursive functions. The readability of a program is always important. However, when writing the code relative to a recursive function it becomes fundamental. It is practically impossible to understand the effects of a recursive function written in an unclean way! The statements with which the recursive calls can be interrupted or those managing the special cases we discussed previously, always need to be clear (to prevent the risk of entering an infinite cycle).

Generally, ending up in an infinite cycle or *loop* during program execution is the least significant of problems, as the program can be interrupted with an *interrupt* command without causing other damage. The problem becomes more serious when during the infinite cycle the program continuously requests new memory space allocation. Indeed, when the computer RAM is exhausted, the operating system uses a portion of the hard disk, the *swap* memory, as auxiliary memory space. Unfortunately, writing on a disk is a time-consuming operation. As a consequence, the computer spends all its time and computing energy on moving the data from RAM to the hard disk and vice versa, thus responding extremely slowly to commands from the mouse or the keyboard. Hence, it may even become difficult to interrupt the program that created such a situation. Sometimes, the only possible, though drastic, solution is to shut down the computer. Thus, lots of care needs to be taken when programming and testing recursive functions.

The Listing 15.4 contains a recursive function for the Quicksort, sorting a `float` type data set. The generalization to include other data types is easy, and we leave it as an exercise to the reader.

The recursive function `quicksort` always works on the same vector containing all the data. The input arguments are a pointer `data` to the data vector, together with indices `first` and `last`, corresponding to the first and last element of the part of the data vector to be sorted (that we call the input vector). On the first call to this function, the one made by the `main` function, these indices take the values 0 and $N - 1$, where N is the size of the vector.

In the present version of the function `quicksort`, we choose $N_{min} = 1$. Thus, the function first of all checks that the input vector contains at least two elements (line 5). If this is not the case, the function is terminated without performing any operation. On line 6 the function chooses the threshold `cut` as the last element of the input vector. On the two following lines the two indices `i` and `j`, which are then used to run along the vector, are initialized. The index `i` runs along the vector from left to right and `j` in the opposite direction, until they reach each other (condition on line 9). From line 10 up to line 24, the vector is rearranged such that all elements with a value equal to or less than `cut` are put on the left, while those larger than `cut` lie on the right. This is achieved in an efficient way by swapping two elements, that were both on the wrong side.

Once all required swaps are performed, the input vector is ready to be partitioned in two subvectors, as prescribed by the algorithm. The partitioning point is determined by the final position of the indices `i` and `j`.

```
1 void quicksort(float *data, int first, int last) {
2    float cut, tmp;
3    int i, j;
4
5    if (first < last) {
6      cut = data[last];
7      i = first;
8      j = last;
9      while (i <= j) {
10        while ((i <= last) && (data[i] <= cut)) {
11          i++;
12        }
13        while (data[j] > cut) {
14          j--;
15        }
16        if (i < j) {
17          tmp = data[i];
18          data[i] = data[j];
19          data[j] = tmp;
20          i++;
21          j--;
22        }
23      }
24      if (i <= last) {
25        quicksort(data, first, j);
26        quicksort(data, i, last);
27      } else {
28        quicksort(data, first, last - 1);
29      }
30    }
31 }
```

Listing 15.4   A recursive function for the Quicksort algorithm.

Exercise 15.4 - The indices of the `quicksort` function

Prove (or at least convince yourself) that when the execution reaches line 24 of the `quicksort` function the indices i and j satisfy the relation $i = j + 1$. There is only one case in which this is not true. Which case it this? What are the values of the indices in this case?

Finally, the last part of the function executes the recursive calls passing as input the two subvectors it just generated; actually the new input values are the pointer to the usual data vector, but a new pair of indices identifying the new input vectors which need to be sorted. As explained in Section 15.3.1, one is allowed to assume that these calls to recursive functions correctly sort the two subvectors. On lines 25 and 26 the typical case, i.e., the one in which both subvectors have a size strictly larger than zero, is treated, while a special case that may occur is treated on line 28.

Because a bad management of these special cases is one of the most common causes of a badly working recursive program, we discuss them in some more detail. The special case we are considering here is when the last element of the input vector `data[last]` is larger than or equal to all other elements of the input. In this case the `while` cycle of line 10 is stopped at the first condition, as i equals `last + 1` (again notice the importance of the order of the conditions). The first subvector that is generated contains all elements of the input, while the second subvector contains none. As has been noted before, this is a dangerous situation, because following the standard rule, `quicksort` should call upon itself using the same identical input, which would generate an endless loop. Thus, it is necessary to manage this case separately. As `data[last]` is larger than or equal to all other elements, it already is in the correct position. Thus, it suffices to call the `quicksort` function for the remainder of the vector. So, one call is made instead of the usual two because the vector has not been split up, but rather has been reduced in size by one element.

Also notice how clear the code is. Although no explicit comments were included (in order to keep the code short and because it is explained in the text), the function is nevertheless well divided in several parts and the number of conditions is limited to those strictly necessary. In this way the flow of the algorithm is kept simple. It would be enough to add a few simple comments in order to provide a complete explaination on how the program works.

15.3.5 *Quicksort analysis*

We now apply the same execution time analysis we performed previously for the Insertion sort algorithm, to the Quicksort algorithm. We want to compute how the execution time, or the number of operations performed by the algorithm, increases with the size N of the input, i.e., the number of data to be sorted. In case of the `quicksort` algorithm, the question of how the memory used by the algorithm depends on the size of the input is easily solved, as it always operates on the same vector. Therefore the used memory space is always equal to the minimum, namely N.

Due to the fact that the `quicksort` function is a recursive function, the computation of the number of performed operations is slightly more complicated. We start by analyzing the special cases. In case the function has to work with a vector of minimal size, $N = N_{min}$, the number of operations n_1 that need to execute is $\mathcal{O}(1)$, since only one single comparison is required in the `quicksort` function of Listing 15.4. Let $T(N)$ be the number of operations, or the computation time, required to execute the function, on an input of size N: then we have $T(N_{min}) = n_1$.

The other special case occurs when the vector last element is also its largest element. In that case, the only cycle that is executed is the one on lines 10-12, which performs $\mathcal{O}(N)$ operations. Apart from that cycle, the function also performs a fixed number of operations. Moreover, on line 28 the function calls itself with an input of size $N - 1$. Thus, we have

$$T_M(N) = n_2 + n_3 N + T(N - 1) \simeq \mathcal{O}(N) + T(N - 1) \, ,$$

where n_2 and n_3 are constants. Note that we have used the notation T_M to indicate that we are treating the special case where the last element also is the largest one.

Finally, let us consider the general case. We assume that the threshold `cut` divides the N elements in xN elements which are smaller than this threshold and $(1 - x)N$ which are larger (x is a uniformly distributed random variable between 0 and 1 for random sequences). The division in two subvectors consists in placing the elements that are smaller than or equal to `cut` in the first xN vector locations and the elements that are larger than `cut` in the other $(1 - x)N$ remaining locations. To this purpose not all of the elements need to be moved, because each of the first xN elements are smaller than or equal to `cut` with probability x (in which case they do not need to be moved). Analogously, each of the last $(1 - x)N$ elements are on the "right side" with probability $(1 - x)$. On average, the number of elements that do not need to be moved are equal to $x \cdot xN + (1 - x) \cdot (1 - x)N$, while the number of elements that do need to be moved are on average $\left(1 - x^2 - (1 - x)^2\right) N = 2x(1 - x)N$. This corresponds to performing $x(1 - x)N$ swaps between element couples.

The two `while` cycles on lines 10-15 always execute $\mathcal{O}(N)$ operations because the indices i and j start at the extremes and stop when they are next to each other. The swaps are performed on lines 17-21 by executing $x(1 - x)\mathcal{O}(N)$ operations. Finally, on lines 25 and 26 the function is called with input sizes xN and $(1 - x)N$. Therefore, we have

$$T_x(N) = c_1 + c_2 N + c_3 x(1 - x)N + T(xN) + T((1 - x)N) \, . \qquad (15.2)$$

This expression contains an explicit dependency on x, or better on the choice of the threshold. By averaging over all possible choices of the threshold, we obtain an estimate of the average time $T(N)$. Consider the threshold is chosen randomly amongst the N elements, the xN elements that end up inside the first subvector may assume values from 1 to N with equal probability[3], i.e., x is uniformly distributed in the interval $[0,1]$. Therefore, the average number of operations required to sort a vector of N data using the `quicksort` function of Listing 15.4 can be obtained by solving the following equation:

$$T(N) = \int_0^1 T_x(N)dx = c_1 + c_2N + c_3 \int_0^1 x(1-x)dx\,N+$$
$$+ \int_0^1 T(xN)dx + \int_0^1 T((1-x)N)dx =$$
$$= c_1 + c_2N + \frac{c_3}{6}N + \frac{2}{N}\sum_{z=N_{\min}}^{N-1} T(z)\,, \quad (15.3)$$

with the initial condition $T(N_{\min}) = n_1$. The limits of the sum in (15.3) reflect the fact that the `quicksort` function with an input of size N can make recursive calls only with input sizes between $N_{\min}$ and $N-1$. The solution of the equation (15.3) is of the type

$$T(N) = a + b\,N + c\,N\,\log(N)\,, \quad (15.4)$$

with $c = 2c_2 + c_3/3$. For large N the third term in Eq. (15.4) clearly dominates the others.

A sorting algorithm with an execution time that grows like $N\log(N)$ is the best possible. The gain with respect to Insertion sort (whose execution time grows like N^2) is due to the use of the D&C strategy and the recursion. The gain is enormous: while an average PC with a clock frequency of some GHz using Insertion sort takes almost half an hour to sort 10^6 data, the same computer manages to do the same job in 5 seconds with Quicksort!

---

[3]Since the case where the threshold corresponds to the largest element is treated separately, the values from 1 to $N-2$ have equal probability, the value $N-1$ has double the probability with respect to these and the value N never occurs. These differences are irrelevant for large N and we do not consider them explicitly.

Exercise 15.5 - Verify the solution of (15.3)

Verify whether the expression (15.4) for $T(N)$ indeed resolves the equation (15.3) if the coefficient c equals $2c_2 + c_3/3$. Suggestion: compare the coefficients of the terms of N and $N \log(N)$ on both sides of the equation.

Exercise 15.6 - Quicksort of sorted sequences

Suppose we pass an already sorted sequence of N data in increasing order to the `quicksort` function. How much time does it take the function to sort it again, or better to understand it was already sorted? Does any special case have to be considered in this analysis?

Exercise 15.7 - Quicksort with fixed division

Imagine to have programmed the Quicksort algorithm in a recursive function, such that the two subvectors that are generated of an input of size N are always of size xN and $(1 - x)N$, i.e., x is fixed. Using equation (15.2) verify that the computation time still grows like $T(N) \simeq c\, N \log(N)$, but with a coefficient equal to

$$c = \frac{c_2 + c_3 x(1 - x)}{-x \log(x) - (1 - x) \log(1 - x)} \, .$$

Is $x = 1/2$ still the optimal choice? What happens for $c_2 = 1$ and increasing c_3?

Suppose we use a `quicksort` function, like the one of Listing 15.4, which takes a lot more time when applied to an already sorted sequence (Exercise 15.6) with respect to random sequences. In this case, it would be desirable to pass to the function mostly random sequences and avoid, even partially, ordered sequences. As the execution times of sorted sequences are very long for large N, it is easy to make mistakes when estimating the total elaboration time (Section 15.2.3) if we are not able to avoid such worst case sequences.

It would be extremely useful to make sure that the typical case coincides with the best case, i.e., that all sequences that are passed to the function are sorted in a time $\mathcal{O}(N \log(N))$. The easiest way to obtain this is by *randomizing the input*, that is by performing a random permutation of the input sequence.

If sorting algorithms were always to be used with fully random sequences, this operation would not improve the algorithm execution time much (rather it would worsen it because of the extra operations). However, in practice it is convenient to randomize the input, because the sequences to be sorted may come from real problems and may have a chance of being already partially sorted. For instance, suppose we need to create a national telephone directory, given telephone directories of all districts. In other words, all the already sorted directories of the districts are supplied to us in electronic format, from which we need to create a sorted directory of all telephone users.

There exists a specific algorithm for this kind of problem which takes a time $\mathcal{O}(N \cdot M)$ where N is the total number of users and M the number of districts. For any fixed value of M and for very large N this algorithm is faster than Quicksort. However, in the specific case of Italy, where the number of users is $N \simeq 10^7$ and the number of districts is $M = 103$, we have that $N \log(N) < NM$, and Quicksort is probably faster than this specific algorithm. In any case the time it takes to program a new algorithm certainly exceeds the few minutes extra it takes Quicksort to sort the data! Therefore, we use Quicksort and pass it a file which is a concatenation of the files containing the separate district telephone directories. This is a typical case for which an initial randomization (i.e., random permutation) of the input data is of great help as it eliminates all partially sorted data which would slow down Quicksort.

Hands on 15.5 - Merge many lists in one

Consider the problem of sorting a list of N data, obtained by merging M already sorted lists. Create an appropriate algorithm which solves this problem in a time $\mathcal{O}(NM)$. Write a program for this algorithm and verify numerically that the execution time grows as predicted. Finally, compare this program to Quicksort in order to determine at which size of the input it is more convenient to quit using Quicksort and use this new specific algorithm.

Finally, let us conclude this chapter with a discussion on the disadvantages of using recursion. Each time a recursive call is made, the operating system needs to save the configuration of the calling function in memory and initialize a new function. These operations take a certain time (which can be avoided in a non recursive program). Nevertheless, in the majority of cases, this extra time is irrelevant if compared to the total execution time.

In order to get convinced that this extra time due to the use of recursive calls is not very relevant, it is enough to compare the execution times of two simple codes. A first one executes a large number of recursive calls (we suggest to use between 2^{20} and 2^{30} recursive calls), while a second computes a similar number of operations using simple nested cycles. The only difference between these codes is the extra time needed to manage the recursion: you should notice this is a negligible execution time. Hence, the extra time in the use of recursive functions should not be considered as a limitation of the recursive method.

Probably the only real case in which recursion works badly, is when it is used in a wrong way! For instance, two such cases are: a badly programmed recursive function (e.g., executing too many operations or allocating too much memory); when using recursive functions is counterproductive. The latter case is well illustrated by the Hands on 15.6 which we strongly recommend the reader to carry out.

Hands on 15.6 - Fibonacci numbers

The Fibonacci numbers F_n are an infinite series of integer positive numbers defined by the following recurrence relation $F_n = F_{n-1} + F_{n-2}$ with $F_1 = F_2 = 1$. Write a program which uses a recursive function generating a generic Fibonacci number F_n, where n is given as an input to the program. Try to compute F_{30}, F_{35}, F_{40}, F_{45} and F_{50}. Estimate how the execution time of this program grows with n. What is the largest Fibonacci number that can be computed within one day by this program?

Write a second program to generate F_n (n is given as an input) without making use of recursion. Does this second version of the program allow one to compute F_{90}? And F_{100}, whose value is 354 224 848 179 261 915 075? Explain the enormous difference between the execution times of the two programs. Suggestion: it is useful to calculate the number of recursive calls that are needed to compute F_n.

Finally, compute the ratio $r_n = F_n/F_{n-1}$ for $n > 100$ and verify whether the result coincides with its analytical prediction (which can be calculated thanks to the recurrence equation by solving a simple quadratic equation). In order to be able to compute r_n for $n > 100$, what should you pay attention to?

Chapter 16

Dynamic data structures

> The universe (which others call the Library) is
> composed of an indefinite, perhaps infinite number
> of hexagonal galleries [...]
> From any hexagon one can see the floors above and
> below—one after another, endlessly.
>
> Jorge Luis Borges, *The Library of Babel* (1941).

Nowadays, computers are more an more in charge of the storage and management of large amounts of data. Think, for instance, of the ongoing digitization of archives and libraries.

We should imagine a data set managed by a computer as a dynamic set, varying in time, on which we can operate. For example, we can insert, delete or search data. Of course there exists a large number of algorithms performing these operations. A complete treatment of this subject would take a lot of time. Instead, in this chapter we show some data structures which are more complex than those described in Chapter 5, but are still relatively simple. We start from the linear data structures and get to the binary tree. In Chapter 13 we already introduced linked lists and binary trees. Here, we treat them in a more complete way.

The aim of this chapter is twofold. First of all, we want to introduce some basic concepts on how to store and manage data on a computer. Second, we want to show how we can efficiently create these structures in C. Once more, we will discover how useful recursive functions can be.

To represent basic, but concrete data, we mostly consider plain integer numbers. The extension to more complicated data is straightforward.

16.1   Linear structures

Following the fundamental rule which recommends to choose always the simplest algorithm solving a given problem, we start by presenting the simplest way to manage data. The *linear data structures* are simple vectors whose elements are added and removed following certain rules. These rules obviously depend on what we want to do with the data.

The first case we consider is a data set without any particular order. Think for example of a data set in a container, such as a *bucket*, not allowing any kind of organization. This structure is generally used when we are only interested in whether a data item is present or not in a set. If one also needs to search for a particular data item, then the bucket structure is not recommended: indeed, such a search can only be done by going through all the data, which is a very inefficient operation!

The only efficient operations[1] on a bin data structure are inserting a data item and randomly extracting a data item (which is then eventually deleted). Let bucket be pointer to the data structure and numData the number of item in the data structure. A new element newItem can be entered with the following statement

```
bucket[numData++] = newItem;
```

To remove an element at the position index we use the statement

```
bucket[index] = bucket[--numData];
```

Note that the position of the unary operators to increase or decrease the variable numData is fundamental.

When using dynamical lists, whose length varies during program execution, we always need to consider the possibility that the number of elements contained in a data structure has reached the size of this data structure. If we know in advance the maximum number $N_{\max}$ of elements to be stored, the easiest solution is to create a structure with a size which is exactly $N_{\max}$. Even if a bit drastic, this solution is optimal in terms of program performance, since, upon execution, no memory needs to be dynamically reallocated, which would inevitably take time. We suggest to opt for this simple solution every time the memory needed is much smaller than the available computer memory.

On the contrary (i.e., if $N_{\max}$ is not known or allocating a data structure of such a length is too heavy) we need an algorithm for resizing the data

---

[1]In general, we consider an operation on a set of N data to be efficient if it takes at most $\log(N)$ elementary operations.

structure. If we do not know the size that will be reached, the best rule is to multiply the length of the structure by a preset factor when we resize it. Generally, a good choice is to double the data structure current length. In this way, we are sure the number of times we resize the data structure only grows logarithmically with its length, which makes it an efficient operation. The lines of code to insert a new element in the bucket data structure are

```
if (numData == size) {
    size *= 2;
    bucket = (dataType*)realloc(bucket,
                            size * sizeof(dataType));
}
bucket[numData++] = newItem;
```

where `size` is the structure current length. Note that we introduced a generic type, `dataType`, for the data which are to be inserted in the data structure. At the beginning of each program using the data structures, the user needs to define the type `dataType` according to the type of objects that are to be managed with these structures. This can be done with a `typedef` command.

Considering we already introduced three variables related to the data structure (the pointer to the data vector, the vector size and the number of data items it contains), it might be useful to define a `struct` with all this information:

```
struct dataStruct {
    dataType *data;
    int size, numData;
};
```

In general, we prefer to immediately define a new type of variable,

```
typedef struct {
    dataType *data;
    int size, numData;
} dataStruct;
```

In this way, we can use the name `dataStruct` to refer to the data structure, which is more concise than the verbose `struct dataStruct`.

Hands on 16.1 - Inserting and removing data in and from a structure

Write two functions to insert and remove an element from the bucket data structure we just defined without using global variables.

The prototypes of the functions are as follows:

```
dataStruct insertInBucket(dataStruct bucket, dataType newItem);
```

```
dataStruct removeFromBucket(dataStruct bucket, int index);
```
What fundamental change is required in the two functions above if we
want the first function to return a `void` (maintaining the ability to resize
the structure) and the second one to read an element which is then removed
from the structure and returned by the calling function?

Reverse Polish notation

The *Reverse Polish Notation* (RPN), also known as the *postfix* notation,
was introduced in 1920 by the Polish mathematician Jan Łukasiewicz.
This arithmetic notation allows one to write any mathematical expression without parentheses, by using a stack containing both the operands
and the results of the operations. The information supplied by the parentheses in the *infix* notation, is given in RPN by the order in which the
operands and the operations are processed. The operands must precede
the operator and are removed from the stack when they are used in the
operation. The operation result is added to the stack and eventually will
serve as a new operand. For example, to carry out the division 9/1.2
with a postfix notation calculator, we first need to insert the number 9,
then the number 1.2 and finally call the division operator. The result is
added to the stack. In the fig-
ure on the right we show the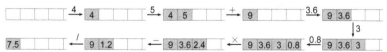
status of the stack throughout
the operations we just described. The advantage of this notation is that
it allows us to calculate complicated expressions in a fast and simple way.
For example, to calculate $(4 + 5)/(3.6 - (3 \times 0.8))$ we just need to insert,
in the given order, 4,5,+,3.6,3,0.8,×,−,/ (with an "enter" command after
each element of the list) to obtain the desired result. The stack status
throughout the calculation should help clarify how this works.

On a calculator without Reverse Polish notation we need to save the intermediate results on paper or in memory (often simple calculators only
have one memory location). So, a computation containing many parentheses is rather inconvenient. Instead, with the Reverse Polish notation,
everything is managed by the stack that contains the partial results of
the computation.

Fig. 16.1 Schematic representation of how the push and pop operations work on a stack of 6 elements. pS is the pointer to the stack. Note how after a pop operation, the extracted element has not physically been removed from the memory. Nevertheless, it is no longer part of the stack (those elements are shown in grey) and can be overwritten with the successive push operations.

16.1.1 Queues and stacks

Two other very common linear data structures are the *queue* and the *stack*. These structures allow one to store data and read (remove) them in a fixed order. The queue is based on a *FIFO* type of strategy, short for *First-In, First-Out*, i.e., the element which is first inserted in the queue is also the first one to leave it when one of its elements is requested. Think of people waiting in queue for example. Instead, in case of a stack we follow a strategy of the *LIFO* type, short for *Last-In, First-Out*, i.e., when an element of the structure is requested, the last stored element is returned. For example, think of a stack of plates (to which we can only add or remove plates on top).

The two basic operations we apply to these types of data structures consist in entering and removing an element. In case of a stack these operations have conventional names: *push* to enter and *pop* to remove. In Listing 16.1 we give an example of functions performing these two operations (neglecting, for the moment, whether we need to resize the structure or not).

```
1 void push(dataStruct *pStack, dataType newItem) {
2   pStack->data[pStack->numData++] = newItem;
3 }
4
5 dataType pop(dataStruct *pStack) {
6   if (pStack->numData > 0) {
7     return pStack->data[--pStack->numData];
8   } else {
9     fprintf(stderr, "ERROR: pop on an empty stack!");
10    exit(EXIT_FAILURE);
11  }
12 }
```

Listing 16.1 Functions to insert and extract a stack element.

The variable numData indicates the size of the stack and also the first empty location for a push operation; `numData-1` indicates the element returned by a pop. In Figure 16.1 we schematically show how the two functions we just described work.

Hands on 16.2 - Calculator with Reverse Polish notation

Write a program simulating a calculator with Reverse Polish notation (box on page 472). The program reads the user's input from the keyboard. The input may consists of any number, the symbols of the 4 basic operations, plus a character terminating the program (for example, q for *quit*). We suggest to use the library function `strtod` to convert a string into a `double` type variable. The data given by the user have to be managed with a stack.

Fig. 16.2   Schematic representation of how a queue works. First we show the result of inserting the number 21 and next, the one after the two elements have been deleted. The arrows indicate the memory locations where to insert (white arrow) or extract (black arrow) an element.

Managing a queue is not any harder than managing a stack. Therefore, we leave it as an exercise for the reader to write the appropriate functions to enter and remove an element from this type of data structure. In Figure 16.2 we schematically show the rules to efficiently manage a queue. Two indices are required, indicating in every moment the location containing the element that can be removed (black arrow) and the location where the next element can be stored (white arrow). Using two indices (instead of one, as we did up to now) allows us to remove an element without having to move the whole queue to the beginning of the vector (which would be inefficient). However, updating the two indices is a more delicate operation. When an index reaches the end of the memory vector containing the queue, we need to redirect it to the beginning of the vector. To this purpose, imagine the vector is folded on itself in a circular shape.

Another delicate issue concerns how to deal with a queue whose size reaches that of the vector containing it. Please note that the queue starting and ending points no longer necessarily coincide with those of the vector. So, we cannot simply add other memory locations to the vector. We also need to copy some elements of the queue in the new piece of vector to re-establish the consecutive order of all the elements in the queue. Copying part of the elements takes $\mathcal{O}(N)$ operations and is a demanding task. We advise to estimate the memory space required to store the queue before-hand, so as to avoid resizing as much as possible. Moreover, if we do need to resize a queue, it is convenient to follow the rule given in Section 16.1 and double its length.

Hands on 16.3 - Managing a queue

 Write two functions to enter and remove an element from a queue. Pay particular attention to the index management, the size of the queue (compare it to the vector size) and all operations required to correctly resize the vector.

16.1.2 *Linked lists*

In Chapter 13 we already introduced and vastly discussed linked lists. We reconsider them here only for completeness. Given they are not a very efficient data structure, we do not dedicate too much space to their description.

Each element of a linked list contains the stored data item and a pointer to the next element. In a doubly linked list, they also have a second pointer to the preceding element. A linked list is an ordered data set. If the order is not required, we can use a bucket which is as efficient as a linked list and easier to program. Figure 16.3 contains some examples of (singly or doubly) linked lists. The pointers allow one to run through the list from head to tail (and the other way around for the doubly linked lists). The head element does not contain any data. So, it cannot be removed from the list. The pointer to the tail element takes the value NULL to indicate no further elements follow next. Sometimes, the last element points to the head of the list, thus creating a circular structure.

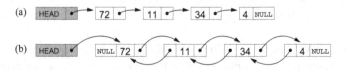

Fig. 16.3 Singly (a) and doubly (b) linked lists. The arrows represent the pointers to the list elements.

Determining the order of the list elements by means of pointers is convenient for two reasons:

- the elements of the lists can be kept in memory with a vector in which they appear in a different order than the one determined by the pointers;
- inserting and removing an element require a number of operations which is independent of the size of the list.

In Figure 16.4 we schematically show how to update pointers of a singly linked list (the operations are analogous for doubly linked ones) when inserting or removing an element. Also in Figure 16.4, on the right, we show one possible way to store the elements of the list in memory. Note that it does not correspond to the order of the list. When a new element is entered, it can be placed at the end of the vector (where there is certainly some free space), even if it occupies a more central location in the list.

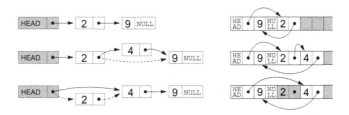

Fig. 16.4   On the left, the elementary operations on the linked list: inserting the element 4 (first to second line) and removing the element 2 (second to third line). On the right, a possible way to store the data in the computer memory is given. The unused locations are colored in gray.

At the price of using pointers, the linked lists offer some advantages with respect to the other linear structures we already discussed. For instance, compared to the bucket structure there is an order. Compared to a queue or stack, we can insert or delete elements at any point of the list and not just at its extremes.

Nevertheless, the linked lists suffer some limitations making them inefficient structures. For example, for a linked list of length N we have that:

- to insert an element in the correct position, we need to run neatly through the list until we reach this position, which necessarily takes $\mathcal{O}(N)$ operations;
- although the list has an order, searching an element in the list

always takes $\mathcal{O}(N)$ operations (the searching procedure must start from the head and run through the list).

To conclude, we remark that this structure does not take advantage of its ordering. Inserting an element in the correct place and searching an element are inefficient operations.

If we are not interested in keeping the data in a certain order, the bucket structure we discussed in the beginning of this chapter should do fine. Otherwise, we recommend to use one of the structures presented in the following sections.

16.2   Priority queues

We saw that linear structures suffer two types of inefficiency. Here, we want to resolve the one related to the slow insertion of an element in a sorted structure. In Section 16.3 we study how to efficiently search an iten in a data structure.

The *priority queues* are data structures where the insertion of an element, as well as the reading/deletion of the highest priority element are easy. The stack and the (simple) queue we saw in Section 16.1.1 are particular examples of priority queues. Let the "age" of an element be the time it passes inside a data structure. Then, in a stack, the priority is inversely proportional to the age of an element (this is why the first one leaving it is the youngest, i.e., the last one entered), while for a queue the priority is proportional to its age (and the first one leaving it is the oldest one). For a generic priority function, we need more flexible structures, such as a *heap* type structure, introduced in Section 16.2.1.

A classic example of priority queues concerns the management of the jobs a processor has to execute. The jobs are put on queue according to the priority they were given. Upon execution, the jobs are extracted, one at a time, from this queue, always giving precedence to the one with highest priority.

16.2.1   *Heaps*

For simplicity, we always consider the data in a structure to be integer positive numbers and the priority of an element to be the value of the data item it contains. So, the element with the highest priority is the biggest one of the structure.

A (binary) *heap* is a vector v[] whose elements have "family ties". The family ties are such that the "parent" of the element v[i] is the element v[(int)(i/2)] and its "children" the elements v[2*i] and v[2*i+1] (if they exist). Note that the indices must start from 1 in order for the family ties to work properly. To create a heap in a C program, the memory location corresponding to the index 0 is best left unused. It is better to waste few memory bytes to maintain the code more readable.

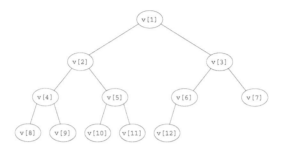

Fig. 16.5   Binary tree representation of a heap with twelve elements.

The family ties of a heap are more evident if we represent the vector elements along a binary tree, as shown in Figure 16.5. Let us stress, though, that a heap is not a tree! Although, we often represent a heap as a binary tree because it is particularly handy, we must keep in mind that a heap is just a vector with family ties, implying priority relations (as we shall see next). For completeness, we recall some tree-related notations: the highest node of a tree (the one without a parent node) is called the *root*; the nodes without any children are called the *leaves*. The *depth* of a node is equal to its distance from the root (by definition, the depth of the root is zero).

The tree representing a heap is always a well-balanced binary tree, since a node of depth h only exists if all those at depth $h - 1$ exist. So, only the last level of the tree may be partially filled, while all others are always completely full. As a consequence, the maximum depth of a heap of N elements is at most $\mathcal{O}(\log N)$.

Exercise 16.1 - Computing the relatives in a heap

Consider the element with index i of a heap. Suppose we want to compute the indices of the elements corresponding to its relatives (parents and children). Can you compute these indices using only boolean and shift operators (described in Chapter

14), working directly on the bits of the number i? Next, consider all elements of a heap at depth h in the binary tree representation. The indices of these elements (or better their binary representations) have a common trait. Which one?

The data contained in a heap have to satisfy the *fundamental heap property*. Namely, the priority of any element should never exceed the one of its parent element. For the type of priority we assumed (the "bigger than" operator), the heap property entails that the relation v[i]<=v[(int)(i/2)] should be satisfied for each index (1<i<=numData). Thus, the root always contains the element with highest priority (the biggest one in our case).

Figure 16.6 contains a couple of examples of correctly filled heaps. It is easy to verify that each child is less than or equal to the parent. Also note that the data of these two heaps are the same, but they are arranged in a different way. Indeed, the way to store data in a heap is not unique. This is due to the fact that the data are only partially sorted. Namely, each element has a higher priority than all those contained in the subtree of which it is the root and has a lower priority than all those found on the path leading to the root. No order is established with respect to all other elements of the structure. In the heap represented by the left tree of Figure 16.6, the element 6 is at a higher level than the element 10. This is allowed because they belong to different branches and therefore there is not a direct comparative relation between them.

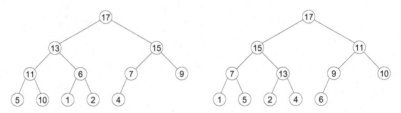

Fig. 16.6   Two different, both valid, ways to maintain the same data in a heap. In a heap type data structure each element has a lower priority (i.e., a lower value in this case) than the parent. However, there does not exist any direct relation between elements belonging to different branches. For example, the elements 6 and 10 occupy different levels in the two heaps.

To prove a heap is a good priority queue, we need to show that it is efficient to enter a new element with any possible priority as well as to read or remove the highest priority element. Reading the highest priority element is easy, because, by construction, this element is always at the tree root, v[1]. Instead, to manage the other two operations we need to introduce some suitable functions.

16.2.2   *Building a heap*

We start by considering how to insert a new element with generic priority inside a heap of length $N - 1$. First of all, the new element is written in the memory location v[N]. However, it could be that it does not satisfy the correct priority relation with the parent element, namely v[N] <= v[(int)(N/2)]. In this case, we need to move the new element inside the heap until it reaches a new position where it does satisfy the priority relations with the parent and the possible children.

In order to place the new element in a correct position, we only consider one kind of move. Namely, we swap it with the parent element if the latter priority is lower than that of the newly inserted element. In Figure 16.7 we show how the iteration of swap moves finally leads to the correct positioning of the new element. Swapping the data between two nodes of the tree allows us to rearrange the data inside the tree without changing its topological structure.

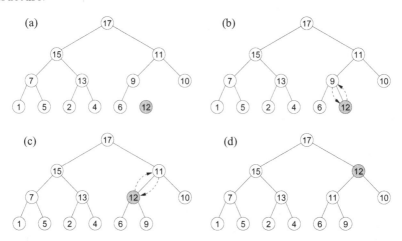

Fig. 16.7   Inserting a new data item (in gray) in a heap type structure. The new element is first written in the last position of the vector (a), and then, with a series of swaps (b-c) moved to the correct position (d).

You may think, for instance, of a heap as if it were the organization chart of a virtuous company, where the supervisors are always more skilled than the subordinate employees. In this company, a new recruited employee initially starts working at the lowest level. With time, if he is more skilled than his supervisor, he takes his place and his ex-supervisor becomes his subordinate. The employee's career comes to a stop when he reaches a more skilled supervisor. From that point on, his position in the company organization chart only changes due to a new hiring (lowering level if the new recruited employee is more skilled) or because one of his supervisors retires (we consider this case later). Because in this company the employees are only compared with their direct supervisor, the skills of employees working at the same level but in different sectors (i.e., in different branches) may vary a lot (see the example of the elements 6 and 10 in Figure 16.6).

The function in Listing 16.2 inserts a new element in a heap data structure.

```
1 void insertInHeap(dataStruct *pHeap, dataType newItem) {
2   int index = ++(pHeap->numData);
3   while (index > 1 &&
4          pHeap->data[(int)(index/2)] < newItem) {
5     pHeap->data[index] = pHeap->data[(int)(index/2)];
6     index = (int)(index / 2);
7   }
8   pHeap->data[index] = newItem;
9 }
```

Listing 16.2   A function inserting a new element in a heap.

Note that, to avoid useless operation and thus optimize the code, we did not physically write `newItem` in the space we created in the heap for the new element (increment of `numData` on line 2). We first moved the elements with a lower priority than `newItem` to the bottom (lines 3–7). The new element is written just once, immediately in the correct position (line 8).

The maximum number of operations the function `insertInHeap` takes to insert a new element in a heap of N elements is equal to its depth, which, by definition, is of order $\mathcal{O}(\log N)$. This worst case occurs when the new element has the highest priority and needs to be moved up to the root of the tree. Instead, in the typical case, the new element to be inserted has a priority which is lower than that of about half of the elements already in the heap. In this typical case, it can be proven that the average number of swaps it takes to correctly place `newItem` is $\mathcal{O}(1)$, even in the limit $N \to \infty$.

To insert N data in a heap structure, we can proceed in the following way. Consider the first data item `v[1]` as a heap consisting of just a single element. Insert the second data item in the heap consisting of only the first one. Next, insert the third in the heap consisting of the first two, then the fourth in the heap consisting of the first three, and so on until all data have been inserted. All these operations can be done on the same original vector. After the kth step, it will contain the first k data items correctly ordered in a heap, while the remaining $N - k$ are in the initial order as they still need to be inserted.

As inserting a new element in a heap of length N typically takes $\mathcal{O}(1)$ operations and at most $\mathcal{O}(\log N)$, we may conclude this algorithm constructing heaps of N elements typically takes $\mathcal{O}(N)$ and at most $\mathcal{O}(N \log N)$ operations. At the end of Section 16.2.3 we discuss a heap construction algorithm which takes $\mathcal{O}(N)$ operations both in the typical as in the worst case scenarios.

16.2.3   *Maintaining a heap*

Apart from inserting a new data item, we also need to quickly reorder the heap structure after the removal of an element. To be concrete, we consider the removal of the highest priority element (contained in the tree root), but the following reasoning remains valid when removing any other element.

Let us again try to think of how a virtuous company is organized. When the president retires, his place is taken by the most skilled of the two vice presidents, maintaining the fundamental heap property. In turn, the empty place one of the vice presidents leaves behind is taken by the most skilled of his subordinates. And so one, until we have reached a tree leaf (Figure 16.8). Unfortunately, this strategy almost never works. Although it maintains the correct priority relationships, it does not maintain the heap topological structure. Indeed, as Figure 16.8(d) clearly shows, the vector locations containing the heap at the end of this process are not always what they should be (i.e., the first locations in the vector).

To avoid this inconvenience, the first operation we perform, when an element is removed from the heap, is to move the heap last element in the vacant location, Figure 16.9(a). In this way, we immediately re-establish the correct topological structure. Next, we restore the correct priority relationships by swapping couples of data, thus leaving the tree topology untouched.

In Figure 16.9(b) we show a typical situation when we just moved the heap last element into the tree root. The priority of this element (in gray in Figure 16.9) is typically too low for the position it occupies and must be moved to a lower place. Note how the remaining priority relationships are

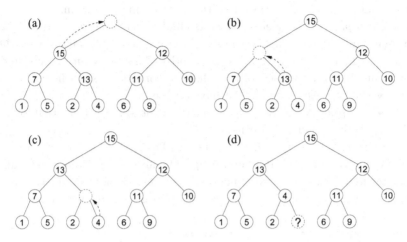

Fig. 16.8   A wrong strategy to delete an element from the heap data structure. After the priority relationships have been updated, the topological structure of the tree (d) does not correspond to that of a heap.

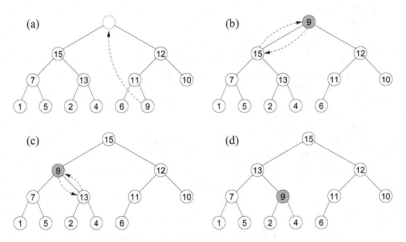

Fig. 16.9   A correct strategy to delete an element from a heap: the first operation (a) is to move its last element into the position of the removed element (the root in this case). Next, the moved element is correctly repositioned in the heap (b-d) by means of a series of swaps with the elements below it.

correct. The only element which is out of place is the gray one. So, we can easily and efficiently reposition it with the following algorithm.

We compare the gray element to its children (if it has any). If at least one of its children has a higher priority, the gray element is swapped with the child with higher priority, see Figure 16.9(b). This procedure is repeated, see Figure 16.9(c), until one of the following conditions is reached:

- the gray element does not have any children any more;
- the priority of the gray element is not smaller than that of its children, as in Figure 16.9(d).

In these cases we are sure the gray element has reached a correct position and we have re-established a good heap. The above algorithm is generally implemented with a recursive function called **heapify** given in Listing 16.3 (we leave as an exercise for the reader to program a nonrecursive one).

```
1  void heapify(int index, dataStruct *pHeap) {
2    int left, right, max;
3    dataType tmp;
4
5    left = 2 * index;
6    if (left <= pHeap->numData) {
7      if (pHeap->data[left] > pHeap->data[index]) {
8        max = left;
9      } else {
10       max = index;
11     }
12     right = left + 1;
13     if (right <= pHeap->numData &&
14         pHeap->data[right] > pHeap->data[max]) {
15       max = right;
16     }
17     if (max != index) {
18       tmp = pHeap->data[index];
19       pHeap->data[index] = pHeap->data[max];
20       pHeap->data[max] = tmp;
21       heapify(max, pHeap);
22     }
23   }
24 }
```

Listing 16.3   A function relocating an element in the heap.

The function name derives from the fact that it restores the heap fundamental property for the element given in input. It assumes the latter has a too low priority for the position it occupies and that the relationships between any other pair of elements are correct. The arguments of the function `heapify` are the pointer to the heap data structure to work on and the index corresponding to the element which potentially has a too low priority (the gray one in Figure 16.9). The indices `left` and `right` (lines 5 and 12) correspond to the children. If these elements exist (conditions on lines 6 and 13) the function compares their values with the element with index `index` (lines 7 and 14) and writes in `max` the index of the element with maximum priority. If `max` results to be different from `index` (line 17), the function swaps the elements with indices `index` and `max` (lines 18-20), thus restoring the heap fundamental property for the element in `index`. Finally, the function calls itself recursively (line 21) with index `max`, corresponding to the element which does not necessarily satisfy the correct priority relationship with its children. This element is to be pushed to the bottom of the tree until it reaches a correct position.

Note that every function `heapify` performs at most a finite number of operations before it possibly calls itself again. Moreover, each new recursive call moves down in the tree the gray element to be repositioned (Figure 16.9). Therefore, the maximum number of recursive calls is equal to the maximum depth of the tree, which, by definition, is $\mathcal{O}(\log N)$. In conclusion, relocating an element requires at most $\mathcal{O}(\log N)$ elementary operations and therefore is an efficient operation.

Since both inserting an element of any possible priority, and removing the highest priority element take at most $\mathcal{O}(\log N)$ operations, we have proved the heap is an efficient priority queue.

However, the function `heapify` can also be used to build a heap in a faster way than the one shown in Section 16.2.2. In this new procedure, we build the heap starting from the elements with a higher index, i.e., starting from the tree leaves.

More precisely, the heap is constructed starting from all isolated elements, i.e., without any family ties between them. Starting from the elements with higher indices, at each step, a new element is added to the heap under construction. The family ties of this element with its children (if it has any) are "activated". In Figure 16.10 the elements which have just been added are colored gray and the lines represent active relationships. Assuming all family ties were correct at the end of the previous step, the only two possible situations that can occur when adding a new element are:

- the element that has just been added has a higher priority than its children, and is therefore, in the correct place;
- the element that has just been added has a too low priority for its current position and can be correctly relocated with a call to

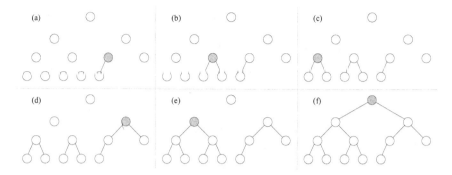

Fig. 16.10 Building a new heap starting from a generic vector of 12 elements. For each new element added to the heap (those in gray) the function `heapify` is called to restore the priority relationship in the subtree of which this element is the root.

function `heapify`, considering all other family ties between the other elements are correct.

Executing the function `heapify` on the element that has just been added, we are sure to leave the heap under construction with all correct active family ties. The latter is needed in order for the construction at the next step to lead to the desired result. In Figure 16.10 we graphically show this building process. Given the elements of the heap have already been written in the vector and only need to be sorted according to the fundamental heap priority, the term "adding an element" should be understood as "the family ties of the element with its children are being activated".

```
1 void buildHeap(dataStruct *pHeap) {
2    int i;
3    for (i = (int)(pHeap->numData / 2); i > 0; i--) {
4      heapify(i, pHeap);
5    }
6 }
```

Listing 16.4   A function sorting a vector into a heap data structure.

To sort a vector of N elements into a heap data structure, the simple function of Listing 16.4 is enough. This function assumes the N data items have already been copied into the structure pointed by **pHeap**, even if they do not have any particular order yet. The heap ordering is generated with a call to **buildHeap**.

Note that, to optimize the code given in Listing 16.4, the index i does not run through all nodes, but only through half of these. This choice is due to the fact that the function `buildHeap` does not perform any operations on the elements without children. So, it is enough to start working on the highest index element having at least one child. This element is the parent of the last element, and thus has index equal to `(int)(N/2)`.

Hands on 16.4 - Two ways to build a heap

Write two programs reading a vector with N data items in input and ordering it into a heap. The first program should implement the algorithm described in Section 16.2.2, while the second one exploits the one we just showed. Compare their performances when varying the length N in case the input vector contains a random sequence of data and in case it contains a sorted sequence in increasing or decreasing order. Before performing the "experimental" measurements, i.e., executing the programs, can you predict, at least at a qualitative level, how the computation time increases in the six considered cases (the two programs with three types of input)?

16.2.4 *Sorting with a heap: Heapsort*

Once you have understood the rules for building and managing a heap data structure, it should not be hard to imagine an efficient algorithm to sort a data set by means of a heap.

Exercise 16.2 - Sorting a heap

Before continuing to read, try to imagine an algorithm that can sort a data set using only a heap data structure. Basically use the functions given in Section 16.2.3. Try to estimate the execution time of this algorithm in the typical, best and worst case scenario.

The algorithm we explain in the following most probably corresponds to the one you have imagined as an answer to the Exercise 16.2. The algorithm *Heapsort* efficiently sorts a data set by simply performing the following two operations (we are sorting the data in an increasing order):

- insert the data to be sorted in a heap, giving the elements with smaller values a higher priority;

- one by one extract the elements from the heap, restoring a correct heap after each extraction.

Thanks to the priority we choose, the first element which is extracted from the heap and returned by the Heapsort algorithm is precisely the smallest one. At each step of the algorithm the smallest element among the remaining ones is returned. In this way, the Heapsort algorithm returns the input data in increasing order.

For the Heapsort algorithm to return the data sorted in increasing order in the *same* vector used to communicate the data in input (as is the case, for example, for the function `quicksort` in Section 15.3.2), we slightly need to change the above algorithm. Namely, the data are sorted in a heap, but giving a higher priority to those with larger value. When removing the elements from the heap, we should imagine the data vector consists of two parts. A first part containing the heap, diminishes by one element at each removal operation. The second part contains the sorted data in increasing order. So, each time an element is removed from the root of the heap, it is placed in the second part of the vector. Consider a vector of length N. When k elements have been extracted from the heap, the first $N - k$ vector elements contain the remaining heap. The extracted elements (the k highest ones) occupy the other k vector locations in the proper order such that the highest element occupies location N. During the next extraction, we want to place the highest element of the heap, contained in the root, in the vector position $N - k$. So, we just need to swap the elements with the indices 1 and $N - k$. This swap also performs the first operation required to reestablish a correct heap after the extraction (Section 16.2.3), namely moving the last element of the heap into its root.

Hands on 16.5 - Heapsort

Write a program using the Heapsort algorithm to sort the data read from a file. Measure the performance of this algorithm by varying the number N of the data to be sorted. Also consider those data sequences which are difficult to sort with the Quicksort algorithm (without doing the initial random permutation).

16.3   Elementary search methods

In this chapter we have analyzed data structures on which we can efficiently perform operations, such as inserting and removing an element. Still, these structures are not adequate to search for one specific member. We now have a look at how to make this operation efficient, i.e., such that it takes at most $\mathcal{O}(\log N)$ elementary operations for a data set consisting of N items.

16.3.1   *Binary search trees*

In Section 5.2.2 we show how the binary search algorithm works. Although the binary search on already sorted data is efficient, it is not such an interesting case, because in practice the actual problem is precisely how to get hold of a sorted structure. Usually, the problem consists in maintaining a dynamic data set in a sufficiently ordered structure, such that elements can be efficiently added, searched and removed.

There exist many data structures allowing to store data such that searching an element is an efficient operation. The majority of these structures have a tree-like topology. As we already partially discovered in Chapter 13 and from what we will see here, the cost of managing a tree-like data structure is at most proportional to its maximum depth. This is why the algorithms that have been invented during the last 50 years mainly aim at maintaining a tree as balanced as possible with the least number of operations. To keep our discussion short and concise, we just focus on the simplest structure, the *binary tree*. We refer the reader to more complete textbooks [Cormen *et al.* (1990)] for the treatment of more complicated algorithms, such as *red-black* trees or Fibonacci heaps.

In a binary tree, such as the one in Figure 16.11, each node has (apart from the data item it contains) three pointers: the first one points to the parent node, and the other two to the child nodes, if they exist. By convention, we assign the value NULL to the pointers pointing to nodes which are not yet present in the tree (for example, the pointer to the parent node of the root and those to the child nodes of the leaves). Considering the fact that the node at the root can change when the tree is updated, it is convenient to keep a variable root pointing to the node serving as root.

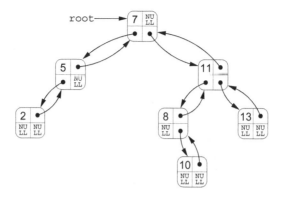

Fig. 16.11   An example of a binary tree. Each node contains the data item to be stored and three pointers defining its family ties. The data have been inserted in the nodes such as to satisfy the fundamental property of a binary search tree.

The structure of the node could be as follows:

```
struct node {
  dataType datum;
  struct node *up, *left, *right;
};
```

where **datum** is a data item stored in the node, **up** points to the parent node, while **left** and **right** to the two child nodes. As usual, we prefer to define a new type **myNode** with the command

```
typedef struct node myNode;
```

to keep the program more concise.

The nodes of a heap structure have a well-defined position in the vector of elements, and therefore also in the physical computer memory. The family ties in a heap are determined entirely by their position in the vector. Instead, in a generic binary tree, the order in which the nodes are written in the memory is irrelevant. Their family ties are made explicit by means of the pointers of each node (analogous to what occurs in linked lists, shown in Figure 16.4). For example, if we want to reserve memory for new nodes, the allocation in memory does not necessary have to be contiguous to the already used one. Nevertheless, it is important to realize that, once a node has been saved in a certain memory location, it cannot be moved, simply because the pointers to that node are using this memory location address. Therefore, we strongly advise to not use the command to dynamically reallocate memory (**realloc**) when the data structure is based on the use of pointers.

In order to design an efficient search operation in a binary tree, its elements should be sorted such that they satisfy the *fundamental property of binary search trees*: if the data item x is stored in the node **n**, all data items stored in the subtree pointed[2] by **n.left** are less than or equal to x, while all those in the subtree pointed by **n.right** are larger than or equal to x.

As for a heap data structure, this sorting property does not uniquely determine the structure of the tree; see for example Figure 16.12. Different trees can be obtained, for example, because the elements have been inserted and removed in a different order.

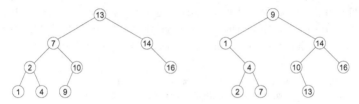

Fig. 16.12 Examples of binary search trees: the same data set can be stored in different ways. Contrary to what occurs in a heap (compare with Figure 16.6), the tree topology identifies the order of the data, whose values increase when read from left to right.

Note however, that in a binary tree, contrary to what happens in a heap, there is a very strong correlation between the value (or the property) of the data and their position in the tree. Indeed, in both the trees of Figure 16.12, the value of the data increases if the nodes are read from left to right (without considering their depth in the tree). This correlation between the value of the data and their position in the tree is what makes the search for an element in a binary tree efficient.

In the following, we schematically show the main operations on a binary search tree. Keep in mind that the described operations take at most a time which is proportional to the tree maximum depth $h_{\max}$ (we leave for the reader to verify this statement), which is typically of the order $\mathcal{O}(\log N)$. So, on average, they are efficient operations.

Moreover, none of the functions we are about to describe allocate memory for the tree nodes. Indeed, we assume a node has been "created", i.e., memory space has been allocated, its data fields have been filled and the NULL value has been assigned to its pointers, before any of the functions we are about to describe are called.

---

[2]Slightly abusing notation, we indicate the subtree whose root is pointed by **p** as the subtree pointed by **p**.

16.3.2   *Inserting and searching in a binary search tree*

The *insertion* of a new data item in the tree is a relatively simple operation.
Compare the new element with the root of the tree and understand in which
subtree it should be placed. Repeat the same operation in the chosen
subtree, until you reach an empty subtree, i.e., a space to put the new
element. The recursive function in Listing 16.5 performs the insertion of a
new node *new, whose pointers have already been initialized to NULL, in a
tree with root *old.

To insert a new node *new in a tree, we just need to call the function
of Listing 16.5 with the pointer to the tree root as a second argument:
insertNode(new, root). In the particular case in which we want to insert
the first node of the tree, the pointer root would be NULL. Therefore we
just need to assign the value new without calling insertNode.

```
1 void insertNode(myNode *new, myNode *old) {
2   if (new->datum <= old->datum) {
3     if (old->left == NULL) {
4       old->left = new;
5       new->up = old;
6     } else {
7       insertNode(new, old->left);
8     }
9   } else {
10    if (old->right == NULL) {
11      old->right = new;
12      new->up = old;
13    } else {
14      insertNode(new, old->right);
15    }
16  }
17 }
```

Listing 16.5   A recursive function to insert a node in a binary tree.

There is a fundamental difference between a heap (that can be represented by a binary tree) and a true binary tree. When representing a heap
as a binary tree, the tree topology is fixed and determined only by the heap
size N. Therefore, we immediately know, for example, which elements correspond to the leaves. Instead, a true binary tree has a dynamic topology
which is not fully determined by the number N of its nodes. In this case,
for example, the nodes without any children cannot immediately be identified. They can be searched by running through the list of nodes or traveling
along the tree from the root down.

In general, while algorithms operating on a heap can start from the root as from the leaves, in a completely equivalent way. Those working on trees have a unique access point, namely its root. Alternatively, we could access a tree from a generic node, but this does not contain any information on the position of that node in the tree.

Exercise 16.3 - Data insertion sequences in a tree

Figure 16.12 contains two different binary trees generated from the same data set, which have been inserted in a different order. Write, for each of the two trees, at least three possible data insertion sequences leading to the filling given in the figure. Note how the insertion sequences compatible with a given binary tree satisfy only partial order relations (which ones?). This should clarify why the trees do not depend only on the data they contain, but also on the way they have been filled.

Exercise 16.4 - Unbalancing when filling a tree

In case we insert elements with the same value in a binary search tree, the function `insertNode` shows a systematic error because it always places these elements to the left of those already present in the tree. This systematic error could result in very unbalanced trees. How can this problem be solved by slightly changing the function `insertNode`? The solution based on pseudorandom numbers is probably the most obvious one. However, there exists an even easier one not using (pseudo)random variables. Which one?

Hands on 16.6 - Depth of binary trees

Write a function computing the depth of a node. After filling a tree with N elements of random value by using the function `insertNode`, measure its maximum depth and the average node depth. Compute the expected value of these two depths by averaging over many different noise samples, i.e., the order in which the nodes are added to the tree. Estimate numerically how these two depths grow with increasing N, by a fitting procedure (possibly a linear fit if you choose the right variables!).

Next, consider only the nodes without children, i.e., the tree leaves. As these nodes appear at the end of each branch, they should give a good estimate of the tree depth. Compute numerically the probability distribution of the leaves depth for various values of N (we suggest you to use values in the interval $10^2 \leq N \leq 10^5$ and to compute the averages considering at least a thousand different noise samples). Numerically estimate the average value $\langle h \rangle$ and the variance $\sigma_h^2 \equiv \langle h^2 \rangle - \langle h \rangle^2$ of these distributions. How do they grow with N? What can you deduce when comparing them to how the average and maximum value of the node increases? Finally, plot the probability distribution of the variable $z \equiv (h - \langle h \rangle)/\sigma_h$ for various values of N. Observe how the distributions for various N are similar, even though their profile is nontrivial as they are, for example, asymmetric with respect to the origin.

```
1 myNode *searchItem(dataType item, myNode *pNode) {
2   if (pNode == NULL || item == pNode->datum) {
3     return pNode;
4   } else if (item < pNode->datum) {
5     return searchItem(item, pNode->left);
6   } else {
7     return searchItem(item, pNode->right);
8   }
9 }
```

Listing 16.6   A recursive function to search a binary tree.

Given a binary search tree filled with data, we now consider a tree search function. To *search* a given element `item` we can use, for example, the recursive function, given in Listing 16.6. The function `searchItem` returns either a pointer to the node containing the searched data item or the value `NULL` if the tree does not contain any such data item. The number of recursive calls is at most equal to the tree maximum depth in case the function `searchItem` is called with second argument `root`.

Hands on 16.7 - Non-recursive functions on binary trees

Write non-recursive versions of the functions inserting a node and searching an element in a binary tree. Keep in mind that for simple functions, such as `insertNode` and `searchItem`, it is sometimes preferable to opt for their non-recursive versions because they are faster and not more difficult to program. Still, remember that the performance of an algorithm may depend much on the computer and compiler one is using.

An element which is easy to find in a binary search tree is the *absolute minimum*, because it always coincides with the leftmost element. The function of Listing 16.7 returns the pointer to the node containing the minimum element of the tree (or subtree) whose root is pointed by pNode. The maximum element is found with a similar function maximumInTree.

```
1 myNode *minimumInTree(myNode *pNode) {
2   while (pNode->left != NULL) {
3     pNode = pNode->left;
4   }
5   return pNode;
6 }
```

Listing 16.7   A function finding the minimum element in a binary tree.

A last function we need finds the node containing the *successive data item* respect to the one contained in the node given as input to the function. A possible version of this function is given in Listing 16.8.

```
1  myNode *nextItem(myNode *pNode) {
2    myNode *pParent = pNode->up;
3    if (pNode->right != NULL) {
4      return minimumInTree(pNode->right);
5    }
6  . while (pParent != NULL && pNode == pParent->right) {
7      pNode = pParent;
8      pParent = pNode->up;
9    }
10   return pParent;
11 }
```

Listing 16.8   A function searching the node containing the immediately successive element.

In the easy case (lines 3-5) the node pointed by pNode has a subtree on the right and its successor is simply the minimum element of that subtree. If the subtree on the right does not exist, it is slightly more complicated because we need to search the successive element in a higher node. In this case (lines 6-10) we need to climb the tree with the following rule. For as long as we are climbing towards the left, smaller elements are found and we need to continue to climb. We only stop when we either reach the root (in this case pParent equals NULL) or if we climb towards the right (in this case pParent->right is different from pNode). In the first case, we may conclude that the element of which we are looking for the immediately successive one is the largest among those present in the tree. Indeed, in this case the next element does not exist and the function returns the value NULL. Instead, in the second case, the next element exists. Namely, it is the one that we find as soon as we start climbing towards to the right. By analogy, it is easy to write the function `previousItem` returning the node containing the immediately preceding element.

16.3.3 *Deleting elements from a binary search tree*

The last operation we need in order to fully manage a binary search tree is the *removal* or *deletion* of an element from the structure. This operation is in general the most complicated one among those needed to manage a data structure, and the binary search tree is no exception to this rule.

Based on the number of children of the node to be removed, we need to use different strategies. A simple strategy takes care of the case when the node has at most one child, while a more complicated strategy is needed in case it has two children. In Figure 16.13 we schematically show the effect of removing the gray node in the three possible cases.

In the simplest case, given Figure 16.13(a), the gray node does not have any children and can be simply removed from the tree. The only operation needed is to update the pointer of the parent node, node 4 in the example of Figure 16.13(a), assigning it the value NULL[3].

In case the gray node has a single child node, as in Figure 16.13(b), such a child node, together with its eventual subtree, takes the place of the deleted node. This might seem a long operation, because an entire subtree is involved. However, if the family ties are managed by means of pointers, we can perform this operation by simply reassigning the pointers of the parent and child nodes of the one we removed (nodes 9 and 4 in Figure 16.13(b)), such that they correctly point to each other. In the subtree with root node 4, the family ties and, as a consequence, the relative pointers remain unchanged. For example, nodes 2 and 7 continue to have node 4 as a parent.

In the third, and most complicated case, the node to be removed has two child nodes, Figure 16.13(c), and we cannot simply delete it. Instead, we need to substitute it with another node taking its place without violating

---

[3]If the tree does not contain any repeated numbers there is a one-to-one correspondence between the tree nodes and the numbers they contain. So, to keep things short, we can indicate the tree nodes by means of the number they contain.

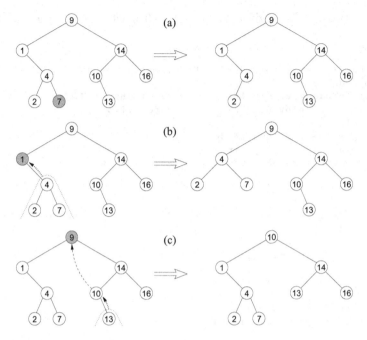

Fig. 16.13 Removing an element from the binary search tree. The gray node is the one we want to delete. We show the three possible cases: the to be removed node has no children (a), has one child (b) or two (c).

the fundamental binary search tree property. This could be either the immediately preceding or the immediately successive one. Without loss of generality, we choose the immediately successive element (node 10 in Figure 16.13(c)). Then the content of the node to be removed is replaced by the content of the immediately successive one and the latter is the one actually removed from the tree. The latter removal can be executed applying the same rules of the preceding case (the one with a single child), thanks to the property stated in the Hands on 16.5.

Exercise 16.5 - Successive elements of a binary search tree

Let x be the node to be deleted with two children and y the one containing the immediately successive element. Prove that y has no children on its left. We advise to prove this by contradiction.

The two functions given in Listing 16.9 delete a node from a binary search tree.

```
1  myNode *deleteNode(myNode *pNode, myNode **pRoot) {
2    myNode *pNext;
3    if (pNode->left == NULL || pNode->right == NULL) {
4      return removeNodeMax1Child(pNode, pRoot);
5    } else {
6      pNext = nextItem(pNode);
7      pNode->datum = pNext->datum;
8      return removeNodeMax1Child(pNext, pRoot);
9    }
10 }
11
12 myNode *removeNodeMax1Child(myNode *pNode, myNode **pRoot) {
13   myNode *pChild;
14   if (pNode->left != NULL) {
15     pChild = pNode->left;
16   } else {
17     pChild = pNode->right;
18   }
19   if (pChild != NULL) {
20     pChild->up = pNode->up;
21   }
22   if (pNode == *pRoot) {
23     *pRoot = pChild;
24   } else if (pNode->up->left == pNode) {
25     pNode->up->left = pChild;
26   } else {
27     pNode->up->right = pChild;
28   }
29   return pNode;
30 }
```

Listing 16.9   Functions deleting a node from a binary search tree.

The function `deleteNode` removes a node pointed by `pNode` from the tree whose root is pointed by `*pRoot`. Please note that we have to pass to the function the pointer `pRoot` to the pointer `root`, because the function may need to change the value of the latter. The cases in which `*pNode` has less than two children are managed by the call to the function `removeNodeMax1Child(pNode, pRoot)` (line 4), which physically deletes the node and possibly adjust the pointers of the parent and child nodes.

The function `removeNodeMax1Child` assumes that the node to be deleted has at most one child. So, in case `*pNode` has two children, the function `deleteNode` first identifies the node containing the immediately successive element, `*pNext`. Then, the content of `*pNext` is copied into `*pNode` and finally `*pNext` is deleted.

In the function `removeNodeMax1Child`, `pChild` is the pointer to the (eventual) single child of `*pNode`. As already said, we also need to supply the function the pointer `pRoot` to the variable `root` pointing to the tree root. Indeed, in case we are deleting the tree root, this variable should be updated.

At the end of the deletion process, the function returns the pointer to the removed node, such that it can be inserted in a list containing all memory locations that are ready to be reused for new nodes. This allows us to keep the memory allocated for the data structure to a minimum.

Binary search trees are very versatile data structures and can be used for countless purposes. When doing the Hands on 16.8 we advise you to write a sufficiently generic program which can be adapted to other problems, as it could turn out to be useful in the future.

Hands on 16.8 - Unbalancing a binary tree

 Repeatedly deleting and inserting elements inside a binary search tree may cause it to become unbalanced. Study this phenomenon while executing a program that analyzes a text with the following operations. Initially the program reads N text words and inserts them in a search tree, sorting them according to the alphabet. Next, perform the following three operations at each time step:

- randomly select a letter;
- remove all words starting with that letter from the tree;
- read new words from the text to bring the number of words inside the tree back to N.

Study as a function of the number of steps executed by the program, how much unbalanced the tree is. For example, measure its maximum and average depth and compare them to the minimum depth (in case of a perfectly balanced tree with the same number N of nodes). Examine different values of N comprised, for example, between 100 and 10^6. Finally, vary the number L of possible letters of the alphabet. Study if and how the tree depth fluctuations change for some values of L, for example, 3, 10, 30 and 100.

Chapter 17

Graphs and graph algorithms

"To find the way out of a labyrinth," William
recited, "there is only one means. At every new
junction, never seen before, the path we have taken
will be marked with three signs. [...]"
"How do you know that? Are you an expert on
labyrinths?"
"No, I am citing an ancient text I once read."
"And by observing this rule you get out?"
"Almost never, as far as I know. But we will try it,
all the same. [...]"

Umberto Eco, *The name of the rose* (1980).

The scientific approach to solve a problem requires in general to construct
abstract representations of the problem, maintaining only the relevant characteristics. In case a system can be considered as a set of "objects" and links
between these, a *graph* representation results to be particularly simple and
useful. In the graph associated to the system the objects are represented
as nodes and the links connecting them as edges between the nodes.

The world surrounding us is full of problems which can be represented as
graphs. For example, to calculate the degree of family relationship between
two persons, we can simply imagine a graph where the nodes are the people
in question and their relatives and draw an edge between each parent-child
couple. The minimum number of edges we need to cross to go from one
person to another is equal to their degree of kinship. Another example
consists in calculating the time to travel by car between two European
cities. It is enough to draw a graph whose nodes are the European cities;

an edge between two nodes is present if there exists a road connecting the corresponding cities in a direct way. In this case, in order to represent the problem, some more information is required: namely, the time needed to travel along each road, that can be written next to the edge representing it. In general, though, a node does not always correspond to a physical object, such as a person or a city. To represent a road map with a graph, the edges are streets and the nodes are their intersections. In what follows we will consider other examples of graphs.

In the first part of this chapter, we introduce graphs, define some of their fundamental properties and show how to manage them with a computer program. Next, we show several graph algorithms, such as those searching for the shortest path between two points, the graph connected components and its minimum spanning tree. In the last part of this chapter, we use these algorithms to study the percolation phenomenon, already introduced in Chapter 13 and here discussed in some more detail.

17.1   Graph definition and its main properties

A *graph* consists of a set of nodes or *vertices* and a set of *edges* connecting the vertices. Mathematically speaking, we write $G = (V, E)$, where G is the graph, V is the set of vertices and E the set of edges. In Figure 17.1 we show examples of graphs consisting of $|V| = 9$ vertices (the circles) and $|E| = 7$ edges (the lines connecting the circles). The symbols $|V|$ and $|E|$ indicate the cardinality of the set of vertices and edges, respectively, i.e., their number of elements. The set V and E of the two graphs of Figure 17.1 are:

$$V = \{1, 2, 3, 4, 5, 6, 7, 8, 9\}, \tag{17.1}$$
$$E = \{(1, 4), (5, 8), (6, 3), (6, 5), (7, 5), (8, 9), (9, 6)\}.$$

Each edge is represented by the couple of vertices it connects.

The difference between the two graphs of Figure 17.1 is that the one on the left is an *undirected* graph, while the one on the right is a *directed* graph. In the former one, an edge between the vertices X and Y can be written either like (X, Y) or, in a completely equivalent way, as (Y, X). Instead, in case of a directed graph, each edge has a certain direction: in the representation (X, Y) the vertex X is the start vertex and Y the end vertex. A famous example of an oriented graph is the *World Wide Web* (WWW) whose vertices are hypertextual pages and the edges are the so-called *hyperlinks* between these pages, which are obviously directed.

The set of all undirected graphs is a subset of the directed graphs as each undirected edge can be viewed as the union of two directed edges between the same vertices, but with opposite directions. Even though the class of directed graphs is more general than that of undirected graphs, we mainly deal with the latter kind in this chapter as they are enough for our purposes. In the following, to introduce some graph properties we refer to the undirected graph in Figure 17.1(a).

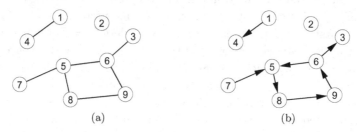

(a)   (b)

Fig. 17.1   Examples of graphs consisting of 9 vertices and 7 edges: an undirected graph (a) and a directed graph (b).

Two vertices are said to be *adjacent* or *neighbors* (or *nearest neighbors*) if there exists an edge directly connecting them. In the example in the figure, the vertices 1 and 4 are adjacent, just like 5 and 6. Instead, the vertices 2 and 3 or 7 and 8 are not adjacent. The *degree* of a vertex is equal to the number of edges incident on that vertex. For example, for the graph in Figure 17.1(a), we have that $c_1 = 1$, $c_2 = 0$, $c_3 = 1$, $c_4 = 1$, $c_5 = 3$, $c_6 = 3$, $c_7 = 1$, $c_8 = 2$ and $c_9 = 2$. The vertex 2 is an isolated vertex. In case of a directed graph, we possibly have to define two different degrees, one counting the edges leaving the vertex (out-degree), and another counting those arriving (in-degree).

A *path* from vertex X to a vertex Y is a sequence $Z_0, Z_1, \ldots, Z_{n-1}, Z_n$ of vertices, such that $Z_0 = X$, $Z_n = Y$ and each couple of successive vertices is connected, i.e., such that $(Z_{i-1}, Z_i) \in E$ for $i = 1, \ldots, n$. For example, the vertex sequence 7-5-6-3 is a path, made of the edges $(7,5)$, $(5,6)$ and $(6,3)$. Not all vertex couples can be the ending point of a path. For example, there does not exist any path between the vertices 4 and 3. Vice versa, when it does exist, the path between two vertices may not be unique. Two other paths between 7 and 3 are the sequences 7-5-8-9-6-3 and 7-5-6-9-8-5-6-3. The first one is a *simple path* because none of its vertices is repeated throughout the sequence.

A graph is said to be *connected* if there exists a path between every couple of vertices belonging to the graph, i.e., if from each vertex we can reach every other vertex by moving along the edges of the graph. A disconnected graph can be decomposed in *connected components* (Section 13.3). Two vertices belong to the same connected component if there exists at least one path between them. The other way around, if such a path does not exist, the vertices belong to different connected components of the graph. The graph in Figure 17.1(a) consists of three connected components: a first one consists of the vertices 1 and 4, a second one is the isolated vertex 2 and finally a third one contains the six remaining vertices.

If the first and last vertex of a path coincide ($Z_0 = Z_n$) it is called a *cycle*. A cycle is *simple* if none of its vertices appear more than once in it. In the figure, the sequence 5-6-9-8-5 is a simple cycle. For each cycle, there exist several equivalent representations: for example, we can also write 5-8-9-6-5 or 8-5-6-9-8 to refer to the same cycle.

A connected and acyclic (not containing any cycles) undirected graph is said to be a *tree*. A set of trees is called a *forest*. The *spanning tree* of a graph G is an acyclic subgraph $G' = (V, E')$, containing all the vertices of the graph G and a subset of edges, $E' \subseteq E$, needed to connect all vertices. In case the graph G has a unique connected component, its spanning tree is indeed a tree. If a graph consists of several connected components, the spanning tree is a forest because it consists of several trees, namely one for each connected component. In case G is a forest, the spanning tree is G itself. In Section 17.3 we consider some examples of spanning trees.

Exercise 17.1 - Trees and forests

Calculate how many edges a tree of N vertices contains. Suppose N vertices form a forest of A trees. How many edges does this forest have? How the forest change if we remove an edge from the forest? And what if we delete k edges?

The execution times of the algorithms which are applied to a graph $G = (V, E)$ grow with the graph size and more in particular, with the number of its vertices $N = |V|$ and the number of its edges $M = |E|$. Often, algorithms performing the same task or solving the same problem take a time growing in a different way. For example, suppose we have two algorithms solving a given problem, and whose execution time grows in one case like $T_1 \propto N^3$ and in the other like $T_2 \propto M^2$. Which one is more

The bridges of Königsberg

It seems the concept of a graph was first used by Euler in 1735 to solve the Königsberg bridge problem. A popular riddle asks whether it is possible to start from a certain point in the city of Königsberg, cross all its bridges only once and return to the starting point. Euler simplified this problem by transforming the city map in a graph maintaining all features relevant to answer the question. As can be seen from the figure, each bridge is transformed in an edge connecting two parts of the city, which are represented by vertices.

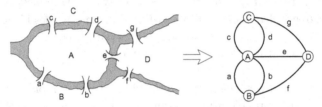

In graph terms, the question is then whether there exists a simple cycle including all edges of the graph (called a *Eulerian circuit*). Given that each time a cycle reaches a vertex it should also leave it, the number of edges belonging to a cycle and passing through one of its generic vertices should be even. So, the degree of each vertex should be even for a cycle containing all edges of the graph. In this way Euler proved, in case of the Königsberg bridges, that it is impossible to cross all bridges one single time to then return to the starting point, as not all vertices of the graph in the figure have an even degree (on the contrary, they all have odd degrees!).

convenient to use depends on the ratio between the two times which in turn depends on the graph to which the algorithm is to be applied. Often, a good answer can be given if we just consider the ratio M/N. Indeed, once this ratio has been fixed, we can write the scaling laws for the execution time as a function of the number of vertices only and understand which execution time grows more slowly with increasing N.

The ratio between the number of edges and the number of vertices is linked to the average degree $\bar{c}$ as in the following equation

$$2\frac{M}{N} = \bar{c} \equiv \frac{1}{N}\sum_{i\in V} c_i \,.$$

The average degree of a graph consisting of N vertices may vary between 0 and $N-1$. The limit cases are a minimally connected graph, which is a set of isolated vertices, $c_i = 0 \; \forall i \in V$, with no edges ($E = \emptyset$), and a maximally connected graph, called a *complete graph*, containing an edge between each couple of vertices. A complete graph of N vertices has precisely $M = N(N-1)/2$ edges and all its vertices have degree $N-1$. We leave it to the reader to verify this relation between the number of vertices N and the number of edges M of a complete graph.

It is useful to define two classes of graphs based on their average degree. *Dense graphs* contain a fraction (not varying with N) of all possible edges, i.e., we have that $M = \mathcal{O}(N^2)$ and $\bar{c} = \mathcal{O}(N)$. *Sparse graphs* have an average degree which does not grow with N or, at most, goes like $\mathcal{O}(\log N)$. Reconsidering the example of two algorithms with execution times T_1 and T_2, we recommend to select the first one for dense graphs and the second to deal with sparse graphs.

When reducing a problem into its equivalent graph representation, we often also need to provide other information apart from the topology (that only specifies which vertices are connected). For example, to compute the shortest cycle passing through all vertices of the graph (the so-called traveling salesman problem), we need to give a number to each edge, called *weight*, representing the distance between the two vertices it connects. If the edges of a graph have a weight, we have a *weighted graph*. In general, an edge weight does not always represent a distance, but a generic cost associated to that edge.

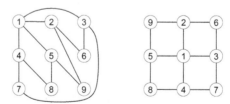

Fig. 17.2   Two different graphic representations of the same graph: the visual aspect of the one on the right is more telling.

We conclude this introduction to graphs with a comment on how they are *graphically represented* i.e. how we can draw them. Remember that a graph only gives us information on the system topology, i.e., which vertices are connected. Its does not tell us anything about their geometry, i.e., how they should be spatially arranged. When drawing a graph on a piece of paper, we need to decide, for each vertex, its coordinates in a two-dimensional space. Given, we do not have any information related to this aspect, there are many ways to do this. Obviously, some graphical representations supply us with more information than other ones. This can be easily seen in Figure 17.2 which contains two different representations of the same graph. Even though the two ways are topologically equivalent, the right one immediately allows us to understand we are dealing with a portion of a two-dimensional square lattice. It would have been even more difficult to realize this, if we had chosen a representation in which the edges intersected. Unfortunately, the latter is often inevitable when trying to "project" a very connected graph on a piece of paper. Finally, we observe that, in the worst possible case, recognizing whether two graphs are the same apart from a permutation of their vertex names (graph isomorphism) is an NP hard problem (see box on page 439). So, in general, it is not easy to immediately know whether there exists a simple graphical representation (for example, one in which only a small number of edges intersect) for a given graph.

Exercise 17.2 - Drawing graphs

 Which complete graphs can you draw on a piece of paper such that none of its edges intersect with each other? If we could use a hologram to represent graphs (i.e., if we could use a three-dimensional space) which complete graphs could we possibly represent without any intersecting edges?

17.2 From graphs to data structures

To represent graph related information in a computer program, it would be enough to write the set V of vertices and the set E of edges in the computer memory. Without loss of generality, we can assume that for a graph of N vertices, the set V is represented by the integer numbers between 0 and $N-1$. Nevertheless, we advise against representing the set E with the mathematical notation used in equation (17.1). Indeed, simply writing the vertex couples corresponding to the graph edges in an array complicates the operations we typically want to perform on graphs. For example, to locate the neighbors of a given vertex we would have to scroll through the entire list.

There basically exist two efficient data structures to represent the set E of edges of a graph. The first one uses an *adjacency matrix* and the second is based on *adjacency lists*. In the following sections, we study the merits and flaws of these two data structures to represent a graph in a computer. We also discuss which one is more convenient depending on the problem under study.

17.2.1   Adjacency matrix

Given a graph with N vertices, the adjacency matrix A is an $N \times N$ matrix such that:

$$A_{ij} = \begin{cases} 1 \text{ if the edge } (i,j) \in E, \\ 0 \text{ otherwise.} \end{cases}$$

On the left side of Figure 17.3 an example of an undirected graph and its corresponding adjacency matrix is given. The adjacency matrix of an undirected graph is always symmetric. It is natural to store the elements of A in a two-dimensional array `A[][]`.

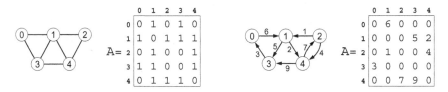

Fig. 17.3   An undirected and unweighted graph (on the left) and a directed and weighted graph (on the right), each with their corresponding adjacency matrix.

The main merit of the adjacency matrix is that it is very easy to write a program using it. For instance, to find out whether two vertices i and j are connected, we just have to read the content of the element `A[i][j]`. Instead, its main flaw is the memory needed to store such a matrix, which is always N^2, independently of the average degree of the graph. Moreover, to determine the neighbors of site i we necessarily need to examin all elements on the ith row. This is why we strongly advise against using it for sparse graphs. Indeed, the matrix would be full of zeros, thus uselessly occupying memory and making it unhandy to work. For these kinds of graphs it is preferable to use adjacency lists (Section 17.2.2).

The adjacency matrix is convenient when working on dense graphs. In this case, the nonzero matrix elements are a reasonable fraction of the total and the size of the matrix, N^2, has the same order of magnitude as the set of edges. So, we are not truly "wasting" memory. Moreover, in case the dense graph is also weighted, the adjacency matrix easily allows us to include this information on the weights: the matrix element A_{ij} is set equal to the weight of the link (i, j) or zero[1] if such a link does not exist. In case of directed graphs, the adjacency matrix allows us to easily distinguish between the edges *leaving* the vertex i (those on the ith row) from those *arriving* at vertex i (those on the ith column). On the right side of Figure 17.3 we included an example of a weighted, directed graph, together with its adjacency matrix representation.

17.2.2 *Adjacency lists*

In order to obtain the adjacency list representing a graph, we build for each of its vertices a list with its neighbors. Each list has a length equal to the corresponding vertex degree. In general, the order in which the neighbors of a given vertex are included in the list is unimportant. So, for each of the N lists we can use the easiest data structure, for example, the bucket described in Section 16.1. Figure 17.4 contains an example of a graph and its representation in terms of adjacency lists: `neigh[]` is an array of pointers (Section 6.5.1) with each element pointing to a list of neighbors. It is convenient to also keep an array `degree[]` with the degrees of the vertices, such that the element `degree[i]` indicates how many neighbors we can read starting from the memory location pointed by `neigh[i]`.

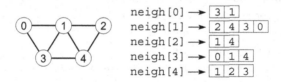

Fig. 17.4 The same undirected and unweighted graph of Figure 17.3 and its representation in terms of adjacency lists.

In total, this graph representation takes $2(N + M)$ memory locations. More precisely, a vector of length N for the degrees, another of the same length for the pointers to the lists and N vectors for the adjacency lists, occupying in total $2M$ memory locations, as for each edge we include two vertices in the adjacency lists. As we already mentioned, the adjacency matrix is typically less efficient to use compared to the adjacency lists.

---

[1]The conventional value of the weight we choose to indicate the absence of a link can be substituted by another one in case 0 is considered a valid weight.

This is why we generally advise to use the latter. In case of a weighted graph, the adiacency lists should also keep hold of the edge weights. To this purpose, we can simply transform each element of the adjacency lists in a **struct** containing both the vertex nearest neighbor as the corresponding edge weight.

Hands on 17.1 - Adjacency lists

 Write a program reading a graph from a file and creating the corresponding adjacency lists. The formatted file contains, on the first line, the number of vertices, and on the following lines, a couple of integer numbers per line corresponding to the vertices joined by an edge. Print the histogram of the vertices degrees.

Hamiltonian cycles

In 1858, the Irish mathematician and physicist Sir William Rowan Hamilton (1805-1865) presented the following problem: given a dodecahedron, is it possible, starting from a given vertex and moving along its edges, to visit all vertices exactly once before returning to the starting vertex? In terms of the equivalent graph, the question is whether there exists a simple cycle passing through all vertices of the graph. In case of the dodecahedron the answer can be found by means of simply trying (a possible solution is included in the figure). For a generic graph it is much harder to answer this question. Only in the first half of the seventies of the XX century, it was discovered that finding Hamiltonian cycles is an NP-complete problem, and thus, very difficult to solve in a worst case scenario.

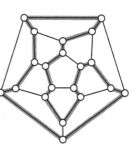

17.3   Graph algorithms

Many interesting problems can be transformed into problems on graphs. For example, we already considered the traveling salesman problem, which consists in determining the minimum weight cycle passing through all the vertices of a weighted graph, and the Eulerian circuit problem, asking whether there exists a cycle containing all edges of a graph exactly once. Other examples are the so-called *Hamiltonian cycle* problem (see box) trying to find a simple cycle passing through all vertices, or the minimum-weight spanning tree, analyzed in Section 17.3.2.

The complexity of these problems is very different. The Eulerian circuit problem and the minimum-weight spanning tree problem belong to the P complexity class, while the traveling salesman problem and the Hamiltonian cycle problem belong to the NP-complete complexity class [Garey and Johnson (1979)]. In this chapter we prefer to deal with algorithms solving polynomial problems: this is why we discuss the minimum-weight spanning tree problem and the problem of listing the connected components of a graph.

For both problems we use the so-called *greedy* solving strategy. To solve a problem, an algorithm makes choices following a predefined strategy. Greedy search algorithms always choose the solution which at that moment seems the best one. The greedy algorithms are in general very fast and easy to program, as they use simple strategies. We strongly advise too use them in all the cases where it can be proven that these algorithms converge to the right solution, as is the case for the problems studied in Sections 17.3.1 and 17.3.2. Unfortunately, for more complex problems, the greedy strategies generally do not give good results. For example, solving the traveling salesman problem with a greedy strategy that moves the traveler to the nearest vertex which has not yet been visited, typically provides a path which is longer than the optimal one.

17.3.1   *Searching a graph*

To answer questions like «Does the graph contain any cycles?», «Is the graph connected?», or «How many connected components does the graph contain?» we need to be able to visit the graph without leaving out any vertex or edge. We present two algorithms for this purpose. Starting from a vertex v, these algorithms visit the connected component to which v belongs to in an exhaustive way. In case the number of visited vertices is less than the total number of vertices N, we need to make sure to restart the algorithm from one of the vertices that have not yet been visited.

The depth-first (DF) search visits the graph following the same strategy that is usually employed to cross a maze[2]: the search goes on visiting new vertices as long as this is possible; when unvisited neighbors are no longer available, the search goes back and choose a different, not yet visited, direction at the last encountered junction. In Figure 17.5 we show the result of a DF search, starting from the vertex D. The gray line indicates the tour made by the DF search algorithm to reach all the vertices of the graph. The number close to the vertices indicates at what time the algorithm passes by that vertex. We label the vertices with letters to avoid any confusion.

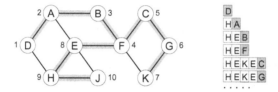

Fig. 17.5   A graph visited with the depth-first search algorithm. The numbers at the vertices indicate the order in which they are visited during the search. The highlighted edges are those the search algorithm travels along. On the right, we show the state of the stack during the first steps of the search: the gray vertex is the one the algorithm is working on.

The algorithm starts from D, lists its non yet visited neighbors (A and H) and selects one of them, for example A (here we adopt the rule of chosing the vertices in alphabetical order). It moves to A, again lists its non visited neighbors (B and E) and chooses B. It continues in this way, until it reaches K, where it gets blocked the first time: K does not have any non visited neighbors, because both F and G have already been visited by the algorithm. So, the algorithm goes back on its steps until it finds a neighbor, among those that have been listed so far, which still needs to be visited, such as the vertex E neighboring F. Moving towards E and analyzing the neighbors of E, it finds out A has already been visited, so it is not even listed, while H and J are included in the list. It continuous along H and finally arrives at J. At this point, it might seem the algorithm has finished its task (from the figure it is obvious that all nodes have been visited). However, the algorithm filled a list of vertices to be potentially visited, and until this list

---

[2]The strategy we describe is equivalent to the well-known *right-hand rule* that allows one to enter, cross and leave any maze by always keeping the right hand on the wall.

is nonempty, the algorithm cannot be terminated. During the last steps, the algorithm reads the vertices still in the list and determines whether they have all been visited or not (think, for instance, of the vertex H initially listed together with A and finally reached by the algorithm coming from E). Note that the final result of this algorithm is a spanning tree (defined in Section 17.1).

To write a non-recursive program for the DF search algorithm we need a stack to store all unvisited neighbors encountered while exploring the graph. At each step of the algorithm, a vertex is extracted from the stack. If it has not yet been visited, its neighbors are analyzed and the unvisited ones are inserted in the stack. On the right of Figure 17.5 we show the status of the stack during the first steps of the algorithm.

It is possible to avoid the explicit use of a stack by programming a recursive DF search function. When it is called on a vertex X, this function analyzes the neighbors of X and calls itself on the neighbors of X which have not yet been visited. In this case, though, we advise against using recursion, because the number of recursive calls opened at the same time could easily become of the order of magnitude of the number of vertices, exceeding the maximum allowed limit.

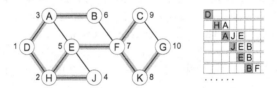

Fig. 17.6   The same graph of Figure 17.5 visited by the breadth-first search algorithm: again, the numbers indicate the order in which the vertices are visited and the highlighted edges are those the algorithm travels along. On the right, the queue used by the search algorithm: the gray vertex is the one the algorithm is working on.

The breadth-first (BF) search, explores the graph in a way similar to how water would fill a set of tanks (vertices) connected by pipelines (edges): first all the nearest neighbor vertices are "flooded", next all their nearest neighbors and so on, until all are totally filled. In Figure 17.6 we show the path followed by the BF procedure to reach all vertices (the number next to each vertex indicates the time at which the algorithm passed by that vertex). The main difference with the DF search is the use of a queue instead of a stack, allowing to analyze the vertices in the order in which they are reached. The other difference might seem a little technical, but sometimes allows us to save a lot of time: in the DF search we need to write in the stack many vertices which are finally reached in other ways (such as the vertices H and E in the preceding example), while in the BF search a vertex is marked as "visited" as soon as it is added to the queue (thus the BF queue contains all vertices just once).

On the right of Figure 17.6 we show the queue content during the first steps of the algorithm: the queue starts with the starting vertex D; at each step, a single vertex (the gray one) is extracted from the queue and its unvisited neighbors are inserted in the queue. Also in this case, the search generates a spanning tree, but with a particular property. Indeed, we can use the spanning tree obtained with the BF search to calculate the distance between the starting vertex and any other vertex of its connected component: this distance is equal to the length of the path connecting the two vertices along the tree (such a path is unique on a tree).

Exercise 17.3 - Graph distances

Compute the distances between the vertex D and the other vertices in Figure 17.6, taking advantage of the gray spanning tree. If we inserted the not visited neighbors of each vertex in alphabetical order in the queue, what would be the resulting spanning tree? On this new spanning tree, are the distances from D to the other vertices the same as on the spanning tree in Figure 17.6?

Hands on 17.2 - Searching the connected components of a graph

---

Write a program computing the number and the dimension of all the connected components of a graph. The graph is given as an input with the format described in the Hands on 17.1. The program should be able to perform both DF as BF search in an equivalent way.

Hands on 17.3 - Distance between the vertices of a graph

Change the program for the BF search such that it also computes the distances between the initial and all other vertices belonging to the same connected component. Use it to measure the distance between all pair of vertices of a given connected graph. To check the code, run it on relatively simple graphs where the distances are known beforehand. For example, consider a linear chain or a two-dimensional lattice.

17.3.2 *Minimum spanning tree*

Given an undirected and weighted graph[3] $G = (V, E)$, the *minimum spanning tree* (MST), is the one whose sum of the edge weights is minimum. In case the edge weights are not all different from each other, the MST may not be unique. In the latter case, the MST search algorithm should find one of them. Figure 17.7 contains a weighted graph with two possible MST: the edges (A, D) and (H, J), as well as (C, F) and (G, K), can be exchanged without changing the spanning tree total weight.

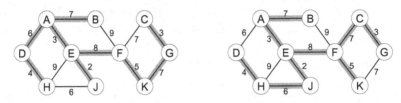

Fig. 17.7   Two possible minimum spanning trees of the same graph.

The MST problem has a broad range of applications. For example, suppose an electricity company needs to build a new distribution network connecting the electric power plant plat and $N - 1$ locations spread out over the territory. Obviously, the company wants to know which of the networks carrying current to all of the locations costs less. This problem can be restated as a MST search problem on a graph whose N vertices correspond to the locations in need of electric power together with the electric power plant. The edge weight reflects the cost to build the electric line between the two locations connected by such an edge. This cost is typically proportional to the distance, but not only (it is more expensive to build a power line in a mountain area than across a flat land).

The most common greedy strategies to search a MST are known as the Prim's algorithm and the Kruskal's algorithm. In both strategies, the MST grows by adding one edge during each step of the algorithm. More precisely, these algorithms generate a sequence of graphs $H_i = (V, E_i)$ with $i = 0, \ldots, N-1$, which are subgraphs of G containing an increasing number of edges $|E_i| = i$: $E_0 = \emptyset \subset E_1 \subset \ldots \subset E_{N-1} \subseteq E$. The sequence starts from H_0 containing only the (isolated) vertices of G, and stops at H_{N-1}, i.e., the MST. At the ith step, given the subgraph H_{i-1}, a new edge (which is certainly part of the MST) is selected and added in order to obtain H_i. Let us discuss these choices in Prim's and Kruskal's algorithms.

---

[3]For simplicity, we consider a connected graph G. Everything discussed in this Section is equally valid for each connected component of G.

In *Prim's strategy* the MST is built, starting from the initial vertex, in a single connected component. So, the graph H_i consists of a "large" connected component of $i + 1$ vertices (the growing MST) containing the initial vertex and other $N - i - 1$ isolated vertices. On the left side of Figure 17.8 we show the graph H_5 obtained after five steps of Prim's algorithm, starting from the vertex D. At the ith step, Prim's algorithm identifies the edges connecting a vertex of the large connected component and an isolated vertex, i.e., those edges connecting the growing MST with the remaining vertices; these are the edges (B, F) and (E, F) in the figure. To expand the MST, we need to add one of these edges to H_i. By choosing the one with the smallest weight, we can be sure to have reached a correct MST at step $N - 1$.

To program an efficient code for Prim's algorithm, it is convenient to use a priority queue (Section 16.2). In the beginning the priority queue contains all vertices with priority zero, except for the vertex from which we want to start building the MST. The priority of the latter is assigned a positive value[4]. The queue contains all vertices which have not yet been inserted in the growing MST. After the first step, the priority of each vertex X is zero in case X is not directly connected to the growing MST or equal to the inverse weight of the edge connecting X to the growing MST. Let us call the ancestor of X the vertex belonging to the growing MST to which X is directly connected. Every vertex in the queue with nonzero priority should also maintain this information regarding who is its ancestor. In the example on the left part of Figure 17.8, the only vertex in the priority queue with nonzero priority is F, appearing twice: with priority 1/8, which is the inverse of the weight of the edge (E, F), and ancestor E; with priority 1/9 and ancestor B. At each step of the algorithm, the vertex with highest priority is extracted, say X, and added to the growing MST together with the edge connecting it to its ancestor. Each neighbor Y of X, still not in the growing MST, is added to the priority queue with a priority equal to the inverse weight of the edge (X,Y) and ancestor X. The case in which the vertex Y is already included in the queue does not create any problem, because the copy of Y with highest priority is picked out first from the queue. The other copies will not be used any more.

The execution time of Prim's algorithm depends on which type of priority queue is used. If a heap (Section 16.2) is used, both the operation of extracting the highest priority element and the one of inserting a new

---

[4]The precise value is irrelevant. Its only purpose is to extract the corresponding vertex at the first step.

element take at most $\mathcal{O}(\log \mathcal{N})$ operations, where $\mathcal{N}$ is the number of elements in the queue. In the Prim's algorithm, the heap may contain at most a number of elements upper-bounded by M, since each edge is used at most once. So, the number of insertion and extraction operations is also upper-bounded by M and the running time of the Prim's algorithm is at most $\mathcal{O}(M \log M) \simeq \mathcal{O}(M \log N)$. With the help of a priority queue, known as the Fibonacci heap [Cormen *et al.* (1990)], we can improve the algorithm performance and achieve an execution time of order $\mathcal{O}(M + N \log N)$. Still, this advantage is irrelevant for sparse graphs for which $M = \mathcal{O}(N)$.

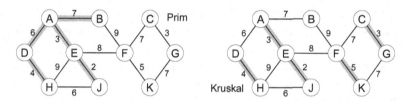

Fig. 17.8 An intermediate state when building the minimum spanning tree with the two algorithms described in the text, Prim's and Kruskal's.

Kruskal's strategy starts from a graph H_0 just consisting of the isolated vertices of G. It examines the edges in order of their increasing weight: every edge which does not close a cycle is added to the growing MST. This rule ensures that at each step of the algorithm, the graph H_i is acyclic and of minimum weight (because the edges are added in order of increasing weight). So, after $N-1$ edges have been added, a MST is certainly reached. On the right side of Figure 17.8 we show the graph H_5 obtained after five steps of Kruskal's algorithm. Note that adopting this strategy, the graphs H_i are generally a forest with many connected components. The algorithm allows us to add a new edge only if it connects two different trees. Instead, it is forbidden to add an edge connecting two vertices of the same tree as it would close a cycle. For example, starting from the graph H_5 depicted on the right of Figure 17.8, the two edges which are then taken under consideration are those with weight 6, i.e. (A, D) and (H, J). The first one of these is added to the growing MST, while the second one is rejected because it would close the cycle A-E-J-H-D-A.

The main problem when implementing this strategy is how to establish quickly whether two vertices belong to the same connected component[5]. To

---

[5]Even though in Kruskal's algorithm each connected component is a tree, we prefer to treat the more general problem in which there might also be cycles present.

this purpose, we need to add a label to the vertices. The algorithm starts from a set H_0 of isolated vertices. Each vertex is a connected component of size one, whose label is give by the vertex' name.

The easiest labeling system is described in Chapter 13, imposing each vertex to carry always the label of the component to which it belongs to. Unfortunately, this strategy is not very efficient. Indeed, when merging two connected components of size N_1 and N_2, it takes $\mathcal{O}(N_1 + N_2)$ number of operations to update the labels and the list of vertices belonging to the resulting connected component. How can we create a more efficient vertex labeling system?

All vertices belonging to a connected component are organized in a (not necessarily binary) tree[6]. The label of each vertex is a pointer to its ancestor on this tree, while the root vertex points to itself. So, to trace from a generic vertex to the root of the tree of which it is part, we just need to follow these pointers until we reach a vertex pointing to itself. Each tree is unambiguously identified by the root vertex on its tree. So, two vertices belong to the same connected component, or tree, if they lead to the same root vertex. An analogous procedure is used for the linked lists in Section 13.5.

So, basically, what we need is to build trees in which we can rapidly reach the root from any of its vertices. This can be done as follows. Initially, we only have isolated vertices: each vertex is a connected component, but it is also the root of this tree and therefore points to itself. Suppose we want to add an edge connecting the vertices X and Y, and the roots of the respective trees, say R_X and R_Y, are different (otherwise we would not need to update any connected component); of course, it is possible that $R_X = X$ or $R_Y = Y$. To merge the two trees in an efficient way, we need to update the pointers of one of the two roots and make it point to the other root vertex. In Figure 17.9 we show the two trees we want to merge (a) and the two possible results of this merging process (b-c).

Which one of the two roots we chose to point to the other one depends on the result we want to obtain. For example, if, in our search for the connected component of a generic vertex, we want to keep the worst case under control, we need to keep the maximum tree depth as low as possible. In this case, it is convenient to keep for each tree the maximum depth, $h_{\max}$, by writing this number in the root vertex. When the two trees are merged, we choose the root vertex with the smallest $h_{\max}$ to point to the

---

[6]This tree is typically very different from the spanning tree obtained with Kruskal's algorithm.

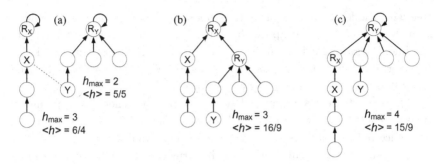

Fig. 17.9 The two possible results of merging the two trees shown in (a): in (b) we minimize $h_{\max}$, while in (c) we keep $\langle h \rangle$ to a minimum.

other root, as in Figure 17.9(b).

Exercise 17.4 - Updating the maximum depth

When merging two trees, we need to update the information on the resulting tree which is kept in its root. Write a formula to update the value of $h_{\max}$ of the resulting tree in function of the values of $h_{\max}$ of the trees which have been merged. Check the formula for the case of Figure 17.9.

Instead, if we want to minimize the average search time for the conected component of a vertex, assuming each vertex is chosen with the same probability, we need to keep the average tree depth, $\langle h \rangle$, as low as possible, where the average is made with respect to the vertices of the tree. When merging two trees of N_1 and N_2 vertices and average depth $\langle h \rangle_1$ and $\langle h \rangle_2$, there are two possible results for the average depth of the resulting tree. If we made the first tree point to the second, we have:

$$\frac{N_1(\langle h \rangle_1 + 1) + N_2 \langle h \rangle_2}{N_1 + N_2} = \frac{N_1 \langle h \rangle_1 + N_2 \langle h \rangle_2}{N_1 + N_2} + \frac{N_1}{N_1 + N_2} \, ,$$

otherwise, we get

$$\frac{N_1 \langle h \rangle_1 + N_2(\langle h \rangle_2 + 1)}{N_1 + N_2} = \frac{N_1 \langle h \rangle_1 + N_2 \langle h \rangle_2}{N_1 + N_2} + \frac{N_2}{N_1 + N_2} \, .$$

In these expressions, the average depth of the tree which points to the other one is increased by one. Indeed, for each vertex of that tree we need one extra step to reach the root after the trees have been merged. The only difference between the two expressions is in the second term on the right-hand side of the equation. We obtain the least average depth by making the tree with the least number of vertices point to the one with more vertices, as in Figure 17.9(c). To apply this strategy, it is convenient to maintain the information regarding the tree size, i.e., its number of vertices, in its root vertex. When merging two trees of sizes N_1 and N_2 we simply need to update the size of the resulting tree to $N_1 + N_2$.

The two strategies we just described typically generate very similar trees. Nevertheless, we presented both in order to stress once more the difference between a worst case and average case analysis.

Computing the execution time of the Kruskal's algorithm is not immediate. Kruskal's strategy always requires to initialize all N vertices as single connected components, taking $\mathcal{O}(N)$ operations, and sort the M edges in $\mathcal{O}(M \log M)$ operations. However, it is not easy to calculate the execution time of the algorithm, when it identifies the connected component of a vertex. Indeed, the average time it takes a vertex to trace back to its root depends on the number and the size of the connected components, which change throughout the program execution. They follow a stochastic process and it is not easy to keep track of them. What we can say is that, adopting the strategy of minimizing the search for the root in the worst case, a single search takes at most $\mathcal{O}(\log M)$ operations. Considering this search is made a number of times equal to the number of edges, the total number of operations needed to find an MST with Kruskal's algorithm is $\mathcal{O}(M \log M)$. The latter derivation does not take the number of operations needed to update the roots of the two trees upon their merging into account, because they are of order M. On a modern computer with a clock frequency of about 3 GHz, this algorithm takes little more than 30 seconds on a graph with $M = 10^7$ edges. However, an eventual programming error causing it to perform $\mathcal{O}(M^2)$ operations upon execution, would be disastrous (it would take a time of the order of a year to complete the job!).

Hands on 17.4 - Minimum spanning tree

      Write a program computing the minimum spanning tree of a weighted graph. The graph is given as an input with the format described in the previous Hands on. Use at least one of the two strategies described above (Prim's and Kruskal's).

17.4 Percolation again

The percolation problem is introduced in Chapter 13. Here, we examin it again with better algorithms to study some of its features in more detail. We focus on a case which can be solved exactly in the limit of very large systems, namely percolation on random graphs. This allows us to show the difference between a simulation of a finite size system and the behavior expected on an infinitely large one.

On a two-dimensional regular lattice (e.g. a square lattice) percolation occurs when at least two vertices on opposite boundaries belong to the same connected component or cluster (Section 13.4); but random graphs have no "opposite boundaries" and the definition of a percolating system needs to be modified. It is useful to imagine percolation as a dynamic process. Initially there are no clusters in the system. At each step, a vertex or an edge is added, until we get a percolating cluster. For reasons which will become clear later on, we focus on the case in which edges are added. So, at the beginning the vertices of the graph are all present, but none are connected.

To study the graph properties during this growth process (think, for instance, of the number and the size of its connected components, and whether one of these percolates the system) we need to observe it at many different "times", i.e., after adding M edges, for various values of M. To this purpose, we want to use an algorithm keeping a list of the graph connected components. Among the strategies described in the previous sections, the ones based on breadth-first or depth-first search (Section 17.3.1) are not convenient because, each time a new edge is added, the algorithm would have to start from scratch. It is much better to keep the information in a form allowing us to update it, rather than recomputing it from scratch, every time a new edge is added. This can be done, for example, if the connected components are described with the algorithm implementing Kruskal's strategy in Section 17.3.2.

Initially, there are no edges and each of the N vertices is a connected component identifiable from the fact that it points to itself. Each time a new edge is added, connecting two vertices belonging to different connected components, these components are merged together with a small number of operations, i.e., roughly independent on the sizes of the two components. This is an efficient strategy to maintain all time-dependent graph information and to understand when percolation takes place.

Hands on 17.5 - Percolation on the square lattice

 Consider a two-dimensional square lattice of size $L \times L$ with open boundary conditions. Estimate the number of randomly placed edges at which the graph percolates, using the strategy described in the text.

17.4.1   *Random graphs*

A *random graph* is a graph generated by a stochastic process. For simplicity, we consider random graphs with a fixed number N of vertices, where the presence or absence of an edge is a random event. Depending on the random process used to generate the edges, we can associate to each graph G the probability $p(G)$ of being created by this process. These probabilities define a *statistical ensemble of random graphs*. The average of a generic quantity $A(G)$ over this ensemble is given by the expression $\sum_G p(G)A(G)$, where the sum is taken over all graphs of N vertices.

In the statistical ensemble of random graphs $\mathcal{G}_{N,M}$ the only graphs with nonzero probability consist of those with N vertices and M edges. The probability associated to each of these graphs is the same and equals the inverse of the total number of these graphs (such that the sum of the probabilities is 1). The number of graphs with N vertices and M edges is given by $\binom{A}{M} \equiv \frac{A!}{M!(A-M)!}$, that is by the number of ways of choosing M edges among the total number $A = N(N-1)/2$ of possible edges between N vertices. To generate a typical random graph belonging to $\mathcal{G}_{N,M}$, we just need to randomly choose M edges, i.e., M couples of vertices. The only things we need to check during this operation is to make sure that (i) each edge connects two distinctive vertices and (ii) no vertex couple is repeated.

Note that in the so-called thermodynamic or infinite volume limit $(N \rightarrow \infty)$ the ensemble $\mathcal{G}_{N,M}$ tends to coincide (in a statistical sense) with the random graph ensemble $\mathcal{G}_{N,p}$ in which each possible edge is selected with probability $p = \frac{2M}{N(N-1)}$. Some graph properties, for example, the probability distribution of the vertex degrees, are more easily calculated in this second ensemble.

The degree of a generic vertex may vary from 0 to $N - 1$, the latter being the maximum number of vertices to which it might be connected. Let us compute the probability f_k that its degree is exactly k. The number of ways to choose k out of $N-1$ edges is given by the binomial coefficient $\binom{N-1}{k}$, multiplied by the probability that the k chosen edges are present, p^k, and the other $N-1-k$ are absent, $(1-p)^{N-1-k}$. Thus, we find

$$f_k = \binom{N-1}{k} p^k (1-p)^{N-1-k} \ .$$

We leave it to the reader to verify the f_k are well-normalized, i.e., $\sum_{k=0}^{N-1} f_k = 1$. Note how the analogous computation in case of the ensemble $\mathcal{G}_{N,M}$ would be more complicated due to the correlations induced by the fact that the number of edges is fixed and equal to M (indeed, in this case, the presence of a high degree vertex makes it more probable for the other vertices to have a degree lower than the average one). On the contrary, in the ensemble $\mathcal{G}_{N,p}$ the presence of an edge does not cause any correlation on the presence of the others.

An interesting case are the random graphs with a finite degree, i.e., which does not diverge with N in the thermodynamic limit. For example, graphs with average degree equal to c can be obtained considering the two random graph ensembles with $M = cN/2$ or $p = c/(N-1)$. In the latter case, the probability distribution of the vertex degrees takes on a particularly simple expression in the thermodynamic limit,

$$f_k = \lim_{N\to\infty} \frac{(N-1)!}{k!(N-1-k)!} \left(\frac{c}{N-1}\right)^k \left(1 - \frac{c}{N-1}\right)^{N-1-k} = \frac{c^k}{k!} e^{-c} \ . \tag{17.2}$$

It is easy to verify the average value of this distribution is equal to $\sum_{k=0}^{\infty} k f_k = c$. The Poisson distribution in Eq. (17.2) implies that in a random graph with average degree c the probability to have a vertex with degree much larger than c decreases exponentially. For large values of c the distribution in Eq. (17.2) tends towards a Gaussian distribution strongly centered around its average value.

In the thermodynamic limit, the evolution of a typical random graphs with increasing average degree c is well-known. For $c < 1$ the typical random graph is a forest consisting of many trees. As c increases from 0 to 1 the trees merge two by two. Still, the typical graph remains acyclic for as long as $c < 1$. Precisely when $c = 1$ (in the thermodynamic limit) the first cycles appear. For $c > 1$ a strictly positive fraction of vertices belongs to the same connected component, called the *giant cluster*. The remaining vertices still form a forest.

17.4.2 *Percolation in random graphs*

It is easy to define the percolation phenomenon in a metric space, i.e., a space in which the notion of a distance has been introduced. As in the case of the square lattice studied in Section 13.4, a graph is considered to be percolating if at least one of its connected components contains points distant enough (in case of a two-dimensional lattice, points located at its opposite borders).

Instead, random graphs cannot in general be embedded in a metric space. For example, when drawing a typical random graph on a piece of paper, most of the edges cross themselves since they connect vertices at large distances. Indeed, in a random graph the topological concept of a connection between two vertices is not necessarily linked to the geometric concept of the distance between them.

If the distance between vertices is not well defined, it does not make any sense to study the percolation phenomenon as the probability that a graph connects vertices at a given distance. We can study an equivalent property though, that we still call percolation, linked to the probability that two randomly chosen vertices are connected, i.e., belong to the same connected component. This probability is appreciably different from zero only when an extensive number, i.e., $\mathcal{O}(N)$, of vertices belong to the same component. So, the phenomenon of percolation in random graphs is linked to the formation of giant clusters. If m is the fraction of vertices belonging to the giant cluster, the probability that two randomly chosen vertices are connected is equal to m^2 (the vertices not belonging to the giant cluster form small trees and give no contribution to this probability). From now on, we consider the terms giant cluster and percolating cluster to be equivalent.

Here, we present some basic results on random graph percolation, following a simple derivation, rather than a fully rigorous one. Let us compute the probability for a generic vertex to belong to the giant cluster in a random graph of average degree c. We consider a random graph of N vertices and $M = cN/2$ edges, to which we add a new vertex. Also this new graph is random (i.e., it is a typical graph of the ensemble $\mathcal{G}_{N,p}$) if each edge between the new vertex and one of the old ones is present with the correct probability $p = c/N$. In this case the degree of the new vertex is a Poissonian random variable with the distribution in Eq. (17.2). The probability m that a vertex belongs to a giant cluster remains unchanged when adding this new vertex[7] and is given by the solution of the equation

$$1 - m = \sum_{k=0}^{\infty} e^{-c} \frac{c^k}{k!} (1 - m)^k .$$

Indeed, this equation tells us that the probability that the new vertex does not belong to the giant cluster, $1-m$, is equal to the sum of the probabilities that this vertex has k neighbors, $e^{-c} c^k / k!$, none of which belong to the giant cluster, $(1 - m)^k$. Summing the series, we get

$$1 - m = e^{-cm} . \tag{17.3}$$

This equations always has the solution $m = 0$, but for $c > 1$ it also has another solution with $m > 0$ indicating the presence of a giant cluster. This second solution cannot be expressed analytically, but we can convince ourselves of its existence by plotting the two sides of Eq. (17.3) in the left part of Figure 17.10. Moreover, for $m \ll 1$, we can expand the right hand side of Eq. (17.3) in Taylor series around $m = 0$ up to the second order. In this way, we obtain two solutions for m:

$$1 - m = 1 - cm + \frac{1}{2} c^2 m^2 \implies \begin{cases} m = 0 , \\ m = 2(c - 1)/c^2 \simeq 2(c - 1) . \end{cases}$$

The second solution tells us when the giant cluster first appears (at $c = c_p = 1$) and how it grows close to the percolating threshold $c_p = 1$. The exact solution of Eq. (17.3) can be easily obtained numerically (for example, with the algorithm given in Section 4.3.2). On the right of Figure 17.10 we show this solution together with this linear approximation we just obtained which is valid close to $c = 1$. In $c = c_p = 1$ the random graph ensemble undergoes a *phase transition*, from a non percolating to a percolating phase: in other words, for $c < c_p$, a typical random graph of $\mathcal{G}_{N,p}$ is not percolating, while, for $c > c_p$, it is percolating. The order parameter of the phase transition is the fraction of vertices of the percolating cluster. The c value where this phase transition occurs is called the *critical point*.

Another interesting quantity tightly related to the phase transition is the average size of the connected components (already introduced in Section 13.4). For $c < 1$, all connected components have a size which does not grow with N and their average does not diverge for $N \to \infty$. Instead, for $c = 1$, i.e., when the giant cluster first appears, we expect the average size to grow with N. Finally, for $c > 1$ the average size is dominated by

---

[7]More precisely, this probability could change by a quantity $\mathcal{O}(1/N)$ which is irrelevant in the thermodynamic limit.

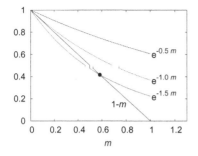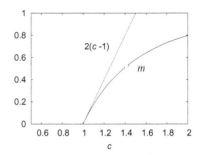

Fig. 17.10   For $c > 1$, the nonzero solution $m(c)$ of equation (17.3) can be found graphically (left figure). This solution is shown in the right figure together with its linear approximation around $c = 1$.

the giant cluster. However, if we exclude the latter, the average size of the other connected components is finite (i.e., does not grow with N) and has a nontrivial decreasing behavior with c (such a behavior is shown in Figure 17.12).

Please note that the average size of the connected components could be defined in more than one way, but only one is meaningful. For example, the average size definition $\tilde{S} \equiv \sum_C S_C / \mathcal{N}_C$, where the sum is over $\mathcal{N}_C$ connected components and S_C is the size of the Cth connected component, does not give us much information about the percolation transition. Indeed, considering that $\sum_C S_C = N$ (the sum of the number of vertices of all connected components is simply the total number of vertices) and that $\mathcal{N}_C = N - M = N(1 - c/2)$ until cycles start appearing, we have that $\tilde{S} = (1 - c/2)^{-1}$ for $c \leq 1$, which does not have a singularity at $c = 1$. The reason why the observable $\tilde{S}$ does not reveal the percolating transition is due to the fact that the sum defining it weights all connected components in the same way. In particular, the largest cluster is counted with the same weight as the other connected components.

A definition of the clusters average size which does behave in the way we described earlier, has been introduced in Section 13.4,

$$\bar{S} \equiv \frac{1}{N} \sum_{i=1}^{N} S_i = \frac{1}{N} \sum_C S_C^2 , \qquad (17.4)$$

where the average is taken over the set of the N vertices and S_i is the size of the connected component to which vertex i belongs. The last expression in Eq. (17.4) is obtained by grouping all vertices belonging to the same cluster. It should be clear that, contrary to $\tilde{S}$, the observable $\bar{S}$ weights much more larger clusters and this is why it can show a divergence at the percolation point $c = 1$ in the thermodynamic limit.

For $c > 1$ the last sum in Eq. (17.4) is dominated by the giant cluster and we want to subtract it. Unfortunately, the giant cluster is well-defined only in the thermodynamic limit. For finite N, the best we can do is to subtract the contribution of the largest connected component and define in this way

$$\bar{S}' \equiv \frac{1}{N} {\sum_{C}}' S_C^2 \, ,$$

where the sum is taken over all clusters, except the largest one. $\bar{S}'$ measures the average size of the non percolating clusters. The average of $\bar{S}'$ over the ensemble of random graphs with average degree c, in the thermodynamic limit, is equal to,

$$\langle \bar{S}' \rangle_c = \frac{1 - m}{1 - c(1 - m)} \, ,$$

where m, solution of Eq. (17.3), is the average fraction of vertices in the giant cluster. For $c \leq 1$, we know that $m = 0$ and the previous expression reduces to $\langle \bar{S}' \rangle_c = \langle \bar{S} \rangle_c = 1/(1 - c)$.

Exercise 17.5 - Growth of the average size

Derive the analytical expression for the average size valid before the percolating point: $\langle \bar{S} \rangle_c = 1/(1 - c)$. Remember that before the percolation point, $c < 1$, a typical random graph is a forest and each edge added typically merges two tree into a new larger tree. Consider also that when two clusters of sizes S_1 and S_2 merge, the average size increases by $\Delta \bar{S} = 2S_1 S_2/N$ and the average degree by $\Delta c = 2/N$ (for large N both increments are very small). Taking the average of these increments over the random graph ensemble, you can obtain a differential equation for $\langle \bar{S} \rangle_c$ as a function of c.

17.5 Numerical percolation study

We discuss now an efficient program to study the percolation phenomenon in random graphs. We consider the so-called Hoshen-Kopelman algorithm [Stauffer and Aharony (1992)]

To keep the list of connected components up-to-date, we use the same strategy of Kruskal's algorithm, described in Section 17.3.2. The following lines of code define the structure corresponding to a connected component. They also contain the declaration of a vector of N connected components.

```
struct connComp {
  struct connComp *parent;
  unsigned int size;
} comp[N];
```

This structure has a pointer **parent** to its ancestor inside the connected component. If the pointer points to the same structure to which it belongs to, then this structure is the root of the connected component. In this case the variable **size** contains the number of vertices belonging to this connected component. This structure is similar to the one we introduced in Section 13.5, while the algorithm we are going to use is more efficient than the two algorithms described in that same section.

The quantities we want to keep track of while the random graph is growing are the size of the largest cluster (which for $N \gg 1$ and $c > 1$ corresponds to the giant cluster) and the average size of clusters $\langle \bar{S} \rangle_c$. To this purpose, we introduce two variables: **largestClusSize**, of **unsigned int** type, storing the number of vertices of the largest cluster; **meanClusSize**, of **unsigned long long int** type, equal to $\sum_C S_C^2 = N \langle \bar{S} \rangle_c$.

Whenever possible, it is advisable to use integer variables instead of rational ones, as operations on the former are not approximated (which is not the case for floating-point operations). The only limit the computer imposes on the use of integer numbers is the maximum value which can be reached given the number of bits of the variable. So, it is a good practice to check always for which parameters of the model under study such a maximum value can be reached. In our case, the size of the largest cluster is at most N, while the value $\sum_C S_C^2$ is at most N^2. Given that the **unsigned int** type has 32 bits, while the **unsigned long long int** has 64 bits, our program allows us to study graphs of size $N < 2^{32}$.

```
1 for (i = 0; i < N; i++) {
2   comp[i].parent = comp + i;
3   comp[i].size = 1;
4 }
5 meanClusSize = N;
6 largestClusSize = 1;
```

Listing 17.1   Initializing the connected components.

The variables are initialized with the code given in Listing 17.1. Since at the beginning each vertex is a connected component, each structure comp[i] points to itself (line 2) and has size one (line 3), as is the case for the largest connected component (line 6). Moreover, we have that $\sum_C S_C^2 = N$ (line 5).

Upon initialization, each vertex is also a connected component (this is why we choose the name comp). It might seem a bit confusing that we keep referring to a vertex with the structure comp of the type connComp even when such a vertex is no longer the root of a connected component. Indeed, we need to keep in mind that the structure connComp effectively represents a connected component (as it is the root of the tree spanning the component) only as long as it points to itself. When this component joins a larger one, its root pointer is assigned to the root of the larger cluster. From that moment on, the structure comp of this vertex, which no longer is a root, becomes redundant (size is no longer used) and slightly misleading. Still, keeping using the structure comp makes the program more efficient, as it requires only a minimum number of variables to be updated.

```
1 pComp1 = componentOf(comp + site1);
2 pComp2 = componentOf(comp + site2);
3 if (pComp1 != pComp2) {
4   meanClusSize += 2 * (unsigned long long int)pComp1->size *
5                                          pComp2->size;
6   newSize = mergeComp(pComp1, pComp2);
7   if (newSize > largestClusSize) {
8     largestClusSize = newSize;
9   }
10 }
```

Listing 17.2   The statements merging two components and updating the observables.

To build the graphs under study, at each step we choose two vertices, site1 and site2 in a random way. The program checks whether they are distinct from each other and whether the edge connecting them is not already part of the growing graph. If both these conditions are satisfied, the corresponding edge is added to the graph. Next, with the lines of code given in Listing 17.2, the program performs the following operations. First of all, with the function componentOf, given in Listing 17.3, it identifies the connected components to which site1 and site2 belong (lines 1-2). If they are distinct from each other, meanClusSize is updated (lines 4-5) and the two components are merged with a function call (line 6) to mergeComp, given in Listing 17.3. Finally, if needed, largestClusSize is

updated (lines 7-9). The values of `largestClusSize` (maximum size) and
`(float)meanClusSize / N` (average size) can be written to a file, with a
frequency chosen by the user, such that they can be analyzed at a later
time.

The expression on lines 4-5 updating `meanCluSize`, derives from the fact
that before the two clusters of size S_1 and S_2 are merged their contribution
to the sum $\sum_C S_C^2$ is equal to $(S_1^2 + S_2^2)$, while afterwards it is equal to
$(S_1 + S_2)^2 = (S_1^2 + S_2^2 + 2S_1S_2)$. It is exactly the difference between these
two expressions that is added to `meanClusSize` on lines 4-5. Also note that,
in order to use this mathematical expression in terms of S_1 and S_2, this
update must be made before the clusters are merged (line 6) and the size
updated to the value $S_1 + S_2$.

A particularly delicate aspect of the expression on lines 4-5 which often
causes errors, is the casting of one of the two variables to the type `unsigned
long long int`. From Listing 17.3 it is clear that `pComp1` and `pComp2` are
pointers to a structure of the type `connComp`, whose element `size` is of the
type `unsigned int`. Writing simply

```
meanClusSize += 2 * pComp1->size * pComp2->size;
```

the result might not always be correct. Indeed, the expression on the right-
hand side of the `+=` is evaluated and temporarily stored in an `unsigned
int` variable. The casting to `unsigned long long int` is carried out only
when added to `meanClusSize`. The problem is that the product of two 32
bit numbers, `pComp1->size * pComp2->size`, might not always be representable with just 32 bit. In the latter case, the most significant bit is lost
and, due to this systematic error, `meanClusSize` would be underestimated.
Explicit casting one of the two operand to 64 bits, enforces the compiler
to store the product result in a 64 bit variable, thus ensuring a correct
operation.

Note that this kind of error is very difficult to track down, as it produces
no warning upon compilation, nor upon execution. The only effect is that it
produces a wrong result, and as a consequence, a wrong description of the
system properties we are studying (which usually are not known, otherwise
we would not be studying them!). We advise, apart from being particularly
careful when casting variables, to check whether the program results are
correct in some limiting cases for which we now what results to expect.
For example, for the case we considered here, we could add all possible
edges and check whether in the end the variables `largestClusSize` and
`meanClusSize` are, respectively, equal to N and N^2. The above mentioned

error would cause a value for meanclusSize lower than the expected one.

The only two functions called in Listing 17.2 are the one identifying the connected component of a given vertex, componentOf, and the one merging two connected components, mergeComp. Both are included in Listing 17.3.

```
1 struct connComp *componentOf(struct connComp *pComp) {
2   while (pComp->parent != pComp) pComp = pComp->parent;
3   return pComp;
4 }
5
6 unsigned int mergeComp(struct connComp *pComp1,
7                        struct connComp *pComp2) {
8   if (pComp1->size < pComp2->size) {
9     pComp1->parent = pComp2;
10    pComp2->size += pComp1->size;
11    return pComp2->size;
12  } else {
13    pComp2->parent = pComp1;
14    pComp1->size += pComp2->size;
15    return pComp1->size;
16  }
17 }
```

Listing 17.3 The functions identifying a vertex' cluster and merging two connected components.

The function componentOf simply follows a vertex' pointer to its ancestor until it reaches a structure pointing to itself.

The function mergeComp is called when two connected components need to be merged. Its arguments are the pointers to the roots of the clusters to be merged. The pointer to the smallest cluster is pointed to the root of the largest one. Moreover, the size of the largest cluster is updated and returned to the calling function, possibly allowing to update largestClusSize (Listing 17.2). By choosing the largest cluster to survive during this merging operation, we can be sure, as we saw in Section 17.3.2, that the *average* time to identify the cluster of a vertex is minimal.

17.5.1 *What, how, how often and when to measure*

The growth of a random graph is a stochastic process, i.e., it depends on a random variable of which we only know the statistical properties. In this case, the stochasticity lies in the choice of the edge which is to be added at each step during the growth. This choice is made such that each edge is chosen with the same probability. This choice ensures us that when adding

M edges to a set of N vertices, each element of $\mathcal{G}_{N,M}$ is obtained with the same probability. So, to perform a statistical average over the ensemble $\mathcal{G}_{N,M}$ we just need to repeat the growth process many times and average the properties of the graphs with N vertices and M edges on the different growth processes, or trajectories (as they are often called).

To compute these averages we can follow two different strategies. The first one consists in calculating the averages directly when executing the program: that is, the program computes many trajectories, but it writes to a file only the ensemble averages, $\langle \bar{S} \rangle_c$ and $\langle S_{\max} \rangle_c$, as a function of $c = 2M/N$. The advantage of this strategy is that it produces small data files.

On the contrary, the second strategy requires to write to file the value of $\bar{S}$ and $S_{\max}$ as a function of c for each trajectory. The ensemble averages, i.e., the averages over the trajectories, are computed a posteriori, with another C program or any other data files manipulator. In particular, the UNIX operating system family allows one to combine system commands and programs (perl, awk, sed, grep, etc.), such that taking these averages is a simple and automatic operation.

This second strategy (which we strongly advise) has several advantages. The trajectories can be analyzed one by one and compared to the average one in order to evaluate the variations from trajectory to trajectory. By writing the trajectories in a file as they are being computed, a possible program interruption does not make us loose all the work that has been done. Moreover, it allows one to change easily the number of trajectories. Indeed, if after the data analysis we understand the number of trajectories was too small, we can run again the same program (with a different seed for the random number generator!), and continue to write *appending* to the same file used before. When performing this operation, we need to pay particular care on how the file is opened and/or the program output is redirected to avoid overwriting the previous results.

Willing to write all trajectories to a file and to average a posteriori, we give a small technical advise, useful in case one also wants to plot the trajectories (which might be very useful to understand, for example, how different the trajectories are from each other or with respect to their average). It is convenient to identify the trajectories in the output file such that the graphics program can distinguish them. For example, with `gnuplot` we just need to include an empty line between two different trajectories. These empty lines do not create any problems when computing the average, but allow one to better visualize the trajectories when plotted.

Now the only thing we still need to decide is for how many values of the average degree c we want to study the system properties. To make this decision we need to take into account that the data file should not become too large and that for each value of c and for each trajectory, we write three numbers $(c, \bar{S}$ and $S_{\max})$ to this file, taking typically about 10 bytes each[8].

Suppose we want to study a set of values for c uniformly distributed between 0 and 2, given that $c_p = 1$. This is equivalent to a number of edges M varying between 0 and N. Moreover, we assume we want to study graphs of up to $N = 10^6$ vertices. Under these hypotheses, if we write on the file each time we add a new edge, a single trajectory for a system of $N = 10^6$ vertices would take 30 MB. In order to obtain good ensemble averages, we need to measure at least a thousand different trajectories. So, the disk space needed would be 30 GB! Even if the available computer capacity is still growing, we advise against writing files of these sizes. First of all, because your operating system could not be able to manage files larger than 2 GB, and, in any case, analyzing them would be particularly time-consuming.

To have files with a maximum size of the order of several tens of megabytes and maintaining the possibility to save up to 10^4 different trajectories in each of them, we can write for each trajectory at most around a hundred different values of c. Given that $c \in [0, 2]$, we choose to write to a file only when c is a multiple of $2 \cdot 10^{-2}$.

This choice of values for c has an extra advantage of being independent of the size of the system, as long as $N > 100$. So, after taking the averages, the files for different sizes N will have the same identical form, thus allowing us to easily study the dependence on N at a fixed value of the average degree c.

17.5.2 *Numerical data analysis: finite size effects*

We assume the data have been collected as suggested in Section 17.5.1 and that the averages have been obtained considering a sufficiently large number of different trajectories. So, we have files containing the values of $\langle \bar{S} \rangle_c$ and $\langle S_{\max} \rangle_c$ for 100 values of the average degree c uniformly distributed between 0 and 2.

From the analysis of Section 17.4.2 we know that in the thermodynamic limit $(N \to \infty)$ in $c_p = 1$ the random graph ensemble undergoes a percolation transition during which a giant cluster forms. Now we want to study how this transition manifests itself in the numerical analysis of

---

[8]The 23 bits of the mantissa corresponds to no more than 7 significant digits in decimal notation. So, if no redundant writing system is used, 10 bytes is a reasonable estimate.

the growth process of a random graph with finite N. We stress once more that in a numerical simulation we can only study systems of finite size N. So, when studying systems with finite, often small, N, it is fundamental to learn how to recognize the signs of a transition, which formally only occurs in the thermodynamic limit.

The case of graph percolation is not the most general possible case, especially because the concept of spatial correlation length ξ, introduced in Section 13.4, is missing. Nevertheless, we want to proceed in small steps and start studying *finite size effects* on a transition about which we know everything in the thermodynamic limit. In Chapters 19 and 20 we show examples of models defined in Euclidean geometric spaces, such as the regular lattices in two and three spatial dimensionsm where the concept of correlation length is more meaningful. In Section 20.3.4 we study in detail the finite size effects of these Euclidean models.

In Figure 17.11(top) we show the fraction of vertices belonging to the connected component with maximum size as a function of the average degree for various values of N. Even though it is hidden by the numerical data with large N, in Figure 17.11(top) we also represent with a thicker line the theoretical behavior of the fraction of vertices of the giant cluster, i.e., the solution $m(c)$ to equation (17.3). Note that the discontinuity in the derivative of the function $m(c)$ in $c = 1$, due to the presence of the phase transition, is not observed for the numerical data. Even if the discontinuity is not present, as N increases, the numerical data resemble more and more the behavior in the infinite volume limit. They clearly indicate a percolating cluster appearing at $c = 1$ in the thermodynamic limit.

The discrepancies between the numerical data with finite N and the behavior in the thermodynamic limit are called finite size effects. These effects may have a not obvious behavior when N is varied. For example, in Figure 17.11(top) the numerical data always overestimate the thermodynamic limit for $c < 1$. However, for $c > 1$, the curve $m(c)$ is reached from the bottom in a non monotonous way, as for small N the numerical data are always larger than the thermodynamic limit. Only near the critical point, the finite size effects are partially predictable. So, only in this region they can be exploited to get information on the system under study (see Section 20.3.4).

The region around the critical point where the finite size effects are more evident is called the *critical region*. The size of the critical region depends on the system size: the larger the system size N, the smaller the critical region. For example, in this case, the size of the critical region decreases

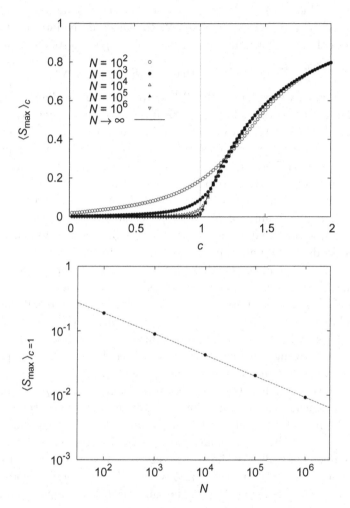

Fig. 17.11 Top: numerical data for the average fraction of vertices in the largest cluster, together with the analytical curve in the thermodynamic limit. Bottom: system size dependence of this average fraction computed at the critical point $c = 1$. The statistical uncertainty on these numerical data is always smaller than the size of the symbol.

proportionally to $N^{-1/3}$.

For $c < 1$ the fraction of vertices belonging to the largest cluster decreases towards zero as N increases, while for $c > 1$ it tends towards the asymptotic value $m(c)$. Note that, precisely at the critical point, the dependence on N is an inverse power of N. In this case, the interpolation of the numerical data, shown in Figure 17.11(bottom), suggests the behavior[9]

$$\frac{\langle S_{\max} \rangle_{c=1}}{N} \propto N^{-1/3} , \quad \text{that is} \quad \langle S_{\max} \rangle_{c=1} \propto N^{2/3} .$$

In Section 20.3.4 we explain in detail how to relate this scaling law to the one explaining the shrinking of the critical region by increasing N.

Instead, in Figure 17.12(top) we show $\langle \bar{S}' \rangle_c$ as a function of the average degree. The curve representing the behavior in the thermodynamic limit is shown with a thick line. It is mostly covered by the numerical data, that perfectly coincide with it far from the critical point. The scale of the y axis is logarithmic to make the data more readable; in a linear scale only the data for the largest values of N would be readable. We use this occasion to remind once more that the choice of the scale to represent the numerical data is of fundamental importance. Indeed, the information extracted from a data set often depend on how these data are graphically presented. There are no fixed rules describing how to proceed when plotting them. Usually, some good sense is enough to get the best results. For example, if the data we are plotting accumulate for small values of one of the variables, it is quite probable we need to use a logarithmic scale for that variable. We suggest the following general rule: the data should occupy a large part of the space available in a way as uniform as possible.

Let us further analyze the data shown in Figure 17.12(top). Note that when c approaches the critical point $c_p = 1$, the numerical data leave the analytical curve $(1 - m)/(1 - c(1 - m))$ representing the behavior in the thermodynamic limit: this is unavoidable given that the mean cluster size is clearly upper bounded by the system size N, while at the critical point, the analytical prediction in the thermodynamic limit diverges according to a power law, $\langle \bar{S}' \rangle_c \simeq 1/|c - 1|$. So, the numerical data cannot follow this curve up to $c = 1$.

Finally, observe in Figure 17.12(bottom) that precisely at the critical point, the growth of $\langle \bar{S}' \rangle_c$ with N follows a power law with exponent $1/3$. This growth, like the one of $\langle S_{\max} \rangle_c$, can be related to the shrinking of the critical region. In Section 20.3.4 we discuss this issue more in detail,

---

[9]In models with long range interactions, the exponents are often simple rational numbers.

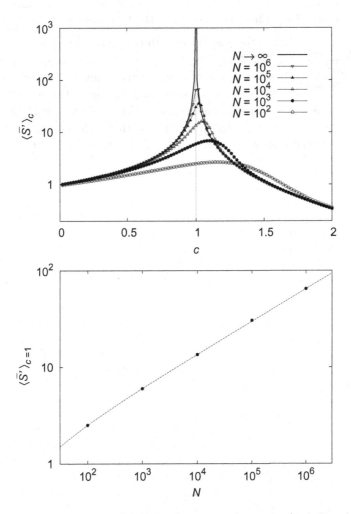

Fig. 17.12   Top: the numerical data for the average cluster size (excluding the largest one), together with the analytical curve in the thermodynamic limit.   Bottom: the dependence of this average size on the total number N of vertices in the system, at the critical point $c = 1$. The statistical uncertainty of the numerical data is always less than the size of the symbol.

studying the scaling laws and showing the relations between the critical exponents.

Hands on 17.6 - Finite size effects in the two-dimensional percolation

Repeat the percolation study described in Sections 17.5.1 and 17.5.2 on a two-dimensional square lattice. Since in this case the percolating cluster is always well-defined, we suggest to measure also the probability that the percolating cluster exists for a given bond density. When plotting this quantity, it should be easy to deduce the power law with which the critical region shrinks. Also study the average size of the non percolating clusters.

Chapter 18

Optimization methods

> The minimum could be defined as the perfection
> that an artefact achieves when it is no longer
> possible to improve it by subtraction.
>
> John Pawson, *Minimum* (1996).

Optimization problems frequently appear in many, not only scientific, disciplines. Mathematically, the optimization of a process is the search for the minimum of a function defining this process in some way. There are numerous examples. Just to quote some, in physics, the problem of determining the parameters of a theory describing the experimental data; in engineering, minimizing production costs of a good; in bioinformatics, searching feasible protein structures. In the first example, we need to minimize the χ^2, defined as the "distance" between the experimentally observed behavior and the one predicted by the theory, as a functions of the theory parameters. The production cost of the second example may be formalized as a function of several variables, each representing the cost of the raw material, the length of the processes, the energy dissipated in each one of these, workforce, etc. Finally, when searching for a protein structure, one needs to minimize the total free energy of the constrained system.

In this chapter, we treat the optimization problem precisely in this way, namely as a search for the minimum of a generic function. In particular, we examine deterministic optimization methods, i.e., those searching for solutions by means of iterations guided by precise criteria. In Sections 18.1 18.2 and 18.3 we treat the case of continuous variables. Section 18.4 is dedicated to the case of discrete variables. We describe the methods based on random searches in Section 20.4. The methods described in the following sections are completely general and can be easily adapted to any specific problem. Finally, we note that searching for the maximum of a function is equivalent to determining its minimum: we just need to change the sign of the measure to be optimized.

18.1 Functions of a single variable

If we need to find the minimum of a function of one single variable, the simplest optimization method is trial and error, just like the bisection method to solve equations, given in Section 4.3.2. The only substantial difference is that, to determine the point $x \in (a, b)$ for which $f(x) = 0$, we just need to compare two values taken by the function in two different points of the interval. Instead, to find a minimum, we need to compare three values of the function, in three different points of the search interval.

From what we have just said, it should be clear that also the optimization problems have the same uncertainty associated to the search of a function root. A solution can only be determined within a certain interval (a, b), established *a priori*, where only one minimum is present. If the function to be minimized has several minima in the chosen interval, the search algorithms generally do not guarantee to determine the absolute one[1] and sometimes do not converge.

Let us show how this works. Given an interval (a, b) where we want to find the minimum of the function $f(x)$, first of all we need to determine a point c, inside the interval $(a < c < b)$, such that

$$f(c) \leq f(a) \quad \text{and} \quad f(c) \leq f(b) . \tag{18.1}$$

These conditions have to be satisfied in order for the minimum to lie inside the interval. If the function minimum is one of the interval endpoints, only one of the two conditions is valid (18.1). In this case, we can reduce the interval enclosing the minimum of $f(x)$ by progressively moving the other endpoint of the interval, until we reach the desired precision. Finally, if we find a single point c inside the interval, for which both conditions (18.1) are violated, we are sure that at least two minima exist for the function inside the interval (a, b).

So, we start with a triplet of points (a, c, b) where a and b are the endpoints of the interval where we are looking for the minimum of the

---

[1]This is particularly true for the deterministic methods. The stochastic methods shown in Section 20.4 suffer less from this problem.

function $f(x)$ and c is a point of the interval satisfying the condition (18.1). A single iteration of the method produces a new triplet of points (a', c', b'), such that the new interval is smaller $(b' - a' < b - a)$ and still contains the function minimum.

In Figure 18.1 we show how to produce the new triplet of points (a', c', b') from the old one (a, c, b). First of all, we introduce another point x inside the interval. Next, we compare the function values in the two internal points, $f(c)$ and $f(x)$. Based on the outcome, we decide which endpoint, a or b, to reject in order to reduce the interval. The rule guiding this choice is such that the internal point is the point where the function takes on its lowest value. In this way the conditions (18.1) remain valid for the new triplet of points. For example, if $f(c) < f(x)$, x becomes the new endpoint of the interval $(b' = x)$ and c remains the internal point $(c' = c)$. This strategy ensures that the function minimum remains within the interval. As a consequence, the algorithm closes down on it with arbitrary precision.

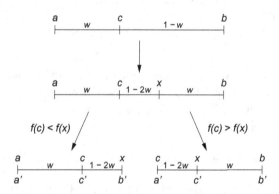

Fig. 18.1 Definition of the measures used in the golden section rule.

The only choice that is missing to make this algorithm usable is the one related to the position of the two internal points. Obviously, an optimal choice would allow the algorithm to converge faster. In Figure 18.1 we see that, based on the result of the comparison between $f(c)$ and $f(x)$, the search process for the minimum bifurcates. In both cases, we want the length of the interval to diminish by a constant multiplicative factor, i.e., such that $(b' - a') = \lambda(b - a)$, with $0 < \lambda < 1$. This choice ensures that the length L of the interval always decreases exponentially with the number n of iterations, $L \propto \lambda^n$. In this way, the number of interactions needed to reach a precision ε only grows logarithmically with the inverse of the precision, $n \propto \ln(1/\varepsilon)$.

Let us consider the triplet of points (a, c, b) before the iteration. We call $w = (c - a)$ the distance between the internal point and the closest interval endpoint; the distances are measured in units of $(b - a)$. In Figure 18.1 we show the case in which c is closer to a than to b, but the argument is perfectly valid also in the case c were closer to b than to a. The position of x is determined by requiring the two possible resulting intervals have the same length,

$$(x - a) = (b - c) \quad \Rightarrow \quad x = a + b - c .$$

From this, we have that $(b - x) = w$ and $(x - c) = 1 - 2w$. Note that x is the symmetric point of c with respect to the centre of the interval (a, b).

The exact value of w is derived imposing that the two possible intervals after the iteration have to be similar to the interval before the iteration. In particular, we need to store the fraction of the interval between the internal point and the endpoint closest to it, which before the iteration is equal to w and after to

$$w' = \frac{1 - 2w}{w + (1 - 2w)} = \frac{1 - 2w}{1 - w} . \tag{18.2}$$

In Figure 18.1 we show all distances between consecutive couples of points, in units of $(b - a)$, from which we can easily derive the expression (18.2) for w'. The equality $w' = w$ determines the value of w by means of the following equation

$$\frac{1 - 2w}{1 - w} = w \quad \Rightarrow \quad w^2 - 3w + 1 = 0 \quad \Rightarrow \quad w = \frac{3 \pm \sqrt{5}}{2} .$$

As $w < 1/2$, only one of the two solutions can be accepted: $w = w^* \equiv \frac{3 - \sqrt{5}}{2} \simeq 0.381966$. Thus, an iteration produces a segment fraction given by $\lambda = 1 - w^* = \frac{\sqrt{5} - 1}{2} \simeq 0.61803$.

The fraction $\lambda = 1 - w$ of the interval (i.e., the largest one of the two) is called the *golden section* or *golden ratio*:

$$\frac{1}{1 - w} = \frac{1 - w}{w} .$$

Hence, the name of this method to search for the minimum, namely *golden section rule*.

The golden section myth

In ancient times, the golden section was considered to be a special length. Introduced around 300 BC by Euclid, the idea that the golden ratio were a special number soon spread. This idea was strengthened by the Italian mathematician Luca Pacioli (1445-1517) who ascribed the golden ratio a magic dimension. Pacioli's *Divina proportione*, illustrated by Leonardo da Vinci, stated that the golden ratio is present in nature in the proportions of the human body and in the finest work of arts made by man, such as the Parthenon, the Egyptian pyramids and some paintings. In this way, the idea was spread that the human mind possessed a mechanism producing pleasure upon seeing elements in golden ratio. In particular, a rectangle whose base and height had a golden ratio was considered to be the utmost perfection. In the XIX century, the psychologist Gustav Theodor Fechner (1801-1887) performed several experiments to verify this theory, confirming it. Successive studies, though, revealed the (at least) partial inconsistency of this thesis. In particular, several articles of a volume of the journal *Empirical Studies of the Arts* [VV. AA. (1997)], published in 1997, fully dedicated to the golden section, show how the human eye prefers rectangles of proportions close, but not equal to the golden ratio. The myth has often been kept alive by the fact that it is easy to find, in any work of art, the ratio one desires. We basically just need to choose the measurement points in an appropriate way.

Hands on 18.1 - Searching with non constant w

 When deriving the value of w, we assumed $w' = w$, i.e., that the value of w is constant during the search. It is interesting to consider what happens when this hypothesis is no longer valid. Consider initially a generic value for w_0 and compute the values of the following w_n based on the equation (18.2):

$$w_n = \frac{1 - 2w_{n-1}}{1 - w_{n-1}}.$$

Note that, if from this equation we got that $w_n > 1/2$, we need to assign w_n the value $(1 - w_n)$, as it is the latter value which corresponds to the distance between the internal point and its closest endpoint.

Does the series of w_n converge to some value? If so, which one? If $w_0 = w^*$, what do you observe? Can you explain this behavior which is seemingly contradictory to the above analytical computation?

The result of the Hands on 18.1 suggests a problem which might arise when executing the golden section rule. Namely, the equation (18.2) has a fixed point in $w = w^*$, which however results to be unstable. If the initial value w_0 is slightly different from the theoretical value w^*, this discrepancy exponentially increases throughout the iterations. By writing $w_n = w^* + \delta_n$ with $|\delta_n| \ll w^*$ and expanding the function $w'(w)$ given in equation (18.2) to the first order in Taylor series around the fixed point w^*, we obtain the rule governing the growth of the discrepancy δ_n:

$$|\delta_n| = \frac{1}{w^*}|\delta_{n-1}| = \left(\frac{1}{w^*}\right)^n |\delta_0| .$$

Remember that, when representing an irrational number, such as w^*, in a computer memory, we always make a rounding error which is at least equal to $|\delta_0| = \mathcal{O}(2^{-m})$, with m being the number of bits of the mantissa. So, it is important to estimate how big this error can get upon program execution. To reach a precision ε, starting from an initial interval of length L_0, the golden section rule calls for a number of iterations n, given by

$$L_0(1 - w^*)^n = \varepsilon \quad \Rightarrow \quad n = \frac{\ln(\varepsilon/L_0)}{\ln(1 - w^*)} .$$

During these n iterations the error on the value of w^* grows up to a value equal to

$$|\delta_n| = |\delta_0| \left(\frac{1}{w^*}\right)^n = |\delta_0| \left(\frac{1}{w^*}\right)^{\frac{\ln(\varepsilon/L_0)}{\ln(1-w^*)}} = |\delta_0| \left(\frac{L_0}{\varepsilon}\right)^2 . \tag{18.3}$$

The last expression is derived knowing that $w^* = (1 - w^*)^2$, which is a direct consequence of how the golden section is defined. The equation (18.3) allows us to verify whether the discrepancy between the numerical value of w and its theoretical one w^* remains sufficiently small when the program is executed. We can and should check this before executing the program, as the expression (18.3) only contains quantities which are known beforehand. Nevertheless, in order to write a function searching the minimum with the golden section rule which works for any value of ε and L_0, we slightly need to alter the algorithm we just described. This change is included in the code of Listing 18.1.

```
 1 double goldenSearch(double (*f)(double), double a, double b,
 2                     double epsilon) {
 3   double fa = f(a), fb = f(b), c, fc, x, fx;
 4
 5   while (b - a > epsilon) {
 6     c = a + W * (b - a);
 7     fc = f(c);
 8     if (fc <= fa && fc <= fb) {
 9       x = a + b - c;
10       fx = f(x);
11       if (fx > fc) {
12         b = x;
13         fb = fx;
14       } else {
15         a = c;
16         fa = fc;
17       }
18     } else if (fc <= fb) {
19       b = c;
20       fb = fc;
21     } else if (fc <= fa) {
22       a = c;
23       fa = fc;
24     } else {
25       error("There are at least two minima in the selected
26             interval");
27     }
28   }
29   return 0.5 * (a + b);
30 }
```

Listing 18.1   Searching a function minimum with the golden section rule.

The function to be minimized has to be passed to the function **gold-enSearch** as a first argument; the following two arguments represent the limits of the interval where the minimum must be searched, while the parameter **epsilon** defines the required precision level. The constant W contains the numeric value of $w^* \simeq 0.381966$. In the program, we defined some variables (**fa**, **fb**, **fc** and **fx**) to store those values of the functions which we use several times, thus minimizing the number of calls to the function to be minimized. Indeed, it might be complex and long to compute the latter.

The **while** cycle on line 5 iterates the algorithm as long as the size of the interval is larger than the desired precision. During each iteration, the internal point (line 6) is computed again, instead of using the one resulting form the previous iteration. This is equal to fixing $w_n = w^*$, thus avoiding problems related to the instability of the fixed point of $w'(w)$. The cost of this change is very small; it only consists in computing c and f(c), on lines 6 and 7.

On line 8 the conditions (18.1), necessary to apply the golden section rule (lines 9-17), are verified. In the case that only one of the two conditions (18.1) is verified, one of the interval endpoints is moved to the internal point (lines 18-23). Finally, if both conditions are false, the function error (line 25) is called which prints a string, given as an argument, on screen, and interrupts the execution of the program.

Hands on 18.2 - Minimizing functions of a single variable

 Write a program which is able to find the minimum of a function of a single variable inside a given interval by means of the golden section rule. Try to determine the maximum precision you can reach by studying functions for which you can analytically determine the extrema.

The function $x \cos x$ has several extrema. In particular, the interval $x \in [-1, 5]$ contains two minima, of different depth. Apply the golden section rule to this function considering various intervals, for istance $(-1, 0)$, $(0, 5)$, $(0, 1)$ and $(0, 2)$. Explain the observed behavior.

18.2 Minimizing functions of more variables

We now consider the problem of finding the minimum of a function of m variables $F(\vec{x})$, with $\vec{x} = (x_1, x_2, \ldots, x_m)$. The methods included here are applicable to functions of any number m of variables. So, they can also be used to optimize functions of a single variable. To make this section more readable, we indicate vectors in bold, i.e., $\boldsymbol{x} \equiv \vec{x}$. The methods described in this section are iterative methods, where the approximation $n+1$ is derived from the approximation n by means of a relation of the type

$$\boldsymbol{x}^{(n+1)} = \boldsymbol{x}^{(n)} + \lambda_n \boldsymbol{u}^{(n)} ,$$

where $\boldsymbol{u}^{(n)}$ is an m-dimensional vector determining the direction where the minimum is searched during the iteration $n + 1$ and λ_n is a parameter establishing the length of the step in the direction $\boldsymbol{u}^{(n)}$. The methods essentially differ in the way $\boldsymbol{u}^{(n)}$ and λ_n are chosen.

18.2.1 *Sequential descent rule*

The easiest optimization method for a function of more than one variable is the *sequential descent rule* or *relaxation method*. Let us assume $x^{(0)} = (x_1^{(0)}, x_2^{(0)}, \ldots, x_m^{(0)})$ is a first approximation to the minimum of $F(x)$ in the considered domain. We define the function

$$G_i^{(n)}(x_i) = F\left(x_i; \left\{x_j = x_j^{(n)}\right\}_{j \neq i}\right) ; \quad i, j = 1, \ldots, m .$$

In other words, $G_i^{(n)}(x_i)$ is the function $F(x)$ in all variables, except for the ith one, fixed to the value given in the nth approximation. So, $G_i^{(n)}(x_i)$ is a function only of x_i. With the golden section rule we can minimize $G_1^{(0)}(x)$ and in this way determine a new approximation of the minimum along the direction of x_1. Starting from this, we can, one at a time, minimize the function with respect to all other variables. Each time, we minimize with respect to a variable, we reach a value of the function $C_{n+1} \equiv F(x^{(n+1)}) < F(x^{(n)})$. The process stops when the relaxation in the m directions no longer produces a significant change of $x^{(n)}$, i.e., when

$$\left| x^{(n+m)} - x^{(n)} \right| < \epsilon . \tag{18.4}$$

In this way, the multidimensional problem has been reduced to a problem in one dimension. In the case of a function of two variables, we can easily "visualize" the algorithm.

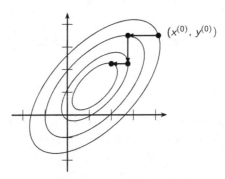

Fig. 18.2   At each step of the sequential descent method, we minimize along the direction of one of the coordinates.

In Figure 18.2 we show the contour lines[2] of a function of two variables. Starting from the point $(x^{(0)}, y^{(0)})$ where $F(x, y) = C_0$, the function F

---

[2]In a Cartesian system (x, y, z), the intersections of a function $z = f(x, y)$ with the planes with constant z are called contour lines.

is considered to be a function only of the variable x. Moving to the left, we reach a minimum in the x direction where the function is equal to $C_1 < C_0$. The minimum can be identified graphically by finding the contour line tangent to the displacement vector. At this point, we have a new approximation from which to start minimizing along the y direction. By iterating this process, we see the solution converges to the extremal point. It is easy to realize this method works well only when the contour lines of the function to be minimized resemble a circle or an ellipse with axes parallel to the coordinate axes. Otherwise (and this is what usually happens) the number of iterations needed to reach the minimum may be very high, as is clear from Figure 18.2. This is why we do not include an algorithm specific to this way of searching for minima. We only showed it because it is rather intuitive and allows us to discuss better the following methods.

18.2.2   *The gradient method*

The algorithm of the previous section is easy. Nevertheless, it is obvious that to reach the minimum it follows a rather winding road. It is surely more efficient to descend towards the minimum along the direction with steepest descent. In a point $\boldsymbol{x}^{(n)}$ this direction is parallel and opposite to those of the function gradient in the considered point. Thus, one way to find the minimum consists in starting from a point $\boldsymbol{x}^{(0)}$ and iterate the equation

$$\boldsymbol{x}^{(n+1)} = \boldsymbol{x}^{(n)} - \lambda_n \boldsymbol{\nabla} F\left(\boldsymbol{x}^{(n)}\right) ,$$

where the gradient operator $\boldsymbol{\nabla}$ is defined as

$$\boldsymbol{\nabla} \equiv \left(\frac{\partial}{\partial x_1}, \frac{\partial}{\partial x_2}, \dots, \frac{\partial}{\partial x_m}\right) .$$

When the minimum has been reached, we have that $\boldsymbol{\nabla} F\left(\boldsymbol{x}^{(min)}\right) = 0$ and $\boldsymbol{x}^{(n+1)} = \boldsymbol{x}^{(n)}$, representing the terminating condition. Actually, due to the usual inevitable approximations, the condition we use is always of the type

$$\left|\boldsymbol{x}^{(n+1)} - \boldsymbol{x}^{(n)}\right| < \epsilon .$$

Once the direction where searching the minimum has been determined, the problem is reduced to a one-dimensional minimization problem. So, we need to find the value of λ_n for which the function F has a minimum in the direction opposite to the one of its gradient. As the function value increases along the gradient direction, we have that

$$F\left(\boldsymbol{x}^{(n)} - \lambda_n \boldsymbol{\nabla} F\left(\boldsymbol{x}^{(n)}\right)\right) \le F\left(\boldsymbol{x}^{(n)}\right) ,$$

i.e., considering F as a function of only λ_n, it should have a minimum for $\lambda_n \geq 0$.

Also for this method it is easy to visualize the descent for a two-variable function. Let us consider, for instance, the function $F(x, y) = x^2 + 4y^2$, which obviously has a minimum in $(0, 0)$. We want to locate this minimum with the gradient method. Starting from the point with coordinates $(x^{(0)}, y^{(0)}) = (2, 1)$, we have that

$$\nabla F(x, y) = \left(\frac{\partial F}{\partial x}, \frac{\partial F}{\partial y} \right) = (2x, 8y) \ . \tag{18.5}$$

F can be written as a function of λ like:

$$F(\lambda) = F\left(x - \lambda \frac{\partial F}{\partial x}, y - \lambda \frac{\partial F}{\partial y} \right) = (x - 2\lambda x)^2 + 4(y - 8\lambda y)^2 \ . \tag{18.6}$$

Imposing that the derivative of F with respect to λ is zero, we find that

$$\lambda = \frac{x^2 + 16y^2}{2x^2 + 128y^2} \ .$$

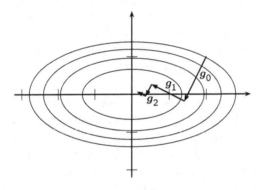

Fig. 18.3 In the gradient method, the descent towards the minimum is along the direction where the function varies the most. The search for the minimum always proceeds in steps which are orthogonal to each other. The displacement vectors $-\lambda \nabla F\left(x^{(i)} \right)$ are indicated with g_i.

Table 18.1 contains the successive steps performed by the algorithm. Starting from the point $(2, 1)$ for which $F = 8$, we move in the direction of the vector $v = (4, 8)$ of $\lambda = 5/34 \simeq 0.15$ and reach the point $(1.71, -0.18)$ for which $F \simeq 3.03$. After few steps we have determined the minimum with the desired precision.

Note how the directions taken at each descent are mutually orthogonal to each other. This is clear from the fact that $\frac{\partial F}{\partial y}$ changes sign at each step.

Table 18.1   Application of the gradient algorithm to find the minimum of the function $F(x, y) = x^2 + 4y^2$.

n	x	y	F	λ	$\frac{\partial F}{\partial x}$	$\frac{\partial F}{\partial y}$	$\left| x^{(n+1)} - x^n \right|$
0	2.00	1.00	8.00	0.15	4.00	8.00	0.00
1	1.41	−0.18	2.12	0.31	2.82	−1.41	1.32
2	0.53	0.26	0.56	0.15	1.06	2.12	0.99
3	0.37	−0.05	0.15	0.31	0.75	−0.37	0.35
4	0.14	0.07	0.04	0.15	0.28	0.56	0.26
5	0.10	−0.01	0.01	0.31	0.20	−0.10	0.09
6	0.04	0.02	0.00	0.15	0.07	0.15	0.07
7	0.03	−0.00	0.00	0.31	0.05	−0.03	0.02
8	0.01	0.00	0.00	0.15	0.02	0.04	0.02
9	0.01	−0.00	0.00	0.31	0.01	−0.01	0.01
10	0.00	0.00	0.00	0.15	0.01	0.01	0.00

This can also be verified by calculating the vectors scalar product. This behavior is presented in Figure 18.3 from which it is clear that the route followed in search for the minimum is a zigzag. The direction taken at each step is always perpendicular to the contour line from which it starts, and each one is also perpendicular to the previous direction.

Indeed, the gradient method is completely analogous to the relaxation method: the only difference lies in the choice of the direction that has to be taken at each new iteration. Even though, at a first sight, the former might seem more efficient, this is not always guaranteed to be the case in any situation. The relaxation method requires that we perform N_{iter} iterations in m different directions. So, we need to compute at least m times the function F during each iteration. With the gradient method we need to compute the function derivatives the same number m of times at each iteration step. Even if the number N_{iter} of iterations can be lower, at each step the function is evaluated twice, to estimate the derivative by finite differences, thus doubling the computation cost[3]. Moreover, the gradient method does not allow us to drastically reduce N_{iter}, because at each step a direction perpendicular to the previous one is taken. So, if we are not dealing with a particularly simple function, the minimum is again approached along a winding road.

To encode this method we decomposed the algorithm in several functions. The resulting code is shown in Listing 18.2. If the functions are

---

[3]This does not imply it is always more convenient to use the analytical derivative. Indeed, for some functions, computing the derivative may be much more demanding than evaluating the finite differences.

well-defined, the code is more comprehensible. However, a decomposition in too many functions may cause the program to perform worse. So, we always need to evaluate carefully whether some function can be eliminated, even by making the code slightly less readable. In the present case, we prefer to make the code more readable, rather than to save on the number of separate functions. Some of these functions are very easy to write, so that we do not include them, and we limit ourselves to describe their tasks.

```
1 #define M 2
2 #define EPSILON 1.E-8
3
4 main() {
5    double x[M], grad[M], xOld[M];
6    double epsilon;
7    int i;
8
9    epsilon = input(x, M);
10   do {
11     copy(x, xOld, M);
12     gradient(myFunction, x, grad, M, EPSILON);
13     opposite(grad, M);
14     dump(grad, M, 0);
15     dump(x, M, 1, myFunction(x, M));
16     printf("\n");
17     linMin(myFunction, x, grad, M, EPSILON);
18   } while (norm(x, xOld, M) > epsilon);
19 }
```

Listing 18.2 Searching a function minimum with the gradient method.

The parameter M represents the number of variables of the function to be minimized. The paremeter EPSILON defines the precision with which we compute the numerical derivatives (Section 7.6). The function input allows the user to provide the coordinates of the initial point and the precision required for the location of the minimum. The latter is returned by that same function and assigned to the variable epsilon. Note that the precision of the minimum cannot be better than EPSILON. The algorithm is iterated as long as the distance between the current iteration and the previous one is higher than the desired precision. This distance is measured with the function norm. Obviously, this distance can be defined in many different ways. By introducing the function norm, we can easily change the definition of the distance without altering the rest of the code. One possible definition is

$$\|\boldsymbol{x} - \boldsymbol{x}'\| = \sqrt{\sum_{i=1}^{m} (x_i - x_i')^2} .$$

At each step, the algorithm carries out the following operations.

(1) The M values of x are copied into xOld by means of the function copy. In this way we store the position at the previous step in memory.

(2) With the function gradient, the gradient of the function myFunction is computed in the point x. The result is returned in the vector grad. The same function uses the parameter EPSILON to numerically compute the derivative as an incremental ratio.

(3) The direction opposite to the one of the gradient is determined by multiplying all components of grad by -1 (function opposite).

(4) The components of grad and x, and the value of the function to be minimized in point x are printed on screen by means of the function dump. Its input parameters are an array, an integer number indicating its length, an integer number c indicating the quantity of optional parameters, followed by c values in double precision. The function dump is described in Section 18.2.3.

(5) The minimum of the function to be optimized is found along the direction defined by the vector grad (remember this is the opposite direction of the one of the gradient), starting from x. The coordinates of this new minimum are assigned to x.

The "core" of the algorithm is the function linMin which, starting form the point x, moves along the direction defined by its third parameter, until it reaches a minimum. The function linMin is shown in Listing 18.3. As the function linMin needs to change the vector x, it copies it in the array xSave to save the original coordinates (line 6). Given the position $\boldsymbol{x}$ and the displacement $\boldsymbol{u}$, represented by the arrays x and u, we need to determine a new position $\boldsymbol{x}' = \boldsymbol{x} + \lambda\boldsymbol{u}$, where F, represented by f in the code, has a minimum, as a function of λ. We find this minimum via the bisection method, by looking for the root of the function derivative with respect to λ[4]. In order to apply this method, we need to find two points a and c where the function derivative with respect to λ has a different sign. In this case, it is not too much difficult to find such points. Indeed, we know that $\lambda \geq 0$. So, one point is $a = 0$ and the other one can be determined starting from

---

[4]We could have used the golden section rule, but we preferred to show an alternative method.

$c = 0$ and adding a positive quantity until the condition is satisfied. Next, we compute the derivate $dF/d\lambda$ in two different points ($a = 0$, $c = \lambda$), along the direction $\boldsymbol{u}$ (lines 7 up to 14), changing each time the value of lambda, that initially takes the value epsilon and is doubled at each step. The point $\boldsymbol{x}'$ where we need to compute the derivative, is determined by adding the vector u multiplied by lambda to the vector x. This task is performed by the function add[5]. As always, we cannot guarantee this process to converge to the correct point. However, if the function to be minimized is smooth enough around the initial point, then we can hope the process will converge.

Once the two points for which the derivative $dF/d\lambda$ has opposite signs has been determined, the point where the derivative cancels out can be found with the bisection method (Section 4.3.2), as shown in the code from line 15 up to line 36. On line 38 the vector x is changed and takes the coordinates of the point $\boldsymbol{x}'$ where the function F is minimal along the direction $\boldsymbol{u}$.

The last function we need to describe is the function dFdLambda, that gives the function derivative along the direction $\boldsymbol{u}$. Once more, this derivative is computed as the incremental ratio of the difference between the value of F in the point $\boldsymbol{x}$ and the point $\boldsymbol{x} + \epsilon\boldsymbol{u}$, and epsilon.

18.2.3 *Functions with a variable number of arguments*

In this section, we show the details of the function dump, which admits a variable number of input arguments, as the smartest readers probably already noticed. For instance, on line 14 of Listing 18.2 the function is used to print M components of the array grad. The third parameter represents the number of optional arguments, which in this case is zero. On line 14 of the same Listing, the same function allows for an extra parameter (namely, the value of the function to be minimized). Indeed, in this case the third argument takes value one.

This is not the first time we discuss functions with a variable number of arguments, i.e., so-called *variadic functions* (such as the functions printf and scanf), in this textbook. However, this is the only chapter where we define one.

---

[5]Note that the coordinates of x change at each step. So, we need to restore its original value before proceeding with the next attempt.

```
 1 void linMin(double (*f)(double *, int), double *x, double *u,
 2              int n, double epsilon) {
 3   double derA, derB, derC;
 4   double lambda = epsilon, lambdaMin, lambdaMax;
 5   double *xSave = (double *)calloc(n, sizeof(double));
 6   copy(x, xSave, n);
 7   derA = dFdLambda((*f), x, u, n, epsilon);
 8   derC = derA;
 9   while ((derA * derC) >= 0) {
10     copy(xSave, x, n);
11     add(x, lambda, u, n);
12     derC = dFdLambda((*f), x, u, n, epsilon);
13     lambda *= 2.;
14   }
15   lambdaMin = 0;
16   lambdaMax = lambda;
17   lambda = 0.5 * (lambdaMin + lambdaMax);
18   do {
19     copy(xSave, x, n);
20     add(x, lambdaMin, u, n);
21     derA = dFdLambda((*f), x, u, n, epsilon);
22     copy(xSave, x, n);
23     add(x, lambda, u, n);
24     derB = dFdLambda((*f), x, u, n, epsilon);
25     copy(xSave, x, n);
26     add(x, lambdaMax, u, n);
27     derC = dFdLambda((*f), x, u, n, epsilon);
28     if ((derA * derB) > 0) {
29       lambdaMin = lambda;
30     } else if ((derA * derB) < 0) {
31       lambdaMax = lambda;
32     } else {
33       lambdaMin = lambdaMax = lambda;
34     }
35     lambda = 0.5 * (lambdaMin + lambdaMax);
36   } while (fabs(lambdaMin-lambdaMax) > epsilon);
37   copy(xSave, x, n);
38   add(x, lambda, u, n);
39   free(xSave);
40 }
```

As all functions, also the variadic ones need to be declared and defined. In C, functions with a variable number of arguments must be defined with at least one fixed argument. In the declaration, the optional arguments are indicated with an ellipsis ..., as in

```
void dump(double *, int, int, ...);
```

The first argument, which is mandatory, represents the pointer to the array to be printed. The second and third argument are also mandatory and are, respectively, the number of components of the array and the number of optional parameters. The ellipsis represent zero or more parameters whose number and type are not defined. The ellipsis necessarily represent the last formal parameter and cannot be followed by other arguments. In the function definition we somehow need to establish how many optional parameters there are. One way is to assign to one of the fixed arguments the role of counter of the optional arguments. In the case of the function dump, the third parameter precisely represents this counter[6]. Once the number of optional parameters is known, we should be able to establish their type. Also this request can be satisfied in different ways. In the case of the function dump we implicitly assume all optional parameters are of the type double. So, we do not need to specify anything. In functions such as printf the type of the optional arguments is obtained from the format description string.

When the function is called, the optional arguments are listed, separated by a comma and between parentheses, as we do for ordinary functions. The values of the parameters are contained in adjacent memory locations. For example, if a **double** and a **char** are passed to a variadic function as optional parameters, their values are represented with nine consecutive bytes in the computer memory; the first eight ones contain the IEEE 754 representation of the first value and the last ones the ASCII code of the second variable. So, in order to know the values of the parameters, we need to know the address of the first memory location, i.e., the first byte of the sequence. To this purpose, a macro va_start is defined in the header file **stdarg.h** (that must be included in the code). This macro assigns the address of the first memory location to a pointer of the type **va_list**. Other two macros are also defined in the file **stdarg.h**. The macro va_arg reads the parameter pointed by the pointer **va_list**, moving the pointer to the next parameter. The macro va_end finishes the operation of reading the parameters list. The usage of these macros is shown in Listing 18.4, which contains the code

---

[6]This is not the only way to know this number. For instance, in functions such as printf, the number of optional arguments is obtained from the format description string.

for the function dump. The function prints with printf the n components of the array x, followed by count double precision values (the format specifier + imposes that the sign of the variable is always written, which otherwise, in the case of positive values, is not shown).

```
1 void dump(double *x, int n, int count, ...) {
2    int i;
3    va_list optionalParameters;
4
5    for (i = 0; i < n; i++) {
6      printf("%+f ", x[i]);
7    }
8    va_start(optionalParameters, count);
9    for (i = 0; i < count; i++) {
10     printf("%+f ", va_arg(optionalParameters, double));
11   }
12   va_end(optionalParameters);
13 }
```

Listing 18.4   Example of a variadic function.

The macro va_start receives as arguments a variable of the type va_list (defined on line 3) and the name of the function last fixed parameter (line 8). The macro assigns the value of optionalParameters, representing in fact the pointer to the memory area containing the optional parameters. The macro va_arg is used to extract the single optional arguments from the parameter list optionalParameters. The macro takes two arguments (line 10): the first one is the pointer to the list of optional arguments; the second one is the name of the type in which the extracted bytes must be converted. At each call, the macro extracts from the memory, initially pointed by optionalParameters, a number of bytes corresponding to the length of the type passed as a second argument. Then converts it into the required type and returns the content. Finally, it changes the value of optionalParameters such that it points to the next parameter.

When the pointer optionalParameters is no longer needed, the macro va_end must be called, as is done on line 12.

18.2.4   *Conjugate gradient method*

In Section 18.2.2 we observed how the choice of descending along the gradient direction is not as efficient as it may seems to be at first sight. The reason is that at each change of direction a 90 degree "turn" is made. From Figure 18.3, which partially reproduces Figure 18.4, it is clear that if the directions g_0 and g_1 form an obtuse angle, the descent would even be faster. The *conjugate gradient method* exactly allows us to choose this kind of trajectory.

Observing Figure 18.4 it is clear that with the gradient method, after the first stretch in the direction g_0, if the perpendicular direction g_1 is followed, the stretch of road at the third iteration is parallel to g_0. If, instead of proceeding in the direction g_1 during the second iteration, we went in the direction $u = g_1 + \gamma_0 g_0$ (with γ_0 an appropriate constant), as given by the dashed arrow in the figure, we would have closed down more directly on the minimum. So, we can avoid to proceed along a direction we already took by following a different direction at each step. This is why we define a series of directions with the relation

$$h_{n+1} = g_{n+1} + \gamma_n h_n \,,$$

where $h_0 = g_0$ and $g_n \equiv -\boldsymbol{\nabla} F\left(\boldsymbol{x}^{(n)}\right)$ is the opposite direction of the one of the gradient of the function to be minimized, evaluated in the point reached at the nth iteration. It can be proven [Press *et al.* (1992)] that

$$\gamma_n = \frac{g_{n+1} \cdot g_{n+1}}{g_n \cdot g_n}$$

is the optimal value. Minimizing the function along this direction, we get a new approximation and the process is iterated until the condition (18.4) is satisfied. So, the point reached at the iteration $n + 1$ is given by

$$\boldsymbol{x}^{(n+1)} = \boldsymbol{x}^{(n)} + \lambda_n h_n \,,$$

where the choice of λ_n should be such that the function is minimal along the direction h_n.

If the function to be minimized is a quadratic form, this algorithm converges in just m steps (m is the size of the vector $\boldsymbol{x}$). When $\boldsymbol{x}^{(n)}$ is close enough to the minimum, the function can be expanded in Taylor series up to the second order and takes the aspect of a quadratic form. So, this result is approximately also valid for functions different from a paraboloid.

In particular, for the function we just studied, the first step is identical to the case in which the descent is along the gradient. So, after the first iteration we reach the point $(1.41, -0.18)$. From here, the next direction we need to take is given by (see Table 18.1)

$$\begin{pmatrix} h_{1,x} \\ h_{1,y} \end{pmatrix} = \begin{pmatrix} -2.82 \\ 1.41 \end{pmatrix} + 0.12 \begin{pmatrix} -4 \\ -8 \end{pmatrix} = \begin{pmatrix} -3.30 \\ 0.45 \end{pmatrix} \,.$$

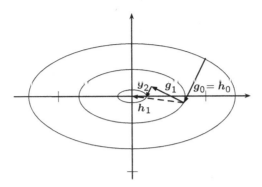

Fig. 18.4 The conjugate gradient method attempts to move along a road towards the minimum, while avoiding those directions which were already taken.

So, the next approximation is searched by minimizing the function along this direction, i.e., imposing that

$$\frac{dF}{d\lambda_n} = xh_{n,x} + 4yh_{n,y} + \lambda_n \left(h_{n,x}^2 + 4h_{n,y}^2 \right) = 0 .$$

By resolving this equation, we find that

$$\lambda_n = -\frac{xh_{n,x} + 4yh_{n,y}}{h_{n,x}^2 + 4h_{n,y}^2} ,$$

which for $n = 1$ gives $\lambda_1 \simeq 0.43$. In this way, the point we reach is

$$\begin{pmatrix} x_2 \\ y_2 \end{pmatrix} = \begin{pmatrix} 1.41 \\ -0.18 \end{pmatrix} + 0.43 \begin{pmatrix} -3.30 \\ 0.45 \end{pmatrix} = \begin{pmatrix} 0.00 \\ 0.01 \end{pmatrix} ,$$

which is exactly the solution to the problem, apart from small rounding errors (we only saved two significant digits).

Once the code for the gradient algorithm has been written, it is easy to change it such that it implements the conjugate gradient method, as can be seen in Listing 18.5. Indeed, by comparing the Listings 18.2 and 18.5, we see that the only differences are the new vectors grad, gOld, h, hOld and the computation of the value of gamma, returned by the function scalar, that computes the scalar product of two vectors of given length.

```
1 #define M 2
2 #define EPSILON 1.E-8
3
4 main() {
5   double x[M] = {2., 1.}, grad[M], xOld[M], gOld[M] = {0., 0.};
6   double h[M] = {0.}, hOld[M] = {0.};
7   double gamma = 0., epsilon, g2;
8   int i;
9
10  epsilon = input(x, M);
11  do {
12    copy(x, xOld, M);
13    gradient(myFunction, x, grad, M, EPSILON);
14    opposite(grad, M);
15    copy(grad, h, M);
16    if ((g2 = scalar(gOld, gOld, M)) != 0.) {
17      gamma = scalar(grad, grad, M) / g2;
18    }
19    add(h, gamma, hOld, M);
20    dump(h, M, 0);
21    dump(x, M, 1, myFunction(x, M));
22    printf("\n");
23    linMin(myFunction, x, h, M, epsilon);
24    copy(h, hOld, M);
25    copy(grad, gOld, M);
26  } while (norm(x, xOld, M) > epsilon);
27 }
```

Listing 18.5 A program minimizing a function with the conjugate gradient method.

18.3 Linear programming

In many important practical cases, the function to be optimized is linear
(or can be linearized) in the problem variables x_i:

$$z = \sum_{i=1}^{m} c_i x_i .$$

The function z is called the *objective function*. Moreover, in the majority of
cases, the variables x_i can be made non negative $(x_i \geq 0, \forall i)$[7]. Often, they
are also *constrained*. Such constraints can be represented by equations or
inequalities establishing the relations existing among the variables. Generally, the variables represent a cost or a quantity. Suppose, for example,
a transportation company has m ways to pack goods, each one having a

---

[7]It is enough that originally they were bounded at the lower end.

different cost c_i, $i = 1, \ldots, m$. If we know the total surface of their warehouse and the surface occupied by each type of package, we can ask which combination of boxes minimizes the cost. In this case, the constraint is represented by the existing relation between the surface of the packages and that of the warehouse:

$$\sum_{i=1}^{m} a_i x_i \leq S,$$

where S is the warehouse total surface, x_i the number of packages of the type i and a_i the surface occupied by a package of type i. The linear programming method, described in this section, was invented by George Dantzig in 1947, precisely to solve planning problems [Dantzig (1951)]. The term *programming* in the name of this method does not have the meaning we usually give it throughout this textbook. At that time, the term *programming* was used as a synonym for *planning*, which is the meaning intended in this context (remember the discussion on the ambiguity of natural language given in Section 2.2).

18.3.1   *Definition of the canonical problem*

In general, the linear programming problem, in the so-called *canonical* or *standard form*, is expressed in terms of a search for the vector $\boldsymbol{x} = (x_1, \ldots, x_m)$, with $x_i \geq 0$, $\forall i$, minimizing the objective function $z = c_1 x_1 + c_2 x_2 + \cdots + c_m x_m = \boldsymbol{c} \cdot \boldsymbol{x}$ in presence of a series of constraints expressed as a system of linear equations

$$A\boldsymbol{x} = \boldsymbol{b},$$

with $\boldsymbol{b} = (b_1, \ldots, b_m)$ and $b_i \geq 0$, $\forall i$. Not all real problems have this form, but they can be easily restated in this way. Usually, the constraints are presented as inequations as

$$a_{i1} x_1 + a_{i2} x_2 + \cdots + a_{im} x_m \leq b_i.$$

In this case, we introduce in each constraint an appropriate nonnegative auxiliary variable, the so-called *slack variable*, transforming the inequality into an equation

$$a_{i1} x_1 + a_{i2} x_2 + \cdots + a_{im} x_m + x_{m+1} = b_i.$$

In the case that the inequality contains a sign $\geq$ a nonnegative auxiliary variable, in this case called the *surplus variable*, is subtracted.

From a geometric viewpoint, the system of equations establishing the constraints, defines an m-dimensional convex polyhedron called the *convex set*. It can be proven that the system possible solutions, called *feasible solutions*, are all contained inside the polyhedron defined in this way. It can also be proven that, if the objective function has a minimum and if the system solution is unique (*optimal solution*), it is a vertex of the convex set (called a *basis*). The proof of this property is beyond the scope of this textbook (for a complete treatment, see, for example, [Garvin (1960)]). However, it is easy to understand it when considering a two-dimensional problem, as shown in Section 18.3.2.

18.3.2   *The simplex method*

A linear programming problem can be solved with the *simplex method* applied in this section to a specific example. Suppose we want to find the maximum of the function

$$z = x_1 + 2x_2$$

in presence of the following constraints:

$$\begin{cases} -x_1 + 3x_2 & \leq +10 \\ -x_1 + x_2 & \geq -6 \\ x_1 & < +10\,, \end{cases}$$

where x_1 and x_2 are nonnegative quantities. From a geometric point of view this is equivalent to searching a solution inside a convex polygon OABCD in the Cartesian plane in Figure 18.5, in which also some curves for which we have $z = C$, with C constant are shown. From the figure it is clear that the maximum value of z is reached when the line $z = C$ passes through the point B, which is one of the polygon vertices. The point B has coordinates $(10, 20/3)$. In this case, the solution to the problem can be easily found graphically. However, when there are more than two variables this becomes difficult.

Therefore, we describe the general method applied to this simple case, in order to show graphically what occurs at each step. First of all, we need to transform the problem in the canonical form. To this purpose, we add a new auxiliary variable to the first and third equation, and subtract one to the second, to transform the system of inequalities to a system of equations. Moreover, we change the sign of the second equation, because its right hand

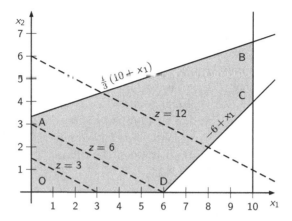

Fig. 18.5   Geometric representation of a linear programming problem. We want to find the minimum of the function $z = x_1 + 2x_2$ inside the polygon **OABCD**. The dashed lines have constant z.

side is negative:

$$\begin{cases} -x_1 + 3x_2 + x_3 & = 10 \\ x_1 - x_2 + x_4 & = 6 \\ x_1 + x_5 & = 10 \,. \end{cases}$$

Finally, as we are searching for the maximum, and not the minimum, value of z, we change the sign of the objective function by defining $z' = -x_1 - 2x_2$. We show the coefficients of the equations in a table, writing the coefficients c_1 and c_2 of the objective function variables (called *cost coefficients*) on the last row:

$$\begin{array}{ccccc|c} -1 & 3 & 1 & 0 & 0 & 10 \\ 1 & -1 & 0 & 1 & 0 & 6 \\ 1 & 0 & 0 & 0 & 1 & 10 \\ \hline -1 & -2 & 0 & 0 & 0 & \end{array}$$

The table lower right element is reserved for the value of the function to be optimized. We now have a system of 3 equations and 5 unknowns, which is not determined and admits for several solutions. A trivial solution is found by searching the columns containing just one coefficient which is different from zero, i.e., the columns 3, 4 and 5. The corresponding variables form a so-called *basis*. In these cases, the solution is obvious: $x_j = b_i/a_{ij}$ (in this specific case, all $a_{ij} = 1$) for the basic variables, while $x_j = 0$ for the other ones. What we found is a basic feasible solution, but not an optimal one.

Geometrically, the solution coincides with the point O of Figure 18.5, and is $(0, 0, 10, 6, 10)$. We note that, in order for z to grow (i.e., z' to decrease), we need to assign a positive value to x_1 or x_2. If we choose to assign x_s a value different from zero, z increases by $c_s x_s$, but at least one of the variables x_3, x_4 and x_5 should vary in order for the system to be fully satisfied. To allow z to vary as much as possible, it is convenient to change the value of the variable with the most negative cost coefficient, i.e., x_2. What is the maximum value of x_2? Obviously it is the one which, substituted in one of the equations, makes another basic variable to be equal to zero. If $x_s \neq 0$, and recalling that by definition $x_i \geq 0$, the equations become

$$x_i = b_i - a_{is} x_s \geq 0 \quad \Leftrightarrow \quad x_s \leq \frac{b_i}{a_{is}} \text{ where } a_{is} > 0 . \tag{18.7}$$

As this relation should be valid for each i, the highest value we can assign to x_s is the minimum of the ratios b_i / a_{is}. If we indicate by r the equation corresponding to this value, we have that

$$x_s = \frac{b_r}{a_{rs}} . \tag{18.8}$$

In the case under study, $s = 2$ and $r = 1$. We can now try to rewrite the system such that $x_s = x_2$ only appears in the first equation (as $r = 1$). To this purpose, we just need to multiply the first equation by the coefficient of x_s of each successive equation, divide it by a_{rs} and subtract the two equations by means of the substitution[8]

$$a_{ij} \rightarrow a_{ij} - a_{is} \frac{a_{rj}}{a_{rs}} . \tag{18.9}$$

By performing this transformation, the system, still expressed as a table, becomes

$$\begin{array}{ccccc|c}
-1 & 3 & 1 & 0 & 0 & 10 \\
\frac{2}{3} & 0 & \frac{1}{3} & 1 & 0 & \frac{28}{3} \\
1 & 0 & 0 & 0 & 1 & 10 \\
\hline
-\frac{5}{3} & 0 & \frac{2}{3} & 0 & 0 & \frac{20}{3}
\end{array}$$

It is easy to see that from this table we can identify a new basis, namely $(0, 10/3, 0, 28/3, 10)$, which geometrically corresponds to the point A of Figure 18.5. Correspondingly, the objective function increases by $c_s x_s = 20/3$. Iterating further, we can increment the value of z, if we include x_1 in the basis. Applying the rule stating that the maximum value of x_1 is determined

---

[8]We are actually applying the Gaussian elimination algorithm to solve systems of linear equations, described in Section 5.3.

by finding the minimum (positive) value of the ratio between b_i and a_{is}, it is immediately clear that in this case, we have $r = 3$ (s naturally equals 1). Transforming the system according to the prescription given in (18.9), the table becomes

$$
\begin{array}{ccccc|c}
0 & 3 & 1 & 0 & 1 & 20 \\
0 & 0 & \frac{1}{3} & 1 & -\frac{2}{3} & \frac{8}{3} \\
1 & 0 & 0 & 0 & 1 & 10 \\
\hline
0 & 0 & \frac{2}{3} & 0 & \frac{5}{3} & \frac{70}{3}
\end{array}
$$

The basis is now $(10, 20/3, 0, 8/3, 0)$ and coincides with the point B of Figure 18.5. Geometrically, we see we have reached the optimal solution. From an algebraic point of view, this is clear from the fact that there are no longer negative cost coefficients, meaning that we can no longer increase the objective function value.

Eventually, the objective function maximum is found, running along the surface of the convex set defined by the constraints, and moving from one vertex to another. To find the road, we just eliminate, at each step, an auxiliary variable from the feasible solution, thus maximizing the variables multiplied by their negative cost coefficient. Indicating the index of this variable by s, this value is found by determining the equation of index r for which the ratio b_r/a_{rs} has the smallest positive value. Displaying the coefficients of the system of the constraint equations together with the equation defining the objective function in tabular form according to the schema given above, and transforming the table elements following the prescription (18.9), a new basis is determined. The variables of the new basis are found by identifying the columns containing only one coefficient which is different from zero. The procedure is iterated as long as all cost coefficients are zero or positive.

The table where all coefficients are displayed is called the *tableau*. To be precise, the term tableau is reserved to a slightly different table, used in the past when calculations were carried out by hand or with the help of a pocket calculator. Here we prefer to use the table in the form we defined, as it is more naturally represented on a computer.

To create a C program able to perform this type of optimization, we need first of all to define an array hosting the coefficients of the tableau and one to store the basis. The most general way to do this, is to define the pointers

```
double **tableau;
double  *basis;
```

In practice, the first represents a matrix consisting of a vector of vectors[9]. The memory space is reserved with `calloc`, as shown in Listing 18.6. The variables `n` and `m` represent, respectively, the number of equations and the number of unknowns. This technique overcomes the problems related to the use of multidimensional static arrays (Section 6.5) and allows us to write completely general functions.

Once the initial tableau is given, it is easy to write the algorithm, consisting of just four steps.

(1) A possible basis is determined.
(2) The value of s is determined by identifying the minimum cost coefficient. If this coefficient is positive, the optimization is concluded, otherwise the value r is determined by identifying the equation with minimum ratio b_i/a_{is}.
(3) The variable with index s is eliminated from the equations with index different from r.

If we define appropriate functions for each of these steps, the algorithm simply consists of the few following lines:

```
do {
    s = minC(tableau[n], m);
    if (s > 0) {
        r = maxC(tableau, n, s);
        removeVariable(tableau, n, m, r, s);
    }
} while (s >= 0);
```

Let us discuss how these functions work. The function `minC` receives in input the last row of the `tableau` (a pointer to a `double` array), containing the cost coefficients. It returns the index of the coefficient with lowest value. This is an extremely simple function we do not discuss in detail. The same goes for `maxC` which receives the entire tableau in input, because it determines the maximum value of x_s by iterating on the equations (columns). The "core" of the program is the function `removeVariable`, that eliminates the variable indicated by the indexes `r` and `s` from the equations with index different from `r`, as in Listing 18.7. The first operation consists in copying the coefficients a_{ij} into the coefficients a'_{ij}, represented by the variable `ap`. On line 3 enough memory space to contain all of the tableau coefficient is reserved. Next, the function `copyTableau` on line 4 is called, which actually copies all elements of `a` in `ap`. With the statement on line 8, the transformation (18.9) is applied to all rows with index different from

---

[9]The same structure is used in Section 17.2.2 to store the adjacency lists.

r. The row with index r is transformed by simply dividing all coefficients by ap[r][s], such that the coefficient of the variable x_s takes on value 1 (line 12). Finally, as the variable ap is no longer useful at that point, we can free its corresponding memory (lines 16 up to 19).

```
1    basis = (double *)calloc(m, sizeof(double));
2    tableau = (double **)calloc(n + 1, sizeof(double*));
3    for (i = 0; i < n; i++) {
4      tableau[i] = (double *)calloc(m + 1, sizeof(double));
5      for (j = 0; j < m; j++) {
6        printf("coeff. %2d, %2d: ", i + 1, j + 1);
7        scanf("%lf", &tableau[i][j]);
8      }
9      printf("known term eq. %2d: ", i + 1, m + 1);
10     scanf("%lf", &tableau[i][m]);
11   }
12   tableau[n] = (double *)calloc(m + 1, sizeof(double));
13   for (j = 0; j < m; j++) {
14       printf("cost coeff. %2d: ", j + 1);
15       scanf("%lf", &tableau[n][j]);
16   }
```

Listing 18.6   One way to allocate memory space for the tableau and the basis and to acquire its contents. The variables n and m are for the number of equations and the number of unknowns.

```
1 void removeVariable(double **a, int n, int m, int r, int s) {
2    int i, j;
3    double **ap = (double **)calloc(n + 1, sizeof(double*));
4    copyTableau(a, ap, n, m);
5    for (i = 0; i <= n; i++) {
6      if (i != r) {
7        for (j = 0; j <= m; j++) {
8          a[i][j] -= ap[i][s] * ap[r][j] / ap[r][s];
9        }
10     } else {
11       for (j = 0; j <= m; j++) {
12         a[i][j] = ap[i][j] / ap[i][s];
13       }
14     }
15   }
16   for (i = 0; i <= n; i++) {
17     free(ap[i]);
18   }
19   free(ap);
20 }
```

Listing 18.7   A function eliminating the unknown with index s from the equations with index different from r in a tableau with n×m components.

18.3.3 *The simplex method in practice*

We should note that there exists no theoretical guarantee stating that the simplex method converges towards the solution. In some cases, the system might enter in an infinite cycle where the solution continuously moves from one vertex of the polyhedron to another. When this occurs, we must change the strategy of choosing the variable which is to be eliminated from the basis. We do not detail this procedure, we just want to stress this difficulty exists. For the complete treatment of these special cases, we refer the reader to the bibliography. Another difficulty which might be encountered, is due to the usual problem of numerical approximations. There exists techniques to circumvent these inconveniences, for which we again refer the reader to specialized texts. They essentially consist in computing at each iteration quantities whose value should be identical to an appropriate combinations of the tableau coefficients. By comparing the values of these control quantities, a possible rounding can be detected and the result is properly corrected.

In practice, the main difficulty is to establish an initial basis. Indeed, the problem is not always presented such that there are enough columns with only one non-zero element. In this case, we just need to add as many *artificial* variables (not to be confused with the *auxiliary* variables) as the columns lacking to create a simple basis. If needed, we can always start from a system whose initial basis consists exclusively of artificial variables. In practice, given a system of n rows and m unknowns, we introduce k artificial variables $x_{m+1}, \ldots, x_{m+k}$, with $k \leq n$ by adding k columns to the characteristic matrix:

$$
\begin{pmatrix}
a_{11} & a_{12} & \cdots & a_{1m} & 1 & 0 & \cdots & 0 \\
a_{21} & a_{22} & \cdots & a_{2m} & 0 & 1 & \cdots & 0 \\
\vdots & & & \vdots & & & & \vdots \\
a_{n1} & a_{n2} & \cdots & a_{nm} & 0 & 0 & \cdots & 1
\end{pmatrix}
$$

The artificial variables only serve to have a simple initial basis, and should be immediately eliminated from the problem. To this purpose, we introduce a measure expressing how artificial the basis is, defined as

$$
w = - \sum_{i=m+1}^{m+k} w_i x_i \, ,
$$

with, initially, $w_i = 1 \; \forall i$. The measure w is added to the objective function, which becomes $z'' = -z - w$. Until $w > 0$, at least one artificial variable is present in the basis and the variable to be eliminated must be chosen among the artificial ones. Thus, the search for the value of s should be limited to $m + 1 \leq s \leq m + k$. When $w = 0$, we have reduced the problem to the original one and we are in the conditions in which we considered the method so far. At that point we may extend the search of the variable to be eliminated to all the other variables.

Hands on 18.3 - The simplex method

 Write a C program implementing the simplex method, considering the case where also artificial variables are taken into account. Then, solve the following optimization problem. A research center distributes data among 4 different labs by means of the Internet. Each one of the labs elaborates the data and makes them available to all the others. Once they have been processed, the data occupy $S(1 + \alpha)$ bytes of disk space, where S is the size of the raw data and α a factor representing the fraction of the original size the data occupy after they have been elaborated. Each lab is connected to the research center with a network with bandwith B_i. They each posses N_i CPU and S_i disk space. The time needed to make a single data item available is given by the sum of time S/B_i needed to transfer it and the elaboration time τ. Determine the relative percentages of data that should be distributed to each center such that the time passing between data acquisition and data elaboration is minimal. Note that we can restate this question by requiring the number of elaborations per time unit is maximal.

18.4   Optimization with discrete variables

In this section we treat a particular case of optimization problems, namely those with variables taking only a discrete set of values. For simplicity, we consider binary variables, such as the spins of the Ising model defined in Section 19.3. Thus, there are 2^N possible system configurations, and the optimization problem consists in finding the one with minimum cost (energy). The time it takes to solve this optimization problem *exactly* typically grows exponentially with the number of variables of the problem (some, much faster, methods finding approximate solutions are discussed in Section 20.4). Nevertheless, in some cases it is absolutely necessary to find the minimum cost function, even if it takes very large computational resources. In these cases, it is useful to know the basic techniques described in the following sections.

18.4.1 *Satisfability problems*

To work on a specific model, we introduce the *satisfability problem* (or *SAT* in short), which is easy to describe, while being very general since the majority of optimization problems can be rewritten as a satisfability problem. A satisfability problem is represented by N boolean variables, assuming only the truth values, false and true, $x_i \in \{0, 1\}$, and M constraints preventing the variables to take certain configurations. It has been proven that each satisfability problem can be written as a logical expression, similar to the following one:

$$F = (x_1 \vee \bar{x}_3) \wedge (x_4) \wedge (x_1 \vee x_2 \vee \bar{x}_4) \wedge (\bar{x}_1 \vee \bar{x}_2) \wedge (\bar{x}_3 \vee x_4) . \quad (18.10)$$

The constraints are represented by the expressions between parentheses. These contain variables or negated variables (those with a bar on top), combined only with the logical OR operator ($\vee$). The formula F results to be true if and only if each constraint has been satisfied, i.e., if each expression between parentheses is true, as these are combined with logical AND operators($\wedge$). In the formula (18.10) we have four variables and five constraints. The second constraint requires x_4 to be true, i.e., $x_4 = 1$, while the first one demands x_1 to be true or x_3 to be false. So, configurations where both $x_1 = 0$ and at the same time $x_3 = 1$ are forbidden.

A configuration $\vec{x} \equiv (x_1, \ldots, x_N)$ is called a solution to the problem if it satisfies all constraints. The solutions to the formula (18.10) are the following three: $(0, 1, 0, 1)$, $(1, 0, 0, 1)$ and $(1, 0, 1, 1)$. To establish an analogy with the minimization problem of a cost function, we also introduce a cost function counting the number of violated clauses in a configuration. So, the solutions are those configurations with zero cost. Generally, when the number of constraints is much larger than the number of variables, the problem no longer admits any solutions. In this case, the optimization problem consists in finding the configuration with minimum cost (which is now positive). We may also add a weight to each constraint (for example, because it is more important that some of them be satisfied rather than others). In this case, we define the cost function as the sum of the weights of the unsatisfied constraints.

It is evident that the search for *one* solution is easier than finding *all* solutions. It is also easier to find one generic solution than the minimum cost configuration, in the case the latter is positive. In the latter case, the difficulty lies in the fact that we do not known what is the value of the minimum cost. Indeed, it is possible we find the minimum cost configuration at the beginning of our search, but to prove it actually has the minimum cost, we need to continue our search until we analyzed all configurations. The techniques shown in Sections 18.4.2 and 18.4.3 attempt to solve the two more difficult problems, though they can also be applied to find a single solution by simply stopping the program if we found one.

18.4.2   *Exhaustive enumeration*

The most direct way to find *all* configurations with (a possibly positive) minimum cost is by means of exhaustive enumeration of all 2^N configurations. There are many ways to program this exhaustive enumeration. We show one of these in Listing 18.8.

In Listing 18.8 we use the expression 1 « N to represent 2^N and the configuration of the N binary variables is stored in the N least significant bits (the rightmost ones) of config. This is why the number of variables N is at most equal to the number of bits reserved for an unsigned long long int (typically 64). This might seem too small. However, the exhaustive search is a very heavy operation. For example, on a computer performing 10^9 operations per second, the case $N = 40$ takes at least one day to complete its execution. On lines 7 and 8 of Listing 18.8 we copy the bits of config in the array x[] storing the configuration. In this way, it can be used to compute, for instance, the cost of the configuration, which we omitted here.

```
1 unsigned long long int config, tmp;
2 int i, x[N];
3
4 for (config = 0; config < (1<<N); config++) {
5   tmp = config;
6   for (i = 0; i < N; i++) {
7     x[i] = tmp % 2;
8     tmp = tmp >> 1;
9   }
10   ...here the array x[] is used...
11 }
```

Listing 18.8   The exhaustive enumeration of 2^N configurations.

The main drawback of the code in Listing 18.8 is that the computation of the configuration cost (or any other observable) is to be repeated from scratch each time `config` changes. Especially, when the cost is the sum of discrete terms (as is the case for the satisfiability problems or the Ising model), it would be much more effcient to change a single variable of the configuration at a time and update only the terms of the cost which changed correspondingly. To this purpose, we must be able to visit the 2^N configurations of N bits in such an order that two successive configurations differ only in a single bit: the Gray code is the solution we are looking for.

An N-bit Gray code is a sorting of binary sequences of N bits where two consecutive sequences differ only by a single bit.

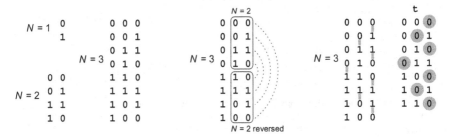

Fig. 18.6   The Gray codes for $N = 1, 2, 3$ (left), building a code with $N = 3$, starting from one with $N = 2$ (center) and an example of the rule to compute the differing bit in two successive strings of the Gray code (right).

In the left part of Figure 18.6 we show a 1, 2 and 3 bit Gray code. Note how all 2^N strings of N bits are sorted such that two consecutive ones differ only by a bit; also the first and last differ only by a single bit. In the central part of Figure 18.6 we show how to build a Gray code for N-bit strings, once the one for strings of $N - 1$ bits is known (in Figure 18.6 we consider $N = 3$, but the reasoning is valid for any value of N). The first 2^{N-1} strings correspond to the Gray code of $N - 1$ bits with an additional 0 in the most significant bit. Instead, the following 2^{N-1} strings are obtained by considering the strings of the $(N - 1)$-bit Gray code *sorted in reversed order*, to which a 1 is added in the most significant bit. It is easy to prove that two consecutive strings of the sequence of N-bit strings we obtain in this way differ only by a single bit (we leave this proof as an exercise to the reader).

To write an efficient program listing all 2^N N-bit strings according to the Gray code, the only thing we should be able to compute fast is the bit which is to be changed to pass from the tth string to the next one. The integer variable t takes values from 0 up to $2^N - 2$. Observing the right part of Figure 18.6, where we included the values of t in binary, next to the Gray code sequence, it is clear that to pass from one string to the next, the bit to be changed is the first 0 we encounter when reading t from right to left. This property, shown in figure for $N = 3$, is valid in general. We apply it in the program of Listing 18.9, where we use the mask `mask` to extract the ith bit of the variable t.

```
1  unsigned long long int t, mask;
2  int i, x[N]={0};
3  ...here we compute the observables
4    depending on the configuration x[]...
5  for (t = 0; t < (1 << N) - 1; t++) {
6    mask = 1; i = 0;
7    while (t & mask) {
8      mask = mask << 1;
9      i++;
10   }
11   x[i] = 1 - x[i];
12   ...here we change the observables depending on x[i]...
13 }
```

Listing 18.9   The Gray code to enumerate 2^N configurations.

Hands on 18.4 - Density of states in the Ising model

With the help of a Gray code, such as the one of Listing 18.9, compute the energy and the magnetization of all configurations of the Ising model, defined in Section 19.3. Consider regular lattices (with periodic boundary conditions) in two and three dimensions. The lattice size needs to be very small, for example, 4×4, 5×5, 6×6 and $3 \times 3 \times 3$. Make a (three-dimensional) plot of the histogram of the number of configurations with a given magnetization and energy. Could you have guessed the observed behavior, at least at a qualitative level? Try to normalize the quantities of the plot such that the results for various system sizes become very similar.

Gray codes

Even though they were already known in the XIXth century, these codes took their name after Frank Gray, the Bell labs researcher who patented them in 1953. The first one using these codes seems to be the French engineer Emile Baudot in 1878 to communicate with the telegraph. They also appear in the solutions to the "Tower of Hanoi" problem proposed in 1883 by the mathematician Edouard Lucas (box on page 453).

At the time when technological devices were mostly mechanical, the Gray codes were widely used to encode any position (for example of a knob) in binary representation by closing and opening a series of electrical contacts. Due to the inevitable mechanical imprecisions of any apparatus, it is practically impossible to open and close two contacts contemporarily. Using the usual binary representation, passing from the value 001 to the next value 010, the device could take on the wrong "intermediate" value (such as 000 or 011). Instead, using a Gray code, only one contact is opened or closed when passing from one position to the next one, thus, eliminating the problem of spurious intermediate states. The successive conversion in standard binary representation is carried out with an appropriate circuit.

18.4.3   *A search by construction*

Another strategy to find all configurations of a system consisting of N binary variables is to *build* each configuration, starting with all undefined variables and fixing them one at a time. This process is easily represented with a so-called *search tree*[10]: its name derives from the main use of this strategy, namely finding a solution. In Figure 18.7 we show the search tree for the satisfiability problem defined by the formula (18.10).

In the tree root, none of the variables has been assigned. When descending from a node to one of its children, we fix the value of one of these undefined variables, taking on the two possible values in the two subtrees. The tree leaves correspond to the system configurations where all N variables are fixed. Instead, all other nodes correspond to partial configurations, where some variables have not yet been assigned.

It is very natural to program this type of search with a recursive func-

---

[10]Even if they have a similar name, these search trees have little to do with those studied in Chapter 16.

tion, such as the one in Listing 18.10. It receives a partial configuration in input, assigns a new variable and calls itself with a new partial configuration. If the variables have all been fixed, the function is called with the first argument equal to N. In the latter case, the function performs the measurement operations on the configuration. Note on line 7, before the function is quit, the variable x[i] is assigned the value NA (a generic integer number, different from 0 and 1), indicating this variable becomes again *not assigned*. At the beginning of the program, all values have the value NA.

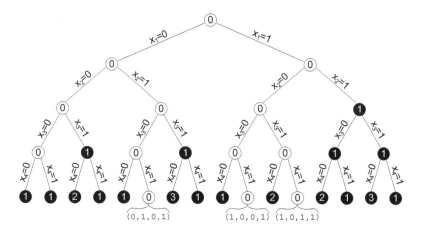

Fig. 18.7   The search tree for the satisfiability problem defined by the formula (18.10). Along the edges we write which assignment is made in descending from the parent to the child node. The number written in the nodes is the cost of the corresponding configuration (possibly partial cost if the node is not a leaf): the black nodes have a nonzero cost.

```
1  void assignVariable(int i, int *x) {
2    if (i < N) {
3      x[i] = 0;
4      assignVariable(i + 1, x);
5      x[i] = 1;
6      assignVariable(i + 1, x);
7      x[i] = NA;
8    } else {
9      ...operations on the configuration...
10   }
11 }
```

Listing 18.10   A recursive function to search all configurations.

The program shown in Listing 18.10 is definitely less efficient than the one of Listing 18.9 to list all 2^N system configurations. Indeed, observe how the number of recursive function calls to `assignVariable` is at least equal to the number of nodes of the search tree, i.e., $2^{N+1} - 1$. Moreover, as we already mentioned several times, a function call is an operation a compiler cannot easily optimize. So, we need to understand in which situations this type of search may be preferable.

Let us again observe Figure 18.7. Each node contains a configuration (possibly partial, if the node is not a leaf), allowing us to compute the (partial) cost. For example, in the case of the satisfiability problems, the cost is equal to the number of violated constraints. For a partial configuration, only the violated constraints where all variables have already been assigned are counted (otherwise there always exists the possibility that a constraint is satisfied thanks to a not yet assigned variable). In Figure 18.7 the number included in each node is the corresponding configuration cost. The black nodes have a nonzero cost. So, the solutions are the configurations in the white leaves (which we explicitly write down).

Also note that the cost of a node is certainly not smaller than the cost of its parent. Indeed, because of the way we define the cost of a partial configuration, the assignment of other variables cannot satisfy constraints that had already been violated. This partial sorting property of the cost in the search tree is important and we can easily take advantage of it. Unfortunately, in the case of other models, it is not always that obvious to define a cost function with this same property.

To find one or more solutions of the satisfiability problem, we can take advantage from the property we just mentioned and avoid to explore subtrees with a black root, as their leaves certainly have a positive cost. In practice, thanks to this rule, the search algorithm performs a number of recursive calls equal to the number of white nodes. For the example in Figure 18.7, this reduces the execution time to less than its half.

From a programming viewpoint, we only need to make few changes to Listing 18.10 in order for it to avoid exploring black subtrees. Namely, on lines 4 and 6, before calling the function `assignVariable` recursively, we check whether the current configuration does not violate any constraints. This can be done, by including, for example, the following lines of code

```
if (checkConfig(x)) assignVariable(i + 1, x);
```

where the function `checkConfig` returns the value 0 if the (possibly partial) configuration violates any constraints of the satisfiability problem.

The searching time can further be improved by choosing a better order

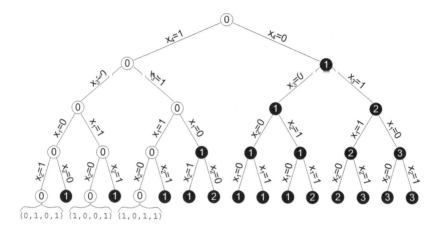

Fig. 18.8   A search tree similar to the one of Figure 18.7, but assigning the variables in a different order.

to assign the variables. In Figure 18.7, a simple sequential order (first we fix x_1, next x_2, and so on up to x_N) was used, which is not the best choice. Indeed, note that the formula (18.10) demand the variable x_4 to be true, otherwise the second constraint is violated. So, it is better to fix that variable to the requested value before assigning any other. In general, the best order to assign the variables depends on the partial configuration reached by the program. So, it may vary from branch to branch along the search tree. The same holds for the first value to assign to the variable we decided to fix.

In Figure 18.8 we show the resulting search tree when assigning the variables in the best possible order. In this case, we assign, in the left branch, the variable which does not increase the cost. Note how the number of white nodes, and thus the number of recursive calls, decreased. Moreover, the wise choice for the first value we assign to each variable (note we do not always assign the value 0 when descending along the left branch and 1 along the right branch) allows us, in this case, to find a solution in the first leaf we reach (the leftmost one); and this is achieved in only N function calls. We also note how the cost of the leaves tends to be smaller for those on the left. In general, a careful choice of which variable to assign at each step in the search allows one to reduce both the time it takes to find a solution and the time to list them all.

The choice of not continuing the search along the subtrees with positive cost, is dictated by the request to reach only configurations with zero cost.

Instead, in the case we want to find the configuration with minimum cost and this cost is *positive*, we need to change strategy with which we discard subtrees. The basic idea is similar to the one we used before. If we are sure there exists a (non partial!) configuration with cost C, the minimum cost is certainly less than or equal to C and all subtrees whose root has a cost higher than C can be rejected. The best value we can assign to C during the search, is the one of the minimum cost found up to that moment. Very often, we do not have any information on the value of C in the beginning. In this case, it is good practice to assign it a very large value in order not to reject any choice before the first configuration is found. Once the latter has been reached, we can assign to C the value of that configuration cost and proceed by following the rule that subtrees with a cost larger than C are discarded. We update the value of C only when we find a configuration with cost less than C, which then becomes the new global minimum. As the process moves along, this kind of search becomes more and more selective, because C tends to decrease to the true global minimum. In this case, a good choice of how the variables are assigned allows one to find the lowest cost configurations at the beginning of the search, thus maintaining a high selectivity during the search and saving a lot of time.

The techniques described in this section can be found under various names in the scientific literature. The two most common ones are *backtracking* and *branch and bound*. The first one refers to an algorithm searching for solutions by assigning the variables one at a time, and in the case a configuration that is incompatible with the solution has been reached(for example, because a constraint is violated), the execution traces back on its track along the search tree. Instead, the term *branch and bound* is used to indicate a generic algorithm searching for the global minimum of a function in a domain by means of the recursive use of two techniques: dividing the domain in subdomains, corresponding to the *branching* of the search tree), and the computation of the lower and upper *bounds* to the function values in each subdomain. This second operation allows one to exclude some subdomains (or subtrees) during the search for the global minimum.

Hands on 18.5 - Random 3-SAT

 The so-called *random 3-SAT* is a satisfiability problem where each constraint contains exactly three randomly chosen variables among the N variables of the problem. Each variable is negated with probability $1/2$ when it is inserted in the constraint. In the limit of large N, the properties of the modelmainly depend on the number of constraints per variable, $\alpha \equiv M/N$, where M is the number of constraints in the problem.

Program a recursive function to search for the problem solutions, by first assigning variables which are forced to take a unique value in the current configuration. Compute the probability $P(\alpha, N)$ that a randomly generated formula with N variables and αN constraints can be satisfied, i.e.., have at least one solution. By analyzing various values of N (we suggest, for example, $N = 10$, 20 and 40), study the behavior of $P(\alpha, N)$ in function of α in the interval $\alpha \in [0, 8]$. Try to identify the value α_c for which, in the large N limit, a phase transition takes place: for $\alpha < \alpha_c$ a problem can usually be satisfied, while for $\alpha > \alpha_c$ it typically does not admit any solution.

Chapter 19

The Monte Carlo method

> That doctrinal piece of literature observed that the
> lottery is an interpolation of chance into the order
> of the world and that to accept errors is not to
> contradict fate but merely to corroborate it.
>
> Jorge Luis Borges, *The Lottery in Babilon* (1941).

Chapters 15, 16 and 17 describe, more or less advanced, deterministic algorithms: these are designed to reach their goal by executing only choices dictated by precise, never random, strategies.

Very often though, it is more convenient (in terms of programming difficulty and execution time) to use algorithms based on stochastic processes that can obtain the same results with analogous precision. Among stochastic algorithms, the Monte Carlo method is certainly the best-known and most widespread. The name Monte Carlo derives from the place where the world's most famous gambling houses reside. It reminds the idea that to correctly apply a stochastic method, we need an enormous amount of random numbers, as the ones generated each night in a casino (if we assume the game is fair!).

After motivating the use of stochastic methods, in Section 19.1, we dedicate a good part of this chapter, in particular Section 19.2, to the basic concepts underlying a dynamic Monte Carlo simulation, i.e., the Markov chains. In Section 19.3, we introduce the Ising model, which is a prototype of problems that can be studied well with the Monte Carlo method. The Ising model (as many other problems) can be resolved in a rigourous way with a deterministic algorithm. Often though, this takes a time which is exponential in the problem size N. Alternatively, a good stochastic algorithm may find an excellent approximation to the solution in a time which is only polynomial in N. As we generally only have a limited amount of computer resources at our disposal, the second approach allows us to study larger systems, albeit in an approximated way. We end this chapter with Section 19.4 where we give a series of general advices on how to optimize a program.

19.1   Numeric integration with the Monte Carlo method

Even if the Monte Carlo method can be applied to a wide range of problems, it is used more often for just some of them: for example, numeric integration (especially in many spatial dimensions) and optimization. We consider the first of these two problems to demonstrate the potential of the Monte Carlo method and leave the discussion of the other to Section 20.4.

In Section 8.3 we discuss how to numerically estimate, with the Monte Carlo method, a definite integral of the type

$$I = \int_a^b f(x)\,dx \;,$$

where $f(x)$ is a generic integrable function. Rewriting the integral as

$$\int_a^b f(x)\,dx = \int_a^b \frac{f(x)}{P(x)} P(x)\,dx = \int_a^b s(x)\,P(x)\,dx \;,$$

where $s(x) \equiv f(x)/P(x)$, we can extract, according to the probability distribution $P(x)$, a set of N random numbers x_i and estimate the integral by the average

$$I \simeq \frac{1}{N} \sum_{i=1}^{N} s(x_i) \;. \tag{19.1}$$

With this method, we are free to choose the probability distribution $P(x)$ to sample the integration interval. This choice is very important, given that the error on the estimate in equation (19.1) depends on the function $s(x)$ we decide to use. Indeed, as the points x_i have been chosen randomly and independently from each other, the terms in the sum of (19.1) are uncorrelated. So, we can apply the central limit theorem to calculate the error on the integral estimate,

$$\sigma_I = \frac{\sigma_s}{\sqrt{N-1}} = \sqrt{\frac{\overline{s^2} - \overline{s}^2}{N-1}} \;, \tag{19.2}$$

where σ_s is the standard deviation of the stochastic variable $s(x)$, whose averages are computed over the measure $P(x)\,dx$, i.e.,

$$\overline{s^k} = \int_a^b s(x)^k\, P(x)\, dx\ .$$

Note that, even though the error of the stochastic Monte Carlo method always decreases with the square root of the number of random extractions, the numerator of expression (19.2) depends on the choice for the function $s(x)$, i.e., the sampling function $P(x)$. This is why it is important to minimize this coefficient.

19.1.1   *Multidimensional integration*

The expression (19.2) for the error on the Monte Carlo estimate of the integral is also valid in the case of multidimensional integrals. In this case, though, the averages $\bar{s}$ and $\overline{s^2}$ are integrals over the multidimensional domain. The fact that this error decreases as $N^{-1/2}$ for any spatial dimension, makes the Monte Carlo integration methods much more efficient than the other integration methods, given in Chapter 8 for large enough number of space dimensions. Indeed, in the case of an integration with the rectangle method (Section 8.2.1) in d spatial dimensions, the integration volume L^d is divided in N cubes of side ϵ such that $N\epsilon^d = L^d$. In each cube, the integration with the rectangle method gives a result which differs at most a quantity of the order $\mathcal{O}(\epsilon^{d+2})$ from the true value. To prove the latter, we consider a cube with side ϵ centered around the origin and develop the integrand to the second order in Taylor series around the origin,

$$\int_{-\epsilon/2}^{\epsilon/2} dx_1 \ldots \int_{-\epsilon/2}^{\epsilon/2} dx_d\, f(\vec{x})$$

$$\simeq \int_{-\epsilon/2}^{\epsilon/2} dx_1 \ldots \int_{-\epsilon/2}^{\epsilon/2} dx_d \left[f(\vec{0}) + \sum_{i=1}^{d} \left.\frac{\partial f(\vec{x})}{\partial x_i}\right|_{\vec{x}=\vec{0}} x_i \right.$$

$$\left. + \frac{1}{2} \sum_{i,j=1}^{d} \left.\frac{\partial^2 f(\vec{x})}{\partial x_i \partial x_j}\right|_{\vec{x}=\vec{0}} x_i x_j \right]\ .$$

The integral of the second term between square brackets is zero because $\int_{-\epsilon/2}^{\epsilon/2} x_i dx_i = 0$. Likewise, also the last term is zero if $i \neq j$. So, only the first term between square brackets and the third term with equal indices, $i = j$, remain.

$$\int_{-\epsilon/2}^{\epsilon/2} dx_1 \dots \int_{-\epsilon/2}^{\epsilon/2} dx_d \, f(\vec{x}) \simeq \epsilon^d f(\vec{0}) + \sum_{i=1}^{d} \epsilon^{d-1} \frac{\epsilon^3}{24} \frac{\partial^2 f(\vec{x})}{\partial^2 x_i} \bigg|_{\vec{x}=\vec{0}} , \quad (19.3)$$

where we have neglected higher order terms, i.e., $\mathcal{O}(\epsilon^{d+4})$, that vanish quicker in the limit $\epsilon \to 0$. Considering that $\epsilon^d f(0)$ is precisely the rectangle method estimate of the integral, the latter term in equation (19.3) is exactly the difference between the true integral and its numeric estimate. By summing this error over all N cubes, we find that the error on the integral estimate is given by a quantity of the order $\mathcal{O}(N\epsilon^{d+2}) = \mathcal{O}(L^{d+2}/N^{2/d})$. A comparison of this expression with the one for the error in the case of a Monte Carlo integration, i.e., $\mathcal{O}(N^{-1/2})$, we find that for $d = 4$ both estimates have an error decaying with the same power of N, while for $d > 4$ the Monte Carlo method is more efficient. Moreover, for very large d, all deterministic methods (in particular, those described in Chapter 8) result to be rather inefficient. The reason is that their error decreases very slowly with the number of measurements, namely as $\sigma = \mathcal{O}(N^{-\omega/d})$ where ω depends on the method, but is always a very small number.

19.1.2   *Uniform sampling*

Let us now tackle the problem of how to choose the sampling distribution $P(x)$ in order to keep the numerator of the expression (19.2) as small as possible. Even if the Monte Carlo integration is mainly used to estimate highly dimensional integrals, we prefer, for simplicity, to study a problem in a small number of dimensions.

We talk about *uniform sampling* when the probability distribution $P(x)$ is uniform in the integration interval. Let us consider a specific example. In order to numerically estimate the integral

$$I = \int_0^L e^{-x} \, dx ,$$

with a uniform sampling of the interval $[0, L]$ we choose the function $P(x) = 1/L$ for $x \in [0, L]$ and $P(x) = 0$ outside of the interval. As a consequence, we have that $s(x) = Le^{-x}$ and the moments of $s(x)$ are given by the expression

$$\overline{s^k} = \frac{1}{L} \int_0^L s(x)^k \, dx = \frac{L^{k-1}}{k} \left(1 - e^{-kL}\right) .$$

Thus, the statistical error on the integral estimate is equal to

$$\sigma_I = \frac{1}{\sqrt{N-1}} \left[\frac{L}{2} \left(1 - e^{-2L}\right) - \left(1 - e^{-L}\right)^2 \right]^{1/2} \underset{N,L \gg 1}{\simeq} \sqrt{\frac{L}{2N}} , \quad (19.4)$$

i.e., it decreases as the inverse of the square root of the number of extracted points. However, it is multiplied by a coefficient which grows with the length of the integration interval.

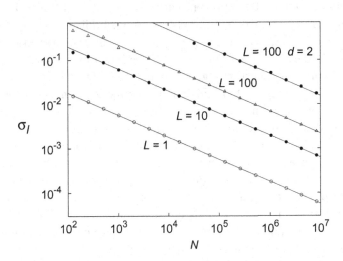

Fig. 19.1 The error of the numerical estimate of the integral defined in the interval $[0, L]$ decreases with the number N of points used for the estimate. The coefficient, however, grows with the interval size. The data on top correspond to a two-dimensional integration.

In Figure 19.1 we show, using a log-log scale, how the error of the estimate of the integral I decreases as the number N of points used for that estimate increases. The points in the plot represent numerical data, while the lines correspond to the result of equation (19.4). Even though the integral we want to calculate is rather simple (it can be easily solved analytically), note how the number of measures needed to get a correct estimate, for example, up to the third decimal digit, is of the order of 10^7 for $L = 10$ and grows linearly with L.

This limitation of the numerical method is even more severe if we consider the integration in more dimensions. For example, the data on top in Figure 19.1 correspond to the error on the estimate of the integral of the function $\exp[-(x_1 + x_2)]$ in the square defined by $0 \leq x_1 \leq 100$ and $0 \leq x_2 \leq 100$: note how 10^7 points do not even allow us to reach a precision of 10^{-2}.

19.1.3   *Importance sampling*

Let us try to understand the origin of this phenomenon and how we can improve our stochastic integration algorithm. We consider the generic integration problem in d spatial dimensions (in Section 19.3 and in Chapter 20 we discuss an integration problem where the number of dimensions grows with the number of problem variables). For simplicity, we focus on the integrand $f(x_1, \ldots, x_d) = \exp[-(x_1 + \cdots + x_d)]$ and the integration domain $0 \le x_i \le L$ in each of the d dimensions. The integrand is sensibly different from zero only in a narrow region around the origin where $x_1 + \cdots + x_d$ is not too large. For $L \gg 1$, this region volume is bounded, while the integration domain volume grows like L^d. So, if we randomly extract points which are distributed uniformly throughout the integration volume, only a fraction of the order $\mathcal{O}(L^{-d})$ ends up in the region around the origin which contributes in a substantial way to the integral. The net result is that a stochastic algorithm, as the one described in Section 19.1.2, spends the majority of its execution time studying regions of the integration domain where the integrand is zero. This does not supply us with much information about the value of the integral we want to calculate. The number of points extracted in the interesting region is $\mathcal{O}(N/L^d)$. So, the error on the integral estimate is $\mathcal{O}(L^{d/2}/N^{1/2})$.

One possible way to solve this problem is to choose the sampling distribution $P(x)$ in a better way. Obviously, this choice cannot be completely arbitrary, because if $P(x)$ were zero in some regions of the integration domain, this could cause a systematic error of the integral estimate.

The aim is to sample the integration domain with a distribution $P(x)$ concentrated in the regions where the integrand $f(x)$ takes on the most significant values, i.e., with highest absolute value. Formally, the optimal solution would be

$$P(x) = \frac{|f(x)|}{\int |f(y)|\, dy} , \tag{19.5}$$

but usually he integral in the denominator is not known analitically. For example, in the case the function $f(x)$ never takes on negative values, the absolute values in expression (19.5) can be omitted, thus obtaining

$$P(x) = \frac{f(x)}{\int f(y)\, dy} \ \Rightarrow\ s(x) = \text{costant} \ \Rightarrow\ \sigma_s = 0 \ \Rightarrow\ \sigma_I = 0 ,$$

i.e., the error is zero! Unfortunately, the integral in the denominator is not known, as it is precisely what we want to estimate numerically!

Typically, a good choice for $P(x)$ is the one of an analytically integrable function which is as similar as possible to the integrand $f(x)$. In one spatial dimension, the knowledge of the primitive function of $P(x)$ allows us to extract random numbers according to the probability distribution $P(x)$, as explained in Section 11.6. Unfortunately, in general (for example, for more complicated integrands or in case the integration domain is multidimensional), it is very difficult to find an integrable function which is a good approximation of the integrand. In all these cases, we advise to use the Monte Carlo method based on Markov chains.

19.2 The Markov chain Monte Carlo method

The Monte Carlo methods based on Markov[1] chains (in short MCMC, *Markov Chain Monte Carlo*) simulate a stochastic dynamical process such that the integration domain regions where the integrand contributes the most to the to integral to be computed are visited with higher probability. If this region is well connected (i.e., it is very probable that the dynamic process moves between two generic points of the region) the MCMC produces excellent results. Instead, for disconnected regions or sparsely connected ones, it is much more difficult to evaluate how successful a MCMC integration is (we discuss this aspect in Section 19.2.5).

In order to simplify the discussion, we prefer to discretize the integration variables and to transform the integrals in summations over all possible configurations C of the system under study. The prototype of the integral we want to compute is

$$\sum_C A(C)P(C) , \quad \text{with} \quad \sum_C P(C) = 1 , \quad \text{and} \quad P(C) \geq 0 \quad \forall C , \quad (19.6)$$

where $P(C)$ is a probability distribution which is very concentrated in an extremely small region of the integration domain, while $A(C)$ is a function which varies little or at least slowly in this domain (more or less like the function $s(x)$ we discuss in Section 19.1.3). Obviously, the sum in equation (19.6) is over a very large number of configurations, otherwise we could just sum the addends without any numerical problem. In the applications we study in Section 19.3 and Chapter 20 the number of addends grows exponentially with the number N of variables in the problem. Instead, here we want to estimate, as well precisely as we can, the sum in Eq. (19.6) with a number of measures growing only as a power of N.

---

[1] Andrej Andreevič Markov, Russian mathematician (1856-1922).

19.2.1   *Markov chains*

We consider a discrete and finite set [2] of configurations or *states* and imagine a dynamic process defined on this set which evolves at discrete time steps. If the evolution is such that the probability to be in a given configuration $C(t+1)$, at time $t+1$, only depends on the configuration $C(t)$ the system takes at the immediately preceding time step and not on the history before that time t, the system forms a *Markov chain*. The main characteristic of a Markov chain is the absence of memory.

We now give some useful definitions and properties of Markov chains. As always, we refer the interested reader to specialized textbooks [Feller (1971); Grimmett and Stirzaker (2001)] for a more complete treatment of this topic. A Markov chain is defined by a set of states and the transition probabilities w_{ij} to go from one generic state i to another state j. A convenient graphical representation of a Markov chain is shown in Figure 19.2, where the graph nodes are the states and the directed edges represent nonzero transition probabilities. For example, being in state 2 at time t, the configuration at time $t+1$ can be the state 4 with probability $w_{24} = 1/3$, or state 7 with probability $w_{27} = 1/15$, or state 2 with probability $w_{22} = 3/5$. In general, the probability to be in a given state i at time $t+1$ is

$$p_i(t+1) = \sum_j p_j(t)\, w_{ji} \,, \tag{19.7}$$

where $p_j(t)$ is the probability to be in state j at the immediately preceding time step and w_{ji} is the transition probability to go from state j to state i during the last step. The probability should be defined such that, at each time instance, $\sum_i p_i(t) = 1$, implying that

$$\sum_j w_{ij} = 1 \qquad \forall i \,. \tag{19.8}$$

Note how the term $p_i(t)w_{ii}$ in the sum of equation (19.7) is the probability that the process is already in state i at time t and remains there for another time step. The equation (19.7) is known as the *master equation* and, if rewritten as

$$p_i(t+1) - p_i(t) = \sum_j p_j(t)w_{ji} - \sum_j p_i(t)w_{ij} \,, \tag{19.9}$$

---

[2]The Markov chain theory is valid also in the case of infinite sets, but here we want to keep the discussion as simple as possible.

it easily allows us to calculate the continuous time limit[3]. The two ways of writing the master equation (19.7) and (19.9), are equivalent thanks to the normalization condition (19.8). Once the initial probability distribution is known, i.e., $p_i(0) \ \forall i$, thanks to the master equation, we can compute the probability to find the dynamical process in any state of the Markov chain at any time. The master equation (19.7) can be rewritten in a more compact way as the product of a probability vector and a transition matrix

$$\vec{p}(t+1) = \vec{p}(t) \cdot \hat{w} \ ,$$

where the vector $\vec{p}(t) \equiv \big(p_1(t), \ldots, p_N(t)\big)$ contains the entire probability distribution at time t and the matrix elements $\hat{w}$ are the transition probabilities w_{ij}. In this notation, it is easy to write the solution at time t, given the initial condition

$$\vec{p}(t) = \vec{p}(0) \cdot \hat{w}^t \ , \tag{19.10}$$

where $\hat{w}^t$ indicates the t-th power of the matrix $\hat{w}$.

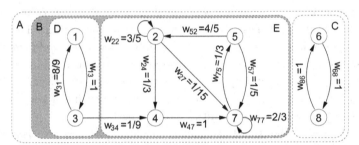

Fig. 19.2 Example of a Markov chain: the graph nodes represent the states and the directed edges the nonzero transition probabilities.

Let us give some more definitions about the Markov chains (Mc in short), based on the example given in Figure 19.2. The Mc A is *decomposable* in two Mc B and C, because no transition is possible between the states of B and those of C. Moreover, the Mc B is *reducible* to the Mc E, because, even if the dynamical process can move from the states of D to those of E, it is not possible to get back to D once it is in E. As a consequence, the probability to find the dynamical process in the states of D decreases towards zero as the number of process steps increases. Instead, the Mc E is

---

[3]To this purpose, we just need to substitute the time $(t+1)$ by $(t+dt)$, divide both members of the equation by dt and consider the w_{ij}/dt as the transition probabilities per time unit. In this way, we obtain, in the limit $dt \to 0$, the differential equation $\dot{p}_i(t) = \sum_j p_j(t) w_{ji} - \sum_j p_i(t) w_{ij}$.

irreducible. Indeed, for each couple of states of E, there exists a sequence of nonzero transition probabilities to go from one state to the other. For long times, the probability is concentrated only on the irreducible part of a Mc, which is hence the most interesting part to study.

Exercise 19.1 - Moving the probability towards irreducible chains.

Consider the Markov chain B in Figure 19.2. Compute how the probability to find the dynamical process in the reducible part, i.e., in one of the states 1 and 3, decreases. Use the master equation and consider the simplified case in which the total probability is initially concentrated in state 3, i.e., $p_3(0) = 1$.

Each state of a Mc can be classified according to their recurrence property, i.e., based on the probability that the dynamical process returns in that state after a large number of steps. We show some of these states, based on Figure 19.2. There exist *periodic* states, for which the return probability is non-zero only for times which are multiples of the period. The period of these periodic states in the Mc C is 2. There also exist *aperiodic* states, such as those in Mc B. Periodic states generally appear only in particular conditions. This is why we just consider the second type. Everything that is valid for aperiodic states is true also for periodic ones if the latter are observed at times which are multiples of the period.

The states of the Mc D are said to be *transient* because their return probability decays to zero at long times. Instead, those in the Mc E are said to be *ergodic* because they have nonzero return probability even in the large time limit. We are mostly interested in the latter, because they are the only ones the dynamical process can reach in the limit $t \to \infty$.

In an irreducible and ergodic Markov chain it is possible to go with nonzero probability from any state to any other. This is precisely what the *ergodicity* property entails in practice. It can be proven [Feller (1971); Grimmett and Stirzaker (2001)] that for such a chain the limit

$$\pi_i = \lim_{t \to \infty} p_i(t)$$

exists and does not depend on the initial condition $p_i(0)$. The vector $\vec{\pi} \equiv (\pi_1, \ldots, \pi_N)$ defines an asymptotic probability distribution, resolving an equation we can obtain from the master equation (19.7) in the long time limit

$$\pi_i = \sum_j \pi_j w_{ji} \, . \tag{19.11}$$

This equation tells us that the probability distribution $\vec{p}(t)$, evolving according to the master equation, does not change in time, once it has reached the asymptotic distribution $\vec{\pi}$. From that moment on, the dynamic process visits all states with the probability given by the time-independent distribution $\vec{\pi}$.

Exercise 19.2 - Asymptotic distribution of a Markov chain

Consider the irreducible and ergodic Markov chain, we indicated with E in Figure 19.2. Using equation (19.11), compute the asymptotic probability distribution $\vec{\pi}$ defined on the states of E.

It is important to stress the dualism we are using when describing the stochastic dynamic process. We can think of this process as a walker following a random route between the states, such that the transition probability from its current state to the next one is given by the w. Alternatively, we can consider the entire probability distribution $p_i(t)$ to find a walker in state i at time t and evolve this probability distribution in time, according to the master equation. The second description is more complete, as it already includes the average over all possible random choices the walker might make. Repeating the simulation of a walker many times, and measuring its position at time t, we can obtain the same information as from $p_i(t)$.

Nevertheless, from the numerical simulation viewpoint, computing the evolution of the entire probability distribution with a master equation is a very demanding task. Indeed, at each time step, it takes a number of operations $\mathcal{O}(d\,M)$, where d is the average degree of the graph corresponding to the Mc and M is the number of states of the chain (typically exponential in N in the interesting cases). Therefore, the only thing we can often do is to study the Markov chain by simulating the random walker. This takes, per time step, an average number of operations equal to the graph average degree (the random walker's possible choices). This is why we always advise to work with Markov chains whose average degree does not grow too much with the number N of problem variables.

19.2.2   *Convergence towards the asymptotic distribution*

The problem of convergence towards the asymptotic distribution is one of the most interesting and at the same time most delicate aspects in the study of Markov chains. Indeed, if we want to measure some properties of the asymptotic distribution $\vec{\pi}$, for example, an average like $\sum_i A_i \pi_i$, we cannot perform these measures as long as $\vec{p}(t) \neq \vec{\pi}$. In statistical mechanics, we talk about the *out-of-equilibrium* regime if $\vec{p}(t) \neq \vec{\pi}$. Instead, if the distribution has reached the asymptotic one, we talk about the *equilibrium* regime. From equation (19.11) it should be clear that starting from an equilibrium distribution, the dynamical systems always remains at equilibrium.

To study how a Mc converges towards its equilibrium it is useful to define a sort of distance between the current distribution and the asymptotic one. Two possible definitions of distance are

$$\delta_1(t) = \sum_i |p_i(t) - \pi_i| \quad \text{and} \quad \delta_2(t) = \sqrt{\sum_i \left(p_i(t) - \pi_i\right)^2} .$$

For our purposes these two definitions are perfectly equivalent.

Formally, we expect that during the evolution the distance $\delta(t)$ tends to zero. In practice, though, we always have to take into account that the computer representations of rational numbers are approximations, which might cause $\delta(t)$ not to really reach zero, but to settle at a very small value (possibly oscillating around it). This small value, which is fully equivalent to zero, is typically at most of the order of 10^{-6} if numbers of the `float` type are used and of the order of 10^{-15} for the `double` type, i.e., more or less one order of magnitude larger than the minimum representable number with the mantissa bits.

If we are studying a Markov chain with a random walker, we do not have direct access to the probability distribution $p_i(t)$. However, we can estimate the latter with time averages of the walker's position. More precisely, we can measure the walker's position in a time interval $[t, t + \Delta t]$ and estimate the probability $p_i(t)$ as the number of times the walker finds himself in the ith state divided by Δt. In Section 20.2 we discuss in detail how to perform the measurements when studying a Markov chain.

Hands on 19.1 - Convergence in a simple Markov chain

Consider the Markov chain indicated with B in Figure 19.2. Numerically study the convergence of the distribution $\vec{p}(t)$ to the asymptotic one $\vec{\pi}$ calculated in the Hands on 19.2. Try to use distributions which are completely concentrated around each one of the chain six states as initial conditions and compare these results. For example, plot their distance from the asymptotic distribution on a graph with logarithmic scale. Relate some of these results to those found in the Hands on 1. Explain the observed behavior when starting from the initial condition $p_1(0) = 0.001$ and $p_2(0) = 0.999$.

Repeat the study for a random walker moving on the same Markov chain. Measure various trajectories starting from each one of the chain six states. How long do two trajectories, starting from different states, "remember" the initial condition, i.e., are different? How "noisy" is the estimate of $p_i(t)$ resulting from this method compared to the one obtained before by evolving $\vec{p}(t)$ directly? How many time steps are needed to estimate the asymptotic distribution $\vec{\pi}$ with a given precision?

We can derive a chain decorrelation time, i.e., the time needed for a chain to "forget" its initial condition, more precisely. It can be proven that the absolute values of the eigenvalues of the matrix $\hat{w}$, whose elements are the transition probabilities w_{ij}, are all less than or equal to 1. Otherwise, the total probability of the entire chain would grow indefinitely throughout the dynamic evolution, contradicting the definition of a probability distribution for which we have (19.8). This probability conservation law also allows one to prove that the eigenvalue with largest absolute value is exactly $\lambda_1 = 1$. The equations (19.8) and (19.11) define the corresponding right, $r_i^{(1)} = 1$, and left, $\ell_i^{(1)} = \pi_i$ eigenvectors [Kuroš (1972)].

For simplicity, we assume the eigenvalues with the largest absolute value are distinct, real and positive: $1 > \lambda_2 > \lambda_3$. This occurs, for example, when there are no periodic modes in the dynamic evolution at very long times. If this is not the case, we simply need to add some terms to the following expressions, but the basic concepts remain the same. We develop, with standard techniques [Kuroš (1972)], the matrix $\hat{w}^t$ in terms of eigenvalues and (right and left) eigenvectors:

$$(\hat{w}^t)_{ji} = r_j^{(1)} \lambda_1^t \ell_i^{(1)} + r_j^{(2)} \lambda_2^t \ell_i^{(2)} + \mathcal{O}(\lambda_3^t) . \tag{19.12}$$

Thanks to the inequality $\lambda_3 < \lambda_2 < 1$, the terms of order $\mathcal{O}(\lambda_3^t)$ become negligible in the very long time limit, $t \to \infty$. By substituting $\lambda_1 = 1$, $r_i^{(1)} = 1$ and $\ell_i^{(1)} = \pi_i$ in (19.12), we obtain the expression

$$(\hat{w}^t)_{ji} = \pi_i + r_j^{(2)} \lambda_2^t \ell_i^{(2)} + \mathcal{O}(\lambda_3^t) .$$

If we insert this in equation (19.10), we get the long time behavior of the

ith component of the probability $\vec{p}(t)$,

$$p_i(t) = \sum_j p_j(0)\,(\hat{w}^t)_{ji} = \sum_j p_j(0)\pi_i + \sum_j p_j(0)r_j^{(2)}\,\lambda_2^t\,\ell_i^{(2)} + \mathcal{O}(\lambda_3^t) =$$

$$= \pi_i + \vec{p}(0)\cdot\vec{r}^{\,(2)}\,\lambda_2^t\,\ell_i^{(2)} + \mathcal{O}(\lambda_3^t)\ .$$

Given that $\lambda_2 < 1$, this equation tells us that, for sufficiently long times, the probability distribution $\vec{p}(t)$ tends to concentrate on the asymptotic one, $\vec{\pi}$, and the difference between the two tends towards zero exponentially with time:

$$p_i(t) - \pi_i \simeq B_i\,e^{-t/\tau}\ , \qquad \text{with} \qquad B_i = \left(\vec{p}(0)\cdot\vec{r}^{\,(2)}\right)\ell_i^{(2)}\ . \qquad (19.13)$$

While the asymptotic distribution $\vec{\pi}$ does not depend on the initial condition $\vec{p}(0)$, the coefficient B_i is proportional to the scalar product $\vec{p}(0)\cdot\vec{r}^{\,(2)}$ (we assume it to be nonzero). The equation (19.13) defines a decorrelation time equal to

$$\tau \equiv \frac{1}{-\log\left(|\lambda_2|\right)}\ .$$

We wrote this expression with the absolute value of the second eigenvalue, $|\lambda_2|$, because in this way it is generally valid for any matrix $\hat{w}$. Note that the decorrelation time diverges in the limit $|\lambda_2| \to 1$. In this limit, the distribution might converge very slowly towards the asymptotic distribution. For example, in the chain indicated by B in Figure 19.2 it is easy to calculate the second eigenvalue which is equal to $|\lambda_2| = \sqrt{1 - w_{34}}$. If the transition probability w_{34} is very small, the convergence time would diverge like $\tau \simeq 2/w_{34}$. This case is easy to interpret. Namely, the probability flux of the transient states, 1 and 3, towards the ergodic ones is very small. This makes the chains transient regime extremely long.

We give a second example of a slow converging chain without transient states in order to show that this is a widespread phenomenon which should always be taken into account. We study a Markov chain of M states forming a ring. The only possible transitions (all with the same probability) are those between first neighbors: $w_{i,i+1} = w_{i,i-1} = 1/2$. This chain asymptotic distribution is uniform over all M states, i.e., $\pi_i = 1/M \ \forall i$.

In Figure 19.3 we show how the distance from the asymptotic distribution diminishes with time in the case we start from a probability concentrated around one unique state. Even though the distance always decreases exponentially with time, we choose a log-log scale in order to clearly distinguish the three curves. A linear scale on the horizontal, and logarithmic

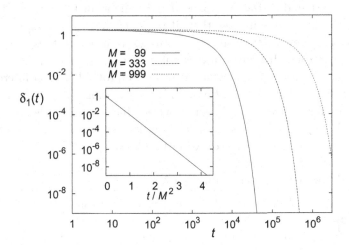

Fig. 19.3   Decreasing of the distance from the asymptotic distribution as a function of time for a linear M-state Markov chain. Insert: if we divide the times by M^2 the curves coincide perfectly.

scale on the vertical axis (lin-log), generally advised to represent an exponential behavior, would have squeezed the curves onto the vertical axis for the two smallest values of M, making them hardly visible. The graph clearly shows that the distance decreases in a way depending on the value of M. A parallel with the random walker problem (studied in Chapter 12) may help us to understand why the decorrelation time grows with M. This Markov chain random walker is exactly the random walker in one spatial dimension described in Section 12.1. Indeed, our random walker moves with with probability $1/2$ either one step to the right or one step to the left. This observation allows us to conclude that the decorrelation time should grow as M^2. The insert of Figure 19.3 shows the same three curves of the main plot. By dividing the time by M^2 they can no longer be distinguished from each other! In this case, we used the lin-log scale and the curves result to be straight lines.

In general, it is reasonable to expect that the decorrelation time from the initial condition (or the convergence time towards the asymptotic distribution) is, among others, linked to the maximum distance between two states of the chain, also called the *diameter*[4]. In the chain we just studied,

---

[4]More precisely, the concept of diameter is defined on a connected graph as the maximum distance between any two vertices of the graph.

two states situated at the antipodes of a ring lie at distance of $M/2$ steps from each other. This implies that, if no other factors slowing down the dynamics are present, the time it takes to go from one state to another is a function of their distance. In particular, the time is $\mathcal{O}(M)$ for a deterministic or ballistic motion (which is rather improbable for an interesting Mc) and $\mathcal{O}(M^2)$ for a stochastic or Brownian motion. Therefore, keep in mind that, for a given Markov chain whose diameter, i.e., the maximum distance between two states, is equal to d, it is reasonable to expect that the relaxation time is at least of the order $\mathcal{O}(d^2)$.

Hands on 19.2 - Oscillations in a Markov chain

A careful reader may have noticed that in Figure 19.3 we only used odd values for the number M of states. The reason is that we wanted to avoid a problem of periodic oscillations between the states of the chain (irrelevant for the study of the convergence). Repeat the study of the same Markov chain for even values of M. Which periodic oscillations are generated in the chain? Using $\pi_i = 1/M$, to what value do the distances $\delta_1(t)$ and $\delta_2(t)$ converge? If the asymptotic value of these distances is nonzero, try to understand why this is so by studying the distribution to which $p_i(t)$ is converging and compare it to the expected one π_i.

The above questions can be answered even without carrying out a numerical study. Try to solve it using only pen and paper before moving to the computer.

19.2.3 *Detailed balance*

We now turn back to the original problem, described at the beginning of Section 19.2. Namely, summing over an enormous number of configurations C with a probability distribution $P(C)$ which is very concentrated around a small subset of these, as in equation (19.6).

We can transform this problem in a Markov chain whose states are the configurations over which we need to sum and whose asymptotic distribution is $\pi_i = P(C_i)$, where C_i indicates the configuration corresponding to the chain ith state. If we manage to build a Markov chain with these properties, we can estimate the sum in equation (19.6) as follows. We simulate a random walker on this Markov chain (the entire distribution cannot be followed because the number of states is too large) for a time t_{eq} which is sufficiently large to reach the equilibrium. In this situation, the walker visits the states precisely with probability π_i. Therefore, the following approximation is valid

$$\sum_C A(C)P(C) \simeq \frac{1}{t_{\max} - t_{\text{eq}}} \sum_{t=t_{\text{eq}}+1}^{t_{\max}} A(C_{i(t)}) \,,$$

where $i(t)$ indicates the walker's state at time t.

The only thing we still need to do, is to create a Markov chain with the proper asymptotic distribution $\vec{\pi}$. There are many ways to choose the transition probabilities w_{ij} generating the same asymptotic distribution. All these choices must satisfy the equation (19.11) which can be rewritten as the so-called *balance equation*

$$0 = \pi_i - \sum_j \pi_j w_{ji} = \sum_j (\pi_i w_{ij} - \pi_j w_{ji}) \quad \forall i \,. \tag{19.14}$$

The simplest choice solving equation (19.14) consists in setting each term between brackets to zero, thus obtaining the so-called *detailed balance equation*

$$\pi_i \, w_{ij} = \pi_j \, w_{ji} \quad \forall i, j \,. \tag{19.15}$$

Equation (19.15) still admits many solutions. For example:

$$\begin{cases} w_{ij} = \pi_j \\ w_{ji} = \pi_i \,, \end{cases} \quad \begin{cases} w_{ij} = 1/\pi_i \\ w_{ji} = 1/\pi_j \,, \end{cases} \quad \begin{cases} w_{ij} = 1 \\ w_{ji} = \pi_i/\pi_j \,, \end{cases} \quad \begin{cases} w_{ij} = \pi_j/\pi_i \\ w_{ji} = 1 \,. \end{cases} \tag{19.16}$$

Not all of these choices are acceptable though. Indeed, let us not forget that the normalization condition, $\sum_j w_{ij} = 1$, should be valid for each state i. Moreover, we note that the detailed balance equation (19.15) is always satisfied for $i = j$: $\pi_i w_{ii} = \pi_i w_{ii}$. As a consequence, we can freely choose w_{ii}, i.e., the probability to remain in the current state.

The first of the four solutions in equation (19.16) can always be created by choosing, for each state i, the following transition probabilities

$$w_{ij} = \pi_j \quad \forall j \neq i \quad \text{and} \quad w_{ii} = 1 - \sum_{j \neq i} w_{ij} = 1 - \sum_{j \neq i} \pi_j \,, \tag{19.17}$$

where w_{ii} is certainly nonnegative thanks to the normalization condition of $\vec{\pi}$. The second solution in equation (19.16) cannot be created, because the inverse of a probability distribution is not a probability distribution ($w_{ij} = 1/\pi_i \geq 1$ and it is not normalized). Finally, the third solution can be created only if $\pi_i < \pi_j$. If not, the fourth solution is to be used. So, the third and the fourth solution can be used together, but with some extra precautions studied in Section 19.2.4.

The other important choice when building a Markov chain concerns the connectivity of the corresponding graph, i.e., the number of states j to which we have access from a state i, i.e., such that $w_{ij} > 0$. A high connectivity allows one to obtain a chain with small diameter, such that the probability $\vec{p}(t)$ diffuses faster along the chain. The other way around, a low connectivity is preferable when considering the computation time per single step, as the number of operations per time step is proportional to the average degree. In general, a good compromise between these two contrasting demands is achieved with a limited average degree or at most of the order $\mathcal{O}(\log M)$, where M is the number of states of the Markov chain. In Section 19.3 we give a concrete example of a Markov chain, clarifying this choice better.

19.2.4   *The Metropolis algorithm*

Even if formally correct (it generates the correct $\vec{\pi}$), the simple choice for the transition probability given in equation (19.17) presents a big shortcoming related to the convergence time. As the π_i are very small (remember that the probabilities are distributed over an enormous amount of states), the w_{ii} result to be very close to 1, causing the random walker to remain most of the time in its current state! Those who are not yet convinced, may try to study the simple M-state Markov chain arranged on a ring with $\pi_i = 1/M$ and compare the results with those shown in Figure 19.3. Choosing the transition probability as in equation (19.17) with $j = i \pm 1$, the dynamical process result to be slower by a factor $M/2$, with respect to what is obtained with $w_{i,i+1} = w_{i,i-1} = 1/2$.

So, an important suggestion is to make the random walker move as much as possible, such as to visit, for a fixed number of steps, the largest number of different states. To this purpose, it is useful to reduce the values of the probabilities w_{ii} of remaining in a state. The Metropolis [Metropolis *et al.* (1953)] algorithm manages to do this. Actually, this is not the main reason why it was introduced in 1953: the main advantage, making the Metropolis algorithm more efficient than others, is that, upon its execution, at each step we need to compute only two probabilities π_i and π_j. As the computation of these probabilities is very heavy, the advantage is clear.

Assuming that at time t the walker is in state i, the *Metropolis algorithm* consists of two stages:

(1) during the first stage, a new state j is *proposed*, randomly chosen according to a symmetric probability u_{ij}, i.e., such that $u_{ij} = u_{ji}$;

(2) during the second stage, the new state j is *accepted* with a probability equal to $\min(1, \pi_j/\pi_i)$ (in this case, the walker moves to the state j at time $t + 1$), otherwise the new state is *rejected* (and the walker remains in the state i also at time $t + 1$).

So, the walker is certain to move if the new proposed state has a higher probability than the current one. Otherwise, the walker only moves with a probability given by the ratio of the states probabilities. As a consequence, it is unlikely that the walker moves onto states with a tiny probability.

Let us analyze the behavior of this important algorithm. We calculate the transition probabilities and verify whether the detailed balance equation is satisfied. Combining the probabilities appearing in the two stages, the transition probability to go from state i to state j is given by

$$w_{ij} = u_{ij} \min\left(1, \frac{\pi_j}{\pi_i}\right) , \tag{19.18}$$

i.e., the probability that state j is proposed, multiplied by the probability that it is also accepted. Inserting the expression (19.18) in the detailed balance equation (19.15), we find that

$$\pi_i \, u_{ij} \min\left(1, \frac{\pi_j}{\pi_i}\right) = \pi_j \, u_{ji} \min\left(1, \frac{\pi_i}{\pi_j}\right) .$$

It is easy to see this equation is correct once the terms u_{ij} and u_{ji}, which are equal to each other by definition, have been canceled out.

The only really delicate aspect when simulating the Metropolis algorithm is the choice of the probabilities u_{ij}. First of all, this probabilities should obey the general rule regarding a Markov chain connectivity, as explained at the end of Section 19.2.3. Moreover, we need to keep the *mean acceptance rate*, i.e., the *average acceptance probability* per time step, under control. The latter is indicated by P_{Acc} and defined as the fraction of proposed moves finally accepted. A golden rule when using the Metropolis algorithm advises to maintain

$$P_{\text{Acc}} \simeq \frac{1}{2} . \tag{19.19}$$

An intuitive explanation of this rule can be given assuming that the function $P(C)$ (to which the Markov chain is converging) is a sufficiently regular function of the configurations C and that the latter belong to a geometric space, where a distance between the configurations is defined. Suppose we are in configuration C_i and we randomly choose the new configuration C_j among those at a fixed distance R from the configuration C_i. We expect the acceptance probability to be a decreasing function in R (Figure 19.4). Indeed, for very small R, we have that $P(C_j) \simeq P(C_i)$, the new configuration is almost always accepted and $P_{\text{Acc}} \simeq 1$. Instead, for large values of R the choice of the new configuration is almost random. So, the possibility to choose a state with a probability which is significantly different from zero, is low.

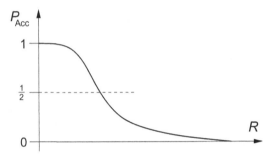

Fig. 19.4   A possible behavior of the average probability to accept a new configuration at a distance R from the current one, with the Metropolis algorithm.

So, we need to avoid, as much as possible, the choices of u_{ij} connecting states with very different probability in order to avoid P_{Acc} to have too many small values and for the walker not to accept any new state. At the same time, even if it might seem less intuitive, it is good practice, to avoid choices producing $P_{\text{Acc}} \simeq 1$. If every newly proposed configuration is accepted, the walker is moving through the configuration space by steps that are too small, and we could have increased the exploration speed with more "risky" choices, i.e., by proposing configurations differing more from the current one. The rule proposed in equation (19.19) is a good compromise, but we should not adhere to it in a too strict way. Values of $P_{\text{Acc}} \in [0.3, 0.7]$ are perfectly acceptable for the majority of practical applications. In Section 19.3 we discuss a first application of the Metropolis algorithm.

Hands on 19.3 - Convergence of the Metropolis algorithm

 Consider a Markov chain whose states are all integer numbers (in theory, these form an infinite set, but the exercise shows this is not a problem) and whose asymptotic distribution is proportional to a Gaussian distribution with zero mean: $\pi_j \propto \exp\left(-(j/\sigma)^2/2\right)$. The walker starts at the origin and moves with the Metropolis algorithm. At each step, a new state is chosen uniformly within a distance R of the currently occupied state. Study the convergence to the asymptotic value of a relevant quantity, such as the walker's mean square displacement, $\langle r^2 \rangle - \langle r \rangle^2$, which should more or less converge to σ^2 (small deviations from this value are due to the discretization of the configuration space). Verify how the convergence time to the asymptotic value varies with the choice of R and has a minimum for the values of R with about $P_{\text{Acc}} \simeq 0.5$. Use a value of σ allowing you to move from a regime where $R \ll \sigma$ to one where $R \gg \sigma$. We suggest, for instance, that $\sigma = 100$, with R varying logarithmically between 1 and 10^5, i.e., $R = 1, 10, 10^2, 10^3, 10^4, 10^5$.

19.2.5 *Barriers ad ergodicity breaking*

We conclude the study of the Markov chains by focusing once more on the problem of their convergence towards the equilibrium distribution. The problem of ergodicity breaking we discuss in this section, is often studied in connection with a specific model (especially those used in statistical mechanics). However, it is a much more general phenomenon, which we therefore study at the level of generic Markov chains.

Let us start from a concrete example. Suppose we have a Markov chain defined on integer numbers and we want the asymptotic probability distribution to be the sum of two Gaussians with unit variance, one centered in $-L$ and the other in L. For simplicity, we only allow for transitions between nearest neighbor states, i.e., between number differing by one. In the simulation, we obviously use the most efficient algorithm among those we know at present, namely the Metropolis algorithm.

In the three plots on top of Figure 19.5 we show the random walker's position, initially starting from the origin, for the first 10^4 steps and for three different values of L. For $L = 2$ the walker goes relatively easily between the two maxima of the distribution. Instead, for $L = 3$ the time between jumps among maxima is already of the order of a thousand of steps (11 crossovers $L \leftrightarrow -L$ can clearly be identified). Finally, for $L = 4$, the walker remains during all the 10^4 steps around the Gaussian maximum with negative average. In the latter case, we need to extend the simulation and consider much longer times in order for the walker to visit both regions where the probability $\vec{\pi}$ is sensibly different from zero.

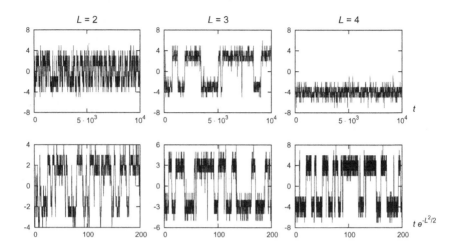

Fig. 19.5   A random walker's position in a Markov chain with an asymptotic probability distribution concentrated in L and $-L$, for three values of L. In the three plots on the bottom, the times are multiplied by a factor $e^{-L^2/2}$.

The cause of this behavior is relatively simple. Any trajectory moving the walker from one maximum of $\vec{\pi}$ to the other one must go through regions where the asymptotic probability is extremely small. In this particular case, this statement might seem obvious and predictable (we are working in one dimension and to go from $-L$ to L or vice versa we need to go through the origin). However, this is general valid also in more complicated cases, such as when dealing with multidimensional integration domains.

In the simple case of the two Gaussian distributions centered in L and $-L$ the asymptotic distribution is

$$\pi_j \propto e^{-(j+L)^2/2} + e^{-(j-L)^2/2} \ .$$

In this case we can estimate the time needed by the walker to go from the negative to the positive states. Going from negative to positive values (and the other way around) only occurs when the walker is at the origin and continues in the opposite direction with respect to where he came from. While the second of these events occurs with probability $1/2$, the first one has probability $\pi_0 = \mathcal{O}(e^{-L^2/2})$. So, this event only occurs every $\tau = 1/\pi_0$ steps and we expect the walker to move from one maximum to the other each $\mathcal{O}(e^{L^2/2})$ time steps.

This argument is formally correct, only in the limit $L \to \infty$ where the probability π_0 tends to zero and the relaxation time diverges. Nevertheless, also for small values of L this leads to excellent results. Indeed, in the lower plots of Figure 19.5 we changed the time scales by a multiplicative factor $\exp(-L^2/2)$, as shown along the horizontal axes. The three resulting curves are very similar (apart from larger fluctuations in the case $L = 2$, where the separation between the maxima is too small to clearly show the effect).

Often, the term *barrier* is used to indicate the region where $\vec{\pi}$ is very small; the random walker needs many attempts to actually cross it.

Please note that in the upper right panel of Fig. 19.5 the number of steps in our simulation were not chosen accurately. Indeed, we cannot be sure to have overcome all barriers in the Markov chain under study. By looking at that plot, we might believe to have reached the asymptotic state, though the walker is only visiting half of the true asymptotic distribution relevant states. Sometimes, the only way to make sure the entire Markov chain has been visited is to increase the length of the numerical simulation. In Section 20.2.1 we explain in greater detail how to study the convergence towards equilibrium of a Markov chain Monte Carlo method.

For any value of L the Markov chain we studied in this section is ergodic, i.e., it is possible to move from any state to any other one (even though the time needed might be very long in some cases). On the contrary, in the limit $L \to \infty$, the relaxation time τ really diverges and the chain decomposes into two subchains, one consisting of the positive states and the other of the negative ones. Indeed, in the limit $L \to \infty$ an *ergodicity breaking* occurs.

Hands on 19.4 - Barrier crossing times

Consider a Markov chain with an asymptotic distribution consisting of two Gaussian distributions centered in L and $-L$ and a barrier around the origin. We just saw that, for the Metropolis algorithm, the transition from one side of the barrier to the other occurs each $\tau = \mathcal{O}(e^{L^2/2})$ steps, i.e., it is a rare dynamical process for large L. Moreover, when this event takes place, it is very quick, as is clear from the rightmost plot on the bottom of Figure 19.5.

Study numerically the time it takes to cross a barrier. To this purpose, compute the length of the random walker's trajectories starting from the position $-L$ and reaching the position L without ever going by the position $-L$ again, and the length of those following the opposite path. Considering that these trajectories last at least $2L$ steps, you should be able to conclude from this analysis, that when the walker decides to cross the barrier, he does so without any delays, following an almost ballistic trajectory!

The system showing ergodicity breaking we have discussed here is very simple. Indeed, it is not difficult to figure out that a different choice of the probabilities u_{ij}, i.e., a different connectivity between the states, can avoid the ergodicity breaking phenomenon. For example, by including the transitions which are symmetric with respect to the origin, i.e., $j \leftrightarrow -j$, among the allowed ones, all dynamical phenomena we described in this section (from the slowing down due to the barrier to the ergodicity breaking) vanish. The transition $j \leftrightarrow -j$ represents a kind of shortcut around the barrier eliminating all these effects. Note how the transition between two states which are symmetric with respect to the origin is always accepted in the Metropolis algorithm, because these states have the same asymptotic probability, $\pi_j = \pi_{-j}$.

The search for these "shortcuts" is one of the most interesting aspects in the development of Markov chain Monte Carlo algorithms. Unfortunately, for more complicated systems than the one discussed in this section, the shortcuts are not at all obvious. For example, the so-called "cluster" algorithms [Newman and Barkema (1999)] do apply some kind of shortcut, but only because of a deep knowledge of the physical-mathematical properties of the Ising model, described in Section 19.3.

19.3   The Ising model

The Ising model is characterized by a set of binary variables placed at the vertices of a regular lattice. These variables are called *spins* because in a typical application of the model they represent elementary magnetic moments. In this section, we study the model defined on a two-dimensional square lattice, such as the one in Figure 19.6. The spins of nearest neighboring vertices, i.e., those connected by an edge, interact with each other, by means of a ferromagnetic interaction attempting to align thse two spins in the same direction. The energy of a configuration $s \equiv (s_1, \ldots, s_N)$ of the system N spins is given by

$$E(s) = - \sum_{(i,j)} J\, s_i\, s_j \ . \tag{19.20}$$

In the expression (19.20) the spin variables can only take on two values $s_i = \pm 1$, the sum is over the pairs of indices $i, j \in \{1, \ldots, N\}$ corresponding to adjacent vertices and the coupling constant[5] J is positive, because the

---

[5]The symbol J we use for the coupling constant should not be confused with the one of the Joule, the measurement unit of energy (which might might actually be the

ferromagnetic interaction fosters the alignment of the spins. The minus sign preceding the sum is needed because the preferred configurations in nature are those minimizing the energy. Indeed, two aligned spins have energy $-J$, while two spins in the opposite direction have energy $+J$. It is easy to generalize this model to other interaction topologies. We can take any graph, place spins on its vertices and have each couple of spins connected by an edge to interact with a coupling term $-Js_is_j$.

We follow the advice of Section 10.4 to use in a simulation the simplest measurement units. As the energy (19.20) is an integer multiple of J (which is typically a small number for real materials), we decide to use precisely J as the measurement unit for the energies. Therefore, we substitute J by 1 in the expression (19.20), keeping in mind that an energy equal to, e.g., -1.73 in our simulation corresponds to an energy of $-1.73\,J$ in the original model.

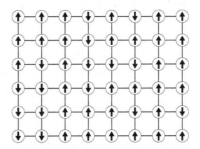

Fig. 19.6   The Ising model on a square two-dimensional lattice.

This model is important in many scientific fields because, even though it is very simply defined (or maybe, exactly thanks to this), and it can be adapted in order to describe very different phenomena. Lenz and Ising introduced this model for the first time in 1924 to study the phenomenon of ferromagnetism. Nevertheless, the model can easily describe a lattice gas of interacting particles (in Section 12.3 we study the case of a non-interacting lattice gas) or the percolation phenomenon (see Chapter 13). Making some small changes, the model can describe very different phenomena, such as the diffusion of an epidemic, how public opinions form or how to reconstruct a black and white picture, damaged by a random noise which inverted the color of some of its pixels (and these are only few among the many possible applications).

---

measurement unit of the coupling constant J, which is an energy).

Another important aspect of these models is the fact that in two spatial dimensions (and more generally for planar graphs) a rigorous analytical solution exists, even if the two-dimensional model presents a nontrivial phase transition. As explained at the beginning of Chapter 20, the phase transitions cover an important role in nature, so to study them it is important to have models which can be mathematically solved. Most of the time, though, a phase transition can only be studied by means of numerical simulations.

In this case we exploit the Ising model analytical results to verify whether the code we write is correct. This is a common procedure. For example, if we just wrote a Monte Carlo program to study a new model which has not yet been analyzed by anybody, we cannot be sure that the results of our simulation reflect the model true behavior, rather than being an artifact of some programming errors. The standard procedure is to verify the program for some particular cases (by changing the code as little as possible!), and compare the numerical results with analytical solutions or previous numeric results (better if obtained by somebody else and with a different code).

In the Ising model, we can associate macroscopic variables (i.e., experimentally observable ones) to each configuration s of microscopic variables (the spins). These macroscopic variables might be the magnetization and the energy which play an important role:

$$m(s) = \frac{M(s)}{N} = \frac{1}{N}\sum_{i=1}^{N} s_i \,, \qquad e(s) = \frac{E(s)}{N} = -\frac{1}{N}\sum_{(i,j)} s_i s_j \,.$$

In general, we use uppercase letters for *extensive* quantities, i.e., quantities which are proportional to the number of model variables, and lowercase letters for the *intensive* ones. The latter tend towards a finite value for $N \to \infty$, i.e., in the so-called *thermodynamic limit* in which the model number of variables increases enormously.

We can easily convince ourselves that $m \in [-1,1]$ and $e \in [-2,2]$ for the model defined on a two-dimensional lattice. The two configurations with all parallel spins have the maximum magnetization, $|m| = 1$, and are fully sorted, i.e., have all satisfied interactions, from which $e = -2$. In nature, physical systems tend to "relax" towards minimum energy states if the temperature is sufficiently low. Instead, at high temperatures, the thermal fluctuations make higher energy configurations probable. To study the properties of the model at temperature T we use the canonical ensemble [Huang (1987)] where each configuration s of N spins has a weight equal to the Gibbs-Boltzmann measure[6]

$$P_{\mathrm{GB}}(\boldsymbol{s}) = \frac{e^{-E(\boldsymbol{s})/T}}{Z} \ , \quad \text{with} \quad Z = \sum_{\boldsymbol{s}} e^{-E(\boldsymbol{s})/T} \ . \tag{19.21}$$

A better known example of this ensemble is the ideal gas at temperature T, in which the molecule velocity follow the Maxwell-Boltzmann distribution

$$P(\vec{v}) \propto e^{-\frac{m|\vec{v}|^2}{2k_B T}} \ ,$$

which is of the form (19.21), if we consider that the energy of a non-interacting moleculeis just its kinetic energy $m|\vec{v}|^2/2$. From expression (19.21), we see that in the high temperature limit, $T \to \infty$, all configurations have the same probability, while in the zero temperature limit, $T \to 0$, the probability distribution is concentrated around the two configurations with minimum energy. The average over the canonical ensemble at temperature T of a generic observable quantity $A(\boldsymbol{s})$ is given by

$$\langle A \rangle_T = \frac{\sum_{\boldsymbol{s}} A(\boldsymbol{s}) e^{-E(\boldsymbol{s})/T}}{\sum_{\boldsymbol{s}} e^{-E(\boldsymbol{s})/T}} = \sum_{\boldsymbol{s}} A(\boldsymbol{s}) P_{\mathrm{GB}}(\boldsymbol{s}) \ , \tag{19.22}$$

where the sum is over all 2^N system configurations.

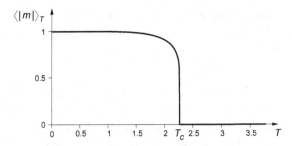

Fig. 19.7   The magnetization of the Ising model on a square lattice.

The mean of the magnetization absolute value in the thermodynamic limit $(N \to \infty)$ in the two-dimensional Ising model is plotted in Figure 19.7. At the critical temperature $T_c = 2/\log(1 + \sqrt{2}) \simeq 2.269$ the model undergoes a phase transition, going from the paramagnetic phase $(T > T_c)$ where

---

[6]In order to use practical measurement units in the simulation, we also fix the Boltzmann constant, k_B, to 1. So, a temperature of 2.5 in the simulation is equivalent to one of $2.5\,k_B/J$ in the physical model.

$\langle |m| \rangle_T$ is zero to the ferromagnetic one $(T < T_c)$ where the system develops a nonzero magnetization equal to

$$\langle |m| \rangle_T - m_0(T) = \left(1 - \left(\operatorname{\sinh} \left(\frac{2}{T} \right) \right)^{-4} \right)^{\frac{1}{8}} . \qquad (19.23)$$

This magnetization can be observed in experiments. For example, it is the one remaining in a piece of iron after it has been placed in contact with a magnet.

It is useful to note that in the Ising model, for $T < T_c$, there exists a kind of barrier between the configurations with positive magnetization and those with negative magnetization. This might cause an ergodicity breaking as explained in Section 19.2.5. In order to visualize how this barrier forms, we can approximate the Gibbs-Boltzmann distribution by putting together all configurations with the same magnetization, m, and associating to this magnetization a probability $\mathcal{P}(m)$ equal to the sum of the weights of all configurations with magnetization m:

$$\mathcal{P}(m) \equiv \sum_{\substack{s: \\ \sum_i s_i = Nm}} P_{\mathrm{GB}}(s) .$$

The typical value of the magnetization corresponds to the maximum of $\mathcal{P}(m)$. The other values of m are much more rare and their probability is generally inversely proportional to the exponential of the number N of variables. This is why the *Landau free energy*, defined by

$$f(m) \equiv -\frac{T \log (\mathcal{P}(m))}{N} ,$$

has a well-defined limit for $N \to \infty$ and its minima correspond to the most probable values of m. A free energy value higher than the one of the minimum indicates a very unprobable magnetization. In Figure 19.8 we schematically show the Landau free energy in the Ising model: for $T < T_c$ it has two minima in $m = \pm m_0(T)$ and a barrier in between. In a dynamical process where only one spin at a time can be inverted (and, thus, m changes in a continuous way, without any jump) the main effect of the barrier is that it makes very difficult the passage from positive to negative magnetizations and vice versa.

The exact solution of the Ising model, i.e., the computation of any mean of the type (19.22), takes a number of operations proportional to 2^N, i.e., exponential in N. Fortunately, we can follow an alternative road. The sum (19.22) defining the average at a given temperature T is exactly of the type

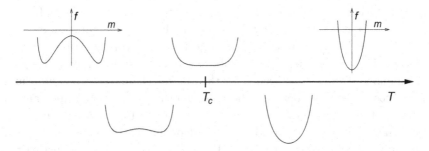

Fig. 19.8 A diagram showing how the profile of the Landau free energy $f(m)$ changes in the Ising model as the temperature is varied.

(19.6) which we know how to integrate with the Monte Carlo method. We just need to choose $P_{\mathrm{GB}}(s)$ to be the Markov chain asymptotic distribution.

We apply the Metropolis algorithm and propose, at each step, a new configuration differing only by a single spin from the current one[7]. This choice is called a *single spin flip* dynamics. In this way, each configuration can be changed in N different ways, depending on which spin variable is chosen. For simplicity, we choose this variable randomly among the N the model consists of.

It is useful to imagine the configurational space as a hypercube in N spatial dimensions (this is why we are dealing with a numeric integration in many dimensions). The 2^N vertices of the hypercube are the model configurations and the edges connect nearest neighbor configurations, i.e., those differing only by a single spin flip. Thus, each vertex is connected to other N vertices.

Before explaining how to write the program, we summarize what we need to do at each time step of the Monte Carlo simulation with the Metropolis algorithm for the Ising model. Let us call s the current configuration.

(1) We randomly choose a spin, s_i, among the N of the model and propose, as a new configuration, s' differing from s only in the value of the spin s_i.

(2) We compute the difference in energy, $\Delta E = E(s') - E(s)$.

(3) If $\Delta E \leq 0$ we accept the new configuration and the time step is finished.

---

[7]The simultaneously flipping of more than one spin generally causes too large variations in energy to be accepted, at least if we do not use a so-called "cluster" algorithm [Newman and Barkema (1999)].

(4) Otherwise, we extract a random number r uniformly in $[0, 1]$:
- if $r \leq \exp(-\Delta E/T)$ we accept the new configuration s';
- if $r > \exp(-\Delta E/T)$ we reject the new configuration.

Considering we need to repeat the above listed operations many times (i e , the number of time steps needed for the Markov chain to reach equilibrium plus those needed to perform the measurements) it is very important to optimize the corresponding lines of code. In Section 19.4 we use the function performing one step of the Metropolis algorithm or the Ising model as a prototype of code to be optimized. However, before reading any further try to do the Hands on 19.5.

Hands on 19.5 - The Metropolis algorithm applied to the Ising model

 Write a function (even if not particularly efficient) carrying out one time step of the Metropolis algorithm for a two-dimensional Ising model. Next, include a second function, computing the magnetization and the energy of the spins configuration. Consider a 10×10 or 20×20 lattice. Starting from a random configuration, study how the magnetization and the energy change with the the number of executed steps. In Section 20.2 we describe in more detail how to study the Ising model.

19.4   Code optimization

In Listing 19.1 we write a function performing one time step of the Metropolis algorithm or the Ising model defined on a generic graph.

The graph is represented by an adjacency list (see Section 17.2.2) stored in the structure of the type `graphStruct`:

```
typedef struct {
  int numNodes, numLinks, *conn, **neigh;
} graphStruct;
```

The spins configuration is kept in the array `s[]`. First of all, we note that the function `oneStep` does not contain any call to other functions and the number of conditional statements is kept as low as possible, as these elements slow down the program execution. As explained in Section 2.4, when a function is called the program execution makes a jump. In practice, the content of the processor registers is copied onto a stack. The processor then executes the machine code corresponding to the function, and once it has finished executing this function, the status of the processor is restored with the stack content.

```
1 void oneStep(int *s, graphStruct *pGraph, float *prob) {
2   int j, site, *pNeigh, siteConn, sum;
3
4   site = (int)(FRANDOM * pGraph->numNodes);
5   pNeigh = pGraph->neigh[site];
6   siteConn = pGraph->conn[site];
7   sum = 0;
8   for (j = 0; j < siteConn; j++, pNeigh++) {
9     sum += s[*pNeigh];
10  }
11  sum *= s[site];
12  if (sum <= 0 || FRANDOM < prob[sum]) {
13    s[site] = -s[site];
14  }
15 }
```

Listing 19.1 The function performing one step of the Metropolis algorithm for the Ising model on a generic graph.

So, calling a function is rather expensive in terms of execution time, compared to the sequential execution of the same statements. Considering that the code readability is one of the main reasons causing us to often use functions, we immediately note that sometimes the requirements of an optimized code are in contrast with those of a maximally comprehensible code. Our aim should be to optimize the code while keeping it comprehensible. To this purpose, the use of comments and explanations in optimized code is essential.

Excessive use of selection structures may cause the execution to slow down, because it does not allow the compiler to organize the statements in an optimal sequence. Indeed, upon compilation, the truth value of the expression in the selection structure is not known. As a consequence, neither are the statements which should be following. By paying a little attention, useless selection structures can be avoided. The following lines of code, where the variable s only takes the values 1 and −1,

```
if (s == 1) {
  a = 2 * b;
} else {
  a = 2 * c;
}
```

can be substituted by the statement a = (b + c) + s * (b - c), providing the same result without using a selection structure.

Let us now briefly explain the code of Listing 19.1. On line 4 the function oneStep randomly chooses a vertex of the graph. The expression FRANDOM is a macro generating a random number uniformly distributed in $[0, 1)$. This expression can be substituted with your preferred pseudorandom number generator, paying attention to the fact that this generator should never return the value 1, since in that case site may take on an invalid value (in a vector of N elements, the index of the last element is $N - 1$).

To compute the difference in energy ΔE between the proposed and the current configuration, we just need to add the contributions of the terms in (19.20) containing the variable s_i we propose to flip,

$$\Delta E = - \sum_{j \in V(i)} \Delta s_i\, s_j = 2 s_i \sum_{j \in V(i)} s_j \,, \qquad (19.24)$$

where $\Delta s_i = -2 s_i$ for a spin flip and $V(i)$ represents the set of nearest neighbors of i. In function oneStep of Listing 19.1 the variable sum is first used to compute the sum $\sum_{j \in V(i)} s_j$ (lines 7-10) and then, from line 11 onward, to store the value of $\Delta E/2$.

The construct if on line 12 checks whether one of the two sufficient conditions to accept the newly proposed configuration is verified. In case it is, the spin s[site] is flipped (line 13). Otherwise, the execution returns to the calling function without changing the configuration of the spins.

The two conditions to accept the new configuration (line 12) are $\Delta E \le 0$, corresponding to the expression sum <= 0, or $r \le \exp(-\Delta E/T)$ which we wrote as FRANDOM < prob[sum]. Note that the order of the conditions guarantees that, if the new configuration has been accepted because $\Delta E \le 0$, no random number is extracted (thus saving time). Moreover, we can use the variable sum in the second condition on line 12 as an index of the array prob[]. Indeed, when the program starts to read prob[sum] the first condition is false and the variable sum certainly takes a positive integer value.

19.4.1   *Use of look-up tables*

We now discuss the form of the second condition of line 12 in more detail. As before, the macro FRANDOM represents a random number in $[0, 1)$, while in the array prob[] we list the values the expression $\exp(-\Delta E/T)$ might take on. Because of the discrete nature of the variable ΔE, the expression $\exp(-\Delta E/T)$ can only take a finite number of different values. Given that sum equals $\Delta E/2$, we just need to assign prob[i] = exp(-2.0 * i

/ `temperature`) once at the beginning of the program. In programming jargon, the array `prob[]` is called a *look-up table* (LUT). This trick is very important because it allows one to save a lot of time during program execution. Indeed, computing the exponential is a complex operation, requiring several elementary operations. Substituting it with a simpler operation, namely the reading a vector element, is always strongly advised any time the argument takes not too many different values.

The same applies for any complex function. Think for example of all complex mathematical functions, whose computation is more demanding than reading an array. Moreover, in the case the LUT is rather short, it is probably kept in the processor most internal registers, because it is frequently used. In these cases, reading the elements of the LUT does not imply any data transfer from the memory to the processor registers, and is therefore an extremely efficient operation (in the example of Listing 19.1 the length of the array `prob[]` is equal to the graph maximum degree).

19.4.2   *Update in random or sequential order*

In a Monte Carlo simulation, the number of time steps needed before the Markov chain reaches equilibrium, increases at least linearly with the number N of the variables of the system under study. Moreover, it is reasonable to expect that the model dynamical behavior (for instance, the relaxation time to reach equilibrium) depends on the number of updates *per* variable. This is why, the simulation time is usually expressed in terms of *Monte Carlo Sweeps* (MCS): one MCS is equivalent to attempt to updating each system variable once, i.e., to N time steps on the Markov chain.

As the times of the Monte Carlo simulation are counted in terms of MCS, it is convenient to substitute the function `oneStep` of Listing 19.1 with a similar function `oneSweep` executing N times the same identical operations contained in the function `oneStep`, thus saving $N - 1$ calls to the main function per MCS. This function `oneSweep` updates the variables in a random order, given that the variable `site` is randomly generated each time. With this type of update, the number of times, a spin is visited in t MCS is a random variable with mean t. For long times, this does not create any problems, but for small times, the dynamics might be different from the one where all spins are updated exactly once during each MCS (take this into account when you want to study precisely the early times dynamics). The advantage of updating in a random order is that no periodic asymptotic regime can set in. Instead, the price we pay is that at each MCS we need to extract N extra pseudorandom numbers. On the contrary, in a sequential update the variables are visited in the order in which the graph vertices are numbered. In Listing 19.2 we present a possible function performing an MCS with this latter type of update.

In the function `oneSweepSeq` the variable `site` scrolls through the N system variables in sequential order (in the program N has been stored in the variable `pGraph->numNodes`). This sequential update has two advantages compared to the random order update. First of all, we do not have to generate N pseudorandom numbers at each MCS. Generating a pseudorandom number is always a demanding operation which might have considerable consequences for the execution time when it has to be repeated this many times. For example, when simulating the Ising model on a two-dimensional lattice with `cap19_IsingSeq.c` whose main function is given in Listing 19.2, the generation of N random numbers per MCS would take about 27 percent more time.

```
1  void oneSweepSeq(int *s, graphStruct *pGraph, float *prob) {
2    int j, site, *pNeigh, siteConn, sum;
3
4    for (site = 0; site < pGraph->numNodes; site++) {
5      pNeigh = pGraph->neigh[site];
6      siteConn = pGraph->conn[site];
7      sum = 0;
8      for (j = 0; j < siteConn; j++, pNeigh++) {
9        sum += s[*pNeigh];
10     }
11     sum *= s[site];
12     if (sum <= 0 || FRANDOM < prob[sum]) {
13       s[site] = -s[site];
14     }
15   }
16 }
```

Listing 19.2   The function to do a MCS by updating the variables in sequential order.

The second advantage is present only when the model is defined on a regular lattice, where the numeration of the vertices follows a preset order, as in Figure 19.9. In theses cases, the sequential update is much more efficient also because it uses optimally the variables transfered from the RAM to the processor registers. On regular lattices we strongly advise to use the sequential update. As far as the onset of periodic asymptotic regimes is concerned, it is our responsibility to check and possibly undertake appropriate action (in any case, we assume that these are rare events, and that, if they occur, they can be easily solved).

19.4.3 *Optimizing the memory accesses*

Let us try to understand better how the regularity of the lattice can optimize the data transfer from the RAM to the processor registers. To keep the problem description simple, we do not take into account the many cache levels present in a modern computer; these intermediate memories, between the RAM and the most internal registers, make the problem optimal solution more complex, but the basic concepts remain the same.

We consider a part of a 30 × 30 lattice, drawn in Figure 19.9. The vertices enumeration scheme is the one described in Section 13.3, i.e., to the vertex with coordinates (ix, iy) we assign the number ix + L * iy. To update the variable s[47] the program needs to know the values of the spins in the vertices 17, 46, 48 and 77. Usually, in a modern computer, the data transfer from the RAM to the processor registers occurs in data packets (for didactical purposes, we assume that data packets consists of 4 32-bits numbers). If the program execution requires the value s[48] be read, several elements of the array s[], for example, from index 48 to index 51, are loaded into the registers, indicated by the gray band in Figure 19.9. The same occurs for the other nearest neighbors of the spin to be updated (if the values were not already loaded in the registers).

The advantage of the regular structure is clear when the program passes on to update the following vertices, those with indices 48 and 49 in Figure 19.9. All required values of the nearest neighboring spins are already present on the registers. This allows the processor to quickly (i.e., at clock frequency) execute a series of operations without having to wait for further data transfers from the RAM which take a much longer time than those of the clock frequency[8].

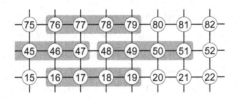

Fig. 19.9 The sequential update exploits the data transfered in packets (the gray rectangles) to the register well.

---

[8]In a modern computer the clock frequency is of the order of several GHz, i.e., 10^9 operations per second. This is a theoretical limit though, not nearly achieved by any program.

It is always difficult to quantify the advantage of the sequential update compared to the random one. The result depends on many hardware features of the computer. It also depends on the way in which the data are transferred into the registers upon execution. In any case, we can approximately estimate the computational advantage, by evaluating how many data are on average transferred from the RAM on the register in a MCS with random update compared to the sequential one (we are still considering the two-dimensional case). In the first case, at each step, we transfer 5 data items (the spin to be update and its 4 nearest neighbors). So, in one MCS we perform about $5N$ transfers. In the second case, the number of transfers is much smaller because the spins belonging to the row we are updating (such as vertices 49, 50 and 51 in Figure 19.9) are first used as right neighbors, then as spins to be updated and finally as left neighbors, before being removed from the registers. This way, we save at least two transfers per variable, resulting in about $3N$ transfers per MCS. Moreover, we need to consider that in this second scheme many useful variables are transferred together. The latter effect is much more difficult to estimate though. Apart form the theoretical estimates, we should always consider the actual computer tests. For a two-dimensional 50×50 lattice, we obtain that the random update takes about 50 percent extra computer time with respect to the sequential one. A considerable amount!

In the function `oneSweepSeq`, given in Listing 19.2, there is one more aspect preventing a good compiler to otpimize in the best possible way the program. The nearest neighbors of vertex `site` are given in terms of the variables stored in the array `neigh[site][]`. At compilation time, the values of these variables are not known as they will be set at execution time. Therefore, the compiler cannot decide any optimized strategy to transfer the variables in the registers and to execute the required operations.

Actually, the use of variables to store the lattice structure is a choice dictated by the request to maintain the program as general as possible. By working with a two-dimensional lattice of size $L \times L$, this request is no longer useful, and we can explicitly write that the neighbors of the vertex `site` are `site-L`, `site-1`, `site+1` and `site+L` (as usual we keep the general case, corresponding to the vertices inside the lattice, while the expressions for those at the boundaries are slightly different and we leave their derivation as an exercise to the reader). In Listing 19.3 we show the functions to update the spins on a two-dimensional $L \times L$ lattice, in which the expressions identifying the nearest neighbors of `site` have been included explicitly.

```
 1 void oneSweep2D(int *s, float *prob) {
 2   int ix, iy, site = 0;
 3
 4   /* case    iy = 0   ix = 0 */
 5   updateOneSpin(s, site, L2, L, 0, 0, prob);
 6   site++;
 7   /* case    iy = 0   0 < ix < L-1 */
 8   for (ix = 1; ix < L-1; ix++, site++) {
 9     updateOneSpin(s, site, L2, 0, 0, 0, prob);
10   }
11   /* case    iy = 0   ix = L-1 */
12   updateOneSpin(s, site, L2, 0, -L, 0, prob);
13   site++;
14   for (iy = 1; iy < L-1; iy++) {
15     /* cases   0 < iy < L-1   ix = 0 */
16     updateOneSpin(s, site, 0, L, 0, 0, prob);
17     site++;
18     /* cases   0 < iy < L-1   0 < ix < L-1 */
19     for (ix = 1; ix < L-1; ix++, site++) {
20       updateOneSpin(s, site, 0, 0, 0, 0, prob);
21     }
22     /* cases   0 < iy < L-1   ix = L-1 */
23     updateOneSpin(s, site, 0, 0, -L, 0, prob);
24     site++;
25   }
26   /* case    iy = L-1   ix = 0 */
27   updateOneSpin(s, site, 0, L, 0, -L2, prob);
28   site++;
29   /* cases   iy = L-1   0 < ix < L-1 */
30   for (ix = 1; ix < L-1; ix++, site++) {
31     updateOneSpin(s, site, 0, 0, 0, -L2, prob);
32   }
33   /* case    iy = L-1   ix = L-1 */
34   updateOneSpin(s, site, 0, 0, -L, -L2, prob);
35 }
36
37 void updateOneSpin(int *s, int site, int offsetS, int offsetW,
38                    int offsetE, int offsetN, float *prob) {
39   int sum = (s[site - L + offsetS] + s[site - 1 + offsetW] +
40         s[site + 1 + offsetE] + s[site + L + offsetN]) * s[site];
41   if (sum <= 0 || FRANDOM < prob[sum]) {
42     s[site] = -s[site];
43   }
44 }
```

Listing 19.3 Functions to perform a MCS for the Ising model on a two-dimensional lattice.

The function **oneSweep2D** analyzes the spins on all lattice vertices by dividing them in nine cases: the four lattice corners (lines 5, 12, 27 and

34), those on the four lattice sides (lines 9, 16, 23 e 31) and the remaining ones inside the lattice (line 20). For each one of these cases, the arguments (from the third to the sixth) in the call to the function `updateOneSpin` are different. These arguments provide the function `updateOneSpin` the values of the so-called *offsets*, i.e., those corrections needed to compute the nearest neighbors, due to the periodic boundary conditions (the letters S, W, E, N with which we indicate the offsets recall the four cardinal directions). For example, for the internal vertices no correction is needed and all offsets are zero (line 20), while for the vertices on the right boundary (line 12, 23 and 34) an offset equal to $-L$ in the eastern direction is needed.

Note that the Listing 19.3 is longer than the Listings 19.1 and 19.2. Unfortunately, this is an (almost inevitable) disadvantage of a well-optimized code: it typically entails much more work for the programmer! Moreover, we note that a shorter program does not always mean it is also quicker. Indeed, the function in Listing 19.2, where the neighbors are addressed by variables, has a 25 percent longer execution time (for a 50×50 lattice) with respect to the version in Listing 19.3.

This result may seem surprising, considering the function `oneSweep2D` performs L^2 calls to the function `updateOneSpin`. Nevertheless, this result is achieved by using a compiler option[9] demanding the content of sufficiently simple functions[10] to be copied in the points where these functions are called (also for recursive functions up to a certain depth). The function `updateOneSpin` is very short and is certainly copied in the points where it is called. In this way, we obtain a fast sequential function `oneSweep2D`.

19.4.4   *Optimizing the sequence of statements*

Willing to generalize the code in Listing 19.3 to study an Ising model defined on a lattice in higher dimensions, we do not want to write explicitly all the particular cases depending on the boundaries (which are 3^d for a lattice in d dimensions). We would like to use a general expression providing the nearest neighbors of `site`: for example, in a two-dimensional lattice we have that `site = ix + L * iy`, as shown in Section 13.3. The function in Listing 19.4 follows this strategy. Note that on line 6 (as on line 7) we cannot write `((iy - 1) % L)` because for `iy = 0` the modulus operation would be ill-defined. The code in Listing 19.4 is much more shorter than the one in

---

[9]For the `gcc` compiler this option is activated with `-finline-functions` and it is also included in the optimization option `-O3`.

[10]The definition of a "simple function" depends on the compiler.

Listing 19.3. Unfortunately, each computation of the nearest neighbor now takes several operations (also for those of the internal vertices, which in principle do not need them). Moreover, the computational cost grows with the lattice dimensionality. As a result, the execution times of the code in Listing 19.4 (at least for the usual example of the 50×50 lattice) are comparable to those of the code in Listing 19.2, where the neighbors are addressed by the variables `neigh`.

```
1  void oneSweep2D(int *s, float *prob) {
2    int ix, iy, sum, site = 0;
3
4    for (iy = 0; iy < L; iy++) {
5      for (ix = 0; ix < L; ix++, site++) {
6        sum = s[site] * (s[ix + L * ((iy + L - 1) % L)] +
7                         s[((ix + L - 1) % L) + L * iy] +
8                         s[((ix + 1) % L) + L * iy] +
9                         s[ix + L * ((iy + 1) % L)]);
10       if (sum <= 0 || FRANDOM < prob[sum]) {
11         s[site] = -s[site];
12       }
13     }
14   }
15 }
```

Listing 19.4 Another function performing a MCS for the Ising model on a two-dimensional lattice.

The function in Listing 19.4 has one feature though (missing in the function of Listing 19.2) which allows it to be optimized by a good compiler exploiting well the *loop unrolling* option. For a computer it is easy to copy L^2 times few lines of code (from line 6 to 12) that appear inside the cycles in Listing 19.4. In this way, the compiler can assign the variables ix and iy to all the values they would take upon program execution. The resulting code is certainly longer (which is no problem whatsoever for the currently available memories). The main advantage though, is that the computation of all indices for the nearest neighbors are carried out during the compilation. This has a twofold advantage: on the one hand, the execution is faster, because the computation of the neighbors has ben already done at compilation time; on the other hand, having fully unrolled the cycles, the compiler can better reorder the statements to make execution faster. In the case of a complete loop unrolling of all cycles in the functions of the Listings 19.3 and 19.4, the corresponding executable programs should have the same execution times.

We now show a last aspect of program execution which can be exploited to improve its performance. A computer processor is an extremely complicated device and inevitably has many latent times. For example, even the outcome of an elementary operation, that in theory requires only a single clock cycle to be executed, may be available only after several clock cycles. You should imagine that a processor works a bit like a passport photo booth. The time needed to take the pictures (i.e., inserting the money, positioning the seat and taking a snapshot) is about one minute. Afterwards, though, we still need to wait for about four more minutes to have the fully developed pictures (for a total of five minutes).

Suppose a group of 10 persons needs to get passport pictures. This would take 50 minutes, if each person were to wait outside of the booth until it stops working before entering it. Fortunately, the passport photo booth is designed to work at different levels. It can take a snapshot, while at the same time the other pictures occupy different levels of the development process. So, the 10 persons can take the pictures sequentially, in a total time of 14 minutes. This is exactly what we want to obtain on a processor, by choosing the most appropriate order for the statements. Unfortunately, sometimes our task is complicated by the dependencies existing between consecutive or nearby statements. For example, the statements

```
a = 2 * b;
c = 1 + a;
```

have a direct dependency, because the second cannot be executed as long as the value of a is not known, i.e., as long as its value is not returned. In this case, we need to consider there will be a latency time between the execution of these two statements. In general, dependencies are created when there exist nearby operations in which the same variable first occurs on the left of the assignment and then on the right.

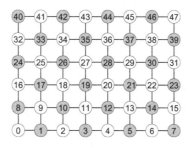

Fig. 19.10   In a checkerboard update, first the variables on all white sites and the all on the gray sites ae updated.

Let us show an exemplar case of how we can reduce the dependencies in the function we are considering in this section, namely the update of the spins on a two-dimensional lattice (this is a specific example, which should clarify the general philosophy though). We color the lattice vertices as a checkerboard (see Figure 19.10) and we write a function updating first all the white vertices, and then all the black ones. In the first part of the function, we only have assignments of the type *white spin* = $\sum$ *black spin*, which have no dependencies since the values of the black spins are only read and never assigned. The same logic applies to the second part of the function that only contains assignments of the kind *black spin* = $\sum$ *white spin*. In principle, in each of the two parts, all statements can be sequentially executed without any latent time. Unfortunately, to exploit at best this kind of optimization, we need to have a deep knowledge of the technical specifications of the processor used to execute the program. The latter are usually not available though.

The optimization tricks we showed throughout the last few sections can be used everywhere in a program, but they are particularly important in those functions representing the "core" of the program (the function executing a MCS is a typical example). Indeed, if we manage to improve, even slightly, the core functions, we might save a lot of execution time. To understand which functions are used more upon execution, there exist special programs, called *profilers*, telling us how much execution time has been spent inside each function. The functions that are executed more rarely, such as the measurement and final check functions, should be maintained to a more readable rather than a particularly optimized level. Obviously, the best thing is to have, at the same time, optimized and comprehensible functions!

Hands on 19.6 - Optimized function for the Metropolis algorithm

Write at least two versions of the function performing a MCS with the Metropolis algorithm for the two-dimensional Ising model. Compare the execution times, by inserting them inside the program written in the Hands on 19.5. Next, change these functions such as to simulate the Ising model defined on a cubic lattice in 3 spatial dimensions. Again measure the execution times and verify how much these times changed in 3 dimensions for the various versions. Some optimization of Section 19.4 do not depend on the topological structure of how the variables interact with each other.

Instead, others do depend on it, because the boundary effects become more important as the dimensions of the space where the spins are embedded increase.

We end this section with a final advice on how to measure the interesting quantities, such as the magnetization and the energy in the Ising model, during the Monte Carlo evolution. The most obvious solution is to write a function that computes everything we are interested in, starting from the system configuration. However, if we want to measure frequently (eventually after each MCS), it would be much more convenient to keep variables with the updated value of the interesting quantities. To this purpose, we can easily change the function performing a MCS for the Ising model. Indeed, we just need to add a few lines of code in the points where the value of the spin s[site] is inverted,

```
if (sum <= 0 || FRANDOM < prob[sum]) {
  s[site] = -s[site];
  *pMag += 2 * s[site];
  *pEner += 2 * sum;
}
```

where **pMag** and **pEner** (passed to the function) are pointers to the variables containing, respectively, the quantities $M(s)$ and $E(s)$, which are always up-to-date in this way. To implement this strategy without making any errors it is strictly necessary to use variables of the integer type. This is because, as explained in Section 4.5, when summing many floating-point variables, we may commit a very large rounding error (and, in order to have an optimized code, it is not wise to use the Kahan algorithm inside the program main function). In the case it is impossible to express the desired quantities in terms of integer variables, we suggest to recompute them each time they are needed, rather them keeping them up-to-date.

Chapter 20

How to use stochastic algorithms

In every art, competence is awesome.

Yoshida Kenkō, *Tsurezuregusa, Essays in Idleness* (1330).

Stochastic algorithms, such as the Monte Carlo method introduced in Chapter 19 or the genetic algorithms discussed in Section 20.4.1, are generally very efficient. However, in order to interpret their results correctly, we need to be more careful than when using deterministic algorithms. In this chapter we discuss some important aspects about the use of stochastic methods.

20.1 Examples where Monte Carlo methods are needed

In Chapter 19 we introduced stochastic methods to compute multidimensional integrals and in Section 19.3 we showed how useful they are to study a simple model in statistical mechanics, the Ising model. In this chapter, we continue using the same Ising model and the computation of the canonical ensemble average (see Section 19.3) as prototypes for Monte Carlo simulations. We want to stress, though, that a method as general and flexible as the Monte Carlo one has many applications. One usually applies it to problems which are difficult to solve analytically, have a large number of system variables and for which a deterministic algorithm would take too much time.

In order to make the discussion a bit more concrete, but still of general interest, we consider the application of the Monte Carlo method to a statistical inference problem common to all scientific disciplines, namely the

Bayesian inference problem. We consider a vector of experimental measurements $\vec{\mu}$ and M different hypotheses H_j describing the experimental observations. Typically, the different hypotheses correspond to M different models or to the same model for M different parameter values. The problem is to understand which hypothesis best describes the experimental data.

Think, for example, of a model for meteorological predictions. Such a model contains a large number of parameters, indicated by $\vec{x}$. We also assume this vector can take M values in a discrete space, even if analogous treatment can be made in the case $\vec{x}$ are continuous variables. The model parameters $\vec{x}$ are the variables of the inference problem, and we want to know which configuration of the variables $\vec{x}$ is more compatible with the experimental measures made by the weather stations. Possible prior information on the hypotheses, i.e., what is known about the values of the variables *before* the experimental measurements are carried out, are represented by the probability distribution $Q(\vec{x})$. One way to conjecture the values of $Q(\vec{x})$ is by analyzing the historical series of measurements of the temperature, pressure and the precipitation levels. The possible constraints, prohibiting some choices for the variables, are included by assigning the value $Q = 0$ to the forbidden configurations. In the case we do not have any prior information, the $Q(\vec{x})$ is constant on the space of variables configurations.

Note that it is not always possible to directly measure the parameters defining the model from the experimental measurements $\vec{\mu}$. Indeed, very often the experimentally measurable quantities are more or less complicated functions of the parameters, i.e., $\mu_i = f_i(\vec{x})$. In the case these functions are invertible, we can easily deduce the influence of the experimental measurements on the model parameters. In the case they are not invertible, we need to address Bayes' formula, that we briefly derive below (for further details we refer the reader to specialized textbooks [Feller (1971); Grimmett and Stirzaker (2001)]).

We indicate with $P(A|B)$ the conditional probability that an event A occurs, knowing that the event B took place. The definition of this conditional probability can be written in terms of the probability $P(A\cap B)$ that both events A and B occur:

$$P(A \cap B) = P(A|B)P(B) = P(B|A)P(A) . \tag{20.1}$$

We now introduce a set of mutually exclusive events, $\{A_i\}$, i.e., $P(A_i\cap A_j) = 0 \ \forall i \neq j$, such that $\sum_i P(A_i) = 1$. In practice, this means one and only one of the events A_i takes pace. The following equalities then hold

$$P(B) = \sum_i P(A_i \cap B) = \sum_i P(B|A_i)P(A_i) . \qquad (20.2)$$

Finally, consider the second equality in equation (20.1) applied to the events A_k and B, and substitute $P(B)$ by the expression given in the last term of equation (20.2), to obtain *Bayes' formula*:

$$P(A_k|B) = \frac{P(B|A_k)P(A_k)}{\sum_i P(B|A_i)P(A_i)} .$$

By applying Bayes' formula to the problem of determining the parameters of the model, we get the following equation:

$$P(\vec{x}|\vec{\mu}) = \frac{P(\vec{\mu}|\vec{x})\,Q(\vec{x})}{Z} , \quad \text{where} \quad Z = \sum_{\vec{x}} P(\vec{\mu}|\vec{x})\,Q(\vec{x}) . \qquad (20.3)$$

The equation (20.3) provides the probability $P(\vec{x}|\vec{\mu})$ that, given the experimental observations $\vec{\mu}$, the parameters of the model take on the values $\vec{x}$, as a function of the prior probability $Q(\vec{x})$ and the probabilities $P(\vec{\mu}|\vec{x})$ that the model with parameters $\vec{x}$ predicts the results $\vec{\mu}$ for the performed measurements.

To use the model for predictions we need to estimate the average, or the most probable, value of some functions of the model parameters (for example, the precipitation level after two days). Once the experimental measurements $\vec{\mu}$ are known, the average value $\langle A \rangle$ of any observable $A(\vec{x})$ of the model, is given by the formula

$$\langle A \rangle = \sum_{\vec{x}} A(\vec{x})\,P(\vec{x}|\vec{\mu}) = \frac{1}{Z}\sum_{\vec{x}} A(\vec{x})\,P(\vec{\mu}|\vec{x})\,Q(\vec{x}) , \qquad (20.4)$$

We can evaluate the expression (20.4) with Monte Carlo methods, precisely because of the form (19.22). Moreover, by introducing a sort of energy function for the Bayesian inference problem variables, i.e., for the parameters $\vec{x}$ of the model,

$$E(\vec{x}) \equiv -\log\left[P(\vec{\mu}|\vec{x})\,Q(\vec{x})\right] ,$$

where the dependency of the measurements $\vec{\mu}$ is implicit, we can rewrite equation (20.4) in the following form

$$\langle A \rangle_{T=1} = \frac{1}{Z}\sum_{\vec{x}} A(\vec{x})e^{-E(\vec{x})} . \qquad (20.5)$$

A comparison with equation (19.22), defining the canonical ensemble average at temperature T [Huang (1987)], reveals that the expression (20.5) is equivalent to a canonical average at temperature $T = 1$. So, we have found a relation between the Bayesian statistical inference problem, which has an enormous amount of applications in all scientific fields, with the estimate of the canonical ensemble average. The latter is the prototype of the problem we want to study in this chapter by means of the Monte Carlo method. Expression (20.5) allows us to understand better the importance of this prototypical problem, beyond the statistical mechanics field.

The definition (20.5) is also particularly useful to calculate the most probable value of $A(\vec{x})$, defined as the value corresponding to the most probable choice of the variables $\vec{x}$. In general, given a probability distribution $P(\vec{x})$, the distribution that is obtained by rising to a power $\beta > 1$, $R(\vec{x}) \propto [P(\vec{x})]^\beta$, is more concentrated around the most probable values of $\vec{x}$. In particular, in the limit $\beta \to \infty$, the distribution $R(x)$ becomes a Dirac delta distribution[1] centered around the most probable value of $\vec{x}$. This observation allows us to compute the most probable value of $A(\vec{x})$ with the following expression

$$\lim_{\beta \to \infty} \frac{1}{Z_\beta} \sum_{\vec{x}} A(\vec{x}) e^{-\beta E(\vec{x})} = \lim_{\beta \to \infty} \langle A \rangle_{T=1/\beta} , \qquad (20.6)$$

where Z_β is the normalization factor of the distribution $\exp[-\beta E(\vec{x})]$. The expression (20.6) tells us that the most probable value of $A(\vec{x})$ is obtained as the average value of the canonical ensemble in the zero temperature limit, $T \to 0$. Computing the average value at zero temperature $\langle A \rangle_{T=0}$ is an optimization problem, as it corresponds to minimizing the function $E(\vec{x})$. We treat this type of problem in more detail in Chapter 18 and in Section 20.4.

As we already mentioned in Section 19.3 for the Ising model, a canonical ensemble average may vary much as a function of the temperature or some other parameter of the model. These variations may be particularly strong near the critical point, i.e., near those values of the parameters and the temperature, where a true phase transition occurs in the thermodynamic limit, i.e., when the number of variables of the model becomes enormous. Due to these strong variations (corresponding to singularities in the average values for $N \to \infty$), it is much more difficult to estimate the averages with the Monte Carlo method near the critical point. We concentrate on these regions because it is important to know how to apply a technique in the worst case in order to be able to tackle the simpler ones without any problem.

---

[1]The Dirac delta distribution, indicated by the Greek letter δ, is defined in terms of the integral $\int \delta(x - x_0) f(x) dx = f(x_0)$ and selects specific values of the integrand.

The other reasons why we concentrate on the study of the critical points are related to their physical interest. The phase transition phenomenon is very widespread in nature. Moreover, it characterizes some of its most interesting aspects. Cooling down water from 28 to 26 degrees Celsius is not very fascinating, but passing from 1 °C to –1 °C causes very interesting effects. Moreover, the models used for numerical simulations often do not imitate the natural phenomenon we want to study in all of its details, but only some of its features, said to be *universal*. For example, the exponent in the expression relating distance and time in a random walk is universal and does not depend on the chosen lattice (see Section 12.2). Analogously, phase transitions can be classified in *universality classes* based on the value of some universal quantities, such as the type of transition and critical exponents (see Section 20.3.3). We can measure the latter only very close to the critical point and they do not depend on the details of the model. In this region, the results of the numerical simulations can be directly compared with the experimental ones, by means of the universality classes. Such a comparison is much more difficult far from the critical point, where no universal quantities can be defined and the observables depend also on the details of the model.

Moreover in all the cases in which not purely physical phenomena are studied, involving a large number of interacting elements (think for example of problems in biology, sociology or economy), we must simplify the problem to define a model which can be simulated with a computer. Therefore, given that the model neglects a whole set of details of the original problem, only the quantities which do not depend on the details, i.e., the universal quantities, may provide us with reliable information on the phenomena we want to study and understand.

20.2 How to run a good Monte Carlo simulation

We choose the estimate of a canonical ensemble average, i.e., the computation of expressions like the one of equation (19.22), as a problem prototype. In order to allow the interested reader to easily reproduce our results, we focus on the study of a simple model, namely the Ising model in two spatial dimensions, defined in Section 19.3. The code simulating this model with the Metropolis algorithm is shown in Section 19.4. We choose to work with a specific model since a good practical example is worth a thousand of general theoretical discussions. Still, we remind the reader that the present discussion can be generalized to the majority of Monte Carlo simulations.

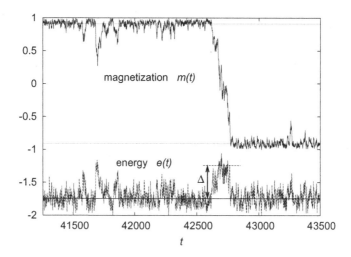

Fig. 20.1   Typical behavior of the magnetization and the energy during a Monte Carlo simulation of the 2-dimensional Ising model ($L = 15$ and $T = 2$). The horizontal lines indicate the analytical values in the limit $L \to \infty$.

One of the first things we observe during the Monte Carlo simulation is the temporal evolution of the interesting observables, those for which we want to compute the averages. To give an idea, we show in Figure 20.1 the behavior of the magnetization and the energy for a two-dimensional Ising model of size $L = 15$ simulated at a temperature $T = 2$ (remember the critical point is at $T_c \simeq 2.27$). The entire simulation is much longer than the several thousands of Monte Carlo sweep (MCS) included in the plot. We limited the time window in Figure 20.1 in order to show the fluctuations of the measured quantities and the correlations between the observables: the magnetization and the energy. Note how the energy visibly grows each time the magnetization is near zero. This is because the lowest energy configurations have the highest (in absolute value) magnetization.

The role of the energy barrier in the single spin flip dynamics should be clear from Figure 20.1 looking around 42 700 MCS. The system manages to pass from configurations with positive magnetization to those with negative magnetization only after many attempts (one occurring around the time 41 700 MCS). When it finally succeeds, the trajectory crosses an energy barrier of about $\Delta \sim 0.5L^2$ (we fixed $J = 1$ and in the plot the energy is normalized by the number of spins $N = L^2$). The energy barriers are the main cause of systematic errors in a Monte Carlo simulation. They dramatically slow down the dynamics the method is based on, increasing the convergence times of the underlying Markov chain (see Section 19.2.2). Their presence forces to simulate up to much longer times. If we do not choose long enough times, the value of the averages we want to estimate is wrong. Therefore, we need to learn how to recognize the effects caused by the presence of energy barriers. To this purpose, the Ising model is good training ground, as we know where it has its highest barriers. Namely, for zero magnetization, $m = 0$, at temperatures lower than the critical one, $T < T_c$ (see Section 19.3).

When performing a Monte Carlo simulation we need to pay attention to several aspects in order to keep possible systematic errors under control:

- we need to make sure we have reached the equilibrium (this problem is also discussed in Section 19.2);
- we need to study the equilibrium correlations in order to compute the uncertainty on the estimate of the average value $\langle A \rangle_T$;
- we need to be able to identify possible phase transitions, because around the critical points we need a higher precision.

The following sections deal with all of these aspects.

20.2.1 *Convergence towards equilibrium*

The first problem we need to tackle consists in understanding whether the dynamics on the Markov chain has reached the equilibrium, i.e., whether the system is visiting all possible configurations with the proper probability distribution $P_{\mathrm{GB}}(s)$. Generally, it is not possible to answer this question just by looking at a single configuration (or just a small number of these). Indeed, as can be seen in Figure 20.1, the values of the observed quantities fluctuate very much, and we can expect nothing else from a method with a stochastic nature!

Therefore, we need to limit ourselves to the observation of average values calculated over reasonably long time intervals. We know that, when the dynamics on the Markov chain reaches equilibrium (for example after t_{eq} MCS), the time average of any observable quantity is equal to its canonical ensemble average,

$$\frac{1}{t_{\mathrm{max}} - t_{\mathrm{eq}}} \sum_{t=t_{\mathrm{eq}}+1}^{t_{\mathrm{max}}} A(s(t)) \simeq \langle A \rangle_T \, ,$$

where $s(t)$ is the configuration at time t of the system evolving with the Monte Carlo algorithm. Moreover, we know this average is independent of the initial condition.

One way to check *thermalization,* i.e., whether the equilibrium has been reached, is to simulate two or more systems starting from very different initial conditions. We assume they have thermalized only when the observables of our interest are the same for both systems (within the thermal fluctuations, which are always present). We immediately stress that this is a necessary, but not a sufficient condition. Thus, we should use it in a wise way. In the case of the Ising model, we consider three independently evolving copies of the system, starting from three different configurations. The first one starts from a random configuration (and therefore with magnetization close to zero), the second from the configuration with $m = 1$ (i.e., all spins are equal to 1) and the third from $m = -1$. In Figure 20.2(top) we show the magnetizations and the energies of these three systems (for $L = 500$ and $T = 2.5$). The energies of the two copies starting from entirely magnetized configurations are very similar and can not be distinguished from each other in the graph. It is easy to understand why: the energy of the Ising model, defined in (19.20), is invariant under a simultaneous flipping of all the spins. Therefore, the two configurations with $|m| = 1$ both have energy $e = -2$. Such a symmetry is roughly mantained also during evolution.

When studying the thermalization times it comes natural to use the logarithmic scale for the time axis. So, we can compute the averages with the following method. We divide the time axis in intervals whose endpoints t_i are more or less equidistant in logarithmic scale. A typical choice is the one in which the interval endpoints coincide with the integer powers of 2, i.e., $t_i = 2^i$. This choice ensures that the values of t_i are integer. In the case we need a larger number of intervals, we can choose a base $1 < b < 2$. In this second case, though, the values of $t_i = b^i$ are rational and we need to round them to integer values. This might cause some limits to overlap, cancelling the corresponding interval. Therefore, we suggest to use the following expression to compute the next endpoint of the interval:

```
measTime = (int)(measTime * b) + 1;
```

where `measTime` is the time at which we want to compute the averages, which should be incremented in a way that it reaches the limit of the next interval. Note that `measTime` always grows at least by one unit, thus avoiding the problem of creating intervals of zero size.

The temperature used in the simulations shown in Figure 20.2(top) is sufficiently higher than the critical one, such that even a large system

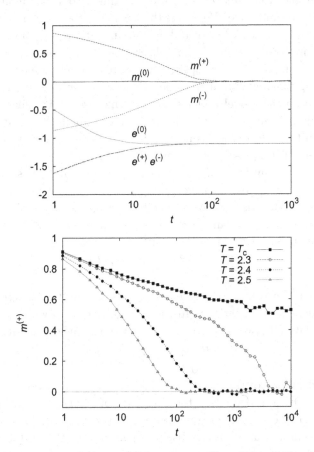

Fig. 20.2 For three two-dimensional Ising systems ($L = 500$ and $T = 2.5$) starting from a random configuration (0), from $m = 1$ (+) and from $m = -1$ (-), we show the convergence towards equilibrium of the magnetization and the energy (top) and the magnetization of the one which started with $m = 1$ at different temperatures (bottom).

quickly converges towards equilibrium. In this case, $t_{eq} \simeq 10^2$ is a reasonable estimate of the thermalization time. In general, we can consider a quantity, which upon reaching the equilibrium coverges towards zero, for example $m^{(+)}$ or $(e^{(0)} - e^{(+)})$, and we estimate t_{eq} as the time at which this quantity reaches the value zero for the first time (from that moment on it will oscillate around zero). We stress that, being a stochastic dynamics, this estimate of t_{eq} may vary between different simulations. We always need to perform more than one simulation, check that the estimate does not vary too much and fix a value for t_{eq} slightly higher than all the measured ones.

Choosing different initial conditions is possible only if we already have information on the model under study. In the case of the Ising model we know the magnetization is the order parameter signaling the phase transition. When this information is not available, we can try to take advantage of some general properties of the model, e.g. its symmetries. For example, if the energy function of the model is invariant under a simultaneous flipping of all the spins, we have that for each temperature $\langle m \rangle_T = 0$ at equilibrium. Otherwise, we can exploit some properties of the canonical ensemble average. For example, by deriving equation (19.22) with respect to the temperature, we obtain the relation

$$\frac{d\langle A \rangle_T}{dT} = \frac{\langle A E \rangle_T - \langle A \rangle_T \langle E \rangle_T}{T^2} , \qquad (20.7)$$

where $\langle A \rangle_T$ is the average of a generic function $A(s)$ and $\langle E \rangle_T$ is the average of the model energy function[2]. In the particular case in which $A = E$, we obtain a relation between the specific heat C_V and the energy fluctuations:

$$C_V \equiv \frac{d\langle E \rangle_T}{dT} = \frac{\langle E^2 \rangle_T - \langle E \rangle_T^2}{T^2} . \qquad (20.8)$$

To take advantage of this relation in checking thermalization, we need to evaluate C_V by approximating the derivative of $d\langle E \rangle_T/dT$ with the difference between the average energies obtained in two simulations performed at nearby temperatures. A very useful aspect of the relation (20.8) is that the left and right members tend towards the same asymptotic value at equilibrium from different sides. More precisely, before thermalizing, i.e., in the *out-of-equilibrium regime*, the specific heat C_V has a value lower than the equilibrium one. On the contrary, the energy fluctuations are higher than those at equilibrium. This property ensures us that the relation (20.8) is true only at equilibrium and not before.

---

[2]We note both these quantities are extensive, i.e., proportional to N. If we want to use intensive quantities, a factor N would appear on the right hand side of equations analogous to (20.7).

The thermalization time might be very large when the system is near the critical point. In Figure 20.2(bottom) we show, for a system with $L = 500$ and starting with $m = 1$, the convergence of the magnetization towards the equilibrium value, $\langle m \rangle_T = 0$, for different temperatures. Note how the convergence becomes more and more slower as the temperature is decreased towards the critical one. At the critical temperature, 10^4 MCS are not enough to thermalize the system. In these cases, we absolutely need to increase the simulation times, reduce the system size, or choose an algorithm converging faster towards equilibrium.

Hands on 20.1 - Thermalization in the Ising model

First of all, check whether your program simulating the Ising model on a two-dimensional lattice works correctly. To this purpose execute it with the same parameters used for Figure 20.2 and compare your results with those shown in the figure. Next, study the thermalization times with the following experiments.

Using $L = 50$ compute the thermalization time for different temperatures. For temperatures higher than T_c you should be able to estimate this time rather well. You can plot the estimated thermalization time as a function of the temperature to study how it grows for $T \to T_c$. Next, estimate the thermalization times exactly at the critical point for various system sizes. As usual, for smaller values of L, the measurements fluctuate more and we need to average over several *thermal histories*, i.e., over several simulations with different random numbers. For $T = T_c$, how does the thermalization time grow with increasing L? Finally, discuss what happens below T_c, especially in respect to the ergodicity breaking and the formation of a barrier between the most probable configurations.

20.2.2 *Correlations at equilibrium*

From now on, we assume to have correctly estimated the thermalization time for the model under study. Therefore, we neglect the Monte Carlo evolution corresponding to the thermalization and we only consider the part of the simulation *at equilibrium*. For simplicity, we move the time origin to the beginning of this part, such that we can write

$$\langle A \rangle_T \simeq \frac{1}{\mathcal{T}} \sum_{t=1}^{\mathcal{T}} A(s(t)) \equiv \frac{1}{\mathcal{T}} \sum_{t=1}^{\mathcal{T}} A_t \equiv \langle\!\langle A \rangle\!\rangle , \qquad (20.9)$$

where $\mathcal{T}$ is the total number of MCS at equilibrium. In order to simplify the notation we introduced the symbol $A_t \equiv A(s(t))$ and the double angular brackets indicate the time average, i.e., over the dynamical equilibrium process. The latter average is the best estimate of the ensemble average and the two coincide in the limit $\mathcal{T} \to \infty$.

The algorithm attempts to update all variables of the model at each MCS. Still, the configurations at two successive time steps may be very correlated, especially near the critical point. This implies we cannot simply calculate the statistical error on the estimate (20.9) of $\langle A \rangle_T$ with the formula

$$\sigma^2_{\langle A \rangle_T} \simeq \frac{1}{\mathcal{T}(\mathcal{T}-1)} \sum_{t=1}^{\mathcal{T}} \left(A_t - \langle\!\langle A \rangle\!\rangle \right)^2 = \frac{\langle\!\langle A^2 \rangle\!\rangle - \langle\!\langle A \rangle\!\rangle^2}{\mathcal{T}-1} ,$$

that assumes two consecutive measurements A_t and A_{t+1} to be completely uncorrelated. To correct the estimate of the statistical error we need to know how strong the correlations between the measurements A_t are. We introduce a function by which we compute these correlations, $C_A(\Delta t) = \phi_A(\Delta t)/\phi_A(0)$ where

$$\phi_A(\Delta t) = \frac{\sum_{t=1}^{\mathcal{T}-\Delta t} A_t A_{t+\Delta t}}{\mathcal{T}-\Delta t} - \left(\frac{\sum_{t=1}^{\mathcal{T}-\Delta t} A_t}{\mathcal{T}-\Delta t} \right) \left(\frac{\sum_{t=1}^{\mathcal{T}-\Delta t} A_{t+\Delta t}}{\mathcal{T}-\Delta t} \right) ,$$

and the averages in $\phi_A(\Delta t)$ are taken over just $\mathcal{T} - \Delta t$ terms. $C_A(\Delta t)$ is called the *connected autocorrelation function* of the observable $A(s)$. This function tells us how correlated two measurements of this quantity are at a distance of Δt MCS. By definition, we have that $C_A(0) = 1$, while $\lim_{\Delta t \to \infty} C_A(\Delta t) = 0$. This is because, for large time differences, in the definition of $\phi_A(\Delta t)$ the terms of the first sum are certainly uncorrelated and their average coincides with the product of the averages given by the other two sums.

In Figure 20.3 we show the equilibrium autocorrelation function of the magnetization, $C_M(\Delta t)$, for two sizes of the model ($L = 20$ and $L = 50$) and various temperatures. From the figure it is clear that the time needed for two magnetization measures to become uncorrelated grows as the temperature is lowered. Moreover, while at $T = 2.5$ the two curves corresponding to the two values of L are very similar, at lower temperatures the finite size effects appear and create a discrepancy between the two curves.

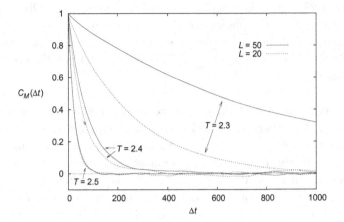

Fig. 20.3 The autocorrelation function of the magnetization $C_M(\Delta t)$ measured at equilibrium for two different system sizes and three different temperatures.

From the function $C_A(\Delta t)$ we can extract the correlation time τ_A in at least two different ways. In the first case, we interpolate $C_A(\Delta t)$ with an exponential function

$$C_A(\Delta t) \simeq \exp\left(-\Delta t / \tau_A^{(\exp)}\right) ,$$

possibly excluding very small values of Δt from the interpolation as they might contain correction terms with respect to the exponential behavior, that should hold for large Δt. In the second case, the correlation time is given by the integral

$$\tau_A^{(\mathrm{int})} \simeq \int_0^\infty C_A(\Delta t)\, d(\Delta t) .$$

In practice this integral is a sum over all possible values of the discrete variable Δt. These two definitions of correlation time coincide in case the correlation function is exactly of the exponential form, $C_A(\Delta t) \propto \exp(-\Delta t/\tau)$.

Hands on 20.2 - Equilibrium correlation times

Compute the correlation times $\tau^{(\exp)}$ and $\tau^{(\mathrm{int})}$ for the autocorrelation function of the magnetization $C_M(\Delta t)$ and the energy $C_E(\Delta t)$. Consider at least two values for the system size (for example, $L = 20$ and $L = 40$) and various temperatures both above and slightly below the critical one (for example, $2.2 \leqslant T \leq 2.5$ is a reasonable interval). Study how much these correlation times vary in changing the temperature and the system size. Observe this depends strongly on the observable that we measure. For example, the measurements of the energy become uncorrelated faster than the magnetization. Explain the numerical results in terms of what you learned about the Ising model.

The correlation time of the energy τ_E has a maximum at the critical temperature. Moreover, for $T = T_c$, τ_E grows with the system size and diverges in the limit $L \to \infty$. Due to this divergence, the single spin flip dynamics in the Ising model presents at T_c a *critical slowing down*. This phenomenon is inevitable (if we do not change algorithm) and it is the determining factor for the duration of this kind of simulation. An analogous phenomenon was observed for the algorithm listing the connected components of Section 13.5.

The correlation time for the magnetization (apart from being much larger than the one of the energy) behaves in a different way. Indeed, as the temperature decreases, τ_M keeps on growing and it has not maximum around T_c. Moreover, for $T < T_c$ it depends in an exponential way on the system size. These observations can be easily explained. Note that, for $T < T_c$, the correlation function $C_M(\Delta t)$ decays if and only if the system magnetization changes several times from positive to negative values. Indeed, for $T < T_c$, due to the ergodicity breaking and the presence of an energy barrier (see Section 19.2.5 and Figures 19.5 and 19.8) the correlation time τ_M grows exponentially with N. In a generic Monte Carlo simulation observables with this kind of correlation times, are more difficult to measure, especially at low temperatures.

The thermalization time of a Monte Carlo simulation is never smaller than (and typically very similar to) the largest equilibrium correlation time. Therefore, we naturally expect it to grow exponentially with the system size, at least for some values of the temperature. If we know which observables have large correlation times, we can take advantage of this similarity to perform an extra check on whether the simulation results are correct. In any case, we note that many observables have correlation times which are much shorter than the thermalization time. Therefore, after having used the first t_{eq} MCS to reach equilibrium, after another time $\mathcal{O}(t_{eq})$ we can perform many uncorrelated measurements of these observables.

Once the right correlation time is obtained for each observable quantity of our interest, we can correctly estimate the statistical error of the average with the formula

$$\sigma^2_{\langle A \rangle_T} = \frac{\langle\!\langle A^2 \rangle\!\rangle - \langle\!\langle A \rangle\!\rangle^2}{\mathcal{T} - 1}(1 + 2\tau_A) \simeq \left(\langle\!\langle A^2 \rangle\!\rangle - \langle\!\langle A \rangle\!\rangle^2\right)\frac{2\tau_A}{\mathcal{T}},$$

where the last expression is valid for $\mathcal{T} \gg 1$ (which is always true) and for $\tau_A \gg 1$ (which is often true). In Section 20.3 we show other methods to correctly estimate the statistical errors of a measurement.

20.2.3 *How to identify a phase transition*

So far, we only measured the average magnetization, $\langle m \rangle_T$, and the average energy $\langle e \rangle_T$. These averages do not give us much information on the existence, and possibly the location, of a critical point though. Indeed, the first average is zero by definition at each temperature, and the second one behaves in a rather regular way with the temperature (plot the data you have gathered so far). Hence, we clearly need to introduce some more significant quantity in order to identify possible critical points.

From the solution of the Ising model, we know that the order parameter of the phase transition, i.e., the quantity measuring how ordered the system is, is the absolute value of the magnetization. So, we could measure $\langle |m| \rangle_T$ or also $\langle m^2 \rangle_T$, because both these averages become nonzero when the temperature decreases below T_c. The main problem when working with these averages is that their value is very small around the critical point. Therefore, the ratio between signal and noise is low. Moreover, the finite size corrections cause these averages to be nonzero even for temperatures well above the critical one.

Additionally we could measure the derivatives of $\langle |m| \rangle_T$, and of $\langle e \rangle_T$ with respect to the temperature. In practice, by taking advantage of the relation (20.7), we should measure the covariance between observables. For the Ising model, in the limit $N \to \infty$, these two derivatives diverge at the critical point, signaling in this way its position. Nevertheless, in a system of finite size no measure can actually diverge. Indeed, the derivatives have a maximum in the vicinity of T_c. In practice, we would need to perform a study of the finite size effects (see Section 20.3.4).

A better choice is to study a quantity that asymptotically tends towards two different values for $T > T_c$ and for $T < T_c$ (for example 0 and 1) and having some particular property at the critical point. To study the transition of the Ising model this quantity is the so-called *Binder parameter*, defined by the expression

$$B(T,L) \equiv \frac{1}{2}\left(3 - \frac{\langle m^4 \rangle_T}{\langle m^2 \rangle_T^2}\right) . \tag{20.10}$$

Observe that for the averages of the magnetization moments we could have used in a completely equivalent way the extensive magnetization. In the definition of the Binder parameter $B(T,L)$ we make explicit its dependence on the temperature T and the system size L. In Figure 20.4(top) we show $B(T,L)$ in a temperature interval around T_c for various values of L. This plot should clarify the advantage of using this parameter. Indeed, $B(T,L)$ varies between 0 and 1, and the curves for different values of L intersect at the critical point! Indeed, a fundamental property of the Binder parameter is that, at the critical point, its value is universal and independent of L in the limit of large L.

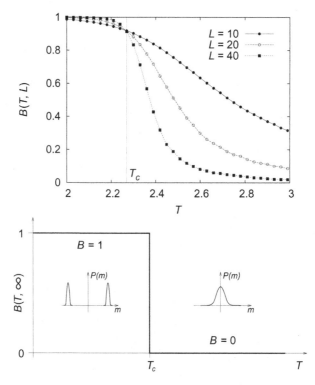

Fig. 20.4   The Binder parameter measured for the Ising model of size $L \times L$ (top) and its behavior in the limit $L \gg 1$ (bottom).

The choice of the factors, $\frac{1}{2}$ and 3, appearing in the definition (20.10) of the Binder parameter is such that $B(T, L)$ tends to zero for $T > T_c$ and tends to one for $T < T_c$. Indeed, for $T > T_c$ the distribution of the magnetization is a Gaussian centered around the origin (at least for large values of L) and for a normal distribution it is known that $\langle m^4 \rangle = 3\langle m^2 \rangle^2$, from which we find that $B(T > T_c, L \gg 1) = 0$. The other way around, for $T < T_c$, the magnetization distribution consists of two parts strongly concentrated around the values of the spontaneous magnetization $\pm m_0$, from which $\langle m^2 \rangle \simeq m_0^2$, $\langle m^4 \rangle \simeq m_0^4$ and $B(T < T_c, L \gg 1) = 1$. The probability distributions of the magnetization, together with the asymptotic value $B(T, \infty)$ are shown in Figure 20.4(bottom).

When studying a phase transition it is very important to know how to identify its position in a precise way. In all these cases it is fundamental that we find a parameter analogous to the Binder one for the Ising model. For example, in the percolation study, a good parameter is the probability that a configuration with density ρ is percolating. This probability varies between 0 and 1 as ρ increases and the curves for various values of the lattice size intersects at the percolating critical point. In Section 20.3.4 we further analyze the importance of this type of parameter when studying the critical region around the transition point.

Hands on 20.3 - Ising model in 3 dimensions

 Repeat for the Ising model in three spatial dimensions (using a cubic lattice with periodic boundary conditions) all studies we carried out in this section for the two-dimensional Ising model. In particular, try to identify the critical point.

20.3 Data analysis

In Section 20.2.2 we study the problem of the time correlations when measuring an observable and how these reduce the precision with which we can compute its average. Unfortunately, the procedure studied in Section 20.2.2 to estimate the correct statistical error is quite demanding. We first need to compute the correlation function and then estimate the correlation time with an interpolation or an integration. An alternative, generally more efficient way is the so-called *block average*.

20.3.1 *Block averages*

We consider a time series of $\mathcal{T}$ measures $\{A_t\}_{t=0,...,\mathcal{T}-1}$ (note we use the indices as in a C array, starting from 0). From this, we want to estimate the true average of the process that generated the data. It is well-known that the best estimator of the true average is the data average value

$$\langle\!\langle A \rangle\!\rangle \equiv \frac{1}{\mathcal{T}} \sum_{t=0}^{\mathcal{T}-1} A_t \ , \quad \text{with error} \quad \sigma_{\langle\!\langle A \rangle\!\rangle} = \sqrt{\frac{\text{var}(A_t)}{\mathcal{T}-1}} \ . \tag{20.11}$$

The expression for the uncertainty of the average estimate $\sigma_{\langle\!\langle A \rangle\!\rangle}$ is correct only if the $\mathcal{T}$ measures are fully uncorrelated from each other. With the symbol $\text{var}(A_t)$ we indicate the variance of the data series defined by

$$\text{var}(A_t) \equiv \frac{1}{\mathcal{T}} \sum_{t=0}^{\mathcal{T}-1} \left(A_t - \langle\!\langle A \rangle\!\rangle \right)^2 = \frac{1}{\mathcal{T}} \sum_{t=0}^{\mathcal{T}-1} A_t^2 - \langle\!\langle A \rangle\!\rangle^2 = \langle\!\langle A^2 \rangle\!\rangle - \langle\!\langle A \rangle\!\rangle^2 \ .$$

If the measures are correlated the expression (20.11) underestimates the statistical uncertainty when determining the average; hence we need a more refined analysis.

Suppose the measures are correlated with a correlation time τ_A. We now show how to proceed in order to get a correct estimate of the error on the average. We group the measures in blocks containing b consecutive measures each and we call $A_t^{(b)}$ the average of the measurements in the tth block,

$$A_t^{(b)} = \frac{1}{b} \sum_{t'=bt}^{b(t+1)-1} A_{t'} \ .$$

The number of blocks, and therefore, the length of the new data sequence $\{A_t^{(b)}\}$ is $\mathcal{T}/b$.[3] In particular, note how the $A_t^{(1)}$ are the original data and that the average value of the data $\langle\!\langle A \rangle\!\rangle$, does not change when these are combined in blocks of equal size (the average value remains the best estimate of the true average).

For $b < \tau_A$, the data of the sequence $\{A_t^{(b)}\}$ are still correlated (with a correlation time of about τ_A/b), while, for $b > \tau_A$, the data become uncorrelated, because the largest part of the temporal correlations is inside the blocks. Let us take advantage of this property in order to correctly estimate the statistical error, $\sigma_{\langle\!\langle A \rangle\!\rangle}$, of the average estimate. We define

$$\sigma_{\langle\!\langle A \rangle\!\rangle}^{(b)} \equiv \sqrt{\frac{\text{var}(A_t^{(b)})}{(\mathcal{T}/b) - 1}} \ ,$$

---

[3]In order to simplify the formulas, we are assuming $\mathcal{T}$ to be multiple of b; otherwise we could have to treat differently the last block, if smaller.

where the variance of the sequence $\{A_t^{(b)}\}$ is defined as before

$$\operatorname{var}(A_t^{(b)}) \equiv \frac{b}{\mathcal{T}} \sum_{t=0}^{\mathcal{T}/b-1} \left(A_t^{(b)}\right)^2 - \langle\!\langle A \rangle\!\rangle^2 .$$

The $\sigma_{\langle\!\langle A \rangle\!\rangle}^{(b)}$ corresponds to the average uncertainty. It is obtained by assuming the data grouped in blocks of size b are uncorrelated. Because of what we just discussed, we expect $\sigma_{\langle\!\langle A \rangle\!\rangle}^{(b)}$ to underestimate the error of the average as long as $b < \tau_A$ and, instead, to provide the correct uncertainty for $b > \tau_A$.

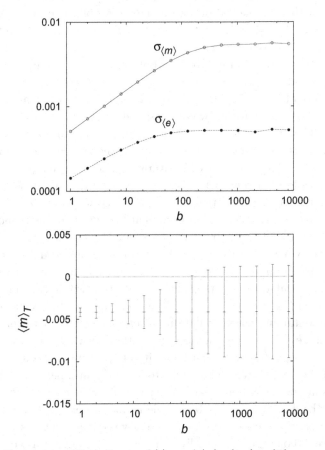

Fig. 20.5 Uncertainty of the estimate of $\langle e \rangle_T$ and $\langle m \rangle_T$ (top) and the average magnetization with its estimated error (bottom) as a function of the number b of measures per block.

In Figure 20.5(top) we show the uncertainties on the estimates of the averages $\langle e \rangle_T$ (below) and $\langle m \rangle_T$ (on top) for the two-dimensional Ising model of size $L = 20$ at temperature $T = 2.4$. The data were obtained from a sequence of 10^6 measurements at equilibrium. Note that the data follow the theoretically predicted behavior. They grow up to a certain value of b, corresponding to the correlation time, after which they stabilize. The value of the *plateau* is the correct error on the average. Also note that the data given in Figure 20.5 fluctuate, given that the variances $\sigma^{(b)}$ are random variables as well.

Having 10^6 available data, we could have combined them in groups using larger values of b than those given in Figure 20.5. This might have obscured our analysis though. Indeed, when the number of blocks becomes too small the value of $\sigma^{(b)}_{\langle\langle A \rangle\rangle}$ possibly fluctuates a lot. Therefore, we advise to use at least about a hundred blocks.

The data presented in Figure 20.5(bottom) should convince us how important a good estimate of the errors is. The figure contains, for various values of the block size b, the average value of the magnetization with its error (the model is still the two-dimensional Ising model with $L = 20$ and $T = 2.4$). The important thing to note is that, if we did not correctly estimate the statistical error, i.e., if we had used the average corresponding to $b = 1$, we would have concluded the average value of the magnetization was not compatible with zero (which is a wrong result, causing us to rethink the entire numerical simulation!). Instead, once we estimated the correct error, the average magnetization is compatible with zero, as it should be.

The data shown in Figure 20.5 are obtained with the function of Listing 20.1, in which the average and the variance of the data sequence is computed to obtain $\sigma^{(b)}_{\langle\langle A \rangle\rangle}$ (lines 6-8). At the same time, the next sequence of data is generated by grouping the current ones two by two (line 9). The function **binning** receives in input the pointer **data** to the beginning of the array containing **numMeas** data items of which we want to compute the block average. Since the function writes the block averages in the same array (more precisely, in its first half), it is important we pass a pointer to a *copy* of the data, if we do not want to loose the original ones.

The statements on lines 11-14 are executed only if **numMeas** is odd, as in this case the cycle on lines 5-10 runs along all data except for the last one. In this case, we loose a data item in the new sequence. This is no problem whatsoever, though, as we usually start from very long data sequences.

```
1  double binning(double *data, int numMeas) {
2    int i, tmp = numMeas / 2;
3    double mean = 0.0, variance = 0.0;
4
5    for (i = 0; i < tmp; i++) {
6      mean += data[2 * i] + data[2 * i + 1];
7      variance += data[2 * i] * data[2 * i] +
8                  data[2 * i + 1] * data[2 * i + 1];
9      data[i] = 0.5 * (data[2 * i] + data[2 * i + 1]);
10   }
11   if (2 * i < numMeas) {
12     mean += data[2 * i];
13     variance += data[2 * i] * data[2 * i];
14   }
15   mean /= numMeas; variance /= numMeas;
16   return sqrt((variance - mean * mean) / (numMeas - 1));
17 }
```

Listing 20.1 The function combining the data in groups to calculate the correct error of the average.

The following lines of code show a possible way to use the function binning.

```
binSize = 1;
while (numMeas >= 100) {
  printf("%i %lg %lg %lg %lg %i\n",
         binSize, aveM, binning(m, numMeas),
         aveE, binning(e, numMeas), numMeas);
  binSize *= 2;
  numMeas /= 2;
}
```

Before executing these lines of code, the arrays m and e have been filled with numMeas values of the magnetization and the energy. The variables aveM and aveE contain the averages of these two data sets. The variable binSize is the size of the block and numMeas represents the length of the current sequence. After each function call to binning these variables are updated, respectively, by multiplying and dividing them by 2. The cycle in these lines of code is executed as long as the number of data items in the sequence is larger than or equal to 100, such that the variance is a stable measure. If we try to decrease this limit, it is easy to convice ourselves we do not gain any extra information because the measurements of $\sigma_{\langle\langle A \rangle\rangle}^{(b)}$ start to fluctuate a lot.

20.3.2   *Jackknife*

The method described in Section 20.3.1 always allows us to produce data sequences which are practically uncorrelated, given a series of equilibrium measurements. For example, grouping with $b = 10^3$ (this is the value of b at which the plateau starts in Figure 20.5) the 10^6 magnetization measurements, we can obtain 10^3 uncorrelated data.

However, we still need to solve a very common problem in data analysis. Namely, we still need to find a correct estimate of the error for the average of complicated function of the measurements. A concrete example, related to what we saw in Section 20.2.3, is the estimate of the uncertainty when computing the Binder parameter defined in equation (20.10). We can easily evaluate the error on the estimate of $\langle m^2 \rangle_T$ and $\langle m^4 \rangle_T$ with the method given in Section 20.3.1, using, respectively, $A_t = m_t^2$ and $A_t = m_t^4$ as data sequences. Once the uncertainties $\sigma_{\langle m^2 \rangle}$ and $\sigma_{\langle m^4 \rangle}$ are known, we could find the one on the estimate of $\langle B(T, L) \rangle_T$ by propagating the errors. This result largely overestimates the true error though. The reason is easy to understand: the second and the fourth moments of the magnetization enter in $B(T, L)$ only through their ratio. So, if the estimate of the numerator $\langle\langle m^4 \rangle\rangle$ fluctuates above the true average, also the denominator estimate $\langle\langle m^2 \rangle\rangle^2$ has a positive fluctuation and the ratio does not change much. Therefore, the fluctuations of the estimate of the ratio are very small compared to those expected from a simple propagation of the errors, which assumes the fluctuations of the numerator and the denominator to be uncorrelated. We show a method allowing one to compute the correct uncertainty also if strong correlations such as these are present.

This method, called *jackknife*, is extremely useful and should always be kept close at hand when analyzing data (just like a jackknife, when going camping for example). The jackknife method allows one to compute the correct uncertainty on the estimate of the average value of any function of the data. For example, given a series of $\mathcal{T}$ uncorrelated measures of the magnetization, the estimate of the average value of the Binder parameter, defined in (20.10), is given by the function

$$B(\{m_t\}) = \frac{1}{2} \left(3 - \frac{\mathcal{T}\sum_t m_t^4}{\left(\sum_t m_t^2\right)^2} \right) .$$

It is not clear though, which error we should associate to this estimate.

The jackknife method is based on the following idea. Suppose all measurements are available but the ith one. With these $\mathcal{T} - 1$ measures we can still estimate the average value of the function. Typically, this estimate is slightly different from the one obtained with all $\mathcal{T}$ measures and the difference between these two estimates precisely give us the information needed to compute the uncertainty of the average estimate.

In slightly more formal terms, suppose the best estimate, μ, of a generic quantity is given by the following function of $\mathcal{T}$ *uncorrelated* measures [4],

$$\mu = f\big(\{x_t\}_{t=1,...,\mathcal{T}}\big) .$$

By defining the averages without measure j as

$$\mu_j = f\big(\{x_t\}_{t \neq j}\big) ,$$

we can determine the uncertainty of μ as

$$\sigma_\mu = \sqrt{\frac{\mathcal{T}-1}{\mathcal{T}} \sum_{j=1}^{\mathcal{T}} (\mu_j - \mu)^2} , \qquad (20.12)$$

that is the spread of the averages μ_j around μ.

Exercise 20.1 - Computation of the average with the jackknife method

In case we want to estimate the sample mean, the best estimator is simply the average value of the measurements

$$\mu = \frac{1}{\mathcal{T}} \sum_{t=1}^{\mathcal{T}} x_t .$$

Prove that in this case, the error resulting from the jackknife method, given by the equation (20.12), is identical to the one we obtain by computing the standard deviation of the measurements, as in the expression (20.11).

Creating a code that computes the error with the jackknife method is easy. We simpy need to write two functions, respectively, returning the value of μ and μ_j. Actually, we can write one single function that, when called with a parameter $j \in [0, \mathcal{T}-1]$, computes the average without the jth measure, while returns the total average, if $j \notin [0, \mathcal{T}-1]$. The drawback of this approach is the number of operations, as the code would contain $\mathcal{T}+1$ function calls performing $\mathcal{O}(\mathcal{T})$ operations each. Performing a number of operations $\mathcal{O}(\mathcal{T}^2)$ is sometimes very heavy (it is not rare to have 10^8 data items and 10^{16} operations are many even for a modern PC) and we need

---

[4]In the case the measures are correlated, we first need to group them in blocks of appropriate size.

more efficient solutions, whenever possible. For example, in the case of the Binder parameter, being the magnetization an integer variable, we can use the function given in Listing 20.2. The latter only takes $\mathcal{O}(2\mathcal{T})$, number of operations because the averages μ_j are computed by subtracting each time a measure from the variables sumM2 and sumM4 containing the sums of all measures. In the case of floating-point variables, the use of expressions like sumM4 - tmp * tmp, where a large quantity sumM4) is compared to a small one, is risky and requires at least the use of Kahan's algorithm (described in Section 4.5).

The function binder given in Listing 20.2 accepts the pointer M to the array containing the magnetization measurements and the number numMeas of these measures as arguments. The other two arguments, pMean and pError, are pointers to the memory locations where the function saves the value of the Binder parameter and its error. The latter is computed with the jackknife method assuming the measures are uncorrelated.

```
1 void binder(int *M, int numMeas,
2                 double *pMean, double *pError) {
3   unsigned long long int tmp, sumM2 = 0, sumM4 = 0;
4   double reducedMean;
5   int i, *pM;
6
7   for (i = 0, pM = M; i < numMeas; i++, pM++) {
8     tmp = (*pM) * (*pM);
9     sumM2 += tmp;
10    sumM4 += tmp * tmp;
11  }
12  *pMean = 0.5*(3.0-(double)numMeas*sumM4/sumM2/sumM2);
13  *pError = 0.0;
14  for (i = 0, pM = M; i < numMeas; i++, pM++) {
15    tmp = (*pM) * (*pM);
16    reducedMean = 0.5 * (3.0 - (double)(numMeas - 1) *
17      (sumM4 - tmp * tmp) / (sumM2 - tmp) / (sumM2 - tmp));
18    *pError += (reducedMean - *pMean)*(reducedMean - *pMean);
19  }
20  *pError = sqrt(*pError * (numMeas - 1) / numMeas);
21 }
```

Listing 20.2 A function computing the error on the estimate of the Binder parameter with the jackknife method.

Hands on 20.4 - Error of the Binder parameter with the jackknife

---

Consider once more the magnetization data obtained when studying the Ising model in 2 and/or 3 dimensions. Combine them in bins of an appropriate size in order to eliminate the correlations. Next, estimate the average value of the Binder parameter and the corresponding error with the jackknife method. Compare this error with the one obtained by the simpler (but less reliable) error propagation.

20.3.3 *Scaling laws and critical exponents*

Very often a Monte Carlo simulation is used to solve a problem with a given number of variables. For example, optimizing a given cost function or computing the average value in a model accurately describing a specific problem. Nevertheless, there exist situations where the interesting result is obtained in the limit in which the number of variables of the model becomes extremely large (in statistical mechanics formally we consider the thermodynamic limit, $N \to \infty$). Think, for example, to those phenomena in nature involving an enormous number of microscopic entities (the number of molecules in gases and solids are of the order of the Avogadro constant $\mathcal{N}_A = 6 \cdot 10^{23}$). In these cases it is impossible to simulate a system of that size. Therefore, we need to know how to obtain the behavior of the model in the thermodynamic limit by simulating a model with a limited (relatively small) number of variables. To this purpose, it is useful to consider the *scaling laws*, that describe how the observable quantities get modified by changing the system size (these are called *finite size effects*). We discuss these topics in this section and the following one. As a premise, we warn the reader that the language adopted in these two sections is inevitably more technical (from a physical-mathematical viewpoint) compared to the rest of the textbook. We are confident that the interested reader should have a good basic knowledge of physics and mathematics.

We consider a model (such as the two-dimensional Ising model) that presents, in the thermodynamic limit, a phase transition with a correlation length diverging at the critical point[5]. An example of a diverging length near the critical point is shown in Section 13.4. In that section we discuss

---

[5]These transitions are typically of the so-called second order.

the percolation phenomenon and the correlation length corresponds to the linear dimension of the connected clusters. In the Ising model, the length diverging at the critical point is defined in terms of the spatial correlation function

$$G(r,T) \equiv \frac{1}{\mathcal{S}_r} \sum_{\substack{i,j: \\ |i-j|=r}} \left(\langle s_i s_j \rangle_T - \langle s_i \rangle_T \langle s_j \rangle_T \right) , \qquad (20.13)$$

where the sum is over all spin couples at a distance r and the factor preceding the sum, equal to the inverse of the number of these couples, normalizes the sum.

The expression (20.13) is not fully correct for temperatures below the critical one[6]. In order for it to be valid at any temperature we need to apply a very small external magnetic field H (without loss of generality, we assume it to be positive). The latter alters the energy of the Ising model with an additional term $-H M = -H \sum_i s_i$, and makes the configurations with negative magnetization very improbable. As a consequence, for $T < T_c$ the average magnetization takes on a positive value, $\langle m \rangle_T = m_0(T)$, defined in equation (19.23). In this and the following section we assume the measurements are always taken in the presence of a very small magnetic field or in the high temperature phase.

It can be proved [Amit and Martin-Mayor (2005)] that near a generic critical point with diverging correlation length the correlation function (20.13) can be rewritten at large distances $r \gg 1$ in the following form:

$$G(r,T \simeq T_c) \propto \frac{\widetilde{G}(r/\xi)}{r^{d-2+\eta}} , \qquad (20.14)$$

where $\widetilde{G}$ typically decays exponentially, $\widetilde{G}(r/\xi) \approx \exp(-r/\xi)$. In this way $\widetilde{G}$ defines the correlation length $\xi(T)$, which depends on the temperature. Two spins at a distance $r < \xi$ fluctuate in a strongly correlated way around their average value, while for $r > \xi$ two spins change in a roughly independent way. Equation (20.14) is obtained by assuming the only characteristic length in the system is the correlation length ξ. In other words equation

---

[6]This is not the right context to exhaustively explain why this is so. We just observe that a correlation function, such as the one in equation (20.13), is well-defined only if it decays to zero in the limit $r \to \infty$. However, for $T < T_c$, we have $\langle s_i \rangle_T = 0$ (because of the spin flip symmetry present at $h = 0$), but $\langle s_i s_j \rangle_T \to m_0^2$ at large distances, where $m_0(T)$ is defined in equation (19.23). The problem does not occur if the average $\langle \cdot \rangle_T$ is made only on half of the configurations, those with a given sign (as if an infinitesimal external field h would be present): in this case, $(\langle s_i \rangle_T)^2 = m_0^2$ would hold and $G(r,T)$ would decay to zero at large distances.

(20.14) holds strictly in the thermodynamic limit, while in a finite size system also its linear size L is a characteristic length. Note that the discretization of the lattice is irrelevant when describing phenomena occurring at large distances.

Hands on 20.5 - The spatial correlation function in the Ising model

 Consider the two-dimensional Ising model. Measure the spatial correlation function $G(r,T)$ for $T > T_c$. At these temperatures you do not have to introduce a magnetic field and you can assume that $\langle s_i \rangle_T = 0$. A practical and fast way to measure $G(r,T)$ is to consider only couples of spins differing by a single spatial coordinate,

$$G(r,T) = \frac{1}{4N} \sum_{x,y} \langle s_{x,y} \left(s_{x+r,y} + s_{x-r,y} + s_{x,y+r} + s_{x,y-r} \right) \rangle_T .$$

In this expression, we explicitly show the two coordinates of each spin and we omitted the complications due to periodic boundary conditions. For example, if the coordinate $x - r$ is negative it should be understood as $L + x - r$. With this definition of $G(r,T)$ the distance r only takes integer values less than $L/2$ (where L is the linear size of the simulated system), due to the periodic boundary conditions.

Estimate the correlation length by interpolating $G(r,T)$ with an exponential function and study how the correlation length $\xi(T)$ grows as $T \to T_c^+$.

Equation (20.14) is called a *scaling law* for the correlation function $G(r,T)$. We want to stress three important aspects of this equation:

- it shows that the dimensions of $G(r,T_c)$ are those of a length to the power $-(d - 2 + \eta)$, given that the argument of $\widetilde{G}(r/\xi)$ is dimensionless;
- it defines a number η, also called the anomalous dimension, which is a *critical exponent* (one of those universal quantities characterizing the phase transition);
- it tells us that, near the critical point, $G(r,T)$ depends on the temperature only through the correlation length $\xi(T)$.

Moreover in the thermodynamic limit, for $T \to T_c$, the correlation length diverges according to the law

$$\xi(T) \propto |T - T_c|^{-\nu} ,$$

defining a second critical exponent, ν. Near the critical point, many critical exponents, all linked to the singular parts of the observable quantities, can be defined[7]. The singular part of the magnetization defines the exponent β through the equation

$$\langle m \rangle_T \propto (T_c - T)^\beta , \qquad \text{with} \quad T < T_c \quad \text{and} \quad \frac{T_c - T}{T_c} \ll 1 .$$

For the two-dimensional Ising model, we can easily derive from the exact expression of the magnetization, given in equation (19.23), the value of the critical exponent, $\beta = 1/8$. Finally, we introduce a quantity which can also be observed experimentally, namely the magnetic susceptibility. The magnetic susceptibility is defined as the variation of the average magnetization when a very small external magnetic field is applied to the system[8],

$$\chi \equiv \frac{\partial \langle m \rangle_T}{\partial H} = \frac{L^d}{T} \left(\langle m^2 \rangle_T - \langle m \rangle_T^2 \right) , \qquad (20.15)$$

where $L^d = N$ is the number of system variables. The divergence of the susceptibility at the critical point defines a critical exponent γ through the formula

$$\chi \propto |T - T_c|^{-\gamma} , \qquad \text{with} \quad \frac{|T - T_c|}{T_c} \ll 1 .$$

The last condition reminds us the fact that the divergence of the singular parts are well-defined only strictly near to the critical point.

Even though it is possible to define many different critical exponents, not all of these are independent. Indeed, there are relations between them which should be respected. For example, in the case of a second order phase transition at finite temperature (such as the one of the Ising model) it can be proved that only two critical exponents are actually independent. We show how to obtain one of the *scaling relations* constraining the values of the critical exponents. In expression (20.15) we substitute the magnetization with its definition, $m = L^{-d} \sum_i s_i$, and obtain

$$\chi = \frac{1}{TL^d} \sum_{i,j} \left(\langle s_i s_j \rangle_T - \langle s_i \rangle_T \langle s_j \rangle_T \right) = \frac{1}{T} \int G(|\vec{r}|, T) \, d\vec{r} \propto$$

$$\propto \int_0^\infty \frac{\widetilde{G}(r/\xi)}{r^{d-2+\eta}} r^{d-1} dr = \xi^{2-\eta} \int_0^\infty \frac{\widetilde{G}(x)}{x^{\eta-1}} dx \propto \xi^{2-\eta} , \qquad (20.16)$$

---

[7]Given a generic function of the temperature, we can always decompose it in a regular and a singular part, $f(T) = f_{\text{reg}}(T) + f_{\text{sing}}(T)$. For $T \to T_c$, the first one is limited, as are all its derivatives, while the singular part has some diverging derivative.

[8]We prefer to define the susceptibility as an intensive quantity, i.e., not growing with the system volume, even though in the majority of textbooks it is defined as an extensive quantity $\chi = \partial \langle M \rangle_T / \partial H$.

where $r = |\vec{r}|$ and $x = r/\xi$. For $T \to T_c$, the first term of equation (20.16) diverges like $\chi \propto |T - T_c|^{-\gamma}$, while the last term diverges like $\xi^{2-\eta} \propto |T - T_c|^{-\nu(2-\eta)}$. By equating the powers of these two diverging laws, we obtain the relation between the critical exponents $\gamma = \nu(2 - \eta)$.

The critical phenomena can be grouped in universality classes, based on their critical exponents. Note that natural phenomena with apparently very different phase transitions may belong to the same universality class. In this case, apart from having the same critical exponents, they might share the same mechanism underlying the phase transition. In this way, we can use a well-studied phenomenon to understand a less-known one. This is the main reason why we want to accurately determine critical exponents and the relative universality class.

20.3.4 *Finite size effects and rescaling*

When attempting to measure the critical temperature and the critical exponents of a model, one of the fundamental problems is that we can only simulate systems of finite size L (which is often also relatively small), while the theory of critical phenomena is only well-defined in the thermodynamic limit. We tackle this problem by showing how we can find out information on the $L \to \infty$ behavior by exploiting the *finite size effects*. In Section 17.5.2 we gave some examples of these kinds of effects in the case of the percolation transition. Here, we consider the general theory with examples from the Ising model.

The entire theory of finite size effects is based on the observation that a system of linear size L behaves as in the thermodynamic limit for temperatures such that $\xi(T) \ll L$, while for $\xi(T) \gg L$ effects due to the limited size L appear; for $\xi(T) \approx L$ a behavior interpolating between the first two, called *crossover*, is observed. The region around the critical point where the correlation length $\xi(T)$ is much larger than the size L of the system is called the *critical region*.

Let us consider a generic observable measured in a system with linear size L, for example, the susceptibility $\chi(T, L)$. In Figure 20.6(top) we show the behavior of $\chi(T, L)$ for three different values of L. Far from the critical point, the three curves coincide. Instead, near T_c the susceptibility values strongly depends on the size of the system. For $L = 10$ and $L = 20$ it is easy to determine the critical region, corresponding to the temperatures at which the data differ from the ones measured in a large system ($L = 40$

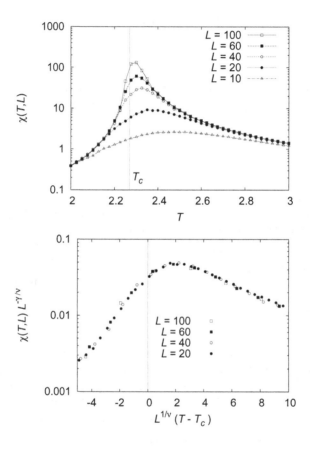

Fig. 20.6   The magnetic susceptibility measured in an Ising model of size $L \times L$ (top) and the same data rescaled (bottom).

in this case). Note that the critical region gets narrow as L increases. As shown in Section 20.3.3, in the limit $L \to \infty$, the singular part of the susceptibility diverges as $\chi \propto \xi^{\gamma/\nu}$. So, by reasoning only in terms of the equations dimensionality[9] we can write

$$\chi \simeq \xi^{\gamma/\nu} \cdot \overline{\chi}\left(\frac{L}{\xi}\right) \qquad \text{with} \quad \overline{\chi}(x) = \begin{cases} \text{costant} & \text{for } x \gg 1, \\ x^{\gamma/\nu} & \text{for } x \ll 1. \end{cases} \qquad (20.17)$$

This expression only depends implicitly on the temperature through $\xi(T)$. We can easily explain the asymptotic behavior of the function $\overline{\chi}$. For $L \gg \xi$, $\overline{\chi}$ should be constant in order to have the thermodynamic behavior $\chi \propto \xi^{\gamma/\nu}$. Instead, in the critical region ($L \ll \xi$), $\overline{\chi}$ needs to cancel out the divergence of the prefactor $\xi^{\gamma/\nu}$, because the susceptibility cannot diverge for finite L.

By substituting $\xi \propto |T - T_c|^{-\nu}$, which is valid near the critical point, we can rewrite the equation (20.17) as

$$\chi(T, L) \simeq |T - T_c|^{-\gamma} \cdot \widetilde{\chi}\left(L^{1/\nu}(T - T_c)\right), \qquad (20.18)$$

where the scaling function $\widetilde{\chi}(x)$ tends towards a constant for $x \to \infty$ and behaves like $\widetilde{\chi}(x) \propto x^{\gamma}$ for $x \ll 1$. The fundamental equation for the analysis of finite size effects is given by (20.18). We can write an analogous equation for each observable quantity. In particular, the equation for the Binder parameter is

$$B(T, L) \simeq \widetilde{B}\left(L^{1/\nu}(T - T_c)\right). \qquad (20.19)$$

In this case, thanks to how the Binder parameter is defined, no term appears in front of the scaling function $\widetilde{B}$. So, the value of $B(T, L)$ does not depend on L at the critical point: $B(T_c, L) = \widetilde{B}(0)$. Moreover, the value of the derivative with respect to the temperature at the critical point is given by

$$\left.\frac{\partial B(T, L)}{\partial T}\right|_{T=T_c} \simeq L^{1/\nu} \cdot \widetilde{B}'\left(L^{1/\nu}(T - T_c)\right)\bigg|_{T=T_c} \simeq \widetilde{B}'(0) \cdot L^{1/\nu}, \qquad (20.20)$$

i.e., it grows as the size of the simulated system increases. We have thus explained analytically why the curves of the Binder parameter for various values of L intersect at the critical point, as is observed for the numerical data shown in Figure 20.4(top).

We finally have all the equations needed to estimate the critical temperature, T_c, and two critical exponents, ν and γ in this case, allowing us to

---

[9]The argument of the function $\overline{\chi}$, providing the finite size correction of the thermodynamic behavior, is dimensionless only if it depends on the ratio of the only two characteristic lengths, $\xi(T)$ and L.

determine the model universality class. The estimate of T_c is obtained from the intersection of the curves $B(T, L)$. The estimate of the exponent ν can be obtained by interpolating the values of the derivatives $\partial B(T, L)/\partial T$ at the critical point, with the power law in the last term of (20.20). In turn, the derivatives can be obtained by interpolating the functions $B(T, L)$ close to T_c: by choosing a very small interval around T_c, even a simple linear interpolation is accurate enough. Finally, we can estimate γ by considering the susceptibility data at the critical point. From equation (20.18), in the limit $T \to T_c$, we obtain $\chi(T_c, L) \propto L^{\gamma/\nu}$, by which we can estimate γ once we know the value of ν.

Once we have estimated T_c, ν and γ, we can again use equations (20.18) and (20.19) to check the obtained results. By plotting the values of $\chi(T, L)L^{-\gamma/\nu}$ or $B(T, L)$ as a function of the rescaled variable $x = L^{1/\nu}(T - T_c)$, we should find that data for various L collapse on a single curve (at least for not too large x). In Figure 20.6(bottom) we show how the rescaled data of $\chi(T, L)$ for the two-dimensional Ising model collapse. The rescaled data of the Binder parameter follow the function $\widetilde{B}(x)$, while the rescaled data of the susceptibility follow the function $\widetilde{\chi}(x)x^{-\gamma}$.

Hands on 20.6 - Computing the critical exponents

Consider once more the data obtained for the Ising model in two or three spatial dimensions. Use them to perform the analysis we just described. Try to get the best possible estimates for the critical temperature and the two critical exponents. Plot the rescaled variables and check how good the rescaling of your data is.

20.4   Optimization with stochastic methods

We talk about optimization problems when we have to minimize a generic *cost function* that depends on N variables. In Chapter 18 we have discussed deterministic methods searching for the minimum. Instead, in this section we show two important stochastic methods to minimize a function.

The expression «Looking for a needle in a haystack» certainly does not do any justice to the typical optimization problem, which is quite a bit harder than searching for a needle! Just to give an idea, the number of pixels in a screen with resolution 1280×854 is about 2^{20}, i.e., equal to the number of configurations of a system with only $N = 20$ binary variables. It is not rare we have to face optimization problems containing between a thousand and a million of variables! For the human mind it is even difficult just to imagine a similar large number of configurations.

In the following sections we briefly describe two of the most used optimization methods, based on stochastic algorithms, namely the genetic algorithms and simulated annealing.

20.4.1 *Genetic algorithms*

John Holland first introduced the technique of the genetic algorithms in the eighties of the XXth century, starting from the research he did on cellular automatons [Holland (1975)]. It is a heuristic optimization method which imitates the evolution mechanisms of species in nature.

Charles R. Darwin (1809-1882) was the first one to realize that the variety of living species is due to an evolutionary process continuously tending to improve a species survival features. This occurs by means of two main phenomena: *mutations* in *reproduction* and *selection* of the most fit individuals by the environment. The maximum efficiency of the evolutionary process is obtained by means of sexual reproduction in which the gene pool of two different individuals is *recombined*. In practice, the children's genes originate partially from one parent, and partially from the other. The generation of individuals with different gene pools allows nature to "explore" different genetic combinations. If the number of individuals is high, the probability to generate children with genetic features which, due to recombination, are more adapt than those of the parents, is rather high. In the course of their lives the organisms have a lower or higher probability to survive which is also a function of their genetic characteristics. In this way, the environment "selects" the fittest individuals which then manage to transmit their genes to the future generations, while the others die before they can generate children. If this were the only mechanism at work, it would not take long before an entirely genetically homogeneous population would have established. In the case of some unfavorable environmental variations, the latter would be doomed to disappear completely, or anyhow, not be able to reach the best conditions. To guarantee the continuous "exploration" of the space of possible gene combinations, nature randomly changes some genes of the new individuals, by means of the mutations. In this way, these new individuals acquire completely new characteristics, not originating from any of the two parents.

By imitating this basic mechanism, the genetic algorithms allow one to find the parameter combination optimizing a certain function, which is the aim of the search. In this case, we talk about maximizing the fitness. However, the problem can be easily transformed into that of minimizing any function. There exist many possible variants of a genetic algorithm. In this section we just explain one particularly simple strategy, and invite the reader to try others.

First of all, we need to define the variables representing the individuals. In the simplest case, the gene pool of an individual consists of a single *chromosome* defined as a set of genes. We can represent the latter in various ways, depending on our needs (from single bits to complicated structures). Each individual should also be given a kind of *score* defining its *fitness*. A chromosome can, for example, be represented as an array of genes, which are represented, in turn, by integer numbers. We can represent an individual by a structure containing its gene pool and a variable representing its score. The aim is then to optimize the score:

```
typedef int GENE;

typedef struct genesAndScore {
  GENE genes[CHROMOSOME_SIZE];
  double fitness;
} individual;
```

The score is determined, starting from the genes contained in the chromosomes, with a problem-specific function. Consider, for example, a particularly simple, easily solvable problem, allowing us to understand what happens during the evolution. Suppose we need to find a sequence of k integer numbers between 0 and 9, whose sum is the largest possible. Obviously, the solution is a simple sequence of 9. With this example, we want to check whether our genetic algorithm works. In this case, the score could be defined as the sum of the values of the genes contained in the chromosome.

To evolve a system, we need to have enough individuals. The initial *population* can be defined as an array of individuals, ordered according to their score, which initially consists of a number N of randomly generated individuals. The array should be defined such that it can host a variable number of individuals between zero and N_{max}. The fact that the number of individuals is limited is certainly a practical choice (we cannot store more individuals than the limited amount of computer memory can possibly contain). There does exist an interesting parallel with what happens in nature, where the organisms live in a environment with limited resources.

If their number grows too much, the resources are not enough to sustain all of them and the weakest individuals will die. The population maximum and initial size should be chosen case by case and we can estimate them by taking the total number of possible gene combinations into account. It obviously does not make any sense to define populations allowing to host all possible combinations. Indeed, in this case, no evolution would take place, as one of these combinations would certainly be the best one. On the other hand, it is inappropriate to start with a too small population, because the evolutionary process would be too slow.

```
Father   ABCD EFGHIJ
Mother   0123 456789

Child 1  ABCD 456789
Child 2  0123 EFGHIJ
```

Fig. 20.7   The crossing-over process consists in "cutting" the chromosomes of the father and mother in a random point (shown with a thick vertical line) and recombining them in order to generate two children. The first child takes the first genes of the father and the remaining ones of the mother, and viceversa for the second.

Once an initial population, sorted by score, has been obtained, the evolution of the system consists essentially in three steps.

(1) At each iteration (generation), the population individuals are *paired up* to generate children. The children are generated by exchanging portions of chromosomes. This phase is called *crossing-over*. In the simplest case each couple of parents A and B gives rise to two children. The crossing-over consists in choosing a random point at which the chromosomes of both parents are "cut". The two children have a chromosome consisting, respectively, of the first portion of chromosome of parent A and the second portion of the chromosome of parent B and vice versa (as shown in Figure 20.7). We can choose the two individuals to be paired in many different ways. For instance, we could recombine each individual with the adjacent one along the array, or we could select two individuals in a random way with a probability proportional to their fitness.

(2) Each generated child could undergo, with a certain probability, genetic mutations. In the easiest case, a mutation consists in a

random variation of any gene, with uniform probability. Also in this case, different variants are possible. For example, if a population has been having a very low average score for a long time, it is preferable to try to improve it by mutating the genes of their children more (*triggered hypermutation*) or to insert entirely new individuals into the population (*random immigration*). Sometimes, we associate to each individual several characters by using the concept of *alleles*, i.e., an alternative form of a gene which is stored as a *recessive character* which, under certain conditions, appears (for example, as a consequence of climate changes or environmental variations). The mutation probability should be sufficiently high in order to guarantee that at each generation combinations, which otherwise would be impossible, are explored. On the other hand, it should be sufficiently low such that the dominating character of the average population is not destroyed. The theory does not give precise indications. The only way to proceed in this case is by trial and error.

(3) The new population, consisting of parents and children, is sorted based on their score. All individuals survive, if their is enough room for all of them and their score is higher than a preset threshold (simulating the possible death in the case of serious malformations). The individuals which cannot enter the population die before giving rise to a new generation.

The process is iterated for a sufficiently long time (also here it is difficult to establish how long *a priori*; the duration is established experimentally) or until we can be sure to have reached the maximum score (obviously we do not always know this value beforehand).

The Listing 20.3 contains the code of a possible evolution function of a species consisting of individuals represented by the above given structure. This code is not the most efficient one, but also in this case we preferred a more comprehensible, rather than a very efficient code. The function takes the array defining the population and its maximum length as input arguments, while the third argument represents the population current size (obviously **size** is less than or equal to **maxSize**). On lines 5 and 6 the space to memorize all individuals present at the end of the generation (double of the current one) is created. Next, the individuals which are already present in the population are copied (lines 8 and 9) and they are made to mate. In this case, we choose each individual to mate with its neighbor in the array **population** (lines 10 and 11).

```
1  int evolve(individual *population, int maxSize, int size) {
2    int i, j, k = 0;
3    double newBornFitness;
4    children newChromosomes;
5    individual *temp = (individual *)calloc(size * 2,
6                                           sizeof(individual));
7    for (i = 0; i < size - 1; i += 2) {
8      temp[i] = population[i];
9      temp[i + 1] = population[i + 1];
10     newChromosomes = crossover(population[i].genes,
11                                population[i + 1].genes);
12     newBornFitness = computeFitness(newChromosomes.offspring1);
13     if (isAlive(newBornFitness)) {
14       for (j = 0; j < CHROMOSOME_SIZE; j++) {
15         temp[size + k].genes[j] = newChromosomes.offspring1[j];
16       }
17       temp[size + k].fitness = newBornFitness;
18       k++;
19     }
20     newBornFitness = computeFitness(newChromosomes.offspring2);
21     if (isAlive(newBornFitness)) {
22       for (j = 0; j < CHROMOSOME_SIZE; j++) {
23         temp[size + k].genes[j] = newChromosomes.offspring2[j];
24       }
25       temp[size + k].fitness = newBornFitness;
26       k++;
27     }
28   }
29   size += k;
30   sort(temp, size);
31   if (size > maxSize) {
32     size = maxSize;
33   }
34   for (i = 0; i < size; i++) {
35     population[i] = temp[i];
36   }
37   free(temp);
38   return size;
39 }
```

Listing 20.3   An evolution function for a population of individuals.

The function **crossover** is given in the Listing 20.4. We defined the structure **children** containing two chromosomes. The function **crossover** returns a variable of this type which is generated by randomly choosing a cutting point **cut** (line 8 of the Listing 20.4) and assigning the first child the genes of the "father" up to **cut-1** and those of the "mother" from **cut** onward. The second child receives the complementary (homologous) genes.

Before returning the structure, the children are subject to a mutation by invoking the function **mutate** which alters some randomly picked genes with a certain probability.

```
1 typedef struct offsprings {
2   GENE offspring1[CHROMOSOME_SIZE];
3   GENE offspring2[CHROMOSOME_SIZE];
4 } children;
5
6 children crossover(GENE *a, GENE *b) {
7   children newBorns;
8   int i, cut = randomGenePos();
9   for (i = 0; i < cut; i++) {
10     newBorns.offspring1[i] = a[i];
11     newBorns.offspring2[i] = b[i];
12   }
13   for (i = cut; i < CHROMOSOME_SIZE; i++) {
14     newBorns.offspring1[i] = b[i];
15     newBorns.offspring2[i] = a[i];
16   }
17   mutate(newBorns.offspring1);
18   mutate(newBorns.offspring2);
19   return newBorns;
20 }
```

Listing 20.4   The function performing a crossing-over of two individuals.

The fitness of each child is evaluated with the function **computeFitness** (which in this case simply returns the sum of the genes). If the score exceeds the survival threshold, the child is added to the population (lines 13 up to 19 and from 21 up to 27 of Listing 20.3). At this point we sort the entire population according to the scores of each individual, The group of individuals which does not exceed the population maximum size passes onto the next generation. The iteration leading to the evolution is something like

```
for (t = 0; t < MAX_TIME; t++) {
  current_size = evolve(population, MAX_POPULATION_SIZE,
                        current_size);
}
```

Once the generations have finished, the individual with index 0 is the "fittest", i.e., has the maximum score.

Hands on 20.7 - Evolution of a species

Write a program to genetically evolve the individuals defined in the text, by completing the described functions. Choose a fully random initial population and print, at each iteration, the maximum score (the one of the individual with index 0), the average score and the population current size. Plot these three quantities as a function of time. For example, try with a maximum population of 100 individuals and an initial population of 10 individuals, chromosomes of 10 genes, for 1000 generations. Study the evolution and the convergence time to reach the optimal result for different mutation probabilities in the entire interval $[0, 1]$. What happens when the mutation probability reduces to zero? And what if it is very large? Does there exist an optimal value of this probability?

Try to change strategy for selecting individuals to pair and to be mutated. Try to define different scores, possibly variable in time, and experiment what effect the existence of *alleles* in the chromosomes have.

The genetic algorithms have some undesirable features. Namely, we cannot predict how long the process takes, the theory does not tell us how to choose the parameters nor can it anticipate which evolutionary schemes are better. On the other hand, apart form being an interesting technique to study evolution, it is particularly useful to solve particularly complex or difficult problems, or even problems which are impossible to solve with traditional techniques. The presence of the mutations guarantees at least that a good deal of the configuration space is explored, allowing the method to "jump out of" possible local, non optimal solutions. In certain cases, the method may provide additional information. For example, by observing the final population, we might find out that the individuals' scores does not depend on the value of certain genes. In this case, the parameters represented by these genes do not have any influence whatsoever and can thus be omitted in the search for solutions. Vice versa, a strong correlation between the value of the genes and the score indicates that the gene in question plays a fundamental role and should be studied in detail.

20.4.2   *The simulated annealing method*

Given a generic cost function, $E(s)$, for which we want to find the minimum, we immediately note that the Gibbs-Boltzmann distribution $P_{GB}(s) \propto \exp[-E(s)/T]$ in the zero temperature, $T \to 0$, is concentrated around the configuration with minimum cost. In the case there exist $\mathcal{M}$ configurations with a cost equal to the minimum one, we have $P_{GB} = 1/\mathcal{M}$ for each one of these. A configuration with a cost which is ΔE higher than the minimum one has a probability proportional to $\exp[-\Delta E/T]$, and therefore becomes extremely improbable for $T \ll \Delta E$.

Thanks to these observations, we could imagine to search the configurations with minimum cost by directly performing a Monte Carlo simulation at $T = 0$. This method typically has a major drawback though. Namely, the dynamics at very low temperatures, and therefore even more at $T = 0$, is slowed down. The reason is that at low temperatures the dynamics does not posses enough thermal agitation to cross the barriers it eventually encounters when relaxing towards low energy configurations. At very low temperatures the time needed to cross an energy barrier of height ΔE is proportional to $\exp[\Delta E/T]$, which diverges for $T \to 0$. Therefore, it is not efficient to directly work at low temperatures. In particular, at $T = 0$ the evolution can never increase the energy, and therefore it cannot cross any barrier. The system inevitably converges towards the first local minimum of the cost or energy function and unlikey the global minimum can be found.

An alternative solution is to start the simulation with a relatively high temperature, which is then lowered during the simulation until it reaches zero at the end of the simulation. This method was introduced in 1983 by Kirkpatrick, Gelatt and Vecchi [Kirkpatrick *et al.* (1983)] and goes by the name of *simulated annealing*. The name derives from the jargon of metallurgy and recalls the process of heating a metal to very high temperatures to then slowly let it cool down in order to obtain an ordered crystalline structure which is more robust.

A difficult optimization problem has many configurations of low cost (even if just one or few of minimum cost). To move between these configurations we typically need to cross high energy barriers. The basic idea of simulated annealing is drawn in a schematic way in Figure 20.8(a), where we reduced the configuration space to one single dimension, while usually it has a huge number of dimensions (one for each problem variable). Initially, when the temperature is high, the dynamics can jump across any barrier and choose the largest region of configuration space (called "valleys" in jargon) with the least average cost. This valley contains with high probability configurations with a low cost. Then, the temperature is decreased, the dynamics becomes more selective and can choose, among the subvalleys of the valley initially chosen, the one with least average cost. If we continue to apply this more and more refined selection mechanism, the dynamics converges towards the minimum cost configuration with high probability. At least if the temperature is decreased in a sufficiently slow way.

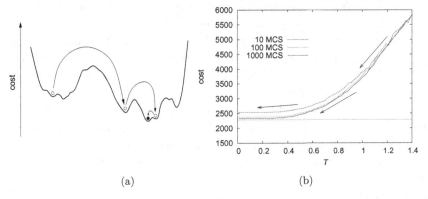

(a)　　　　　　　　　　(b)

Fig. 20.8　A simple scheme of how a simulated annealing searching for the minimum of a cost function evolves (top) and the average cost measured with three different cooling schemes (bottom).

In simulated annealing, the temperature works a bit like a microscope. At high temperature we see the set of configurations in a coarse way. Instead, at low temperatures, we can identify the small details of the cost function, but only in a narrow region of the configuration space (exactly like when we enlarge a detail with a microscope).

We should not forget that, as in all stochastic processes, we can also have bad luck when performing a simulated annealing. Indeed, a bad choice for the initial valley could produce a poor final result. This is why we need to perform the search several times, keeping the configuration with lowest cost we found as a final result.

Designing a simulated annealing we only need to make few choices. Once we decided the type of Monte Carlo dynamics at fixed temperature (for example, the Metropolis algorithm), we just need to determine the scheme by which lowering the temperature. Let us call T_{max} the initial temperature, which should be sufficiently high in order for the system to move more or less freely throughout the entire configuration space.

We choose a cooling scheme in which the system evolves for $\mathcal{T}$ MCS at each temperature. The temperatures are discretized and we call $T_n^{(\mathrm{SA})}$ the nth temperature. Our choice has some advantages compared to performing one single MCS at each temperature and changing T in a denser way.

- We can make the cooling infinitely slow by simply sending $\mathcal{T} \to \infty$. In this limit, the Markov chain has the time to thermalize at each finite temperature, thus providing the right thermodynamic result.

- We can determine the averages of the observables over the $\mathcal{T}$ MCS at each temperature. These averages converge towards the thermodynamic averages in the limit $\mathcal{T} \to \infty$.

- If we are using a look-up table (see Sec. 19.4.1), each time the temperature is changed we need to recompute the table entries. Therefore, it is preferable that this occurs only a limited number of times (also for very large $\mathcal{T}$).

The only thing we need to choose before starting the simulated annealing is the temperature sequence $T_n^{(\mathrm{SA})}$. Obviously, there exist an infinite number of choices for $T_n^{(\mathrm{SA})}$. The two most common cooling schemes are the linear and the geometric one, defined respectively by the following expressions

$$T_n^{(\mathrm{SA})} = T_{n-1}^{(\mathrm{SA})} - \Delta T \iff T_n^{(\mathrm{SA})} = T_{\max} - n \cdot \Delta T \ , \ \text{with } 0 < \Delta T \ll T_{\max} \ ,$$

$$T_n^{(\mathrm{SA})} = T_{n-1}^{(\mathrm{SA})} \cdot \alpha \iff T_n^{(\mathrm{SA})} = T_{\max} \cdot \alpha^n \ , \qquad \text{with } 0 < 1 - \alpha \ll 1 \ .$$

In the first case (linear scheme) the temperature is decreased by subtracting each time a fixed ΔT, which should be much smaller than $T_{\max}$ in order for the number of different temperatures to be large. In the second case (geometric scheme) the temperature decreases because it is multiplied at each step by a factor α less than 1. In order to have a large number of different temperatures upon cooling, we need to choose a value of α close to 1. Note that in the second scheme the temperature never reaches zero. Therefore, we need to fix a minimum temperature below which the simulated annealing should stop. This is not difficult to do, as for temperatures close to zero, a further lowering of the temperature does not significantly change the costs of the configurations reached by the Monte Carlo dynamics (for example, observe Figure 20.8(b) for $T \lesssim 0.2$). So, it is advisable to stop the simulated annealing when this region is reached.

At the end of the cooling, is always advisable to perform some MCS exactly at zero temperature. In the dynamics at $T = 0$ the proposed configurations are only accepted if they do not increase the cost. As a consequence, the dynamics quickly converges towards a local minimum of the cost function (in case it was not already there).

As an indication, a reasonable cooling scheme may contain around a hundred different temperatures. Nevertheless, the ideal cooling scheme strongly depends on the optimization problem. Therefore, it is difficult to give more accurate, and still general, prescriptions than the ones given here.

Theoretically speaking, if the number of MCS made during the simulated annealing is sufficiently large, the stochastic dynamics would reach equilibrium for each temperature $T_n^{(SA)}$. In this case, we would be sure that the average values measured during the simulated annealing do correspond to the average values in the canonical ensemble. In particular, at $T = 0$ the system would reach the minimum cost configuration. Unfortunately, in practice this case is difficult to occur. For a typical difficult optimization problem, the thermalization times are of the order of the exponential of the number of variables divided by the temperature, i.e., $\log(t_{eq}) \propto N/T$. Therefore, at low temperatures, especially for a system with a large number of variables, the time we can run a simulation is definitely much smaller than the one needed to thermalize.

We need to keep in mind that the simulated annealing is a non-equilibrium process that can approximate very well the equilibrium probability distribution in a much shorter execution time. Once the cooling scheme has been established, the execution times of the simulated annealing grow linearly with the number N of variables. Instead, the exact solution (or the thermalization at very low temperatures) takes an exponential time in N, making it unreachable in the majority of practical cases. Moreover, in many situations it is better to have a good approximation of the true solution in little time, rather than to find exactly the optimum after a very long time.

In Figure 20.8(b) we show the typical behavior of the average cost measured during a simulated annealing. At each temperature we report the value of $\mathcal{T}^{-1} \sum_t E(s(t))$, i.e., the average value of the cost of the configurations obtained at temperature T. In this case, the problem has $N = 10^4$ variables and we chose a linear cooling scheme with $T_{max} = 1.5$ and $\Delta T = 0.02$. the curves correspond to various values of the cooling velocity, with $\mathcal{T} = 10, 100, 1000$ MCS at each temperature. The horizontal dashed line is an estimate, obtained with pseudoanalytical methods, of what should be the minimum cost function (we use the conditional tense as we are dealing with a difficult optimization problem, not fully understood yet). Note in Figure 20.8(b) that for $T \gtrsim 1.1$ the average cost curves coincide, at least for the two slowest cooling schemes. This clearly shows that in this temperature range we have reached the equilibrium (the average cost does not change as the simulation time increases). Therefore, the choice of $T_{\max}$ is correct as it falls in the region of high temperatures, where we are able to reach the equilibrium. On the contrary, for $T \lesssim 1$, the value of the average energy depends on $\mathcal{T}$ and probably also for the slowest cooling scheme the system is out of equilibrium. Finally, note that for $T \lesssim 0.2$ the average value of the cost does not change with the temperature. Probably the system has reached a local minimum (but not the global one) of the cost function and the temperature is too low to leave it. Once this region has been reached, we may interrupt the simulated annealing.

Appendix A

The main C statements

A program always starts with the function `main`.

The main types of variables are `int`, `float`, `double` and `char`. Respectively, they refer to integer variables (`int`), variables representing rational numbers (`float` and `double`) and characters (`char`), p. 68.

The arithmetic operators are `+`, `-`, `*`, `/`. The logical operators `&&`, `||`, `!` and the relational operators are discussed on p. 77. The `sizeof()` operator returns the number of bytes allocated in memory for an expression or a type, p. 79.

The cast operator explicitly converts one type of variable into another, within the scope of the expression in which it is used, as shown on p. 79.

To write messages to the standard output (generally on screen) use the `printf` function, as in

```
printf(" Message number %d \n", msg);
```

where the string `%d` is an output format specifier. Table 3.7 on p. 81 contains the most frequently used format specifiers, in which case the header file `<stdio.h>` should be included.

The `scanf` function reads the value of one or more input variables from the standard input (usually the keyboard), as in

```
scanf("%d", &msg);
```

The `scanf` format specifiers are listed in Table 3.8.

The directive `#define` allows to define a macro as shown on p. 87.

The selection control structure is achieved with the `if` statement, p. 100, possibly followed by the `else` clause. If the statement condition is true, the program executes the statements enclosed between the first couple of curly brackets. Otherwise, the statements following the `else` clause are executed, in case the latter is present.

```
if (i > 0) {
   printf("i positive");
} else {
   printf("i negative");
}
```

Sometimes the ? operator is used, p. 102. This operator returns either the expression to the left or the right of the colon : depending on the truth value (true or false) of the expression preceding the operator:

```
sign = (i > 0) ? 1 : -1;
```

In order to execute one or more statements until a certain condition is verified, use the while command, p. 104, and do statements, p. 105. With the while statement the lines of code enclosed between the curly brackets are executed for as long as the condition between parentheses remains true.

```
double S = 10.;
/* reads a value x which is subtracted from S until
   S becomes negative or zero */
while (S > 0) {
   ...
   scanf("%f", &x);
   ...
   S -= x;
}
```

Also with the do statement the lines of code included between the curly brackets are executed for as long as the condition between the parentheses is true. However, in this case the condition is checked only after the block of statements has been executed at least once.

```
do {
   printf("Insert either 1 or 2: ");
   scanf("%d", &i);
} while ((i != 1) && (i != 2));
```

To execute a cycle controlled by an index it is better to use the for statement, p. 107. The for statement has three expressions, separated by a semicolon ;, each one of which may be omitted. The first one is an expression which is evaluated just once before entering the cycle; the second is a logical expression, causing the cycle to be interrupted when false; the third is an expression which is evaluated at the end of each cycle.

```
int S = 0;
/* computes the sum of the first 100 integer numbers */
for (i = 0; i < 100; i++) {
   S += i;
}
```

A one-dimensional array is declared as in

```
double a[5];
```

a two-dimensional array as in

```
double a[5][7];
```

An array can be explicitly filled during the declaration phase by specifying the number of elements, p. 125.

A string is an array of characters. Its length may be defined upon its declaration, p. 140.

A pointer is declared as following

```
double *pd;
```

The reference operator & applied to a variable returns the pointer to that variable; the indirection or dereference operator * applied to a pointer returns the value of the pointed variable. Their use is shown on p. 151.

The name of an array is a pointer to the array initial position.

The const qualifier ensures a variable cannot be changed. It is particularly useful when applied to pointers, p. 157.

In the C language a file becomes accessible to read or write operations by a pointer to FILE. A file always needs to be opened with the fopen function, p. 169. You can read from a file with the fread function and write to it with the fwrite function (Listing 6.11).

A function must be declared before it is defined, p. 178. The declaration may contain the names of the formal parameters as in

```
unsigned long long int factorial(int n);
```

or not, as in

```
unsigned long long int factorial(int);
```

The definition is given in the body of the function, p. 185, as in

```
double squareSum(double a, double b) {
  return (a * a + b * b);
}
```

An array can be passed to a function only by passing the value of the pointer to the array itself, p. 190.

A function returns a value with the return statement.

The structures, struct, allow to group data that are possibly of a different type, p. 259:

```
struct point{
  double x;
  double y;
};
struct point point1;
struct point *pPoint2;
```

In order to select a member of a structure, you can either start from the structure itself and use the `.` operator, or from the pointer to the structure and use the `->` operator:

```
double a = point1.x;
double b = pPoint2->x;
```

The function `system`, p. 280, allows to execute commands of the operating system within the C code:

```
i = system("rm badFile.txt");
if (i != 0) {printf("Removal error.\n");}
```

Memory can be allocated dynamically (without initializing it to zero) with `malloc`, p. 280:

```
void *malloc(size_t numberOfBytes);
```

There also exists a memory allocation function initializing all allocated bytes to zero, p. 282:

```
void *calloc(size_t numberOfWords, size_t sizeOfWord);
```

The dynamically allocated memory needs to be freed with the function `free`, p. 283:

```
void free(void *p);
```

A dynamically allocated memory space can be enlarged with the function `realloc`, p. 283:

```
void *realloc(void *p, size_t totalSize);
```

It is possible to rename a variable type, p. 285:

```
typedef float position;
```

The syntax of a `union` is similar to the one of a `struct`, but it retains only one of its possible members (namely, the one which was last given a value). Thus, the memory space allocated to a `union` has a size equal to the one needed for its largest component, p. 370:

```
union chameleon{
  double green;
  int red;
```

```
    char yellow;
} theChameleonJohn, theChameleonMary;
```

The function `fgetc` (when used include `<stdio.h>`) allows to read the next character of a file, p. 378:

```
int fgetc(FILE *pointerToFile);
```

The function `strlen` (include `<string.h>` when using this or either one of the following functions) returns the number of characters in a string (without counting the terminating character) `\0` , p. 379:

```
size_t strlen(const char *myString);
```

The function `strcpy` copies a string, p. 379:

```
char *strcpy(char *destination, const char *source);
```

The function `strcmp` compares two strings, `string1` and `string2`. It returns a null value if the two strings are the same, a negative value if `string1` is less than `string2` and a positive value if `string1` is larger than `string2`, p. 381:

```
int strcmp(const char *string1, const char *string2);
```

The operator `&` performs the bitwise AND of two variables, p. 406:

```
unsigned int a, b, c;
a = 11;
b = 13;
c = a & b;
```

The operator `|` returns the bitwise OR of two variables, p. 407:

```
c = a | b;
```

The operator `^` performs the bitwise XOR of two variables, p. 407:

```
c = a ^ b;
```

In the following example, the left shift operator `<<` shifts the bits composing the word `myWord`, `numberOfBits` bits to the left , p. 409:

```
c = myWord << numberOfBits;
```

Instead, the right shift operator `>>` shifts the bits composing the word `myWord`, `numberOfBits` bits to the right , p. 409:

```
c = myWord >> numberOfBits;
```

The operator `~` returns the bitwise NOT of a single variable, p. 409:

```
b = ~ a;
```

Appendix B

The ASCII codes

Table B.1   Codes and characters in the ASCII standard. The code in base 10 is shown in column *Dec*, the one in base 16 in columnn *Hex* and the related character is shown in column *C*.

Dec	Hex	C	Dec	Hex	C	Dec	Hex	C	Dec	Hex	C
000	00	NUL	001	01	SOH	002	02	STX	003	03	ETX
004	04	EOT	005	05	ENQ	006	06	ACK	007	07	BEL
008	08	BS	009	09	HT	010	0a	LF	011	0b	VT
012	0c	FF	013	0d	CR	014	0e	SO	015	0f	SI
016	10	DLE	017	11	DC1	018	12	DC2	019	13	DC3
020	14	DC4	021	15	NAK	022	16	SYN	023	17	ETB
024	18	CAN	025	19	EM	026	1a	SUB	027	1b	ESC
028	1c	FS	029	1d	GS	030	1e	RS	031	1f	US
032	20		033	21	!	034	22	"	035	23	#
036	24	$	037	25	%	038	26	&	039	27	'
040	28	(	041	29	)	042	2a	*	043	2b	+
044	2c	,	045	2d	-	046	2e	.	047	2f	/
048	30	0	049	31	1	050	32	2	051	33	3
052	34	4	053	35	5	054	36	6	055	37	7
056	38	8	057	39	9	058	3a	:	059	3b	;
060	3c	<	061	3d	=	062	3e	>	063	3f	?
064	40	@	065	41	A	066	42	B	067	43	C
068	44	D	069	45	E	070	46	F	071	47	G
072	48	H	073	49	I	074	4a	J	075	4b	K
076	4c	L	077	4d	M	078	4e	N	079	4f	O
080	50	P	081	51	Q	082	52	R	083	53	S
084	54	T	085	55	U	086	56	V	087	57	W
088	58	X	089	59	Y	090	5a	Z	091	5b	[
092	5c	\	093	5d	]	094	5e	^	095	5f	_
096	60	`	097	61	a	098	62	b	099	63	c
100	64	d	101	65	e	102	66	f	103	67	g
104	68	h	105	69	i	106	6a	j	107	6b	k
108	6c	l	109	6d	m	110	6e	n	111	6f	o
112	70	p	113	71	q	114	72	r	115	73	s
116	74	t	117	75	u	118	76	v	119	77	w
120	78	x	121	79	y	122	7a	z	123	7b	{
124	7c			125	7d	}	126	7e	~	127	7f	DEL

Bibliography

Abramowitz, M. and Stegun, I. (1965). *Handbook of Mathematical Functions* (Dover).

Amit, D. J. and Martin-Mayor, V. (2005). *Field Theory, the Renormalization Group, and Critical Phenomena* (World Scientific).

ANSI (1995). *Programming Languages — C — Amendment 1: C Integrity (ISO/IEC 9899:1990/AMD 1:1995)*.

Babbage, C. (1822). A note respecting the application of machinery to the calculation of astronomical tables, *Mem. Astron. Soc.* **1**, p. 309.

Bachvalov, N. S. (1977). *Numerical Methods* (Mir Publishers).

Bohm, C. and Jacopini, G. (1966). Flow diagrams, Turing machines, and languages with only two formation rules, *Commun. of the ACM* **9**, 5, pp. 366–371.

Carpenter, B. E. and Doran, R. W. (1986). *A. M. Turing's ACE Report of 1946 and Other Papers* (MIT press), http://www.turingarchive.org. First published in 1946 as internal note of National Physics Laboratory with n. DSIR 10/385.

Cormen, T. H., Leiserson, C. E. and Rivest, R. L. (1990). *Introduction to Algorithms* (MIT press and McGraw-Hill, Cambridge, MA and New York).

Dantzig, G. B. (1951). Maximization of a linear function of variables subject to linear inequalities, in T. C. Koopmans (ed.), *Activity Analysis of Production and Allocation* (John Wiley & Sons, New York), pp. 339–347.

Deitel, H. M. and Deitel, P. J. (2011). *C++: How to Program*, 8th edn. (Prentice Hall).

Dolya, A. (2003). Interview with Brian Kernighan, *Linux Journal* Available at http://www.linuxjournal.com/article/7035.

ENIAC (1946). *A Report on the ENIAC (Electronic Numerical Integrator and Computer)*, The University of Pennsylvania.

Feller, W. (1971). *An Introduction to Probability Theory and its Applications* (John Wiley & Sons, New York).

Gardner, M. (1970). The fantastic combinations of John Conway's new solitaire game life, *Scientific American* **23**, pp. 120–123.

Garey, M. R. and Johnson, D. S. (1979). *Computers and Intractability: A Guide to the Theory of NP-completeness* (Freeman, New York).

Garvin, W. W. (1960). *Introduction to Linear Programming* (McGraw-Hill).

Gihman, I. I. and Skorohod, A. V. (1972). *Stochastic Differential Equations* (Springer-Verlag).

Goldberg, D. (1991). *What Every Computer Scientist Should Know About Floating-Point Arithmetic* (Association for Computing Machinery Inc).

Gough, B. J. (2005). *An Introduction to GCC* (Network Theory Ltd).

Grimmett, G. and Stirzaker, D. (2001). *Probability and Random Processes* (Oxford University Press, Oxford).

Gutzwiller, M. C. (1990). *Chaos in Classical and Quantum Mechanics* (Springer-Verlag, Berlin).

Hellekalek, P. (2009). plab: Theory and practice of random number generation, `http://random.mat.sbg.ac.at/`.

Holland, J. H. (1975). *Adaptation in Natural and Artificial Systems* (MIT Press).

Huang, K. (1987). *Statistical Mechanics* (Wiley).

ISO (1999). *Programming Languages — C (ISO/IEC 9899:1999)*.

James, F. (1994). RANLUX: A fortran implementation of the high-quality pseudorandom number generator of Luescher, *Computer Phys. Commun.* **79**, pp. 111–114.

Kahan, W. (1965). Further remarks on reducing truncation errors, *Communications of the ACM* **8**, 1, p. 40.

Kaplan, R. (2000). *The Nothing that Is: A Natural History of Zero* (Oxford University Press).

Kelley, A. and Pohl, I. (1998). *A Book on C: Programming in C* (Addison Wesley).

Kernighan, B. W. and Ritchie, D. M. (1988). *The C Programming Language*, 2nd edn. (Prentice Hall).

Kirkpatrick, S., Gelatt, C. D. and Vecchi, M. P. (1983). Optimization by simulated annealing, *Science* **220**, pp. 671–680.

Knuth, D. E. (1969). *The Art of Computer Programming, Volume 2: Seminumerical Algorithms* (Addison-Wesley).

Koenig, A. and Moo, B. E. (2000). *Accelerated C++* (Addison-Wesley).

Kuroš, A. G. (1972). *Higher Algebra* (Mir Publisher).

Luescher, M. (1994). A portable high-quality random number generator for lattice field theory simulations, *Computer Phys. Commun.* **79**, pp. 100–110.

Marinari, E., Parisi, G., Ruelle, D. and Windey, P. (1983). Random walk in a random environment and $1/f$ noise, *Phys. Rev. Lett.* **50**, pp. 1223–1225.

MARKI (1946). *A Manual of Operation For The Automatic Sequence Controlled Calculator*, Oxford University Press.

Marsaglia, G. (1999). Some good(?) random number generators, with C code, comparisons, Tech. Rep. Newsgroups: sci.stat.math, sci.math, a copy can be found on the web site `http://www.scientificprogramming.org/doc/marsaglia.html`.

Metropolis, N., Rosenbluth, A. W., Rosenbluth, M. N., Teller, A. H. and Teller, E. (1953). Equations of state calculations by fast computing machine, *J. Chem. Phys.* **21**, pp. 1087–1091.

Mittelbach, F. and Goosens, M. (2004). *The LaTeX Companion* (Addison-Wesley).

Morse, P. M. and Feshbach, H. (1953). *Methods of Theoretical Physics* (McGraw — Hill).

Newman, M. E. J. and Barkema, G. T. (1999). *Monte Carlo Methods in Statistical Physics* (Clarendon Press, Oxford).

Press, W. H., Teukolsky, S. A., Vetterling, W. T. and Flannery, B. P. (1992). *Numerical Recipes in C* (Cambridge University Press), http://www.nr.com/.

Richards, M. (1967). The bcpl reference manual, Tech. Rep. MIT Project MAC Memorandum M-352, MIT, http://cm.bell-labs.com/cm/cs/who/dmr/bcpl.pdf.

Sinai, Y. G. (1982). in R. Schrader, R. Seiler and D. A. Uhlenbrock (eds.), *Proceedings of the Berlin Conference on Mathematical Problems in Theoretical Physics* (Springer-Verlag), p. 12.

Smirnov, S. (1964). *A Course of Higher Mathematics* (Pergamon Press).

Stauffer, D. and Aharony, A. (1992). *Introduction to Percolation Theory* (Taylor & Francis).

Taylor, J. R. (1996). *An Introduction to Error Analysis* (University Science Books).

The Unicode Consortium (2003). *The Unicode Standard — Version 4.0* (Addison-Wesley), http.//www.unicode.org.

Thompson, K. (1972). Technical memorandum 1/1/1972, Tech. Rep. MM-72-1271-1, Bell Labs, http://cm.bell-labs.com/cm/cs/who/dmr/kbman.pdf.

Urban, M. and Tiemann, B. (2001). *FreeBSD Unleashed* (SAMS), available at http://www.freebsd.org.

von Mises, R. (1964). *Mathematical Theory of Probability and Statistics* (Academic Press).

von Neumann, J. (1946). The principles of large-scale computing machines, *IEEE Annals of the History of Computing* **3**.

von Neumann, J. and Burks, A. (1966). *Theory of Self-Reproducing Automata* (University of Illinois Press, Urbana).

VV. AA. (1997). *Empirical Studies of the Arts* **15**, 2, pp. 111–255.

Wakerly, J. F. (1989). *Microcomputer Architecture and Programming* (John Wiley & Sons).

Wall, L., Christiansen, T. and Orwant, J. (2000). *Programming Perl*, 3rd edn. (O'Reilly).

Wolfram, S. (2002). *A New Kind of Science* (Wolfram Media Inc).

Index